SpringBoard®
English
Language Arts

STUDENT EDITION   ENGLISH I

About The College Board

The College Board is a mission-driven not-for-profit organization that connects students to college success and opportunity. Founded in 1900, the College Board was created to expand access to higher education. Today, the membership association is made up of over 6,000 of the world's leading educational institutions and is dedicated to promoting excellence and equity in education. Each year, the College Board helps more than seven million students prepare for a successful transition to college through programs and services in college readiness and college success—including the SAT® and the Advanced Placement Program®. The organization also serves the education community through research and advocacy on behalf of students, educators, and schools. For further information, visit collegeboard.org.

ISBN: 978-1-4573-1295-3

1 2 3 4 5 6 7 8   20 21 22 23 24 25 26

Printed in the United States of America

Acknowledgements

The College Board gratefully acknowledges the outstanding work of the classroom teachers who have been integral to the development of this program. The end product is testimony to their expertise, understanding of student learning needs, and dedication to rigorous and accessible English Language Arts instruction.

Lance Balla
Everett School District
Everett, Washington

Carisa Barnes
San Diego Unified School
District
San Diego, California

Leia Bell
Hillsborough County Public
Schools
Tampa, Florida

Alysa Broussard
Lafayette Parish School
System
Lafayette, Louisiana

Robert J. Caughey
San Dieguito Union High
School District
San Diego, California

Susie Challancin
Bellevue School District 405
Bellevue, Washington

Doug Cole
Cherry Creek School District
Greenwood Village, Colorado

Cari Davis
Rio Rancho Public School
District
Rio Rancho, New Mexico

Paul De Maret
Poudre School District
Fort Collins, Colorado

Sylvia Ellison
Hillsborough County Public
Schools
Hillsborough, Florida

Karen Fullam
Hillsborough County Public
Schools
Tampa, Florida

Michael Gragert
Plano Independent School
District
Plano, Texas

Nancy Gray
Brevard County Schools
Viera, Florida

Charise Hallberg
Bellevue School District 405
Bellevue, Washington

T.J. Hanify
Bellevue School District 405
Bellevue, Washington

Jessi Hupper
Peninsula School District
Gig Harbor, Washington

Nimat Jones
ICEF Public Schools, Los
Angeles, California

Karen Kampschmidt
Fort Thomas Independent
School District
Fort Thomas, Kentucky

Karen Kennedy
Peninsula School District
Peninsula, Washington

LeAnn Klepzig
Bradley County Schools
Cleveland, Tennessee

Susie Lowry
Volusia County School
District
Deland, Florida

Michelle Lewis
Spokane Public School
Spokane, Washington

John Marshall
Mead School District
Mead, Washington

Cassandra Mattison
Hillsborough County Public
Schools
Tampa, Florida

Glenn Morgan
San Diego Unified School
District
San Diego, California

John Murray
Garland Independent School
District
Sachse, Texas

Kristen J. Ohaver
Charlotte-Mecklenburg
Schools
Charlotte, North Carolina

Amanda Olinger
Harrisburg School District
Harrisburg, South Dakota

Julie Pennabaker
Quakertown Community
School District
Quakertown, Pennsylvania

Bryan Sandala
School District of Palm Beach
County
West Palm Beach, Florida

Angela Seiler
Rio Rancho Public School
District
Rio Rancho, New Mexico

Amanda Shackelford
Lafayette Parish School
System
Lafayette, Louisiana

Kimberlyn Slagle
Lafayette Parish School
System
Lafayette, Louisiana

Sarah Smith Arceneaux
Lafayette Parish School
System
Lafayette, Louisiana

Holly Talley
Hillsborough County Public
Schools
Ruskin, Florida

Derek Thomas
Hillsborough County Public
Schools
Tampa, Florida

Maria Torres-Crosby
Hillsborough County Public
Schools
Tampa, Florida

Susan Van Doren
South Lake Tahoe, California

JoEllen Victoreen
San José Unified School
District
San José, California

Rebecca Wenrich
Peninsula School District
Gig Harbor, Washington

Research and Planning Advisors

We also wish to thank the members of our SpringBoard Advisory Council and the many educators who gave generously of their time and their ideas as we conducted research for both the print and online programs. Your suggestions and reactions to ideas helped immeasurably as we created this edition. We gratefully acknowledge the teachers and administrators in the following districts.

ABC Unified School District
Cerritos, California

Allen Independent School District
Allen, Texas

Bellevue, School District 405
Bellevue, Washington

Burnet Consolidated Independent School District
Burnet, Texas

Community Unit School District 308
Oswego, Illinois

Fresno Unified School District
Fresno, California

Frisco Independent School District
Frisco, Texas

Garland Independent School District
Garland, Texas

Grapevine-Colleyville Independent School District
Grapevine, Texas

Hamilton County Schools
Chattanooga, Tennessee

Hesperia Unified School District
Hesperia, California

Hillsborough County Public Schools
Tampa, Florida

ICEF Public Schools
Los Angeles, California

IDEA Public Schools
Weslaco, Texas

Irving Independent School District
Irving, Texas

Keller Independent School District
Keller, Texas

KIPP Houston
Houston, Texas

Lafayette Parish Schools
Lafayette Parish, Louisiana

Los Angeles Unified School District
Los Angeles, California

Lubbock Independent School District
Lubbock, Texas

Mansfield Independent School District
Mansfield, Texas

Midland Independent School District
Midland, Texas

Milwaukee Public Schools
Milwaukee, Wisconsin

New Haven School District
New Haven, Connecticut

Ogden School District
Ogden, Utah

Rio Rancho Public Schools
Rio Rancho, New Mexico

San José Unified School District
San José, California

Scottsdale Unified School District
Scottsdale, Arizona

Spokane Public Schools
Spokane, Washington

Tacoma Public Schools
Tacoma, Washington

SpringBoard English Language Arts

Lori O'Dea
Executive Director
Content Development

Natasha Vasavada
Executive Director
Pre-AP & SpringBoard

Doug Waugh
VP, SpringBoard & Pre-AP
Programs

Sarah Balistreri
Senior Director
ELA Content Development

Florencia Duran Wald
Senior Director
ELA Content Development

Julie Manley
Senior Director
Professional Learning

Joely Negedly
Senior Director
Pre-AP Humanities

Jessica Brockman
Product Manager
English Language Arts

Suzie Doss
Director
SpringBoard Implementation

Jennifer Duva
Director
English Language Arts

Spencer Gonçalves
Director
Digital Content Development

Rebecca Grudzina
Senior Editor
English Language Arts

Georgia Scurletis
Senior Instructional Writer
Pre-AP English Language Arts

Abigail Johnson
Editor
English Language Arts

Casseia Lewis
Assistant Editor
English Language Arts

Natalie Hansford
Editorial Assistant
English Language Arts

Table of Contents

CONTENTS

CONTENTS

CONTENTS

Resources

Texts not included in these materials.

Introduction to SpringBoard English Language Arts

About SpringBoard ELA

SpringBoard was built around a simple belief: if you give students and teachers the best materials, engaging methods, and ongoing support, then student success will surely follow. Developed by teachers, SpringBoard brings your classroom to life with materials that help you practice the skills and learn the knowledge you need to excel in high school and beyond. Read on to find out how SpringBoard will support your learning.

Instructional Materials

SpringBoard English Language Arts supplies a Student Edition and Teacher Edition, in print and digital form, for grades 6–12. In addition to using the English Language Arts curriculum, you can sharpen your reading, writing, and language skills with materials including Language Workshop, Close Reading Workshop, and Writing Workshop.

Design that Begins with the End in Mind

- Based on the Understanding by Design model, SpringBoard teaches the skills and knowledge that matter most to meet AP and college and career readiness standards.

- You will start each unit by unpacking the assessment, so you know where you're heading and why the skills you're developing matter.

- Each activity starts with clear, standards-aligned learning targets.

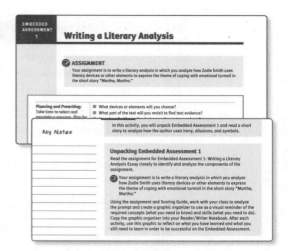

UNIT 1

VISUAL PROMPT
In stories and images, small details work together to create meaning, convey the author or artist's message, and affect the audience. What small details do you notice in this painting?

TELLING DETAILS

In the living room the voice-clock sang, *Tick-tock, seven o'clock, time to get up, time to get up, seven o'clock!* as if it were afraid that nobody would. The morning house lay empty. The clock ticked on, repeating and repeating its sounds into the emptiness. ...
In the kitchen the breakfast stove gave a hissing sigh and ejected from its warm interior eight pieces of perfectly browned toast, eight eggs sunny side up, sixteen slices of bacon, two coffees, and two cool glasses of milk.

–from "There Will Come Soft Rains" by Ray Bradbury

The Practice of Reading Closely

- SpringBoard puts a special focus on close reading, giving you strategies and structure for developing this key skill.

- You will encounter compelling texts—fiction, nonfiction, poetry, drama, visuals, and film.

Poem

"Bilingual/Bilingüe"

by **Rhina P. Espaillat**

My father liked them separate, one there,
one here (allá y aquí), as if aware

that words might cut in two his daughter's heart
(el corazón) and lock the alien part

5 to what he was—his memory, his name
(su nombre)—with a key he could not claim.

"English outside this door, Spanish inside,"
he said, "y basta¹." But who can divide

the world, the word (mundo y palabra) from

About the Author

Zadie Smith (b. 1975) is a British author of English and Jamaican heritage. Born Sadie Smith, she changed the spelling of her first name to Zadie when she was 14. She published her first novel when she was in college, which put her on *Granta* magazine's list of 20 best young authors. Smith writes stories that delve into race, religion, class, and cultural identity. Her novels often contain eccentric characters and witty dialogue.

Short Story

Martha, Martha (Part 1)

by Zadie Smith

1 Though the telephone is a perfectly useless indicator of most human qualities, it's pretty precise about age. From her tiny office on the third floor, Pam Roberts looked through a window and correctly identified the Martha Penk she was waiting for, a shrimpish girl pushing twenty-two, lost down there. She had on a red overcoat and cream snow boots, putting her weight on their edges like an ice skater; she seemed to waver between two doorways. Pam

A Living System of Learning

- SpringBoard puts you and your classmates in charge of your learning to create a more dynamic classroom experience.

- With a flexible design and rich library of tools and resources, SpringBoard helps your teacher personalize instruction for your class.

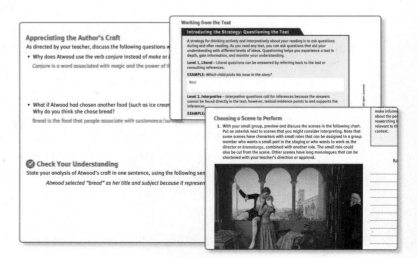

Appreciating the Author's Craft
As directed by your teacher, discuss the following questions w...
- Why does Atwood use the verb *conjure* instead of *make* or b...
  Conjure is a word associated with magic and the power of th...

- What if Atwood had chosen another food (such as ice cream...
  Why do you think she chose bread?
  Bread is the food that people associate with sustenance/survival...

Check Your Understanding
State your analysis of Atwood's craft in one sentence, using the following sen...
  Atwood selected "bread" as her title and subject because it represen...

Working from the Text

Introducing the Strategy: Questioning the Text

A strategy for thinking actively and interpretively about your reading is to ask questions during and after reading. As you read any text, you can ask questions that aid your understanding with different levels of ideas. Questioning helps you experience a text in depth, gain information, and monitor your understanding.

Level 1, Literal – Literal questions can be answered by referring back to the text or consulting references.

EXAMPLE: Which child picks his nose in the story?
  Rizvi

Level 2, Interpretive – Interpretive questions call for inferences because the answers cannot be found directly in the text; however, textual evidence points to and supports the inferences.

EXAMPLE:

Choosing a Scene to Perform
1. With your small group, preview and discuss the scenes in the following chart. Put an asterisk next to scenes that you might consider interpreting. Note that some scenes have characters with small roles that can be assigned to a group member who has only a small part in the staging or who wants to work as the director or dramaturge, combined with another role. The small role could also be cut from the scene. Other scenes have long monologues that can be shortened with your teacher's direction or approval.

make inform...
about the pe...
researching is...
relevant to th...
context.

Bringing the Classroom to Life

When you enter a SpringBoard classroom you don't hear a teacher talking in the front of the room. You hear a buzz of excitement, with students working together and taking charge of how they learn. That's what the teachers who designed SpringBoard wanted for their classrooms, so they created a curriculum and materials that are focused on real classroom needs, encouraging teacher and student involvement.

SpringBoard translates the expectations of state standards into engaging daily lessons. We believe that reading, writing, speaking, and listening should all be learned together. You'll see examples of our integrated approach throughout our materials. And we put a special focus on close reading, giving you strategies and structure for developing this key skill.

Our Approach to Reading

In SpringBoard ELA, we move right into compelling texts—fiction, nonfiction, poetry, drama, visuals, and film—and offer the tools, supports, and approaches that will help you get the most out of every reading.

The Practice of Reading Closely

Texts take center stage in the SpringBoard ELA classroom, where you will prepare for close, critical reading of a wide range of materials. With guidance from your teacher, you will develop the habits of close reading that will serve you for a lifetime.

- **As You Read:** You prepare to read and annotate the text for notable elements like genre characteristics, important use of words, and text structures.

- **First Reading:** You read on your own, with a partner, in a group, or with the class. You annotate the text as you begin to uncover its meaning.

- **Making Observations:** Your teacher guides you to pause during or right after the first reading to observe the small details within a text in order to arrive at a deeper understanding of the whole.

- **Returning to the Text:** You continue to deepen your understanding of the text by responding to a series of text-dependent questions. You will use text evidence, speak with new vocabulary words, reflect on your classmates' ideas, and make connections among texts, ideas, and experiences.

- **Working from the Text:** You use the text as a source as you move from reading and analysis to productive work, including academic discussion and writing.

Reading Independently

As a SpringBoard student, you'll practice good reading habits in class so that you can read challenging texts in other classes and on your own. Independent reading is an integral part of every SpringBoard English Language Arts unit. At the beginning of the year, you will learn how to make a plan for independent reading. **Independent Reading Lists** for each unit give you a jump-start on selecting texts by offering a list of suggested titles, including a number of Spanish-language titles, that connect to the themes, genres, and concepts of the SpringBoard unit.

While you work your way through each unit, you will respond to **Independent Reading Links** that lead you to make connections between the reading you're doing on your own and the skills and knowledge you're developing in class. Twice per unit, **Independent Reading Checkpoints** give you a chance to reflect on and synthesize your independent reading in an informal writing assignment or discussion.

Reading to Build Knowledge

SpringBoard units are designed so that you can delve deeply into an overarching topic, theme, or idea. Each unit will pose essential questions that relate to the ideas and texts within the unit, and you will return to these questions again and again, each time refining your responses with new understanding and new evidence to support your point of view.

You will also deepen your knowledge of key topics by conducting both on-the-spot and extended research, asking and answering questions, evaluating multiple sources, and synthesizing your findings.

Twice a unit you will go on a **Knowledge Quest**. Each Knowledge Quest begins with a Knowledge Question and supporting questions to focus your reading. After reading several texts that explore a topic, theme, or idea, you will get to return to the Knowledge Question and show your growing understanding of the topic by responding to a writing prompt or engaging in a discussion.

At the end of a Knowledge Quest, you will be encouraged to continue building your knowledge of the topic by going to **Zinc Reading Labs** and finding related texts to read. Zinc Reading Labs offers a variety of informational and literary texts that you can choose based on your interests. Vocabulary sets for each text let you learn new words and practice using them.

Your independent reading can also enhance your understanding of the topics you are studying in class if you want it to. SpringBoard's **Independent Reading Lists** include suggested books that relate to the topics and themes from each unit. By choosing those books you can see a different side of the topic, learn new words, and find other topics you want to learn more about.

Reading to Gain Perspectives

Gaining Perspectives features use a text as a jumping off point for examining an issue relevant to you. You will be asked to consider the perspectives of others and to empathize with others who have different points of view. You will also be asked to think about social and ethical norms and to recognize the family, school, and community resources available to you. Each Gaining Perspectives feature concludes with a writing task in which you will summarize the discussion you have with your classmates.

Our Approach to Writing

SpringBoard English Language Arts provides you with the support you need to write in all the major modes, emphasizing argumentative, informational, and narrative. You will write often, and you will learn to become a critical reviewer of your own and your peers' work through frequent opportunities for revision and editing. You will learn to plan with purpose, audience, topic, and context in mind; develop drafts with engaging ideas, examples, facts and commentary; revise for clarity, development, organization, style, and diction; and edit using the conventions of the English language.

The Craft of Writing

As you read texts by skilled authors, you will observe the many choices those authors make. You'll tune in to the ways authors purposefully use words, sentences, and structures to convey meaning. After analyzing and critiquing others' work, you will learn to apply your understanding of author's craft to your own writing. A few SpringBoard features help you do just that:

- **Writing prompts** lead up to the Embedded Assessments and give you practice with writing texts in multiple genres, including personal narratives, argumentative essays, letters, research papers, and more. Writing to Sources writing prompts drive you back to texts you have read or viewed to mine for evidence.

- **Focus on the Sentence** tasks help you process content while also practicing the craft of writing powerful sentences.

- **Grammar & Usage** features highlight interesting grammar or usage concepts that appear in a text, both to improve your reading comprehension and to help you attend to these concepts as you craft your own texts.

- **Language & Writer's Craft** features address topics in writing such as style, word choice, and sentence construction.

- **Language Checkpoints** offer in-depth practice with standard English conventions and guide you to develop an editor's checklist to use as a reference each time you check your own or a peer's written work.

Modes of Writing

SpringBoard helps you become a better academic writer by giving you authentic prompts that require you to use sources, and showing you how to work through the writing process. Over the course of the year you will have the chance to write narratives, arguments, and informational texts, and you will develop a wide range of writing skills:

- Consider task, audience, and purpose when structuring and organizing your writing.

- Incorporate details, reasons, and textual evidence to support your ideas.

- Generate research questions, evaluate sources, gather relevant evidence, and report and cite your findings accurately.

- Use research-based strategies that will guide you through the writing process.

Writing with a Focus on the Sentence

SpringBoard English Language Arts leverages sentence writing strategies that were developed by The Writing Revolution. These evidence-based strategies are part of the Hochman Method, the Writing Revolution's system for helping students learn to write across all content areas and grades. The Writing Revolution emphasizes the importance of embedding writing and grammar instruction into content. That's why SpringBoard's Focus on the Sentence tasks integrate sentence-level writing into the curriculum. These tasks not only help you learn and practice important grammar concepts and sentence forms, but they also provide a chance for you to process and demonstrate your understanding of texts, images, class discussions, and other content.

Our Approach to Vocabulary

Vocabulary is threaded throughout each unit and developed over the course of the SpringBoard English Language Arts year. You will have ample opportunities to read and hear new words, explore their meanings, origins, and connotations, and use them in written and oral responses.

- Important academic and literary terms that you will need to actively participate in classroom discussions are called out in your book.

- Challenging vocabulary terms found in reading passages are glossed at the point of use.

- Periodic Word Connections boxes guide you through the process of exploring a word with multiple meanings and nuances, an interesting etymology, a telling root or affix, a helpful Spanish cognate, a relationship to another word, or a connection to another content area.

Zinc Reading Labs

Zinc Reading Labs combines the best features of a typical vocabulary program with those of a typical reading program and makes reading and learning new words a game. Zinc offers a variety of nonfiction and fiction texts that you can choose from based on individual needs and interest. Each article has a corresponding vocabulary set that pre-teaches challenging words through spaced repetition, to help you genuinely learn and internalize the vocabulary. Additional vocabulary games focus on SAT/ACT power words and foundational words for English language learners.

Pre-AP Connections

SpringBoard shares Pre-AP's core principles and encourages you to build skills that you will use in high school and beyond. These principles are evident in every SpringBoard activity.

Close Observation and Analysis
... to notice and consider

When reading, your teacher will guide you to pause to make observations and notice details in the text before analyzing or explaining. Only after you have noticed and enjoyed elements of the text do you then return to the text for deeper analysis and inferential thinking. This close reading sequence helps you interact and engage with the text in increasingly meaningful ways.

Evidence-Based Writing
... with a focus on the sentence

SpringBoard offers varied and frequent writing opportunities, with specific attention to developing complex and precise sentences as the building block to sophisticated paragraph and essay length writing. Instead of being isolated from reading, sentence-level grammar and writing exercises are integrated into the curriculum to enhance your comprehension and your ability to compose a variety of texts.

Higher-Order Questioning
... to spark productive lingering

Each unit opens with two essential questions that relate to the topics, themes, and texts within that unit. You return to these questions throughout the unit and refine your answers as new evidence is presented. SpringBoard also encourages you to craft your own questions, and to dig deeply into the texts you read. After each reading passage, you evaluate the meaning of the text and examine the choices that the author made when writing it.

Academic Conversations
... to support peer-to-peer dialogue

SpringBoard classrooms are places where students like you engage in collaborative learning. You will participate in discussion groups, writing groups, debates, Socratic seminars, literature circles, and oral interpretations and performances. These activities create an environment where you can share, compare, critique, debate, and build on others' ideas to advance your learning.

PSAT/SAT Connections

We want you to be rewarded for the hard work you do in your English Language Arts courses, including when you sit down to take important assessments. Therefore, SpringBoard English Language Arts focuses on the same essential knowledge and skills that are the center of the Evidence-Based Reading and Writing sections of the SAT Suite of Assessments (SAT, PSAT/NMSQT, PSAT™ 10, and PSAT™ 8/9). To make our alignment transparent, we conducted a research study, the results of which showed strong to exemplary alignment between the SpringBoard ELA courses and the corresponding SAT Suite tests. This means that you are getting ready for the SAT, PSAT/NMSQT, PSAT™ 10, and PSAT™ 8/9 in the classroom every day.

Tools and Supports

SpringBoard Digital

SpringBoard puts you in charge of what you learn and gives students and teachers the flexibility and support they need. SpringBoard Digital is an interactive program that provides always-available online content that's accessible from any device—desktop computer, laptop, tablet, or interactive whiteboard. The student edition allows you to interact with the text, respond to prompts, take assessments, and engage with a suite of tools, all in the digital space. Teachers get access to a correlations viewer that embeds correlations at point of use, a lesson planner, progress reports, grading, messaging, and more.

Zinc Reading Labs

All SpringBoard users have access to Zinc Reading Labs, where you can find a huge library of reading material chosen specifically to align with the SpringBoard English Language Arts curriculum.

Zinc offers:

- Fresh and engaging nonfiction and fiction content for independent reading.
- Interactive games, quizzes, and tasks that build skills and confidence.
- Freedom of choice: Zinc's massive and ever-growing library means that all students should find texts they want to read.

Turnitin Revision Assistant

When you develop drafts of an available Embedded Assessment through SpringBoard Digital, you can use a tool called Turnitin Revision Assistant. This online tool gives instant feedback to students as they write so they can polish their drafts and practice their revision skills. The feedback model Revision Assistant uses is based on scoring by SpringBoard teachers, and it's trained to assess the same rubric areas that they assess.

Revision Assistant offers:

- A template to help you create an outline.
- Actionable, instant feedback in specific areas such as structure, use of language, and ideas.
- Identification of strengths and weakness in your writing.

A Letter to the Student

Dear Student,

Welcome to the SpringBoard program! We created this program with you in mind: it puts you and your classmates at the center of your learning and equips you with the skills and knowledge you need to excel in high school, and beyond.

The energy and excitement you bring to class helps you and your classmates learn. You will explore compelling themes through readings, classroom discussions, and projects. You will dive into fascinating texts—some of which you'll choose on your own—from different genres including myths, poems, biographies, plays, and films. You will engage in lively discussions, debates, and performances so that you become confident sharing and presenting your ideas. You will write frequently to sharpen your ability to craft effective sentences, paragraphs, and longer texts. And you'll start each unit with a clear understanding of where you're headed by unpacking the skills and knowledge you'll need to do well on the assessment at the end.

SpringBoard helps you make connections between the concepts you're reading and writing about in class and the real world. Instead of just memorizing how to do things, you'll draw on your own and your classmates' experiences and knowledge to come to new and deeper understandings. When questions arise from the materials you're studying in class, you'll learn how to do both quick and longer-term research to find answers. Plus, you'll have access to tools and resources that are built right into the program, including powerful learning strategies, independent reading lists to help you select texts to read outside of class, and digital tools that you can access any time from any device—desktop computer, laptop, or tablet.

We want students to be rewarded for the hard work they do in their English Language Arts course. That's why the SpringBoard program focuses on the essential knowledge and skills that will prepare you for the challenging work you'll do in your high school classes, in AP courses, and in college.

Students from around the country are talking about how much they like the SpringBoard approach to learning. We hope you enjoy learning with SpringBoard, too.

Sincerely,

The SpringBoard Team

VISUAL PROMPT
In stories and images, small details work together to create meaning, convey the author or artist's message, and affect the audience. What small details do you notice in this painting?

TELLING DETAILS

In the living room the voice-clock sang, *Tick-tock, seven o'clock, time to get up, time to get up, seven o'clock!* as if it were afraid that nobody would. The morning house lay empty. The clock ticked on, repeating and repeating its sounds into the emptiness. ...

In the kitchen the breakfast stove gave a hissing sigh and ejected from its warm interior eight pieces of perfectly browned toast, eight eggs sunny side up, sixteen slices of bacon, two coffees, and two cool glasses of milk.

–from "There Will Come Soft Rains" by Ray Bradbury

ACTIVITY	CONTENTS	

My Independent Reading List

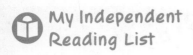

My Independent
Reading List

_____
_____
_____
_____
_____
_____
_____
_____
_____
_____
_____
_____
_____
_____
_____
_____
_____
_____
_____
_____
_____
_____
_____
_____
_____
_____
_____
_____
_____
_____
_____
_____
_____
_____
_____
_____
_____
_____
_____
_____
_____

Previewing the Unit

Learning Targets

- Preview the big ideas for the unit.
- Create a plan for reading independently.

Preview

In this activity, you will explore the big ideas and tasks of Unit 1 and make plans for your own independent reading.

About the Unit

With this unit's focus on telling details, you will be exploring how even the smallest detail can unlock the meaning of a short story. You will also learn about some of the devices authors use to create worlds and engage their readers, and you will use those devices to create your own short story.

Essential Questions

Based on your current thinking, how would you answer these questions?

1. How do telling details work together to convey meaning?

2. How are writing and reading connected?

3. What tools do authors use to create meaning and affect their readers?

🎲 Planning Independent Reading

The focus of this unit is telling details, and you will have the opportunity to look for telling details in a wide range of short stories in class. In your independent reading, you have the opportunity to read a longer story with telling details, a story either real (nonfiction) or imagined (fiction). By reading a longer work, you will experience how authors use telling details to create rich worlds over a sustained period. To help you choose the right book, use the following questions as a guide.

4. What have you enjoyed reading in the past? What is your favorite book or favorite type of book? Who is your favorite author?

5. When you select a potential book, preview it. What do you notice about the front cover design? What type of visual is shown? What types of fonts and colors are used? What information is on the back cover? Are there awards or blurbs that tell you about the book?

6. Read the first few pages. Are they interesting? How does the author try to hook you to keep reading? What can you tell about the characters and setting so far? Does the book seem too hard, too easy, or just right?

My Notes

Reading Discussion Groups

Participate in a book pass and group discussion with your classmates. Practice previewing each book by looking at the covers and reading the first few pages.

7. In your Reader/Writer Notebook, record each book's title and author, something from your previewing that stands out to you, and your rating of the book.

8. After previewing each book and thinking about the goals of this unit, do you want to continue reading the book you brought to the group or choose something else?

9. Create an Independent Reading Plan to help you set personal reading goals. Keep this plan in your Reader/Writer Notebook.

   I have chosen to read _____

   by (author) _____

   because (reason after previewing) _____

   _____.

   I will set aside time to read at (time, place) _____.

   I should finish this text by (date) _____.

10. Record your daily reading pace in your Independent Reading Log. Write a brief daily report in your log responding to what you have read. Include questions about what you have read.

11. Respond to the Independent Reading Links you encounter throughout the unit.

Whose Room Is This?

Making Inferences
Note-taking

Learning Targets

- Consider the telling details in a series of photographs and make inferences about the subjects.
- Adjust responses as new information surfaces.
- Integrate ideas from multiple images to build knowledge and vocabulary about a topic.

Preview

In this activity, you will analyze a series of similarly-framed photographs of rooms to observe the details they contain and connect your observations to an understanding of the people who inhabited the rooms.

My Notes

About the Photographer

Mitch Epstein (b. 1952) is an American fine-art photographer who helped pioneer and redefine color photography as an art form in the 1970s. Influenced by photographers Garry Winogrand and William Eggleston's use of color, his large-format images draw deep meaning from places and objects. Epstein does not use a digital camera to shoot his subjects. Instead, he uses film because he believes he gets superior tonal rendering and detail for his large prints. He has published ten books that are based on many of his photography projects and has worked as a director, cinematographer, and production designer on numerous films. Epstein's photographs are part of several major museum collections and have been exhibited around the world.

Directions: Closely observe the working environment and the details in the image and record your observations.

Photo 1: Mitch Epstein, 2016

KNOWLEDGE QUEST

Knowledge Question:

What do our working environments reveal about us?

In Activity 1.2, you will examine a series of photographs on the topic of working environments. While you view them and build knowledge about the topic, think about your answer to the Knowledge Question.

What details about this room and its contents reveal how this person works?

_____

_____

_____

What else might the objects in the room and on the walls reveal about the person who works here?

_____

_____

_____

Directions: Closely observe the working environment and the objects in the image and record your observations.

Photo 2: Mitch Epstein, 2016

What details about this room and its contents reveal how this person works?

_____

_____

_____

What else might the objects in the room and on the walls reveal about the person who works here?

_____

_____

_____

_____

Directions: Closely observe the working environment and the objects in the image and record your observations.

Photo 3: Mitch Epstein, 2016

What details about this room and its contents reveal how this person works?

_____

_____

_____

What else might the objects in the room and on the walls reveal about the person who works here?

_____

_____

_____

Directions: Closely observe the working environment and the objects in the image and record your observations.

Photo 4: Mitch Epstein, 2016

What details about this room and its contents reveal how this person works?

_____

_____

_____

What else might the objects in the room and on the walls reveal about the person who works here?

_____

_____

_____

Returning to the Images

- Return to the photographs as you respond to the following questions. Use evidence from the photographs to support your responses.
- Write any additional questions you have about the photographs in your Reader/Writer Notebook.

1. **KQ** The photographs show different people's working *environments*. What is the meaning of the word *environment* as it is used to describe the photographs?

_____

_____

_____

_____

2. The first and fourth photographs appear to have many similarities, but what differences in the details do you notice?

_____

_____

_____

_____

3. What is the effect of photographing the rooms without people? Why might the photographer make that choice?

_____

_____

_____

_____

4. **KQ** What central idea about working environments is the photographer trying to convey in this series of photographs? Use details from the photographs in your answer.

_____

_____

_____

_____

⊘ Knowledge Quest

Use your knowledge about working environments from viewing the four photographs and consider your own working environment. With a small group, discuss what our working environments reveal about us. Be sure to:

- Set rules with your classmates to facilitate a collegial discussion of the topic.
- Ask and respond to questions to broaden the discussion, connect ideas, and draw others into the conversation.
- Respond thoughtfully to the various perspectives that classmates offer and summarize points of agreement and disagreement.

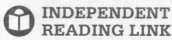

INDEPENDENT READING LINK

You can continue to build your knowledge about working environments by reading other articles at ZINC Reading Labs. Search for keywords such as *jobs* or *office*.

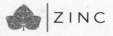

☑ Focus on the Sentence

Choose one of the photographs to reexamine. Do some research about the room's owner, and use that information to help you decide which of the room's details are particularly revealing about his or her identity. Write three or four sentences that connect those details to traits you learned about the room's owner.

You can use the following sentence frame to help you write each of your sentences:

The _____ is a detail that reveals _____ .

_____

_____

_____

_____

"Bread" and the Power of Imagination

Learning Strategies

Marking the Text
Note-taking

My Notes

Learning Targets

- Determine how an author's language choices contribute to the meaning of a work.
- Use sentence expansion to create robust sentences filled with relevant, specific details.

Preview

In this activity, you will read and analyze a short literary essay through discussion and writing detailed sentences.

As You Read

- Use the My Notes section to number and label each room or setting your mind visits.
- Circle unknown or multiple-meaning words or phrases and use context as a clue to determine their meanings. Check your inferred meanings in a print or digital dictionary.

About the Author

Margaret Atwood (b. 1939) is an award-winning Canadian author of more than forty books of fiction, poetry, and critical essays—including the best-selling dystopian novel *The Handmaid's Tale*. Atwood explores questions of morality in many of her novels and believes that cultural attitudes in novels are not usually invented by the novelist; they are reflections of something the novelist sees in the society around her. She is known for the specificity of details in her writing and relies on the particulars of actual places to create a space for her characters to inhabit. Atwood has said she can invent characters, but she cannot invent settings. In order to write about a place, she needs to have visited it.

Essay

Bread

by **Margaret Atwood**

1   Imagine a piece of bread. You don't have to imagine it, it's right here in the kitchen, on the breadboard, in its plastic bag, lying beside the bread knife. The bread knife is an old one you picked up at an auction; it has the word BREAD carved into the wooden handle. You open the bag, pull back the wrapper, cut yourself a slice. You put butter on it, then peanut butter, then honey, and you fold it over. Some of the honey runs out onto your fingers and you lick it off. It takes you about a minute to eat the bread. This bread happens to be brown, but there is also white bread, in the refrigerator, and a **heel** of rye you got last week, round as a full stomach then, now going moldy. Occasionally you make bread. You think of it as something relaxing to do with your hands.

2   Imagine a famine. Now imagine a piece of bread. Both of these things are real but you happen to be in the same room with only one of them. Put yourself into a different room, that's what the mind is for. You are now lying on a thin mattress in a hot room. The walls are made of dried earth, and your sister, who is younger than you, is in the room with you. She is starving, her belly is bloated, flies land on her eyes; you brush them off with your hand. You have a cloth too, filthy but damp, and you press it to her lips and forehead. The piece of bread is the bread you've been saving, for days it seems. You are as hungry as she is, but not yet as weak. How long does this take? When will someone come with more bread? You think of going out to see if you might find something that could be eaten, but outside the streets are infested with scavengers and the stink of corpses is everywhere.

Should you share the bread or give the whole piece to your sister? Should you eat the piece of bread yourself? After all, you have a better chance of living, you're stronger. How long does it take to decide?

heel: a crusty end piece of a loaf of bread

3　Imagine a prison. There is something you know that you have not yet told. Those in control of the prison know that you know. So do those not in control. If you tell, thirty or forty or a hundred of your friends, your comrades, will be caught and will die. If you refuse to tell, tonight will be like last night. They always choose the night. You don't think about the night however, but about the piece of bread they offered you. How long does it take? The piece of bread was brown and fresh and reminded you of sunlight falling across a wooden floor. It reminded you of a bowl, a yellow bowl that was once in your home. It held apples and pears; it stood on a table you can also remember. It's not the hunger or the pain that is killing you but the absence of the yellow bowl. If you could only hold the bowl in your hands, right here, you could withstand anything, you tell yourself. The bread they offered you is **subversive**, it's treacherous, it does not mean life.

4　There were once two sisters. One was rich and had no children, the other had five children and was a widow, so poor that she no longer had any food left. She went to her sister and asked her for a mouthful of bread. "My children are dying," she said. The rich sister said, "I do not have enough for myself," and drove her away from the door. Then the husband of the rich sister came home and wanted to cut himself a piece of bread, but when he made the first cut, out flowed red blood.

Everyone knew what that meant.

This is a traditional German fairy tale.

5　The loaf of bread I have conjured for you floats about a foot above your kitchen table. The table is normal, there are no trap doors in it. A blue tea towel floats beneath the bread, and there are no strings attaching the cloth to the bread or the bread to the ceiling or the table to the cloth, you've proved it by passing your hand above and below. You didn't touch the bread though. What stopped you? You don't want to know whether the bread is real or whether it's just a hallucination I've somehow **duped** you into seeing. There's no doubt that you can see the bread, you can even smell it, it smells like yeast, and it looks solid enough, solid as your own arm. But can you trust it? Can you eat it? You don't want to know, imagine that.

Making Observations
- How many rooms or settings do you notice?
- What details stand out to you?
- What questions does this text raise for you?

subversive: intended to weaken or destroy a political system, organization, or authority
duped: tricked

Working from the Text

1. Look back at the notes you took and identify the settings. How much bread is there in each setting?

Room/Setting	How Much Bread
Setting 1:	
Setting 2:	
Setting 3:	
Setting 4:	
Setting 5:	

2. Turn to a partner and discuss the following questions: How does the amount of bread in each setting affect the bread's value or importance? What other factors or circumstances change the value of the bread throughout the story?

☑ Focus on the Sentence

Follow your teacher's instructions and use sentence expansion to describe how the value of bread changes throughout the essay, paragraph by paragraph.

Paragraph 1

Kernel: It loses value.

What? The Bread

Where? in the Kitchen

Why? there's soo much of it that I I got Moldy

Expanded sentence:

In the Kitchen, the Bread Loses value Because you have so much of it that it got Moldy

Textual evidence to support the why:

".. and a heel of The Rye you got Last week, Round as full stomach Then, now going moldy."

Paragraph 2

Kernel: It gains value.

What? The Bread

Where? in The kitchen

Why? They Both need it To survive.

Expanded sentence:

in the kitchen The Bread gains value Because They Both need it To survive

Textual evidence to support the why:

should you Share The Bread or give it to your sister.?

Paragraph 3

Kernel: It gains value.

What? the Bread

Where? In Prison

Why? he was hungry.

Expanded sentence:

The Bread gains valu Becaus he was hungry.

Textual evidence to support the why:

Paragraph 4

Kernel: It gains value.

What?

Where?

Why?

Expanded sentence:

Textual evidence to support the why:

Paragraph 5

Kernel: It gains value.

What? -

Where? -

Why? -

- -

Expanded sentence:

_____

_____

Textual evidence to support the why:

_____

_____

Appreciating the Author's Craft

As directed by your teacher, discuss the following questions with your classmates.

- Why does Atwood use the verb *conjure* instead of *make* or *bake*?

- What if Atwood had chosen another food (such as ice cream) instead of bread as her subject? Why do you think she chose bread?

☑ Check Your Understanding

State your analysis of Atwood's craft in one sentence, using the following sentence frame.

Atwood selected "bread" as her title and subject because it represents _____ .

A Study in Characterization

Learning Strategies

Close Reading
Rereading
Skimming/Scanning
Summarizing

Learning Targets

- Analyze how a writer can develop characters through a narrator.
- Understand the ways in which language choices can be made to achieve intended effects.

Preview

In this activity, you will read a short story and analyze what the telling details reveal about one of the story's main characters.

My Notes

📝 Opening Writing Prompt

Read the first paragraph of "The First Day" and respond to the following question.

> Based on the details and language in the first paragraph, how do you know that this is not just another ordinary day in the narrator's life?

As You Read

- Use the story's details to create a mental image of the characters and setting.
- Circle unfamiliar words or phrases. Use context clues or a dictionary to determine their meanings.

About the Author

American novelist and short-story writer Edward P. Jones (b. 1950) is a writer of place—mainly segregated Washington, D.C.—where he grew up. His work depicts the effects of slavery in antebellum America and the lives of working-class African Americans. Most of his characters are fictional, but Jones believes it is important to place them in real houses and places, except for when he wrote the Pulitzer Prize-winning novel, *The Known World*, and created the fictional world of Manchester County, Virginia. Unlike many writers, Jones does not write a lot of things down when he creates a new piece; instead, he writes much of his work in his head. In addition to winning the Pulitzer Prize, for fiction, Jones received a MacArthur Fellowship in 2004.

Short Story

The First Day

by **Edward P. Jones**

1   On an otherwise unremarkable September morning, long before I learned to be ashamed of my mother, she takes my hand and we set off down New Jersey Avenue to begin my very first day of school. I am wearing a checkeredlike blue-and-green cotton dress, and scattered about these colors are bits of yellow and white and brown. My mother has uncharacteristically spent nearly an hour on my hair that morning, plaiting and replaiting so that now my scalp tingles. Whenever I turn my head quickly, my nose fills with the faint smell of Dixie Peach hair grease. The smell is somehow a soothing one now and I will reach for it time- and time again before the morning ends. All the **plaits**, each with a blue barrette near the tip and each twisted into an uncommon sturdiness, will last until I go to bed that night, something that has never happened before. My stomach is full of milk and oatmeal sweetened with brown sugar. Like everything else I have on, my pale green slip and underwear are new, the underwear having come three to a plastic package with a little girl on the front who appears to be dancing. Behind my ears, my mother, to stop my whining, has dabbed the stingiest bit of her gardenia perfume, the last present my father gave her before he disappeared into memory. Because I cannot smell it, I have only her word that the perfume is there. I am also wearing yellow socks trimmed with thin lines of black and white around the tops. My shoes are my greatest joy, black patent-leather miracles, and when one is nicked at the toe later that morning in class, my heart will break.

2   I am carrying a pencil, a pencil sharpener, and a small ten-cent tablet with a black-and-white speckled cover. My mother does not believe that a girl in kindergarten needs such things, so I am taking them only because of my insistent whining and because they are presents from our neighbors, Mary Keith and Blondelle Harris. Miss Mary and Miss Blondelle are watching my two younger sisters until my mother returns. The women are as precious to me as my mother and sisters. Out playing one day, I have overheard an older child, speaking to another child, call Miss Mary and Miss Blondelle a word that is brand new to me. This is my mother: When I say the word in fun to one of my sisters, my mother slaps me across the mouth and the word is lost for years and years.

3   All the way down New Jersey Avenue, the sidewalks are **teeming** with children. In my neighborhood, I have many friends, but I see none of them as my mother and I walk. We cross New York Avenue, we cross Pierce Street, and we cross L and K, and still I see no one who knows my name. At I Street, between New Jersey Avenue and Third Street, we enter Seaton Elementary School, a timeworn, sad-faced building across the street from my mother's church, Mt. Carmel Baptist.

plaits: braids
teeming: filling up and overflowing

My Notes

4 Just inside the front door, women out of the advertisements in *Ebony* are greeting other parents and children. The woman who greets us has pearls thick as jumbo marbles that come down almost to her navel, and she acts as if she had known me all my life, touching my shoulder, cupping her hand under my chin. She is enveloped in a perfume that I only know is not gardenia. When, in answer to her question, my mother tells her that we live at 1227 New Jersey Avenue, the woman first seems to be picturing in her head where we live. Then she shakes her head and says that we are at the wrong school, that we should be at Walker-Jones.

5 My mother shakes her head **vigorously**. "I want her to go here," my mother says. "If I'da wanted her someplace else, I'da took her there." The woman continues to act as if she has known me all my life, but she tells my mother that we live beyond the area that Seaton serves. My mother is not convinced and for several more minutes she questions the woman about why I cannot attend Seaton. For as many Sundays as I can remember, perhaps even Sundays when I was in her womb, my mother has pointed across I Street to Seaton as we come and go to Mt. Carmel. "You gonna go there and learn about the whole world." But one of the guardians of that place is saying no, and no again. I am learning this about my mother: The higher up on the scale of respectability a person is—and teachers are rather high up in her eyes—the less she is liable to let them push her around. But finally, I see in her eyes the closing gate, and she takes my hand and we leave the building. On the steps, she stops as people move past us on either side.

6 "Mama, I can't go to school?"

7 She says nothing at first, then takes my hand again and we are down the steps quickly and nearing New Jersey Avenue before I can blink. This is my mother: She says, "One monkey don't stop no show."

8 Walker-Jones is a larger, newer school and I immediately like it because of that. But it is not across the street from my mother's church, her rock, one of her connections to God, and I sense her doubts as she absently rubs her thumb over the back of her hand. We find our way to the crowded auditorium where gray metal chairs are set up in the middle of the room. Along the wall to the left are tables and other chairs. Every chair seems occupied by a child or adult. Somewhere in the room a child is crying, a cry that rises above the buzz-talk of so many people. Strewn about the floor are dozens and dozens of pieces of white paper, and people are walking over them without any thought of picking them up. And seeing this lack of concern, I am all of a sudden afraid.

9 "Is this where they register for school?" my mother asks a woman at one of the tables.

10 The woman looks up slowly as if she has heard this question once too often. She nods. She is tiny, almost as small as the girl standing beside her. The woman's hair is set in a mass of curlers and all of those curlers are made of paper money, here a dollar bill, there a five-dollar bill. The girl's hair is arrayed in curls, but some of them are beginning to droop and this makes me happy.

vigorously: forcefully

My Notes

11 On the table beside the woman's pocketbook is a large notebook, worthy of someone in high school, and looking at me looking at the notebook, the girl places her hand possessively on it. In her other hand she holds several pencils with thick crowns of additional erasers.

12 "These the forms you gotta use?" my mother asks the woman, picking up a few pieces of the paper from the table. "Is this what you have to fill out?"

13 The woman tells her yes, but that she need fill out only one.

14 "I see," my mother says, looking about the room. Then: "Would you help me with this form? That is, if you don't mind."

15 The woman asks my mother what she means.

16 "This form. Would you mind helpin' me fill it out?"

17 The woman still seems not to understand.

18 "I can't read it. I don't know how to read or write, and I'm askin you to help me." My mother looks at me, then looks away. I know almost all of her looks, but this one is brand new to me. "Would you help me, then?"

19 The woman says Why sure, and suddenly she appears happier, so much more satisfied with everything. She finishes the form for her daughter and my mother and I step aside to wait for her. We find two chairs nearby and sit. My mother is now diseased, according to the girl's eyes, and until the moment her mother takes her and the form to the front of the auditorium, the girl never stops looking at my mother. I stare back at her. "Don't stare," my mother says to me. "You know better than that."

20 Another woman out of the *Ebony* ads takes the woman's child away. Now, the woman says upon returning, let's see what we can do for you two.

21 My mother answers the questions the woman reads off the form. They start with my last name, and then on to the first and middle names. This is school, I think. This is going to school. My mother slowly enunciates each word of my name. This is my mother: As the questions go on, she takes from her pocketbook document after document, as if they will support my right to attend school, as if she has been saving them up for just this moment. Indeed, she takes out more papers than I have ever seen her do in other places: my birth certificate, my baptismal record, a doctor's letter concerning my bout with chicken pox, rent receipts, records of immunization, a letter about our public assistance payments, even her marriage license—every single paper that has anything even remotely to do with my five-year-old life. Few of the papers are needed here, but it does not matter and my mother continues to pull out the documents with the purposefulness of a magician pulling out a long string of scarves. She has learned that money is the beginning and end of everything in this world, and when the woman finishes, my mother offers her fifty cents, and the woman accepts it without hesitation. My mother and I are just about the last parent and child in the room.

pocketbook: purse

My Notes

22 My mother presents the form to a woman sitting in front of the stage, and the woman looks at it and writes something on a white card, which she gives to my mother. Before long, the woman who has taken the girl with the drooping curls appears from behind us, speaks to the sitting woman, and introduces herself to my mother and me. She's to be my teacher, she tells my mother. My mother stares.

23 We go into the hall, where my mother kneels down to me. Her lips are quivering. "I'll be back to pick you up at twelve o'clock. I don't want you to go nowhere. You just wait right here. And listen to every word she say." I touch her lips and press them together. It is an old, old game between us. She puts my hand down at my side, which is not part of the game. She stands and looks a second at the teacher, then she turns and walks away. I see where she has **darned** one of her socks the night before. Her shoes make loud sounds in the hall. She passes through the doors and I can still hear the loud sounds of her shoes. And even when the teacher turns me toward the classrooms and I hear what must be the singing and talking of all the children in the world, I can still hear my mother's footsteps above it all.

Making Observations
- What telling details stand out to you?
- What are your initial observations about the mother?

darned: mended by hand

Working from the Text

1. Skim the story and underline all the instances when the narrator uses the words "this is my mother" to announce definitive moments that capture the essence of her mom. List the quotes in the following table and create a simple sentence for each quote by choosing an adjective to describe the narrator's mother.

"This Is My Mother" Quotes	Simple Sentences
	The narrator's mother is _____ .
	The narrator's mother is _____ .
	The narrator's mother is _____ .
	The narrator's mother is _____ .

2. Now use the following sentence frame to complete a sentence that includes the four adjectives you listed.

Based on the narrator's comments, she views her mother as _____ ,
_____ , _____ , *and* _____ .

3. Is there another side to the narrator's mother—when her actions show something about who she is on the inside—that these quotes and adjectives don't capture? Highlight the moments in the text, and list the quotes in the table. Then create a simple sentence for each quote, using an adjective to describe the narrator's mother.

Quotes	Simple Sentences
	The narrator's mother is _____ .
	The narrator's mother is _____ .
	The narrator's mother is _____ .
	The narrator's mother is _____ .

LANGUAGE & WRITER'S CRAFT:
Subordinating Conjunctions and Complex Sentences

Complex sentences join an independent clause and a dependent clause and show a particular kind of relationship. Beginning sentences with certain subordinating conjunctions (i.e., *although, even though, while*) will signal to readers that there will be contrasting or contradictory information coming up later in the sentence, which will appear after the comma.

Subordinating Conjunctions that Signal a Contrast

although	even though	whereas
though	even if	while

Example: *Even though the narrator is young, she is wise beyond her years.*

PRACTICE Read the following pairs of sentences and determine which subordinating conjunction could be used to combine each pair. Rewrite each pair as a single complex sentence.

The woman is stubborn. / The woman is loving.

The girl is turned away from a school. / Her mother persists.

☑ Check Your Understanding

Consider the contrasting traits you unearthed in the narrator's depiction of her mother in "The First Day." What subordinating conjunction could you use to signal that contrast? Write a sentence that captures two contradictory traits of the mother.

Appreciating the Author's Craft

Discuss the following questions with your classmates.

- How would the story be different if Jones had the sound of the mother's footsteps "fade into the distance"?

- Why does the narrator hear her mother's footsteps "above it all"?

Analyzing and Writing a Complex Sentence

Learning Strategies

Think-Pair-Share

Learning Targets

- Create complex sentences by combining clauses to show the relationships between ideas.
- Understand the ways in which language choices can be made to achieve intended effects.

Preview

In this activity, you will learn to recognize dependent and independent clauses and construct complex sentences.

Independent and Dependent Clauses

An independent clause has a subject and a predicate and can stand on its own as a sentence.

A dependent clause, also known as a subordinate clause, is a group of words that has a subject and a predicate but does not express a complete thought and cannot stand on its own as a sentence. It needs to be combined with an independent clause to make a sentence.

1. The following clauses come from the first sentence of "The First Day." Label each clause as independent or dependent. Then explain your reasoning.

    a. down New Jersey Avenue

    _____

    _____

    _____

    b. she takes my hand

    _____

    _____

    _____

    c. to begin my very first day of school

    _____

    _____

    _____

    d. long before I learned to be ashamed of my mother

    _____

    _____

    _____

My Notes

e. and we set off

_____

_____

_____

f. on an otherwise unremarkable September morning

_____

_____

_____

_____

2. With a partner, determine which question each clause answers: _Who does what? When? Where? Why?_

   a. down New Jersey Avenue

   _____

   b. she takes my hand

   _____

   c. to begin my very first day of school

   _____

   d. long before I learned to be ashamed of my mother

   _____

   e. and we set off

   _____

   f. on an otherwise unremarkable September morning

   _____

3. Now use the clauses from steps 1 and 2 to reconstruct the complex sentence from "The First Day." Be sure to include commas where necessary.

_____

_____

_____

_____

4. Notice that the clauses in the sentence from step 3 follow this pattern: When / Who Does What / Where / Why. Now write an original complex sentence following the same pattern and label each part of the sentence. The sentence can be based on an event in your own life or an event that happened to someone else.

_____

_____

_____

Assess and Reflect

Read the historical background about this well-known image and use the information you learn to complete the exercise that follows. Then use what you know about ordering clauses to expand the kernel sentence into an informative caption.

Historical Background

The United States had been fighting in World War II for four years as part of the Allied powers. The Allies had defeated Germany three months earlier, but Japan did not surrender until August 14, 1945. People all across America celebrated when they heard the news, including Alfred Eisenstaedt who took this photograph at New York's Times Square. To this day, this is one of the most famous pictures associated with the end of World War II.

Kernel: _____

When? _____

Where? _____

Why? _____

_____

Expanded sentence:

_____

_____

_____

Intention and Craft

Learning Targets

- Analyze how the setting of a short story influences its theme.
- Analyze how suspense is built over the course of a story.
- Consider details that show how characters change.

Preview

In this activity, you will read and analyze a short story through discussion and by writing a detailed sentence.

Opening Writing Prompt

Read "What Happened During the Ice Storm" and respond to the following question.

If you were to turn the title "What Happened During the Ice Storm" into a question, what would your answer be?

As You Read

- Underline descriptions that help you visualize the setting and better understand the characters.
- Circle unknown or multiple-meaning words or phrases and use context as a clue to determine their meanings. Check your inferred meanings in a print or digital dictionary.

About the Author

Jim Heynen (b. 1940) is an author of short fiction, as well as poetry, novels, and nonfiction. Some of Heynen's best-loved stories are about a group of farm boys, whose adventures were inspired by the author's own childhood spent in rural Iowa. Says Heynen, "Good stories from the imagination are waiting to be born from the good characters of our experience." Although his farm-boy stories are not autobiographical, they do contain details from his own life and the lives of people he knew.

In addition to being a prolific writer, Heynen is also a teacher. He has served on the faculty of St. Olaf College in Minnesota and Pacific Lutheran University, and he continues to give lectures and workshops on writing.

My Notes

Short Story

What Happened During the Ice Storm

by **Jim Heynen**

1   One winter there was a freezing rain. How beautiful! people said when things outside started to shine with ice. But the freezing rain kept coming. Tree branches glistened like glass. Then broke like glass. Ice thickened on the windows until everything outside blurred. Farmers moved their livestock into the barns, and most animals were safe. But not the pheasants. Their eyes froze shut.

2   Some farmers went ice-skating down the gravel roads with clubs to harvest the pheasants that sat helplessly in the roadside ditches. The boys went out into the freezing rain to find pheasants too. They saw dark spots along a fence. Pheasants, all right. Five or six of them. The boys slid their feet along slowly, trying not to break the ice that covered the snow. They slid up close to the pheasants. The pheasants pulled their heads down between their wings. They couldn't tell how easy it was to see them huddled there.

3   The boys stood still in the icy rain. Their breath came out in slow puffs of steam. The pheasants' breath came out in quick little white puffs. Some of them lifted their heads and turned them from side to side, but they were blindfolded with ice and didn't **flush**. The boys had not brought clubs, or sacks, or anything but themselves. They stood over the pheasants, turning their own heads, looking at each other, each expecting the other to do something. To pounce on a pheasant, or to yell Bang! Things around them were shining and dripping

flush: suddenly fly off

with icy rain. The barbed wire fence. The fence posts. The broken stems of grass. Even the grass seeds. The grass seeds looked like little yolks inside gelatin whites. And the pheasants looked like unborn birds glazed in egg white. Ice was hardening on the boys' caps and coats. Soon they would be covered with ice too.

4   Then one of the boys said, Shh. He was taking off his coat, the thin layer of ice splintering in flakes as he pulled his arms from the sleeves. But the inside of the coat was dry and warm. He covered two of the crouching pheasants with his coat, rounding the back of it over them like a shell. The other boys did the same. They covered all the helpless pheasants. The small gray hens and the larger brown cocks. Now the boys felt the rain soaking through their shirts and freezing. They ran across the slippery fields, unsure of their footing, the ice clinging to their skin as they made their way toward the warm blurry lights of the house.

Making Observations
- What are some details of the setting of this story?
- What happens in the story?

Returning to the Text

- Return to the text as you respond to the following questions. Use evidence from the text to support your responses.
- Write any additional questions you have about the short story in your Reader/Writer Notebook.

1. What are the effects of the freezing rain throughout the first paragraph?

_____

_____

_____

_____

2. Reread paragraph 2. Why do the farmers leave their houses? What sentence from the text supports your response? Why do the boys leave their houses?

_____

_____

_____

_____

3. Write two sentences from the text that support the inference that the boys' intentions toward the pheasants may differ from those of the farmers.

_____

_____

_____

_____

4. How are the beautiful and destructive results of the ice storm reflected in the actions of the farmers and the boys?

_____

_____

_____

_____

Working from the Text

5. Reread the first three paragraphs of the story and work with a partner to answer the following question: How does a sense of danger to the pheasants gradually build as the story unfolds? Discuss the cumulative impact of details expressed through the author's word choice on the the overall tone for the pheasants.

☑ Focus on the Sentence

Write multiple sentences that tell why readers might become more and more nervous about what will happen to the pheasants. You can use the following sentence frame to help you write each of your sentences:

The sense of danger to the pheasants gradually builds because of _____ .

_____

_____

_____

_____

After you have finished writing your sentences, combine them into one longer complex sentence. Use parallel structure in your longer sentence.

_____

_____

_____

_____

Appreciating the Author's Craft

Participate in a collaborative discussion of the following questions with your classmates.

- In paragraph 3, how does the author link the boys and the pheasants? In what ways do the boys begin to feel like the pheasants?

- How would the story's ending be different if the author removed "unsure of their footing" in the final sentence? Would you be more or less likely to think the boys will continue to behave empathetically, or sensitively, now that they've had this experience with the pheasants?

☑ Check Your Understanding

State your analysis of the author's craft by completing the following sentence frame:

Heynen shows how the boys developed empathy for the pheasants by _____ .

Telling Details of Transformation

Learning Targets

- Use telling details to make inferences about the emotional state of a story's main character.
- Analyze how a story's theme is developed through characterization.
- Discuss how specific word choices impact the meaning and tone of a text.

Preview

In this activity, you will read a short story and analyze how its complex main character develops over the course of the story.

My Notes

📝 Opening Writing Prompt

From the moment the bank clerk in "The Red Fox Fur Coat" spots the coat in the shop window, she is emotionally affected. Some of her emotions are directly stated, while others are indirectly expressed. Read the first paragraph of "The Red Fox Fur Coat" and use the My Notes section to list the directly-stated and inferred emotions the bank clerk experiences.

1. In the following chart, write the emotions that were indirectly stated in paragraph 1 of "The Red Fox Fur Coat." For each emotion you list in the chart, write the telling details that caused you to infer that the bank clerk was feeling it.

Emotion	Detail from the Text

As You Read

- Underline telling details about the main character.
- Circle unknown words and phrases. Try to determine the meaning of the words by using context clues, word parts, or a dictionary.

About the Author

Teolinda Gersão (b. 1940) is a Portuguese novelist and short story writer, as well as a former professor of German and comparative literature. Gersão has received a number of awards for her writing, including the Pen Club Prize for the Novel in 1981 and 1989 and the Portuguese Writer's Association Short-Story Prize in 2001. Among the themes Gersão likes to explore in her writing are those of metamorphosis and the struggle against societal conventions.

Short Story

The Red Fox Fur Coat

by **Teolinda Gersão**

1   On her way home one day, a humble bank clerk happened to see a red fox fur coat in a furrier's shop window. She stopped outside and felt a shiver of pleasure and desire run through her. For this was the coat she had always wanted. There wasn't another one like it, she thought, running her eyes over the other coats hanging from the metal rack or delicately draped over a **brocade** sofa. It was rare, unique; she had never seen such a color, golden, with a coppery sheen, and so bright it looked as if it were on fire. The shop was closed at the time, as she discovered when, giving in to the impulse to enter, she pushed at the door. She would come back tomorrow, as early as possible, in her lunch break, or during the morning; yes, she would find a pretext to slip out during the morning. That night she slept little and awoke feeling troubled and slightly feverish. She counted the minutes until the shop would open; her eyes wandered from the clock on the wall to her wristwatch and back, while she dealt with various customers. As soon as she could, she found an excuse to pop out and run to the shop, trembling to think that the coat might have been sold. It had not, she learned, been sold; she felt her breath return, her heartbeat ease, felt the blood drain from her face and resume its measured flow.

2   "It could have been made for you," said the saleswoman when the bank clerk put the coat on and looked at herself in the mirror. "It fits perfectly on the shoulders and at the waist, and the length is just right," she said, "and it really suits your skin tone. Not that I'm trying to pressure you into buying it," she added hurriedly, "obviously you're free to choose anything you like, but if you

---

brocade: fabric with a rich, raised design

don't mind my saying so, the coat really does look as if it had been made for you. Just for you," she said again, with the hint of a smile.

3   "How much is it?" the bank clerk asked, half turning round—thus setting the hem of the coat swinging—because she found it hard to take her eyes off her own image in the mirror.

4   She recoiled, stunned, when she heard the reply. It cost far more than she had thought, five times more than she could possibly afford.

5   "But we can spread out the payment if you like," said the saleswoman kindly.

6   She could always sacrifice her holidays, the bank clerk thought. Or divert some of the money intended for a car loan. She could use less heating, eat smaller meals. It would do her good, really, because she was beginning to put on a bit of weight.

7   "All right," she said, doing rapid calculations in her head. "I'll give you a deposit and start paying next week. But it's definitely mine now, isn't it?"

8   "Absolutely," said the saleswoman, attaching a "Sold" label to the coat. "You can take it away with you when you've paid the third installment."

9   She started visiting the shop at night, when it was closed and no one would see her, in order to gaze at the coat through the window, and each time it brought her more joy, each time it was brighter, more fiery, like red flames that did not burn, but were soft on her body, like a thick, ample, enfolding skin that moved when she moved …

10   It would be admired, as would she, people would turn to stare after her, but it was not this that provoked a secret smile; rather, she realized, it was an inner satisfaction, an obscure certainty, a sense of being in harmony with herself, that spilled over in all kinds of small ways. It was as if the rhythm of her breathing had changed, had grown calmer and deeper. She realized too, perhaps because she no longer felt tired, that she moved more quickly, that she could walk effortlessly now, at twice her usual speed. Her legs were agile, her feet nimble. Everything about her was lighter, quicker; her back, shoulders, and limbs all moved more easily.

11   It must be all the keep-fit I've been doing, she thought, because for some reason she had started taking regular exercise. For a few months now she had been spending two hours a week running at the track. But what she liked most was to go running in the forest, on the outskirts of the city, feeling the sand crunch beneath her feet, learning to place her feet on the ground in a different way—in direct, perfect, intimate contact with the earth. She was intensely aware of her body; she was more alive now, more alert. All her senses were keener too, she could hear, even from some distance away, infinitesimal sounds which, before, would have gone unnoticed: a lizard scurrying through the leaves, an invisible mouse making a twig crack, an acorn falling, a bird landing on a bush; she could sense atmospheric changes long before they happened: the wind turning, a rise in humidity, an increase in air pressure that would

culminate in rain. And another aspect of all the things to which she had now become sensitized was the discovery of smells, a whole world of smells; she could find paths and trails purely by smell; it was strange how she had never before noticed that everything has a smell: the earth, the bark of trees, plants, leaves, and that every animal can be distinguished by its own peculiar smell, a whole spectrum of smells that came to her on waves through the air, and which she could draw together or separate out, sniffing the wind, **imperceptibly** lifting her head. She suddenly became very interested in animals and found herself leafing through encyclopedias, looking at the pictures—the hedgehog's pale, soft, tender underbelly; the swift hare, of uncertain hue, leaping; she pored over the bodies of birds, fascinated, pondering the softness of the flesh behind their feathers; and a single word kept bobbing **insistently** about in her mind: predator.

12 She seemed to be hungrier too, she thought, as she put away her books and went into the kitchen, and this negative aspect to all the physical exercise displeased her greatly. She tried to find a way to avoid putting on weight and prowled, dissatisfied, past patisseries, never finding what she was looking for, because the smell of coffee was repellent to her and made her feel nauseous. No, she was hungry for other things, although she didn't quite know what, fruit perhaps; this might be an opportunity to lose a little weight. She bought a vast quantity of grapes and apples and ate them all in one day, but still she felt hungry, a hidden hunger that gnawed at her from inside and never stopped.

13 She was cheered by an unexpected invitation to a party, welcoming any diversion that would make her forget that absurd hunger. She reveled in getting dressed up and in painting her lips and nails scarlet. Her nails, she noticed, were very long, and even her hands seemed more sensitive, more elongated. Anyone she touched at the party that night would remain eternally in her power, she thought, smiling at herself in the mirror—a feline smile, it seemed to her. She narrowed her eyes and widened the smile, letting it spread over her face, which took on a pleasingly triangular shape that she further emphasized with make-up.

14 In the middle of the party, she noticed someone slicing up some meat, cooked very rare—roast beef, she thought, although these words had suddenly ceased to have any meaning. She reached out her hand and devoured a whole slice. Ah, she thought, the taste of almost raw meat, the action of sinking her teeth into it, of making the blood spurt, the taste of blood on her tongue, in her mouth, the innocence of devouring the whole slice, and she took another slice, already sensing that using her hand was now a pointless waste of time, that she should just pick it up directly with her mouth.

15 She burst out laughing and began to dance, waving her bloodstained hands in the air, feeling her own blood rise, as if some tempestuous inner force had been unleashed, a malign force that she could transmit to others, a plague or a curse, but this idea was nevertheless sweet, quiet, almost joyful, she felt, as she swayed, slightly drunk, listening to the echo of her own laughter.

imperceptibly: ever so slightly
insistently: in a manner that demands attention

16 She would spend the night obeying all these newly released forces and, in the morning, she would go and fetch the coat, because the day had come when it would be hers; it was part of her; she would know it even with her eyes closed, by touch alone, the soft, thick pelt burning her skin, cleaving to her, until she could no longer tell skin from skin …

17 "It could have been made for you," the saleswoman said again, as she removed it from the coat hanger.

18 The coat cleaving to her, until she could no longer tell skin from skin, as she could see in the mirror, as she turned the collar up around her head, her face disfigured, suddenly thinner, made up to look longer, her eyes narrow, restless, burning…

19 "Goodbye, then, and thanks," she said, rushing out of the shop, afraid that time was getting short and that people would stop in alarm to stare at her, because suddenly the impulse to go down on all fours and simply run was too strong, reincarnating her body, rediscovering her animal body; and as she fled, as she left the city behind her and simply fled, it took an almost superhuman effort to get into her car and drive to the edge of the forest, keeping tight control of her body, keeping tight control of her **tremulous** body for just one more minute, before that slam of the door, that first genuine leap on feet free at last, shaking her back and her tail, sniffing the air, the ground, the wind, and, with a howl of pleasure and joy, plunging off into the depths of the forest.

Making Observations

- What does the saleswoman observe about the bank clerk each time she tries on the red fox fur coat?
- The main character begins the story as a "humble bank clerk." What does she end the story as?

tremulous: trembling

Working from the Text

2. Think about how the bank clerk character develops over the course of the story. At what point do you know that the red fox fur coat is changing her physically, as well as emotionally?

_____

_____

_____

_____

3. In your Reader/Writer Notebook, write a short first-person narrative from the perspective of the bank clerk, describing her physical evolution throughout the course of the story. Report telling details about the change she is experiencing, almost as if you are reporting physical symptoms to a doctor.

4. Share the narrative you wrote in your Reader/Writer Notebook with a partner. Note and compare which physical changes each of you highlighted as telling details and discuss which parts of the text the details come from. Use the My Notes section to mark where you and your partner found each detail.

5. Work independently to answer the following questions.

a. In paragraph 11, the word *predator* keeps "bobbing insistently about" in the bank clerk's mind. Do you think this is because the bank clerk is truly a predator? Or, do you think the bank clerk is actually prey—a victim of some external force? Explain your answer.

_____

_____

_____

_____

b. How can telling details lead you to an answer about the clerk being a predator? What does the textual evidence most strongly suggest?

_____

_____

_____

_____

c. After the bank clerk claims her coat, her transformation into a fox is swift. What does the narrator say about how it feels to be inside the bank clerk's body?

_____

_____

_____

_____

d. In the About the Author section of this activity, you read that Gersão likes to write about characters who struggle against societal conventions. Do you think the bank clerk struggled to live within the norms of city life before she saw the red fox fur coat? What details from the story support your inference?

_____

_____

_____

_____

6. Share your ideas with your partner. Work together to capture each of your responses in complex sentences that begin with the subordinating conjunction *although*. Write one sentence for each of you.

_____

_____

_____

_____

Appreciating the Author's Craft

As directed by your teacher, discuss the following questions with your classmates.

- Why does Gersão use the word *reincarnating* instead of *transforming* in the last paragraph?

- How does Gersão plant seeds from the very beginning of the story to indicate that the bank clerk is destined to return to her "foxy" self?

- Revisit the Essential Question about telling details. What are some of the telling details that contribute to the meaning of the story?

My Notes

Learning Targets

- Use telling details to gain insights into the main character's emotional state.
- Analyze the text for different ways the author builds suspense.

Preview

In this activity, you will read the first half of a short story and find telling details that allow you to delve into the main character's mind.

Opening Writing Prompt

Read the first seven paragraphs of "Lamb to the Slaughter" and respond to the following question.

How has Mary set the stage for her husband's return from work, and what is her emotional state?

As You Read

- Highlight telling details that reveal Mary's emotions.
- Circle unknown words and phrases. Try to determine the meaning of the words by using context clues, word parts, or a dictionary.

About the Author

Roald Dahl (1916–1990) was a British novelist, short story writer, poet, and screenwriter. However, before all of this, he was a World War II fighter pilot—and it may be this experience that he had to thank for the start of his literary career. Surprisingly, he didn't always think of himself as a writer, and he may not have become one if C. S. Forester, a writer for the *Saturday Evening Post*, had not asked to interview him about his flying adventures during the war. Dahl found it difficult to order his thoughts for the interview and asked if he could send Forester some notes about what happened instead. Forester agreed—and then sent what Dahl wrote directly to the *Saturday Evening Post's* editors, who in turn sent Dahl $1,000 for the right to publish them as a story. Over the years following, Dahl became a prolific and well-paid writer. Although his best-known works include children's novels, such as *Matilda* and *Charlie and the Chocolate Factory*, Dahl also wrote darkly humorous stories for adults.

Short Story

Lamb to the Slaughter (Part 1)

by **Roald Dahl**

1 The room was warm and clean, the curtains drawn, the two table lamps alight—hers and the one by the empty chair opposite. On the sideboard behind her, two tall glasses, soda water, whisky. Fresh ice cubes in the Thermos bucket.

2 Mary Maloney was waiting for her husband to come home from work.

3 Now and again she would glance up at the clock, but without anxiety, merely to please herself with the thought that each minute gone by made it nearer the time when he could come. There was a slow smiling air about her, and about everything she did. The drop of the head as she bent over her sewing was curiously tranquil. Her skin—for this was her sixth month with child—had acquired a wonderful translucent quality, the mouth was soft, and the eyes, with their new placid look seemed larger, darker than before.

4 When the clock said ten minutes to five, she began to listen, and a few moments later, punctually as always, she heard the tires on the gravel outside, and the car door slamming, the footsteps passing the window, the key turning in the lock. She laid aside her sewing, stood up, and went forward to kiss him as he came in.

5 "Hallo, darling," she said.

6 "Hallo," he answered.

7 She took his coat and hung it in the closet. Then she walked over and made the drinks, a strongish one for him, a weak one for herself and soon she was back again in her chair with the sewing, and he in the other, opposite, holding the tall glass with both his hands, rocking it so the ice cubes tinkled against the side.

8 For her, this was always a blissful time of day. She knew he didn't want to speak much until the first drink was finished, and she, on her side, was content to sit quietly, enjoying his company after the long hours alone in the house. She loved to luxuriate in the presence of this man, and to feel—almost as a sunbather feels the sun—that warm male glow that came out of him to her when they were alone together. She loved him for the way he sat loosely in a chair, for the way he came in a door, or moved slowly across the room with long strides. She loved the intent, far look in his eyes when they rested on her, the funny shape of the mouth, and especially the way he remained silent about his tiredness, sitting still with himself until the whisky had taken some of it away.

9 "Tired, darling?"

10 "Yes," he said. "I'm tired." And as he spoke, he did an unusual thing. He lifted his glass and drained it in one swallow although there was still half of

it, at least half of it, left. She wasn't really watching him, but she knew what he had done because she heard the ice cubes falling back against the bottom of the empty glass when he lowered his arm. He paused a moment, leaning forward in the chair, then he got up and went slowly over to fetch himself another.

11 "I'll get it!" she cried, jumping up.

12 "Sit down," he said.

13 When he came back, she noticed that the new drink was dark amber with the quantity of whisky in it.

14 "Darling, shall I get your slippers?"

15 "No."

16 She watched him as he began to sip the dark yellow drink, and she could see little oily swirls in the liquid because it was so strong.

17 "I think it's a shame," she said, "that when a policeman gets to be as senior as you, they keep him walking about on his feet all day long."

18 He didn't answer, so she bent her head again and went on with her sewing; but each time he lifted the drink to his lips, she heard the ice cubes clinking against the side of the glass.

19 "Darling," she said. "Would you like me to get you some cheese? I haven't made any supper because it's Thursday."

20 "No," he said.

21 "If you're too tired to eat out," she went on, "it's still not too late. There's plenty of meat and stuff in the freezer, and you can have it right here and not even move out of the chair."

22 Her eyes waited on him for an answer, a smile, a little nod, but he made no sign.

23 "Anyway," she went on, "I'll get you some cheese and crackers first."

24 "I don't want it," he said.

25 She moved uneasily in her chair, the large eyes still watching his face. "But you must have supper. I can easily do it here. I'd like to do it. We can have lamb chops. Or pork. Anything you want. Everything's in the freezer."

26 "Forget it," he said.

27 "But, darling, you must eat! I'll fix it anyway, and then you can have it or not, as you like."

28 She stood up and placed her sewing on the table by the lamp.

29 "Sit down," he said. "Just for a minute, sit down."

30 It wasn't till then that she began to get frightened.

31 "Go on," he said. "Sit down."

32 She lowered herself back slowly into the chair, watching him all the time with those large, bewildered eyes. He had finished the second drink and was staring down into the glass, frowning.

33 "Listen," he said. "I've got something to tell you."

34 "What is it, darling? What's the matter?"

35 He had now become absolutely motionless, and he kept his head down so that the light from the lamp beside him fell across the upper part of his face, leaving the chin and mouth in shadow. She noticed there was a little muscle moving near the corner of his left eye.

36 "This is going to be a bit of a shock to you, I'm afraid," he said. "But I've thought about it a good deal and I've decided the only thing to do is tell you right away. I hope you won't blame me too much."

37 And he told her. It didn't take long, four or five minutes at most, and she sat very still through it all, watching him with a kind of dazed horror as he went further and further away from her with each word.

38 "So there it is," he added. "And I know it's kind of a bad time to be telling you, but there simply wasn't any other way. Of course I'll give you money and see you're looked after. But there needn't really be any fuss. I hope not anyway. It wouldn't be very good for my job."

Making Observations
- What telling details stand out to you?
- What are your initial observations about Mary and her husband?

Working from the Text

1. Reread paragraphs 8–38 and search for details showing that Mary has certain expectations for her Thursday evening.

2. With a partner, revisit paragraphs 8–38 and use the My Notes section to mark places in the text where Mary's husband goes "off script."

 Focus on the Sentence

Work with your partner to write a series of sentences about events that Mary did not expect to happen this particular evening. Use the following sentence frame:

Mary didn't expect her husband to _____ .

_____

_____

_____

_____

Gaining Perspectives

In the short story "Lamb to the Slaughter," Mary and her husband are having marital problems. Think about the effect of her husband's news on Mary's mental, emotional, physical, and social health. With a partner, role-play a conversation between Mary and a friend, where Mary shares the conversation she had with her husband. How would Mary describe the effects? How could her friend help? When you have finished, present the outcome of your discussion with another group.

Appreciating the Author's Craft

Discuss the following questions with your classmates, citing strong evidence from the text that supports your analysis of the text itself and the inferences you draw from the text.

- As Mary's husband passes along his news to Mary, what is stated in the story and what must be inferred?

- Why does Dahl choose to avoid directly stating Mary's husband's news within the dialogue?

- What do you think Mary's husband told her? What evidence supports your speculation?

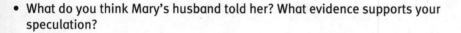

> **INDEPENDENT READING LINK**
>
> **Read and Discuss**
>
> What kind of information is stated and unstated in the text you are reading independently? Think about times you have had to make inferences while reading in order to fully understand what the author is writing about. In a small group, discuss different reasons authors may have for omitting information from a story or text. As you discuss, remember to listen actively to your peers and build on their ideas.

Learning Strategies

Marking the Text
Rereading

My Notes

Learning Targets

- Consider what telling details reveal about shifts in a main character's state of mind.
- Analyze a story's use of dramatic irony.
- Analyze how an author creates different effects for readers.

Preview

In this activity, you will read the second half of "Lamb to the Slaughter" and analyze how Dahl creates tension and humor in his writing.

As You Read

- Underline words and phrases that hint at Mary's state of mind.
- Circle unfamiliar words or phrases. Use context clues or a dictionary to determine their meanings.

Short Story

Lamb to the Slaughter (Part 2)

by **Roald Dahl**

39 Her first instinct was not to believe any of it, to reject it all. It occurred to her that perhaps he hadn't even spoken, that she herself had imagined the whole thing. Maybe, if she went about her business and acted as though she hadn't been listening, then later, when she sort of woke up again, she might find none of it had ever happened.

40 "I'll get the supper," she managed to whisper, and this time he didn't stop her.

41 When she walked across the room she couldn't feel her feet touching the floor. She couldn't feel anything at all—except a slight nausea and a desire to vomit. Everything was automatic now—down the steps to the cellar, the light switch, the deep freeze, the hand inside the cabinet taking hold of the first object it met. She lifted it out, and looked at it. It was wrapped in paper, so she took off the paper and looked at it again.

42 A leg of lamb.

43 All right then, they would have lamb for supper. She carried it upstairs, holding the thin bone-end of it with both her hands, and as she went through the living-room, she saw him standing over by the window with his back to her, and she stopped.

44 "For God's sake," he said, hearing her, but not turning around. "Don't make supper for me. I'm going out."

45 At that point, Mary Maloney simply walked up behind him and without any pause she swung the big frozen leg of lamb high in the air and brought it down as hard as she could on the back of his head.

46 She might just as well have hit him with a steel club.

47 She stepped back a pace, waiting, and the funny thing was that he remained standing there for at least four or five seconds, gently swaying. Then he crashed to the carpet.

48 The violence of the crash, the noise, the small table overturning, helped bring her out of the shock. She came out slowly, feeling cold and surprised, and she stood for a while blinking at the body, still holding the ridiculous piece of meat tight with both hands.

49 All right, she told herself. So I've killed him.

50 It was extraordinary, now, how clear her mind became all of a sudden. She began thinking very fast. As the wife of a detective, she knew quite well what the penalty would be. That was fine. It made no difference to her. In fact, it would be a relief. On the other hand, what about the child? What were the laws about murderers with unborn children? Did they kill them both—mother and child? Or did they wait until the tenth month? What did they do?

51 Mary Maloney didn't know. And she certainly wasn't prepared to take the chance.

52 She carried the meat into the kitchen, placed it in a pan, turned the oven on high, and shoved it inside. Then she washed her hands and ran upstairs to the bedroom. She sat down before the mirror, **tidied** her face, touched up her lips and face. She tried a smile. It came out rather peculiar. She tried again.

53 "Hallo, Sam," she said brightly, aloud.

54 The voice sounded peculiar too.

55 "I want some potatoes please, Sam. Yes, and I think a can of peas."

56 That was better. Both the smile and the voice were coming out better now. She rehearsed it several times more. Then she ran downstairs, took her coat, went out the back door, down the garden, into the street.

57 It wasn't six o'clock yet and the lights were still on in the grocery shop.

58 "Hallo, Sam," she said brightly, smiling at the man behind the counter.

59 "Why, good evening, Mrs Maloney. How're you?"

60 "I want some potatoes please, Sam. Yes, and I think a can of peas."

61 The man turned and reached up behind him on the shelf for the peas.

62 "Patrick's decided he's tired and doesn't want to eat out tonight," she told him. "We usually go out Thursdays, you know, and now he's caught me without any vegetables in the house."

63 "Then how about meat, Mrs Maloney?"

64 "No, I've got meat, thanks. I got a nice leg of lamb, from the freezer."

65 "Oh."

66 "I don't much like cooking it frozen, Sam, but I'm taking a chance on it this time. You think it'll be all right?"

tidied: cleaned, or made neat

67 "Personally," the grocer said, "I don't believe it makes any difference. You want these Idaho potatoes?"

68 "Oh yes, that'll be fine. Two of those."

69 "Anything else?" The grocer cocked his head on one side, looking at her pleasantly. "How about afterwards? What you going to give him for afterwards?"

70 "Well—what would you suggest, Sam?"

71 The man glanced around his shop. "How about a nice big slice of cheesecake? I know he likes that."

72 "Perfect," she said. "He loves it."

73 And when it was all wrapped and she had paid she put on her brightest smile and said, "Thank you, Sam. Good night."

74 "Good night, Mrs Maloney. And thank you."

75 And now, she told herself as she hurried back, all she was doing now, she was returning home to her husband and he was waiting for his supper; and she must cook it good, and make it as tasty as possible because the poor man was tired; and if, when she entered the house, she happened to find anything unusual, or tragic, or terrible, then naturally it would be a shock and she'd become frantic with grief and horror. Mind you, she wasn't expecting to find anything. She was just going home with the vegetables. Mrs Patrick Maloney going home with the vegetables on Thursday evening to cook supper for her husband.

76 That's the way, she told herself. Do everything right and natural. Keep things absolutely natural and there'll be no need for any acting at all.

77 Therefore, when she entered the kitchen by the back door, she was humming a little tune to herself and smiling.

78 "Patrick!" she called. "How are you, darling?"

79 She put the parcel down on the table and went through into the living-room; and when she saw him lying there on the floor with his legs doubled up and one arm twisted back underneath his body, it really was rather a shock. All the old love and longing for him welled up inside her, and she ran over to him, knelt down beside him, and began to cry her heart out. It was easy. No acting was necessary.

80 A few minutes later she got up and went to the phone. She knew the number of the police station, and when the man at the other end answered, she cried to him, "Quick! Come quick! Patrick's dead!"

81 "Who's speaking?"

82 "Mrs Maloney. Mrs Patrick Maloney."

83 "You mean Patrick Maloney's dead?"

84 "I think so," she sobbed. "He's lying on the floor and I think he's dead."

85 "Be right over," the man said.

86 The car came very quickly, and when she opened the front door, two policemen walked in. She knew them both—she knew nearly all the men at that precinct—and she fell right into Jack Noonan's arms, weeping hysterically. He put her gently into a chair, then went over to join the other one, who was called O'Malley, kneeling by the body.

87 "Is he dead?" she cried.

88 "I'm afraid he is. What happened?"

89 Briefly, she told her story about going out to the grocer and coming back to find him on the floor. While she was talking, crying and talking, Noonan discovered a small patch of congealed blood on the dead man's head. He showed it to O'Malley who got up at once and hurried to the phone.

90 Soon, other men began to come into the house. First a doctor, then two detectives, one of whom she knew by name. Later, a police photographer arrived and took pictures, and a man who knew about fingerprints. There was a great deal of whispering and muttering beside the corpse, and the detectives kept asking her a lot of questions. But they always treated her kindly. She told her story again, this time right from the beginning, when Patrick had come in, and she was sewing, and he was tired, so tired he hadn't wanted to go out for supper. She told how she'd put the meat in the oven—"it's there now, cooking"—and how she'd slipped out to the grocer for vegetables, and come back to find him lying on the floor.

91 "Which grocer?" one of the detectives asked.

92 She told him, and he turned and whispered something to the other detective who immediately went outside into the street.

93 In fifteen minutes he was back with a page of notes, and there was more whispering, and through her sobbing she heard a few of the whispered phrases—" ... acted quite normal ... very cheerful ... wanted to give him a good supper ... peas ... cheesecake ... impossible that she ... "

94 After a while, the photographer and the doctor departed and two other men came in and took the corpse away on a stretcher. Then the fingerprint man went away. The two detectives remained, and so did the two policemen. They were exceptionally nice to her, and Jack Noonan asked if she wouldn't rather go somewhere else, to her sister's house perhaps, or to his own wife who would take care of her and put her up for the night.

95 No, she said. She didn't feel she could move even a yard at the moment. Would they mind awfully if she stayed just where she was until she felt better? She didn't feel too good at the moment, she really didn't.

96 Then hadn't she better lie down on the bed? Jack Noonan asked.

97 No, she said. She'd like to stay right where she was, in this chair. A little later perhaps, when she felt better, she would move.

98 So they left her there while they went about their business, searching the house. Occasionally one of the detectives asked her another question. Sometimes Jack Noonan spoke to her gently as he passed by. Her husband, he

My Notes

Etymology

The word **spanner** is a British word for "wrench." It first appeared around 1790 and comes from the German word *spannen*, meaning "to stretch." Here the detectives are looking for a conventional weapon, which means they don't suspect the leg of lamb cooking in the oven.

premises: property; site
chink: opening

told her, had been killed by a blow on the back of the head administered with a heavy blunt instrument, almost certainly a large piece of metal. They were looking for the weapon. The murderer may have taken it with him, but on the other hand he may've thrown it away or hidden it somewhere on the **premises**.

99 "It's the old story," he said. "Get the weapon and you've got the man."

100 Later, one of the detectives came up and sat beside her. Did she know, he asked, of anything in the house that could've been used as the weapon? Would she mind having a look around to see if anything was missing—a very big spanner, for example, or a heavy metal vase.

101 They didn't have any heavy metal vases, she said.

102 "Or a big spanner?"

103 She didn't think they had a big spanner. But there might be some things like that in the garage.

104 The search went on. She knew that there were other policemen in the garden all around the house. She could hear their footsteps on the gravel outside, and sometimes she saw the flash of a torch through a **chink** in the curtains. It began to get late, nearly nine she noticed by the clock on the mantel. The four men searching the rooms seemed to be growing weary, a trifle exasperated.

105 "Jack," she said, the next time Sergeant Noonan went by. "Would you mind giving me a drink?"

106 "Sure I'll give you a drink. You mean this whisky?"

107 "Yes, please. But just a small one. It might make me feel better."

108 He handed her the glass.

109 "Why don't you have one yourself," she said. "You must be awfully tired. Please do. You've been very good to me."

110 "Well," he answered. "It's not strictly allowed, but I might take just a drop to keep me going."

111 One by one the others came in and were persuaded to take a little nip of whisky. They stood around rather awkwardly with the drinks in their hands, uncomfortable in her presence, trying to say consoling things to her. Sergeant Noonan wandered into the kitchen, came out quickly and said, "Look, Mrs Maloney. You know that oven of yours is still on, and the meat still inside."

112 "Oh dear me!" she cried. "So it is!"

113 "I better turn it off for you, hadn't I?"

114 "Will you do that, Jack? Thank you so much."

115 When the sergeant returned the second time, she looked at him with her large, dark, tearful eyes. "Jack Noonan," she said.

116 "Yes?"

117 "Would you do me a small favour—you and these others?"

118 "We can try, Mrs Maloney."

119 "Well," she said. "Here you all are, and good friends of dear Patrick's too, and helping to catch the man who killed him. You must be terribly hungry by now because it's long past your supper time, and I know Patrick would never forgive me, God bless his soul, if I allowed you to remain in his house without offering you decent hospitality. Why don't you eat up that lamb that's in the oven? It'll be cooked just right by now."

120 "Wouldn't dream of it," Sergeant Noonan said.

121 "Please," she begged. "Please eat it. Personally I couldn't touch a thing, certainly not what's been in the house when he was here. But it's all right for you. It'd be a favour to me if you'd eat it up. Then you can go on with your work again afterwards."

122 There was a good deal of hesitating among the four policemen, but they were clearly hungry, and in the end they were persuaded to go into the kitchen and help themselves. The woman stayed where she was, listening to them through the open door, and she could hear them speaking among themselves, their voices thick and sloppy because their mouths were full of meat.

123 "Have some more, Charlie?"

124 "No. Better not finish it."

125 "She wants us to finish it. She said so. Be doing her a favour."

126 "Okay then. Give me some more."

127 "That's the hell of a big club the guy must've used to hit poor Patrick," one of them was saying. "The doc says his skull was smashed all to pieces just like from a sledgehammer."

128 "That's why it ought to be easy to find."

129 "Exactly what I say."

130 "Whoever done it, they're not going to be carrying a thing like that around with them longer than they need."

131 One of them belched.

132 "Personally, I think it's right here on the premises."

133 "Probably right under our very noses. What you think, Jack?"

134 And in the other room, Mary Maloney began to giggle.

Making Observations

- In what ways does Mary surprise you in this part of the story? Why are you surprised?
- What assumptions do the police officers make about Patrick's murderer and the murder weapon?

My Notes

_____
_____
_____
_____
_____
_____
_____
_____

VOCABULARY

LITERARY

Dramatic irony is a literary device that authors use to create humor and tension in a story. Dramatic irony is when the audience (or reader) knows more about what is happening than at least one of the characters in the story.

_____
_____
_____
_____
_____
_____
_____
_____
_____
_____
_____
_____
_____
_____
_____
_____

Working from the Text

1. Do you think Mary stays in control throughout the story? If so, how? If not, where do you see her sense of control shift?

_____
_____
_____
_____

2. With a partner, reread the story to note instances where one character knows something that another character does not. Highlight specific words and phrases that indicate that a particular character is unaware of something another character is aware of. In the My Notes section, write what you would whisper to the characters who are unaware of certain information.

3. Now write a sentence to describe two moments of **dramatic irony** that you found in step 2. Use the words _although_, _while_, or _even though_ at the beginning of each sentence.

_____
_____
_____
_____

Appreciating the Author's Craft

Dahl chose to end the story with the final detail: "And in the other room, Mary Maloney began to giggle." Use your annotations to respond to the following prompt.

How would the story be different if Dahl had chosen to end with Mary crying instead of giggling? What is telling about the detail that she is giggling?

_____
_____
_____
_____
_____

☑ Check Your Understanding

State your analysis of Dahl's craft by writing one sentence, using the following sentence frame:

In "Lamb to the Slaughter," Dahl conveys _____ by/through _____ .

Writing a Literary Analysis Paragraph

My Notes

Learning Targets

- Develop and strengthen writing by planning and revising text in order to address what is most significant for a specific purpose.
- Write explanatory texts that analyze and communicate complex ideas clearly and accurately.

Preview

In this activity, you will plan, draft, and revise a literary analysis paragraph by creating complete sentences, adding transition words and phrases, and adding context for direct quotations.

Using a Single-Paragraph Outline

1. Use the following single-paragraph outline to plan a paragraph about how Roald Dahl conveys humor in "Lamb to the Slaughter."

T.S. _____

_____

_____

_____

1. _____

_____

2. _____

_____

3. _____

_____

4. _____

_____

C.S. _____

_____

_____

_____

Revising an Unelaborated Paragraph

2. Use what you have learned about effective sentences to **revise** the following paragraph. Add more specific details with quotations from the text and combine sentences, add sentence variety, and incorporate a variety of transitions to improve the flow. Write your revised paragraph on the lines provided.

In "Lamb to the Slaughter," Dahl conveys humor by transforming dinner to murder weapon and then back to dinner. Mary desperately wants to serve her husband dinner. "But, darling, you must eat!" Mary decides to serve dinner in a different way. She smashes the back of his head with a frozen leg of lamb. Mary serves the lamb again. The detectives are searching for the murder weapon. "Probably right under our very noses." It was funny in a shocking way when Mary used the frozen lamb as a murder weapon; it's even funnier when Dahl employs dramatic irony and has Mary serve the lamb again—as the detectives' dinner!

ACADEMIC

To **revise** is to rework or reorganize a piece of writing to improve its logic and flow. The term comes to English from the Latin root *revisere*, which means, "to look at again." Revising happens when you complete a piece of writing and then look at it again.

VOCABULARY

_____

_____

_____

_____

_____

_____

_____

_____

_____

_____

_____

_____

_____

_____

_____

_____

_____

_____

_____

_____

Assess and Reflect

As you did with the paragraph you revised earlier in this activity, use what you have learned about effective sentences and paragraphs and make revisions so that this simple, unelaborated paragraph becomes an effective, analytical paragraph.

In "Lamb to the Slaughter," Dahl conveys dramatic irony through Mary's dialogue with the detectives. Dramatic irony is when the reader knows something that at least one of the characters does not. Mary offers the detectives dinner. "It'd be a favour to me if you'd eat it up." Mary knows the lamb is the murder weapon. Dahl's readers know the lamb is the murder weapon. Detective Noonan doesn't know the lamb is the murder weapon. The detectives eat the lamb. "Probably right under our very noses."

_____
_____
_____
_____
_____
_____
_____
_____
_____
_____
_____
_____
_____
_____
_____
_____
_____
_____
_____
_____
_____
_____

Studying Words, Making Predictions

Learning Strategies

Predicting
Previewing

Learning Targets

- Use print and digital reference materials to clarify meanings of words.
- Analyze the connotations of words.
- Make predictions about the tone and content of a text based on its use of language.

Preview

In this activity, you will define and analyze a group of words to help you build knowledge about a topic and make predictions about a short story.

My Notes

Defining and Categorizing the Words

1. Work together with a group of your classmates to sort the following words into categories based on the words' meaning(s) and connotations. Consult print and digital resources, such as a dictionary, a thesaurus, and an encyclopedia, as you create categories. Then list the categories, including each word and its definition(s), in your Reader/Writer Notebook.

civilian	uncanny	sentinel	oscillation
vigorously	velocity	secessionist	soldier
Yanks	evade	ineffable	stunning
latter	current	northward	South
dignity	vortex	former	ludicrous
elude	dignitary	gray-clad	Federal army
interval	deference		

Making Predictions

2. Based on your work with the words, answer the following questions about the short story they come from.

- Do you predict the short story will be historical fiction or science fiction? Write your answer and tell which words support your response.

_____

_____

_____

_____

_____

- Do you predict the short story will include more adventure or romance? Write your answer and tell which words support your response.

_____

_____

_____

_____

_____

- Do you predict the tone of the short story will be solemn or humorous? Write your answer and tell which words support your response.

_____

_____

_____

_____

☑ Check Your Understanding

Make a prediction about the story based on what you've inferred from words that come from it. Use the following sentence frame to help you write your prediction:

I predict that the short story will be about _____ because _____ .

A Lesson in Perspective

Learning Targets

- Analyze the ways in which a narrator's perspective can shift.
- Use telling details to gain insights into the main character's traits and state of mind.

Preview

In this activity, you will read the first part of a short story and analyze how the author uses shifts in tone and perspective to create a desired effect.

Opening Writing Prompt

Read Part 1 of "An Occurrence at Owl Creek Bridge" and think of the narrator as being physically present in the setting.

- Where is the narrator positioned as he or she portrays the scene in each of the first seven paragraphs? Is the narrator moving around or staying in one place?
- What are your clues? Underline them or make annotations in the My Notes section next to each paragraph in Part 1.

About the Author

Ambrose Bierce (1842–1914) was a journalist, poet, novelist, and short story writer. He began his career in journalism as a teenager by working as an apprentice on a small abolitionist newspaper. Then he enlisted in the Union Army's 9th Indiana Infantry, in 1861, at the outset of the American Civil War. During his service as a soldier, he witnessed some of the Civil War's deadliest battles and nearly died himself, after sustaining a serious head injury.

Many of Bierce's short stories reflect the brutality of war and undermine romantic notions about its "glories." However, Bierce wrote about other topics as well, including politics and crime. After the American Civil War, he settled in San Francisco for a time and resumed his journalism career, becoming well known for his witty and sarcastic writing style. In addition to being famed as a short story writer, Bierce is also noted for his crime reporting, his scathingly critical articles about public figures, and his compilation of satirical word definitions entitled *The Devil's Dictionary*.

My Notes

Short Story

An Occurrence at Owl Creek Bridge (Part 1)

by **Ambrose Bierce**

1   A man stood upon a railroad bridge in northern Alabama, looking down into the swift water twenty feet below. The man's hands were behind his back, the wrists bound with a cord. A rope closely encircled his neck. It was attached to a stout cross-timber above his head and the slack fell to the level of his knees. Some loose boards laid upon the ties supporting the rails of the railway supplied a footing for him and his executioners—two private[1] soldiers of the Federal[2] army, directed by a sergeant[3] who in civil life may have been a deputy sheriff. At a short remove upon the same temporary platform was an officer in the uniform of his rank, armed. He was a captain.[4] A sentinel[5] at each end of the bridge stood with his rifle in the position known as "support," that is to say, vertical in front of the left shoulder, the hammer resting on the forearm thrown straight across the chest—a formal and unnatural position, enforcing an erect carriage of the body. It did not appear to be the duty of these two men to know what was occurring at the center of the bridge; they merely blockaded the two ends of the foot planking that traversed it.

2   Beyond one of the sentinels nobody was in sight; the railroad ran straight away into a forest for a hundred yards, then, curving, was lost to view. Doubtless there was an outpost farther along. The other bank of the stream was open ground—a gentle slope topped with a stockade of vertical tree trunks, loopholed for rifles, with a single embrasure[6] through which protruded the muzzle of a brass cannon commanding the bridge. Midway up the slope between the bridge and fort were the spectators—a single company of infantry in line, at "parade rest," the butts of their rifles on the ground, the barrels inclining slightly backward against the right shoulder, the hands crossed upon the stock. A lieutenant[7] stood at the right of the line, the point of his sword upon the ground, his left hand resting upon his right. Excepting the group of four at the center of the bridge, not a man moved. The company faced the bridge, staring stonily, motionless. The sentinels, facing the banks of the stream, might have been statues to adorn the bridge. The captain stood with folded arms, silent, observing the work of his **subordinates**, but making no

---

[1] A private is someone serving in the military at the lowest rank.

[2] Something described as "Federal" is related to a union's central government, as opposed to one of its local governments.

[3] A sergeant is someone in the military who serves in a position of authority. A sergeant is lower in rank than a captain.

[4] A captain is someone in the military who is in charge of carrying out certain tasks.

[5] A sentinel is a guard.

[6] An embrasure is an opening in a wall through which weapons are fired.

[7] A lieutenant is someone in the military who serves in a position of authority. A lieutenant is lower in rank than a captain and higher in rank than a sergeant.

subordinates: assistants to someone who is in a position of authority

sign. Death is a dignitary who when he comes announced is to be received with formal **manifestations** of respect, even by those most familiar with him. In the code of military etiquette silence and fixity are forms of deference.

3 The man who was engaged in being hanged was apparently about thirty-five years of age. He was a civilian, if one might judge from his habit, which was that of a planter. His features were good—a straight nose, firm mouth, broad forehead, from which his long, dark hair was combed straight back, falling behind his ears to the collar of his well fitting frock coat. He wore a moustache and pointed beard, but no whiskers; his eyes were large and dark gray, and had a kindly expression which one would hardly have expected in one whose neck was in the hemp. Evidently this was no vulgar assassin. The liberal military code makes provision for hanging many kinds of persons, and gentlemen are not excluded.

4 The preparations being complete, the two private soldiers stepped aside and each drew away the plank upon which he had been standing. The sergeant turned to the captain, saluted and placed himself immediately behind that officer, who in turn moved apart one pace. These movements left the condemned man and the sergeant standing on the two ends of the same plank, which spanned three of the cross-ties of the bridge. The end upon which the civilian stood almost, but not quite, reached a fourth. This plank had been held in place by the weight of the captain; it was now held by that of the sergeant. At a signal from the former the latter would step aside, the plank would tilt and the condemned man go down between two ties. The arrangement commended itself to his judgement as simple and effective. His face had not been covered nor his eyes bandaged. He looked a moment at his "unsteadfast footing," then let his gaze wander to the swirling water of the stream racing madly beneath his feet. A piece of dancing driftwood caught his attention and his eyes followed it down the current. How slowly it appeared to move! What a sluggish stream!

My Notes

manifestations: public displays

5   He closed his eyes in order to fix his last thoughts upon his wife and children. The water, touched to gold by the early sun, the brooding mists under the banks at some distance down the stream, the fort, the soldiers, the piece of drift—all had distracted him. And now he became conscious of a new disturbance. Striking through the thought of his dear ones was sound which he could neither ignore nor understand, a sharp, distinct, metallic percussion like the stroke of a blacksmith's hammer upon the anvil; it had the same ringing quality. He wondered what it was, and whether immeasurably distant or near by—it seemed both. Its recurrence was regular, but as slow as the tolling of a death knell. He awaited each new stroke with impatience and—he knew not why—apprehension. The intervals of silence grew progressively longer; the delays became maddening. With their greater infrequency the sounds increased in strength and sharpness. They hurt his ear like the thrust of a knife; he feared he would shriek. What he heard was the ticking of his watch.

6   He unclosed his eyes and saw again the water below him. "If I could free my hands," he thought, "I might throw off the noose and spring into the stream. By diving I could evade the bullets and, swimming vigorously, reach the bank, take to the woods and get away home. My home, thank God, is as yet outside their lines; my wife and little ones are still beyond the invader's farthest advance."

7   As these thoughts, which have here to be set down in words, were flashed into the doomed man's brain rather than evolved from it the captain nodded to the sergeant. The sergeant stepped aside.

Making Observations
- What is about to happen to the man who stands upon the railroad bridge?
- What do you know about the man, so far?

Returning to the Text

- Return to the text as you respond to the following questions. Use evidence from the text to support your responses.
- Write any additional questions you have about the short story in your Reader/Writer Notebook.

1. From what he has seen, what does the man think of the mechanism by which he'll be hanged?

_____

_____

_____

_____

2. In paragraph 4, how does the narrator describe the stream? What does the man think about the stream? What does this tell you about the man's state of mind?

_____

_____

_____

_____

3. In paragraph 5, what specific things does the man remember about the river's water and banks as he closes his eyes, and why do you think he notices these things?

_____

_____

_____

_____

4. In paragraph 6, how do the man's surroundings inspire a plan for his survival?

_____

_____

_____

_____

Appreciating the Author's Craft

Before joining a group discussion, respond to the first question in one sentence. Start your sentence with the word *if*.

- How would the story be different if the man were blindfolded?

- How does the shift to the gaze upon the water affect the overall tone of the story in Part 1?

☑ Check Your Understanding

Think about the prediction you made in Activity 1.11. Then use the following paragraph frame to revise your prediction, as needed, to reflect what you have learned so far about the main character of "An Occurrence at Owl Creek Bridge."

I predicted that the short story would be about _____ because _____ .
Based on what I've learned about the main character of this story, I now think _____ because _____ .

Filling in Farquhar's Backstory

Learning Strategies

Predicting
Rereading

Learning Targets

- Consider telling details that give insights into the main character of a story.
- Analyze how the author's use of flashback creates tension.

Preview

In this activity, you will continue to read, discuss, and write about "An Occurrence at Owl Creek Bridge."

My Notes

✍ Opening Writing Prompt

Read Part 2 of "An Occurrence at Owl Creek Bridge." Use the words you sorted during Activity 1.11 to answer the following question:

How is Peyton Farquhar tricked? How do you know?

Words: secessionist, South, civilian, soldier, gray-clad, Yanks, northward, Federal scout

As You Read

- Underline telling details that help you better understand the character of Peyton Farquhar.
- Circle unknown words and phrases. Try to determine the meaning of the words by using context clues, word parts, or a dictionary.

My Notes

_____
_____
_____
_____
_____
_____
_____
_____
_____
_____
_____
_____
_____
_____
_____
_____
_____
_____
_____
_____
_____
_____
_____

Short Story

An Occurrence at Owl Creek Bridge (Part 2)

by **Ambrose Bierce**

8   Peyton Farquhar was a well to do planter, of an old and highly respected Alabama family. Being a slave owner and like other slave owners a politician, he was naturally an original **secessionist** and ardently devoted to the Southern cause. Circumstances of an imperious nature, which it is unnecessary to relate here, had prevented him from taking service with that gallant army which had fought the disastrous **campaigns** ending with the fall of Corinth, and he chafed under the **inglorious restraint**, longing for the release of his energies, the larger life of the soldier, the opportunity for distinction. That opportunity, he felt, would come, as it comes to all in wartime. Meanwhile he did what he could. No service was too humble for him to perform in the aid of the South, no adventure too perilous for him to undertake if consistent with the character of a civilian who was at heart a soldier, and who in good faith and without too much qualification **assented** to at least a part of the frankly villainous **dictum** that all is fair in love and war.

9   One evening while Farquhar and his wife were sitting on a rustic bench near the entrance to his grounds, a gray-clad soldier rode up to the gate and asked for a drink of water. Mrs. Farquhar was only too happy to serve him with her own white hands. While she was fetching the water her husband approached the dusty horseman and inquired eagerly for news from the front.

10   "The Yanks are repairing the railroads," said the man, "and are getting ready for another advance. They have reached the Owl Creek bridge, put it in order and built a stockade on the north bank. The **commandant** has issued an order, which is posted everywhere, declaring that any civilian caught interfering with the railroad, its bridges, tunnels, or trains will be summarily hanged. I saw the order."

11   "How far is it to the Owl Creek bridge?" Farquhar asked.

12   "About thirty miles."

13   "Is there no force on this side of the creek?"

14   "Only a picket post half a mile out, on the railroad, and a single sentinel at this end of the bridge."

15   "Suppose a man—a civilian and student of hanging—should elude the picket post and perhaps get the better of the sentinel," said Farquhar, smiling, "what could he accomplish?"

16   The soldier reflected. "I was there a month ago," he replied. "I observed that the flood of last winter had lodged a great quantity of driftwood against

secessionist: someone in favor of seceding, or breaking away from the union; a Confederate

campaigns: planned military activities that have a specific goal

inglorious: not bringing glory

restraint: a rule that limits one's freedom to make a decision for himself or herself

assented: agreed

dictum: an opinion held by someone who is considered to be an expert

commandant: an officer in command of a military unit

the wooden pier at this end of the bridge. It is now dry and would burn like tinder."

17 The lady had now brought the water, which the soldier drank. He thanked her ceremoniously, bowed to her husband and rode away. An hour later, after nightfall, he repassed the plantation, going northward in the direction from which he had come. He was a Federal scout.

Making Observations

- What telling details about Farquhar's character stand out to you?
- How does Farquhar serve the "Southern cause"?
- Who is the gray-clad soldier?

scout: a person who watches for something to happen

Returning to the Text

- Return to the text as you respond to the following questions. Use evidence from the text to support your responses.
- Write any additional questions you have about the short story in your Reader/Writer Notebook.

1. What do you learn about Farquhar's character in Part 2?

_____

_____

_____

_____

2. What information does the Federal scout share with Farquhar?

_____

_____

_____

_____

3. Why does the Federal scout share inside information with Farquhar about what the Union soldiers are doing? Is the information he shares truthful?

_____

_____

_____

_____

Appreciating the Author's Craft

Discuss the following questions with your classmates.

- In linear plot development, the events of a story happen in chronological order. In non-linear plot development, events happen out of order. For example, plots that include a flashback interrupt the sequence of a story by telling about an event that happened before the story began. How is Part 2 of "An Occurrence at Owl Creek Bridge" an example of a flashback?

- How might Bierce's story be different if he had begun it with the scene in Part 2?

- Why do you think Bierce chose to use non-linear plot development in this story?

INDEPENDENT READING LINK

Read and Respond

Think about the structure of the text you are reading independently, whether it is fiction or nonfiction. Do events and facts unfold in a linear or non-linear way? Write a paragraph that tells the structure of the text you are reading and explains why the author chose to order it in this way. Remember to cite strong and thorough text evidence to support your response.

☑ Check Your Understanding

Think about the prediction you made in Activity 1.11. Then use the following sentence frame to revise your prediction to reflect what you have learned so far in "An Occurrence at Owl Creek Bridge."

I predicted that the short story would be about _____ , but _____ .

Bierce and the Language of Sensation

My Notes

Learning Targets

- Identify sensory details that give insights into the main character's state of mind.
- Analyze how different language choices can shift the tone of a text.
- Confirm or correct predictions made at the beginning of reading.

Preview

In this activity, you will read the ending of "An Occurrence at Owl Creek Bridge" and discuss the story's themes.

As You Read

- Underline text that describes what Farquhar sees, feels, and hears.
- Circle unknown words and phrases. Try to determine the meaning of the words by using context clues, word parts, or a dictionary.

Short Story

An Occurrence at Owl Creek Bridge (Part 3)

by **Ambrose Bierce**

18   As Peyton Farquhar fell straight downward through the bridge he lost consciousness and was as one already dead. From this state he was awakened—ages later, it seemed to him—by the pain of a sharp pressure upon his throat, followed by a sense of suffocation. Keen, poignant agonies seemed to shoot from his neck downward through every fiber of his body and limbs. These pains appeared to flash along well defined lines of **ramification** and to beat with an inconceivably rapid **periodicity**. They seemed like streams of pulsating fire heating him to an intolerable temperature. As to his head, he was conscious of nothing but a feeling of fullness—of congestion. These sensations were unaccompanied by thought. The intellectual part of his nature was already **effaced**; he had power only to feel, and feeling was torment. He was conscious of motion. **Encompassed** in a luminous cloud, of which he was now merely the fiery heart, without material substance, he swung through unthinkable arcs of **oscillation**, like a vast pendulum. Then all at once, with terrible suddenness, the light about him shot upward with the noise of a loud splash; a frightful roaring was in his ears, and all was cold and dark. The power of thought was **restored**; he knew that the rope had broken and he had fallen into the stream. There was no additional strangulation; the noose about his neck was already suffocating him and kept the water from his lungs. To die of hanging at the bottom of a river!—the idea seemed to him ludicrous. He opened his eyes

ramification: branching out
periodicity: happening again and again, at intervals
effaced: erased
encompassed: surrounded
oscillation: going from one extreme to another again and again
restored: brought back to its original condition

in the darkness and saw above him a gleam of light, but how distant, how **inaccessible**! He was still sinking, for the light became fainter and fainter until it was a mere glimmer. Then it began to grow and brighten, and he knew that he was rising toward the surface—knew it with reluctance, for he was now very comfortable. "To be hanged and drowned," he thought, "that is not so bad; but I do not wish to be shot. No; I will not be shot; that is not fair."

19 He was not conscious of an effort, but a sharp pain in his wrist apprised him that he was trying to free his hands. He gave the struggle his attention, as an idler might observe the feat of a juggler, without interest in the outcome. What splendid effort!—what magnificent, what superhuman strength! Ah, that was a fine endeavor! Bravo! The cord fell away; his arms parted and floated upward, the hands dimly seen on each side in the growing light. He watched them with a new interest as first one and then the other pounced upon the noose at his neck. They tore it away and thrust it fiercely aside, its undulations resembling those of a water snake. "Put it back, put it back!" He thought he shouted these words to his hands, for the undoing of the noose had been succeeded by the direst pang that he had yet experienced. His neck ached horribly; his brain was on fire, his heart, which had been fluttering faintly, gave a great leap, trying to force itself out at his mouth. His whole body was racked and wrenched with an insupportable anguish! But his disobedient hands gave no heed to the command. They beat the water vigorously with quick, downward strokes, forcing him to the surface. He felt his head emerge; his eyes were blinded by the sunlight; his chest expanded convulsively, and with a supreme and crowning agony his lungs engulfed a great draught of air, which instantly he expelled in a shriek!

20 He was now in full possession of his physical senses. They were, indeed, **preternaturally** keen and alert. Something in the awful disturbance of his organic system had so exalted and refined them that they made record of things never before **perceived**. He felt the ripples upon his face and heard their separate sounds as they struck. He looked at the forest on the bank of the stream, saw the individual trees, the leaves and the veining of each leaf—he saw the very insects upon them: the locusts, the brilliant bodied flies, the gray spiders stretching their webs from twig to twig. He noted the prismatic colors in all the dewdrops upon a million blades of grass. The humming of the gnats that danced above the eddies of the stream, the beating of the dragon flies' wings, the strokes of the water spiders' legs, like oars which had lifted their boat—all these made audible music. A fish slid along beneath his eyes and he heard the rush of its body parting the water.

21 He had come to the surface facing down the stream; in a moment the visible world seemed to wheel slowly round, himself the pivotal point, and he saw the bridge, the fort, the soldiers upon the bridge, the captain, the sergeant, the two privates, his executioners. They were in silhouette against the blue sky. They shouted and gesticulated, pointing at him. The captain had drawn his pistol, but did not fire; the others were unarmed. Their movements were grotesque and horrible, their forms gigantic.

inaccessible: not able to be reached, entered, or obtained
preternaturally: in a supernatural way
perceived: sensed or detected

My Notes

22 Suddenly he heard a sharp **report** and something struck the water smartly within a few inches of his head, spattering his face with spray. He heard a second report, and saw one of the sentinels with his rifle at his shoulder, a light cloud of blue smoke rising from the muzzle. The man in the water saw the eye of the man on the bridge gazing into his own through the sights of the rifle. He observed that it was a gray eye and remembered having read that gray eyes were keenest, and that all famous marksmen had them. Nevertheless, this one had missed.

23 A counter-swirl had caught Farquhar and turned him half round; he was again looking at the forest on the bank opposite the fort. The sound of a clear, high voice in a monotonous singsong now rang out behind him and came across the water with a distinctness that pierced and subdued all other sounds, even the beating of the ripples in his ears. Although no soldier, he had frequented camps enough to know the dread significance of that deliberate, drawling, aspirated chant; the lieutenant on shore was taking a part in the morning's work. How coldly and pitilessly—with what an even, calm intonation, presaging, and enforcing tranquility in the men—with what accurately measured interval fell those cruel words:

24 "Company!…Attention!…Shoulder arms!…Ready!…Aim!…Fire!"

25 Farquhar dived—dived as deeply as he could. The water roared in his ears like the voice of Niagara, yet he heard the dull thunder of the volley and, rising again toward the surface, met shining bits of metal, singularly flattened, oscillating slowly downward. Some of them touched him on the face and hands, then fell away, continuing their descent. One lodged between his collar and neck; it was uncomfortably warm and he snatched it out.

26 As he rose to the surface, gasping for breath, he saw that he had been a long time under water; he was **perceptibly** farther downstream—nearer to safety. The soldiers had almost finished reloading; the metal ramrods flashed all at once in the sunshine as they were drawn from the barrels, turned in the air, and thrust into their sockets. The two sentinels fired again, independently and ineffectually.

27 The hunted man saw all this over his shoulder; he was now swimming vigorously with the current. His brain was as energetic as his arms and legs; he thought with the rapidity of lightning:

28 "The officer," he reasoned, "will not make that **martinet's** error a second time. It is as easy to dodge a volley as a single shot. He has probably already given the command to fire at will. God help me, I cannot dodge them all!"

29 An appalling splash within two yards of him was followed by a loud, rushing sound, DIMINUENDO, which seemed to travel back through the air to the fort and died in an explosion which stirred the very river to its deeps! A rising sheet of water curved over him, fell down upon him, blinded him, strangled him! The cannon had taken a hand in the game. As he shook his head free from the commotion of the smitten water he heard the deflected

report: a sharp explosive noise
perceptibly: noticeably
martinet: someone who follows rules exactly
diminuendo: gradual decrease in loudness

shot humming through the air ahead, and in an instant it was cracking and smashing the branches in the forest beyond.

30   "They will not do that again," he thought; "the next time they will use a charge of grape. I must keep my eye upon the gun; the smoke will apprise me—the report arrives too late; it lags behind the missile. That is a good gun."

31   Suddenly he felt himself whirled round and round—spinning like a top. The water, the banks, the forests, the now distant bridge, fort and men, all were commingled and blurred. Objects were represented by their colors only; circular horizontal streaks of color—that was all he saw. He had been caught in a vortex and was being whirled on with a velocity of advance and gyration that made him giddy and sick. In few moments he was flung upon the gravel at the foot of the left bank of the stream—the southern bank—and behind a projecting point which concealed him from his enemies. The sudden arrest of his motion, the abrasion of one of his hands on the gravel, restored him, and he wept with delight. He dug his fingers into the sand, threw it over himself in handfuls and audibly blessed it. It looked like diamonds, rubies, emeralds; he could think of nothing beautiful which it did not resemble. The trees upon the bank were giant garden plants; he noted a definite order in their arrangement, inhaled the fragrance of their blooms. A strange roseate light shone through the spaces among their trunks and the wind made in their branches the music of **Aeolian harps**. He had not wish to perfect his escape—he was content to remain in that enchanting spot until retaken.

32   A whiz and a rattle of grapeshot among the branches high above his head roused him from his dream. The baffled cannoneer had fired him a random farewell. He sprang to his feet, rushed up the sloping bank, and plunged into the forest.

33   All that day he traveled, laying his course by the rounding sun. The forest seemed interminable; nowhere did he discover a break in it, not even a woodman's road. He had not known that he lived in so wild a region. There was something uncanny in the revelation.

34   By nightfall he was fatigued, footsore, famished. The thought of his wife and children urged him on. At last he found a road which led him in what he knew to be the right direction. It was as wide and straight as a city street, yet it seemed untraveled. No fields bordered it, no dwelling anywhere. Not so much as the barking of a dog suggested human habitation. The black bodies of the trees formed a straight wall on both sides, **terminating** on the horizon in a point, like a diagram in a lesson in perspective. Overhead, as he looked up through this rift in the wood, shone great golden stars looking unfamiliar and grouped in strange constellations. He was sure they were arranged in some order which had a secret and malign significance. The wood on either side was full of singular noises, among which—once, twice, and again—he distinctly heard whispers in an unknown tongue.

35   His neck was in pain and lifting his hand to it found it horribly swollen. He knew that it had a circle of black where the rope had bruised it. His eyes felt

Aeolian harps: stringed instruments that make music when wind blows against them
terminating: ending

congested; he could no longer close them. His tongue was swollen with thirst; he relieved its fever by thrusting it forward from between his teeth into the cold air. How softly the turf had carpeted the untraveled avenue—he could no longer feel the roadway beneath his feet!

36 Doubtless, despite his suffering, he had fallen asleep while walking, for now he sees another scene—perhaps he has merely recovered from a delirium. He stands at the gate of his own home. All is as he left it, and all bright and beautiful in the morning sunshine. He must have traveled the entire night. As he pushes open the gate and passes up the wide white walk, he sees a flutter of female garments; his wife, looking fresh and cool and sweet, steps down from the veranda to meet him. At the bottom of the steps she stands waiting, with a smile of ineffable joy, an attitude of matchless grace and dignity. Ah, how beautiful she is! He springs forwards with extended arms. As he is about to clasp her he feels a stunning blow upon the back of the neck; a blinding white light blazes all about him with a sound like the shock of a cannon—then all is darkness and silence!

37 Peyton Farquhar was dead; his body, with a broken neck, swung gently from side to side beneath the timbers of the Owl Creek bridge.

Making Observations

- What settings does Farquhar visit?
- In what ways does Farquhar's state of mind change over the course of Part 3?
- What pushes Farquhar to keep trying to survive?

Working from the Text

1. Revisit the sensory descriptions you underlined while reading Part 3 of this story and copy examples of what Farquhar feels, sees, and hears into the following chart.

Farquhar feels ...	Farquhar sees ...	Farquhar hears ...

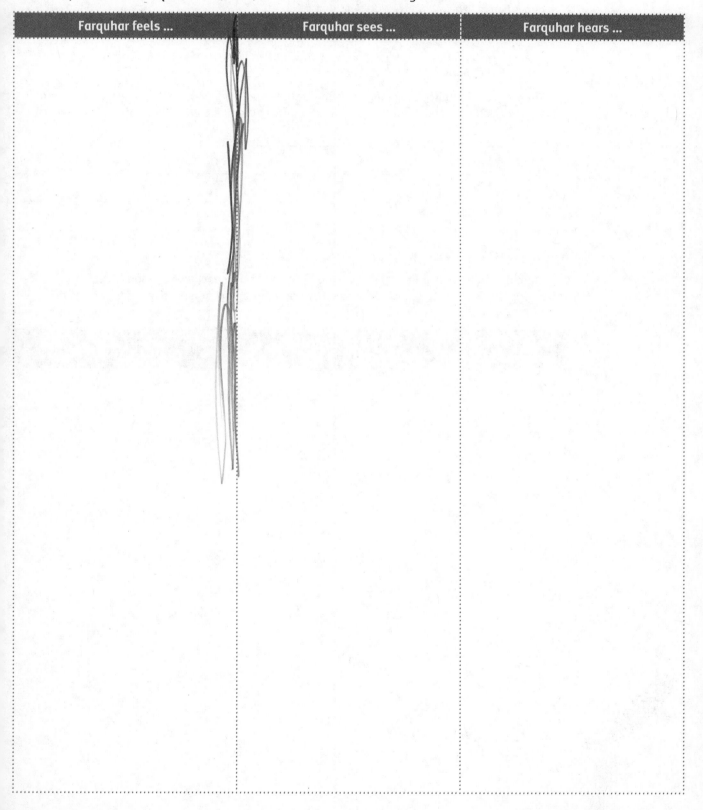

2. Contrast the final two sentences from the story:

"As he is about to clasp her he feels a stunning blow upon the back of the neck; a blinding white light blazes all about him with a sound like the shock of a cannon — then all is darkness and silence!"

vs.

"Peyton Farquhar was dead; his body, with a broken neck, swung gently from side to side beneath the timbers of the Owl Creek bridge."

Then write a sentence beginning with the word *while* to tell about how the word choice and sensory details in the penultimate sentence differ from those in the final sentence.

_____

_____

_____

_____

Appreciating the Author's Craft

Complete the following outline by identifying from whose perspective each part of "An Occurrence at Owl Creek Bridge" is told. Include notes on whether and how perspective shifts within each part of the story.

"An Occurrence at Owl Creek Bridge"	Notes on Perspective	
Part 1		
Part 2		
Part 3		
Final Sentence		

Discuss the following questions with your classmates.

• How would the story be different if it ended with "all is darkness and silence"?

• Did Farquhar achieve his goal of living the "larger life of a soldier" by attempting to destroy the bridge in order to thwart the Union forces?

• Revisit the Essential Question about telling details. Which details in the story did you find most telling when trying to understand Farquhar and his situation?

☑ Check Your Understanding

Think about the prediction you made about "An Occurrence at Owl Creek Bridge" in Activity 1.11. How did the perspective shifts affect the accuracy of your prediction?

Literary Analysis Paragraph

Learning Strategies

Drafting
Outlining

My Notes

Learning Targets

- Use an outline to plan a literary analysis paragraph.
- Generate a topic sentence that includes a claim.
- Draft a literary analysis paragraph.

Preview

In this activity, you will use an outline to help you develop and write a literary analysis paragraph about how the language used in "An Occurrence at Owl Creek Bridge" connects to the overall message of the story.

Writing to Sources: Informational Text

Write a literary analysis paragraph about how Ambrose Bierce uses shifts in language to make a statement about the nature of war or another aspect of "An Occurrence at Owl Creek Bridge" of your choice. Use a single-paragraph outline to plan your writing.

Writing a Topic Sentence

1. Begin your outline by generating a topic sentence that connects something you have observed about "An Occurrence at Owl Creek Bridge" to a theory you have about the story's overall meaning. An effective topic sentence will:

   - State an argument to support a claim about the story.
   - Be supportable with evidence from the story, while also being debatable.

T.S. _____

_____

_____

_____

1. _____

2. _____

3. _____

4. _____

C.S. _____

_____

_____

_____

Completing the Outline

2. Return to the story and find evidence that supports your claim. Add the most compelling evidence to the outline's numbered lines. Remember that you don't need to use complete sentences, but quoted text should be kept intact.

3. Craft a concluding statement that follows from and supports the explanation you present and connects your evidence to your topic sentence.

Assess and Reflect

Use the outline you created to develop an analytical paragraph about how Ambrose Bierce uses shifts in language to make a larger statement in the story. As you develop your paragraph, be sure to:

- Support the claim in your topic sentence with details and evidence from the story.
- Use quotation marks around text that comes directly from the story.
- Use a variety of complete sentences.

Shared Gifts: Introducing Irony

Learning Strategies

Close Reading
Drafting
Marking the Text
SIFT
Skimming/Scanning

My Notes

Learning Targets

- Unpack the requirements for Embedded Assessment 1.
- Explain how images signify the literal and symbolic importance of objects to the development of complex characters.
- Explain how situational irony contributes to a theme.

Preview

In this activity, you will unpack Embedded Assessment 1 and read a short story to analyze how the author uses irony, allusions, and symbols.

Unpacking Embedded Assessment 1

Read the assignment for Embedded Assessment 1: Writing a Literary Analysis Essay closely to identify and analyze the components of the assignment.

 Your assignment is to write a literary analysis in which you analyze how Zadie Smith uses literary devices or other elements to express the theme of coping with emotional turmoil in the short story "Martha, Martha."

Using the assignment and Scoring Guide, work with your class to analyze the prompt and create a graphic organizer to use as a visual reminder of the required concepts (what you need to know) and skills (what you need to do). Copy the graphic organizer into your Reader/Writer Notebook. After each activity, use this graphic to reflect on what you have learned and what you still need to learn in order to be successful on the Embedded Assessment.

As You Read

- Underline names or ideas that come from other stories.
- Circle unknown words and phrases. Try to determine the meaning of the words by using context clues, word parts, or a dictionary.

About the Author

 William Sydney Porter (1862–1910), whose pen name was O. Henry, was born in Greensboro, North Carolina. Porter left school at the age of 15 and moved to Texas, where he wrote a humorous weekly paper. When that failed, he worked as a reporter and columnist for the *Houston Post*. He was later convicted of embezzling money (although there is some doubt about his guilt) and was sentenced to jail. While in jail, he started writing short stories. After serving his sentence, Porter moved to New York City, where he wrote under his pen name for the magazine *New York World*. Porter became a prolific writer, publishing more than 600 short stories.

Short Story

The Gift of the Magi

by **O. Henry**

1   One dollar and eighty-seven cents. That was all. And sixty cents of it was in pennies. Pennies saved one and two at a time by bulldozing the grocer and the vegetable man and the butcher until one's cheeks burned with the silent **imputation** of **parsimony** that such close dealing implied. Three times Della counted it. One dollar and eighty-seven cents. And the next day would be Christmas.

2   There was clearly nothing to do but flop down on the shabby little couch and howl. So Della did it. Which instigates the moral reflection that life is made up of sobs, sniffles, and smiles, with sniffles predominating.

3   While the mistress of the home is gradually subsiding from the first stage to the second, take a look at the home. A furnished flat at $8 per week. It did not exactly beggar description, but it certainly had that word on the lookout for the mendicancy squad.

4   In the **vestibule** below was a letter-box into which no letter would go, and an electric button from which no mortal finger could coax a ring. Also appertaining thereunto was a card bearing the name "Mr. James Dillingham Young."

5   The "Dillingham" had been flung to the breeze during a former period of prosperity when its possessor was being paid $30 per week. Now, when the income was shrunk to $20, the letters of "Dillingham" looked blurred, as though they were thinking seriously of contracting to a modest and unassuming D. But whenever Mr. James Dillingham Young came home and reached his flat above he was called "Jim" and greatly hugged by Mrs. James Dillingham Young, already introduced to you as Della. Which is all very good.

6   Della finished her cry and attended to her cheeks with the powder rag. She stood by the window and looked out dully at a gray cat walking a gray fence in a gray backyard. Tomorrow would be Christmas Day, and she had only $1.87 with which to buy Jim a present. She had been saving every penny she could for months, with this result. Twenty dollars a week doesn't go far. Expenses had been greater than she had calculated. They always are. Only $1.87 to buy a present for Jim. Her Jim. Many a happy hour she had spent planning for something nice for him. Something fine and rare and sterling—something just a little bit near to being worthy of the honor of being owned by Jim.

7   There was a pier-glass between the windows of the room. Perhaps you have seen a pier glass in an $8 flat. A very thin and very agile person may, by observing his reflection in a rapid sequence of longitudinal strips, obtain a fairly accurate conception of his looks. Della, being slender, had mastered the art.

WORD CONNECTIONS

Etymology
The word **mendicancy** first appeared in 1790 and means the "state or condition of being a beggar." The narrator is trying to amuse the reader by making mention of the *mendicancy squad*, which was a group of police who arrested beggars and homeless people.

My Notes

imputation: accusation
parsimony: thriftiness
vestibule: hallway

8   Suddenly she whirled from the window and stood before the glass. Her eyes were shining brilliantly, but her face had lost its color within twenty seconds. Rapidly she pulled down her hair and let it fall to its full length.

9   Now, there were two possessions of the James Dillingham Youngs in which they both took a mighty pride. One was Jim's gold watch that had been his father's and his grandfather's. The other was Della's hair. Had the queen of Sheba lived in the flat across the airshaft, Della would have let her hair hang out the window some day to dry just to **depreciate** Her Majesty's jewels and gifts. Had King Solomon been the janitor, with all his treasures piled up in the basement, Jim would have pulled out his watch every time he passed, just to see him pluck at his beard from envy.

10   So now Della's beautiful hair fell about her rippling and shining like a cascade of brown waters. It reached below her knee and made itself almost a garment for her. And then she did it up again nervously and quickly. Once she faltered for a minute and stood still while a tear or two splashed on the worn red carpet.

11   On went her old brown jacket; on went her old brown hat. With a whirl of skirts and with the brilliant sparkle still in her eyes, she fluttered out the door and down the stairs to the street.

12   Where she stopped the sign read: "Mme. Sofronie. Hair Goods of All Kinds." One flight up Della ran, and collected herself, panting. Madame, large, too white, chilly, hardly looked the "Sofronie."

13   "Will you buy my hair?" asked Della.

14   "I buy hair," said Madame. "Take yer hat off and let's have a sight at the looks of it."

15   Down rippled the brown cascade.

16   "Twenty dollars," said Madame, lifting the mass with a practiced hand.

17   "Give it to me quick," said Della.

18   Oh, and the next two hours tripped by on rosy wings. Forget the hashed metaphor. She was ransacking the stores for Jim's present.

19   She found it at last. It surely had been made for Jim and no one else. There was no other like it in any of the stores, and she had turned all of them inside out. It was a platinum fob chain simple and **chaste** in design, properly proclaiming its value by substance alone and not by **meretricious ornamentation**—as all good things should do. It was even worthy of The Watch. As soon as she saw it she knew that it must be Jim's. It was like him. Quietness and value—the description applied to both. Twenty-one dollars they took from her for it, and she hurried home with the 87 cents. With that chain on his watch Jim might be properly anxious about the time in any company. Grand as the watch was, he sometimes looked at it on the sly on account of the old leather strap that he used in place of a chain.

---

depreciate: lessen the value of
chaste: pure, simple
meretricious ornamentation: gaudy or flashy decoration

My Notes

20 When Della reached home her intoxication gave way a little to prudence and reason. She got out her curling irons and lighted the gas and went to work repairing the ravages made by generosity added to love. Which is always a tremendous task, dear friends—a mammoth task.

21 Within forty minutes her head was covered with tiny, close-lying curls that made her look wonderfully like a **truant** schoolboy. She looked at her reflection in the mirror long, carefully, and critically.

22 "If Jim doesn't kill me," she said to herself, "before he takes a second look at me, he'll say I look like a Coney Island chorus girl. But what could I do—oh! what could I do with a dollar and eighty-seven cents?"

23 At 7 o'clock the coffee was made and the frying-pan was on the back of the stove hot and ready to cook the chops.

24 Jim was never late. Della doubled the fob chain in her hand and sat on the corner of the table near the door that he always entered. Then she heard his step on the stair away down on the first flight, and she turned white for just a moment. She had a habit of saying a little silent prayer about the simplest everyday things, and now she whispered: "Please God, make him think I am still pretty."

25 The door opened and Jim stepped in and closed it. He looked thin and very serious. Poor fellow, he was only twenty-two—and to be burdened with a family! He needed a new overcoat and he was without gloves.

26 Jim stopped inside the door, as immovable as a **setter** at the scent of quail. His eyes were fixed upon Della, and there was an expression in them that she could not read, and it terrified her. It was not anger, nor surprise, nor disapproval, nor horror, nor any of the sentiments that she had been prepared for. He simply stared at her fixedly with that peculiar expression on his face.

27 Della wriggled off the table and went for him.

28 "Jim, darling," she cried, "don't look at me that way. I had my hair cut off and sold because I couldn't have lived through Christmas without giving you a present. It'll grow out again—you won't mind, will you? I just had to do it. My hair grows awfully fast. Say 'Merry Christmas!' Jim, and let's be happy. You don't know what a nice—what a beautiful, nice gift I've got for you."

29 "You've cut off your hair?" asked Jim, **laboriously**, as if he had not arrived at that **patent** fact yet even after the hardest mental labor.

30 "Cut it off and sold it," said Della. "Don't you like me just as well, anyhow? I'm me without my hair, ain't I?"

31 Jim looked about the room curiously.

32 "You say your hair is gone?" he said, with an air almost of idiocy.

33 "You needn't look for it," said Della. "It's sold, I tell you—sold and gone, too. It's Christmas Eve, boy. Be good to me, for it went for you. Maybe the hairs of my head were numbered," she went on with sudden serious sweetness, "but nobody could ever count my love for you. Shall I put the chops on, Jim?"

truant: absent from school
setter: hunting dog
laboriously: with difficulty
patent: obvious

My Notes

34 Out of his trance Jim seemed quickly to wake. He **enfolded** his Della. For ten seconds let us **regard with discreet scrutiny** some inconsequential object in the other direction. Eight dollars a week or a million a year—what is the difference? A mathematician or a wit would give you the wrong answer. The magi brought valuable gifts, but that was not among them. This dark **assertion** will be illuminated later on.

35 Jim drew a package from his overcoat pocket and threw it upon the table.

36 "Don't make any mistake, Dell," he said, "about me. I don't think there's anything in the way of a haircut or a shave or a shampoo that could make me like my girl any less. But if you'll unwrap that package you may see why you had me going a while at first."

37 White fingers and nimble tore at the string and paper. And then an ecstatic scream of joy; and then, alas! a quick feminine change to hysterical tears and wails, necessitating the immediate employment of all the comforting powers of the lord of the flat.

38 For there lay The Combs—the set of combs, side and back, that Della had worshipped long in a Broadway window. Beautiful combs, pure tortoise shell, with jeweled rims—just the shade to wear in the beautiful vanished hair. They were expensive combs, she knew, and her heart had simply craved and yearned over them without the least hope of possession. And now, they were hers, but the tresses that should have adorned the coveted adornments were gone.

39 But she hugged them to her bosom, and at length she was able to look up with dim eyes and a smile and say: "My hair grows so fast, Jim!"

40 And then Della leaped up like a little singed cat and cried, "Oh, oh!"

41 Jim had not yet seen his beautiful present. She held it out to him eagerly upon her open palm. The dull precious metal seemed to flash with a reflection of her bright and ardent spirit.

42 "Isn't it a dandy, Jim? I hunted all over town to find it. You'll have to look at the time a hundred times a day now. Give me your watch. I want to see how it looks on it."

43 Instead of obeying, Jim tumbled down on the couch and put his hands under the back of his head and smiled.

44 "Dell," said he, "let's put our Christmas presents away and keep 'em a while. They're too nice to use just at present. I sold the watch to get the money to buy your combs. And now suppose you put the chops on."

45 The magi, as you know, were wise men—wonderfully wise men—who brought gifts to the Babe in the manger. They invented the art of giving Christmas presents. Being wise, their gifts were no doubt wise ones, possibly bearing the privilege of exchange in case of duplication. And here I have lamely related to you the uneventful chronicle of two foolish children in a flat who most unwisely sacrificed for each other the greatest treasures of their house.

enfolded: wrapped arms around
regard with discreet scrutiny: look at closely but not in an obvious way
assertion: declaration or statement, often without proof

But in a last word to the wise of these days let it be said that of all who give gifts these two were the wisest. Of all who give and receive gifts, such as they are wisest. Everywhere they are wisest. They are the magi.

What details in this image, "Adoration of the Magi," relate to themes and ideas presented in the short story "The Gift of the Magi?"

Making Observations

- What characters do we meet in the story?
- What does each character want?

Returning to the Text

- Return to the text as you respond to the following questions. Cite text evidence to support your responses.
- Write any additional questions you have about the text in your Reader/Writer Notebook.

1. What evidence has O. Henry provided in the text to support the inference that Della and Jim do not have a lot of money?

_____

_____

_____

_____

2. By the end of paragraph 6, the reader has met the two main characters—Della and Jim—and has a sense of their relationship. How does understanding their relationship underscore the story's central idea? What is the central idea?

_____

_____

_____

_____

3. O. Henry chooses specific words and phrases to point to the story's historical setting. Reread paragraphs 19–20. Which phrases give a sense of the story's time and place?

_____

_____

_____

_____

4. From what point of view is the story told? Reread paragraph 45. What do you notice about the story's point of view in this paragraph?

_____

_____

_____

_____

5. How does the author's use of language contribute to the narrator's voice in the story?

_____

_____

_____

_____

Identifying Literary Devices: Irony and Allusion

Authors of short stories use a wide variety of literary devices to achieve different effects. Two common literary devices are irony and allusion.

There are three main forms of irony: verbal, situational, and dramatic. Verbal irony is when an author uses words that mean something different from what they seem to mean to create a specific tone or show a certain attitude. It is important to understand the context of verbal irony so that you don't take it literally. For example, a woman driving to work gets a flat tire and says, "Great! My day couldn't start off any better!"

6. In your Reader/Writer Notebook, briefly describe one example of verbal irony you have read or seen.

Situational irony is when what happens is different from what was expected to happen. Authors use situational irony as a way to surprise readers and disrupt their expectations, which usually has a large impact on the theme of the story.

7. In your Reader/Writer Notebook, briefly describe one example of situational irony you have read or seen.

Dramatic irony is when the audience (or reader) knows more about what is happening than the characters in the story do. Authors use dramatic irony to build suspense and keep the audience (or readers) interested. Recall the moments of dramatic irony in "Lamb to the Slaughter."

8. In your Reader/Writer Notebook, briefly describe one other example of dramatic irony you have read or seen.

Allusions are references an author makes to other works of literature, historical events, or other common cultural knowledge. Many allusions refer to people, places, and events that take place in the Bible and classical mythology. Authors create allusions when they draw on or transform source material, such as the Bible, and bring significance to specific parts of their stories.

9. How does understanding the allusion to the magi help with understanding O. Henry's purpose in writing this story?

_____

_____

Working from the Text

Introducing the Strategy: SIFT

The acronym SIFT stands for Symbol, Imagery, Figurative Language, and Tone or Theme. You can use this strategy to "sift" through the parts of a story in order to explore how a writer uses literary elements and stylistic techniques to convey meaning or theme. Identifying these elements is the key to helping you understand the author's purpose and commentary on life—the story's theme.

VOCABULARY

LITERARY

Irony is a literary device that plays on readers' expectations by portraying events in a way that is actually different from reality.

An allusion is a reference that a writer makes to a well-known person, event, or place from history, music, art, or another literary work.

ACADEMIC

Commentary in a narrative text further develops the theme or main idea the author wants to convey. Sometimes it is directly stated in the text, and sometimes it must be inferred by examining elements like character, plot, and tone. In an essay, commentary refers to the explanations and interpretations an author writes to support an opinion or an analysis.

10. After reading the story, go back and scan for examples of symbols, imagery, figurative language, and tone/theme and complete the SIFT graphic organizer. Record examples from "The Gift of the Magi" for each of the SIFT elements.

Literary Element	Text Details	Effects or Meanings of Details
Symbol		
Imagery		
Figurative Language		
Tone/Theme		

Determining Theme: A Review

Remember that to determine theme, you must consider how all elements work together within a story and what ideas about life these elements present. Also, keep the following points in mind when writing about the theme of a story.

A theme is not:

- a topic, such as "love" or "sacrifice."
- a summary, such as "two people sell their valuables to show their love for each other."
- a moral, such as "if you love someone, you will do anything for him or her."

A theme is a general statement about life (e.g., "people show their love for each other by making sacrifices").

11. With a partner, brainstorm other themes that are developed through the characters and plot of this short story. Choose one and work together to create a thematic statement that states the theme and briefly explains how that theme is developed through characterization or plot.

_____

_____

_____

_____

_____

_____

INDEPENDENT READING LINK

Read and Respond

Think about the themes that are emerging in the text you are reading independently, whether it is fiction or nonfiction. Choose one and write a thematic statement that states the theme and briefly explains how it emerges and is shaped and refined by specific details in the text.

☑ Check Your Understanding

In a few sentences, explain what effect O. Henry's use of irony achieves.

_____

_____

_____

_____

📝 Writing to Sources: Informational Text

Write a paragraph that analyzes the effect of the author's use of a literary device or element. Be sure to:

- Begin with a topic sentence that responds to the prompt and states the literary device or element.
- Provide details from the text as supporting evidence.
- Respond using precise language and literary terminology and in a formal style and an objective tone.

Language Checkpoint:
Using Punctuation Within Sentences

Learning Targets
- Understand the purposes of punctuation within a sentence.
- Demonstrate command of commas, colons, semicolons, and dashes.
- Revise writing to correct the use of punctuation within a sentence.

Preview

In this activity, you will recognize and use correct punctuation within a sentence.

Understanding Punctuation Within Sentences

Punctuation within sentences makes ideas clearer. Varied—and correct—use of punctuation adds interest to your writing and helps readers follow your ideas.

Read the following sentence from "The Gift of the Magi."

> A very thin and very agile person may, by observing his reflection in a rapid sequence of longitudinal strips, obtain a fairly accurate conception of his looks.

Reread the same sentence, this time without commas.

> A very thin and very agile person may by observing his reflection in a rapid sequence of longitudinal strips obtain a fairly accurate conception of his looks.

1. Which version of the sentence is clearer? Why?

Commas

Commas are used in sentences for several reasons, including:

- to separate two independent clauses when one of them starts with *and, but, or, nor, so,* or *yet.*
- to set off introductory clauses and phrases.
- to set off information that is not necessary to understand a sentence.
- to shift into or out of a quotation.
- to prevent possible confusion or misreading.

2. Read the following sentences and describe why the comma was used.

> **a.** "Give it to me quick," said Della.
>
> **b.** Had King Solomon been the janitor, with all his treasures piled up in the basement, Jim would pull out his watch every time he passed.
>
> **c.** Then she heard his step on the stair away down the first flight, and she turned white for just a moment.
>
> **d.** Instead of obeying, Jim tumbled down on the couch and put his hands under the back of his head and smiled.

Colons, Semicolons, and Dashes

Colons, semicolons, and dashes are, like commas, used to help organize information in sentences.

The **colon** is used to introduce an explanation, a list of items, or a quotation.

> The truth was clear: they had each hoped to surprise the other.

> She moved quickly to pile on clothes for the weather: boots, sweater, overcoat, scarf and knit cap.

> She read a sign: "Mme. Sofronie. Hair Goods of All Kinds."

The **semicolon** is used to join two or more independent clauses. An independent clause can stand on its own as a complete sentence. A semicolon is used only when the ideas in the independent clauses are closely related.

> On went her old brown jacket; on went her old brown hat.

3. How are these two independent clauses related?

A **dash** is longer than a hyphen (–) and is used to emphasize or set off information.

> He looked thin and very serious. Poor fellow, he was only twenty-two—and to be burdened with a family!

4. Why does O. Henry use a dash in this instance?

Recognizing Punctuation Within Sentences

5. For each of these sentences, add a punctuation mark that makes the sentence clear.

   a. Della reveals her plan with a question _____ "Will you buy my hair?"

   b. "But what could I do _____ oh! what could I do with a dollar and eighty-seven cents?"

   c. Della and Jim each made a sacrifice for the other _____ she sells her hair and he sells his watch.

   d. It was a platinum fob chain simple and chaste in design, properly proclaiming its value by substance alone and not by meretricious ornamentation _____ as all good things should do.

   e. For there lay The Combs—the set of combs _____ side and back _____ that Della had worshipped long in a Broadway window.

Revising

6. Read the paragraph in the left column, which is a student's reflection about "The Gift of the Magi." For every number, identify the revision in the right column that would work best.

[1] "The Gift of the Magi" the widely-read short story by O. Henry is a beautiful story of love. [2] Jim and Della love each other and they want to give each other nice gifts for Christmas. [3] Though neither of them has much money to go shopping, they each own something that is valuable. [4] Della possesses beautiful hair, Jim owns a nice watch. [5] They both use their possessions, their dearest possessions to show how much they love each other.

1. **a.** NO CHANGE
   b. "The Gift of the Magi;" the widely-read short story by O. Henry is a beautiful story of love.
   c. "The Gift of the Magi," the widely-read short story by O. Henry, is a beautiful story of love.
   d. "The Gift of the Magi," the widely-read short story by O. Henry is a beautiful story of love.

2. **a.** NO CHANGE
   b. Jim and Della love each other, and they want to give each other nice gifts for Christmas.
   c. Jim and Della love each other; and they want to give each other nice gifts for Christmas.
   d. Jim and Della love each other—and they want to give each other nice gifts for Christmas.

3. **a.** NO CHANGE
   b. Though neither of them has much money to go shopping; they each own something that is valuable.
   c. Though neither of them has much money to go shopping—they each own something that is valuable.
   d. Though, neither of them has much money to go shopping, they each own something that is valuable.

4. **a.** NO CHANGE
   b. Della possesses beautiful hair—Jim owns a nice watch.
   c. Della possesses beautiful hair; Jim owns a nice watch.
   d. Della possesses beautiful hair, Jim, owns a nice watch.

5. **a.** NO CHANGE
   b. They both use their possessions—their dearest possessions to show how much they love each other.
   c. They both use their possessions; their dearest possessions to show how much they love each other.
   d. They both use their possessions—their dearest possessions—to show how much they love each other.

☑ Check Your Understanding

What questions can you ask yourself whenever you write to ensure that you are using your knowledge of punctuation to make your writing clear? How can you remind yourself to correctly use commas, colons, semicolons, and dashes? Add the questions to your Editor's Checklist.

Practice

Reread the paragraph you wrote in Activity 1.16 aloud. As you read, listen for where you naturally pause within your sentences. If you pause and there's no punctuation on the page, consider whether adding punctuation within the sentence would make it clearer. Add commas, colons, semicolons, and dashes to clarify your ideas.

"Games at Twilight": Use the Evidence

My Notes

Learning Targets

- Closely read a story to find details about complex characters' traits and feelings.
- Cite strong and thorough text evidence to analyze the author's purpose.
- Pose various levels of questions to foster an academic discussion.

Preview

In this activity, you will read and analyze a short story through discussion and writing detailed sentences.

As You Read

- Use the My Notes section to note the characters' traits and feelings.
- Circle unknown words and phrases. Try to determine the meaning of the words by using context clues, word parts, or a dictionary.

About the Author

Anita Desai (b. 1937) is an award-winning Indian author of many novels, short stories, and children's stories, including the best-selling novel *Fire on the Mountain*. Desai's novels and short stories often focus on family and use rich visual imagery and details. Her characters often show signs of heroism and strength, simply by surviving everyday life experiences. Desai says that writing is a necessity for her and is as instinctive as breathing. In her work she explores how gender issues are central, not only in the family, but to the nation as well. Desai states that her novels are not a reflection of Indian society, but a part of her private effort to communicate her feelings about life.

Short Story

Games at Twilight

by **Anita Desai**

1   It was still too hot to play outdoors. They had had their tea, they had been washed and had their hair brushed, and after the long day of confinement in the house that was not cool but at least a protection from the sun, the children strained to get out. Their faces were red and bloated with the effort, but their mother would not open the door, everything was still curtained and shuttered in a way that stifled the children, made them feel that their lungs were stuffed with cotton wool and their noses with dust and if they didn't burst out into the light and see the sun and feel the air, they would choke.

2   "Please, ma, please," they begged. "We'll play in the veranda and porch—we won't go a step out of the porch."

3   "You will, I know you will, and then—"

4   "No—we won't, we won't," they wailed so horrendously that she actually let down the bolt of the front door so that they burst out like seeds from a crackling, overripe pod into the veranda, with such wild, maniacal yells that she retreated to her bath and the shower of talcum powder and the fresh sari that were to help her face the summer evening.

5   They faced the afternoon. It was too hot. Too bright. The white walls of the veranda glared stridently in the sun. The bougainvillea hung about it, purple and magenta, in livid balloons. The garden outside was like a tray made of beaten brass, flattened out on the red gravel and the stony soil in all shades of metal—aluminum, tin, copper, and brass. No life stirred at this arid time of day—the birds still drooped, like dead fruit, in the papery tents of the trees; some squirrels lay limp on the wet earth under the garden tap. The outdoor dog lay stretched as if dead on the veranda mat, his paws and ears and tail all reaching out like dying travelers in search of water. He rolled his eyes at the children—two white marbles rolling in the purple sockets, begging for sympathy—and attempted to lift his tail in a wag but could not. It only twitched and lay still.

6   Then, perhaps roused by the shrieks of the children, a band of parrots suddenly fell out of the eucalyptus tree, tumbled frantically in the still, sizzling air, then sorted themselves out into battle formation and streaked away across the white sky.

7   The children, too, felt released. They too began tumbling, shoving, pushing against each other, frantic to start. Start what? Start their business. The business of the children's day which is—play.

8   "Let's play hide-and-seek."

9   "Who'll be It?"

My Notes

10 "You be It."

11 "Why should I? You be—"

12 "You're the eldest—"

13 "That doesn't mean—"

14 The shoves became harder. Some kicked out. The motherly Mira intervened. She pulled the boys roughly apart. There was a tearing sound of cloth, but it was lost in the heavy panting and angry grumbling, and no one paid attention to the small sleeve hanging loosely off a shoulder.

15 "Make a circle, make a circle!" she shouted, firmly pulling and pushing till a kind of vague circle was formed. "Now clap!" she roared, and, clapping, they all chanted in melancholy unison: "Dip, dip, dip—my blue ship—" and every now and then one or the other saw he was safe by the way his hands fell at the crucial moment—palm on palm, or back of hand on palm—and dropped out of the circle with a yell and a jump of relief and jubilation.

16 Raghu was It. He started to protest, to cry "You cheated—Mira cheated—Anu cheated—" but it was too late, the others had all already streaked away. There was no one to hear when he called out, "Only in the veranda—the porch—Ma said—Ma said to stay in the porch!" No one had stopped to listen, all he saw were their brown legs flashing through the dusty shrubs, scrambling up brick walls, leaping over compost heaps and hedges, and then the porch stood empty in the purple shade of the bougainvillea, and the garden was as empty as before; even the limp squirrels had whisked away, leaving everything gleaming, brassy, and bare.

17 Only small Manu suddenly reappeared, as if he had dropped out of an invisible cloud or from a bird's claws, and stood for a moment in the center of the yellow lawn, chewing his finger and near to tears as he heard Raghu shouting, with his head pressed against the veranda wall, "Eighty-three, eighty-five, eighty-nine, ninety . . ." and then made off in a panic, half of him wanting to fly north, the other half counseling south. Raghu turned just in time to see the flash of his white shorts and the uncertain skittering of his red sandals, and charged after him with such a bloodcurdling yell that Manu stumbled over the hosepipe, fell into its rubber coils, and lay there weeping, "I won't be It—you have to find them all—all—All!"

18 "I know I have to, idiot," Raghu said, superciliously kicking him with his toe. "You're dead," he said with satisfaction, licking the beads of perspiration off his upper lip, and then stalked off in search of worthier prey, whistling spiritedly so that the hiders should hear and tremble.

19 Ravi heard the whistling and picked his nose in a panic, trying to find comfort by burrowing the finger deep—deep into that soft tunnel. He felt himself too exposed, sitting on an upturned flowerpot behind the garage. Where could he burrow? He could run around the garage if he heard Raghu come—around and around and around—but he hadn't much faith in his short legs when matched against Raghu's long, hefty, hairy footballer legs. Ravi had

crucial: important

a frightening glimpse of them as Raghu combed the hedge of crotons and hibiscus, trampling delicate ferns underfoot as he did so. Ravi looked about him desperately, swallowing a small ball of snot in his fear.

20   The garage was locked with a great heavy lock to which the driver had the key in his room, hanging from a nail on the wall under his workshirt. Ravi had peeped in and seen him still sprawling on his string cot in his vest and striped underpants, the hair on his chest and the hair in his nose shaking with the vibrations of his phlegm-obstructed snores. Ravi had wished he were tall enough, big enough to reach the key on the nail, but it was impossible, beyond his reach for years to come. He had sidled away and sat dejectedly on the flowerpot. That at least was cut to his own size.

21   But next to the garage was another shed with a big green door. Also locked. No one even knew who had the key to the lock. That shed wasn't opened more than once a year, when Ma turned out all the old broken bits of furniture and rolls of matting and leaking buckets, and the white anthills were broken and swept away and Flit sprayed into the spider webs and rat holes so that the whole operation was like the looting of a poor, ruined, and conquered city. The green leaves of the door sagged. They were nearly off their rusty hinges. The hinges were large and made a small gap between the door and the walls—only just large enough for rats, dogs, and, possibly, Ravi to slip through.

22   Ravi had never cared to enter such a dark and depressing mortuary of defunct household goods seething with such unspeakable and alarming animal life but, as Raghu's whistling grew angrier and sharper and his crashing and storming in the hedge wilder, Ravi suddenly slipped off the flowerpot and through the crack and was gone. He chuckled aloud with astonishment at his own temerity so that Raghu came out of the hedge, stood silent with his hands on his hips, listening, and finally shouted, "I heard you! I'm coming! Got you!" and came charging round the garage only to find the upturned flowerpot, the yellow dust, the crawling of white ants in a mud hill against the closed shed door—nothing. Snarling, he bent to pick up a stick and went off, whacking it against the garage and shed walls as if to beat out his prey.

23   Ravi shook, then shivered with delight, with self-congratulation. Also with fear. It was dark, spooky in the shed. It had a muffled smell, as of graves. Ravi had once got locked into the linen cupboard and sat there weeping for half an hour before he was rescued. But at least that had been a familiar place, and even smelled pleasantly of starch, laundry, and, reassuringly, of his mother. But the shed smelled of rats, anthills, dust, and spider webs. Also of less definable, less recognizable horrors. And it was dark. Except for the white-hot cracks along the door, there was no light. The roof was very low. Although Ravi was small, he felt as if he could reach up and touch it with his fingertips. But he didn't stretch. He hunched himself into a ball so as not to bump into anything, touch or feel anything. What might there not be to touch him and feel him

temerity: recklessness

as he stood there, trying to see in the dark? Something cold, or slimy—like a snake. Snakes! He leapt up as Raghu whacked the wall with his stick—then, quickly realizing what it was, felt almost relieved to hear Raghu, hear his stick. It made him feel protected.

24 But Raghu soon moved away. There wasn't a sound once his footsteps had gone around the garage and disappeared. Ravi stood frozen inside the shed. Then he shivered all over. Something had tickled the back of his neck. It took him a while to pick up the courage to lift his hand and explore. It was an insect—perhaps a spider—exploring him. He squashed it and wondered how many more creatures were watching him, waiting to reach out and touch him, the stranger.

25 There was nothing now. After standing in that position—his hand still on his neck, feeling the wet splodge of the squashed spider gradually dry—for minutes, hours, his legs began to tremble with the effort, the inaction. By now he could see enough in the dark to make out the large solid shapes of old wardrobes, broken buckets, and bedsteads piled on top of each other around him. He recognized an old bathtub—patches of enamel glimmered at him, and at last he lowered himself onto its edge.

26 He contemplated slipping out of the shed and into the **fray**. He wondered if it would not be better to be captured by Raghu and be returned to the milling crowd as long as he could be in the sun, the light, the free spaces of the garden, and the familiarity of his brothers, sisters, and cousins. It would be evening soon. Their games would become legitimate. The parents would sit out on the lawn on cane basket chairs and watch them as they tore around the garden or gathered in knots to share a loot of mulberries or black, teeth-splitting jamun from the garden trees. The gardener would fix the hosepipe to the water tap, and water would fall lavishly through the air to the ground, soaking the dry yellow grass and the red gravel and arousing the sweet, the intoxicating scent of water on dry earth—that loveliest scent in the world. Ravi sniffed for a whiff of it. He half-rose from the bathtub, then heard the despairing scream of one of the girls as Raghu **bore down** upon her. There was the sound of a crash, and of rolling about in the bushes, the shrubs, then screams and accusing sobs of "I touched the den—" "You did not—" "I did—" "You liar, you did not" and then a fading away and silence again.

27 Ravi sat back on the harsh edge of the tub, deciding to hold out a bit longer. What fun if they were all found and caught—he alone left unconquered! He had never known that sensation. Nothing more wonderful had ever happened to him than being taken out by an uncle and bought a whole slab of chocolate all to himself, or being flung into the soda man's pony cart and driven up to the gate by the friendly driver with the red beard and pointed ears. To defeat Raghu—that **hirsute**, hoarse-voiced football champion—and to be the winner in a circle of older, bigger, luckier children—that would be thrilling beyond imagination. He hugged his knees together and smiled to himself almost shyly at the thought of so much victory, such laurels.

fray: intense competition, battle, or fight
bore down: advanced in a threatening manner
hirsute: shaggy; hairy

28 There he sat smiling, knocking his heels against the bathtub, now and then getting up and going to the door to put his ear to the broad crack and listening for sounds of the game, the pursuer and the pursued, and then returning to his seat with the dogged determination of the true winner, a breaker of records, a champion.

29 It grew darker in the shed as the light at the door grew softer, fuzzier, turned to a kind of crumbling yellow pollen that turned to yellow fur, blue fur, gray fur. Evening. Twilight. The sound of water gushing, falling. The scent of earth receiving water, **slaking** its thirst in great gulps and releasing that green scent of freshness, coolness. Through the crack Ravi saw the long purple shadows of the shed and the garage lying still across the yard. Beyond that, the white walls of the house. The bougainvillea had lost its lividity, hung in dark bundles that quaked and twittered and seethed with masses of homing sparrows. The lawn was shut off from his view. Could he hear the children's voices? It seemed to him that he could. It seemed to him that he could hear them chanting, singing, laughing. But what about the game? What had happened? Could it be over? How could it when he was still not found?

30 It then occurred to him that he could have slipped out long ago, dashed across the yard to the veranda, and touched the "den." It was necessary to do that to win. He had forgotten. He had only remembered the part of hiding and trying to elude the seeker. He had done that so successfully, his success had occupied him so wholly, that he had quite forgotten that success had to be clinched by that final dash to victory and the ringing cry of "Den!"

31 With a whimper he burst through the crack, fell on his knees, got up, and stumbled on stiff, benumbed legs across the shadowy yard, crying heartily by the time he reached the veranda so that when he flung himself at the white pillar and bawled, "Den! Den! Den!" his voice broke with rage and pity at the disgrace of it all, and he felt himself flooded with tears and misery.

32 Out on the lawn, the children stopped chanting. They all turned to stare at him in amazement. Their faces were pale and triangular in the dusk. The trees and bushes around them stood inky and sepulchral, spilling long shadows across them. They stared, wondering at his reappearance, his passion, his wild animal howling. Their mother rose from her basket chair and came toward him, worried, annoyed, saying, "Stop it, stop it, Ravi. Don't be a baby. Have you hurt yourself?" Seeing him attended to, the children went back to clasping their hands and chanting, "The grass is green, the rose is red. . . ."

33 But Ravi would not let them. He tore himself out of his mother's grasp and pounded across the lawn into their midst, charging at them with his head lowered so that they scattered in surprise. "I won, I won, I won," he bawled, shaking his head so that the big tears flew. "Raghu didn't find me. I won, I won—"

34 It took them a minute to grasp what he was saying, even who he was. They had quite forgotten him. Raghu had found all the others long ago. There had been a fight about who was to be It next. It had been so fierce that their

My Notes

slaking: satisfying

mother had emerged from her bath and made them change to another game. Then they had played another and another. Broken mulberries from the tree and eaten them. Helped the driver wash the car when their father returned from work. Helped the gardener water the beds till he roared at them and swore he would complain to their parents. The parents had come out, taken up their positions on the cane chairs. They had begun to play again, sing and chant. All this time no one had remembered Ravi. Having disappeared from the scene, he had disappeared from their minds. Clean.

35 "Don't be a fool," Raghu said roughly, pushing him aside, and even Mira said, "Stop howling, Ravi. If you want to play, you can stand at the end of the line," and she put him there very firmly.

36 The game proceeded. Two pairs of arms reached up and met in an arc. The children trooped under it again and again in a lugubrious circle, ducking their heads and intoning

37 "The grass is green,

38 The rose is red;

39 Remember me

40 When I am dead, dead, dead, dead…"

41 And the arc of thin arms trembled in the twilight, and the heads were bowed so sadly, and their feet tramped to that melancholy refrain so mournfully, so helplessly, that Ravi could not bear it. He would not follow them, he would not be included in this funereal game. He had wanted victory and triumph—not a funeral. But he had been forgotten, left out, and he would not join them now. The ignominy of being forgotten—how could he face it? He felt his heart go heavy and ache inside him unbearably. He lay down full length on the damp grass, crushing his face into it, no longer crying, silenced by a terrible sense of his insignificance.

Making Observations

- What characters do we meet in the story?
- Where does this story take place? What details about the setting grab your attention?
- What questions does this story raise for you?

lugubrious: mournful; gloomy
ignominy: shame and dishonor

☑ Focus on the Sentence

Use details from the story to complete the following sentences.

Ravi wants to win the game because _____

_____

Ravi wants to win the game, but _____

_____

Ravi wants to win the game, so _____

_____

Returning to the Text

- Return to the text as you respond to the following questions. Use text evidence to support your responses.
- Write any additional questions you have about the text in your Reader/Writer Notebook.

1. What telling details reveal Ravi's feelings toward Raghu?

_____

_____

_____

_____

2. From what point of view is this story written? What effect does the chosen point of view have on the story?

_____

_____

_____

_____

3. What bitter lesson does Ravi learn at the end of the story?

_____

_____

_____

_____

4. In this story, Desai uses language to portray images of death. Cite a few examples of this imagery, and explain how it relates to the story.

_____

_____

_____

_____

5. What is one theme of the story? Cite strong textual evidence to support your response.

_____

_____

_____

_____

Working from the Text

Introducing the Strategy: Questioning the Text

A strategy for thinking actively and interpretively about your reading is to ask questions during and after reading. As you read any text, you can ask questions that aid your understanding with different levels of ideas. Questioning helps you experience a text in depth, gain information, and monitor your understanding.

Level 1, Literal – Literal questions can be answered by referring back to the text or consulting references.

EXAMPLE: *Which child picks his nose in the story?*

Level 2, Interpretive – Interpretive questions call for inferences because the answers cannot be found directly in the text; however, textual evidence points to and supports the inferences.

EXAMPLE: *Why is Raghu able to triumph over other players?*

Level 3, Universal – Universal questions go beyond the text. What are the larger issues or ideas raised by the text?

EXAMPLE: *What theme is expressed by the last line of the story?* He lay down full length on the damp grass, crushing his face into it, no longer crying, silenced by a terrible sense of his insignificance.

6. Review the questions you have already responded to in this activity, including the Making Observations and Returning to the Text questions. Identify which level each question addresses. Then look through any questions you have asked yourself and classify those as well.

7. To prepare for a group discussion, generate two Level 2 questions and two Level 3 questions about "Games at Twilight." The Level 2 questions should guide your group through the process of making inferences based on evidence from the story. The Level 3 questions should lead to open-ended discussion about the themes and universal ideas present in the story. Record your questions and your initial responses to them in the following chart.

Level 2 Question:	My Initial Response and Evidence:
Level 2 Question:	My Initial Response and Evidence:
Level 3 Question:	My Initial Response and Evidence:
Level 3 Question:	My Initial Response and Evidence:

8. In your groups, review each participant's questions to determine if there are duplicate or similar questions that can be discussed simultaneously. Then take turns posing your questions to the group, carefully taking notes when your questions are under discussion. Be sure to participate collaboratively by following these guidelines:

- Make sure you are prepared with questions and evidence from the text to use to contribute to a thoughtful, well-reasoned discussion.

- Work with your group to set rules for a respectful discussion, including how to disagree with someone's ideas.

- Contribute relevant information and incorporate the ideas of others into your responses by clarifying, agreeing with, or challenging ideas and conclusions.

- Be respectful of diverse perspectives by accurately summarizing views that you agree or disagree with while defending or altering your own views in light of the discussion.

9. After the discussion, reflect on whether your group members participated effectively. Do you think that following the discussion guidelines benefited your understanding of the text?

INDEPENDENT READING LINK

Read and Discuss

Write at least two Level 3 questions for the text you are reading independently. In your discussion group, share your questions and determine if your text offers an answer to someone else's question. Discuss any similarities or differences you discover.

LANGUAGE & WRITER'S CRAFT: Parallel Structure

Parallel structure is the use of a repeated word pattern. It is used to show the reader that two or more things are of equal importance. A sentence has parallel structure when related ideas are expressed in the same grammatical form. By using parallel structure, writers can create sentences that communicate even complex ideas very clearly. Some writers use parallel structure deliberately, thinking about the syntax, or arrangement of words and grammatical elements, in their sentences. Parallel structure can also occur naturally in sentences, when a writer puts words together in a way that sounds clear, balanced, and powerful. As you will see in the examples that follow, the parallelism in a sentence can be found at the word level, phrase level, or clause level. You will also see examples of parallelism among sentences.

The Word Level

Nouns: *But the shed smelled of rats, anthills, dust, and spider webs.*

Adjectives: *to be the winner in a circle of older, bigger, luckier children*

Gerunds: *It seemed to him that he could hear them chanting, singing, laughing.*

The Phrase Level

crumbling yellow pollen that turned to yellow fur, blue fur, gray fur

"You cheated—Mira cheated—Anu cheated—"

The Clause Level

Helped the driver wash the car when their father returned from work. Helped the gardener water the beds.

And the arc of thin arms trembled in the twilight, and the heads were bowed so sadly, and their feet tramped to that melancholy refrain so mournfully, so helplessly, that Ravi could not bear it.

PRACTICE Using what you have learned about parallelism, revisit "Games at Twilight" and look for further examples of parallelism at the word level, phrase level, and clause level. Record them in the space provided.

Learning Targets

- Analyze symbolism, imagery, and figurative language in a short story to understand the story's tone and theme.
- Determine the impact of an author's language choices on meaning and tone.
- Use literary elements, such as imagery, sequencing, and telling details to write a narrative from the limited point of view.

Preview

In this activity, you will read a short story and use the SIFT strategy to determine what the author is conveying through his literary choices.

About the Author

Ray Bradbury (1920–2012) is remembered mostly as a fantasy writer, although he also wrote horror, science fiction, and mysteries. He is best known for his novels *Fahrenheit 451*, *The Martian Chronicles*, and *The Illustrated Man*. He loved reading and at an early age became obsessed with science fiction when a guest at his parents' boarding house left behind some science fiction magazines. When Bradbury was twelve years old, a magician touched his head with an electrically charged sword and said, "Live forever." That one moment inspired him to start writing, and he wrote every day from that point on. Bradbury published more than thirty books, close to 600 short stories, and numerous poems, essays, and plays. Many of his works have been adapted into television shows or films.

Learning Strategies

Marking the Text
Note-taking
Skimming/Scanning
SIFT

My Notes

111

Short Story

There Will Come Soft Rains

by **Ray Bradbury**

1 In the living room the voice-clock sang, Tick-tock, seven o'clock, time to get up, time to get up, seven o'clock! as if it were afraid that nobody would. The morning house lay empty. The clock ticked on, repeating and repeating its sounds into the emptiness. *Seven-nine, breakfast time, seven-nine!*

2 In the kitchen the breakfast stove gave a hissing sigh and ejected from its warm interior eight pieces of perfectly browned toast, eight eggs sunny side up, sixteen slices of bacon, two coffees, and two cool glasses of milk.

3 "*Today is August 4, 2026,*" said a second voice from the kitchen ceiling, "*in the city of Allendale, California.*" It repeated the date three times for memory's sake. "*Today is Mr. Featherstone's birthday. Today is the anniversary of Tilita's marriage. Insurance is payable, as are the water, gas, and light bills.*"

4 Somewhere in the walls, relays clicked, memory tapes glided under electric eyes.

5 *Eight-one, tick-tock, eight-one o'clock, off to school, off to work, run, run, eight-one!* But no doors slammed, no carpets took the soft tread of rubber heels. It was raining outside. The weather box on the front door sang quietly: "*Rain, rain, go away; umbrellas, raincoats for today…*" And the rain tapped on the empty house, echoing.

6 Outside, the garage chimed and lifted its door to reveal the waiting car. After a long wait the door swung down again.

7 At eight-thirty the eggs were shriveled and the toast was like stone. An aluminum wedge scraped them into the sink, where hot water whirled them down a metal throat which digested and flushed them away to the distant sea. The dirty dishes were dropped into a hot washer and emerged twinkling dry.

8 *Nine-fifteen,* sang the clock, *time to clean.*

9 Out of **warrens** in the wall, tiny robot mice darted. The rooms were a crawl with the small cleaning animals, all rubber and metal. They thudded against chairs, whirling their moustached runners, **kneading** the rug nap, sucking gently at hidden dust. Then, like mysterious invaders, they popped into their burrows. Their pink electric eyes faded. The house was clean.

10 Ten o'clock. The sun came out from behind the rain. The house stood alone in a city of rubble and ashes. This was the one house left standing. At night the ruined city gave off a radioactive glow which could be seen for miles.

11 Ten-fifteen. The garden sprinklers whirled up in golden founts, filling the soft morning air with scatterings of brightness. The water pelted window panes, running down the charred west side where the house had been burned, evenly free of its white paint. The entire west face of the house was black, save

warrens: mazelike places
kneading: massaging

for five places. Here the **silhouette** in paint of a man mowing a lawn. Here, as in a photograph, a woman bent to pick flowers. Still farther over, their images burned on wood in one **titanic** instant, a small boy, hands flung into the air; higher up, the image of a thrown ball, and opposite him a girl, hands raised to catch a ball which never came down.

12   The five spots of paint - the man, the woman, the children, the ball—remained. The rest was a thin charcoaled layer.

13   The gentle sprinkler rain filled the garden with falling light.

14   Until this day, how well the house had kept its peace. How carefully it had inquired, "Who goes there? What's the password?" and, getting no answer from lonely foxes and whining cats, it had shut up its windows and drawn shades in an old-maidenly preoccupation with self-protection which bordered on a mechanical **paranoia**.

15   It quivered at each sound, the house did. If a sparrow brushed a window, the shade snapped up. The bird, startled, flew off! No, not even a bird must touch the house!

16   Twelve noon.

17   A dog whined, shivering, on the front porch.

18   The front door recognized the dog voice and opened. The dog, once huge and fleshy, but now gone to bone and covered with sores, moved in and through the house, tracking mud. Behind it whirred angry mice, angry at having to pick up mud, angry at inconvenience.

19   For not a leaf fragment blew under the door but what the wall panels flipped open and the copper scrap rats flashed swiftly out. The offending dust, hair, or paper, seized in miniature steel jaws, was raced back to the burrows. There, down tubes which fed into the cellar, it was dropped into the sighing vent of an incinerator which sat like evil Baal in a dark corner.

20   The dog ran upstairs, hysterically yelping to each door, at last realizing, as the house realized, that only silence was here.

21   It sniffed the air and scratched the kitchen door. Behind the door, the stove was making pancakes, which filled the house with a rich baked odor and the scent of maple syrup.

22   The dog frothed at the mouth, lying at the door, sniffing, its eyes turned to fire. It ran wildly in circles, biting at its tail, spun in a frenzy, and died. It lay in the parlor for an hour.

23   *Two o'clock,* sang a voice.

24   Delicately sensing decay at last, the regiments of mice hummed out as softly as blown gray leaves in an electrical wind.

25   Two-fifteen.

26   The dog was gone.

---

silhouette: outline drawing
titanic: huge or powerful
paranoia: unreasonable feeling that you are in danger

27 In the cellar, the incinerator glowed suddenly and a whirl of sparks leaped up the chimney.

28 Two thirty-five.

29 Bridge tables sprouted from patio walls. Playing cards fluttered onto pads in a shower of pips. Martinis manifested on an oaken bench with egg-salad sandwiches. Music played.

30 But the tables were silent and the cards untouched.

31 At four o'clock the tables folded like great butterflies back through the paneled walls.

32 Four-thirty.

33 The nursery walls glowed.

34 Animals took shape: yellow giraffes, blue lions, pink antelopes, lilac panthers cavorting in crystal substance. The walls were glass. They looked out upon color and fantasy. Hidden films clocked through well-oiled sprockets, and the walls lived. The nursery floor was woven to resemble a crisp, cereal meadow. Over this ran aluminum roaches and iron crickets, and in the hot still air butterflies of delicate red tissue wavered among the sharp aroma of animal spoors! There was the sound like a great matted yellow hive of bees within a dark bellows, the lazy bumble of a purring lion. And there was the patter of okapi feet and the murmur of a fresh jungle rain, like other hoofs, falling upon the summer-starched grass. Now the walls dissolved into distances of parched grass, mile on mile, and warm endless sky. The animals drew away into thorn brakes and water holes. It was the children's hour.

35 Five o'clock. The bath filled with clear hot water.

36 Six, seven, eight o'clock. The dinner dishes **manipulated** like magic tricks, and in the study a click.

37 In the metal stand opposite the hearth where a fire now blazed up warmly, a cigar popped out, half an inch of soft gray ash on it, smoking, waiting.

38 Nine o'clock. The beds warmed their hidden circuits, for nights were cool here.

39 Nine-five. A voice spoke from the study ceiling: *"Mrs. McClellan, which poem would you like this evening?"* The house was silent.

40 The voice said at last, *"Since you express no preference, I shall select a poem at random."*

41 Quiet music rose to back the voice. *"Sara Teasdale. As I recall, your favorite…*

42 *There will come soft rains and the smell of the ground,*
And swallows circling with their shimmering sound;

43 *And frogs in the pools singing at night,*
And wild plum trees in tremulous white;

manipulated: moved; controlled

44 *Robins will wear their feathery fire,*
Whistling their whims on a low fence-wire;

45 *And not one will know of the war, not one*
Will care at last when it is done.

46 *Not one would mind, neither bird nor tree,*
If mankind perished utterly;

47 *And Spring herself, when she woke at dawn*
Would scarcely know that we were gone."

48 The fire burned on the stone hearth and the cigar fell away into a mound of quiet ash on its tray. The empty chairs faced each other between the silent walls, and the music played.

49 At ten o'clock the house began to die.

50 The wind blew. A falling tree bough crashed through the kitchen window. Cleaning solvent, bottled, shattered over the stove. The room was ablaze in an instant!

51 *"Fire!"* screamed a voice. The house lights flashed, water pumps shot water from the ceilings. But the solvent spread on the linoleum, licking, eating, under the kitchen door, while the voices took it up in chorus: *"Fire, fire, fire!"*

52 The house tried to save itself. Doors sprang tightly shut, but the windows were broken by the heat and the wind blew and sucked upon the fire.

53 The house gave ground as the fire in ten billion angry sparks moved with flaming ease from room to room and then up the stairs. While scurrying water rats squeaked from the walls, pistoled their water, and ran for more. And the wall sprays let down showers of mechanical rain.

54 But too late. Somewhere, sighing, a pump shrugged to a stop. The quenching rain ceased. The reserve water supply which had filled baths and washed dishes for many quiet days was gone.

55 The fire crackled up the stairs. It fed upon Picassos and Matisses in the upper halls, like **delicacies**, baking off the oily flesh, tenderly crisping the canvases into black shavings.

56 Now the fire lay in beds, stood in windows, changed the colors of drapes!

57 And then, reinforcements. From attic trapdoors, blind robot faces peered down with faucet mouths gushing green chemical.

58 The fire backed off, as even an elephant must at the sight of a dead snake.

59 Now there were twenty snakes whipping over the floor, killing the fire with a clear cold venom of green froth.

60 But the fire was clever. It had sent flame outside the house, up through the attic to the pumps there. An explosion! The attic brain which directed the pumps was shattered into bronze shrapnel on the beams.

61 The fire rushed back into every closet and felt of the clothes hung there.

My Notes

delicacies: special foods

62 The house shuddered, oak bone on bone, its bared skeleton cringing from the heat, its wire, its nerves revealed as if a surgeon had torn the skin off to let the red veins and capillaries quiver in the scalded air. *Help, help! Fire! Run, run!* Heat snapped mirrors like the first brittle winter ice. And the voices wailed. *Fire, fire, run, run,* like a tragic nursery rhyme, a dozen voices, high, low, like children dying in a forest, alone, alone. And the voices fading as the wires popped their sheathings like hot chestnuts. One, two, three, four, five voices died.

63 In the nursery the jungle burned. Blue lions roared, purple giraffes bounded off. The panthers ran in circles, changing color, and ten million animals, running before the fire, vanished off toward a distant steaming river... Ten more voices died.

64 In the last instant under the fire avalanche, other choruses, oblivious, could be heard announcing the time, cutting the lawn by remote-control mower, or setting an umbrella frantically out and in, the slamming and opening front door, a thousand things happening, like a clock shop when each clock strikes the hour insanely before or after the other, a scene of maniac confusion, yet unity; singing, screaming, a few last cleaning mice darting bravely out to carry the horrid ashes away! And one voice, with sublime disregard for the situation, read poetry aloud in the fiery study, until all the film spools burned, until all the wires withered and the circuits cracked.

65 The fire burst the house and let it slam flat down, puffing out skirts of spark and smoke.

66 In the kitchen, an instant before the rain of fire and timber, the stove could be seen making breakfasts at a psychopathic rate, ten dozen eggs, six loaves of toast, twenty dozen bacon strips, which, eaten by fire, started the stove working again, hysterically hissing!

67 The crash. The attic smashing into kitchen and parlor. The parlor into cellar, cellar into sub-cellar. Deep freeze, armchair, film tapes, circuits, beds, and all like skeletons thrown in a cluttered mound deep under.

68 Smoke and silence. A great quantity of smoke.

69 Dawn showed faintly in the east. Among the ruins, one wall stood alone. Within the wall, a last voice said, over and over again and again, even as the sun rose to shine upon the heaped rubble and steam:

70 *"Today is August 5, 2026, today is August 5, 2026, today is..."*

Making Observations
- Who are the characters in this story?
- What details about the setting stand out to you?

oblivious: unaware

Returning to the Text

- Return to the text as you respond to the following questions. Cite text evidence to support your responses.
- Write any additional questions you have about the text in your Reader/Writer Notebook.

1. What is the organizational structure of the story? What effect does the structure of the text create on the story itself? Provide evidence from the text to support your response.

_____

_____

_____

_____

2. In the lines, "In the living room, the voice-clock sang ... as if it were afraid that nobody would," what literary device is Bradbury using? What effect does Bradbury achieve by using this device?

_____

_____

_____

_____

3. What is ironic about the author's description of the house as having a "mechanical paranoia"?

_____

_____

_____

_____

4. What is the significance of the repeated references to rain throughout the story?

_____

_____

_____

_____

Working from the Text

5. With a partner, go back and scan the story for examples of symbols, imagery, figurative language, and tone/theme to complete the SIFT graphic organizer.

Literary Element	Text Details	Effects or Meanings of Details
Symbol		
Imagery		
Figurative Language		
Tone/Theme		

☑ Check Your Understanding

Describe Bradbury's message in "There Will Come Soft Rains." How is that message conveyed through literary elements and tone? Use evidence from the text to support your response.

_____

_____

_____

_____

_____

✍ Writing Prompt: Literary

Reread the final paragraphs of "There Will Come Soft Rains," in which one lone wall stands after fire has destroyed the house. Think about the feeling this imagery has created for both the reader and the house. Using the story starter that follows, write a continuation of the narrative that shows what happens next. Use narrative techniques, such as dialogue, pacing, and description, and deliberate sentence structure to develop events and emulate Bradbury's style. You may want to devise an alternative resolution. Be sure to:

- Include telling details and vivid imagery to engage the reader.
- Include parallel constructions that add variety and clarity to your writing.
- Maintain the limited point of view to show the remaining wall's perspective.
- Use dialogue, description, or reflection to introduce and develop new events or characters.
- Sequence events using details that build on the rest of the story to create a coherent whole.

    _"Today is August 5, 2026, today is August 5, 2026, today is …" the lone wall kept repeating over and over. In the distance, a figure emerged and _____ ._

The Leap into the Future

My Notes

Learning Targets

- Identify examples of plot devices in a short story.
- Analyze how an author uses text structure for a specific purpose.

Preview

In this activity, you will explore some structural elements of a short story and analyze why the author chose to use those text structures.

Introducing the Strategy: Visualizing

Visualizing settings, characters, objects, and situations as you read helps deepen your understanding of texts by allowing you to remember details and keeping you engaged to the end of the text. Some texts offer a lot of visual information, and other texts require more work to create a good mental image. Either way, visualizing is a strategy that can help you read closely.

Opening Writing Prompt

Read the opening paragraph of "The Leap" and, in the My Notes section, write a brief description of the character you visualized.

As You Read

- Use the My Notes area to identify shifts in time within the story.
- Circle unknown words and phrases. Try to determine the meaning of the words by using context clues, word parts, or a dictionary.

About the Author

Louise Erdrich (b. 1954) is a contemporary Native American novelist. Her fiction reflects her mixed heritage: German, French, and Ojibwa. Prior to her writing career, she worked many different jobs, including lifeguarding, waitressing, cooking, construction, and farming. Her grandparents and parents were rich storytellers, and listening to these family stories led her to begin her writing career. Her father encouraged all his children to write stories, even paying them a nickel for every story they wrote. Erdrich's mother supported the effort by creating book covers from simple materials for those early manuscripts. Today, Erdrich continues to write novels, poetry, and children's books. She also owns a bookstore in Minneapolis, Minnesota.

Short Story

The Leap

by **Louise Erdrich**

1   My mother is the surviving half of a blindfold trapeze act, not a fact I think about much even now that she is sightless, the result of **encroaching** and stubborn cataracts. She walks slowly through her house here in New Hampshire, lightly touching her way along walls and running her hands over knickknacks, books, the drift of a grown child's belongings and castoffs. She has never upset an object or as much as brushed a magazine onto the floor. She has never lost her balance or bumped into a closet door left carelessly open.

2   It has occurred to me that the catlike **precision** of her movements in old age might be the result of her early training, but she shows so little of the drama or flair one might expect from a performer that I tend to forget the Flying Avalons. She has kept no sequined costume, no photographs, no feathers or posters from that part of her youth. I would, in fact, tend to think that all memory of double somersaults and heart-stopping catches had left her arms and legs were it not for the fact that sometimes, as I sit sewing in the room of the rebuilt house in which I slept as a child, I hear the crackle, catch a whiff of smoke from the stove downstairs and suddenly the room goes dark, the stitches burn beneath my fingers, and I am sewing with a needle of hot silver, a thread of fire.

3   I owe her my existence three times. The first was when she saved herself. In the town square a **replica** tent pole, cracked and splintered, now stands cast in concrete. It commemorates the disaster that put our town smack on the front page of the Boston and New York tabloids. It is from those old newspapers, now historical records, that I get my information. Not from my mother, Anna of the Flying Avalons, nor from any of her in-laws, nor certainly from the other half of her particular act, Harold Avalon, her first husband. In one news account it says, "The day was mildly overcast, but nothing in the air or temperature gave any hint of the sudden force with which the deadly gale would strike."

4   I have lived in the West, where you can see the weather coming for miles, and it is true that out here we are at something of a disadvantage. When extremes of temperature collide, a hot and cold front, winds generate instantaneously behind a hill and crash upon you without warning. That, I think, was the likely situation on that day in June. People probably commented on the pleasant air, grateful that no hot sun beat upon the striped tent that stretched over the entire center green. They bought their tickets and surrendered them in anticipation. They sat. They ate caramelized popcorn and roasted peanuts. There was time, before the storm, for three acts. The White Arabians of Ali-Khazar rose on their hind legs and waltzed. The Mysterious Bernie folded himself into a painted cracker tin, and the Lady of the Mists made herself appear and disappear in surprising places. As the clouds gathered

---

GRAMMAR & USAGE

Grammar & Usage

Erdrich uses several parallel constructions to transmit telling details in the opening of this story. For example: *She walks slowly through her house here in New Hampshire, lightly touching her way along walls and running her hands over knickknacks, books, the drift of a grown child's belongings and castoffs.*

What parts of this sentence are parallel? What effect does Erdrich achieve by using parallel structures? Find other examples of parallel structure as you read.

My Notes

---

encroaching: advancing slowly
precision: accuracy or exactness
replica: copy of an original

outside, unnoticed, the ringmaster cracked his whip, shouted his introduction and pointed to the ceiling of the tent, where the Flying Avalons were perched.

5 They loved to drop gracefully from nowhere, like two sparkling birds, and blow kisses as they threw off their **plumed** helmets and high-collared capes. They laughed and flirted openly as they beat their way up again on the trapeze bars. In the final vignette of their act, they actually would kiss in midair, pausing, almost hovering as they swooped past one another. On the ground, between bows, Harry Avalon would skip quickly to the front rows and point out the smear of my mother's lipstick, just off the edge of his mouth. They made a romantic pair all right, especially in the blindfold sequence.

6 That afternoon, as the anticipation increased, as Mr. and Mrs. Avalon tied sparkling strips of cloth onto each other's face and as they puckered their lips in mock kisses, lips destined "never again to meet," as one long breathless article put it, the wind rose, miles off, wrapped itself into a cone, and howled. There came a rumble of electrical energy, drowned out by the sudden roll of drums. One detail not mentioned by the press, perhaps unknown—Anna was pregnant at the time, seven months and hardly showing, her stomach muscles were that strong. It seems incredible that she would work high above the ground when any fall could be so dangerous, but the explanation—I know from watching her go blind—is that my mother lives comfortably in extreme elements. She is one with the constant dark now, just as the air was her home, familiar to her, safe, before the storm that afternoon.

7 From opposite ends of the tent they waved, blind and smiling, to the crowd below. The ringmaster removed his hat and called for silence, so that the two above could concentrate. They rubbed their hands in chalky powder, then Harry launched himself and swung, once, twice, in huge **calibrated** beats across space. He hung from his knees and on the third swing stretched wide his arms, held his hands out to receive his pregnant wife as she dove from her shining bar.

8 It was while the two were in midair, their hands about to meet, that lightning struck the main pole and sizzled down the guy wires, filling the air with a blue radiance that Harry Avalon must certainly have seen through the cloth of his blindfold as the tent buckled and

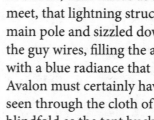

plumed: decorated with feathers
calibrated: standardized or carefully measured

the edifice toppled him forward, the swing continuing and not returning in its sweep, and Harry going down, down into the crowd with his last thought, perhaps, just a prickle of surprise at his empty hands.

9 My mother once said that I'd be amazed at how many things a person can do within the act of falling. Perhaps, at the time, she was teaching me to dive off a board at the town pool, for I associate the idea with midair somersaults. But I also think she meant that even in that awful doomed second one could think, for she certainly did. When her hands did not meet her husband's, my mother tore her blindfold away. As he swept past her on the wrong side, she could have grasped his ankle, the toe-end of his tights, and gone down clutching him. Instead, she changed direction. Her body twisted toward a heavy wire and she managed to hang on to the braided metal, still hot from the lightning strike. Her palms were burned so terribly that once healed they bore no lines, only the blank scar tissue of a quieter future. She was lowered, gently, to the sawdust ring just underneath the dome of the canvas roof, which did not entirely settle but was held up on one end and jabbed through, torn, and still on fire in places from the giant spark, though rain and men's jackets soon put that out.

10 Three people died, but except for her hands my mother was not seriously harmed until an overeager rescuer broke her arm in extricating her and also, in the process, collapsed a portion of the tent bearing a huge buckle that knocked her unconscious. She was taken to the town hospital, and there she must have hemorrhaged, for they kept her confined to her bed, a month and a half before her baby was born without life.

11 Harry Avalon had wanted to be buried in the circus cemetery next to the original Avalon, his uncle, so she sent him back with his brothers. The child, however, is buried around the corner, beyond this house and just down the highway. Sometimes I used to walk there just to sit. She was a girl, but I rarely thought of her as a sister or even as a separate person really. I suppose you could call it the egocentrism of a child, of all young children, but I considered her a less finished version of myself.

12 When the snow falls, throwing shadows among the stones, I can easily pick hers out from the road, for it is bigger than the others and in the shape of a lamb at rest, its legs curled beneath. The carved lamb looms larger as the years pass, though it is probably only my eyes, the vision shifting, as what is close to me blurs and distances sharpen. In odd moments, I think it is the edge drawing near, the edge of everything, the unseen horizon we do not really speak of in the eastern woods. And it also seems to me, although this is probably an idle fantasy, that the statue is growing more sharply etched, as if, instead of weathering itself into a porous mass, it is hardening on the hillside with each snowfall, perfecting itself.

13 It was during her confinement in the hospital that my mother met my father. He was called in to look at the set of her arm, which was complicated. He stayed, sitting at her bedside, for he was something of an armchair traveler and had spent his war quietly, at an air force training grounds, where he became a specialist in arms and legs broken during parachute training

egocentrism: quality of being self-centered or selfish

exercises. Anna Avalon had been to many of the places he longed to visit—Venice, Rome, Mexico, all through France and Spain. She had no family of her own and was taken in by the Avalons, trained to perform from a very young age. They toured Europe before the war, then based themselves in New York. She was illiterate.

14 It was in the hospital that she finally learned to read and write, as a way of overcoming the boredom and depression of those weeks, and it was my father who insisted on teaching her. In return for stories of' her adventures, he graded her first exercises. He bought her her first book, and over her hold letters, which the pale guides of the penmanship pads could not contain, they fell in love.

15 I wonder if my father calculated the exchange offered: one form of flying for another. For after that, and for as long as I can remember, my mother has never been without a book. Until now, that is, and it remains the greatest difficulty of her blindness. Since my father's recent death, there is no one to read to her, which is why I returned, in fact, from my failed life where the land is flat. I came home to read to my mother, to read out loud, read long into the dark if I must, to read all night.

16 Once my father and mother married, they moved onto the old farm he had inherited but didn't care much for. Though he'd been thinking of moving to a larger city, he settled down and broadened his practice in this valley. It still seems odd to me, when they could have gone anywhere else, that they chose to stay in the town where the disaster had occurred, and which my father in the first place had found so constricting. It was my mother who insisted upon it, after her child did not survive. And then, too, she loved the sagging farmhouse with its scrap of what was left of a vast acreage of woods and hidden hay fields that stretched to the game park.

17 I owe my existence, the second time then, to the two of them and the hospital that brought them together. That is the debt we take for granted since none of us asks for life. It is only once we have it that we hang on so dearly.

18 I was seven the year the house caught fire, probably from standing ash. It can rekindle, and my father, forgetful around the house and perpetually exhausted from night hours on call, often emptied what he thought were ashes from cold stoves into wooden or cardboard containers. The fire could have started from a flaming box, or perhaps a buildup of creosote inside the chimney was the culprit. it started right around the stove, and the heart of the house was gutted. The baby-sitter, fallen asleep in my father's den on the first floor, woke to find the stairway to my upstairs room cut off by flames. She used the phone, then ran outside to stand beneath my window.

19 When my parents arrived, the town volunteers had drawn water from the fire pond and were spraying the outside of the house, preparing to go inside after me, not knowing at the time that there was only one staircase and that it was lost. On the other side of the house, the superannuated extension ladder broke in half. Perhaps the clatter of it falling against the walls woke me, for I'd been asleep up to that point.

20 As soon as I awakened, in the small room that I now use for sewing, I smelled the smoke. I followed things by the letter then, was good at memorizing instructions, and so I did exactly what was taught in the second-grade home fire drill. I got up, I touched the back of my door before opening it. Finding it hot, I left it closed and stuffed my rolled-up rug beneath the crack. I did not hide under my bed or crawl into my closet. I put on my flannel robe, and then I sat down to wait.

21 Outside, my mother stood below my dark window and saw clearly that there was no rescue. Flames had pierced one side wall, and the glare of the fire lighted the massive limbs and trunk of the vigorous old elm that had probably been planted the year the house was built, a hundred years ago at least. No leaf touched the wall, and just one thin branch scraped the roof. From below, it looked as though even a squirrel would have had trouble jumping from the tree onto the house, for the **breadth** of that small branch was no bigger than my mother's wrist.

22 Standing there, beside Father, who was preparing to rush back around to the front of the house, my mother asked him to unzip her dress. When he wouldn't be bothered, she made him understand. He couldn't make his hands work, so she finally tore it off and stood there in her pearls and stockings. She directed one of the men to lean the broken half of the extension ladder up against the trunk of the tree. In surprise, he complied. She ascended. She vanished. Then she could be seen among the leafless branches of late November as she made her way up and, along her stomach, inched the length of a bough that curved above the branch that brushed the roof.

23 Once there, swaying, she stood and balanced. There were plenty of people in the crowd and many who still remember, or think they do, my mother's leap through the ice-dark air toward that thinnest extension, and how she broke the branch falling so that it cracked in her hands, cracked louder than the flames as she vaulted with it toward the edge of the roof, and how it hurtled down end over end without her, and their eyes went up, again, to see where she had flown.

24 I didn't see her leap through air, only heard the sudden thump and looked out my window. She was hanging by the backs of her heels from the new gutter we had put in that year, and she was smiling. I was not surprised to see her, she was so matter-of-fact. She tapped on the window. I remember how she did it, too. It was the friendliest tap, a bit tentative, as if she was afraid she had arrived too early at a friend's house. Then she gestured at the latch, and when I opened the window she told me to raise it wider and prop it up with the stick so it wouldn't crush her fingers. She swung down, caught the ledge, and crawled through the opening. Once she was in my room, I realized she had on only underclothing, a bra of the heavy stitched cotton women used to wear and step-in, lace-trimmed drawers. I remember feeling light-headed, of course, terribly relieved, and then embarrassed for her to be seen by the crowd undressed. I was still embarrassed as we flew out the window, toward earth, me in her lap, her toes pointed as we skimmed toward the painted target of the fire fighter's net.

My Notes

breadth: width

25 I know that she's right. I knew it even then. As you fall there is time to think. Curled as I was, against her stomach, I was not startled by the cries of the crowd or the looming faces. The wind roared and beat its hot breath at our back, the flames whistled. I slowly wondered what would happen if we missed the circle or bounced out of it. Then I wrapped my hands around my mother's hands. I felt the brush of her lips and heard the beat of her heart in my ears, loud as thunder, long as the roll of drums.

Making Observations

- What are the different events that the narrator tells us about?
- What visual details of the characters or settings stand out to you?
- What questions does this text raise for you?

Returning to the Text

- Return to the text as you respond to the following questions. Cite text evidence to support your responses.
- Write any additional questions you have about the text in your Reader/Writer Notebook.

1. Based on the opening paragraphs, how has the mother changed since her early years as a circus performer?

2. What character traits does the mother display with her circus performances and her actions when the accident takes place?

3. What attracts the narrator's father to her mother?

4. What are two literal leaps in the story? What is an example of a figurative leap?

5. From what point of view is this story written? What effect does the chosen point of view have on the story?

6. The narrator owes her mother her existence "three times." What are those three times? Use text evidence to support your response.

_____

_____

_____

_____

Working from the Text

7. Turn to a partner and discuss the following questions:

- What parts of the story are most suspenseful? How does foreshadowing contribute to the suspense?

- How did the author structure this story? What does the author achieve by using this structure?

☑ Check Your Understanding

State your analysis of Erdrich's craft in one sentence using the following stem.

Erdrich uses flashbacks to tell this story because _____ .

LANGUAGE & WRITER'S CRAFT: Understanding Pronoun-Antecedent Agreement

Pronouns are words that take the place of nouns (names for people, places, things, and ideas). Sometimes they take the place of other pronouns. Pronouns should agree with their antecedents in gender (male, female, or neuter) and number (singular or plural). When a pronoun doesn't agree with its antecedent, the sentence may be confusing.

Jose was happy with **his** book choice.

In this sentence, the pronoun *his* refers to the antecedent *Jose*. Both the pronoun and its antecedent are singular and masculine, so they agree.

Each time **Alyssa** talked to Jada, **she** carefully chose **her** words.

In this sentence, the pronouns *she* and *her* refer to the antecedent *Alyssa*. Both pronouns and the antecedent are singular and feminine, so they agree.

When a pronoun agrees with a compound antecedent (an antecedent joined by a conjunction such as *and* or *or/nor*), follow these rules:

When the parts of the antecedent are joined by *and*, the antecedent is plural.

Alyssa and **Jada** carefully closed **their** door.

In this sentence, the pronoun *their* refers to the antecedents *Alyssa* and *Jada*. The antecedent is plural, so the pronoun is plural as well.

When singular parts of the antecedent are joined by *or/nor*, the antecedent is singular.

Is **Adam** or **Mario** sensitive about **his** short hair?

In this sentence, the pronoun *his* refers to *Adam* or *Mario*. The antecedent is singular, so the pronoun is singular.

PRACTICE Revise each of the following sentences to correct errors in pronoun-antecedent agreement.

a. Two acrobats flipped through the air, its arms joining perfectly.

b. Neither Anna nor her mother said they would come to help.

WORD CONNECTIONS

Etymology

The word **antecedent** is made up of the Latin prefix *ante-* (meaning "before") and the Latin root *cedere* (meaning "to go").

Understanding Verb Tense and Voice

Verbs are the engines of sentences. They express action (e.g., *run, jump, think*) or a state of being (e.g., *is, was*). Verbs have qualities called *tense* and *voice* that provide additional information.

Verb Tense refers to the expression of a verb's time. Verbs do more than express action or a state of being; they also tell when something happened—in the past, present, or future. In your writing, use tenses consistently unless you are deliberately expressing differences in time or sequence.

> **Inconsistent:** *I was talking to my mother, and I say, "You'd be amazed at how many things a person can do within the act of falling."*

> **Consistent:** *I was talking to my mother, and I said, "You'd be amazed at how many things a person can do within the act of falling."*

Verb Voice refers to whether the verb is active or passive. In a sentence using active voice, the subject of the sentence performs the action expressed by the verb. In a sentence using passive voice, the subject of the sentence receives the action.

> **Active Voice:** *Louise Erdrich wrote the short story "The Leap."*

> **Passive Voice:** *The short story "The Leap" was written by Louise Erdrich.*

Active voice is more direct and less wordy than passive voice, so you should use active voice in most cases. In some cases, though, the passive voice is preferable. For instance, a writer might want to emphasize the recipient of the action, may want to avoid naming who or what performs an action, or may think that the performer of the action is not important.

Exploring Verb Tense

1. Read the following excerpt from "The Leap." Identify and underline each verb.

> I owe her my existence three times. The first was when she saved herself. In the town square a replica tent pole, cracked and splintered, now stands cast in concrete. It commemorates the disaster that put our town smack on the front page of the Boston and New York tabloids. It is from those old newspapers, now historical records, that I get my information. Not from my mother, Anna of the Flying Avalons, nor from any of her in-laws, nor certainly from the other half of her particular act, Harold Avalon, her first husband. In one news account it says, "The day was mildly overcast, but nothing in the air or temperature gave any hint of the sudden force with which the deadly gale would strike."

2. With a partner, decide whether the verbs are in the past, present, or future tense. Why do you think Erdrich uses this tense?

Avoiding Unnecessary Shifts in Verb Tense

Writers may choose to use a variety of tenses to narrate details about events that have happened in the past, to describe realities of the moment, and to express wishes for the future. Using a variety of tenses can be a powerful narrative tool, but switching tenses unintentionally can make writing unclear. In your writing, use tenses consistently, unless you have a good reason to switch them.

3. Look at this sentence from "The Leap." Underline the verbs. Discuss with a partner what you notice about the verbs' tenses.

> She walks slowly through her house here in New Hampshire, lightly touching her way along walls and running her hands over knickknacks, books, the drift of a grown child's belongings and castoffs.

4. What do you notice about the verbs in these two clauses? With a partner, look at the sentence, and make an observation about the verbs' tenses.

They bought their tickets, and then surrender them in anticipation.

Exploring Verb Voice

5. Read the following sentence, which uses active voice. Then briefly describe why you think the writer chose the active voice.

My mother tore her blindfold away.

6. Now read this sentence, which is written in passive voice. How does the passive voice change the meaning and effect of the sentence?

   The blindfold was torn away.

Avoiding Unnecessary Shifts in Verb Voice

Writers may choose to use active and passive voice for different effects, but they should avoid unnecessary shifts in voice.

7. Look at this sentence from a student's essay about "The Leap." Underline the verbs.

   The narrator recalls her childhood, and the pain is remembered.

8. What do you notice about the verbs in these two clauses? With a partner, look at the sentence, and make an observation about the verbs' voices.

Revising

9. Read the following passage from a student's essay about "The Leap." Work with a partner to check whether the verbs maintain an appropriate and consistent tense. Look for changes in the writer's voice. Circle any mistakes you notice, and then mark the text to correct the mistakes.

   [1] Louise Erdrich, the author of "The Leap," uses a series of flashbacks to tell this story. [2] The narrator recalled stories of her mother's life, which she learns about from old newspapers. [3] According to the newspapers, her mother was the surviving half of a blindfold trapeze act; her athleticism and quick thinking help her escape death. [4] While in the hospital after the tragic accident, she met the narrator's father, a doctor who cares for the mother [5] I'm telling you, this story was great and you should stop what you are doing right now and read it.

☑ Check Your Understanding

Imagine you are editing a classmate's writing, and you notice incorrect shifts in verb tense and voice. In your own words, write an explanation to help your classmate understand how to identify shifts and how to correct them. Then add items to your Editor's Checklist to help you remember how to revise your writing to use verb tense and voice consistently and appropriately.

Practice

Return to a text you have written in this unit and check your use of verb tense. Then check it for verb voice. Is the text consistent and clear? If not, edit it.

Analyzing Martha

Learning Strategies

Graphic Organizer
Marking the Text
Note-taking

My Notes

Learning Targets

- Analyze how complex characters are developed over the course of a story.
- Recognize important details in a short story.

Preview

In this activity, you will read the first part of a short story and analyze the literary techniques the author uses to develop characters.

As You Read

- Use the My Notes section to jot down pieces of information you read about the characters that help develop your mental image of them.
- Circle unknown words and phrases. Try to determine the meaning of the words by using context clues, word parts, or a dictionary.

About the Author

Zadie Smith (b. 1975) is a British author of English and Jamaican heritage. Born Sadie Smith, she changed the spelling of her name to Zadie when she was 14. She published her first novel when she was in college, which put her on *Granta* magazine's list of 20 best young authors. Smith writes stories that delve into race, religion, class, and cultural identity. Her novels often contain eccentric characters and witty dialogue.

Short Story

Martha, Martha (Part 1)

by **Zadie Smith**

1   Though the telephone is a perfectly useless indicator of most human qualities, it's pretty precise about age. From her tiny office on the third floor, Pam Roberts looked through a window and correctly identified the Martha Penk she was waiting for, a shrimpish girl pushing twenty-two, lost down there. She had on a red overcoat and cream snow boots, putting her weight on their edges like an ice skater; she seemed to waver between two doorways. Pam opened her mouth to call out 'Miss Penk!' but never got to make the curious sound—abruptly the girl turned the corner and headed back down Apple towards the river. Pam went to her own door, opened it, worried her chapped lips with a finger, closed it again. The cold was just too extreme; today the first snows were due, opening performance of a show that would last a dreary, relentless four months. Besides, she had her slippers on. Miss Martha Penk,

who appeared to believe that two bedrooms and a garden could be had for a thousand dollars a month, would figure out her second mistake soon enough, come back, discover the bell. The confusion was common; it arose from the higgledy-piggledy arrangement of the ground floor—a busy bookshop and a swing-doored optician obscured the sign that told you of the dentist, the insurers, the accountant and Pam's own dinky realty business at the top of the building; also the antique elevator that would take you to them. Pam tapped her door with a knuckle, warning it she would return, and crossed the room to the filing cabinet. On tiptoes she slid open the top drawer and began flicking through files, her Mozart swelling behind her. She sang along with that section of the *Requiem* that sounds so very like 'OH I SEE YOU WILL GO *DOWN!* AND I SEE YOU WILL GO ALSO!', although it could not be this for the words are Latin. As she sang she ground one of her Chinese slippers rhythmically into the carpet and pressed herself into the metal drawer to reach for something at the very back: 'OH I SEE YOU WILL GO DOWN, OH! I SEE YOU WILL GO DOWN! ALSO! ALSO!'

2   Pam found what she wanted, closed the cabinet suddenly with an elbow and sat down in a fat armchair opposite a lithograph of Venice. She put a foot in her hand and said 'Phee-yoo! Now, there you go,' pressing relief into a sore instep. She started picking out every third sheet or so from the listings and laying them on the floor before her in a small pile. At the opening of the 'Lacrimosa' she removed her slipper entirely, but then hearing someone gallop up the stairs, replaced it and quickly rose to greet a large, dark, bearded man in a sheepskin overcoat, who stood bent at the knees like a shortstop, trying to recover his breath in the hallway. He took a step towards her, looked up and frowned. He paused where he was, supporting himself with a hand on the door frame. Pam knew exactly why he had come and the two spoke at the same time.

3   'This temping agency?' he asked, a heavy accent, quickly identified by Pam as Middle-Easterny. A Middle-Easterny scarf, too, and a hat.

4   'No dear, no,' said Pam, and let her glasses fall to her chest from their chain, 'It's above the other Milliner's Books, right? There's two Milliner's Books—you need the one on the corner of Apple and Wallace—this is the wrong Milliner's, this is above the children's Milliner's—I don't know why they just don't say that to people—' The man groaned pleasantly and hit his temple with the hub of his palm.

5   'I make mistake. Sorry, please.'

6   'No, they just didn't say, they never do. It's not you, dear, it's them—people always come here by mistake, it's not you. It's two minutes from here. Now, you go back down, turn left, then immediately right, you can see it from there. I've got somebody who just did the exact same, but exactly—only vice versa—she's gone to…'

7   A further thundering on the stairs and three more men, younger, also bearded. They stood bent like their friend, panting, one man crying the involuntary tears of a Massachusetts winter. They stared at Pam who stared

My Notes

frankly back at them, with her hands on her makeshift hips, up there where her black linen trousers began, high under the breasts. A black T-shirt and cardigan finished the thing off. Pam was a recognized doodlenut when it came to clothes, buying the same things over and over, black and loose, like a fat Zen monk. She didn't mind. Her moustache was moist and visible—oh, so let 'em stare was how Pam felt about it. Young men did not register with Pam any more.

8 'My friends,' explained the man, and with his friends began the descent, emptying out a **demotic** mystery language into the stairwell. Miss Penk must have passed them on the bend. A moment later she was in the room apologizing for her lateness.

9 'Sorry I'm late, I'm sorry,' she said, but did not look sorry. Her face, very black, could not blush, and her accent, to Pam's ears very English, could not apologize. She stood in the center of the room, clumsily **divesting** herself of the loud red coat. She was short, but more muscular, more solid than she had appeared from three floors up. A cheap-looking grey trouser suit and some fake pearls were conspiring to make her older than she was. The buttons on the jacket looked like rusty spare change.

10 'No, I saw you, you see,' began Pam warmly, coming forward to catch what was falling, a scarf, a woolly hat, 'There's two Milliner's—did you see those men? On the stairs? They did the exact same thing—and I saw you down—' 'The lift's broken, it don't work,' said Martha, and now lifted her head and reached out a hand. Pam felt faintly interrupted, but took the hand and gave it a double-handed shake.

11 'Pam Roberts, we spoke on the phone. It's so good to *meet* you!'

12 'I'm Martha,' she replied and quickly freed herself. She passed a smoothing hand over her own short ironed hair, cut in a flapper's style, a helmet brilliant with some kind of polish. A concrete kiss curl had been plastered on to her left cheek. Pam had never seen anything quite like it in her office before.

13 'Well. Now, did you come from far? Are you nearby?' Pam asked, a question that had a little business in it.

14 'Near, yeah,' said the girl, firmly. She stood oddly, hands by her sides, feet together, 'A hotel, it's called The Charles? It's just like by the river—it's just if you go down by—'

15 'Oh, I know where it is—it's *very* nice.'

16 'It costs too much, man,' said Martha, tutting loudly, removing a pair of childish mittens, 'But I came right from London and I didn't have any place arranged—I just arksed the taxi to take me to the nearest hotel—I been there a week, but I can't afford it for much longer, you know?'

17 Usually Pam would use these minutes in the office to **ascertain** something about likely wealth, class, all very gently— what kind of house, what kind of taste, what kind of price—but she had been wrong about English

demotic: relating to language used by ordinary people
divesting: ridding
ascertain: find out

accents before, not knowing which were high class, which not. Or whether high class meant money at *all*—if you watched PBS as Pam did you soon found out that in England it could, often did, mean the exact opposite.

18   'It is such a nice place, The Charles. They really do things properly there, don't they? They really make the best of that location, I think. I stayed there once for a realty conference, and I really appreciated the standard of the breakfasts. People talk about pool this, steam-room that, but in actual fact it's the little things, like a *breakfast*. A good hot *breakfast*. But my *God* the price isn't any fun—Martha, we'll have you out of there in no time, I promise, especially if we find something empty—'

19   'Yes,' said Martha, but rather too quick, too desperate, 'How long would it be before I could move in somewhere?' Pam felt herself immediately on surer ground and slipped down a gear into patter, 'Well, as I'm saying, dear, it depends on whether the place has people in it at the moment—but even then, we can turn it around very very quickly. It just needs to happen so that everybody wants to make it work, that's all. Don't worry, we'll find something that works. And if it doesn't work, we'll cut it loose and go on to the next,' she said loudly, clapping her hands and glancing at a clock on the wall, 'Now, I've got about two hours free—it's really very dry at the moment so there's *plenty* to show.' She bent down to scoop the remembered listings from the floor, 'I think I understand what you're looking for, Martha, I received your letter, I have it right here—Wait—' Pam reached over to her stereo like a woman with one foot each in two drifting boats; she punched at a couple of buttons to no **avail**, 'Sometimes it gets a little loud. Funny little machine. It's completely wireless! It's like a single unit stereo for single people, very liberating. You can't really adjust it without the remote, though, which is a little frustrating. And I find it gets louder sometimes, do you know? Sort of when you don't expect it?'

20   'Classical,' said Martha, and looked at Pam and the surrounding office with determined reverence, 'I want to listen to more classical music. I want to know more about it. It's on my list.'

21   And this she said in such a way that Pam had no doubt that there was such a list, and that renting an apartment *today* was somewhere on it. The girl had a manner that was all itinerary, charmless and determined, and Pam, a Midwesterner by birth, had the shameful idea that she might go far, this Martha Penk, here on the East Coast.

22   'Oh! Well, I don't know what there is to *know*, really. I mean, I don't know anything at *all*. It's the violins that do it for me, I guess, the way they sound like somebody's crying? The "Lacrimosa" means crying, I'm pretty sure. Lachrymose—that's from the eye, isn't it? But are you at the university?'

23   'No!' said Martha but her face at last released a flood of undisguised pleasure, as when a girl is told she could be a model or an actress or do whatever she does amateurishly, professionally, 'I wish! Maybe one day. I'm looking for that next level—qualifications, getting forward, raising myself, my consciousness. But that's like a dream, yeah, for me at this stage?'

My Notes

avail: use, advantage, or value

24 She looked serious again, began enlisting her hands in her speech, drawing out these 'levels' in the air, 'It's about stepping a bit further, I mean, for me, I really want to improve myself while I'm here, go up a bit, like listening to different music, like that.'

…

25 'Now,' said Pam, struggling a little, 'From your letter I understood you were thinking around the thousand mark—but that's really a little *low*—I mean, I'll show you those places, Martha, but I can't guarantee you're going to *like* them. I mean, they're not there to be *liked*,' Pam said patiently, and gathered up her car keys from her desk, 'But we'll find something that works—we just need to get a handle on it. I'd like to show you a big place that's going for two thousand, maybe—maybe lower—it's negotiable with the present owner. In more vibrant times, it's worth at least three. It'll give us some idea anyway. I'm here to make it work for you, so, I'm going to be led by you…'

26 Outside a plane roared low like some prehistoric bird, Pam shuddered; Martha did not move. Pam tried jostling her keys expectantly in her hand; Martha put down the CD case leaving the notes unfolded and walked over to the window. From behind she was an even more neatly made girl than from the front, everything tight and defined, fighting slightly against the **banal** restraint of polyester.

27 'We'll take my car, if that's all right,' tried Pam, anxious that Martha should not open a window but unwilling to ask her not to. It was hot in the room, but it was that time of year: you either fried or you froze. But Martha had already tugged on the sash, in a second her head was out there in the open air. Pam winced. She hated to see people lean all the way out of a window like that.

28 'Do you get a lot of university people? Students?'

29 'Oh, *yes*. At the beginning of a semester, certainly. Students around here have some money to spare, if you know what I mean.'

30 Martha took her plastic pearls in her hand and twisted them. 'They must be amazing. Focused people.'

31 'Oh! Well, yes, I suppose. Certainly, they're *bright*. There's just no denying that. But I'm afraid,' said Pam in her own, overused, comic whisper, 'They can be pretty *obnoxious* as well.'

32 'There aren't any black students,' Martha said in a tone somewhere between statement and question. Pam, who was in the middle of forcing her arm though a recalcitrant coat sleeve, stopped in her position like a scarecrow, 'Well, of *course* there are students of color, dear! I see them all the time—I mean, even before the affirmative action and all of that—I mean, there's always been the basketball scholarships and the rest—though it's much, much better now of course. They're *completely* here on their own steam *now*. Lots of Chinese young people too, and Indian, many. Many! Oh, there's plenty, *plenty* of people of color here, you'll see,' said Pam and switched off her desk lamp. 'But have

banal: ordinary and boring

you been to America before?' 'Only Florida when I was twelve. I didn't like it—it's quite **vulgar**?' said Martha, and the word was most definitely borrowed in her mouth. Pam, who also occasionally borrowed words, recognized the habit and tried to look kindly upon it.

33 'Florida and Nigeria are the only places I've been, really, out of England,' continued Martha, leaning yet further out, gazing across the square, 'And now here.'

34 'Oh, are you Nigerian?' Pam asked, kicked off her slippers and began to replace them with treasured walking boots. When people remarked that Pam had become 'so *hard*' recently or suggested that she'd turned into a doodlenut since her divorce, they often meant these boots and nothing more than these boots.

35 'My parents.'

36 'Penk, it's very unusual, isn't it?' said Pam to Martha's back, 'Is that a Nigerian name?'

37 'No.'

38 Nothing further came. Discovering her remote control behind a coffee cup, Pam stopped the CD and then approached, reaching briskly around Martha to close the window. Clearly, the girl blew hot and cold; in the end Pam just needed her name on a contract, nothing more. Even that was not essential—plenty of people take up your whole afternoon and never call again; Pam called them her one-day stands.

39 'Look at that sky. It's gonna snow any minute. You know, we should try to get going before it really starts to come down…'

40 With a simple, businesslike nod Pam indicated the coat that Martha had left draped over the photocopier.

Making Observations

- What do we know about the characters so far?
- What details of the setting stand out to you?

vulgar: lacking good taste

☑ Focus on the Sentence

Choose one character from "Martha, Martha" and write two statements and two questions about her or him. Be sure that you have evidence from the text to support your statements and questions.

Statement 1: _____

_____

Statement 2: _____

_____

Question 1: _____

_____

Question 2: _____

_____

Returning to the Text

- Return to the text as you respond to the following questions. Cite text evidence to support your responses.
- Write any additional questions you have about the text in your Reader/Writer Notebook.

1. The two main characters, Pam and Martha, are seemingly very different. What do the story's telling details reveal about them? How does their relationship reflect a theme developing in the story?

_____

_____

_____

_____

2. What text evidence supports the idea that Martha is trying to escape from something and start over in America? What inferences can you make based on this evidence?

_____

_____

_____

_____

Working from the Text

3. When you analyze characters, you look closely at their words, thoughts, and actions to better understand why they do what they do and say what they say. Analyzing the main characters in "Martha, Martha" will also aid you in the literary analysis you will write. Review your notes from "Martha, Martha" and complete two versions of the following chart, one for Pam and the other for Martha.

Pam's Attributes	Telling Details from the Text	What the Telling Details Reveal About the Character
Character's Appearance		
Character's Words		
Character's Thoughts		
Character's Actions		
What Others Say/Think About the Character		

Martha's Attributes	Telling Details from the Text	What the Telling Details Reveal About the Character
Character's Appearance		
Character's Words		
Character's Thoughts		
Character's Actions		
What Others Say/Think About the Character		

4. The author was born in London, England, her father was British, and her mother is Jamaican. Smith is a professor at a university in New York City. How are these experiences with multiculturalism reflected in her literary work, "Martha, Martha"? Cite text evidence to support your analysis.

_____

_____

_____

_____

_____

_____

5. One of the literary devices authors can use to create believable, well-developed characters is the character foil. In "Martha, Martha," the two main characters, Pam and Martha, are very different from one another. With a partner, discuss their similarities and differences. Which one has characteristics that are easier to identify? Make a T-Chart to record your ideas.

LITERARY

A **character foil** is a character who contrasts with another character, often the protagonist. Characters and their foils can either be entirely different or similar with just a key difference. In either case, the way the character and the foil contrast leads to some insight about each.

VOCABULARY

☑ Check Your Understanding

In a few sentences, describe both Pam and Martha. What are they like, and what do you think is motivating them? Which telling details contribute to your understanding of the characters?

✍ Writing to Sources: Informational Text

Write a paragraph that analyzes the author's use of foils to create believable characters. Be sure to:

- Begin with a topic sentence that responds to the prompt.
- Cite details from the text as supporting evidence.
- Respond using literary terminology and in an appropriately formal register, tone, and voice.

Learning Strategies

Graphic Organizer
Marking the Text
Note-taking

My Notes

Learning Targets

- Use new information to revisit and revise a character analysis.
- Analyze an author's use of literary devices in a short story.

Preview

In this activity, you will finish reading "Martha, Martha" and begin composing a literary analysis for Embedded Assessment 1.

As You Read

- Use the My Notes section to jot down pieces of information you read about the characters that help develop your mental image of them.
- Circle unknown words and phrases. Try to determine the meaning of the words by using context clues, word parts, or a dictionary.

Short Story

Martha, Martha (Part 2)

by **Zadie Smith**

[Pam and Martha visit a large, old home being rented out by a professor. Martha feels that the house feels sad and dank and tells Pam that it is out of her price range. It has begun to snow.]

41 *'Okay...*well, now I wanted to ask about money,' said Pam slowly, coming to the opening and hugging herself against the chill, 'I mean, are we talking about savings? You're very young. Or will you be working? Just so I have some *idea* of how much space we have to maneuver.'

42 Martha stayed where she was in the garden but put both hands out in front of her, awaiting whatever came. The flakes were massive, consistent and quick, as if the snow was not merely falling but being delivered, like manna, because people needed it.

43 'I've been left some,' said Martha quietly, 'In a will. My uncle passed. Basically, it's enough for a year. A thousand a month, two bedrooms and a garden, yeah? Maybe a bit more, maybe. I need space for people. To come.' She paused. 'If they want.' Suddenly she seemed agitated, even panicked; she attacked her bottom lip with her teeth and looked up and over into the next garden, 'People who might visit, you get me? But this is too too big, I can't afford it. I can't. Don't you have anything I can *afford?'*

44 It looked for a moment that the girl was about to cry—out of instinct Pam hurried towards her—but by the time she stepped outside Martha had already recovered herself, turning to peer now over the back wall towards the piercing towers and stark white crosses of the university. She seemed calmly framed by them and remote, a figure in a plastic snowstorm.

45 'Something a bit further out, maybe,' offered Pam a minute later as they climbed back into the car.

46 'If I had all that education,' said Martha, fastening her seat belt, 'Believe me, I wouldn't live somewhere like *that*.'

47 'Oh no?'

48 'I'd live somewhere *new*.'

49 'I see,' said Pam tersely, starting the car and welcoming the automatic resuscitation of the stereo, Mozart and his death song as background filler. 'Well, each to their own, I suppose, Martha, that's what this business is about, of course. Actually, I used to live on this street, at the top end, at this end, in the more modern architecture, and I must say I found it very pleasant for a long time. Though I also enjoy—I have a sort of apartment now, downtown, and that's also very nice, in a different way.'

50 'You used to live in one of these big houses?' Martha asked, with unseemly incredulity, and as she spoke they drove past the very house. For the first time in months Pam resisted the urge to inspect the curtains, the lawn, the little things he'd changed for somebody else.

51 'Why'd you go?'

52 'Circumstances. My circumstances changed. I guess you could say that.'

53 'How?'

54 'My *gosh*, you are a nosy parker. I'll guess I'll have to tell you my dress size next.'

55 'I'm just arksing, you don't have to answer.'

56 'You should be a lawyer or something, it's like being cross-*examined*.' 'So why'd you go?'

57 Pam sighed, but in fact she had, some time ago, designed a speech to answer the question, whoever it came from, 'Well, I suppose at my age, Martha, and especially in the light of the events of last September, I just think you have to make things work for you, work for you *personally*, because life is really too short, and if they don't work, you just have to go ahead and cut them loose, and that's basically—'

58 'I'd love to be a lawyer,' interrupted Martha, 'My friend is a lawyer. She has a house like that. Big-up house. We used to get the bus together to school. Now she's a big lawyer. That's like the best thing you can be.'

59 'You know what?' said Pam, drumming the steering wheel and preparing to lie, 'I like what I do. I don't think I'd change it to be a lawyer for all the tea in China. I really don't. I guess that's just me.'

60 Martha pulled down the passenger mirror, licked her finger and began to reshape her kiss curl.

My Notes

61 'She's my role model, Kara—she definitely took it to the next level—as a young black woman, you know? She didn't get caught up in a lot of the things you can get caught up in—kids and that. She took it forward. That's where I'm aiming for—if you don't aim high, there's no point, really.'

62 Martha wound down the window that Pam had just closed and Pam felt she might just scream if the girl kept letting the outside in everywhere they went.

63 'Now, *good* for her! And good for you, too. God knows, when I was your age, all I did was have children, oh *my*. I've three girls. But it's such a different world. I wouldn't even want to bring up children in this world now. My *gosh*, it's really snowing. That's a couple of inches since we left the office.'

64 They drove twenty minutes and then parked a street from the one they wanted so Martha would have an opportunity to see a bit of this new neighborhood by foot. It was cold beyond cold.

65 Everything laid out like a promise, delayed for summer; bleached porches, dead gardens, naked trees, a sky-blue clapboard house, its rose-pink neighbor. Part of the East Coast realtor's skill is to explain what places will look like when the sun finally comes.

66 'And this just goes the most *incredible* orange when the fall comes. It's like the whole city is on fire. Just life, life, life *everywhere*. Now: the couple we're about to see,' said Pam, walking briskly ahead, 'They are just darling. Yousef and Amelia. He's Moroccan and so handsome and she's American, just American, and they have such a beautiful daughter, Lily.'

67 'Where they going to go, then, if I move in?'

68 'They're moving to Morocco. It's just what we were saying, they don't really want to bring up children in this country, I'm afraid. And frankly, I can understand that. They're *artists* too, so, they're a little bit flaky. But *very* sophisticated. So witty, and they make you feel comfortable right away, you know? Now, Martha, I've shown so many people this house, but it's a little too small for a family and a little too big for a single person, so it's awkward—but it's *perfect* for you—now, what is that—'

69 There had been a babbling noise the past minute or so, excited foreign voices, and as they turned the corner Martha saw some snow come flying and guessed at children, but the next second revealed the depth of the voices—these were bearded men, with dark, ashen skins—and the argument was over design, a snowman. It was incompetently begun, a tall upturned cone upon which a future head would never sit. And now work had stopped entirely; at the sight of the two women, the men froze and looked at their gloved hands and seemed to find themselves ridiculous.

70 'But those are the men!' cried Pam when they were not five yards out of hearing range, 'From my office. They just came just before you. But isn't that *weird*? They're making a snowman!'

71 'Is that what they were doing?' asked Martha, and dug into her pocket for a mint she had quietly lifted from the bowl of same in Pam's office.

72 'Well, what *else* were they doing. You know, Martha, they've probably never seen snow. Isn't that amazing—what a thing to see!'

73 'Grown men playing in the snow,' said Martha, but Pam could not be dissuaded from the romance of it, and it was the first anecdote she told as they walked through the door of 28 Linnaean, a canary-yellow first-floor apartment with two porches, front and back, nestled behind a nineteenth-century police station.

…

74 Amelia said, 'Hey there, Martha. Do you think you'll take this place off our hands? *Please* won't you, please? We're totally desperate!'

75 'I don't know yet, do I?' said Martha very fiercely and made the odd, contemptuous noise with her teeth again. Lily reached out a doughy pink hand for Martha's face; she flinched from it.

76 'Oh,' said Amelia, reddening, and battling Lily's tiny kicking legs, 'I didn't mean to—'

77 Pam almost blew up right there—she just *could not* understand what kind of a girl this was, where she came from, what kind of conversation was normal for her. She drummed her fingers on the patch of wall behind her—as close an expression of **suppressed** fury as Pam ever managed.

78 'Martha, I'm sure Amelia only meant—'

79 'I was really joking, I didn't—' said Amelia, putting an incautious hand on Martha's shoulder, feeling a taut, inflexible muscle. She soon retracted it, but Martha continued to look and speak to the spot where the hand had been, 'I didn't mean that, I mean I meant I think I want to be nearer the university, nearer all of that, yeah? It's very alone up here, if you're alone, isn't it?'

80 'Well, you know, there's a very convenient bus—' said Amelia, looking over Martha to Pam who was performing a minimal mime with her thumbs to the effect that she did not know the girl well nor could she explain her.

81 'I'll look around,' said Martha, and walked away from them both, down the hall.

…

82 At the other end of the apartment, Martha's walk changed; she was alone. She moved through the two big bedrooms, loose and alert, examining the strange foreign things in them: Arabic writing, meaningless paintings, and all those touches that rich people seem to use to look poor: wood floors, threadbare rugs, no duvets, all blankets, nothing matching. Old leather instead of new, fireplaces instead of central heating, everything wrong. Only the bathroom was impressive; very clean, white tiled. It had a mirror with a movie star's bald light bulbs circling it. Martha locked herself in here, ran both of

suppressed: bottled up

My Notes

the taps full blast, and sat on the closed toilet seat. She took a worn-looking, folded photograph from her coat pocket and wept. She was crying even before she had unfolded it, but flattening it out now against her knee made it almost impossible for her to breathe. In the picture a grinning, long-lashed boy, about eighteen months old, with a head like a polished ackee nut, sat on the lap of a handsome black man. Neither the picture nor their mutual beauty was in any way marred by the fact that both of them had sellotaped their noses to their foreheads to give the impression of pigs' snouts. Martha turned over the photograph and read what was written there.

83 Martha, Martha, I love U

84 And I'm trying 2 tell U true

85 For this New Year 2002

86 I am going to be there for U

87 I know that U have many dreams

88 And life is not always how it seems

89 But I want U 2 put me 2 the test

90 And I will do all the rest

91 Together we will get so much higher

92 Through my love and our desire

93 Don't give up on what we've got

94 Cos Ben and Jamal love U a lot!

95 It took another five minutes to recover herself. She rinsed her face in the sink and flushed the toilet. She came close up to the mirror and gave thanks to God for her secretive skin that told nobody anything; no flush, no puffiness. She could hear a great deal of laughter the other side of the door and wondered what they were saying about her; especially *him,* who was probably the worst, because he'd married like that and those ones that marry white always feel even more superior. She hadn't expected this. She didn't know what she'd expected.

96 'Martha!' cried Pam as she appeared again in the kitchen-lounge, 'I thought you'd been eaten by something. Eaten by a bear.'

97 'Just looking around. It's nice.'

…

98 'So you've had a good look around—she's had a good look around, Yousef, so that's something. Now,' said Pam, reaching down to the floor to get her bag, 'I don't want to hurry anybody. It always helps to get to know each other a little bit, I think. How can we make this work, for everybody?'

99 'But I don't know if I—I can't—'

100 'Martha, *dear,*' said Pam, returning a pen and pad she was holding back to her bag, 'There's no hurry whatsoever, that's not the way this works at all.'

WORD CONNECTIONS

Roots and Affixes

Superior has the Latin root *super,* which means "placed above." This root is found as a prefix in many English words, including *superb, superlative, supreme, supervise, superintendent,* and *supernatural.*

101 'You know what?' replied Martha. With trembling fingers, she undid and then retied the waistband of her coat, 'I've got to go.'

102 'Well—' said Pam, completely astonished, and shook her head, 'But—if you'll give me—just wait a minute, I'll—'

103 'I'll walk. I want to walk—I need some air.'

104 Pam put down her coffee cup, and smiled awkwardly between Yousef and Amelia on the one hand and Martha on the other, increasing, as only Pam knew how, the awkwardness on both sides.

105 'I think I want a one bedroom thing,' mumbled Martha, her hand already on the doorknob, 'One bedroom would be more...' she said but could not finish. 'I'm sorry,' she said, and again Pam could not tell if she meant it. You can't tell anything about a one-day stand. They aren't there to be known. Pam shunted herself off the stool and put her hands out as if for something falling but Martha had already backed on to the porch. She struggled down the snowy steps, felt the same panic that rightly belongs to a fire escape. She could hear the clamor of snowman builders, speaking in tongues, laughing about something.

Making Observations
- What details stand out to you?
- How do the characters relate to one another?

My Notes

WORD CONNECTIONS

Roots and Affixes
The word clamor comes from a Latin word meaning "to call out." The root *clam*, also spelled *claim*, appears in *exclaim* and *exclamation*, *proclaim* and *proclamation*.

Returning to the Text

- Return to the text as you respond to the following questions. Use text evidence to support your responses.
- Write any additional questions you have about the short story in your Reader/Writer Notebook.

1. What can you infer from the message on the back of the photograph? What evidence supports your understanding?

_____

_____

_____

_____

2. Why does Martha want to live near the university?

_____

_____

_____

_____

3. What causes Martha to panic and want to leave the yellow apartment?

_____

_____

_____

_____

4. What inference can you make about what happened to Martha in her past? Find textual evidence to support your answer.

_____

_____

_____

_____

Working from the Text

5. With a small group, brainstorm a list of the literary elements you have studied in this unit and take turns explaining their meanings. Review the stories you have read and analyze the effect these devices have on the stories in which they are used.

_____

_____

_____

_____

_____

_____

_____

_____

_____

_____

6. Conduct a close reading of paragraphs 82–101 of "Martha, Martha." Use sticky notes to annotate the text with your interpretation and analysis.

7. How are the author's experiences with multiculturalism reflected in Part 2 of her literary work, "Martha, Martha"? Revisit your initial response to Activity 1.20, step 4, and incorporate new details. Then in a small group, discuss your ideas of how multiculturalism is reflected in the story.

☑ Check Your Understanding

Revisit your response to the Check Your Understanding task in Activity 1.20. Revise it in light of the information presented in the second half of the short story.

_____

_____

_____

_____

ⓘ Independent Reading Checkpoint

You are going to participate in book talks in small groups to share insights into the books you have each read. You should consider how the author creates a rich world in your independent reading book. Is the world that the author creates real or imagined? What telling details does the author use to sustain your interest throughout the book?

Writing a Literary Analysis

ASSIGNMENT

Your assignment is to write a literary analysis in which you analyze how Zadie Smith uses literary devices or other elements to express the theme of coping with emotional turmoil in the short story "Martha, Martha."

Planning and Prewriting: Take time to select and annotate a passage. Plan for your response.	▪ What devices or elements will you choose? ▪ What part of the text will you revisit to find text evidence? ▪ How does Smith use the devices or elements you chose?
Drafting: Determine the structure of your essay and how to incorporate necessary elements.	▪ How will you organize your essay? What tools will you use to help you organize? ▪ What is your claim? ▪ What textual evidence do you need to support your claim? How will you include implicit and explicit information from the text?
Evaluating and Revising: Create opportunities to review and revise to produce your best work.	▪ How will you ask for feedback on your draft? Whom will you ask? ▪ How will you ensure you have included a logical structure, effective order, and transitions? ▪ How will you revise your work to make your sentences more effective? ▪ How can you incorporate parallel structures?
Checking and Editing for Publication: Confirm that the final draft is ready for publication.	▪ How will you proofread and edit your draft to demonstrate a command of the conventions of standard English (capitalization, punctuation, spelling, grammar, and usage)? ▪ How will you ensure pronoun-antecedent agreement? ▪ How will you ensure you are using verb tense and voice consistently and clearly? ▪ How will you use the Scoring Guide to be sure you have met all the criteria for this assignment?

Reflection

Describe how you have grown as a reader, and as a writer, in the process of creating this literary analysis. Have you discovered anything new about yourself as a reader? As a writer? If so, what? If not, why not?

Writing a Literary Analysis

SCORING GUIDE

Scoring Criteria	Exemplary	Proficient	Emerging	Incomplete
Ideas	The response • shows thorough comprehension of the source text and is free from errors of interpretation • shows a perceptive analysis of the explicit and implicit meanings found in the text • includes relevant, sufficient, and strategically chosen support for claims.	The response • shows effective comprehension of the source text and is free from significant errors of interpretation • shows a reasonable analysis of the explicit and implicit meanings found in the text • includes relevant support for claims.	The response • shows a basic or general comprehension of the text and has some errors of interpretation • shows a limited or unconvincing analysis of the explicit and implicit meanings found in the text • includes limited or weak support for claims.	The response • shows little or no comprehension of the source text and has numerous errors of interpretation • shows little or no analysis of the explicit and implicit meanings found in the text • includes little or no support for claims.
Structure	The response • presents a cohesive and logical organizational structure, with an insightful claim, effective order, and clear transitions.	The response • presents a cohesive and logical organizational structure, with a plausible claim, effective order, and transitions.	The response • presents an incohesive and inadequate organizational structure, with an unclear claim and a lack of adequate transitions.	The response • lacks cohesion and presents a missing or inadequate structure, with no identifiable claim and few, if any, transitions.
Use of Language	The response • uses highly effective diction and sentence variety • demonstrates a strong command of the conventions of standard written English, with almost no errors.	The response • uses purposeful diction and sentence variety • demonstrates an adequate command of the conventions of standard written English, with only slight errors that do not interfere with meaning.	The response • uses inappropriate diction and has limited sentence variety • contains several errors in the conventions of standard written English that interfere with meaning.	The response • uses diction that is inaccurate and inappropriate and has little to no sentence variety • contains many errors in the conventions of standard written English that interfere with meaning.

My Notes

Learning Targets

- Reflect on previous learning about the writing process and make connections to new learning.
- Identify and analyze the skills and knowledge necessary to complete Embedded Assessment 2.

Preview

In this activity you will revisit the Essential Questions that you have been thinking about over the course of the unit. You will also unpack Embedded Assessment 2 and start thinking about the short story you will write.

Essential Questions

You have explored telling details and the effect they have on your experience of a short story. You have also looked at several tools that authors can use to transmit their messages. Revisit your initial responses to the first two Essential Questions and revise them to incorporate your new learning. Then draft a response to the third question.

1. How do telling details work together to convey meaning?

2. What tools do authors use to create meaning and affect their readers?

3. How are writing and reading connected?

Unpacking Embedded Assessment 2

Read the assignment for Embedded Assessment 2: Writing a Short Story closely to identify and analyze the components of the assignment.

 Your assignment is to write an original short story from real or imagined experiences or events. Your story must include a variety of narrative techniques—such as plot structure, setting, point of view, characterization, and conflict—as well as telling details and a well-structured sequence of events.

Using the assignment and Scoring Guide, analyze the prompt and create a graphic organizer to use as a visual reminder of the required concepts (what you need to know) and skills (what you need to do). Copy the graphic organizer in your Reader/Writer Notebook.

Planning for Embedded Assessment 2

4. In your Reader/Writer Notebook, make a three-column chart and label the columns "Settings," "Characters," and "Conflicts." In each column, brainstorm some ideas you might like to write about.

5. After brainstorming, meet with a partner to discuss your ideas. Take turns listening, giving feedback, and asking questions to clarify your ideas. Use the Web Organizer to make decisions about your ideas for possible settings, characters, and conflicts.

Reading About Writing

Learning Strategies

Close Reading
Diffusing
Marking the Text
Rereading

Learning Targets

- Determine how an author's language choices contribute to the meaning of the work.
- Learn about the writing process of professional writers and make connections to your own process.
- Integrate ideas from multiple texts to build knowledge and vocabulary about professional writers.

Preview

In this activity, you will read and think about essays in which writers reflect on their writing processes, giving you the opportunity to reflect on your own writing process.

As You Read

- Highlight details that remind you of your own writing process.
- Circle unknown words and phrases. Try to determine the meaning of the words by using context clues, word parts, or a dictionary.

Introducing the Strategy: Diffusing

Diffusing is a process you can use to define, clarify, or validate your understanding of words. To diffuse a word, circle it, use context clues or a reference to define it, and write a synonym that you are more familiar with in the margin near it. If you use context clues to define the word, be sure to use a reference, like a dictionary, to ensure you are correct.

About the Author

John McPhee (b. 1931) is an American author of more than twenty-five books of nonfiction. He was nominated for the Pulitzer Prize four times, ultimately winning it after the fourth nomination. While contemporary writers were heading in one journalistic direction, McPhee went in another direction, incorporating more literary elements in his writing, such as thorough characterization and lively details. He is known for investigating and writing about a wide variety of his own interests, including the Alaskan wilderness, basketball, and everything related to oranges. McPhee is a writing professor at Princeton University, and has stated that he painstakingly outlines and organizes the structure of his ideas before he begins to write. Often, his works don't follow a linear timeline, but instead mimic a fictional style in which he chooses how and when to reveal information to the reader.

My Notes

KNOWLEDGE QUEST

Knowledge Question:

Why is revision an essential part of professional writing?

In Activity 1.23 you will read two essays that examine the topic of professional writers. While you read and build knowledge about the topic, think about your answer to the Knowledge Question.

My Notes

_____
_____
_____
_____
_____
_____
_____
_____
_____
_____
_____
_____
_____
_____
_____
_____
_____
_____
_____
_____
_____
_____
_____
_____
_____
_____
_____
_____

Essay

from "Draft No. 4"

by **John McPhee,** *The New Yorker,* **April 29, 2013**

1   First drafts are slow and develop clumsily, because every sentence affects not only those before it but also those that follow. The first draft of a long piece on California geology took two gloomy years; the second, third, and fourth drafts took about six months altogether. That four-to-one ratio in writing time—first draft versus the other drafts combined—has for me been consistent in projects of any length, even if the first draft takes only a few days or weeks. There are psychological differences from phase to phase, and the first is the phase of the pit and the pendulum. After that, it seems as if a different person is taking over. Dread largely disappears. Problems become less threatening, more interesting. Experience is more helpful, as if an amateur is being replaced by a professional. Days go by quickly, and not a few could be called pleasant, I'll admit.

. . .

2   When Jenny [McPhee's daughter] was a senior at Princeton High School and much put out by the time it was taking her to start an assigned piece of writing, let alone complete it, she told me one day as I was driving her to school that she felt incompetent and was worried about the difficulty she was having getting things right the first time, worried by her need to revise. I went on to my office and wrote her a note. "Dear Jenny: The way to do a piece of writing is three or four times over, never once. For me, the hardest part comes first, getting something—anything—out in front of me. Sometimes in a nervous frenzy I just fling words as if I were flinging mud at a wall. Blurt out, heave out, babble out something—anything—as a first draft. With that, you have achieved a sort of nucleus. Then, as you work it over and alter it, you begin to shape sentences that score higher with the ear and eye. Edit it again—top to bottom. The chances are that about now you'll be seeing something that you are sort of eager for others to see. And all that takes time. What I have left out is the interstitial time. You finish that first awful blurting, and then you put the thing aside. You get in your car and drive home. On the way, your mind is still knitting at the words. You think of a better way to say something, a good phrase to correct a certain problem. Without the drafted version—if it did not exist—you obviously would not be thinking of things that would improve it. In short, you may be actually writing only two or three hours a day, but your mind, in one way or another, is working on it twenty-four hours a day—yes, while you sleep—but only if some sort of draft or earlier version already exists. Until it exists, writing has not really begun."

. . .

3   It is toward the end of the second draft, if I'm lucky, when the feeling comes over me that I have something I want to show to other people, something that seems to be working and is not going to go away. The feeling is more than

welcome, yes, but it is hardly euphoria. It's just a new lease on life, a sense that I'm going to survive until the middle of next month. After reading the second draft aloud, and going through the piece for the third time (removing the tin horns and radio static that I heard while reading), I enclose things in boxes for Draft No. 4. If I enjoy anything in this process it is Draft No. 4. I go searching for replacements for the words in the boxes. The final adjustments may be small-scale, but they are large to me, and I love addressing them. You could call this the copy-editing phase if real copy editors were not out there in the future prepared to examine the piece. The basic thing I do with college students is pretend that I'm their editor and their copy editor. In preparation for conferences with them, I draw boxes around words or phrases in the pieces they write. I suggest to them that they might do this for themselves.

4   You draw a box not only around any word that does not seem quite right but also around words that fulfill their assignment but seem to present an opportunity. While the word inside the box may be perfectly O.K., there is likely to be an even better word for this situation, a word right smack on the button, and why don't you try to find such a word? If none occurs, don't linger; keep reading and drawing boxes, and later revisit them one by one. If there's a box around "sensitive," because it seems pretentious in the context, try "**susceptible**." Why "susceptible"? Because you looked up "sensitive" in the dictionary and it said "highly susceptible." With dictionaries, I spend a great deal more time looking up words I know than words I have never heard of—at least ninety-nine to one. The dictionary definitions of words you are trying to replace are far more likely to help you out than a scattershot wad from a thesaurus. If you use the dictionary after the thesaurus, the thesaurus will not hurt you. So draw a box around "wad." Webster: "The cotton or silk obtained from the Syrian swallowwort, formerly cultivated in Egypt and imported to Europe." Oh. But read on: "A little mass, tuft, or bundle ... a small, compact heap." Stet[1] that one. I call this "the search for the mot juste," because when I was in the eighth grade Miss Bartholomew told us that Gustave Flaubert walked around in his garden for days on end searching in his head for *le mot juste*. Who could forget that? Flaubert seemed heroic. Certain kids considered him weird.

5   This, for example, came up while I was writing about the Atchafalaya, the huge river swamp in southern Louisiana, and how it looked from a small plane in the air. Land is growing there as silt arrives from the north. Parts of the swamp are filling in. From the airplane, you could **discern** where these places were, because, seen through the trees, there would be an interruption of the reflection of sunlight on water. What word or phrase was I going to use for that reflection? I looked up "sparkle" in my old Webster's Collegiate. It said: "See 'flash.' " I looked up "flash." The definitions were followed by a presentation of synonyms: "flash, gleam, glance, glint, sparkle, glitter, scintillate, coruscate, glimmer, shimmer mean to shoot forth light." I liked that last part, so I changed the manuscript to say, "The reflection of the sun races through the trees and shoots forth light from the water."

---

[1] **stet:** a Latin term meaning "let it stand."

susceptible: easily influenced or impressed
discern: perceive or figure out

Knowledge Quest
- What are some words you would use to describe McPhee's revision process?
- What is one essential edit McPhee makes to create his fourth draft?

Returning to the Text
- Return to the text as you respond to the following questions. Use evidence from the text to support your responses.
- Write any additional insights you have about the essay in your Reader/Writer Notebook.

1. **KQ** What does McPhee mean when he says, "Stet that one" in the context of the passage?

_____

_____

_____

_____

2. What does McPhee's use of the French phrase *le mot juste* mean in the context of the passage?

_____

_____

_____

_____

3. How many drafts does it usually take John McPhee to write an essay he is pleased with? What is his advice to writers when they get to the final draft stage?

_____

_____

_____

_____

4. How does McPhee engage his audience in paragraphs 1 and 2?

_____

_____

_____

_____

5. What if McPhee did not use the "boxing" method for "Draft No. 4"? How would his writing be different?

_____

_____

_____

_____

6. **KQ** Does McPhee think revision is an essential part of the writing process? Use evidence from the text in your response.

_____

_____

_____

_____

7. What insight do you gain about McPhee's process from the telling details in the essay?

_____

_____

_____

_____

Working from the Text

8. Reread the essay, paying close attention to the author's writing process and how he resolves problems. Work with a partner to analyze what problem McPhee presents in each section of the essay and the solution(s) he offers.

Problem	Solution
Paragraph 1:	
Paragraph 2:	

Problem	Solution
Paragraphs 3–5:	

As You Read

- Highlight details that remind you of your own writing process.
- Circle unknown words and phrases. Try to determine the meaning of the words by using context clues, word parts, or a dictionary.

About the Author

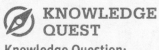

Donald M. Murray (1924–2006) was a Pulitzer Prize-winning American journalist and professor at the University of New Hampshire. He was well known for his books on writing and teaching and acted as a writing coach for different national newspapers. For Murray, writing was a way to discover and declare who he was and to understand his own life. Even after becoming a teacher, he still viewed himself as continuing to learn to write well. He encouraged writers to consider their voice and style above all else through word choice and point of view. He also believed that perhaps many people have writing talent, but the hard work they invest in their writing and rewriting is the key to true success.

✍ KNOWLEDGE QUEST

Knowledge Question:

Why is revision an essential part of professional writing?

Essay

Write Badly to Write Well

from *Write to Learn*

by **Donald M. Murray**

1   The only truly failed draft is a blank page. My closest writing friend, Chip Scanlan, to whom I always turn when I am stuck, reminds me that we have to "write badly to write well." When I start to write, I want a final draft first, but that isn't possible; it isn't even desirable. It would mean I was trying to pawn off a preowned piece of thinking as an original. Slick, glib writing should not be the goal; I should be seeking writing that is turning up unexpected, undeveloped meanings. My early drafts should be filled with accident, awkwardness, possibility, potential.

2 When building, reconstructing, or painting a house, the workers have to erect a jumble of ladders and levels on which they can stand. This scaffolding is essential to the building of the house, but it is not the house itself.

3 As a writer I have to construct drafts that are not the final draft. They help me build the house of prose or poetry. They are essential tools, but after I am through I take them down and the reader never sees them. As I work on the scaffolding, I have to remind myself that the false starts, clumsy sentences, undeveloped paragraphs, false trails, wrong words, mistakes in syntax and spelling are all scaffolding that will be taken down in the revision and editing process. Now I have to build the house.

⊘ Knowledge Quest

- Which words does Murray use to describe his drafts that surprise you?
- After reading this essay, what is something new you learned about professional writing?

Returning to the Text

- Return to the text as you respond to the following questions. Use evidence from the text to support your responses.
- Write any additional insights you have about the essay in your Reader/Writer Notebook.

9. Explain the connection Murray makes between writing a draft and building or painting a house. In what other ways can you connect his concept of scaffolding to your writing or to other areas of your life?

_____

_____

_____

_____

10. What does Murray mean by referring to the advice that "we have to 'write badly to write well'"?

_____

_____

_____

_____

11. What effect do Murray's words "accident, awkwardness, possibility, potential" have on the voice of the text?

_____

_____

_____

_____

12. **KQ** Based on context, what is the meaning of the word "syntax" in paragraph 3?

_____

_____

_____

_____

13. **KQ** What is Murray's goal for his writing? How does revision help get him there? Cite textual evidence in your response.

_____

_____

_____

_____

_____

INDEPENDENT READING LINK

You can continue to build your knowledge about professional writers by reading other articles at ZINC Reading Labs. Search for keywords such as *art of writing* or *professional writer*.

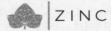 Z I N C

Knowledge Quest

Use your knowledge of the two essays to consider the writing and revision processes of professional writers. Write an essay for future professional writers that explains why revision is an essential part of professional writing. Be sure to:

- Select and convey essential ideas from both essays.
- Organize information clearly and effectively.
- Accurately paraphrase and objectively summarize content.

Check Your Understanding

Think about your own writing process and write a brief response, comparing your process to both John McPhee's and Donald M. Murray's. How is it like or different from theirs? What tactics of theirs would you want to try?

Reviewing the Elements of Plot

Learning Targets

- Identify the elements of a plot in previously-read texts.
- Analyze non-linear plot development and compare it to linear plot development.

Preview

In this activity, you will learn to recognize the different elements of a plot in order to organize the plot of your own short story.

Learning Strategies

Brainstorming
Close Reading
Marking the Text

LITERARY

The **exposition** in a narrative text gives the reader the background information needed to understand a story. In the exposition, the author introduces the characters, describes the setting, and begins to reveal the conflict.

The **resolution** (or denouement) in a narrative is the ending in which the main conflict is finally resolved.

Elements of a Plot

Well-written stories—fiction, non-fiction, novels, short stories, and plays—incorporate the elements of a plot. A plot most often begins with **exposition**, or an introduction to the characters, setting, and possible conflicts. To keep the audience's interest, the plot continues with rising action, typically based on the conflicts that the author introduces during the exposition. A plot moves toward a climax, the moment when the conflict is at its peak. Then it descends through falling action to the **resolution**.

1. Work with a partner to label the elements on the Plot Diagram.

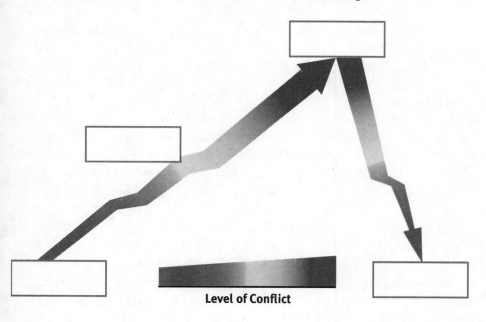

Level of Conflict

2. With your partner, use the Text Structure Stairs graphic organizer to map out the plot of a familiar story. Identify where in the story each plot element occurs.

Linear vs. Non-Linear Plot Development

A linear plot consists of a series of events with a clear beginning, middle, and end in chronological order. Sometimes authors use a non-linear plot structure in which the events of the story are told non-chronologically. These types of stories may contain elements such as flashback, foreshadowing, subplot, or parallel plot. The stories in this unit use a range of plot structures.

Linear

from "The Gift of the Magi"

One dollar and eighty-seven cents. That was all. And sixty cents of it was in pennies. Pennies saved one and two at a time by bulldozing the grocer and the vegetable man and the butcher until one's cheeks burned with the silent imputation of parsimony that such close dealing implied. Three times Della counted it. One dollar and eighty-seven cents. And the next day would be Christmas.

There was clearly nothing to do but flop down on the shabby little couch and howl. So Della did it.

Non-Linear

from "The Leap"

It has occurred to me that the catlike precision of her movements in old age might be the result of her early training, but she shows so little of the drama or flair one might expect from a performer that I tend to forget the Flying Avalons. She has kept no sequined costume, no photographs, no feathers or posters from that part of her youth. I would, in fact, tend to think that all memory of double somersaults and heart-stopping catches had left her arms and legs were it not for the fact that sometimes, as I sit sewing in the room of the rebuilt house in which I slept as a child, I hear the crackle, catch a whiff of smoke from the stove downstairs and suddenly the room goes dark, the stitches burn beneath my fingers, and I am sewing with a needle of hot silver, a thread of fire.

I owe her my existence three times. The first was when she saved herself. In the town square a replica tent pole, cracked and splintered, now stands cast in concrete. It commemorates the disaster that put our town smack on the front page of the Boston and New York tabloids. It is from those old newspapers, now historical records, that I get my information. Not from my mother, Anna of the Flying Avalons, nor from any of her in-laws, nor certainly from the other half of her particular act, Harold Avalon, her first husband. In one news account it says, "The day was mildly overcast, but nothing in the air or temperature gave any hint of the sudden force with which the deadly gale would strike."

3. Reread the excerpts and underline the words or sentences that indicate whether the plot is linear or non-linear. What are the characteristics of each type of plot structure?

   a. Linear

   _____

   _____

   _____

   b. Non-Linear

   _____

   _____

   _____

INDEPENDENT READING LINK

Read and Respond

Create a plot diagram or Text Structure Stairs graphic organizer to identify the plot elements and techniques used in the text you have been reading independently. Below the chart, write a few sentences to explain how these elements contribute to the theme of the text that you are reading.

4. Skim "The Gift of the Magi" and "The Leap," paying attention to the effects of each story's plot structure. Create a T-chart in your Reader/Writer Notebook to point out specific parts of the text that reflect flashback, foreshadowing, subplot, and their effects. Compare your chart with a partner and discuss.

5. What are the advantages and disadvantages of each plot structure? Work with your partner to create a list.

   a. Linear

   _____

   _____

   _____

   b. Non-Linear

   _____

   _____

   _____

6. Think about what kind of plot structure would best support your favorite story ideas from those you brainstormed for Embedded Assessment 2. In a small group, discuss your ideas and explain your choices.

☑ Check Your Understanding

Quickwrite: Why might an author choose to tell a story using a non-linear plot structure?

Reviewing the Elements of Setting and Characterization

Learning Strategies

Close Reading
Graphic Organizer
Marking the Text

Learning Targets

- Analyze the connections between theme, characterization, and setting.
- Connect prior knowledge to the genre of short story.

Preview

In this activity, you will analyze elements of setting and characterization in familiar texts in order to organize and plan your own short story.

My Notes

Setting and Theme

In literature, the setting is where and when a story takes place. Setting can play a small or large role in influencing the action or theme of a story. A character in the British countryside during the 18th century will have a different experience from a character on a different planet in the distant future. Setting can also influence the theme of a story through the experience of the characters. For example, a story set during the Civil War would likely influence themes about power and justice.

1. When you hear the word *setting*, what comes to mind? Refer back to one short story you read in this unit and describe its setting.

2. Find a partner or small group based on the short story you chose. As a group, discuss the themes of the story and make a chart, diagram, or illustration that shows how the setting influences the story's themes.

3. Work with your group to complete the "Setting" column in the following chart.

Characterization and Theme

The way an author uses characterization also influences how themes in a story are portrayed. An author can telegraph themes by showing a character's *internal*, or inner, conflict, which occurs when a character struggles between opposing needs, desires, or emotions within his or her own mind. The author can also show characterization through *external* conflict, which occurs when a character struggles against an outside force. This force may be another character, a societal expectation, or something in the physical world.

4. When you hear the word *characterization*, what comes to mind? Refer back to one short story you read in this unit and describe the author's characterization of the main character, including her or his internal and external conflicts.

5. Make a list of the story's themes. With a partner, share your insight on how the characterization of the character you chose influences the story's themes.

6. With your partner, complete the "Main Characters" column in the following chart. Together analyze how the settings and characters of the Unit 1 stories influence the themes and fill out the "Thematic Statement" column.

Story	Setting	Main Characters	Thematic Statement
"The First Day" by Edward P. Jones			
"An Occurrence at Owl Creek Bridge" by Ambrose Bierce			
"Games at Twilight" by Anita Desai			
"There Will Come Soft Rains" by Ray Bradbury			
"Martha, Martha" by Zadie Smith			

Developing Believable Characters and Conflicts

The stories you have read in this unit introduce a wide variety of characters of different backgrounds in different settings. In each case, the main characters are believable, causing the reader to want to continue reading in order to discover how the characters develop and resolve conflicts. We usually find characters believable when they are three-dimensional, flawed, relatable, and confronted with a problem. To develop a believable character in your own writing, consider your character's relationships to the other characters in the story and what their purpose and backstory are. Wanting something is a believable quality in a character—what does your character want or need? What is standing in the way? How will your character change over time?

7. Look back over the characterization you identified in step 4. With a partner, discuss what about this character does or does not feel believable. Try to identify the character's wants, desires, obstacles, and how he or she changes over the course of the story.

8. After concluding your discussion, work independently to describe the conflicts that arise in each story. Label whether the conflict is internal or external.

Story	Conflict
"The Gift of the Magi" by O. Henry	
"Games at Twilight" by Anita Desai	
"There Will Come Soft Rains" by Ray Bradbury	
"The Leap" by Louise Erdrich	
"Martha, Martha" by Zadie Smith	

📝 Drafting Embedded Assessment 2

Consider plot structure, setting, characterization, and theme. Choose one story idea to write about in your Reader/Writer Notebook and create an outline for your narrative. Brainstorm the following elements for your outline:

- Describe the plot structure you will use.
- Write a description of the setting and one or more characters.
- Describe the central conflicts, including at least one internal and one external conflict.

Point of View and Style

Learning Strategies

Close Reading
Marking the Text

Learning Targets

- Review and analyze the three main points of view in literary writing.
- Analyze various authors' use of narrative techniques, such as point of view, diction, and syntax.

Preview

In this activity, you will explore the points of view present in the short stories you have read in this unit, and analyze an author's style to emulate.

My Notes

Comparing Points of View

The point of view is the position from which a story is told. When writing, an author consciously chooses a point of view that best supports the plot elements and characterization. The point of view can be used in different ways, and each way has its advantages and limitations in telling a story.

First Person

from "The Leap"

I didn't see her leap through air, only heard the sudden thump and looked out my window. She was hanging by the backs of her heels from the new gutter we had put in that year, and she was smiling. I was not surprised to see her, she was so matter-of-fact. She tapped on the window. I remember how she did it, too. It was the friendliest tap, a bit tentative, as if she was afraid she had arrived too early at a friend's house. Then she gestured at the latch, and when I opened the window she told me to raise it wider and prop it up with the stick so it wouldn't crush her fingers. She swung down, caught the ledge, and crawled through the opening. Once she was in my room, I realized she had on only underclothing, a bra of the heavy stitched cotton women used to wear and step-in, lace-trimmed drawers. I remember feeling light-headed, of course, terribly relieved, and then embarrassed for her to be seen by the crowd undressed. I was still embarrassed as we flew out the window, toward earth, me in her lap, her toes pointed as we skimmed toward the painted target of the fire fighter's net.

Third-Person Limited

from "Lamb to the Slaughter"

The room was warm and clean, the curtains drawn, the two table lamps alight—hers and the one by the empty chair opposite. On the sideboard behind her, two tall glasses, soda water, whisky. Fresh ice cubes in the Thermos bucket.

Mary Maloney was waiting for her husband to come home from work.

Now and again she would glance up at the clock, but without anxiety, merely to please herself with the thought that each minute gone by made it nearer the time when he could come. There was a slow smiling air about her, and about everything she did. The drop of the head as she bent over her sewing was curiously tranquil. Her skin—for this was her sixth month with child—had acquired a wonderful translucent quality, the mouth was soft, and the eyes, with their new placid look seemed larger, darker than before.

Third-Person Omniscient

from "Games at Twilight"

It was still too hot to play outdoors. They had had their tea, they had been washed and had their hair brushed, and after the long day of confinement in the house that was not cool but at least a protection from the sun, the children strained to get out. Their faces were red and bloated with effort, but their mother would not open the door, everything was still curtained and shuttered in a way that stifled the children, made them feel that their lungs were stuffed with cotton wool and their noses with dust and if they didn't burst out into the light and see the sun and feel the air, they would choke.

"Please, ma, please," they begged. "We'll play in the veranda and porch—we won't go a step out of the porch."

"You will, I know you will, and then—"

"No—we won't, we won't" they wailed so horrendously that she actually let down the bolt of the front door so that they burst out like seeds from a crackling, overripe pod into the veranda, with such wild, maniacal yells that she retreated to her bath and the shower of talcum powder and the fresh sari that were to help her face the summer evening.

1. Reread the excerpts and underline the words or sentences that help you determine points of view. What are the characteristics of each point of view?

   a. First Person

   _____

   _____

   _____

   b. Third-Person Limited

   _____

   _____

   _____

   c. Third-Person Omniscient

   _____

   _____

   _____

2. Reread the texts "Lamb to the Slaughter" and "Games at Twilight," paying attention to the effects of each story's point of view. Create a T-chart in your Reader/Writer Notebook to analyze the specific points of view and their effects. Compare your chart with a partner and discuss.

3. What are the advantages and disadvantages of each point of view? Work with a partner to create a list.

   a. First Person

   _____

   _____

   _____

   b. Third-Person Limited

   _____

   _____

   _____

   c. Third-Person Omniscient

   _____

   _____

   _____

4. Examine and discuss the differences among the three points of view.

5. Think about what point of view might work best in your short story and discuss your idea with a partner. Add your decision to your Reader/Writer Notebook.

Writer's Style

You have learned by reading the stories in this unit that all writers have a unique style or voice, which they develop through elements such as **diction**, **syntax**, and point of view. Review these elements to be sure you understand and can define them.

6. Certain stories grab the reader's attention and maintain it by using a unique style. Reread the opening paragraph of "The Gift of the Magi" by O. Henry, then complete the following tasks.

   • Circle the images that stand out in the passage.
   • Underline the sentence fragments and annotate the text to describe what effect the author creates with these fragments.

7. Compare the opening of "The Gift of the Magi" to the opening of "Games at Twilight" by Anita Desai as you annotate the Desai passage.

   • Circle the images that stand out in the passage.
   • Annotate the text to describe your impression of the setting Desai creates.

> **LITERARY VOCABULARY**
>
> **Diction** is the way in which a writer makes word choices in his or her writing. A writer's diction often conveys voice and tone.
>
> **Syntax** is the way a writer arranges words and grammatical elements to create phrases, clauses, and sentences.

8. Notice how the syntax affects the pacing of the action. Which story has a faster pace? How does each writer create tension differently?

_____

_____

_____

_____

Emulate a Writer's Style

Just as the writers you have read in this unit have unique and varied styles, you will also develop your own style as you develop your writing skills. One way to develop and strengthen your writing is to try a new approach, including emulating another writer. To emulate another writer is to imitate the writer's style, including how he or she constructs sentences. For example, here is a sample paragraph written as an emulation of the opening of "The Gift of the Magi":

Sample

5:42 a.m. Too early. And work would start in less than an hour. Work that demanded Ava stay on her feet for six hours at a time until she was certain she would collapse, aching and exhausted and all used up. Two times she hit the snooze button. 5:50 a.m. 5:58 a.m. Have to get up.

☑ Check Your Understanding

Find a paragraph from a Unit 1 short story that you would like to emulate. Write an opening paragraph for your short story in the same style. Be sure to:

- Emulate the style of the author you chose by focusing on what is most significant about the writer's style.
- Introduce a character, a setting, and a conflict in the opening and include telling details that develop your reader's interest in and understanding of the story.
- Vary your sentence types to create an effect (or to affect the pacing of the narrative).

Working Through the Writing Process

Learning Strategies

Brainstorming
Mapping
Outlining

Learning Targets
- Review the concepts of audience and purpose.
- Develop and strengthen writing by planning and organizing ideas.

Preview
In this activity, you will draft and revise the short story that you have been planning, and learn about the steps it will take to make it a final product.

My Notes

The Writing Process

Writing is a process with steps—the most challenging being the drafting step—that can be repeated over and over as a writer explores ideas and concepts, and until the writer is satisfied. Think back to the essays on the writing process written by John McPhee and Donald M. Murray. Both authors discuss how their unique writing processes produce final drafts that satisfy them.

Audience

Determining the audience for your writing is essential for your story to have an impact on your reader. The language you choose must reflect the reader, or audience, you have in mind. As you work through the writing process, you will continue to make adjustments to your writing to ensure that it addresses your audience and purpose.

1. Revisit the essays by McPhee and Murray. Who are their intended audiences, and how do the writers' language choices reflect those audiences?

2. Determine the audience you have in mind for your story. Will your audience be your peers, young children, or a grandparent? All of these? Make notes about your intended audience and some of the language you will use to reach it.

Authors must also consider the topic and context for writing. For example, McPhee engages his audience by explaining his own writing process, choosing specific phrases and anecdotes to entertain, but also to share with fellow writers in the difficulties and victories of the writing process. In "Games at Twilight," Desai uses vivid descriptions and imagery to immerse her audience in the story, occasionally including startling anecdotes to inform readers of particular characters' motivations.

3. What types of details, language, or organizational structure will you use to convey your topic and the context of your narrative?

_____

_____

_____

Continuing the Writing Process for Your Narrative

You have drafted an outline for your short story, taking into consideration crucial elements such as plot structure, characterization, setting, and conflict.

4. Review the Unit 1 activities, your outline, and your Reader/Writer Notebook, and confirm the choices you have made so far. Then use the Text Structure Stairs graphic organizer to help you plan the order of events in your short story for Embedded Assessment 2.

5. Swap outlines and graphic organizers with a partner. Provide feedback by asking questions and offering advice. Make changes to your own writing based on your partner's feedback.

6. Begin your draft by describing the setting and characters with rich telling details. Incorporate a point of view that makes sense with the story and reveals just enough about the characters. Include internal and external conflict, narrative techniques such as pacing, irony, flashback, or multiple plot lines, and a conclusion that reflects a resolution of the conflict.

7. After you have written your draft, reread it for clarity, development, organization, style, diction, and sentence effectiveness. Annotate your draft for the following issues:

   • places where you need to add dialogue, telling details, and sensory language to create a more vivid picture of the setting, events, and characters

   • unclear or unresolved internal and external conflict

   • plot structure (linear or non-linear) that does not reinforce the content and/or syntax that does not support the actions and theme

8. Swap drafts with your partner and check your partner's draft against the Scoring Guide and your Editor's Checklist. Provide thoughtful, constructive feedback to each other.

9. Compile the feedback from your partner as well as the notes you have made for yourself. Then revise your short story based on the information you have gathered.

☑ Check Your Understanding

Draft a brief statement explaining the audience and purpose for your narrative, providing a short summary of your story and the techniques you will use to tell it.

🎁 Independent Reading Checkpoint

Meet with a small group to discuss the following questions related to your independent reading.

• How does an author's use of telling details differ between short stories and longer works?

• What have you learned from your observations about an author's use of telling details that will help you as you complete Embedded Assessment 2?

• How can you use your reading to strengthen your short story?

Writing a Short Story

 ASSIGNMENT

Your assignment is to write an original story from real or imagined experiences or events. Your story must include a variety of narrative techniques—such as foreshadowing, point of view, figurative language, imagery, symbolism, and/or irony—as well as telling details and a well-structured sequence of events.

Planning and Prewriting: Plan your narrative.	▪ Review the unit activities and your Reader/Writer Notebook for ideas. What activities have you completed that will help you as you create a short story with the required narrative techniques? ▪ What events or experiences do you want to write about? What prewriting strategies can you use to help you create ideas?
Drafting: Determine the structure and how to incorporate the elements of a short story.	▪ What setting will you use? Point of view? Characters? ▪ What telling details will you include to develop your story? ▪ Which additional narrative techniques will you use? Have you thought about including irony or foreshadowing to create a sense of mystery, surprise, and tension? ▪ How does the story structure you created develop the events, characters, and plot of your story so that it engages your readers?
Evaluating and Revising: Create opportunities to review and revise to produce your best work.	▪ When and how will you share your work with others to get feedback on all elements of your narrative? ▪ What words, phrases, dialogue, telling details, and sensory language have you used to create a vivid picture of the setting, events/experiences, and characters? ▪ Is your story developing as you want it to? Are you willing to change your story if you must? Once you get suggestions, are you creating a plan to include revision ideas in your draft? ▪ Does your conclusion reflect on experiences in the narrative and provide an effective resolution? ▪ Have you used the Scoring Guide to help you evaluate how well your draft includes the required elements of the assignment?
Checking and Editing for Publication: Confirm that the final draft is ready for publication.	▪ How will you check for grammatical and technical accuracy? Cohesion?

Reflection

After completing Embedded Assessment 2, think about how you set out and accomplished the tasks for this assignment. Write a reflection explaining how your reading and rereading of short stories helped you as a writer. What did you do to review and revise your story, and how has your writing improved by going step-by-step through the writing process?

Writing a Short Story

SCORING GUIDE

Scoring Criteria	Exemplary	Proficient	Emerging	Incomplete
Ideas	The narrative • sustains focus on setting, character, events, and/or ideas to strengthen the unity of the story • presents thought-provoking details, conflict, and resolution to heighten reader interest • develops engaging and authentic characters who grow in complexity throughout the story.	The narrative • generally focuses on setting, character, events, and/or ideas to maintain the unity of the story • includes appropriate details and well-developed conflict and resolution to sustain reader interest • develops believable characters who grow in depth throughout the story.	The narrative • does not sustain a focus on setting, character, events, and/or ideas, limiting the unity of the story • includes few or no details and an unfocused conflict and resolution • contains characters who are not developed or are not believable.	The narrative • does not contain a setting, character(s), events, and/or ideas • does not include details or provide conflict or resolution • does not contain believable characters.
Structure	The narrative • follows the structure of the genre • engages the reader and uses a variety of techniques to sequence events and create a coherence • provides an insightful conclusion with a clear and reasonable resolution.	The narrative • follows the structure of the genre • orients the reader and includes a sequence of events that create a coherent whole • provides a conclusion and clear resolution.	The narrative • may follow only parts of the structure of the genre • presents disconnected events with limited coherence • contains an underdeveloped conclusion with little or no resolution.	The narrative • does not follow the structure of the genre • includes few if any events and no coherence • does not contain a conclusion or does not provide a resolution.
Use of Language	The narrative • purposefully uses precise language, telling details, and sensory language to enhance mood or tone • effectively uses a range of narrative techniques and literary devices to enhance the plot • demonstrates technical command of spelling and standard English conventions.	The narrative • uses precise language and sensory details to define the mood or tone • uses a range of narrative techniques and literary devices to establish the plot • demonstrates general command of conventions and spelling; minor errors do not interfere with meaning.	The narrative • uses limited sensory details resulting in an unfocused or vague mood or tone • contains few or no narrative techniques or devices • demonstrates limited command of conventions and spelling; errors interfere with meaning.	The narrative • uses no sensory details to create mood or tone • contains few or no narrative techniques or devices • contains numerous errors in grammar and conventions that interfere with meaning.

VISUAL PROMPT
How is the experience of watching
a performance of a play, such as
Romeo and Juliet, different from
reading the play on the page?

PIVOTAL WORDS
AND PHRASES

My father liked them separate, one there,
one here (allá y aquí), as if aware

that words might cut in two his daughter's heart
(el corazón) and lock the alien part

–from "Bilingual/Bilingüe," by Rhina P. Espaillat

GOALS

- To read poetry and drama to analyze both their meaning and the author's craft.
- To work collaboratively to analyze a play and prepare a thoughtful performance of a scene.
- To plan, write, revise, edit, and publish poems and analytical reviews of poems using genre characteristics and craft.

VOCABULARY

ACADEMIC
lede
motive
nut graf
strategize

LITERARY
anaphora
aside
block
dramaturge
found poem
monologues
ode
poetic structure
prosody
rhyming couplet
sestina
soliloquy
sonnet
stage directions
subtext

ACTIVITY	CONTENTS	

CONTENTS

My Independent Reading List

Learning Strategies

Previewing
Skimming/Scanning

My Notes

Learning Targets

- Preview the big ideas for the unit.
- Create a plan for reading independently.

Preview

In this activity, you will explore the big ideas and tasks of Unit 2 and make plans for your own independent reading.

About the Unit

As you explore the work of poets, performers, and dramatists, you will focus on the meaning and impact of individual words and phrases. By exploring a wide range of poetry, you will gain an appreciation for word choice and revision, and by performing a drama, you will acquire firsthand knowledge of how delivery can affect the way dialogue is interpreted by an audience. Throughout this unit, you will craft poems, write critical reviews, draft multiple-paragraph works of literary analysis, and present dramatic interpretations.

Essential Questions

Based on your current thinking, how would you answer these questions?

1. How do authors use words and phrases to move the emotions, thoughts, and actions of readers?
2. Why do authors revise their work?
3. How does the mode of communication change the meaning of what is being communicated?

🎁 Planning Independent Reading

The focus of this unit is on pivotal words and phrases, and you will have the opportunity to look for pivotal words and phrases in poems and plays in class. Find a longer work about a poet, playwright, or other creator who interests you to read independently. You can choose a biography, a memoir, a published collection of letters, a full-length play, or a poetry anthology. Reading a longer work will help you see the subject in a new way. To find a book you will like, consider these questions.

- What kind of poetry have you enjoyed reading in the past? What is your favorite type of poetry? Do you have a favorite poet?
- Have you ever seen a live performance of a drama? Have you read the drama that you saw performed? Which do you enjoy more: comedy or tragedy?
- Do you know if any of your favorite movies or television shows are based on a play or novel?
- When you find a book you might like, flip through the first section. Does it seem interesting? Does it seem too easy, too hard, or just right?

Finding Poetry in Prose

Learning Strategies

Marking the Text
Skimming/Scanning

Learning Targets

- Analyze the use of pivotal words and phrases in a found poem.
- Search a short story for examples of poetic language.
- Write a found poem based on a familiar piece of prose.

Preview

In this activity, you will compare and contrast a found poem with a piece of prose and then create a found poem of your own.

My Notes

Exhibit A

Predator
Pored over
the bodies
of birds.

Pondering
the softness
flesh
behind
feathers.

A
single

word

bobbing

       bobbing
bobbing
       about
in her mind:
predator.

Exhibit B

And another aspect of all the things to which she had now become sensitized was the discovery of smells, a whole world of smells; she could find paths and trails purely by smell; it was strange how she had never before noticed that everything has a smell: the earth, the bark of trees, plants, leaves, and that every animal can be distinguished by its own peculiar smell, a whole spectrum of smells that came to her on waves through the air, and which she could draw together or separate out, sniffing the wind, imperceptibly lifting her head. She suddenly became very interested in animals and found herself leafing through encyclopedias, looking at the pictures—the hedgehog's pale, soft, tender underbelly; the swift hare, of uncertain hue, leaping; she pored over the bodies of birds, fascinated, pondering the softness of the flesh behind their feathers; and a single word kept bobbing insistently about in her mind: predator.

My Notes

Working from the Text

1. What makes Exhibit A poetic?

2. Who is the subject of Exhibit A? Which words act as telling details?

3. Reread the final sentence from Exhibit B. What do you notice about the language?

4. Now draw a line through every word from the final sentence of Exhibit B that the poet omitted.

5. What words did the poet leave out of Exhibit A and why?

6. Follow these instructions to create your own **found poem**, based on the short story "What Happened During the Ice Storm." When you complete your poem, write it in your Reader/Writer Notebook.

- **Reread:** Return to "What Happened During the Ice Storm" from Unit 1 and underline language that "shows" instead of "tells."
- **Focus:** Decide to focus on one aspect of the narrative for your found poem.
- **Copy:** Find words, phrases, and lines from the story that relate to what you want to write about. Copy them onto a fresh sheet of paper, leaving plenty of room between lines, so that you can study the language easily. Or, cut apart the words and phrases you've copied to form individual slips that you can physically manipulate.
- **Cut:** Eliminate any words that seem unnecessary, do not sound quite right, or are distracting from your poem's focus.
- **Don't:** You are not allowed to add your own language; you have to work with the words from the story.
- **Do:** You have the freedom to repeat language, change punctuation, change capitalization, change line breaks, and experiment with spacing.
- **Read aloud:** Read aloud your found poem, pausing briefly at the line ends, line breaks, and punctuation (commas, semicolons, periods). If something sounds wrong, edit the line breaks, punctuation, or spacing.

- **Title:** Give your found poem a title. "What Happened During the Ice Storm" is already taken!
- **Finalize:** Write the final version of your poem in the following space.

7. Read your poem aloud to a partner and invite feedback. Focus the feedback discussion on these questions:

- Does the found poetry mirror the themes or tones of the original work?
- Which words or phrases in the found poems are especially interesting or vivid?

☑ Check Your Understanding

As you have observed, composing a found poem entails making a lot of decisions about what words to cut and what words to keep. While constructing your found poem, which words did you keep? Why did they seem important? What words did you cut, and why? What other decisions did you make while constructing your found poem?

_____

_____

_____

_____

_____

_____

_____

_____

_____

_____

_____

The Art of Poetry Revision

My Notes

Learning Targets

- Trace the development of a poem through several drafts.
- Analyze how adding, deleting, and preserving words and phrases changes the overall effect of a poem.
- Understand that the revision process removes roadblocks to understanding the meaning of a piece of writing.

Preview

In this activity, you will read an essay about how the revision process helps poets unlock the essence of a poem, then analyze the changes among various drafts of an award-winning poem.

📝 Opening Writing Prompt

In the previous activity, you reflected on the process of constructing a found poem from an existing piece of short fiction. Essentially, you crafted a retelling of the original story in poetic form.

> If you were creating your own poem instead of retelling a story, how would your writing process change? How might it be the same as or different from creating a found poem?

About the Author

Rasma Haidri is an essayist, blogger, and award-winning poet living in Norway. The daughter of a Norwegian mother and an Indian father, Haidri grew up in Tennessee without a feeling of being from "anywhere in particular." However, after moving around the United States for a time, she finally found the sense of "home" that she'd been searching for in the land of her ancestors.

Haidri teaches British and American Studies and writes on themes of family, motherhood, politics, love of the written word, and hope in the face of mortality. She won the Mandy Poetry Prize for her poem "Lottery" and has also received the Southern Women Writers Association Emerging Writer Award in Creative Nonfiction and the Wisconsin Academy of Arts, Letters, and Science Poetry Award.

Essay

from **Lottery**

by **Rasma Haidri**

1   William Wordsworth's famous definition of poetry as the "spontaneous overflow of powerful feelings from emotions **recollected** in tranquility" appears at first to argue against revision. Something in the word *spontaneous* seems **antithetical** to revision, or so I thought when I first learned about Wordsworth back in college. At that time, I imagined he meant he lounged dreamily on a **divan** until, with a gold nib **quill**, he set about drafting the lines of a poem.

2   I believe part of this may have been right. Not the part about lounging dreamily, but the part about drafting. In this essay, I want to explore how through the hard work of revision over a long time, I was able to recollect the "spontaneous overflow of powerful feelings" that were central to my poem "Lottery."

3   The incident that spurred my poem was a time I took my mother grocery shopping, and she unexpectedly asked me to help her buy a lottery ticket. I was moved by the event and felt a need to tell about it. Now, I could have gone home and told my spouse about what happened and how it made me feel, but this retelling wouldn't have been a poem. In order to get at the poem, I needed to grasp the deepest feelings the incident aroused in me. In other words, I needed to get to what Wordsworth meant by recollecting a "spontaneous overflow of powerful feelings."

4   The problem with words about feelings or emotions is that they are abstract. Any word I might insert into the phrase "It made me feel _____" is going to be **theoretical**, as if we are talking about the emotion. In poetry, we need to recollect the emotion itself. In doing so, we come up with a rendering of an ordinary event that is somehow bigger than the sum of its parts.

5   Sometimes beginning writers feel that to take a poem through many drafts is to apply some sort of censorship to it, to tame its spirited individuality and make it **conform**. They resist revision because they fear editing away the poem's essence. Experience has taught me that revision can be the very means by which I recollect in tranquility. Each revision removes **hindrances** until the poem's "spontaneous overflow of powerful feelings" is released.

Making Observations
- What purpose does the author establish for this essay?
- What ideas grab your attention?

recollected: remembered

antithetical: sharply contrasted

divan: long sofa that usually has no back

quill: pen made from a bird's feather

theoretical: concerned with theories, or explanations for things that have not yet been proved true

conform: become similar to something else

hindrances: obstacles

Returning to the Text

- Return to the text as you respond to the following questions. Use text evidence to support your responses.
- Write any additional questions you have about the essay in your Reader/Writer Notebook.

1. What spurred Haidri to write the poem "Lottery"?

_____

_____

_____

2. In Haidri's opinion, what is the difference between a retelling and a poem?

_____

_____

_____

3. Why does Haidri think it is difficult to describe feelings?

_____

_____

_____

4. According to Haidri, how does one "recollect the emotion itself"?

_____

_____

_____

5. According to Haidri, how do some beginning writers feel about revising poetry?

_____

_____

_____

6. How does Haidri see the revision of poetry?

_____

_____

_____

Working from the Text

7. In your group, read these three versions of Haidri's poem "Lottery": Journal Entry, Draft 2, and Final Draft. Then answer the questions in the chart that follows. Include text evidence with each of your answers.

Journal Entry

That's 6 and a half million a year after taxes you tell me, of the man who won $111 million. That's more than Trump! I have our lottery tickets in here you pt to your black billfold
with the brown ribbing. Rummage further into your handbag. Kleenex, bent envelopes,
a crumpled single dollar rising over your wrist as you dig. The lottery tickets are two weeks old. Bought on the eve of my departure for California when I took her to Woodman's to buy everything she needed while I was gone. Two cartons of ciggarettes, 3 gal. of milk, rice cakes and black bellied bottles of diet rite—I want to buy a lottery ticket you said, and weaved your way, half blind, exhausted, sore knees from side to side pushed the weight of your body to the far end of the store, by videos and ice cream and packaged liquor.

You had your numbers picked out, written large and clear on a tear of scrap cardboard, bright yellow.

Neither of us knew how to go about it. Mother could not teach daughter. Daughter could not get it done. I rubbed in the dots for you. Bought a computer generated one for me—only lingering slightly over your numbers. Trying to register their significance—and not seeing any immediately didn't dare intrude into their origin—ask on what you are basing your luck. Just as now I don't ask you if you know how they decided how many years to divide $111 million by to make this man rich for the rest of his life, or what (I don't want to ask) you would do with the money—could it buy back your teeth, your eyesight, your light strong bones and lean flesh.

You didn't check our numbers that night I was on vacation But no one else has claimed it you tell me as if that's all it takes to mean everything, all of it, is out there waiting for us to win, to call claim, start celebrating.

My Notes

Draft 2

Everything you would need
the week of my vacation
could be found at Woodman's:
two cartons of cigarettes
three gallons of milk
unsalted rice cakes and
six black bottles of diet cola.

I want to
buy a lottery ticket,
you added and weaved worn-out,
stiff-kneed, half-blind,
to the far end of the store
near the videos, ice cream,
and packaged liquor

Neither of us knew how to go about it.

You had already chosen your numbers,
written them in large cursive
on a tear of yellow cardboard.

I fumbled, rubbing in the dots for you,
lingered slightly over your numbers
to register their significance, but found none.

You did not check the ticket while I was gone,
and look for it now in the depths of your purse,
kleenex, envelopes, a dollar bill
rising over your wrists as you dig.

That's six and a half million a year for life!
you tell me of the man who won last winter,
and I do not ask how they figured
the number of years in his life, nor do I ask
what you would do with the money
Buy back your teeth? Your eyesight,
light bones and lean flesh?
Buy back the Tennessee summers
you played squirt guns with us
and caught fireflies we could sell to science
for thirty cents a hundred?

No one else has claimed it!
you say, as if that alone
makes everything possible,
and all of it is out there waiting for you
to start up this celebration.

Final Draft

Everything my mother needs
can be found at Woodman's:
two cartons of cigarettes
a gallon of milk,
unsalted rice cakes and
six black bottles of diet cola.

I want to buy a lottery ticket.
she adds and weaves stiff-kneed,
half-blind, to the far end of the store
near the videos and packaged liquor.

She has already chosen the numbers,
written them in large cursive
on a scrap of yellow cardboard.

Neither of us knows how to go about it.

I fumble, rubbing in the dots,
lingering slightly over her numbers
but find no significance.

That's six and a half million a year <u>for life!</u>
she says of the man who won last winter
and I do not ask how one figures
the number of years left in his life.
Nor do I ask if she will buy back
her teeth, eyes, strong bones and lean flesh.
Buy back the summers
she played squirt guns with us
and caught fireflies I could sell to science
for thirty cents a hundred.

No one has claimed it!
she whispers, as if everything
is still possible.

Revision Categories	Journal Entry → Draft 2 → Final Draft
How did the point of view change?	
How did the verb tense change?	
What was cut?	
What was preserved?	
What was added?	

Appreciating the Author's Craft

Discuss the following questions with your classmates.

- Think about the words and phrases Haidri refused to cut from "Lottery." How are they essential for communicating the poem's meaning?

- Think about the words and phrases Haidri decided to edit out of her poem. How were they "hindrances" to understanding the poem's meaning?

- Think about the words Haidri added to her poem. What function do they serve?

Crafting an Analytical Paragraph About Revision

8. Think of one significant addition or deletion that Haidri made to her poem "Lottery." Then write a paragraph about it that answers the question: *Why did Haidri make this revision, and what effect did the revision have on the overall meaning of the poem?*

Before you begin writing, take time to answer these questions:

- Which specific revision of "Lottery" most interests you?
- Is it a revision that involved cutting words or phrases? Is it a revision that highlighted some of the original language?
- Why did Haidri make the revision? What quote from her essay best supports your point or provides added insight about the revision?
- How do you think the revision contributes to the poem's overall effect? How does the revision make the poem more powerful or clear?

Also, consider using one of the following sentence frames to write your topic sentence.

- *In Rasma Haidri's final version of her poem "Lottery," her decision to cut _____ leaves the reader with a sense of _____.*
- *In Rasma Haidri's final version of her poem "Lottery," her decision to preserve _____ gives the reader a sense of _____.*

_____

_____

_____

_____

_____

_____

_____

_____

_____

_____

_____

_____

_____

_____

☑ Check Your Understanding

Think about the pivotal words and phrases Haidri valued in her final version of "Lottery." Were they there from the beginning or were they added later in the writing process? What do they contribute to the overall effect of the poem?

Word Choice That Matters

Learning Targets

- Analyze language use in a short poem.
- Make connections to specific words and phrases in order to understand a text more deeply.
- Analyze how punctuation contributes to a poem's meaning and impact.

Preview

In this activity, you will consider how an author's word and punctuation choices affect the meaning and impact of a poem.

As You read

- Underline words and phrases that help you visualize the objects and events described in the poem.
- Circle unknown words and phrases. Try to determine the meanings of the words by using context clues, word parts, or a dictionary.

About the Author

John Montague (1929–2016) was born in Brooklyn, New York, the son of Irish immigrants who had come to the United States to escape political strife and pursue the American Dream. Unfortunately, their arrival coincided with the beginning of the Great Depression. When Montague was four years old, his parents sent him back to Ireland to live with family. There he lived the life of a farm boy until he was sent to boarding school and was introduced to the long tradition of Irish poetry. Initially uninterested in learning about poetry, Montague eventually found inspiration and began writing his own poems.

Montague devoted many years to being a writer and scholar. In addition to poems, he wrote short stories, memoirs, and translations of French poetry. He became one of the world's best known Irish poets, winning many awards and achieving the high honor of being named the first occupant of the Ireland Chair of Poetry in 1998.

Poem

The Fight

by **John Montague**

When I found the swallow's
Nest under the bridge—
Ankle-deep in the bog stream,
Traffic drumming overhead—

My Notes

5   I was so pleased, I ran
To fetch a school companion
To share the nude fragility
Of the shells, lightly freckled
With colour, in their cradle
10 Of feathers, twigs, earth.

It was still breast warm
Where I curved in my hand
To count them, one by one
Into his cold palm, a kind
15 Of trophy or offering. Turn-
Ing my back, to scoop out
The last, I heard him run
Down the echoing hollow
Of the bridge. Splashing
20 After, I bent tangled in
Bull wire at the bridge's
Mouth, when I saw him take
And break them, one by one
Against a sunlit stone.

25 For minutes we fought
Standing and falling in
The river's brown **spate**,
And I would still fight
Though now I can forgive.

30 To worship or destroy beauty—
That double edge of impulse
I recognise, by which we live;
But also the bitter **paradox**
Of betraying love to harm,
35 Then lungeing, too late,
With fists, to its defence.

My Notes

_____

_____

_____

_____

_____

_____

bull wire: type of wire used in fences

spate: sudden forceful flow of water

paradox: situation that has contradictory aspects

Making Observations
- How does the speaker feel?
- Why does the speaker fight his friend?

Working from the Text

1. Summarize the story of "The Fight" in no more than two sentences.

   _____

   _____

2. Reread the poem "The Fight" with a partner. What language does Montague use to refer to the eggs without using the word eggs?

   _____

   _____

   _____

   _____

3. Find language about the eggs from the first and second stanzas, and then record your associations with the descriptions. Which words stand out to you and why? How does word choice contribute to your feelings about the swallow's eggs?

Language Describing the Eggs	Sample Associations with Words and Phrases
First Stanza:	
Second Stanza:	
Second Stanza:	

My Notes

☑ Check Your Understanding

Use the following sentence frame to write a sentence about one of Montague's descriptions for the eggs.

> *Montague's use of the word / phrase* _____ *in "The Fight" suggests to the reader that the eggs are* _____ .

Appreciating the Author's Craft

Discuss the following questions about this excerpt from "The Fight" with your classmates.

> ... Turn-
> Ing my back, to scoop out
> The last, I heard him run
> Down the echoing hollow
> Of the bridge. Splashing
> After, I bent tangled in
> Bull wire at the bridge's
> Mouth, when I saw him take
> And break them, one by one
> Against a sunlit stone.

- Do you see anything peculiar in the punctuation? Why is it remarkable here?

- How would this moment in the poem be different if Montague had placed the entire word *turning* on the next line?

- What affect does Montague's punctuation of the word "Turn- / Ing" have on the way his audience reads the poem?

- Why does Montague want his audience to pay attention to this moment?

Gaining Perspectives

In the poem "The Fight," one of the children destroys a living thing. Is this kind of aggression normal? Today, many people blame media for contributing to the normalization of violence. With a partner, briefly search online to see what types of media habits can lead to the normalization of violence. Consider whether you agree or disagree with what your research reveals. Then discuss with your partner two ways to influence children to protect nature instead of destroy it. Present your solutions to the class.

My Notes

My Notes

Learning Targets

- Analyze two texts for examples of language that implies impulsiveness.
- Use an outline to plan a multiple-paragraph response.
- Draft a multiple-paragraph response.

Preview

In this activity, you will use an outline to help you develop and write a multiple-paragraph response about how pivotal words and phrases illustrate the unpredictability of human impulse in the face of nature.

Opening Writing Prompt

Reread the last stanza of John Montague's poem "The Fight." Then answer the following question.

How is this stanza different from the rest of the poem?

Revisiting "The Fight"

1. Sometimes writers use a semicolon (;) to connect two complete thoughts, while also creating a dramatic pause between them. Reread the last stanza of "The Fight" and write one sentence for each half of the stanza, translating the poetic verse into prose.

2. When Montague refers to the "double edge of impulse," what does he mean?

Writing to Sources: Informational Text

Both the short story "What Happened During the Ice Storm" and the poem "The Fight" tell stories about the unpredictability of human impulse in the face of nature. How does each writer use pivotal words and phrases to develop this theme? Use the following process to outline and plan your writing.

Gathering Evidence

3. Reread both texts, noting language that implies impulsive or unpredictable action toward nature. Write each example of this language in the chart, along with notes about why you think the example shows that someone is acting impulsively.

Title	Language	Notes
"What Happened During the Ice Storm"		
"The Fight"		

Forming a Multiple-Paragraph Outline

4. Use the following multiple-paragraph outline to plan a response to literature about how pivotal words and phrases from "What Happened During the Ice Storm" and "The Fight" illustrate the unpredictable nature of human impulse in the face of nature. In the left column of the outline, state the main idea of each paragraph, and in the right column, list details that support each main idea.

Multiple-Paragraph Outline	
Main Idea	**Details**
Introduction Paragraph 1	• • •
Heynen Paragraph 2	• • •
Montague Paragraph 3	• • •

Composing a Multiple-Paragraph Analysis

5. Use the evidence that you gathered as well as the notes in your multiple-paragraph outline to help you write your analysis. As you develop your draft, be sure to:

   • Write an introduction that tells the theme of your response and states a thesis.
   • Include in your introduction the title and author for each literary work your analysis will explore.
   • Support your thesis with details and evidence from "What Happened During the Ice Storm" and "The Fight."
   • Use quotation marks around language that comes directly from the texts.
   • Use a variety of complete sentences.
   • Use a semicolon to link independent clauses that are closely related.
   • Include a transitional sentence at the beginning of the third paragraph that tells readers how this paragraph connects the ones that came before it.
   • Include a concluding statement that connects the details and evidence you have provided to the thesis in your introductory paragraph.

To help you write sentences for your second and third paragraphs, you may use the following sentence frame:

The writer's use of the word / phrase _____ suggests to the reader that _____ .

Performance Punctuating Meaning

Learning Strategies

Close Reading
Marking the Text

Learning Targets

- Analyze how a poem's speaker changes or shifts his perspective.
- Plan and draft a multiple-paragraph response about the performance of a poem.
- Understand how adding or deleting words and phrases can change the impact of a poem.
- Integrate ideas from multiple texts to build knowledge and vocabulary about sign language.

Preview

In this activity, you will read a poem and then observe a live performance of it, considering how the poem's meaning is enhanced by its performance.

📝 Opening Writing Prompt

Similar to "The Fight," "Tamara's Opus" tells a story of experience and change. Read "Tamara's Opus" and trace the speaker's development. Then respond to the following questions.

How does he change or shift perspective over the course of the poem? What words or phrases best illustrate these changes or shifts in perspective?

As You Read

- Underline words and phrases that relate to sign language and communication.
- Circle unknown words and phrases. Try to determine the meaning of the words and verify your definitions by using context clues, word parts, or a dictionary.

About the Author

Joshua Bennett is a poet, a scholar, and an artist who is well known for his spoken-word performances. Bennett grew up in the Bronx in a family of six children and wrote his first poem at the age of five. He went on to receive degrees from Penn State University and Princeton University, and he was a junior fellow in the Society of Fellows at Harvard University. He also won the National Poetry Series Award for his collection *The Sobbing School* in 2015.

My Notes

2.6

My Notes

Poem

Tamara's Opus

by **Joshua Bennett**

Tamara has never listened
to hip-hop
Never danced
to the rhythm of raindrops
5 or fallen asleep to a chorus of chirping crickets
she has been Deaf
for as long as I have been alive
and ever since the day that I first turned five
My father has said:
10 "Joshua. Nothing is wrong with Tamara.
God just makes
some people different."
And at that moment
those nine letters felt like hammers
15 swung gracefully by unholy hands
to shatter my stained-glass innocence
into shards that could never be pieced back together
or do anything more
than sever the ties between my sister and I.
20 I waited
was patient numberless years
anticipating the second
her ears would open like lotuses
and allow my sunlight sentences to seep
25 into her insides
make her remember all those conversations
we must have had in Heaven
back when God hand-picked us
to be sibling souls centuries ago
30 I still remember her 20th birthday
readily recall my awestruck eleven-year old eyes
as I watched Deaf men and women of all ages
dance in unison to the vibrations
of speakers booming so loud

35 that I imagined angels chastising us

for disturbing their worship

with such beautiful blasphemy

until you have seen

a Deaf girl dance

40 you know nothing of passion.

There was a barricade between us

that I never took the time to destroy

never for even a moment

thought to pick up a book and look up

45 the signs for *sister*

for *family*

for *goodbye, I will see you again some day*

remember the face of your little brother.

It is only now I see

50 that I was never willing

to put in the extra effort to love her properly

So as the only person in my family

who is not fluent in sign language

I have decided to take this time

55 to apologize

Tamara, *I am sorry*

for my silence.

But true love knows no frequency

So I will use these hands

60 to speak volumes

that could never be contained

within the boundaries of sound waves

I will shout at the top of my fingertips

until digits dance and relay these messages

65 directly to your soul

I know

that there is no poem

that can make up for all the time that we have lost

but please, if you can,

70 *just listen*

My Notes

KNOWLEDGE QUEST

Knowledge Question:
How might knowing sign language affect you and the people around you?

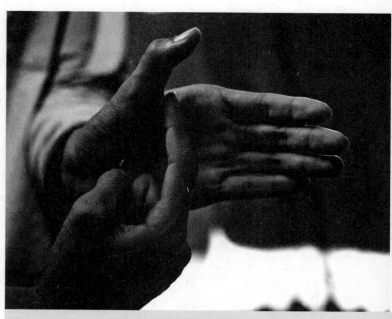

Sign language is not universal. Different sign languages are used in different regions, similar to the way spoken languages vary. American Sign Language (ASL) is used in the United States.

Observing Shifts in Perspective

1. As your classmates read their written responses to the Opening Writing Prompt, complete the chart by noting examples of how the poem's speaker changes or shifts his perspective. Include words and phrases from the text that give evidence of the shifts.

Change or Shift in Perspective	Text Evidence of the Change

Knowledge Quest

Think about how knowing sign language affects you and the people around you. With a partner, briefly research articles about the effects of using sign language. In a small group, discuss whether you think people who use sign language have a different culture than people who do not use sign language. Explain your reasoning. Be sure to:

- Prepare for the discussion, and use your research as evidence in the discussion.
- Ask and respond to questions that relate to language and culture.
- Summarize comments from all points of view, and make new connections based on others' ideas and evidence.

 INDEPENDENT READING LINK

You can continue to build your knowledge about sign language by reading other articles at ZINC Reading Labs. Search for keywords such as *ASL* or *human interaction*.

 ZINC

Working from the Text

2. Watch Bennett's performance of "Tamara's Opus." What are your first impressions?

_____

_____

_____

3. As you view "Tamara's Opus" for a second time, pay attention to all the ways that Bennett's physicality and his vocalization of the words change during the performance. Make notes on the following lines about the kinds of changes you see.

_____

_____

_____

4. Work with a group to choose three types of physical and/or vocal changes that Bennett undergoes during his performance of "Tamara's Opus." Focus on these kinds of changes as you watch his performance for a third time. Make notes in the chart about how the changes coincide with the poem's words and phrases and how they affect and enhance the audience's understanding of the poem.

Change 1: _____	Change 2: _____	Change 3: _____

5. What do you feel were the effects of Bennett's performance choices?

_____

_____

_____

✍ Writing to Sources: Informational Text

How does Bennett use performance techniques to demonstrate and emphasize the change that he (or the speaker) goes through over the course of the poem? Use evidence from the poem and the performance to support your thinking. Organize your writing using the following multiple-paragraph outline. Be sure to:

- Write an introduction that includes a general statement addressing the topic of spoken word poetry and then follows with a thesis statement that specifically mentions Bennett and the title of his poem.
- Support your thesis with evidence from the poem and performance.
- Include transitional phrases at the beginnings of paragraphs to help readers follow the chronology of Bennett's performance.
- Use quotation marks around text that comes directly from the poem and include slash marks to indicate the ends of lines within a piece of quoted text.

Multiple-Paragraph Outline	
Main Idea	**Details**
Introduction Paragraph 1	 • • •
Paragraph 2	 • • •
Paragraph 3	 • • •

Appreciating the Author's Craft

In Bennett's White House performance of "Tamara's Opus," he chooses to end the poem signing and saying the words "just listen." However, in another version of the poem, published on the Disability Studies Quarterly website, the poem has several more lines. It ends as follows:

> *just listen*
> as I play you a symphony
> on the strings of my heart
> made for no other ears on this Earth
> but yours.

Discuss the following questions about this ending with a partner.

- What if these two versions were reversed?

- How might Bennett's White House performance have been different if he had added these final four lines after "just listen"?

- Which provides more of a dramatic flourish for a live ending? Explain your answer.

- Does the written version of the poem feel unfinished with its ending "just listen"? Why or why not?

☑ Check Your Understanding

Revisit the Essential Question, "How does the mode of communication change the meaning of what is being communicated?" Explain why some words and phrases in the live performance of a piece of writing may differ from those in its printed version.

Writing a Review of the White House Poetry Jam

Learning Targets

- Use an outline to plan and draft a multiple-paragraph review.
- Use sentence expansion to develop a lede and write a nut graf that states a claim.

Learning Strategies

Graphic Organizer
Outlining
Rereading

Preview

In this activity, you will use an outline to help you develop and write a multiple-paragraph review of Joshua Bennett's performance.

ACADEMIC

In journalism, the **lede** is the opening of an article, or the sentence that tells what happened. It is followed by the **nut graf**, or a statement that tells why readers should care about what happened. *Lede* is an alternative spelling of the word *lead* that was devised to distinguish the opening of a story from the molten lead used in typesetting machines. *Nut graf* is an abbreviation of the term *nutshell paragraph*.

Preparing to Write a Review

1. Pretend that instead of watching video coverage of the 2009 White House poetry jam, you actually are in attendance as a journalist. Your job is to recap and critically review the evening for those who are not in attendance. You will need to include enough detail so that your readers can imagine what it was like to be in the audience and experience "Tamara's Opus." In your review, you need to address the subject matter of the piece and the language and performance choices made by the artist and relate them to the live audience's reactions.

Forming a Multiple-Paragraph Outline

2. Decide how many paragraphs your review will require at a minimum. Then create a multiple-paragraph outline in your Reader/Writer notebook to plan your review.

- Begin your outline with notes for an introductory paragraph that includes a **lede** and a **nut graf**. Give an overview of the White House event and then make a claim about the performance you will review.

- Develop the remaining paragraphs of your outline with notes about the language and performance choices made by the artist whose work you are reviewing.

☑ Focus on the Sentence

Follow your teacher's instructions and use sentence expansion to write your lede.

Kernel: He performed.

Who? _____

What? _____

Where? _____

When? _____

Why? _____

Expanded sentence:

_____

_____

My Notes

Asserting Opinion and Focus in the Review

3. Think about what you want to say about the performance you are reviewing. Did you have a positive, negative, or mixed reaction to it? Decide what your claim about the performance will be and how you will support it with evidence. Then write your nut graf.

_____

_____

_____

_____

Writing a Multiple-Paragraph Response

4. Use your notes from the previous activities in this unit, along with the notes in your multiple-paragraph outline, to help you write your review. As you develop your draft, be sure to:

   • Support your claim with the most convincing details and evidence from the work you are reviewing.

   • Use quotation marks around text that comes directly from the poem.

   • Use a variety of complete sentences.

   • Include transitional sentences at the beginning of the second and third paragraphs that help readers understand how these paragraphs relate to the lede and to each other.

Assess and Reflect

Choose a video of a musical or spoken-word event that features interesting language and performance choices. Then write a review of the performance modeled after the review you wrote about Bennett's performance. Use sentence expansion to help you write the lede for your review. Make sure your review states a claim and includes supporting evidence from the poem.

Kernel: He performed. / She performed. _____

Who? _____

What? _____

Where? _____

When? _____

Why? _____

Expanded sentence:

_____

_____

_____

Taking Sides in Verona

Learning Targets

- Use context clues and knowledge of sentence structure to aid understanding of unfamiliar words and phrases.
- Analyze characters in a play.

Preview

In this activity, you will analyze a scene from *Romeo and Juliet* and participate in a choral reading of it.

My Notes

📝 Opening Writing Prompt

Read the first four lines of *Romeo and Juliet*, which make up one long sentence of the prologue. Reduce these four lines to their kernel subject and predicate. Then answer the following question.

What do you think the last line, in particular, is saying about the setting of *Romeo and Juliet*?

Two households, both alike in dignity
(In fair Verona, where we lay our scene),
From ancient grudge break to new mutiny,
Where civil blood makes civil hands unclean.

Exploring a Multiple-Meaning Word

The adjective *civil* is used twice in the final line of the prologue for *Romeo and Juliet*. This word has many denotations. They include:

i. of or occurring within the state or between or among citizens of the state

ii. applying to ordinary citizens as contrasted with the military

iii. not rude; marked by satisfactory (or especially minimal) adherence to social usages and sufficient but not noteworthy consideration for others

iv. (of divisions of time) legally recognized in ordinary affairs of life

1. Which definition applies to the first instance of "civil," and what context clues help you know this is the intended meaning?

   _____

   _____

   _____

   _____

2. Which definition applies to the second use of "civil," and what context clues help you know this is the intended meaning?

   _____

   _____

   _____

   _____

Get to Know the Characters

3. You will begin your study of *Romeo and Juliet* by first reading and performing a pivotal scene from the middle of the play that features the characters Romeo, Mercutio, Tybalt, and Benvolio. Find out more about your assigned character by reading the descriptions that follow. Don't worry about missing anything. You will go back to the beginning of the play later.

Character	Description and Affiliation
Romeo	*Who is he, and what is he all about?* Romeo Montague is a big deal. After all, this play is called *Romeo and Juliet*, and in our culture his name—Romeo—is forever connected with being a lady's man. Bottom line: He is a romantic and rash guy. He loves easily and angers easily, but even the head of the Capulet family considers him honest and well behaved. Sometimes we judge people not just by who they are and the way they behave but also by their friends. Romeo has two buddies: Benvolio and Mercutio. Benvolio is gentle and loyal, and Mercutio is a lot of fun, but he is also a little wacky and unstable. *Where does he stand on Verona's war between the households?* It is complicated! As a Montague, his family is one of the two powerful, warring "households" mentioned in the prologue, but he secretly runs off and gets married to a (gulp) Capulet. Long story short: Benvolio drags him to a party, and he falls hard for Juliet. He even leaves the party to sneak into her family's garden. Luckily, she does not think he is a stalker; instead, she asks him to marry her. Now that he is secretly married to a Capulet, he just wishes the households would make up.

Character	Description and Affiliation
Mercutio	*Who is he, and what is he all about?* Mercutio's name is a big clue to his character and style. Like mercury (an unstable element that can explode or burst into flames easily), he is easily provoked and hot-headed. But he is also funny, quick to laugh, and quick to joke. He loves playing with words, and when he talks with people, he uses his language as he uses his sword—to attack, defend, and be playful. In other words, he is fun, but he can be a danger to others and himself, and sometimes things get out of hand. *Where does he stand on Verona's war between the households?* His two best friends are Romeo and Benvolio. Although he is not a member of the Montague family, he considers himself a close ally and friend of the family.
Tybalt	*Who is he, and what is he all about?* Tybalt is proud, tough, and aggressive, and he has a reputation for being one of the best sword fighters around. Like Mercutio, he gets angry quickly, but he has none of the fun-loving mischief that Mercutio has. He cannot seem to forgive and forget. Once he has made enemies, they stay enemies; Tybalt never stops trying to get even. *Where does he stand on Verona's war between the households?* Since he is a nephew to the head of the Capulet family, he is very protective of his clan. For example, at a party that Romeo and his friends crash, he immediately suspects that Romeo and his friends are trying to make fun of him and his family. Touchy, touchy!
Benvolio	*Who is he, and what is he all about?* Benvolio's name sounds like the word *benevolent*, and that is no accident. Like all things "bene," he is considered good and kind. When his buddy Romeo is pouting, Benvolio takes him to the party where he flirts with Juliet. (Well, maybe that is not such a good idea.) He is also friends with Mercutio, which is a good thing. When Mercutio gets all wound up, Benvolio tries hard to calm him down. In fact, just a few minutes ago, he had to work his magic—let's see how long that lasts. *Where does he stand on Verona's war between the households?* He is one of Romeo's best friends. He is not a fighter by nature, but he considers himself part of Team Montague. Somehow, even though he is a peacemaker by nature, he gets sucked into at least two fights, each time trying to stop the fight before it gets out of hand.

Director's
Notes

Drama

Romeo and Juliet
Act III, Scene I, lines 38–95
by **William Shakespeare**

BENVOLIO: Two households, both alike in dignity
(In fair Verona, where we lay our scene),
From ancient grudge break to new mutiny,
Where civil blood makes civil hands unclean.[1]

TYBALT: Follow me close, for[2] I will speak to them.—
Gentlemen, good e'en[3]. A word with one of you.

40 **MERCUTIO:** And but one[4] word with one of us? Couple it[5]
with something. Make it a word and a blow[6].

TYBALT: You shall find me apt[7] enough to that, sir, an[8]
you will give me occasion[9].

MERCUTIO: Could you not take some occasion without
45 giving?

TYBALT: Mercutio, thou consortest[10] with Romeo.

MERCUTIO: Consort? What, dost thou make us minstrels[11]?
An thou make minstrels of us[12], look to[13] hear

---

[1] This is the first quatrain of the prologue. This is an adaptation of the original play to set the
 stage for the tension between the characters.
[2] *for:* because, since
[3] *good e'en:* good evening (or here, good day)
[4] *but one:* only one
[5] *couple it:* put it together
[6] *blow:* hit
[7] *apt:* willing
[8] *an:* if
[9] *give me occasion:* give me a reason
[10] *consortest:* spend time, or play music
[11] *minstrels:* musicians (low-grade people)
[12] *make minstrels of us:* if you call us minstrels
[13] *look to:* expect to

nothing but[14] discords[15]. Here's my fiddlestick[16], here's

50 that shall make you dance. Zounds[17], consort!

BENVOLIO: We talk here in the public haunt[18] of men.

Either withdraw[19] unto some private place,

Or reason coldly[20] of your grievances[21],

Or else depart. Here all eyes gaze on us.

55 **MERCUTIO:** Men's eyes were made to look, and let them gaze.

I will not budge[22] for no man's pleasure[23], I.

Enter Romeo.

TYBALT: Well, peace be with you, sir. Here comes my man[24].

MERCUTIO: But I'll be hanged[25], sir, if he wear your livery[26].

Marry, go before to field[27], he'll be your follower.

60 Your Worship[28] in that sense may call him "man."

TYBALT: Romeo, the love I bear[29] thee can afford[30]

No better term than this: thou art a villain[31].

ROMEO: Tybalt, the reason that I have to love thee

Doth much excuse the appertaining[32] rage

65 To such a greeting[33]. Villain am I none.

Therefore farewell. I see thou knowest me not.

[14] *nothing but:* only
[15] *discords:* out of tune music, or the sounds of an argument
[16] *fiddlestick:* violin bow, or sword
[17] *Zounds:* an old exclamation meaning "God's wounds"
[18] *haunt:* place where people gather
[19] *withdraw:* move to another place
[20] *coldly:* calmly
[21] *grievances:* disagreements
[22] *budge:* move
[23] *for no man's pleasure:* to please some other man
[24] *my man:* the man I am looking for
[25] *I'll be hanged:* I'd be amazed
[26] *livery:* uniform of a servant indicating what family he serves
[27] *go before to field:* a place where they might have a duel, away from people's view
[28] *Worship:* a title used for important people, here used sarcastically by Mercutio
[29] *bear:* have
[30] *afford:* give
[31] *villain:* low-born, bad person, criminal
[32] *appertaining:* accompanying
[33] *such a greeting:* the things that Tybalt just said to Romeo

Director's Notes

2.8

TYBALT: Boy[34], this shall not excuse the injuries
That thou hast done me. Therefore turn and draw.

ROMEO: I do protest I never injured thee
70 But love thee better than thou canst devise[35]
Till thou shalt know the reason of my love.
And so, good Capulet, which name I tender[36]
As dearly as mine own, be satisfied.

MERCUTIO: O calm, dishonorable, vile[37] submission[38]!
75 *Alla stoccata*[39] carries it away[40]. *[Draws.[41]]*
Tybalt, you ratcatcher, will you walk[42]?

TYBALT: What wouldst thou have with me[43]?

MERCUTIO: Good king of cats[44], nothing but one of your
nine lives, that I mean to make bold withal[45], and,
80 as you shall use me hereafter, dry-beat[46] the rest of the
eight. Will you pluck your sword out of his pilcher[47]
by the ears[48]? Make haste[49], lest[50] mine be about your
ears ere it be out.

TYBALT: I am for you[51]. *[He draws.]*

85 **ROMEO:** Gentle Mercutio, put thy rapier up[52].

---

[34] *Boy:* a very disrespectful way to address an adult
[35] *devise:* imagine
[36] *tender:* hold
[37] *vile:* disgusting
[38] *submission:* surrender
[39] *Alla stoccata:* name for a specific sword thrust, but can also suggest a cutting remark.
[40] *carries it away:* wins the argument
[41] *Draws:* pulls out his sword
[42] *walk:* fight with me
[43] *have with me:* want from me
[44] *king of cats:* A cat has nine lives, and Mercutio wants to take one of them.
[45] *make bold withal:* have my way with
[46] *dry-beat:* very heavily hit
[47] *pilcher:* sheath
[48] *ears:* hand-grip
[49] *make haste:* be quick
[50] *lest:* in case
[51] *I am for you:* I will fight you
[52] *Put thy rapier up:* put away your sword

MERCUTIO: Come, sir, your *passado*[53]. *[They fight.]*

ROMEO: Draw[54], Benvolio, beat down their weapons. *[Romeo draws.]*
Gentlemen, for shame forbear[55] this outrage!
Tybalt! Mercutio! The Prince expressly[56] hath
90 Forbid this bandying[57] in Verona streets.
Hold[58], Tybalt! Good Mercutio!
[Romeo attempts to beat down their rapiers. Tybalt stabs Mercutio.]

MERCUTIO: I am hurt.
A plague o' both houses![59] I am sped[60].
95 Is he gone and hath nothing[61]?

The Royal Shakespeare Company's 2004 production of *Romeo and Juliet*

---

[53] *passado:* a style of sword lunge
[54] *Draw:* pull out your sword (in this case not to fight, but to stop the fight)
[55] *forbear:* stop
[56] *expressly:* clearly
[57] *bandying:* sword fighting
[58] *Hold:* stop
[59] *A plague o' both houses:* let a plague infect both your families. That is, I curse all of you.
[60] *sped:* finished
[61] *hath nothing?:* hasn't been wounded?

Preparing for the Role

Follow your teacher's directions and work with a group of classmates to read your character description, read the scene, and answer the following questions about your character. After you have finished answering the questions, practice reading aloud the speaking parts for your character in a way that reflects an understanding of what he is saying.

4. Romeo

   a. Tybalt calls Romeo a villain. How does Romeo try to convince Tybalt that he is not?

_____

_____

_____

_____

   b. What words does Romeo use to hint to Tybalt that he is married to Juliet?

_____

_____

_____

_____

   c. What does Romeo mean when he tells Mercutio to "put thy rapier up"? Does Mercutio follow his advice? How do you know?

_____

_____

_____

_____

5. Mercutio

   a. How does Mercutio respond when Tybalt asks to have "a word" with him?

_____

_____

_____

_____

b. What is Mercutio calling his "fiddlestick"? How does he plan to use it to make Tybalt "dance"? What did Tybalt say that prompted Mercutio to start making all the musical references?

_____

_____

_____

_____

c. Why does Mercutio say "a plague o' both houses"? What houses is he talking about? Why both?

_____

_____

_____

_____

6. Tybalt

a. When Mercutio challenges Tybalt to "a word and a blow," how does Tybalt respond? How is he using the word "occasion"?

_____

_____

_____

_____

b. What words does Tybalt use to show his feelings toward Romeo?

_____

_____

_____

_____

c. What does Tybalt mean when he tells Romeo to "turn and draw"?

_____

_____

_____

_____

7. Benvolio

a. Does Benvolio tell Mercutio and Tybalt not to fight? If not, what choice is he offering them?

_____

_____

_____

_____

b. What does Benvolio mean when he says "all eyes gaze on us"? Why does he care?

_____

_____

_____

_____

c. In this entire scene, Benvolio speaks only once. What could that tell you about his character?

_____

_____

_____

_____

☑ Check Your Understanding

What are some things an actor should do before making choices about how to deliver a character's lines?

_____

_____

_____

_____

_____

_____

Putting Words into Play

Learning Strategies

Close Reading
Marking the Text

Learning Targets

- Collaborate with peers to perform a scene from a play, analyzing the characters and following the stage directions.
- Use the dialogue of a play to make inferences about performance needs, such as setting, props, costumes, and stage directions.
- Write a character aside.

Preview

In this activity, you will work with some classmates to create a personalized performance of a scene from *Romeo and Juliet*.

My Notes

📝 Opening Writing Prompt

Reread the excerpted exchange between Benvolio and Mercutio. Then answer the following question.

How do you think Benvolio would deliver the words "here all eyes gaze on us," and how do you think Mercutio would serve back the words "let them gaze"?

BENVOLIO: We talk here in the public haunt of men.
Either withdraw unto some private place,
And reason coldly of your grievances,
Or else depart; here all eyes gaze on us.

MERCUTIO: Men's eyes were made to look, and let them gaze;
I will not budge for no man's pleasure, I.

As You Read

- Underline key phrases or intense lines for the character whose part you will be reading.
- Circle unknown words and phrases. Try to determine the meaning of the words by using context clues. Refer back to the footnotes in Activity 2.8 as needed.

Director's Notes

About the Author

Known as the Bard of Avon, William Shakespeare was a poet, playwright, actor, and businessman who is commonly considered the most famous writer in the English language. Although he wrote at the turn of the 17th century, people around the world are still reading and performing his work today, as well as quoting it—sometimes without even knowing that they're doing so! Shakespeare's turns of phrase are so ingrained in the English language that the only work thought to be quoted more often than Shakespeare's plays and poetry is the Bible. Some phrases you may use that come straight from Shakespeare's writing include "heart of gold," "good riddance," "vanish into thin air," and "seen better days." Shakespeare's clever way with words and his ability to capture the wide-ranging emotions of people from all walks of life have enabled his writing to endure and remain relevant to audiences for hundreds of years. It is thought that he wrote 37 plays, including comedies, histories, and tragedies, as well as more than 150 poems.

Drama

Romeo and Juliet
Act III, Scene I, Lines 38–95

by **William Shakespeare**

> **BENVOLIO:** Two households, both alike in dignity
> (In fair Verona, where we lay our scene),
> From ancient grudge break to new mutiny,
> Where civil blood makes civil hands unclean.
>
> **TYBALT:** *[to his companions]*
> Follow me close, for I will speak to them.—
> Gentlemen, good e'en. A word with one of you.
>
> 40   **MERCUTIO:** And but one word with one of us? Couple it
> with something. Make it a word and a blow.
>
> **TYBALT:** You shall find me apt enough to that, sir, an
> you will give me occasion.

MERCUTIO: Could you not take some occasion without
45 giving?

TYBALT: Mercutio, thou consortest with Romeo.

MERCUTIO: Consort? What, dost thou make us minstrels?
An thou make minstrels of us, look to hear
nothing but discords. Here's my fiddlestick; here's
50 that shall make you dance. Zounds, consort!

BENVOLIO: We talk here in the public haunt of men.
Either withdraw unto some private place,
Or reason coldly of your grievances,
Or else depart. Here all eyes gaze on us.

55 **MERCUTIO:** Men's eyes were made to look, and let them gaze.
I will not budge for no man's pleasure, I.

Enter Romeo.

TYBALT: Well, peace be with you, sir. Here comes my man.

MERCUTIO: But I'll be hanged, sir, if he wear your livery.
Marry, go before to field, he'll be your follower.
60 Your Worship in that sense may call him "man."

TYBALT: Romeo, the love I bear thee can afford
No better term than this: thou art a villain.

ROMEO: Tybalt, the reason that I have to love thee
Doth much excuse the appertaining rage
65 To such a greeting. Villain am I none.
Therefore farewell. I see thou knowest me not.

TYBALT: Boy, this shall not excuse the injuries
That thou hast done me. Therefore turn and draw.

ROMEO: I do protest I never injured thee
70 But love thee better than thou canst devise
Till thou shalt know the reason of my love.
And so, good Capulet, which name I tender
As dearly as mine own, be satisfied.

Director's
Notes

Director's Notes

MERCUTIO: O calm, dishonorable, vile submission!
75 *Alla stoccata* carries it away. *[He draws.]*
Tybalt, you ratcatcher, will you walk?

TYBALT: What wouldst thou have with me?

MERCUTIO: Good king of cats, nothing but one of your
nine lives, that I mean to make bold withal, and, as
80 you shall use me hereafter, dry-beat the rest of the
eight. Will you pluck your sword out of his pilcher
by the ears? Make haste, lest mine be about your
ears ere it be out.

TYBALT: I am for you. *[He draws.]*

85 ROMEO: Gentle Mercutio, put thy rapier up.

MERCUTIO: Come, sir, your *passado. [They fight.]*

ROMEO: Draw, Benvolio, beat down their weapons. *[Romeo draws.]*
Gentlemen, for shame forbear this outrage!
Tybalt! Mercutio! The Prince expressly hath
90 Forbid this bandying in Verona streets.
Hold, Tybalt! Good Mercutio!
[Romeo attempts to beat down their rapiers. Tybalt stabs Mercutio.]

PETRUCHIO: Away, Tybalt!

[Tybalt, Petruchio, and their followers exit.]

MERCUTIO: I am hurt.
A plague o' both houses! I am sped.
95 Is he gone and hath nothing?

VOCABULARY

LITERARY
Stage directions are notes that the playwright includes in the script about how characters should behave and move across the stage. Often these notes are set in brackets or parentheses or in a different style of type than the rest of the script. In this version of *Romeo and Juliet*, the stage directions are in italics and bracketed.

Making Observations

- What do the **stage directions** say about each character's movements and behavior?
- What character movements and behaviors are implied in the dialogue?

Working from the Text

Reread the scene from *Romeo and Juliet*. Then work with your classmates to answer the following questions about how your group will choose to perform the scene.

1. What is your character's name? _____

2. Think about who your character is.

   a. What is his main **motive** during the scene, and how do you know?

   _____

   _____

   b. What does your character's dialogue show about how he wants the other characters to view him?

   _____

   _____

   c. What attitude should your character project when he speaks? What are ways that you can use the volume and pitch of your voice to portray this attitude?

   _____

   _____

3. Think about your character's movements on the stage.

   a. Before or during which lines does your character come onto the stage?

   _____

   _____

   b. Once your character is onstage, where should he stand? Also, will he remain in the same place throughout the scene or move to different parts of the stage?

   _____

   _____

   c. The play's stage directions are in italics and bracketed. What (if anything) do the play's stage directions say about how your character should move across the stage?

   _____

   _____

   d. What does your character's dialogue imply about how your character should move across the stage?

   _____

   _____

ACADEMIC

Motive is a character's reason for behaving in a certain way. The term is also used in reference to the behavior of real people, including when people commit crimes. The word comes from the Latin *movēre*, which means "to move."

My Notes

4. Think about ways to make the scene come alive.

   a. What do you know about the setting from the characters' dialogue, and what can you use to create this setting onstage?

   _____

   _____

   b. What do you think your character is wearing, and why do you think this?

   _____

   _____

   c. What props, if any, does your character need? For example, should your character have a sword? Why or why not?

   _____

   _____

   d. How might you use music and lighting to create atmosphere, help audience members know where to focus their attention, or make certain parts of the scene more dramatic?

   _____

   _____

Writing an Aside

5. Work with your classmates to write an **aside** for your character to deliver during your performance of the scene from *Romeo and Juliet*. As inspiration for your aside, think about the following questions.

   • Does your character have a secret? If so, what is it?
   • How does your character want the scene to play out, and how is this different from what is actually happening?
   • Is there something your character feels that he doesn't want to show? What is he feeling and why doesn't he want to show it?

☑ Check Your Understanding

What were you able to infer from the text of *Romeo and Juliet* about the setting, props, costumes, and stage movements needed for your performance? Elaborate on one inference you made and include evidence from the text for support.

_____

_____

VOCABULARY

LITERARY

In a play, an **aside** is something spoken by a character that is not meant to be heard by the other characters. Sometimes the audience is directly addressed in the aside, and other times the aside is simply the character's internal narration.

Reflecting on Performance Choices

Learning Strategies

Graphic Organizer
Outlining
Rereading

Learning Targets

- Formulate two possible interpretations of the same text and develop director's notes about how to tailor performance choices to each.
- Use an outline to plan and draft a multiple-paragraph analysis.

Preview

In this activity, you will use an outline to help you develop and write a multiple-paragraph analysis of an excerpt from *Romeo and Juliet*.

Preparing to Write an Analysis

1. Read the following passages and then choose one of the passages to use as the subject of your analysis. For your analysis, you will describe two different ways you could (as a director) interpret and perform the passage's lines, keeping their context in mind. For example, you could choose a funny approach, a tense approach, a loud approach, or a subtle approach. When you explain your two interpretations, describe how and why you would emphasize certain words in order to express your intent.

Passage One

> MERCUTIO: Consort! What, dost thou make us minstrels?
> An thou make minstrels of us, look to hear
> nothing but discords. Here's my fiddlestick, here's
> that shall make you dance. Zounds, consort!

Passage Two

> BENVOLIO: We talk here in the public haunt of men.
> Either withdraw unto some private place,
> And reason coldly of your grievances,
> Or else depart. Here all eyes gaze on us.

Passage Three

> ROMEO: Tybalt, the reason that I have to love thee
> Doth much excuse the appertaining rage
> To such a greeting. Villain am I none.
> Therefore farewell. I see thou knowest me not.

My Notes

_____

_____

_____

_____

_____

_____

_____

_____

_____

_____

_____

_____

_____

_____

_____

_____

_____

_____

_____

_____

_____

_____

_____

_____

_____

_____

_____

_____

_____

Forming a Multiple-Paragraph Outline for a Dramatic Interpretation

2. Create a multiple-paragraph outline in your Reader/Writer Notebook to plan your analysis.

- Begin your outline with notes for an introductory paragraph, including a general overview of the nature of dramatic interpretation and information about the line-delivery options you will describe.
- Develop the remaining paragraphs of your outline by including notes about the language and performance choices a director might recommend in order to ensure that each delivery option would express the intended interpretation.

✍ Writing to Sources: Informational Text

Use your notes from past lessons, along with your multiple-paragraph outline, to help you write your analysis. As you develop your draft, be sure to:

- Write an introduction that includes a general statement addressing the topic of dramatic interpretation, followed by a thesis statement that specifically mentions the scene, character, and line delivery options.
- Support your thesis with well-chosen, relevant facts and quotations.
- Use quotation marks around text that comes directly from the play.
- Use a variety of complete sentences.
- Include transitions at the beginning of the second and third paragraphs to link the major sections of the text. You may use the following sentence frame to form one transitional sentence: *In the _____ interpretation of the scene, I would _____.*
- Write a concluding statement that supports the information you have provided.

Assess and Reflect

Think of a specific word, phrase, or line you delivered during your performance of a character from *Romeo and Juliet*. Then write a brief paragraph about the meaning of that word, phrase, or line in the greater context of the scene, and how you chose to deliver it. Consider the Essential Question, "How does the mode of communication change the meaning of what is being communicated?"

Setting the Stage

Learning Strategies

Marking the Text
Previewing
Visualizing

Learning Targets

- Reread and analyze the prologue to *Romeo and Juliet* by examining the word choice and structure.
- Define *drama* and *tragedy* in the context of the play.

Preview

In this activity, you will take a much closer look at all fourteen lines of the prologue of *Romeo and Juliet* as you prepare to read the rest of the play.

Revisiting the Essential Questions

Based on what you learned in the first part of this unit, how would you respond to these questions now?

1. How do authors use words and phrases to move the emotions, thoughts, and actions of readers?

2. Why do authors revise their work?

3. How does the mode of communication change the meaning of what is being communicated?

Unpacking Embedded Assessment 1

Read the assignment for Embedded Assessment 1: Presenting a Dramatic Interpretation.

Your assignment is to work collaboratively with your acting company to interpret, rehearse, and perform a scene from William Shakespeare's *Romeo and Juliet*. In preparation, each member of the acting company will create a staging notebook providing textual evidence and commentary on the planned interpretation. Finally, you will write a reflection evaluating your final performance.

In your own words, summarize what you will need to know to complete this assessment successfully. With your class, create a graphic organizer to represent the skills and knowledge you will need to complete the tasks identified in the Embedded Assessment.

As You Read

- Place a star next to any parts that are still unclear.
- Circle unfamiliar words or phrases. Try to determine the meanings of the words by using context clues, word parts, or a dictionary.

WORD CONNECTIONS

Roots and Affixes
The word **prologue** comes from the Greek word *prologos*, containing the prefix *pro-* (before) and root *logos* (saying). This literally translates to "before the speech" or "before the play."

My Notes

My Notes

Drama

Romeo and Juliet
Prologue

by **William Shakespeare**

Enter Chorus

Two households, both alike in **dignity**
(In fair Verona, where we lay our scene),
From ancient grudge break to new **mutiny**,
Where civil blood makes civil hands unclean.
5   From forth the fatal loins of these two foes
A pair of **star-crossed lovers** take their life;
Whose misadventured **piteous** overthrows
Doth with their death bury their parents' strife.
The fearful passage of their death-marked love
10 And the continuance of their parents' rage,
Which, but their children's end, naught could remove,
Is now the two hours' traffic of our stage;
The which, if you with patient ears attend,
What here shall miss, our **toil** shall strive to mend.

Making Observations

- What details stand out to you in the prologue?
- What questions does this text raise for you?

dignity: rank
mutiny: rebellion against authority
star-crossed lovers: lovers destined for an unhappy end
piteous: pathetic
toil: hard work

Returning to the Text

- Return to the text as you respond to the following questions. Use evidence from the text to support your responses.

- Write any additional questions you have about the prologue in your Reader/Writer Notebook.

4. You examined lines 1–4 in Activity 2.9. Now paraphrase each of the other sets of lines: lines 5–8, lines 9–12, and lines 13–14.

_____

_____

_____

_____

5. What is the main purpose of the prologue?

_____

_____

_____

_____

6. List words that you associate with the term *tragedy*. Add a few key words from the prologue.

_____

_____

_____

_____

Poetic Form: Sonnet

A play's prologue serves as an introductory speech in which an actor, in this case probably just one man called the "Chorus," provides the audience with a brief outline of the plot.

In this play, the prologue is a 14-line poem with a defined structure that is called an English or Shakespearean **sonnet**. Note that this sonnet, like all of Shakespeare's sonnets, uses iambic pentameter to create a distinct rhythm. The most noticeable feature of this rhythmic pattern is the use of pentameter, which means that each line includes 10 syllables or 5 feet (pairs of syllables).

7. Count the number of syllables for each line. Label the lines of the prologue to show its rhythm and rhyme scheme.

8. How would you describe the rhyme scheme of the prologue? Which words rhyme with each other?

_____

_____

LITERARY

A **sonnet** is a 14-line lyric poem, usually written in iambic pentameter and following a strict pattern of rhyme. English sonnets contain three quatrains (four lines that rhyme) and one couplet (two lines that rhyme).

VOCABULARY

My Notes

9. Assign a letter of the alphabet to each word in a rhyming pair. How would you represent the rhyme scheme of the prologue using only letters?

Working from the Text

10. A *tableau* is a purposeful arrangement of characters frozen as if in a painting or a photograph. After you are assigned a character name, work with your class to create a tableau based on the information provided in the prologue and in the cast of characters in your copy of *Romeo and Juliet*. Think about the following as you prepare to assume your role in the class tableau.

    - Body positions (whom you stand next to, distance)
    - Postures and poses
    - Facial expressions and gestures

☑ Check Your Understanding

Based on your reading of the prologue and the definition of *tragedy*, as well as your performance of Act III, Scene I, generate questions you have about *Romeo and Juliet*. Use evidence from the prologue and Act III, Scene I, to write initial responses. Revisit your questions after you have read the rest of the play to check your understanding.

What Is the Conflict?

Learning Strategies

Close Reading
Diffusing
Marking the Text
Skimming/Scanning
Visualizing

Learning Targets

- Read the opening scene of *Romeo and Juliet* and identify the relationships between characters.
- Annotate the text for vocal and visual delivery to communicate meaning in a performance.

Preview

In this activity, you will read Act I, Scene I, from *Romeo and Juliet* and annotate the text in order to present a vocal and visual performance.

As You Read

- Underline words and phrases that seem to be insults.
- Circle unknown words and phrases. Try to determine the meaning of the words by using context clues, word parts, or a dictionary.

Diffusing Shakespeare's Language

1. Working with a partner, skim and scan the text of the excerpt from Act I, Scene I, and diffuse some of Shakespeare's unfamiliar language using the following translation table. What other resources could you use to help diffuse Shakespeare's language?

Shakespeare	Translation	Shakespeare	Translation
Thee/Thou	You	Ay	Yes
Thy/Thine	Your	Would	Wish
Hath	Has	Alas	Unfortunately
Art	Are	'Tis	It is
Wilt/Wouldst	Will/Would	Marry	Really
An	If	Canst/Didst/Hadst/Dost	Can/Did/Has/Does

INDEPENDENT READING LINK

Read and Respond

Skim the text you are reading independently and try to find words that are technical or specific to the subject's discipline. Write a list of these words, and use context clues to write a definition for each word. Then use a reference, such as a glossary or dictionary, to validate your definitions. Clarify your definition as needed, and make sure your definition reflects the precise and appropriate meaning of the word in its context.

My Notes

Drama

Romeo and Juliet
Act I, Scene I, Lines 34–73

by **William Shakespeare**

SAMPSON: My naked weapon is out. Quarrel, I will back
35 thee.

GREGORY: How! Turn thy back and run?

SAMPSON: Fear me not.

GREGORY: No, marry. I fear thee!

SAMPSON: Let us take the law of our sides; let them
40 begin.

GREGORY: I will frown as I pass by, and let them take it
as they list.

SAMPSON: Nay, as they dare. I will bite my thumb at
them, which is a disgrace to them, if they bear it. *[He bites his thumb.]*

Enter ABRAHAM and BALTHASAR

45 **ABRAHAM:** Do you bite your thumb at us, sir?

SAMPSON: I do bite my thumb, sir.

ABRAHAM: Do you bite your thumb at us, sir?

SAMPSON: *[Aside to GREGORY]* Is the law of our side, if I
say "Ay"?

50 **GREGORY:** *[Aside to SAMPSON]* No.

SAMPSON: No, sir, I do not bite my thumb at you, sir,
but I bite my thumb, sir.

GREGORY: Do you quarrel, sir?

ABRAHAM: Quarrel, sir? No, sir.

55 **SAMPSON:** If you do, sir. I am for you. I serve as
good a man as you.

ABRAHAM: No better.

SAMPSON: Well, sir.

GREGORY: *[Aside to SAMPSON]* Say "better"; here comes
60 one of my master's kinsmen.

SAMPSON: Yes, better, sir.

quarrel: fight
kinsmen: relatives

ABRAHAM: You lie.

SAMPSON: Draw if you be men.—Gregory, remember
thy swashing blow.

They fight. Enter BENVOLIO

65 BENVOLIO: Part, fools!
Put up your swords. You know not what you do. *[Beats down their
swords.]*

Enter TYBALT, drawing his sword

TYBALT: What, art thou drawn among these heartless hinds?
Turn thee, Benvolio; look upon thy death.

BENVOLIO: I do but keep the peace. Put up thy sword,
70   Or manage it to part these men with me.

TYBALT: What, drawn and talk of peace? I hate the word
As I hate hell, all Montagues, and thee.
Have at thee, coward! *[They fight.]*

Making Observations

- What started the fight?
- What words show how the characters feel about each other?

swashing: violent

Returning to the Text

- Return to the text as you respond to the following questions. Use text evidence to support your responses.
- Write any additional questions you have about the scene in your Reader/Writer Notebook.

2. How does this opening scene help set the stage for the play?

_____

_____

_____

_____

3. How does Benvolio's attitude shift at the end of the scene?

_____

_____

_____

_____

Working from the Text

4. In your groups, choose or assign the characters' roles. As you reread the scene, take notes to paraphrase what your assigned character is saying.

5. After you feel comfortable with the meaning, prepare for a dramatic reading with your group by annotating the text with tone cues to indicate the appropriate vocal delivery (for example: angry, confused, bragging, laughing). Use punctuation as cues, taking note of commas, semicolons, colons, and periods. Make notes where question marks and exclamation marks appear.

6. As you read the scene aloud with your group, visualize how the scene could be performed on stage. How would the actors use movement and gestures to communicate meaning to the audience? Where would the actors stand on the stage? Add annotations to the text to indicate appropriate visual delivery for your character.

☑ Check Your Understanding

What parts of the text are important to consider when deciding how to deliver a scene?

📝 Writing Prompt: Informational

Work with a small group to write a paragraph explaining how you would stage this scene. Refer back to the scene as necessary. Explain why you think your staging ideas would be effective, based on your intended interpretation. Be sure to:

- Include an explanation about how you developed your ideas.
- Support your explanation with text evidence from the scene.
- Explain your ideas using reflective commentary.

All by Myself

Learning Targets

- Make inferences about characters from textual evidence.
- Explore symbols, imagery, and figurative language within monologues.

Preview

In this activity, you will revisit Act I of *Romeo and Juliet* and analyze how monologues are used to further understanding of the play.

Learning Strategies

Discussion Groups
Graphic Organizer
SIFT
Skimming/Scanning

LITERARY

Monologues are long speeches in a play, or other kind of performance, delivered by one actor. The character can be speaking to other characters or speaking to the audience.

Finding the Monologues: Act I

1. Skim and scan Act I of Romeo and Juliet looking for examples of **monologues**. Note the acts, scenes, and lines. List those you find in the following space.

Working from the Text

2. In Act I, Scene III, Lady Capulet has a monologue in which she uses figurative language. Reread the monologue and select textual evidence that reveals how Lady Capulet wants Juliet to view Paris. Make inferences about why Lady Capulet favors the match.

Textual Evidence	Inferences

3. Choose another monologue from Act I. Who is speaking to whom? What is the speaker trying to communicate via the monologue? Work in small groups to complete the graphic organizer. Support your answer by citing textual evidence and logical inferences.

Textual Evidence	Inference

4. Rehearse and present your interpretation of a monologue from Act I to students in another group, each of whom has analyzed a different monologue from Act I.

☑ Check Your Understanding

What function do monologues serve?

✎ Writing to Sources: Informational Text

Write a literary analysis in which you explain how Shakespeare uses the speaker's words and phrases to convey a theme or message. Be sure to:

- Include relevant support for your claim, details, examples, and commentary.
- Use transitional words and phrases, as well as a variety of sentence types, to create cohesion.

Acting Companies

Learning Targets

- Discuss and evaluate possible scenes for performance.
- Explore the theatrical tool of Staging Notebooks.
- Establish acting companies.

Preview

In this activity, you will choose a scene from *Romeo and Juliet* for performance. Then you will form an acting company and use your selected scene to create a Staging Notebook.

Choosing a Scene to Perform

1. With your small group, preview and discuss the scenes in the following chart. Put an asterisk next to scenes that you might consider interpreting. Note that some scenes have characters with small roles that can be assigned to a group member who wants a small part in the staging or who wants to work as the director or dramaturge, combined with another role. The small role could also be cut from the scene. Other scenes have long monologues that can be shortened with your teacher's direction or approval.

Learning Strategies

Brainstorming
Discussion Groups
Sketching

LITERARY

A **dramaturge** is a member of an acting company who helps the director and actors make informed decisions about the performance by researching information relevant to the play and its context.

"Romeo and Juliet Farewell" by Eleanor Fortescue-Brickdale (1872–1945)

My Notes

Act and Scene	Description	Characters	Research Suggestions
Act I, Scene I lines 153–232 *from "Good morrow, cousin" to "die in debt."* (80 lines total)	Benvolio tries to cheer up Romeo, who pines for Rosaline.	Benvolio Romeo	family relationships, courtship, convents
Act I, Scene II entire scene (103 lines total)	Paris asks Lord Capulet for Juliet's hand in marriage. Benvolio and Romeo find out about the Capulets' party from Peter, a servant.	Lord Capulet Paris Peter Benvolio Romeo	servants, marriage customs, patriarchy
Act I, Scene III entire scene (107 lines total)	Lady Capulet and the Nurse are discussing Paris with Juliet before the party.	Juliet Lady Capulet Nurse Peter	marriage customs, nobility, nursemaids
Act I, Scene IV lines 1–116 *from "What, shall this speech" to "Strike, drum."* (116 lines total)	Romeo is worried about going to the party because he had a bad dream, and Mercutio is teasing him.	Romeo Mercutio Benvolio	superstitions, festivities
Act I, Scene V lines 41–141 *from "Oh, she doth teach" to "all are gone."* (101 lines)	Romeo and Juliet meet and fall in love; meanwhile, Tybalt complains to Lord Capulet about Romeo crashing the party.	Romeo Juliet Tybalt Capulet Nurse	festivities, courtship, dancing
Act II, Scene II lines 33–137 (105 lines total)	Romeo visits Juliet after the party and overhears her declaring her love on the balcony.	Romeo Juliet	courtship, architecture
Act II, Scene III entire scene (94 lines total)	Romeo visits the Friar to tell him about his love for Juliet and ask him to perform the wedding.	Romeo Friar Lawrence	friars, herbal medicine

Act and Scene	Description	Characters	Research Suggestions
Act II, Scene IV lines 1–85 (85 lines total)	Mercutio and Benvolio discuss Tybalt's challenge and give Romeo a hard time.	Mercutio Benvolio Romeo	dueling
Act III, Scene III lines 1–108 (108 lines total)	Romeo receives word of his banishment, and the Friar is trying to calm him when the Nurse arrives.	Romeo Friar Nurse	friars, banishment laws
Act IV, Scene I lines 1–122 *from "On Thursday, sir?"* *to "tell me not of fear!"* (122 lines total)	Juliet meets Paris on the way to church. The Friar gives her a potion to fake her death and avoid marriage.	Paris Friar Lawrence Juliet	burial vaults, herbal portions
Act IV, Scene V lines 1–95 *from "Mistress" to* *"crossing their high will."* (95 lines total)	The Nurse thinks Juliet is dead, and she informs the household.	Nurse Capulet Lady Capulet Friar Paris	funeral customs, astrology
Act V, Scene I entire scene (88 lines total)	Balthasar tells Romeo of Juliet's "death." Romeo buys poison to kill himself.	Romeo Balthasar Apothecary	apothecary, poisons
Act V, Scene III lines 84–170 *from "For here lies Juliet"* *to "let me die."* (87 lines total)	Romeo and Juliet commit suicide.	Romeo Juliet	burial customs

INDEPENDENT READING LINK

Read and Respond

Think about the language that the writer uses in the text you are reading independently, whether it is fiction or nonfiction. Choose some pivotal words and phrases and write a few sentences that briefly explain how the author uses them to communicate ideas.

My Notes

_____

_____

_____

_____

_____

_____

_____

_____

_____

_____

_____

_____

_____

_____

_____

LITERARY

To **block** a scene means to create the plan for how actors will position themselves on the stage in relation to one another, the audience, and the objects on the stage.

VOCABULARY

2. After you have selected your scene, brainstorm possible interpretations. Film adaptations of *Romeo and Juliet* have included traditional interpretations as well as unique interpretations such as rival gangs in *West Side Story*, garden gnomes in *Gnomeo and Juliet*, and kung fu cops and mobsters in *Romeo Must Die*. Consider the style of performance your group would like to present.

3. In Shakespeare's day, acting companies named themselves, just as musical groups do today. Shakespeare belonged first to the Lord Chamberlain's Men and later to the King's Men. Your acting company should come to a consensus on a name that reflects the characteristics of your group.

   Create a contract, using the frame that follows, and sketch a rough draft of a poster design advertising your performance. Include a performance date, cast (characters and student names), director, and dramaturge, as well as words and images that reflect your interpretation.

   We, the _____ (name of acting company), pledge to plan, rehearse, and perform _____ (act and scene) from William Shakespeare's *Romeo and Juliet*.

4. Every member of the acting company will complete a Staging Notebook. Based on your primary role in the performance, prepare an Actor's Notebook or a Director's Notebook. Read the description of your notebook, highlighting key elements. Create a "To Do" list that you can go back to as you work with your acting company.

Director's Notebook

- **Interpretation:** After you have selected your scene from the chart, brainstorm possible interpretations, such as choosing a funny approach, tense approach, loud approach, or subtle approach. Consider the time, place, and characters that would enhance your interpretation. Write a paragraph describing the interpretation you have chosen for your scene. Provide textual evidence to explain the reasoning and plan for the theatrical elements that will create your interpretation.

- **Visuals:** Decide whether you will use visuals for your scene (posters, large photographs, etc.), and create them or enlist the help of others who do not have large roles in the group.

- **Text:** Print a copy of your scene and annotate it with suggestions for your actors' vocal and visual delivery. Be sure to describe interactions and reactions you want to emphasize based on the pivotal words and phrases. The more information you can give the actors, the better.

- **Set Diagram:** Sketch the scene from the audience's perspective as well as an aerial view. Use your sketches to create a "playbook" approach to **block** your scene for character placement and movement.

- **Lighting, Sound, and Props:** Create a plan for lighting and sound (effects or music) that will enhance your acting company's performance. Include an explanation of your intended effect. Make a list of the props for your scene and where you will get them.

- **Introduction:** Write an introduction that provides context (what happened prior to your scene) and previews the content of your scene. Memorize and present the introduction before your performance.

- **Meeting Log:** After every meeting, you will be responsible for writing a dated log that records how the meeting went. Some questions you might answer in your log include the following:

- What did the group accomplish?
- What obstacles were identified?
- Which problems have been resolved? How?
- What needs to be done before and at the next meeting?

- **Director's "To Do" List:** This will be the first entry in your Director's Staging Notebook.

Actor's Notebook

- **Interpretation:** Several interpretations of *Romeo and Juliet* have been created throughout the years. After you have selected your scene from the chart, write a paragraph describing the interpretation you have chosen for your character. Provide textual evidence to explain the reasoning and plan for the theatrical elements that will create your interpretation.

- **Text:** Print out or make a copy of your scene and highlight your lines. Paraphrase each of your lines and annotate them with your plan for vocal and visual delivery. Annotate the other characters' lines with notes on your nonverbal reactions.

- **Costume:** Decide on an appropriate costume for your character. Sketch, photograph, cut out of a magazine, or print out an online image of both your ideal costume and your real costume.

- **Character Analysis:** Create a visual representation of your character's thoughts, desires, actions, and obstacles. Focus on your scene, but you can include evidence from other parts of the play.

- **Actor's "To Do" List:** This will be the first entry in your Actor's Staging Notebook.

Dramaturge's Notebook

- **Research Questions:** Generate research questions related to the scene. In addition to the suggestions in this activity, consider the history and context of the play, unfamiliar references or vocabulary in your scene, and theater and performance in Shakespeare's time. Conduct research to answer questions and take careful notes on note cards.

- **Annotated Bibliography:** Create a bibliography of the works you consulted in your research. Include annotations that summarize what you learned, and provide commentary on how this information enhances your understanding of Shakespeare, *Romeo and Juliet*, and/or your scene.

- **Suggestions:** Based on your research findings, prepare a list of suggestions for the director and the actors. Present them to the group and be prepared to explain your reasons for the suggestions.

- **Interpretation:** Write an explanation of how your research helped the acting company interpret its scene. Cite specific sources and quotes from your research. Memorize this explanation and present it after the performance.

- **Dramaturge's "To Do" List:** This will be the first entry in your Dramaturge's Staging Notebook.

☑ Check Your Understanding

Why is it important for each person in an acting company to have a Staging Notebook?

My Notes

Learning Strategies

Choral Reading
Chunking the Text
Oral Reading
Rereading

My Notes

Learning Targets

- Analyze how an author draws on source material to create a new work.
- Analyze a key scene in two different artistic mediums.

Preview

In this activity, you will analyze an excerpt from the script of *West Side Story*. This scene is an adaptation of the balcony scene from *Romeo and Juliet*.

Shakespeare's Influence on Modern Works

One of the best-known modern works that draws on Shakespeare's *Romeo and Juliet* is the musical *West Side Story*. The story of feuding families in *Romeo and Juliet* becomes the story of warring street gangs in 1950s New York City. The Montagues and Capulets of Shakespeare's play become the Jets and Sharks of the West Side neighborhood. The Jets are white teenagers of European descent, while the Sharks are teens of Puerto Rican ancestry. Each group is determined to protect its side of the neighborhood.

As You Read

- Highlight any similarities and differences between this scene and *Romeo and Juliet*.
- Circle unknown words and phrases. Try to determine the meaning of the words on your own, then verify the meanings by checking a dictionary.

About the Author

Arthur Laurents (1918–2011) was considered one of American theater's greatest writers for musical theater. Among the well-known plays he wrote are *West Side Story* (1957), *Gypsy* (1959), *The Way We Were* (1973), and *The Turning Point* (1977). Laurents grew up in Brooklyn, New York, and began his career by writing scripts for radio programs. After a stint in the Army during World War II, where he wrote training films, he wrote musicals for Broadway.

Script

from West Side Story

by **Arthur Laurents**

SCENE FIVE. Maria and Tony have just met at a dance. They danced and kissed and now Tony is looking for Maria.

11:00 P.M. A back alley. A suggestion of buildings; a fire escape climbing to the rear window of an unseen flat. As Tony sings, he looks for where Maria lives, wishing for her. And she does appear, at the window above him, which opens onto the fire escape. Music stays beneath most of the scene.

TONY [*sings*]: Maria, Maria ...

MARIA: Ssh!

TONY: Maria!

MARIA: Quiet!

5　TONY: Come down.

MARIA: No.

TONY: Maria ...

MARIA: Please. If Bernardo—

TONY: He's at the dance. Come down.

10　MARIA: He will soon bring Anita home.

TONY: Just for a minute.

MARIA [*smiles*]: A minute is not enough.

TONY [*smiles*]: For an hour then.

MARIA: I cannot.

15　TONY: Forever!

MARIA: Ssh!

TONY: Then I'm coming up.

WOMAN'S VOICE [*from the offstage apartment*]: Maria!

MARIA: Momentito, Mama ...

20　TONY [*climbing up*]: Maria, Maria—

MARIA: Cállate! [*reaching her hand out to stop him*] Ssh!

TONY [*grabbing her hand*]: Ssh!

MARIA: It is dangerous.

TONY: I'm not "one of them."

25　MARIA: You are; but to me, you are not. Just as I am one of them—[*She gestures toward the apartment.*]

TONY: To me, you are all the—[*She covers his mouth with her hand.*]

MAN'S VOICE [*from the unseen apartment*]: Maruca!

MARIA: Sí, ya vengo, Papa.

TONY: Maruca?

30 MARIA: His pet name for me.

TONY: I like him. He will like me.

MARIA: No. He is like Bernardo: afraid. [*suddenly laughing*] Imagine being afraid of you!

TONY: You see?

MARIA [*touching his face*]: I see you.

35 TONY: See only me.

MARIA [*sings*]:

Only you, you're the only thing I'll see forever.

In my eyes, in my words and in everything I do,

Nothing else but you

40 Ever!

TONY:

And there's nothing for me but Maria,

Every sight that I see is Maria

MARIA: Tony, Tony . . .

45 TONY:

Always you, every thought I'll ever know,

Everywhere I go, you'll be.

MARIA [*And now the buildings, the world fade away, leaving them suspended in space.*]:

All the world is only you and me!

50 Tonight, tonight,

It all began tonight,

I saw you and the world went away.

Tonight, tonight,

There's only you tonight,

55 What you are, what you do, what you say.

TONY:

Today, all day I had the feeling

A miracle would happen—

I know now I was right.

60 For here you are

And what was just a world is a star

Tonight!

BOTH:

Tonight, tonight,

65 The world is full of light,

With suns and moons all over the place.

Tonight, tonight,

The world is wild and bright,

Going mad, shooting stars into space.

70 Today the world was just an address,

A place for me to live in,

No better than all right,

But here you are

And what was just a world is a star

75 Tonight!

MAN'S VOICE [*off stage*]: Maruca!

MARIA: Wait for me! [*She goes inside as the buildings begin to come back into place.*]

TONY [*sings*]:

Tonight, tonight,

80 It all began tonight,

I saw you and the world went away.

MARIA [*returning*]: I cannot stay. Go quickly!

TONY: I'm not afraid.

MARIA: They are strict with me. Please.

85 TONY [*kissing her*]: Good night.

MARIA: Buenas noches.

TONY: I love you.

MARIA: Yes, yes. Hurry. [*He climbs down.*] Wait! When will I see you? [*He starts back up.*] No!

90 TONY: Tomorrow.

MARIA: I work at the bridal shop. Come there.

TONY: At sundown.

MARIA: Yes. Good night.

TONY: Good night. [*He starts off.*]

95 MARIA: Tony!

TONY: Ssh!

MARIA: Come to the back door.

TONY: Sí. [*Again he starts out.*]

MARIA: Tony! [*He stops. A pause.*] What does Tony stand for?

100 TONY: Anton.

MARIA: Te adoro, Anton.

TONY: Te adoro, Maria.

My Notes

_____

_____

_____

_____

_____

_____

_____

_____

_____

_____

_____

_____

_____

_____

_____

_____

_____

_____

_____

_____

_____

_____

_____

_____

_____

_____

_____

_____

_____

_____

_____

_____

_____

My Notes

[*Both sing as music starts again:*]

Good night, good night,

105 Sleep well and when you dream,

Dream of me

Tonight.

[*She goes inside; he ducks out into the shadows just as Bernardo and Anita enter.*]

Making Observations

- What happens in this scene?
- What lines stand out to you most?
- What emotions do you feel while reading this scene?

Returning to the Text

- Return to the text as you respond to the following questions. Use text evidence to support your responses.
- Write any additional questions you have about the scene in your Reader/Writer Notebook.

1. Why is it significant that Tony and Maria repeat the phrase "tonight, tonight" over and over in their song?

_____

_____

_____

_____

2. What is the significance of the setting where Maria and Tony agree to meet next? Why might Laurents have chosen this setting?

_____

_____

_____

_____

3. What comparisons can be made between the relationships of Romeo and Juliet and Tony and Maria?

_____

_____

_____

_____

4. How does Laurents draw on the theme of the importance of names and families in the scene in *Romeo and Juliet*? Use text evidence in your response.

_____

_____

_____

_____

Working from the Text

5. Compare this scene from *West Side Story* with the scene in *Romeo and Juliet*. How are the scenes similar? How are they different? Use the following table to record ideas.

	Romeo and Juliet, Act II Scene II	*West Side Story*, Scene V
Summarize the plot of each scene.		
Describe the setting.		
List and describe the characters.		
Describe the dialogue, including imagery.		

6. Think about the similarities and differences in each version of the scene.

   a. What is emphasized in each version?

_____

_____

_____

_____

   b. What is absent in each version?

_____

_____

_____

_____

_____

☑ Check Your Understanding

How did Laurents use Shakespeare's play as inspiration for this scene from *West Side Story*?

✍ Writing to Sources: Informational

Write a review stating a preference for one of the balcony scenes you have read. Compare and contrast how the setting, dialogue, and stage directions contribute to an emotional impact. Provide commentary on both scenes. Be sure to:

- Clearly introduce your preference in a topic sentence or thesis.
- Develop the topic using concrete details and quotations from the scenes to support comparisons and contrasts that you draw.
- Include appropriate transitions.
- Write a concluding statement that follows from the explanation you have presented.

Learning Strategies

Chunking the Text
Oral Reading
Sketching

My Notes

Learning Targets

- Analyze the relationships between the protagonists and their foils, and emphasize interactions in vocal and visual delivery.
- Create a visual representation of a character's motivation: thoughts, desires, actions, and obstacles.

Preview

In this activity, you and your acting company will conduct an oral reading of a scene from Act II from *Romeo and Juliet*.

Reading Act II of *Romeo and Juliet*

1. With your group, choose one of the following scenes from Act II that you are not performing for your Embedded Assessment and do an oral reading.

   a. Act II, Scene III: Romeo and Friar Lawrence

   b. Act II, Scene IV: Mercutio, Benvolio, Romeo (until the Nurse enters)

   c. Act II, Scene V: Juliet and the Nurse

As You Read

- Use your Reader/Writer Notebook to log any physical interactions between the characters. For example, note when one character shoves another.
- Also record facial reactions one character could have to the words or actions of another character. For example, write "eye-rolling" when the character is bored or frustrated.
- Circle words and phrases that you aren't sure how to pronounce.

Working from the Text

2. Who is the protagonist in your scene? Which character is serving as a foil by illustrating traits that are very different from the protagonist's? (Review the term *character foil* from Unit 1 if needed.)

3. Rehearse the scene with an emphasis on the interactions between the protagonist and the foil and their reactions to each other. Perform your scene for at least one other group.

4. Choose one of the characters in your scene. On separate paper, create a visual representation of your character's motivation. See the following example for Tybalt. Sketch an outline and annotate it with your analysis on the corresponding body parts as follows:

   - Head: your character's thoughts
   - Heart: your character's desires
   - Arms: your character's actions
   - Legs: your character's obstacles

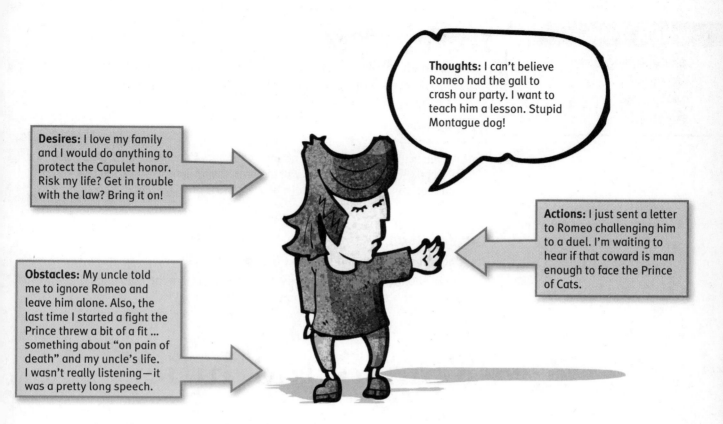

Thoughts: I can't believe Romeo had the gall to crash our party. I want to teach him a lesson. Stupid Montague dog!

Desires: I love my family and I would do anything to protect the Capulet honor. Risk my life? Get in trouble with the law? Bring it on!

Actions: I just sent a letter to Romeo challenging him to a duel. I'm waiting to hear if that coward is man enough to face the Prince of Cats.

Obstacles: My uncle told me to ignore Romeo and leave him alone. Also, the last time I started a fight the Prince threw a bit of a fit ... something about "on pain of death" and my uncle's life. I wasn't really listening—it was a pretty long speech.

Focus on the Sentence

Write "S" if the words form a complete sentence. Capitalize and punctuate the sentences. Write "F" if the words are a sentence fragment. Change the fragments into complete sentences using what you learned about characters and their foils.

_____ is a character that differs from a story's protagonist, either completely or in one key trait

_____

_____ foils are used for characterization

_____

✏️ Writing to Sources: Informational Text

Choose one of the friend/foil relationships you read in Act II, Scene III or Scene V. Write a paragraph that explains how the protagonist interacts with the foil. Explain the purpose that the foil serves. Be sure to:

- Identify the scene, and name the protagonist and the foil.
- Include direct quotations and specific examples from the text to support your explanation.
- Use a coherent organizational structure and make connections between specific words, images, and the ideas conveyed.

Learning Strategies

Chunking the Text
Discussion Groups
Oral Reading
Sketching

My Notes

Learning Targets

- Analyze a scene for dramatic irony and character motivation.
- Analyze characters' interactions and evaluate how their conflicting motives advance the plot.

Preview

In this activity, you and your acting company will conduct an oral reading of Act II, Scene VI. Then you will analyze how dramatic irony and the motivations of characters (both hidden and blatant) affect a scene.

As You Read

- Underline text that foreshadows the end of the play.
- Circle unknown words and phrases. Try to determine the meanings of the words by using context clues, word parts, or a dictionary.

Drama

Romeo and Juliet
Act II, Scene VI

by **William Shakespeare**

    FRIAR: So smile the heavens upon this holy act
That after-hours with sorrow chide us not.

    ROMEO: Amen, amen. But come what sorrow can,
It cannot countervail the exchange of joy
5   That one short minute gives me in her sight.
Do thou but close our hands with holy words,
Then love-devouring death do what he dare,
It is enough I may but call her mine.

    FRIAR: These violent delights have violent ends
10   And in their triumph die, like fire and powder,
Which, as they kiss, consume. The sweetest honey
Is loathsome in his own deliciousness
And in the taste confounds the appetite.
Therefore love moderately. Long love doth so.

countervail: equal
moderately: cautiously

15   Too swift arrives as tardy as too slow.

Enter JULIET

Here comes the lady. O, so light a foot
Will ne'er wear out the everlasting flint.
A lover may **bestride** the **gossamers**
That idles in the **wanton** summer air,
20   And yet not fall, so light is vanity.

JULIET: Good even to my ghostly confessor.

FRIAR: Romeo shall thank thee, daughter, for us both.

JULIET: As much to him, else is his thanks too much.

ROMEO: Ah, Juliet, if the measure of thy joy
25   Be heaped like mine, and that thy skill be more
To **blazon** it, then sweeten with thy breath
This neighbor air, and let rich music's tongue
Unfold the imagined happiness that both
Receive in either by this dear encounter.

30   **JULIET:** Conceit, more rich in matter than in words,
Brags of his substance, not of ornament.
They are but beggars that can count their worth,
But my true love is grown to such excess
I cannot sum up sum of half my wealth.

35   **FRIAR:** Come, come with me, and we will make short work;
For, by your leaves, you shall not stay alone
Till Holy Church incorporate two in one.

Exit

"Romeo and Juliet Before Friar Lawrence" by Carl Ludwig Friedrich Becker (1820–1900)

My Notes

_____
_____
_____
_____
_____
_____
_____
_____
_____
_____
_____
_____
_____
_____

Making Observations
- What happens in this scene?
- What questions do you have after reading the scene?

bestride: walk
gossamers: spiderwebs
wanton: playful
blazon: proclaim

Returning to the Text

- Return to the text and use text evidence to respond to the following questions.
- Write any additional questions you have about the scene in your Reader/Writer Notebook.

1. What does Romeo mean when he says the following to Friar Lawrence?

> Amen, amen. But come what sorrow can,
> It cannot countervail the exchange of joy
> That one short minute gives me in her sight.
> Do thou but close our hands with holy words,
> Then love-devouring death do what he dare,
> It is enough I may but call her mine

_____

_____

_____

_____

2. Review the term *dramatic irony* from Unit 1. Why are Romeo's words an example of dramatic irony?

_____

_____

_____

_____

3. How does Shakespeare's use of language contribute to the dramatic irony of the scene?

_____

_____

_____

_____

Working from the Text

4. Read the Friar's final words to Romeo before Juliet arrives. Highlight phrases that reveal the Friar's true feelings about the wedding.

> These violent delights have violent ends
> And in their triumph die, like fire and powder,
> Which, as they kiss, consume. The sweetest honey
> Is loathsome in its own deliciousness
> And in the taste confounds the appetite.
> Therefore love moderately. Long love doth so.
> Too swift arrives as tardy as too slow.

5. How does the Friar really feel about Romeo and Juliet's wedding? Why do the Friar and Nurse, adults who care deeply about the young lovers, allow Romeo and Juliet to act so quickly on their feelings?

_____

_____

_____

_____

6. Act II, Scene VI ends just as Romeo and Juliet are heading to church to be married. Why does Shakespeare have the wedding take place off stage?

_____

_____

_____

_____

7. Examine the painting "Romeo and Juliet Before Friar Lawrence." Write two interpretive questions about the painting and how it represents Act II, Scene VI.

_____

_____

_____

_____

8. The painting is communicating a scene from the play in a different medium. What is emphasized and absent in both the scene and the painting?

_____

_____

_____

_____

☑ Check Your Understanding

With your acting company, write brief responses to the following questions. Include your responses in your Staging Notebook.

a. What kind of theatrical elements, such as set design, sound, music, and lighting, would you use to indicate the mood of the scene?

b. How do the motives of the characters in this scene advance the plot of the drama?

Learning Strategies

Chunking the Text
Quickwrite
Skimming/Scanning
TWIST

VOCABULARY

LITERARY

A soliloquy is a long speech delivered by an actor alone on the stage, usually representing his or her internal thoughts. The word comes from the Latin roots *solus* (alone) and *loqui* (speak) and means "talking to oneself."

My Notes

Learning Targets

• Analyze soliloquies and monologues for performance cues.
• Examine how complex characters develop a theme.

Preview

In this activity, you will analyze and compare monologues and soliloquies from Acts II and III of *Romeo and Juliet*.

Talking Alone

1. Review the literary term *monologue*. In your own words, explain the difference between a soliloquy and a monologue.

_____

_____

_____

_____

2. Work with your acting company to skim and scan Acts II and III to find examples of soliloquies and monologues; add them to the following graphic organizer. Identify them by act, scene, speaker, and first line as in the examples. Try to find two more of each.

Monologues in Acts II and III	Soliloquies in Acts II and III
Act III, Scene II, Juliet: "Shall I speak ill of him that is my husband?"	Act II, Scene III, Friar Lawrence: "The grey-eyed morn smiles on the frowning night."

My Notes

3. With your acting company, choose a soliloquy that is not part of the scene you are performing in the Embedded Assessment.

4. Read the soliloquy several times, and discuss with your group what the speaker is communicating. Annotate the text for vocal and visual delivery that would convey the meaning to an audience.

Performing a Soliloquy

5. Select a short but important segment of the soliloquy to deliver from memory. Try some of these strategies to help you memorize lines:

   a. Visualize the lines by creating word pictures in your head in response to the imagery and diction.

   b. Chunk the text into phrases and lines. Learn them one chunk at a time, building on what you have memorized.

   c. Say the lines out loud using the vocal and visual delivery that you would use in performance.

   d. Write down the lines several different times during the process of committing them to memory.

6. After you have rehearsed, perform your lines for your acting company.

7. **Quickwrite:** Choose at least one of the following prompts to respond to in writing.

   • What performance clues does Shakespeare provide within the language of your chosen soliloquy?

   • What other purposes does a soliloquy serve? Why does Shakespeare include them?

   • What does the audience learn from watching characters struggle aloud with conflicting motives?

☑ Focus on the Sentence

Identify several themes that Shakespeare develops in the soliloquies in Acts II and III to complete the following sentences.

Nature is _____

Adults cannot _____

Young love is _____

Learning Targets

- Analyze the subtext of a passage to determine the true meaning and impact of a character's words.
- Plan, rehearse, and perform exaggerated visual delivery to communicate meaning to an audience.

Preview

In this activity, you will read the beginning of Act IV. In this scene, Juliet seeks advice from Friar Lawrence.

Cause and Effect

1. Many works of literature focus on young people "coming of age." Part of the process of coming of age is learning and accepting that sometimes parents and other trusted adults make mistakes. After all, they are only human. Complete the following graphic organizer to identify how the adults in Juliet's life are making mistakes that contribute to her frustration by the end of Act III.

Adult Decision or Advice	Effect on Juliet
Juliet's father threatens to disown her if she refuses to marry Paris.	She has the impossible choice of breaking her wedding vows or losing her family and starving on the streets.
Juliet's mother...	
The Nurse...	

- Leading up to this scene, Juliet becomes more alienated from her family and friends. She relies more frequently on the audience to understand the **subtext**. Revisit the passage in Act III, Scene V, in which Lady Capulet visits Juliet's bedroom immediately after Romeo has left.

  Summarize her statements to her mother about Romeo.

  _____

  _____

  Summarize the subtext of her statements (what she really means).

  _____

  _____

My Notes

As You Read

- Mark with a star places where Juliet does not give Paris a direct answer.
- Circle unknown words and phrases. Try to determine the meaning of the words by using context clues, word parts, or a dictionary.

Drama

Romeo and Juliet
Act IV, Scene I, Lines 18–37

by **William Shakespeare**

PARIS: Happily met, my lady and my wife.

JULIET: That may be, sir, when I may be a wife.

20 **PARIS:** That "may be" must be, love, on Thursday next.

JULIET: What must be shall be.

FRIAR LAWRENCE: That's a certain text.

PARIS: Come you to make **confession** to his father?

JULIET: To answer that, I should confess to you.

25 **PARIS:** Do not deny to him that you love me.

JULIET: I will confess to you that I love him.

PARIS: So will you, I am sure, that you love me.

JULIET: If I do so, it will be of more price
Being spoke behind your back than to your face.

30 **PARIS:** Poor soul, thy face is much abused with tears.

JULIET: The tears have got small victory by that,
For it was bad enough before their **spite**.

PARIS: Thou wrong'st it, more than tears with that report.

JULIET: That is no **slander**, sir, which is a truth,
35 And what I spake, I spake it to my face.

PARIS: Thy face is mine, and thou hast slandered it.

JULIET: It may be so, for it is not mine own.

---

confession: an admission of sins
spite: hatred
slander: maliciously false statement

My Notes

Making Observations

- What do you notice about the characters in this scene?
- How do Paris and Juliet speak to each other?

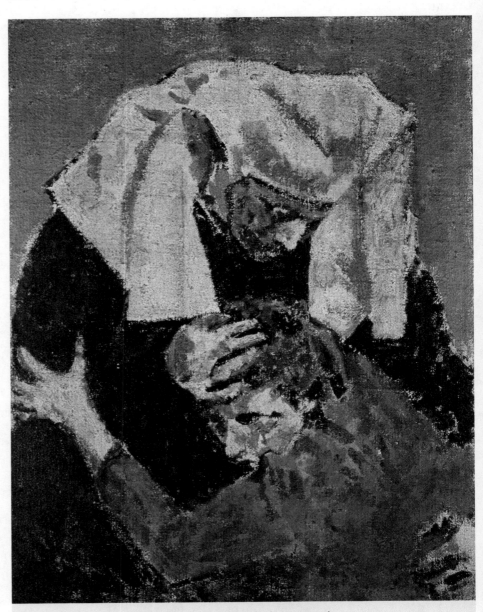

"Juliet and Her Nurse" by Walter Richard Sickert (1860–1942)

Returning to the Text

- Return to the text as you respond to the following questions. Use text evidence to support your responses.
- Write any additional questions you have about the scene in your Reader/Writer Notebook.

2. Why does Juliet refuse to give Paris a direct answer to any of his questions?

_____

_____

_____

_____

3. How does Paris feel about Juliet?

_____

_____

_____

_____

Working from the Text

4. In a small group, conduct an oral reading of the passage. In addition to Paris, Juliet, and Friar Lawrence, assign one group member the role of Juliet's subtext. After Juliet speaks, that group member will say aloud or pantomime Juliet's true thoughts.

5. In an actual performance, subtext has to be expressed through vocal or visual delivery. Use the following graphic organizer to make a plan for visual delivery as you read the rest of Act IV, Scene I.

What Juliet Would Rather Do Than Marry Paris: Textual Evidence	Plan for Visual Delivery (movements, expressions, gestures)
The Friar's Plan for Juliet: Textual Evidence	Plan for Visual Delivery (movements, expressions, gestures)

6. As you continue to read Act IV, look for other examples of subtext.

☑ Check Your Understanding

Quickwrite: Why is it important to keep the subtext in mind when you are performing a scene?

The Fault in Their Stars

Learning Targets

• Plan an interpretation that emphasizes the emotional impact and dramatic irony of Act V.

Preview

In this activity, you will collaborate with your acting company to analyze the end of *Romeo and Juliet* and practice planning your dramatic interpretation.

My Notes

Victims of Fate

1. In the prologue, Shakespeare calls Romeo and Juliet "star-crossed lovers." In Act V, when Romeo thinks Juliet is dead, he declares, "Then I defy you, stars!" What accidental and unfortunate events in the play support the theme that Romeo and Juliet are the victims of fate, or "the stars"?

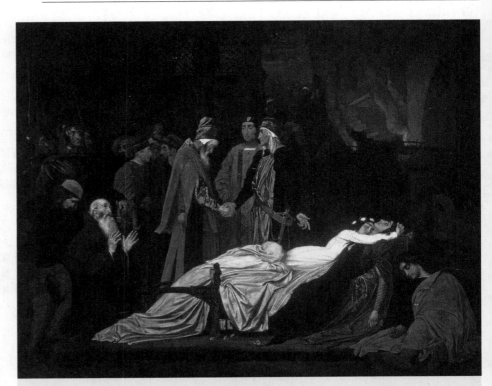

"The Reconciliation of the Montagues and the Capulets over the Dead Bodies of Romeo and Juliet," by Frederic Leighton (1830–1896)

Act V of Romeo and Juliet

2. **Scenes I and II:** Look for more evidence that Romeo and Juliet are victims of fate. What key events happen in these scenes?

_____

_____

3. Before you reread Scene III, review the definition of *dramatic irony*. What key information does the audience have that Romeo doesn't know?

_____

_____

4. **Scene III:** Think like a director and take notes in the following graphic organizer on how you would use vocal and visual delivery as well as other theatrical elements to intensify the emotional impact and emphasize the dramatic irony.

Theatrical Element/ My Choices as Director	How My Choices Would Intensify the Emotional Impact	How My Choices Would Emphasize the Dramatic Irony
Vocal Delivery:		
Visual Delivery:		
Other Theatrical Elements:		

My Notes

☑ **Focus on the Sentence**

Change the sentence fragments into complete sentences, using what you learned about *Romeo and Juliet*. Use correct capitalization and punctuation.

victims of fate because

_____

_____

uses dramatic irony in *Romeo and Juliet* to

_____

_____

📝 **Writing Prompt: Informational**

Now that you have read and analyzed the play *Romeo and Juliet*, revisit your response to the Essential Question: How do authors use words and phrases to move the emotions, thoughts, and actions of readers? Write a paragraph explaining how your response has grown, changed, and developed throughout this unit. Be sure to:

• Include a summary of your initial response to the Essential Question.

• Give examples that clearly compare and contrast your earlier thoughts with your current thoughts.

• Include reflective commentary.

Presenting a Dramatic Interpretation

🔊 ASSIGNMENT

Your assignment is to work collaboratively with your group to interpret, rehearse, and perform a scene from William Shakespeare's *Romeo and Juliet*. In preparation, each member of the group will create a staging notebook providing textual evidence and commentary on the planned interpretation. Finally, you will write a reflection evaluating your final performance.

Planning: Take time to make a performance plan.	■ How will you prepare a staging notebook that reflects your primary role in the production? (See activity 2.14 for guidelines.) ■ How will your group effectively integrate theatrical elements such as vocal and visual delivery, blocking, props, costumes, lighting, music, sound, and set design into your final performance? ■ As an actor, how will you learn your lines and prepare vocal and visual delivery? ■ As a director, how will you guide the acting company and prepare theatrical elements? ■ As a dramaturge, how will you research to provide background information?
Rehearsing: Collaborate with your acting company to polish your performance.	■ When and where will you meet to rehearse your scene several times? ■ How can the director's and dramaturge's feedback enhance the group's performance? ■ How could you use a video recording of one of your rehearsals to help you improve the quality of the performance? ■ How can another group help you rehearse by providing feedback on your performance?
Performing: Perform your scene for an audience of your peers.	■ How will the director introduce the scene? ■ Who will prompt actors who need assistance with their lines? ■ After the performance, how will the dramaturge explain how the performance reflects his or her research?
Evaluating: Write an evaluation of your group's final performance.	■ What were the strengths of your performance? What challenges did you face? ■ How can you use the Scoring Guide to ensure your understanding of the criteria for this piece?

Reflection

After completing this Embedded Assessment, think about how you accomplished this task, and respond to the following questions:

- How did different groups use visual and vocal delivery to enhance their performance in memorable ways?
- How did performing a scene help you understand or appreciate the play?

Presenting a Dramatic Interpretation

SCORING GUIDE

Scoring Criteria	Exemplary	Proficient	Emerging	Incomplete
Performance	The performance • represents an insightful interpretation of the scene and clearly communicates the intended effect to the audience • includes a reflection that represents the creative thinking of the entire acting company, with insightful commentary on the challenges and the final performance.	The performance • represents a clear interpretation of the scene and communicates it effectively to the audience • includes a reflection on the process of preparing for and performing the scene, including commentary on challenges faced and an evaluation of the final performance.	The performance • shows an attempt to interpret the scene • may not clearly communicate the scene to the audience • includes a reflection that summarizes the process rather than the thinking behind the interpretation and the performance.	The performance • is not coherent and does not clearly communicate the scene to the audience • includes a reflection that is minimal and simply lists the steps in the process; it does not reflect the thinking of the group or the effect of the performance.
Staging Notebook	The staging notebook • is detailed and shows evidence of a high degree of collaboration • thoroughly reflects a high degree of planning for visual and vocal delivery.	The staging notebook • is detailed and shows evidence of an adequate degree of collaboration • adequately reflects planning for visual and vocal delivery.	The staging notebook • shows little evidence of collaboration • reflects a limited amount of planning for visual and vocal delivery.	The staging notebook • is sparse and does not show evidence of collaboration • does not adequately reflect prior planning for visual and vocal delivery.
Delivery	The delivery • demonstrates a creative use of diction to communicate the scene • demonstrates skillful use of speaking rate, volume, enunciation, and purposeful gestures.	The delivery • includes appropriate and effective vocal and visual delivery of dialogue • demonstrates effective use of speaking rate, volume, enunciation, and gestures.	The delivery • includes some appropriate vocal and visual delivery of dialogue • demonstrates uneven use of speaking rate, volume, enunciation, and gestures.	The delivery • lacks appropriate vocal and visual delivery of dialogue • lacks appropriate speaking rate, volume, enunciation, or gestures.

Pivoting Back to Poetry

Learning Targets

- Reflect on previous learning about the writing process and vocabulary and make connections to new learning.
- Identify and analyze the skills and knowledge necessary to complete Embedded Assessment 2.

Preview

In this activity, your focus of study will pivot from Shakespeare and plays to poetry of all kinds. You will revisit the Essential Questions that you have been thinking about, familiarize yourself with Embedded Assessment 2, brainstorm ideas in your new group, and strategize the work you will do for your Poetry Project.

Revisiting the Essential Questions

At this point in Unit 2, you have read and created poems, watched and performed scenes from a play, and examined the connection between words on the page and words on a stage. You have seen poems become performances ("Tamara's Opus"), and read poems within plays (the prologue to *Romeo and Juliet*). Now you will return to poetry to examine closely how other poets make choices about words and structures in order to convey their messages. How would you respond to each of these questions now?

1. How do authors use words and phrases to move the emotions, thoughts, and actions of readers?

2. Why do authors revise their work?

3. How does the mode of communication change the meaning of what is being communicated?

Unpacking Embedded Assessment 2

Closely read the following Embedded Assessment assignment to identify and analyze its components.

Your group assignment is to create a poetry project that will include original works and analytical reviews of published works. Each group member must contribute three items to the project: either two original pieces and one analytical review or one original piece and two analytical reviews. Original works can include poems, illustrations of poems, or recorded spoken performances of original or published poems. Use multimedia to create your project and present it in a polished format.

Learning Strategies

Brainstorming
Discussion Groups
Mapping

ACADEMIC

To **strategize** is to plan the actions you will take to complete a task. Think about how this verb relates to the strategies you use to unpack Embedded Assessment 2 or the strategic thinking you will use to plan your Poetry Project with your group.

VOCABULARY

My Notes

Participating Collaboratively

You have worked in acting companies for a few weeks, and now you will be regrouping into poetry project groups. It will be important that you find ways to work together productively because Embedded Assessment 2 will require everyone's input. Some important guidelines for working collaboratively are:

- **Engage in respectful discourse.** Listen actively, respond in an appropriate tone, and transition from one speaker to the next in an orderly way. Adjust your communication style as needed to meet the needs of the group and task.

- **Engage in meaningful discourse.** Build on the ideas your group members present and be sure that the information you contribute is relevant.

- **Develop a plan for consensus building.** Decide how your group will handle disagreements or conflicts, ensuring that everyone works together to discuss and develop solutions that the entire group finds acceptable.

- **Set ground rules for decision making.** Decide on a method that ensures everyone understands what decision is being made or voted on, and be sure that everyone can live with the result.

4. Before starting work on the poetry project, develop your plan for consensus building within your group. Use the Internet or other sources to investigate different methods and decide which one will suit your group.

5. Work with your group to brainstorm themes or topics for your project.

6. Create a chart to review different poetry structures that can be used as possible models for your original poetry. In the chart, include a list of the poems in Unit 2 that could be used as pieces for analysis.

☑ Check Your Understanding

Quickwrite: What aspects of working in a group have been successful for you in the past? What are some skills you can focus on developing over the course of this project?

Simple but Powerful Poetic Language

Learning Strategies

Close Reading
Diffusing
Marking the Text
Paraphrasing
Rereading
TP-CASTT

Learning Targets

- Explain how poetic structure and word choice affect meaning in poetry.
- Describe connections between poems and your own experiences, society, and other texts from around the world.

Preview

In this activity, you will learn and use a new strategy to analyze and compare features in two different poems. You will also write a short essay closely examining a particular poetic element across poems and highlighting what you determine to be the best examples.

Revisiting Poetry

As you discovered at the beginning of this unit, poetry comes in many forms. It has been a form of written expression for thousands of years. Poetry can rhyme or be written in free verse, but what makes it different from prose or drama is the fact that lines and stanzas separate its ideas. A poet organizes lines and ideas through poetic structure. Poetic structure can be as strict as a Shakespearean sonnet, or it can be as sprawling as an epic poem. Poets also use prosody to convey their message, which becomes clear when they are read aloud.

As You Read

- Put a star next to any visual elements, like word positions, that jump out at you.
- Circle unknown words and phrases. Try to determine the meaning of the words by using context clues, word parts, or a dictionary.

About the Poet

Wisława Szymborska (1923–2012) was a Polish poet who received international recognition when she won the Nobel Prize for Literature in 1996. She also received the Polish PEN Club Prize, the Goethe Prize, and the Herder Prize during her career. Her poems are known for their wit and simplicity, as well as her references to Polish history from World War II through Joseph Stalin's regime. She lived in Krakow, Poland, and studied Polish literature and sociology at Jagiellonian University. When World War II broke out in 1939, she continued her education in underground classes, and avoided being deported to Germany by working as a railroad employee. The prolific Szymborska published more than fifteen books of poetry and prose.

VOCABULARY

LITERARY

Poetic structure is the organization of words, lines, and images, as well as ideas, in a poem. It can be characterized by the use of different elements such as rhyme, line length, and metrical patterns.

The pattern and rhythm of sounds in poetry is called **prosody**, and includes the use of stress and intonation.

My Notes

Poem

Some Like Poetry

by **Wisława Szymborska**
translated by **Regina Grol**

Some -

thus not all. Not even the majority of all but the minority.

Not counting schools, where one has to,

and the poets themselves,

5　there might be two people per thousand.

Like -

but one also likes chicken soup with noodles,

one likes compliments and the color blue,

one likes an old scarf,

10　one likes having the upper hand,

one likes stroking a dog.

Poetry -

but what is poetry.

Many shaky answers

15　have been given to this question.

But I don't know and don't know and hold on to it

like to a sustaining railing.

Making Observations

- What stands out most to you in this poem?
- How does Szymborska incorporate the words from the title into the poem?

Introducing the Strategy: TP-CASTT

This reading strategy is used to conduct an analysis of a literary text by identifying and discussing each topic in the acronym: Title, Paraphrase, Connotation, Attitude, Shifts, Theme, and Title again. It is most effective if you begin at the top and work your way down the elements. However, you will find that as you study one element, you will naturally begin to explore others. For example, a study of connotation often leads to a discussion of tone and shifts. Revisiting the title often leads to a discussion of the theme.

1. With a partner, use the TP-CASTT strategy to analyze the poem.

Title What do you think the title means before you read the poem?	
Paraphrase What is the poem about? Translate the poem in your own words.	
Connotation What is the association of key words beyond their literal meanings?	
Attitude How does the author feel about the speaker, other characters, or the subject?	
Shifts Where do shifts in tone, setting, voice, etc., occur? Look for keywords, punctuation, stanza divisions, and changes in line length or rhyme. What is the purpose of the shift? How does the shift contribute to effect and meaning?	
Theme What overall message or idea comes through the literal and metaphorical layers of the poem?	
Title (again) What do you think it means now, after reading the poem?	

VOCABULARY

LITERARY

Anaphora is a particular kind of repetition in which the same word or group of words is repeated at the beginnings of two or more clauses or lines. The term comes from a Greek word that means "the act of carrying back."

Returning to the Text

- Return to the poem as you respond to the following questions. Use text evidence to support your responses.
- Write any additional questions you have about the poem in your Reader/Writer Notebook.

2. What is the effect of **anaphora** in this poem?

_____

_____

_____

_____

3. Szymborska writes, "But I don't know and don't know and hold on to it / like to a sustaining railing." What is her purpose in writing this? How does her use of this language achieve her purpose?

_____

_____

_____

_____

4. Look at stanza 1. What pivotal words or phrases does Szymborska use? How does this language contribute to the tone of the text?

_____

_____

_____

_____

Working from the Text

5. What connections can you make from this poem to your own experiences? To society? To points of view presented in other texts from around the world? Fill out the following chart independently, then compare your answers with a classmate.

Personal Experiences	Society	Other Texts

6. Discuss the following question: Szymborska conjures up the scent of chicken soup and the image of an old scarf in stanza 2. Does her use of these everyday items diminish what it means to like poetry? Why or why not?

As You Read

- Highlight words that rhyme with a word you already read.
- Circle unknown words and phrases. Try to determine the meaning of the words by using context clues, word parts, or a dictionary.

About the Poet

W. B. Yeats (1865–1939) is regarded as one of the most influential poets of the 20th century. Although he lived much of his life in England, he identified as Irish and embraced his Irish roots and nationality. This pride led him to feature many Irish legends and heroes in his poems. Yeats published his first poem in 1885 in the *Dublin University Review*. Yeats cultivated a deep interest in theosophy (a blend of theology and philosophy), the occult, and mysticism—and even joined a secret society that practiced ritual magic. Despite his fascination with mysticism, much of Yeats's poetry focuses on ordinary traditions, as well as the contrast between art and life. Yeats was appointed to the Irish senate in 1922 and won the Nobel Prize for Literature in 1923.

My Notes

My Notes

Poem

An Irish Airman Foresees His Death

by **W. B. Yeats**

I know that I shall meet my fate
Somewhere among the clouds above;
Those that I fight I do not hate,
Those that I guard I do not love;
5 My country is Kiltartan Cross[1],
My countrymen Kiltartan's poor,
No likely end could bring them loss
Or leave them happier than before.
Nor law, nor duty **bade** me fight,
10 Nor public man, nor cheering crowds,
A lonely impulse of delight
Drove to this **tumult** in the clouds;
I balanced all, brought all to mind,
The years to come seemed waste of breath,
15 A waste of breath the years behind
In balance with this life, this death.

Making Observations

- Who do you think is narrating the poem?
- Which pair of lines is most striking to you?
- What emotions do you feel while reading this poem?

British biplanes intercepting
a German squadron during
World War I.

bade: commanded
tumult: confusion or disorder

[1] **Kiltartan Cross:** A barony, or division of land, in County Galway, Ireland

7. With a partner, use the TP-CASTT strategy to analyze the poem.

Title	
Paraphrase	
Connotation	
Attitude	
Shift	
Theme	
Title (again)	

Returning to the Text

- Return to the poem as you respond to the following questions. Use text evidence to support your responses.
- Write any questions you have about the poem in your Reader/Writer Notebook.

8. What is the tone of this poem? What words contribute to the tone?

_____

_____

_____

_____

9. Why does the speaker see his life as "a waste of breath"?

_____

_____

_____

_____

10. What are some of the pivotal words or phrases Yeats uses? How do they contribute to the mood of the poem and help the reader understand the poem more clearly? Use evidence from the text to support your response.

_____

_____

_____

_____

Working from the Text

11. What effect does the poet's use of prosody have on the theme of the poem?

_____

_____

_____

_____

12. What connections can you make from this poem to your own experiences? To society? To points of view in other texts from around the world? Fill out the following chart independently, then compare your answers with a classmate.

Personal Experiences	Society	Other Texts

Appreciating the Poet's Craft

As directed by your teacher, discuss the following question.

• What connections can you make between "Some Like Poetry" and "An Irish Airman Foresees His Death"? How do the poets use poetic structure and prosody to convey their meaning? What TP-CASTT elements are similar or different across the poems?

 Check Your Understanding

Review your notes and observations about the two poems. How do the poets' word choices contribute to the themes of the poems?

 Writing to Sources: Informational Text

Select one of the poetic elements you have studied in this activity and explain how one of the poets uses that element and what effect the element has on the poem. Be sure to:

• Write a focused claim.

• Select strong examples of the chosen element in the poem and explain how each example illustrates the element you have chosen.

• Include original commentary that clearly demonstrates your understanding of the poem and develops your claim.

INDEPENDENT READING LINK

Read and Discuss

You have read plays and poems and observed how writers use pivotal phrases in order to convey a specific meaning or create an effect. In your independent reading, you have had the opportunity to read a work of your choice, which has exposed you to how a variety of writers use pivotal language. Meet with a small group to share and present a few examples of pivotal words and phrases you have come across so far and describe how the language is effective.

Sound, Rhythm, and Themes in Poetry

Learning Strategies

Close Reading
Diffusing
Marking the Text
Paraphrasing
Rereading
Summarizing

Learning Targets

- Analyze a poet's use of prosody and structure to achieve her purpose.
- Analyze poetry for visual elements and theme.

Preview

In this activity, you will analyze poetic elements and craft in the poem "Prayer to the Pacific." You will also compare the themes of poems from this unit and analyze and evaluate one poem in a short essay.

My Notes

As You Read

- Use the My Notes section to jot down observations you have about the poet's choices with regard to text structure.
- Circle unknown words and phrases. Try to determine the meanings of the words by using context clues, word parts, or a dictionary.

About the Poet

American novelist and poet Leslie Marmon Silko (b. 1948) is regarded as one of the most important contemporary Native American writers. Her work is renowned for portraying the life, struggles, and culture of modern Native Americans. Silko comes from mixed ancestry but identifies with her Laguna Pueblo heritage. She grew up on the edge of the Laguna Pueblo reservation, where she attended elementary school, learning about Laguna spirituality, traditions, and myths. After fifth grade, she transferred to a Catholic school that banned her from speaking her native language. This transition profoundly affected her, and her struggle to find her identity between two cultures resonates deeply in her work. In addition to poetry, Silko has published novels and essays that explore Native American identity and themes.

Poem

Prayer to the Pacific

by **Leslie Marmon Silko**

I traveled to the ocean
                    distant
                            from my southwest land of sandrock
                            to the moving blue water
5   Big as the myth of origin.
Pale
pale water in the yellow-white light of
                            sun floating west
                                    to China
10   where ocean herself was born.
Clouds that blow across the sand are wet.

Squat in the wet sand and speak to the Ocean:
            I return to you turquoise the red coral you sent us,
                            sister spirit of Earth.
15 Four round stones in my pocket I carry back the ocean
                        to suck and to taste.

Thirty thousand years ago
                    Indians came riding across the ocean
                    carried by giant sea turtles.
20 Waves were high that day
            great sea turtles waded slowly out
                    from the gray sundown sea.
Grandfather Turtle rolled in the sand four times
            and disappeared
25   swimming into the sun.
And so from that time
            immemorial,
                    as the old people say,
            rain clouds drift from the west
30   gift from the ocean.

immemorial: in the distant past

My Notes

Green leaves in the wind
Wet earth on my feet
     swallowing raindrops
        clear from China.

Making Observations

- What do you notice about the way that words are positioned in this poem?
- What is the setting of the poem?

Returning to the Text

- Return to the poem as you respond to the following questions. Use text evidence to support your responses.
- Write any additional questions you have about the poem in your Reader/Writer Notebook.

1. Describe visual elements that the poet uses and explain how effective her use of these elements is in achieving her purpose.

_____

_____

_____

_____

2. How does the poet's use of words referencing time contribute to the poem's theme and voice?

_____

_____

_____

_____

3. What pivotal words or phrases does Silko use? How do they help the reader understand the poem more clearly?

_____

_____

_____

_____

Working from the Text

4. In your Reader/Writer Notebook, write a summary of the poem.

5. With a partner, take turns reading the poem aloud to each other, focusing on emphasizing the sounds, pauses, and rhythms in the text. The first person should read the poem by pausing at each line break, and the second person should read the poem by pausing at the punctuation breaks. While your partner reads, jot down the words you hear stressed or emphasized.

With Line Breaks	With Punctuation

6. What is the effect of the author using only one word on certain lines throughout the poem?

_____

_____

_____

_____

7. Turn to a partner and discuss the following questions: How does this poem reflect Silko's connection to her Native American culture? What message is she conveying?

_____

_____

_____

_____

☑ Check Your Understanding

Review your notes and observations on the poem. Explain how the poet's use of structure and prosody affects the theme of the poem.

Comparing Poetic Themes

Recall that a theme is a general statement about life, such as, "all people experience ups and downs in life, but an individual's reactions to these events define who she or he is." Revisit notes that you have made in the TP-CASTT charts or elsewhere regarding the themes of "Some Like Poetry," "An Irish Airman Foresees His Death," and "Prayer to the Pacific" and answer the following questions with a partner.

• Which of the poets are more explicit in revealing the themes of their poems, and which reveal themes more implicitly?

• The themes of all three poems are quite personal. Which one strikes you most profoundly, and why?

• In each poem, note lines or phrases that do much of the work in broadcasting the poem's theme and explain why they are effective.

Structure and Imagery in Poetry

Learning Strategies

Close Reading
Diffusing
Discussion Groups
Marking the Text
Paraphrasing
Rereading

My Notes

About the Poet

Elizabeth Bishop (1911–1979) was a respected yet not well known poet during her lifetime. Since her death, her reputation has risen and she is now considered one of the greatest 20th-century American poets. After the death of her father when she was one year old and the institutionalization of her mother when she was five years old, Bishop was raised by both sets of her grandparents, one in Nova Scotia and one in Massachusetts. She rarely delved into her personal life in her poetry; instead, Bishop preferred to focus on the physical world, drawing from her travels all over the globe. A perfectionist when it came to revisions, Bishop published only 101 poems during her writing career. She received the Pulitzer prize in 1956 and the National Book Award in 1970, when she also began teaching at Harvard University.

My Notes

_____
_____
_____
_____
_____
_____
_____
_____
_____
_____
_____
_____
_____
_____

almanac: annual calendar containing important dates, astronomical information, and tide tables

equinoctial: happening at or near the time of an equinox (when the length of day is equal to night)

Poem

Sestina

by **Elizabeth Bishop**

September rain falls on the house.
In the failing light, the old grandmother
sits in the kitchen with the child
beside the Little Marvel Stove,
5 reading the jokes from the almanac,
laughing and talking to hide her tears.

She thinks that her equinoctial tears
and the rain that beats on the roof of the house
were both foretold by the almanac,
10 but only known to a grandmother.
The iron kettle sings on the stove.
She cuts some bread and says to the child,

It's time for tea now; but the child
is watching the teakettle's small hard tears
15 dance like mad on the hot black stove,
the way the rain must dance on the house.
Tidying up, the old grandmother
hangs up the clever almanac

on its string. Birdlike, the almanac
20 hovers half open above the child,
hovers above the old grandmother
and her teacup full of dark brown tears.
She shivers and says she thinks the house
feels chilly, and puts more wood in the stove.

25 It was to be, says the Marvel Stove.
I know what I know, says the almanac.
With crayons the child draws a rigid house
and a winding pathway. Then the child
puts in a man with buttons like tears
30 and shows it proudly to the grandmother.

But secretly, while the grandmother
busies herself about the stove,
the little moons fall down like tears
from between the pages of the almanac
35 into the flower bed the child
has carefully placed in the front of the house.

Time to plant tears, says the almanac.
The grandmother sings to the marvelous stove
and the child draws another inscrutable house.

A hot cup of tea warms this grandmother's hands. Having tea with a family member is a comforting daily ritual that can strengthen family bonds.

⊘ Knowledge Quest

- Which detail about the grandmother and the child stands out to you?
- How would you describe the relationship between the grandmother and the child?

inscrutable: impossible to interpret

LITERARY

A **sestina** is a poem in which the words that end each line of the first stanza are used as line endings in each of the following stanzas, rotated in a set pattern. All six words appear in the closing triplet:

A B C D E F
F A E B D C
C F D A B E
E C B F A D
D E A C F B
B D F E C A
(F A) (B D) (C E)

A sestina is usually unrhymed, and in place of a rhyme scheme the use of repetition creates the poem's prosody or rhythm.

Poetic Form: Sestina

A poet makes structural choices carefully, measuring the weight of each line, line break, and word for emphasis. Some poets choose to work within a structure with specific rules, such as the **sestina**. Attributed to a 12th-century troubadour named Arnaut Daniel, a sestina is a complex structure, and its effects can be seen through its use of unlikely repetition. A sestina contains six stanzas of six lines each, and each line ends in one of six words, which alternate. It closes with a final triplet in which all six words appear.

1. Why do you think the poet chose the structure of the sestina for this poem? What effect does the repetition have on the theme?

_____
_____
_____
_____

2. What is the role of imagery in the poem?

_____
_____
_____
_____

3. **Discussion Group:** How does this poem use repetition to make connections between ideas and images? What message does it seem to be conveying? To help you determine your answers, use the following graphic organizer to map out the repeated words and the images they bring to mind.

Repeated Word	Image

4. Discussion Group: What other words or phrases contribute to the tone of the poem? Why might the poet have made these language choices?

5. Discussion Group: What is the effect of the structure and imagery in the poem? How would the poem be different if the poet was not required to repeat certain words?

As You Read

- Underline words that illustrate the family dynamics revealed in the poem.
- Circle unknown words and phrases. Try to determine the meanings of the words by using context clues, word parts, or a dictionary.

About the Poet

Rhina P. Espaillat (b. 1932) was born in the Dominican Republic. Her family settled in New York City after being exiled during the regime of the dictator Rafael Trujillo in 1939. As a young girl, Espaillat began writing poetry in both Spanish and English, and her works have since been published in both languages in eleven poetry collections. She graduated from Hunter College in 1953 and went on to teach English in New York City public schools for many years. She was inspired by the everyday events of life, and they served as a source of ideas for her poems. Espaillat has translated the poetry of Robert Frost and Richard Wilbur into Spanish, and her work has been published in many poetry anthologies. She won the T. S. Eliot Prize in 1998 and several other awards for her poetry and Spanish translations.

KNOWLEDGE QUEST

Knowledge Question:
How do our family relationships help determine who we are?

My Notes

Poem

"Bilingual/Bilingüe"

by **Rhina P. Espaillat**

My father liked them separate, one there,
one here (allá y aquí), as if aware

that words might cut in two his daughter's heart
(el corazón) and lock the alien part

5   to what he was—his memory, his name
(su nombre)—with a key he could not claim.

"English outside this door, Spanish inside,"
he said, "y basta[1]." But who can divide

the world, the word (mundo y palabra) from
10 any child? I knew how to be dumb

and stubborn (testaruda); late, in bed,
I hoarded secret syllables I read

until my tongue (mi lengua) learned to run
where his stumbled. And still the heart was one.

15 I like to think he knew that, even when,
proud (orgulloso) of his daughter's pen,

he stood outside mis versos[2], half in fear
of words he loved but wanted not to hear.

Knowledge Quest

- Why does the daughter describe herself as "stubborn"?
- What do you notice about the family described in the poem that someone else might miss?

---

[1] **y basta:** Spanish term meaning "and enough"
[2] **mis versos:** Spanish term meaning "my verses"

Poetic Form: Rhyming Couplet

A poet might choose to use rhyming couplets in order to create prosody, or rhythm and rhyme, inside a complete thought. Rhyming couplets are typically short and succinct and can be used for dramatic effect or to give the reader a sense of completion as they read the poem.

LITERARY

In a poem, a rhyming couplet is a pair of lines that rhyme, have the same rhythm (or meter), and are of similar length. One famous rhyming couplet can be found in Shakespeare's *Macbeth*:

Double, double, toil and trouble;

Fire burn and cauldron bubble.

6. Why might Espaillat have chosen the structure of rhyming couplets? How does this poem use repetition to make connections between ideas and images?

_____

_____

_____

_____

_____

_____

My Notes

_____

_____

7. What is the relationship between the title of the poem and the content of the poem?

_____

_____

_____

_____

_____

_____

_____

_____

8. What is the effect of Espaillat including Spanish words alongside their English counterparts?

_____

_____

_____

_____

_____

_____

_____

_____

9. **Discussion Groups:** How does this poem use rhyming couplets and language to create tension? What message does it seem to convey? To help you determine your answers, use the following graphic organizer to map out and organize your thoughts.

Rhyming Couplet	Tension and Message
My father liked them separate, one there, one here (allá y aquí), as if aware	
that words might cut in two his daughter's heart (el corazón) and lock the alien part	
to what he was—his memory, his name (su nombre)—with a key he could not claim.	
"English outside this door, Spanish inside," he said, "y basta." But who can divide	
the world, the word (mundo y palabra) from any child? I knew how to be dumb	
and stubborn (testaruda); late, in bed, I hoarded secret syllables I read	
until my tongue (mi lengua) learned to run where his stumbled. And still the heart was one.	
I like to think he knew that, even when, proud (orgulloso) of his daughter's pen,	
he stood outside mis versos, half in fear of words he loved but wanted not to hear.	

10. **Discussion Groups:** How does the author's choice of words and placement of them reinforce the message of the poem?

11. **Discussion Groups:** Explain the effect of the poet's use of parentheses in the poem. What effect does this graphic element have on the message?

☑ **Check Your Understanding**

What is the theme or message of each of these poems?

> ✍ **Writing to Sources: Informational Text**
>
> Revisit the forms of the poems you have read so far in Unit 2. What choices have the poets made with regard to form and structure to best convey the poems' themes? Choose two poems to analyze and compare in a short essay. Be sure to:
>
> - Clearly demonstrate your understanding of the poems.
> - Write with academic vocabulary used to analyze poetry.
> - Include relevant evidence from each poem and original commentary in your analysis.

My Notes

⬡ **INDEPENDENT READING LINK**

Read and Connect

Think about the themes that are revealing themselves in the text you are currently reading independently. Write about some of the connections you can make between any of these themes and the themes that you have found in the poetry in this unit.

Language Checkpoint: Using Pronouns

- Understand the relationship between pronouns and their antecedents.
- Revise writing to improve and clarify pronoun use.
- Maintain pronoun-antecedent agreement in writing.

Preview

In this activity, you will explore how pronouns are used in writing and learn how to check your own work for clear pronoun usage.

Understanding Pronoun-Antecedent Agreement

Pronouns are words that take the place of nouns (names for people, places, things, and ideas) in a sentence. Sometimes they take the place of other pronouns. Pronouns should agree with their antecedents in gender (male, female, or neuter) and number (singular or plural). When a pronoun does not agree with its antecedent, the sentence may be confusing.

> In the failing light, the old **grandmother**
> sits in the kitchen with the child
> beside the Little Marvel Stove,
> reading the jokes from the almanac,
> laughing and talking to hide **her** tears.

In this sentence, the pronoun *her* refers to the antecedent *grandmother*. Both the pronoun and its antecedent are singular and feminine, so they agree.

When a pronoun refers to a compound antecedent (an antecedent joined by a conjunction such as *and* or *or*), follow these rules:

When the singular parts of a compound antecedent are joined by *and*, the antecedent is plural.

> **The grandmother** and **the child** warmed up **their** tea.

In this sentence, the pronoun *their* refers to *The grandmother* and *the child*. The antecedent is plural, so the pronoun is plural as well.

When singular parts of a compound antecedent are joined by *or* or *nor*, the antecedent is singular.

> Neither **the grandmother** nor the **child** wants **her** tea served hot.

In this sentence, the pronoun *her* refers to *the grandmother* or *the child*. The antecedent is singular, so the pronoun is singular.

1. Revise each of the following sentences to correct errors in pronoun-antecedent agreement.

   a. But secretly, while the grandmother busied herself about the stove, it thought about the past and cried.

   _____

   _____

   b. The almanac hovers half open above the child and rains his seasonal facts and forecasts down upon the floor.

   _____

   _____

Using Pronouns Clearly

When writing, make sure that it is always clear to whom or what your pronouns refer. Sometimes you may need to revise your writing in order to make it clear.

Unclear: The grandmother spoke to the child and then she walked away.
[*Who walked away?*]
Clear: The grandmother spoke to the child and then walked away.
Clear: The grandmother spoke to the child, who then walked away.

Unclear: The grandmother and the child drew houses. They were quiet.
[*Were the grandmother and child quiet, or were the houses quiet?*]
Clear: The grandmother and the child quietly drew houses.
Clear: The grandmother and the child drew quiet houses.

2. For each sentence, think about what makes the sentence unclear. Then write a question about what is unclear. Rewrite the sentence to make it clear.

   a. The grandmother and the child talked. She delighted in hearing her response.

   _____

   _____

   b. The grandmother told the child to draw quietly. She said she was sorry.

   _____

   _____

Using Pronouns with Collective Nouns

So far you have practiced creating agreement between both singular and plural pronouns and their antecedents. Another typical pronoun error concerns agreement with collective nouns. A **collective noun** is a singular noun that names two or more people, animals, or things. Some examples of collective nouns include the following: *army, audience, class, family, flock, public, team.*

A collective noun is considered singular when it refers to a single group whose members act all together, or in unison.

> The family prepared **its** dinner together on the stove.
> [*All family members are preparing the dinner together.*]

When the members of the group act as individuals (all performing different actions), the collective noun is plural, and it requires a plural pronoun.

> The family chose different options for **their** meals.
> [*Each family member makes his or her own choice.*]

Deciding whether a collective noun is singular or plural can be tricky, so keep in mind these guidelines:

- If the group members are acting as one, then the collective noun is singular.
- If the group members are acting separately from each other, then the collective noun is plural.

3. Revise each of the following sentences to correct agreement between a pronoun and a collective noun.

a. The family consulted their almanac to see the weather forecast for autumn.

_____

_____

b. The family differed in its opinion on when it would stop raining.

_____

_____

Editing

Read the student's summary of "Sestina" in the left column. For each sentence, indicate what, if any, change is necessary.

[1] "Sestina" is a poem about a grandmother and child who is drinking tea. [2] The family makes tea on their stove on a rainy day. [3] The grandmother and the child wants her tea with milk. [4] The child asked the grandmother for its crayon. [5] The grandmother and the child checks the almanac and listens to the rain on their roof.

1. **a.** NO CHANGE
   b. "Sestina" is a poem about a grandmother and child who are drinking tea.
   c. "Sestina" is a poem about a grandmother or a child who are drinking tea.
   d. "Sestina" is a poem about a grandmother and child who drinks tea.

2. **a.** NO CHANGE
   b. The family makes tea on her stove on a rainy day.
   c. The family makes tea on its stove on a rainy day.
   d. The family make tea on their stove on a rainy day.

3. **a.** NO CHANGE
   b. The grandmother or the child wants their tea with milk.
   c. The grandmother and the child wants her tea with milk.
   d. The grandmother and the child want their tea with milk.

4. **a.** NO CHANGE
   b. The child asked the grandmother for her crayon.
   c. The child asked the grandmother for their crayon.
   d. The child asked it for her crayon.

5. **a.** NO CHANGE
   b. The grandmother and the child checks the almanac and listens to the rain on its roof.
   c. The grandmother and the child check the almanac and listen to the rain on their roof.
   d. The grandmother and the child check the almanac and listen to the rain on her roof.

☑ Check Your Understanding

What question(s) can you ask yourself whenever you write in order to ensure that you are using pronouns clearly and correctly? Add the question(s) to your Editor's Checklist.

Practice

Reread the analysis you wrote in Activity 2.24. As you reread, pay attention to your use of pronouns. Underline the pronouns and circle their antecedents, making sure each pronoun agrees with its antecedent. Revise as necessary to ensure clear and correct pronoun usage.

Learning Strategies

Close Reading
Diffusing
Discussion Groups
Marking the Text
Paraphrasing
Rereading

My Notes

Learning Targets

- Identify pivotal phrases in a poem and analyze the poet's language choices in relation to the poem's meaning.
- Make connections between poems and your experiences, other texts, and society.
- Integrate ideas from multiple texts to build knowledge and vocabulary about family dynamics.

Preview

In this activity, you will learn about different ways a poet can express meaning through the poetic form of an ode. You will also write a poem with the structure of your own choosing.

As You Read

- Underline vivid words and phrases.
- Circle unknown words and phrases. Try to determine the meanings of the words by using context clues, word parts, or a dictionary.

About the Poet

Sandra Cisneros (b. 1954) grew up in Chicago and has lived in many places around the world, spending most of her time in Texas. Cisneros has written extensively about the experiences of growing up as a Latina. In talking about her writing, Cisneros says she creates stories from things that have touched her deeply: "in real life a story doesn't have shape, and it's the writer that gives it a beginning, middle, and an end." In addition to poetry, Cisneros has written short stories, novels, and essays and was awarded the National Medal of Art in 2016. She is a dual citizen of the United States and Mexico.

Poem

Abuelito Who

by **Sandra Cisneros**

KNOWLEDGE QUEST

Knowledge Question:

How do our family relationships help determine who we are?

Abuelito[1] who throws coins like rain
and asks who loves him
who is dough and feathers
who is a watch and glass of water
5 whose hair is made of fur
is too sad to come downstairs today
who tells me in Spanish you are my diamond
who tells me in English you are my sky
whose little eyes are string
10 can't come out to play
sleeps in his room all night and day
who used to laugh like the letter k
is sick
is a doorknob tied to a sour stick
15 is tired shut the door
doesn't live here anymore
is hiding underneath the bed
who talks to me inside my head
is blankets and spoons and big brown shoes
20 who snores up and down up and down up and down again
is the rain on the roof that falls like coins
asking who loves him
who loves him who?

My Notes

Knowledge Quest

- What are your first thoughts about the speaker's feelings toward Abuelito?
- Which detail confuses you about the relationship between Abuelito and the speaker?

---

[1] **Abuelito:** Spanish term for "grandfather"

Returning to the Text

- Return to the poem as you respond to the following questions. Use text evidence to support your responses.
- Write any additional questions you have about the poem in your Reader/Writer Notebook.

1. What is the significance of the poem's title?

_____

_____

_____

_____

2. What type of relationship does the speaker of the poem have with the subject (her *abuelito*)?

_____

_____

_____

_____

3. What pivotal words or phrases does Cisneros use? How do they help the reader understand the poem and its tone more clearly?

_____

_____

_____

_____

4. **KQ** Think about the meaning of the phrase *family dynamics*. What tension do you notice in the family dynamics in this poem?

_____

_____

_____

_____

5. Identify examples of the poem's prosody, or rhythm.

_____

_____

_____

_____

6. Select a few lines of the poem. What are the implicit and explicit meanings of the lines?

_____

_____

_____

_____

_____

7. **KQ** Reflect on the family relationships in "Sestina," "Bilingual/Bilingüe," and "Abuelito Who." What themes emerge regarding relationships between adult family members and children and the closeness and space in those relationships?

_____

_____

_____

_____

_____

_____

 Knowledge Quest

Think about the family dynamics in the three poems. How do the people communicate and interact? Then, write a paragraph describing how our family relationships help determine who we are. Be sure to:

- Clearly state a topic sentence that sets up your analysis.
- Expand on your topic with well-chosen evidence from the poems.
- Use precise language to convey your understanding of the theme of family dynamics.

INDEPENDENT READING LINK

You can continue to build your knowledge about family dynamics by reading poetry at ZINC Reading Labs. Select the **fiction and poetry** filters and **family relationships** in the **Search all ZINC articles** field.

 ZINC

LITERARY

An **ode** is a lyric poem expressing the feelings or thoughts of a speaker, often celebrating a person, an event, or a thing. "Ode" comes from the Greek words *oide* and *aeidein*, which mean to sing or chant.

VOCABULARY

Poetic Form: Ode

A poet might choose to use the poetic form of an **ode** when he or she wishes to dedicate the work to a person, place, event, or thing. Roman poets reserved it as a form to be used only when trying to convey their strongest feelings. As a result, odes tend to be full of emotion—joy, sorrow, love, or awe.

8. **Discussion Groups:** Why can this poem be categorized as an ode? How does this poem use repetition to emphasize ideas and feelings? What message does it convey to you? To help you determine your answers, use the following chart to analyze the poem as an ode.

Subject of the Ode	Repeated Words or Images	Feelings the Speaker Has About the Subject

9. **Discussion Groups:** What is the effect of the speaker repeating the word "who" throughout the poem?

10. Create a list of your favorite people, places, things, or experiences. Share your list with a partner and discuss what might qualify or disqualify each item as the subject of an ode. Choose one subject and then write your feelings about it.

Topic	My Feelings About It

☑ Check Your Understanding

How does the poem's tone reflect its message?

_____

_____

_____

_____

📝 Writing Prompt: Literary

Choose a subject you would like to write a poem about. It could be one of the connections you have made to a poem in this unit, or some other subject. Then choose an appropriate poetic form to convey your subject. To generate ideas, reread some of the Unit 2 poems, discuss ideas with your project group, or flip through a journal you are keeping. Be sure to:

- Have your purpose and audience in mind.
- Use implicit meaning to communicate tone and mood.
- Use words and phrases that convey the tone, voice, and mood you want.
- Use structure, prosody, line length, or word position to convey your message.

Creating a Poetry Project

Learning Targets

- Write an analytical review that examines theme, structure, diction, and style of a published poem.
- Create an original poem and revise it based on peer feedback.

Preview

In this activity, you will work collaboratively to plan, draft, and revise your group's multimedia poetry project.

Planning

1. Revisit the planning documents you began in Activity 2.21, which include the list of brainstormed ideas and your plan for consensus building. Continue to brainstorm possible themes or topics that will make your project cohesive, and make a final selection, using your consensus-building method if needed.

2. Fill out the following chart to help your group distribute responsibilities and decide what pieces each group member will contribute.

Theme	Original Works	Analytical Reviews

Drafting

3. Begin drafting your pieces of the project independently, using the relevant steps that follow.

- **Analytical Review:** Select a poem and review its elements using the TP-CASTT method. Once you have identified the different elements of the poem, organize the textual evidence you have found to include in your analysis. Use the following chart to organize your notes. Then write a draft of your analysis in your Reader/Writer Notebook.

Poetic Element	Textual Evidence	Analysis

- **Original Poem:** Choose a topic that interests you and works with your group topic or theme. Then review the different poetic structures and forms you have read and choose one that works with your topic and message. Decide how you will incorporate characteristics of the form into your poem. Draft your poem or poems in your Reader/Writer Notebook.

- **Illustration of a Poem:** Revisit poems that you have read in the past or find a new poem that addresses your group's topic or theme and that creates a vivid mental image for you. Use that image to create a piece of art that illustrates the meaning and/or tone of the poem. Include the text of the poem next to or within your illustration.

- **Recorded Spoken Performance of a Poem:** Revisit poems that you have read in the past, find a new poem, or use an original poem that addresses your group's topic or theme and that appeals to you when read aloud. Use a dictionary to confirm the pronunciation of any unfamiliar words. Practice reading the poem aloud in a manner that expresses your interpretation of it, using punctuation as a guide. Practice reading it again with appropriate speaking rate, volume, and enunciation before completing your recording.

4. As a group, decide which additional pieces will benefit from being presented with illustrations, recorded spoken pieces, or other kinds of multimedia. Discuss the imagery presented in each piece and how it can best be translated into a multimedia format.

Piece	Imagery	Presentation Method	Reason	Resources Needed

Revising and Rehearsing

5. When you have written your parts of the project, review your writing thoroughly for clarity, development, organization, style, diction, and sentence effectiveness. Work with a group member to edit each other's written pieces. Use the following checklist.

Question	Advice for Revision
Does the piece fit with the group's theme?	
Is the piece clear and well thought out?	
Are the ideas in the piece engaging and well developed through the use of specific details, examples, and original commentary?	
Is the piece well organized?	
Is the style/diction of the piece appropriate to the audience and purpose?	
Are the sentences in the piece effective?	

6. Use your group member's feedback and advice to revise your written pieces.

7. If your project includes a recorded spoken performance of a poem, rehearse your performance in front of your group. Ask for constructive feedback and practice any changes you need to make before recording your performance.

8. After revising and rehearsing, come back together as a group to organize the project. Use the following questions to guide your organization.

   - Have you peer-edited all the written pieces in the project?
   - Have you rehearsed and recorded all the spoken performances?
   - Have you determined the best order for the pieces?
   - Have you written introductions and transitions?

Order of the Pieces in the Presentation	Introductions or Transitions

☑ Check Your Understanding

What are the key elements of the Poetry Project assignment? How will you complete it? What are your group members responsible for?

ⓘ Independent Reading Checkpoint

You have read a wide variety of poetry, drama, and novels and observed how writers use pivotal words and phrases in order to be more concise and create interesting writing. In your independent reading, you have had the opportunity to read additional texts containing pivotal language. Meet with a small group to discuss the following questions.

- How might a poet's use of pivotal words and phrases differ from other authors'?
- What have you read that will help you as you complete Embedded Assessment 2?

Presenting a Poetry Project

ASSIGNMENT

Your group assignment is to create a poetry project that will include original works and analytical reviews of published works. Each group member must contribute three items to the project: either two original pieces and one analytical review or one original piece and two analytical reviews. Original works can include poems, illustrations of poems, or recorded spoken performances of original or published poems. Use multimedia to create your project and present it in a polished format.

Planning: Collaborate with your group to create a project plan.	■ How will you come to consensus on a theme or topic for your project so that it seems cohesive? ■ Have you reviewed the different poetry structures presented in the unit as possible models for your original poetry? ■ How will you find published poems to include? ■ Have you decided what pieces each group member will contribute?
Drafting: Write original poems and analytical reviews, and plan illustrations and recorded performances.	■ How will you incorporate characteristics of genre into your creative and analytical writing? ■ How will you incorporate adequate, relevant evidence from the text in your reviews? ■ How will you analyze published poems to create illustrations and/or perform and record them?
Revising: Finalize the pieces of the project.	■ Have you peer-edited all the pieces in the project? ■ Have you determined the best order for the pieces? ■ Have you written necessary introductions or transitions? ■ Have you rehearsed and recorded spoken performances?
Publishing: Create the final multimedia format of the project.	■ Which digital tools will you use to compile the pieces of the project? ■ How will you make the project cohesive and visually appealing ■ Where will you publish your project so your audience can access it?

Reflection

How effective was your group's collaboration? Which interactions went well and which ones could have gone better? How effective were your plan for consensus building and ground rules for decision making?

Presenting a Poetry Project

SCORING GUIDE

Scoring Criteria	Exemplary	Proficient	Emerging	Incomplete
Ideas	The project • represents a thorough comprehension of the source texts • is free from errors of interpretation • includes a perceptive analysis of the explicit and implicit meanings of the texts.	The project • represents an effective comprehension of the source texts • is free from significant errors of interpretation • includes a reasonable analysis of the explicit and implicit meanings of the texts.	The project • shows a very basic or general comprehension of the source texts • shows possible errors of interpretation • shows a limited analysis of the explicit and implicit meanings of the texts.	The project • shows little to no comprehension of the source texts • shows numerous errors of interpretation • shows little or no analysis of the explicit and implicit meanings of the texts.
Structure	The project • is effectively organized and cohesive, and shows evidence of a high degree of collaboration • includes multimedia resources that are used creatively to enhance understanding of the topic.	The project • is organized and cohesive, and shows evidence of collaboration • uses multimedia effectively to support information about the topic.	The project • is loosely organized and shows minimal evidence of collaboration • uses multimedia choices that are distracting and do not serve the project's purpose.	The project • is not organized and shows little to no evidence of collaboration • does not use multimedia
Use of Language	The project • demonstrates a creative and effective logical order through the use of introductions and transitions.	The project • demonstrates appropriate logical order through the use of introductions and transitions.	The project • attempts a logical order through the use of introductions and transitions.	The project • lacks introductions and transitions and has an illogical order.

VISUAL PROMPT
Work means different things to different people. How do you view work right now? Why do you view it that way?

COMPELLING EVIDENCE

Then one day, alone in the kitchen with my father, I let drop a few whines about the job. I gave him details, examples of what troubled me, yet although he listened intently, I saw no sympathy in his eyes. No "Oh, you poor little thing." Perhaps he understood that what I wanted was a solution to the job, not an escape from it. In any case, he put down his cup of coffee and said, "Listen. You don't live there. You live here. With your people. Go to work. Get your money. And come on home."

—from "The Work You Do, the Person You Are," by Toni Morrison

UNIT 3

Compelling Evidence

CONTENTS

My Independent Reading List

Compelling Evidence

Previewing the Unit

Learning Targets
- Preview the big ideas for the unit.
- Create a plan for reading independently.

Preview
In this activity, you will explore the big ideas and tasks in Unit 3 and make plans for your own independent reading.

About the Unit
With this unit's focus on compelling evidence, you will explore the difference between what authors are saying in their arguments and what they are doing as writers. Initially you will read and analyze essays and arguments about the value of work, bringing writers into conversation with one another as they describe lessons learned during their first work experiences. Then you will read arguments about the value of post-secondary education, ultimately writing an argument of your own. The unit closes with a research project in which you will choose a career that you find interesting, find reliable sources of information about that career, and present your findings.

Essential Questions
Based on your current thinking, how would you answer these questions?

1. What makes an argument convincing?
2. What makes a piece of evidence compelling?
3. What is the value of work for teenagers?
4. What is the value of a college education?

Planning Independent Reading
The focus of this unit is compelling evidence, and you will read and write arguments in class. During your independent reading, you have the opportunity to read a longer argument on a topic that interests you. You can read a nonfiction text about the topic or a fiction text that deals with the topic as an overarching theme. Reading a longer work will allow you to see how an author develops an argument using a wide range of tools, and ultimately evaluate how effective the argument is. To find a book you will like, consider these questions.

- What topics or causes interest you?
- Is there someone local or elsewhere whom you admire?
- What current events or news items have been interesting to you?
- Read the first few pages of the text. Do you agree with the author's argument? How does the author try to convince you to keep reading?

My Notes

A Study in Contrasts

My Notes

Learning Targets

- Analyze the structure of an essay and present your findings.
- Discuss how the structure of a text connects to the author's message.
- Integrate ideas from multiple texts to build knowledge and vocabulary about getting a job.

Preview

In this activity, you will read and discuss a personal essay and analyze its use of contrast as a tool for helping readers understand the essay's message.

📝 Opening Writing Prompt

Read the first paragraph of "The Work You Do, the Person You Are" by Toni Morrison. List all the things "She" had that the narrator did not. Then respond to the following questions.

> What do you think these physical objects might say about the setting the narrator is describing? What do you think the narrator's relationship to "Her" is?

As You Read

- Underline details about "Her."
- Circle unfamiliar words or phrases. Try to determine the meaning of the words by using context clues, word parts, or a dictionary.

About the Author

Toni Morrison (1931–2019) was a writer who authored novels, children's books, short stories, plays, essays, and even the libretto for an opera. In addition, she was a professor and editor whose work played a vital role in bringing books by black authors to mainstream audiences. Morrison wrote about the African American experience and believed that literature is a singularly powerful tool for challenging the mindsets of people in the dominant culture. Her work is appreciated and studied worldwide, and it has earned her numerous awards, including the Nobel Prize for Literature, the Pulitzer Prize for Fiction, and the Presidential Medal of Freedom. Her most highly acclaimed novels include *The Bluest Eye, Song of Solomon,* and *Beloved,* which became a major motion picture in 1998.

Essay

The Work You Do, the Person You Are

by **Toni Morrison**

The pleasure of being necessary to my parents was profound. I was not like the children in folktales: burdensome mouths to feed.

KNOWLEDGE QUEST

Knowledge Question:
What motivates people to find and keep jobs?

Across Activities 3.2 and 3.3, you will read two essays on getting a job. While you read and build knowledge about the topic, think about your answer to the Knowledge Question.

1   All I had to do for the two dollars was clean Her house for a few hours after school. It was a beautiful house, too, with a plastic-covered sofa and chairs, wall-to-wall blue-and-white carpeting, a white enamel stove, a washing machine and a dryer—things that were common in Her neighborhood, absent in mine. In the middle of the war, She had butter, sugar, steaks, and seam-up-the-back stockings.

2   I knew how to scrub floors on my knees and how to wash clothes in our zinc tub, but I had never seen a Hoover vacuum cleaner or an iron that wasn't heated by fire.

3   Part of my pride in working for Her was earning money I could squander: on movies, candy, paddleballs, jacks, ice cream cones. But a larger part of my pride was based on the fact that I gave half my wages to my mother, which meant that some of my earnings were used for real things—an insurance-policy payment or what was owed to the milkman or the iceman. The pleasure of being necessary to my parents was **profound**. I was not like the children in folktales: burdensome mouths to feed, nuisances to be corrected, problems so severe that they were abandoned to the forest. I had a status that doing routine chores in my house did not provide—and it earned me a slow smile, an approving nod from an adult. Confirmations that I was adultlike, not childlike.

4   In those days, the forties, children were not just loved or liked; they were needed. They could earn money; they could care for children younger than themselves; they could work the farm, take care of the herd, run errands, and much more. I suspect that children aren't needed in that way now. They are loved, doted on, protected, and helped. Fine, and yet …

5   Little by little, I got better at cleaning Her house good enough to be given more to do, much more. I was ordered to carry bookcases upstairs and, once, to move a piano from one side of a room to the other. I fell carrying the bookcases. And after pushing the piano my arms and legs hurt so badly. I wanted to refuse, or at least to complain, but I was afraid She would fire me, and I would lose the freedom the dollar gave me, as well as the standing I had at home—although both were slowly being eroded. She began to offer me her clothes, for a price. Impressed by these worn things, which looked simply gorgeous to a little girl who had only two dresses to wear to school, I bought a few. Until my mother asked me if I really wanted to work for castoffs. So I

My Notes

profound: deeply felt, both emotionally and intellectually

learned to say "No, thank you" to a faded sweater offered for a quarter of a week's pay.

6   Still, I had trouble summoning the courage to discuss or object to the increasing demands She made. And I knew that if I told my mother how unhappy I was she would tell me to quit. Then one day, alone in the kitchen with my father, I let drop a few whines about the job. I gave him details, examples of what troubled me, yet although he listened intently, I saw no sympathy in his eyes. No "Oh, you poor little thing." Perhaps he understood that what I wanted was a solution to the job, not an escape from it. In any case, he put down his cup of coffee and said, "Listen. You don't live there. You live here. With your people. Go to work. Get your money. And come on home."

7   That was what he said. This was what I heard:

1. Whatever the work is, do it well—not for the boss but for yourself.
2. You make the job; it doesn't make you.
3. Your real life is with us, your family.
4. You are not the work you do; you are the person you are.

8   I have worked for all sorts of people since then, geniuses and morons, quick-witted and dull, bighearted and narrow. I've had many kinds of jobs, but since that conversation with my father I have never considered the level of labor to be the measure of myself, and I have never placed the security of a job above the value of home.

Ø Knowledge Quest

- Which detail about the author's house cleaning job stands out to you?
- What motivates the author to keep her job?

Working from the Text

1. For each paragraph, identify a quote that demonstrates contrast, identify any words in the quote that specifically signal contrast, answer the additional question addressing word choice or style (if there is one), and write an analytical sentence that incorporates the quote and reveals a greater message.

a. **Paragraph 1**

Quote demonstrating contrast:

Contrast clue word(s):

_____

Analytical sentence incorporating quote (or part of quote):

_____

_____

_____

b. **Paragraph 2**

Quote demonstrating contrast:

Contrast clue word(s):

_____

Rhetorical strategy question: What is the effect of Morrison naming the brand of vacuum cleaner?

_____

_____

_____

Analytical sentence incorporating quote (or part of quote):

_____

_____

_____

c. Paragraph 3

Quote demonstrating contrast:

Contrast clue word(s):

_____

Word-choice question: Morrison uses the verb _squander_ to describe how she sometimes chose to spend her money. Why didn't she use the word _spend_ instead? How is _squander_ different from _spend_?

_____

_____

_____

Analytical sentence incorporating quote (or part of quote):

_____

_____

_____

d. Paragraph 4

Quote demonstrating contrast:

Contrast clue word(s):

_____

Punctuation question: How is an ellipsis (…) usually used? Do you think that is how it is being used here? Explain.

_____

_____

_____

Analytical sentence incorporating quote (or part of quote):

_____

_____

_____

e. **Paragraph 5**

Quote demonstrating contrast:

Contrast clue word(s):

_____

Multiple-meaning word question: You may have seen the word *erode* being used in science, meaning to physically wear away or deteriorate over time (e.g., a cliff being eroded by the sea). How is Morrison using a slightly different connotation of the word *erode* when she refers to her freedom and standing as "slowly being eroded"?

_____

_____

_____

Analytical sentence incorporating quote (or part of quote):

_____

_____

_____

f. **Paragraph 6**

Quote demonstrating contrast:

Contrast clue word(s):

_____

Rhetorical strategy question: What is the effect of the simple language and repetition that Morrison's father uses?

_____

_____

_____

Analytical sentence incorporating quote (or part of quote):

_____

_____

_____

g. **Paragraph 7**

Quote demonstrating contrast:

Contrast clue word(s):

_____

Rhetorical strategy question: What is the relationship between this contrast and the essay's title?

_____

_____

Analytical sentence incorporating quote (or part of quote):

_____

_____

h. **Paragraph 8**

Quote demonstrating contrast:

Contrast clue word(s):

_____

Vocabulary across texts question: In the short story "The Red Fox Fur Coat," you saw the word *narrow* used literally to describe how the protagonist's eyes changed as she transformed into a fox: "her face disfigured, suddenly thinner, made up to look longer, her eyes narrow. ..." How is Morrison using another meaning of the word *narrow* when she contrasts it with *bighearted*?

_____

_____

Analytical sentence incorporating quote (or part of quote):

_____

_____

_____

Informal Presentation

2. Work with a group to informally present your analysis of one paragraph to the class. As you present, be sure to:

- Present information and supporting evidence clearly and logically.
- Ensure that listeners can follow your line of reasoning.
- Use formal English and conventions of language to effectively communicate your ideas.

☑ Focus on the Sentence

Summarize Morrison's essay in three sentences using the following sentence frames.

Morrison valued work because _____

_____

Morrison valued work, but _____

_____

Morrison valued work, so _____

_____

An Alternative Perspective on Work and Home

My Notes

Learning Targets

- Visualize important moments from a scene in an essay.
- Analyze an author's language and text structure choices.
- Compare and contrast the messages of two essays on the same theme.
- Integrate ideas from multiple texts to build knowledge and vocabulary about a getting a job.

Preview

In this activity, you will read another essay about work and identity and create a storyboard for one of its pivotal scenes. Then you will write a paragraph from the point of view of the essay's author.

Envisioning Pivotal Scenes

1. Analyze this image that originally accompanied Danial Adkison's essay and make predictions about the contents of the essay.

a. What details in this image reveal how this person works?

_____

_____

b. Why do you think the artist does not show how tall the stacks of dishes are?

_____

_____

c. What prediction can you make about the subject of the essay based on this image?

_____

_____

📝 Opening Writing Prompt

Read the first three paragraphs of "Drowning in Dishes, but Finding a Home." Then respond to the following questions.

How do parents in Adkison's hometown view the issue of teenagers working part-time jobs? How does Adkison's personal reason for wanting to work differ from the community's point of view?

_____

_____

_____

_____

As You Read

- Underline details that show how the author feels about his job.
- Circle unknown words and phrases. Try to determine the meaning of the words by using context clues, word parts, or a dictionary.

About the Author

Although Danial Adkison publishes his own writing on occasion, he spends most of his work hours helping journalists and editors release news articles that shine and come in on time. Adkison is an assistant news editor and a former copy chief who has contributed to a variety of publications, including *The Village Voice, The New York Times, Condé Nast Portfolio, Time* magazine, and *City Limits,* among others.

It may not be surprising that, as an editor, one of Adkison's main mottoes is "neatness counts." Says Adkison, "In journalism, the product is credibility, and if you're making mistakes, you're losing it." It is for this reason that Adkison believes in the value of checking for typos and working to find just the right turn of phrase, or order of words, for expressing an idea clearly and memorably.

KNOWLEDGE QUEST

Knowledge Question:
What motivates people to find and keep jobs?

My Notes

Essay

Drowning in Dishes, but Finding a Home

by **Danial Adkison**

1   The people who make a difference in your life come in all types. Some write on a chalkboard. Some wear a sports uniform. Some wear a suit and tie. For me, that person wore a tie with a Pizza Hut logo on it.

2   I started working at Pizza Hut in December 1989, when I was a freshman in high school. Parents in my small western Colorado town encouraged teenagers to work in the service industry after school and on weekends. It kept us out of trouble.

3   Having a job also kept me out of the house. I grew up mostly with my mother, and I never knew my biological father. My younger sister, younger brother and I went through a series of stepfathers. My relationship with those men was almost always **fraught**, and I was always looking for reasons to be away from home.

4   The Pizza Hut was old, and in the back it had three giant sinks instead of a dishwasher. One basin was for soapy water, one for rinsing and the other for sanitizing, using a tablet that made me cough when I dropped it into the hot water. All new employees started by washing dishes and busing tables. If they proved their **mettle**, they learned to make pizzas, cut and serve them on wooden paddles and take orders.

5   On my first night, the dishes piled up after the dinner rush: plates, silverware, cups and oily black deep-dish pans, which came clean only with a lot of soap and scrubbing in steaming-hot water. I couldn't keep up, and stacks of dishes formed on all sides of me. Every time I made a dent in the pile, the call came back for help clearing tables out front, and I returned with brown tubs full of more dirty dishes.

6   At home, the chore I hated most was dishes. A few years earlier, my mother's then boyfriend instilled a loathing of that task by making me scrub the Teflon off a cookie sheet, believing that it was grease, while he sat on the couch and smoked cigarettes. That boyfriend was gone, but another with a different set of problems had taken his place.

7   My shift was supposed to end at 9 p.m., but when I asked to leave, the manager, Jeff, shook his head. "Not until the work is done," he said. "You leave a clean station." I was angry and thought about quitting, but I scrubbed, rinsed and sanitized until after 10 that night.

8   I stayed on dish duty for weeks. My heart sank every time I arrived at work and saw my name written next to "dishes" on the position chart. I spent

fraught: difficult or troubled
mettle: willingness and ability to persevere through a challenge

my shifts behind those steel sinks, being splashed with greasy water. After work, my red-and-white checked button-up shirt and gray polyester pants smelled like onions, olives and oil. At home, I sometimes found green peppers in my socks. I hated every minute I spent on dish duty, and I wasn't afraid to let everyone around me know it.

9   One slow midweek night, when I managed to catch up on dishes and clean out the sinks early, I asked Jeff when I could do something different. "Do you know why you're still doing dishes?" he asked. "Because you keep complaining about it." Nobody likes to work with a complainer, he said. But, he promised, if I continued to leave a clean station and not complain, next week he would put me on the "make table," where pizzas were assembled before being put into the oven.

10   A few days later, when I reported for my after-school shift, I saw my name penciled not in the "dishes" box but in the "make table" box. I was ecstatic.

11   Jeff had a special way of running his restaurant. From a crop of teenagers, he assembled a team of employees who cared about their work—and one another. Most of my best friends from high school also worked at Pizza Hut, and some of my best memories were made under that red roof.

12   Pizza Hut became not only my escape from home but also, in many ways, an alternate home. In my real home, I felt unstable and out of control. At work, the path seemed clear: Work hard and do things right, and you will succeed. This model had not seemed possible before.

13   For one of the first times in my life, I felt empowered. By the time I was in 11th grade, Jeff had promoted me to shift manager. By my senior year, I was an assistant manager, responsible for much of the bookkeeping, inventory and scheduling. I was in charge when Jeff was away.

14   Our staff was like a second family. We had all-day staff parties that started with rafting trips and ended with dinner and movies. Most of us played on a softball team. We went camping together. We had water fights in the parking lot and played music on the jukebox, turned up to full blast, after all the customers had left.

15 Jeff was the leader of this unlikely family. He was about 15 years older than me and had recently gone through a divorce. I never considered it at the time, because he seemed to be having as much fun as everyone else, but if I was using my job to create the family I wish I'd had, it was possible that he was, too.

16 Senior year arrived, and though I loved that job, I knew I would go to college the next fall. I was an A student in class but probably about a C-minus in applying to schools. My mom hadn't gone to college, and I didn't have a lot of logistical or financial support at home. I had received a pile of brochures from colleges, but I didn't know where to start—and, at $40, every application fee cost me half a day's pay.

17 A guidance counselor persuaded me to apply to Boston University, which seemed great, primarily because of its distance from Colorado. The scholarship application had to be in by the end of November—and I was definitely not going there without a big scholarship. But maybe because of the fee or because of my sheer cluelessness, I kept putting off the application.

18 I still had not mailed it the day before it was due. At work that day, I offhandedly mentioned to Jeff that an application was due the next day but that I hadn't mailed it. He opened a drawer and took out an overnight envelope. He told me to stop what I was doing, leave work and send the application immediately. I protested about the expense of overnight postage, but he said he would cover it.

19 I ended up getting into B.U., with a scholarship, but I still had never even visited Boston. Though my mom worked hard to take care of my siblings and me, there just was no room in the budget to send me on a college visit. So I figured I would just see the school when I got there in August.

20 Jeff surprised me with an early graduation present: a trip to Boston. He paid for the hotel, the car and the plane tickets. We toured campus and visited Fenway Park and did some sightseeing around New England. We ate at a lot of Pizza Huts, and we judged them against ours. The verdict: None of them seemed to be very much fun.

21 Before I headed to college, I told Jeff that I would come back to work over winter break. While I was away, he was promoted to regional manager, and a different person was put in charge of our store. I went back anyway, and though I did my best to enjoy it, the magic was gone. The family had **dispersed**, and I felt free to shift my mind-set to college and the future.

22 I have kept in touch with Jeff over the years. We usually meet for lunch when I'm in town. Sometimes we even have pizza.

dispersed: moved away from each other

23 Washing dishes for Jeff was grueling, greasy work. But then again, making a pizza, or driving a truck, or baking a cake, or any of countless other jobs are not always enjoyable in themselves, either. Out of all the lessons I learned from that guy in the Pizza Hut tie, maybe the biggest is that any job can be the best job if you have the right boss.

 Knowledge Quest

- What words does Adkison use to describe his boss?
- What additional knowledge about what motivates people to find and keep jobs did you gain from this essay?

 Knowledge Quest

Use your knowledge about "The Work You Do, the Person You Are" and "Drowning in Dishes, but Finding a Home" to discuss with a partner the topic of getting and keeping a job.

Be sure to:

- Prepare for the discussion and cite text evidence in your comments.
- Summarize points you agree on and points you disagree on, and make new connections based on your partner's ideas.
- After the discussion, write notes about the ideas you discussed.

My Notes

INDEPENDENT READING LINK

You can continue to build your knowledge about getting a job by reading other articles at ZINC Reading Labs. Search for keywords such as *employment* or *working*.

 ZINC

VOCABULARY

ACADEMIC

A scene is a situation that plays out among a story's characters.

A storyboard is a visual layout of a story. It includes pictures of scenes from the story, along with captions that briefly tell what is happening in each scene. Storyboards are often used during the planning phases for movies, television shows, and commercials.

A thumbnail sketch is a small drawing made to plan the composition of a more detailed or finished image that will be created later. The purpose of a thumbnail sketch is similar to that of an outline for a piece of writing; it shows the subject and important details of the image's visual story.

Working from the Text

2. Work with your classmates to identify pivotal scenes from "Drowning in Dishes, but Finding a Home" to include in a storyboard of the essay. As you consider what moments to depict, think about which ones are easiest for you to visualize or connect to. Then make a thumbnail sketch of the scene, write a quick description of what the thumbnail sketch depicts, and include a supporting quote for the scene from the text. Copy the format of the storyboard that follows in your Reader/Writer Notebook or another sheet of paper to customize the size and number of scenes.

Shot 1

Image Description:

_____

_____

_____

Supporting Quote:

_____

_____

_____

Shot 2

Image Description:

_____

_____

_____

Supporting Quote:

_____

_____

_____

Shot 3

Image Description:

_____

_____

_____

Supporting Quote:

_____

_____

_____

Shot 4

Image Description:

_____

_____

_____

Supporting Quote:

_____

_____

_____

3. Discuss the following questions with your classmates after you have reviewed each other's storyboards.

a. What sentences from the essay best support Jeff's prominent role in the visual stories?

_____

_____

_____

_____

b. In the essay, Adkison doesn't mention Jeff's name until the seventh paragraph. How would the effect of the essay be different if the narrator had introduced him in the first paragraph, as "my manager Jeff," instead of "that person [who] wore a tie with a Pizza Hut logo on it"?

_____

_____

_____

_____

☑ Check Your Understanding

In the essay's final paragraph, how does Adkison generalize the role Jeff played in his personal life in order to make a broader comment about the nature of work?

INDEPENDENT READING LINK

Read and Respond

Think about the text you are reading independently. Does it include any moments that play out in your mind like a movie scene? Or, does the text have a message you can connect to in visual ways? Choose the moment or message you are best able to envision and plot it out in a storyboard, similar to the one you are creating for "Drowning in Dishes, but Finding a Home." Remember to include three or four shots that help tell the scene's story or communicate the text's message and include a thumbnail sketch, an image description, and a supporting quote for each. Then share your completed storyboard with a group of your peers.

✍ Writing Prompt: Informational

Reread paragraphs 6–8 from "The Work You Do, the Person You Are" by Toni Morrison and think about how Adkison might respond to the paragraphs. What do you think he would have to say about how Morrison interpreted and internalized her father's advice? Write a paragraph or two from Adkison's point of view. Before you write, consider the following questions: _With which of the four points listed at the end of Morrison's essay would Adkison most likely agree? Why? With which of the four points would Adkison most likely disagree? Why?_ Be sure to:

- Include evidence from Adkison's essay to support your stance.
- Use a variety of effective sentence structures.

Comparing and Contrasting Morrison's and Adkison's Essays

My Notes

Learning Targets

• Compare and contrast the structures and messages of two essays on the same theme.

• Gather evidence from informational texts to support your analysis.

• Use an outline to plan an informational essay.

Preview

In this activity, you will analyze thematic and structural similarities and differences between "The Work You Do, the Person You Are," by Toni Morrison, and "Drowning in Dishes, but Finding a Home," by Danial Adkison. Then you will plan and write a text-based response to these essays.

Distinguishing Between What Writers Say and What Writers Do

1. Work with your classmates to complete a Venn diagram showing how Morrison's and Adkison's essays are alike and different. As you work, consider these two questions:

   • What does each writer say that is unique?

   • What does each writer do that is unique?

   Then share your group's Venn diagram with the class.

2. As groups share their diagrams with the class, use the following Venn diagram to record notes from the whole-group discussion.

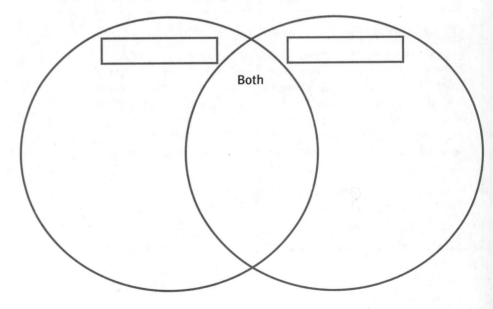

Both

Writing to Sources: Informational Text

You just read two personal essays written by adults reflecting back on their early work experiences as teenagers and the lessons they learned about work from authority figures in their lives. In a written response, explain the extent to which those lessons agree or disagree with one another and why. Support your position by showing how each writer uses personal anecdotes and different strategies to express his or her perspective.

Gathering Evidence

3. Reread "The Work You Do, the Person You Are," by Toni Morrison, and "Drowning in Dishes, but Finding a Home," by Danial Adkison. As you read the essays, use the following charts to record notes about language you may want to quote directly or paraphrase in your response.

Morrison's "The Work You Do, the Person You Are"
What is she saying?
What is she doing?

Supporting evidence/quotations	How this quote relates back to the greater point

Adkison's "Drowning in Dishes, but Finding a Home"
What is he saying?
What is he doing?

Supporting evidence/quotations	How this quote relates back to the greater point

Developing a Multiple-Paragraph Outline

4. Use the following multiple-paragraph outline to plan your informational essay.

- Begin your outline by generating details for an introductory paragraph. This paragraph should include a general statement about the theme you are exploring, a more specific statement that refers to the two essays you will be discussing, and a thesis statement about how each of the writers gets her or his point across through subtly different methods.

- Develop the remaining paragraphs of your outline by generating details that support your thesis statement. Use paragraph 2 to focus on details from Morrison's essay and paragraph 3 to focus on details from Adkison's essay.

Multiple-Paragraph Outline	
Main Idea	**Details**
Introduction Paragraph 1	• • •
Morrison Paragraph 2	• • •
Adkison Paragraph 3	• • •

Writing a Text-Based Response

5. Reread the writing prompt posed earlier in this activity. Use notes from your Venn diagram and Supporting Evidence/Quotations charts, along with the notes in your multiple-paragraph outline, to help you write your response. As you develop your draft, be sure to:

   • Write an introduction that includes a general statement about the theme you are exploring, a more specific statement about the two essays you are responding to, and a thesis statement about how each author gets his or her point across.

   • Support your thesis with the best supporting evidence available from the Venn diagram and charts you completed.

   • Use quotation marks around text that comes directly from an essay.

   • Use a variety of complete sentences.

   • Include a transitional sentence at the beginning of the second and third paragraphs to help readers understand how these paragraphs relate to your thesis and each other.

   • Write a conclusion that revisits, without simply restating, the ideas from your introductory paragraph.

Assess and Reflect

Imagine that Toni Morrison and Danial Adkison are having a conversation about the value of work for teenagers. Write a dramatic dialogue that tells what they might say to each other on this subject, making sure that each author speaks at least three times and takes into account the viewpoints expressed by the other author.

When Anecdote Becomes Argument

Learning Strategies

Graphic Organizer
Marking the Text
Predicting

My Notes

Learning Targets

- Compare and contrast the purposes of multiple texts on the same theme.
- Analyze how an author's claims are developed by particular language and structure choices in an argumentative text.

Preview

In this activity, you will read and analyze a personal essay that includes a call to action. Then you will use the essay as inspiration as you write the script for a one-minute public service announcement.

📝 Opening Writing Prompt

Read the following list of titles. You will recognize the first two from your recent reading. The third title is a text you are about to read. Then answer the following question: How is the third title different from the first two?

- "The Work You Do, the Person You Are"
- "Drowning in Dishes, but Finding a Home"
- "What to Do with the Kids This Summer? Put' Em to Work"

Making Predictions

1. Based on the title "What to Do with the Kids This Summer? Put 'Em to Work," who is the audience? What are your clues?

2. How might this piece of writing be different from Morrison's and Adkison's essays?

As You Read

- Underline criticisms the author states about kids and parenting today.
- Circle unknown words and phrases. Try to determine the meaning of the words by using context clues, word parts, or a dictionary.

About the Author

Ben Sasse (b. 1972) is a history scholar and former professor and university president who has served as a United States senator since 2015. Sasse also served as an assistant secretary in the U.S. Department of Health and Human Services from 2007 to 2009.

Though he is not primarily a writer, Sasse believes in the importance of books and has authored two of his own on American culture and political philosophy. On the subject of reading, he wrote this in his *The New York Times* Bestseller *The Vanishing American Adult: Our Coming-of-Age Crisis—and How to Rebuild a Culture of Self-Reliance*: "America's Founders understood literacy as a prerequisite for freedom and our form of self-government. Once we know how to read, what we read matters." Sasse suggests choosing books that are deeply engaging and then having conversations about them. Says Sasse, "It is not only the content of a book that changes you but the shared community of those who have read it, discussed it, argued about it."

Essay

What to Do with the Kids This Summer? Put 'Em to Work

by **Ben Sasse**

1   Summer break 1985 was defined by my 4:30 a.m. alarm. The bus rolled up at 5, and my friends and I stumbled on, fighting off sleep until we arrived at the fields. Detasseling corn was a rite of passage in this Nebraska town: In order to cross-pollinate top-notch seed corn in those days, you needed people, lots of them, to walk through the fields to pull corn tassels manually from individual rows.

2   The job stank. It's wet and chilly in the field that early. Giant sprinklers called center pivots often got stuck and flooded acres with ankle-deep cold water. We'd start out wearing sweatshirts underneath trash bag ponchos, but by 10, as temperatures approached triple digits, we'd shed layers. For the rest of the day, our bare skin would brush against sharp corn leaves until it was marked with innumerable paper cuts.

3   We would get home covered in nasty rashes, caked in mud and bone-tired. I'd go to bed in the late afternoon and sleep straight through till the alarm sounded again, for weeks on end.

4   That was our summer vacation. What do our kids do today?

5   It's not an idle question. Nearly a quarter-century on, when I became the president of Midland University back in this same Nebraska town, one of the

My Notes

idle: valueless or purposeless

first things I noticed was how few of our students had done any hard physical work before college. Detasseling corn, like a lot of agricultural work, is now done mostly by machine.

6   And parents, on the whole, had fewer household labor needs and could afford to spare their kids the less pleasant experiences of their own childhoods, while providing them with things they wish they'd had, as well as opportunities to cultivate new skills. The time our students didn't spend in school was mostly spent consuming: products, media and entertainment, especially entertainment.

7   Another thing I noticed was an unnerving passivity. When I saw students doing their campus jobs, they seemed to have a tough time. Over and over, faculty members and administrators noted how their students' limited experience with hard work made them oddly fuzzyheaded when facing real-world problems rather than classroom tests.

8   I was worried. How would these kids survive once they left home for good? And how would an America built on self-discipline and deferred gratification survive?

9   Adolescence is a great thing, but we've made it too long. It's supposed to be a protected space in which kids who've become biologically adult are not obligated to immediately become emotionally, morally and financially adult. Done right, adolescence is a greenhouse phase, but adolescence should not be an escape from adulthood; it should be when we learn how to become adults.

10   We're parenting too much, too long. Our efforts to protect our kids from hurt feelings, tedious chores, money worries and the like are well intentioned. But many of us, perhaps especially middle-class parents, are unwittingly enabling many of our kids to not grow up.

11 What can we do about it—especially during these long summer months when our kids expect to be entertained? What's the modern equivalent of detasseling corn?

12 My wife, Melissa, and I, together with our neighbors, try to create experiences for our kids that build character. We want our kids to exercise their muscles and their minds.

13 Last year, we sent our eldest child, Corrie, then 14, to spend a month working on a cattle ranch. When we dropped her off, she was nervous but eager. Between checking cows for pregnancies—a job that involves a shoulder-length glove—and bottle-feeding orphaned heifers, she loved it and hated it. But she knew that her mild suffering was also a formative experience for a lifetime.

14 Not everyone lives in a big cattle state, and younger kids require more parental supervision. I also don't romanticize agrarian life—there's too much manure around for it to be truly idyllic—but meaningful work for kids is less about any particular task than the habits the hours teach. The effort involved and the struggles, once overcome, become the scar tissue of future character.

15 Look around your neighborhood and see what ways your kids could serve their community. Even in this digital age, lawns need to be mowed and lemonade stands can break even.

16 Older folks will benefit from the help, and your kids will gain from the perspective of people who've been on the planet longer than they have. Younger kids can work alongside Mom and Dad, too (just know that everything will take twice as long). The point isn't how perfect your neighbor's lawn looks; the point is that your kids can learn to work toward making a contribution to their community.

17 We should also encourage our kids to travel. I'm not talking about the grand European tour or the Chevy Chase road trip. Travel is simply an opportunity to help our kids to get out of their comfort zones, learn to see different social and economic arrangements. I remember my wife (then my college girlfriend) tugging me along to volunteer on a re-entry preparation program for Boston inmates.

18 Start close to home and visit a different neighborhood—you don't have eyes to see your own community until you've visited another. Travel need not be about changing locations, but reaching across generations to break out of the artificial age segregation of our era. Getting out of one's own bubble can be dramatic.

19 Few experiences help our kids discover the distinction between needs and wants like the great outdoors. It doesn't have to be a hike through the Yukon, but just living out of a backpack for a long weekend where they take an active role in planning meals, buying food, picking a site and setting up the tent. The key thing is not to have been passive consumers on someone else's trip. They'll have been the planners, the decision makers and the

My Notes

My Notes

WORD CONNECTIONS

Allusion

The phrase **Teddy Roosevelt-like vigor** alludes to Theodore Roosevelt, the 26th president of the United States. Theodore Roosevelt, whose nickname was Teddy, is remembered not only for the role he played in American history but also for the energy and persistence with which he pursued interests, such as boxing and horseback riding. When people think of Teddy Roosevelt, they think of someone who was bold and action-oriented.

risk calculators, while you're still there to make sure nothing goes too far off the rails.

20 We also want our kids to travel into literature. So we work with our children to build reading lists of books that they will wrestle with and be shaped by for the rest of their lives. Becoming a reader grows our horizons, our appetite for the good, the true and the beautiful, and our empathy.

21 Not everything will work for every family. The challenge of adolescence is not going to be solved in a single summer. The health of our republic depends on shared principles like the First Amendment, but it is also built on the Teddy Roosevelt-like vigor of its citizens and local self-reliance. This should be a gift of these long summer days to our children.

22 My grandfather had a saying from the farm that "every hour of sleep before midnight is worth two hours of sleep after midnight." I don't know about the science of that, yet I know what he meant: that you should get up and out to work early enough that you're tired enough to feel the value of being able to get to bed early again.

23 I learned that lesson in 1985. If my kids get nothing else from this summer, I hope they learn it, too.

Making Observations

- What kinds of work does the author think today's teenagers should be encouraged to do?
- What does the author think is the value of work for teenagers?

Returning to the Text

- Return to the text as you respond to the following questions. Use evidence from the text to support your responses.
- Write any additional questions you have about the essay in your Reader/Writer Notebook.

3. Before reading, you made a prediction about the audience of "What to Do with the Kids This Summer? Put 'Em to Work." How did your reading confirm or contradict your prediction?

_____

_____

_____

_____

4. How is the purpose of "What to Do with the Kids This Summer? Put 'Em to Work" similar to those of Morrison's and Adkison's essays? Explain your answer.

_____

_____

_____

_____

5. How is the purpose of "What to Do with the Kids This Summer? Put 'Em to Work" different from those of Morrison's and Adkison's essays? Explain your answer.

_____

_____

_____

_____

Working from the Text

6. The following chart divides Sasse's essay into seven sections. Work with your classmates to complete the chart.

Paragraphs	What the Author Says and Does
1–4	**Says**
	Does

Paragraphs		What the Author Says and Does
5–7	Says	
	Does	
8	Says	
	Does	
9–10	Says	
	Does	
11	Says	
	Does	
12–20	Says	
	Does	

Paragraphs	What the Author Says and Does
21–23	**Says**
	Does

Main Argument:

7. At what point in the argument does Sasse get to his claim?

_____

8. Which words best state Sasse's claim?

_____

_____

_____

Write a Public Service Announcement

9. Reread paragraphs 12–20 of "What to Do with the Kids This Summer? Put 'Em to Work." In these nine paragraphs, Sasse gives a call to action to fellow parents. Use Sasse's parenting advice as inspiration for a minute-long public service announcement that answers the following question: "What to do with the kids this summer?" As you write the script, be sure to:

- Include a call to action.
- Give reasons and examples that support or explain your call to action.
- Use language that will appeal to your audience.
- Incorporate some of the catchiest sound-bite-like phrases from Sasse's essay.

☑ Check Your Understanding

Quickwrite: How would Sasse respond to the question, "What is the value of work for teenagers?"

_____

_____

_____

_____

VOCABULARY

ACADEMIC

A **sound bite** is a short excerpt from the recording of a speech or piece of music. The purpose of a sound bite is to capture the essence of the longer recording. Speakers or writers can plant sound bites in their arguments so their audience can walk away and pass the message along.

What Do You Have to Say About Summer?

My Notes

Learning Targets

- In a written response, defend, challenge, or qualify an author's claims.
- Plan and draft an argument.

Preview

In this activity, you will react to the essay "What to Do with the Kids This Summer? Put 'Em to Work" by Ben Sasse. You will analyze Sasse's main points and then decide whether and why you agree or disagree with them.

Preparing to Argue

1. Reread "What to Do with the Kids This Summer? Put 'Em to Work" and review the notes you made in the chart about what Sasse said and did in his essay. Then respond to the following questions: How many different voices or perspectives do you hear during the course of his argument? Whose voices or perspectives do you think are missing?

2. Read the following writing prompt. You will prepare to respond to it over the course of this activity.

✍ Writing Prompt: Argumentative

You just read about how Ben Sasse feels teenagers should spend their summer. As a teenager, what is your reaction to Sasse's recommendations? How do you feel about his suggestions and assumptions? Do you mostly agree, mostly disagree, or agree with some parts but disagree with others? In a brief argument, defend, challenge, or qualify Sasse's overall claim that summer jobs are the best way to build self-reliance among teenagers. Take a position and then support it with evidence from personal experience, observations, and knowledge from other sources. Be sure to:

- Write an introduction that articulates your claim and broadly addresses any sub-claims you want to assert.
- Support your claim with the best quotes from your chart about your stance on Sasse's main points. Follow each quote with sentences that explain your reaction to it.
- Use quotation marks around text that comes directly from the essay.
- Use a variety of complete sentences.
- Write a conclusion that reasserts your claim and recasts Sasse's ideas through the lens of your personal experience.

Find Your Stance

3. Skim Sasse's essay for five main points that support his claim that teenagers' lack of summer employment is a problem. In the following chart, quote text from the essay that represents each point. Then place an "X" in the "Agree" column, if you fully agree with the point, or place an "X" in the "Disagree" column if you disagree or only partially agree with the point. Finally, write notes that explain why you agree, disagree, or only partially agree.

Sasse's Point or Quote	Agree	Disagree	Why do you say so?

4. As preparation for writing your argument, write a complex sentence that states your overall claim about Sasse's essay. Choose from the following sentence frames to help you articulate your stance.

Sentence frames for defending a claim:

- *Sasse argues _____, and I agree because _____.*
- *I agree with Sasse that _____ because my experience, _____, confirms it.*

Sentence frames for challenging a claim:

- *I disagree with Sasse's view that _____ because, as my personal experiences have demonstrated, _____.*
- *Sasse's claim that _____ rests on the questionable assumption that _____.*

Sentence frames for qualifying a claim:

- *My feelings on the issue of _____ are _____. On one hand, I agree that _____; however, based on my personal experience, _____.*
- *I am of two minds on Sasse's claim that _____. On one hand, I agree that _____. On the other hand, I am not sure if _____.*

Creating a Multiple-Paragraph Outline

5. Use the following multiple-paragraph outline to plan your argument.

- Begin your outline by generating details for an introductory paragraph. Include a modified version of the complex sentence you wrote to articulate your claim. Then broadly address other sub-claims you will assert in the course of your argument.

- Develop the remaining paragraphs of your outline by generating details that support your claim. Focus your argument on two of Sasse's main points. Use paragraph 2 to focus on one of the points and paragraph 3 to focus on the other. Then use paragraph 4 to write a conclusion for your argument that reasserts your claim and recasts Sasse's argument through the lens of your own personal experiences.

Multiple-Paragraph Outline	
Main Idea	**Details**
Introduction *Overall claim and rationale* Paragraph 1	• • •
Sasse's point A and your reaction Paragraph 2	• • •
Sasse's point B and your reaction Paragraph 3	• • •
Conclusion *Reassert claim and recast Sasse's argument through the lens of your experiences* Paragraph 4	• • •

Writing Your Argument

6. Using your multiple-paragraph outline as a guide, draft the first paragraph of your argument. Be sure to:

- Include a modified version of the complex sentence you wrote to articulate your claim.
- Broadly address other sub-claims you will assert in the course of your argument.

7. Draft the body paragraphs of your argument, based on details you included in your multiple-paragraph outline. Be sure to:

- Address at least two of Sasse's main points.
- For each paragraph, introduce one main point and then tell about your reaction to it.
- Use valid reasoning and sufficient evidence to support your reaction.

_____

_____

_____

_____

_____

_____

_____

_____

_____

_____

_____

_____

_____

_____

_____

_____

_____

_____

_____

_____

_____

_____

_____

_____

_____

_____

_____

_____

_____

_____

_____

_____

8. Draft a conclusion for your argument. Be sure to:

- Reassert your overall claim.
- Recast Sasse's argument in light of your own experiences or observations.

_____

_____

_____

_____

_____

_____

_____

_____

_____

_____

_____

_____

_____

_____

_____

_____

_____

_____

My Notes

Learning Targets

- Create an objective summary of a text.
- Analyze how an author's claim is developed and refined by text structure and language choices in an argumentative text.

Preview

In this activity, you will read and analyze another argument about the value of work. Then you will work with your classmates to interpret the author's stance about who is to blame for the decline of jobs held by American teenagers.

✍ Opening Writing Prompt

Read the first paragraph of "The Decline of the American Teenager's Job." Then answer the following questions.

Do you agree or disagree with the statement, "The author probably thinks readers should respect Ronald Reagan"? What evidence from the paragraph makes you say so?

Focusing on Language

1. If a reader agrees that we should respect Ronald Reagan, which word choices have a positive connotation to support that?

2. Based on the Reagan story alone, how do you think Lexington would answer the question, "What is the value of work for teenagers?"

3. Do you see parallels between Reagan's and Adkison's experiences?

As You Read

- Highlight phrases and sentences that reveal the author's stance.
- Circle unknown words and phrases. Try to determine the meaning of the words by using context clues, word parts, or a dictionary.

About the Author

Lexington is the name of a column in *The Economist*, and it also serves as a pen name for the writers of that column. *The Economist* is a weekly newspaper published in Great Britain, and its Lexington writers specialize in argumentative writing about business and politics in the United States. The Lexington column was named for Lexington, Massachusetts, which is the site of the beginning of the American Revolutionary War.

Argument

The Decline of the American Teenager's Summer Job

by **Lexington**

It is striking how often self-made Americans have stories to tell about boring summer jobs.

1   The first time that Ronald Reagan appeared on a newspaper front page was as a teenage lifeguard, hailed for saving a drowning man from a fast-flowing river. The future president was not yet "Ronnie", America's reassuring, twinkling, optimist-in-chief. He was still "Dutch", to use his childhood nickname: a slim, bespectacled youth, serious to the point of **priggishness**. A biographer, Garry Wills, unearthed a high school yearbook in which Reagan scolded swimmers he pulled from the cool, treacherous Rock River, near his boyhood home of Dixon, Illinois. "A big hippopotamus with a sandwich in each hand, and some firewater tanked away," Reagan wrote of one. Each summer from 1927 to 1932 the teenager would rise early to collect a 300lb block of ice and hamburger supplies before driving in his employer's van to the river, working 12 hours a day, seven days a week. The post offered responsibility, money for college and stability in a childhood blighted by frequent moves, brushes with financial ruin and his father's drinking. There was glory, too: in all he saved 77 lives. A picture of the Rock River hung in Reagan's Oval Office.

2   Strikingly often, self-made Americans have stories to share about teenage jobs, involving alarm clocks clanging before dawn, aching muscles, stern bosses and soul-fortifying hours of boredom. In 1978, a record year in the annals of the Bureau of Labour Statistics, 72% of all teenagers were employed in July, the peak month for youthful ice-cream scooping, shelf-stacking and burger-flipping. But for two decades the traditional summer job has been in decline, with 43% of teens working in July 2016.

3   Lexington decided to head to Dixon to ask why. This being an anxious and **litigious** age, Reagan's river beach is closed now. But the YMCA that

priggishness: being extremely proper
litigious: easily provoked to start a lawsuit

My Notes

trained him in lifesaving (and where he paraded as a drum major) still hires lifeguards. This summer finds one of them, Lexi Nelson, 18, between high school and community college, where she will study dental hygiene. Perhaps a quarter of her friends are working this season. The rest have mixed views of her job, which can start at five in the morning. "When I get up early they bash on it," Miss Nelson reports, "but most of the time they're jealous of the money." Lifeguarding in an indoor pool is not the most exciting job, she concedes, but that teaches patience.

4   The story of the vanishing job is not a simple one. Ask teenagers, their employers and the mayor of Dixon—a business-owner who hires teenagers each summer at a pair of sandwich shops and a frozen yogurt store—and they point to two main causes: well-meaning adults and a changing economy.

5   Reagan's stirring example is still taught in Dixon, a trim, conservative town, with an equestrian statue of the president on its riverfront and loudspeakers on lamp-posts that play the Carpenters and other easy-listening classics. But many parents discourage teens from working, it is widely agreed. Parents instead tell their children to study, take summer courses, volunteer or practise for sports that might help them compete for college places.

6   Local keepers of the Reagan flame see a town still filled with opportunities for self-advancement. Patrick Gorman, director of the Ronald Reagan Boyhood Home, a museum that preserves a house rented by the president's family in Dixon, is confident that anyone who wants a job can find one, even if it might be "detasseling" corn—picking pollen tassels from growing corn cobs, an arduous summer task traditionally reserved for the young, involving cold mornings, baking middays and scratches from corn leaves. Mr Gorman easily found six teenagers to volunteer as museum guides: "Good kids migrate to good kids," he **beams**.

7   Not all teenagers have the same needs. The three lifeguards interviewed at the YMCA are either college-bound or plan to be, and part-time work suits them. Bosses at the "Y" note that youngsters with only a high-school education typically have a different goal: landing a full-time job with health insurance and benefits.

8   Liandro Arellano Jr., Dixon's mayor, argues that teenage job prospects have been complicated by well-intentioned politicians raising the state-wide minimum wage to $8.25 an hour. For that pay it is both tempting and possible to hire college students or older workers with a proven job record, references and the ability to turn up on time, says Mr Arellano, a Republican. The youngest workers, below 18, earn $7.75 but need more training, and those aged 15 need work permits and cannot touch slicers or big bread knives. Larger economic forces have buffeted Dixon, too. After the credit crunch of 2008, a flood of laid-off factory workers and experienced adults wanted to work for Mr Arellano. With unemployment rates now below 5% in Dixon, applicants for entry-level jobs are getting younger again. Teenagers can be fine summer helpers, he says—"They're very excited about their first job"—though keeping them off smartphones is "a constant battle".

beams: smiles widely

Buy That Teenager an Alarm Clock

9   Nationwide, **affluent** white teenagers have historically been much more likely to take summer jobs than lower-income, non-white youths. Family connections help, and it is easier to find work at a golf course or tennis club than amid inner-city blight. Though big cities like Chicago, 100 miles from Dixon, have government-run schemes that prod employers to offer summer work, demand exceeds supply: last year 77,000 Chicago youths applied for 31,000 summer jobs or internships. For all that, some of Mr. Arellano's worst staff have been youngsters who do not need the money or want a job reference: they are the ones who quit without warning to go on a family holiday. Well-off parents are not always "super-supportive", he sighs.

10   Some parents may question the value of manual work in an age of high-tech change. But an elite education counts for little without self-discipline and resilience. Drudgery can teach humility: when hauling boxes, a brain full of algebra matters less than a teen's muscles. At best, it can breach the social barriers that harm democracy. Summer jobs are called all-American for a reason.

Making Observations

• What did Ronald Reagan gain from his job as a teenager?
• Why don't more teenagers have summer jobs these days?

affluent: financially well off

Working from the Text

4. For each section of the article, summarize Lexington's words (what Lexington says), and then describe what the writer accomplishes or does in that section. For the "says" part, write in first person, as if you were Lexington. For the "does" part, write in third person as you describe Lexington's moves as a writer. In the "main argument" section at the end, summarize Lexington's central claim.

Paragraphs	What the Author Says and Does	
Title and Subtitle	Says	
	Does	
1	Says	
	Does	
2–3	Says	
	Does	
4–8	Says	
	Does	
Subheading	Says	
	Does	

Paragraphs	What the Author Says and Does
9–10	**Says**
	Does
Main Argument:	

Appreciating the Author's Craft

5. Discuss the following questions with your classmates.

- What is Lexington's main claim, and where is it stated or implied in the article?

- Where in the article does Lexington's tone shift?

- How would the article be different if the subhead "Buy That Teenager an Alarm Clock" were changed to "Let's Encourage Kids to Try Working" or "The Value of Manual Work"?

INDEPENDENT READING LINK

Read and Connect

As you consider how the tone varies in Sasse's essay and Lexington's article, think also about the tone of the text you are reading independently. Is it more similar to that of Sasse's essay or Lexington's article? Or, do you think the tone of your text is completely different from the other texts? Write a paragraph that identifies the tone of your text and explains how you determined it. Then tell how the tone of your text is similar to and/or different from that of Sasse's and Lexington's texts. Finally, tell how the tone of your text affects its overall message.

Exploring the Final Paragraph

6. The following words are from the final paragraph of "The Decline of the American Teenager's Summer Job." Write a definition for each of the words, consulting a print or online dictionary for help.

value _____

manual _____

elite _____

resilience _____

drudgery _____

humility _____

breach _____

social _____

barrier _____

democracy _____

7. Paraphrase the final paragraph of "The Decline of the American Teenager's Summer Job," using the word knowledge you gained. Be sure to maintain the text's meaning and present information in a logical order.

Weighing the Author's Use of Evidence

8. Over the course of the article, Lexington assigns blame to various groups or entities for the decline of the American teenager's summer job. Who or what do you think is most responsible for the decline? Complete the following chart about how Lexington assigns blame to parents, teenagers, and other groups or entities you may identify. Rank who or what you think is most responsible by assigning a "1" to that group or entity. Assign a "2" to the second most responsible and a "3" to the least responsible. Then gather evidence from the article to justify your rankings.

Teenagers
Rank:
Evidence for rank:

Parents
Rank:
Evidence for rank:

Other: _____
Rank:
Evidence for rank:

Interpreting a Stance

9. Share your completed rankings chart with your classmates and see whether you all agreed about the amount of blame Lexington's article assigns to teenagers, parents, and other parties. If you did not agree, give each of your classmates a chance to explain the reasoning behind his or her rankings. Then work with your classmates to reach a consensus about the correct rankings and write the results on the following lines. (Assign a "1" to that group or entity that is most responsible, a "2" to the second most responsible, and a "3" to the least responsible.)

_____ Teenagers

_____ Parents

_____ Other parties

> ### 📝 Writing Prompt: Argumentative
>
> Use notes from your rankings chart and class discussion about who is most to blame for the decline in American teenage jobs to help you write a paragraph explaining your interpretation of Lexington's stance. Be sure to:
>
> - Include a topic sentence that introduces your subject and purpose.
> - Identify whom you think Lexington assigns the most blame to, and support your claim with evidence from the article.
> - Name other groups or entities to whom blame is also assigned, and include evidence from the article to explain why you think Lexington holds them less responsible.

Assess and Reflect

Revisit the argument you wrote about "What to Do with the Kids This Summer? Put 'Em to Work" by Ben Sasse. Use the following chart to divide your argument into sections, using whatever number of sections is appropriate. Next, answer the questions about each section by paraphrasing what you said, as the narrator of the essay, and then telling what you did as a writer, or how you built your argument and used language to appeal to your audience. In the "main argument" section, summarize your central claim.

Section 1: _____
What did you say?
What did you do?

Section 2: _____
What did you say?
What did you do?

Section 3: _____
What did you say?
What did you do?

Section 4: _____
What did you say?
What did you do?

Main Argument

Think about the strategies you used in crafting your argument. If you were to revise your argument, what additional strategies could you incorporate to strengthen it?

_____

_____

_____

_____

_____

_____

_____

_____

_____

Letting the Data Do the Talking

Learning Strategies

Predicting
Previewing

My Notes

Learning Targets

- Interpret graphs and use them to make predictions about a text.
- Interpret statistics represented in a graph and synthesize information from several graphs.

Preview

In this activity, you will preview the title, subtitle, and several informational graphics from an argument you will read in the next activity. Then you will analyze the graphs and use the information from them to help you predict claims the author of the argument has made.

📝 Opening Writing Prompt

Read the following quote. Then answer the question: What do you think Lindblom means by "every statistic tells a tale in shorthand"?

"Anecdotes can be just as valid as evidence as statistics, even though statistics tend to have a better reputation as objective fact. But every statistic is really a form of anecdote; every statistic tells a tale in shorthand."

—Ken Lindblom (Stony Brook University)

Interpreting Data

1. The following informational graphics appear in an argument you will be reading in the next activity. Work with your classmates to interpret the data presented in each graph and answer the questions that follow it. Then write a response to this question in your Reader/Writer Notebook:

   Based on the four graphs, what are possible claims you might find in the written text of the article?

   Use the following sentence frame to describe the trend you notice in the data.

   Based on this graph, I can see that there has been a trend among

   _____ *to work* _____

   during _____ .

Graph 1:

Civilian Labor Force Participation Rate: 16-to-19-Year-Olds

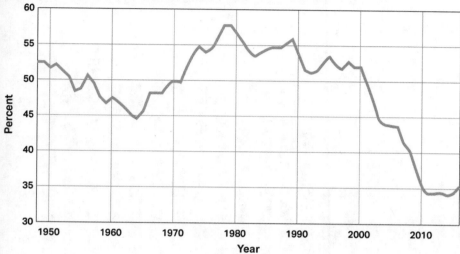

Graph 2:

Teen-Labor Participation Rates vs. Share of New High School Graduates in College Courses

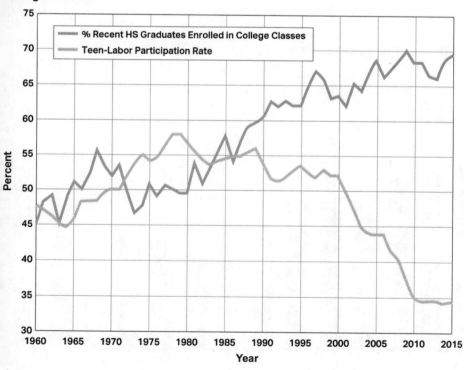

Graph 3:

Share of Teenagers Taking Summer Courses

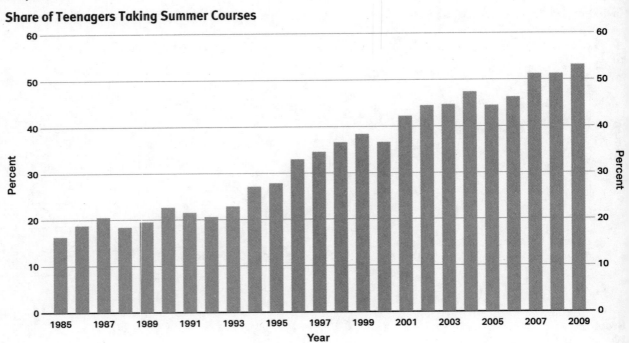

Graph 4:

Share of Non-Working Teens Who Say They Wish They Were Working

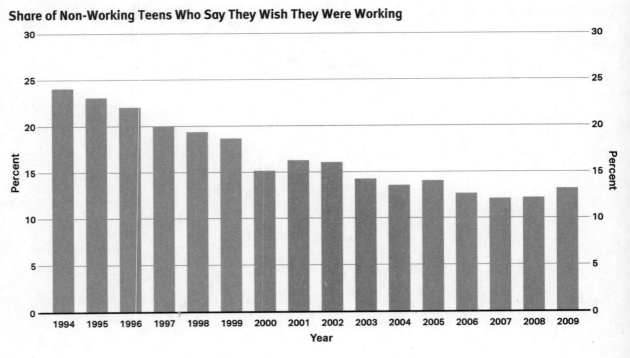

Synthesizing the Data

2. Use your notes about the graphs from "Teenagers Have Stopped Getting Summer Jobs—Why?" to help you write a few sentences that answer the following question: Based on the graphic representations of data you interpreted in your small group, what story could you tell?

_____

_____

_____

_____

_____

_____

_____

_____

☑ Check Your Understanding

Read the following quote from the beginning of "Teenagers Have Stopped Getting Summer Jobs—Why?" and respond to the questions. "Most [teenagers] used to work in July and August. Now the vast majority don't. Are they being lazy, or strategic?" Why?

_____

_____

_____

Changing the Conversation

My Notes

Learning Targets

- Analyze the text structure and language choices in an argumentative text.
- Relate a claim to its supporting evidence.

Preview

In this activity, you will read, analyze, and discuss an argument that includes statistics about how teenagers spend their time during the summer.

Opening Writing Prompt

Read the first four paragraphs from Derek Thompson's article "Teenagers Have Stopped Getting Summer Jobs—Why?" Then answer this question:

> If Ben Sasse and Lexington started a conversation about the decline in summer employment among teenagers, how is Thompson changing that conversation? In other words, what new idea does Thompson contribute to our ongoing conversation in the first four paragraphs of his article?

As You Read

- Highlight sentences that supply reasons that support the claim.
- Circle unfamiliar words or phrases. Try to determine the meaning of the words by using context clues, word parts, or a dictionary.

About the Author

In addition to being the senior editor at *The Atlantic* and the author of the national bestselling book *Hit Makers: How to Succeed in an Age of Distraction*, Derek Thompson is also a business columnist, podcast host, news analyst, and speaker who has been called "one of the brightest new voices in American journalism." Some keys to Thompson's success as a writer are that he is a talented investigator and his writing style is highly relatable—not only does he ask great questions and thoroughly research their answers, but he explains his findings in a way that is easy to understand. Thompson received the Best in Business Award in 2016 for Columns and Commentary from the Society of American Business Writers and Editors.

Argument

Teenagers Have Stopped Getting Summer Jobs— Why?

by **Derek Thompson**

Most used to work in July and August. Now the vast majority don't. Are they being lazy, or strategic?

1   The summer job is considered a rite of passage for the American Teenager. It is a time when tossing newspaper bundles and bussing restaurant tables acts as a rehearsal for weightier adult responsibilities, like bundling investments and bussing dinner-party plates. But in the last few decades, the summer job has been disappearing. In the summer of 1978, 60 percent of teens were working or looking for work. Last summer, just 35 percent were.

2   Why did American teens stop trying to get summer jobs? One typical answer is: They're just kids, and kids are getting lazier.

3   One can rule out that **hypothesis** pretty quickly. The number of teens in the workforce has collapsed since 2000, as the graph below shows. But the share of NEETs—young people who are "Neither in Education, Employment, or Training"—has been extraordinarily steady. In fact, it has not budged more than 0.1 percentage point since the late 1990s. Just 7 percent of American teens are NEETs, which is lower than France and about the same as the mean of all advanced economies in the OECD. The supposed laziness of American teenagers is unchanging and, literally, average.

Civilian Labor Force Participation Rate: 16-to-19-Year-Olds

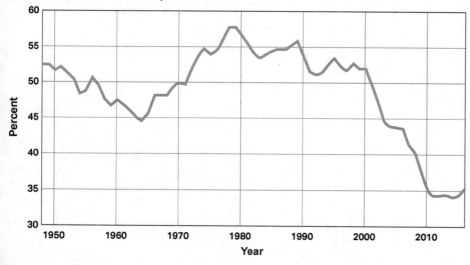

4   A better answer is that teenagers aren't spending more time on the couch, but rather spending more time in the classroom. Education is to blame, rather

My Notes

hypothesis: testable guess or theory

than **indolence**. Teens are remaining in high school longer, going to college more often, and taking more summer classes. The percent of recent high-school graduates enrolled in college—both two-year and four-year—has grown by 25 percentage points. That is almost exactly the decline in the teenage labor-force participation rate.

Teen-Labor Participation Rates vs. Share of New High School Graduates in College Classes

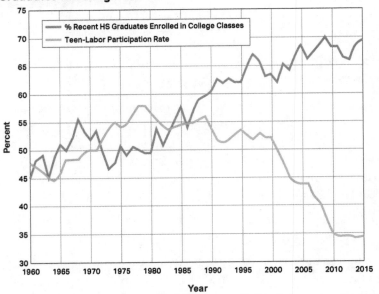

5 With tougher high-school requirements and greater pressure to go to college, summer classes are the new summer job. The percent of 16-to-19-year-olds enrolled in summer school has tripled in the last 20 years, according to the Bureau of Labor Statistics. The rise may be directly related to the fact that parents and high schools are encouraging students to take on more classwork, according to Ben Steverman, a *Bloomberg* reporter who covers teen employment. He finds that the percentage of high-school grads completing at least four years of English, three years of science, math, and social science, and two years of foreign language has *sextupled* since the early 1980s.

Share of Teenagers Taking Summer Classes

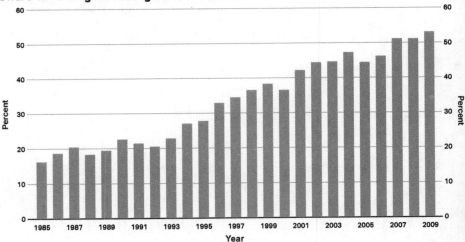

indolence: laziness

My Notes

6   The second reason why teens work less today is that employers are more reluctant to hire them. First, the rise of low-skill immigration in the last few decades has created more competition for exactly the sort of jobs that teenagers used to do, like grocery-store cashiers, restaurant servers, and retail salespeople. Second, older Americans stay in the workforce longer than ever, and many of them wind down their careers in office secretary and retail jobs, which used to be the province of 16-year-olds in the summer. Third, the number of federally funded summer jobs, where students work temporarily with their local government, has declined. At the same time, the minimum wage has grown, which may have discouraged bosses from taking on young inexperienced workers who are only "worth" hiring at a salary that's become illegal. Together, these policies have reduced the number of temporary paid jobs for teenagers in the public and private sector. Fourth, companies have caught on to the fact that if they want to hire teenagers, they don't have to pay them, at all: There has been an extraordinary rise in unpaid internships over the last decade. Although these teenage interns are clearly working, they don't show up in the official employment statistics, because they're not getting paid.

7   The last big-picture explanation for the demise of teen summer jobs is cultural. Teenagers are exquisitely sensitive to the social norms of their peers. If they see cool older teenagers scooping ice cream during their freshman summer, they'll really look forward to a job scooping ice cream during their sophomore summer. But any social feedback loop can spin both ways. Recently, the cultural norm is shifting toward summer classes and unpaid internships rather than summer jobs. Since the mid-1990s, the share of teenagers who say they wish they were working has fallen by about 50 percent, according to the BLS. That suggests—although it cannot prove—that summer jobs have lost cultural cachet, as the norm has shifted away from working.

Share of Non-Working Teens Who Say They Wish They Were Working

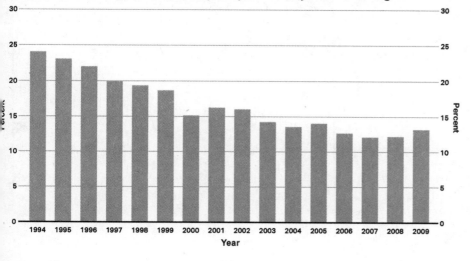

8   It's important to note that it's probably white adults who feel the strongest nostalgia for summer jobs. Here's a look at the teen participation rate for the last two full years for whites, Hispanics, and blacks. Each July and August sees

sector: part of the national economy

cachet: prestige or superior status

a 10-point jump in the number of white teenage workers, a 5-point jump in the number of Hispanic teen workers, and hardly any movement among black teenagers. (There is evidence that Asian teens are more like white teens in this regard.)

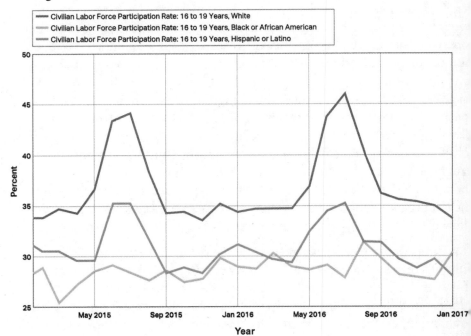

9   Compare that to 1978 and 1979, the statistical peak of the teen summer job. In July and August in the late 1970s, 30 percent of white teens flooded into the labor force, along with 20 percent of Hispanics. Again, black teen participation hardly budged.

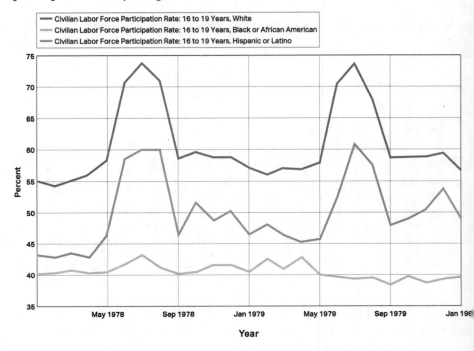

10 Putting these two graphs together, two things are clear. First, the summer-job bump has declined for all ethnicities in the last 40 years. Second, summer jobs are the province of the white and wealthy. Children of richer families are more likely to take part-time summer jobs, according to a report from the Center for Labor Market Studies at Northeastern University. But black and low-income teens are less likely to work, not only because their neighborhoods have fewer opportunities, but also because their families have fewer connections to companies with internships and part-time jobs. Altogether, summer jobs may be yet another **vector** through which privilege becomes inherited from one generation to the next.

11 Is there any good reason to be nostalgic for teen summer jobs? Don't they teach kids responsibility, "soft skills," and a humbling tolerance for the tedium of office life? There are several studies that show summer jobs for teens pay a long-term dividend in higher earnings and reduced crime. But there are even more studies hailing the benefits of high-school completion and college attendance, and many teens have to choose between education and work. (It will be interesting to see if the summer job has a **resurgence** in the new low-unemployment economy.)

12 The mysterious disappearance of the summer job for teenagers turns out to be a perfect **parable** for the flexibility of the workforce. Many of the jobs that teenagers used to do no longer exist; they've gone to older Americans and new immigrants. But rather than use the **fallow** months to quintuple their video-game time, teenagers are taking the time to invest in their educational future. This is hardly the place to expend America's finite national anxiety.

Making Observations
- What is the author's answer to the question posed in the title?
- What is your initial impression of the author?

Working from the Text

1. The following chart divides Thompson's essay into six sections. Work with your classmates to read each section and then answer the questions about it in the chart. To answer the questions, first paraphrase what Thompson says as the narrator of the essay. Then write a sentence or two about what he does as a writer—tell how he builds his argument and uses language to appeal to his audience. In the "main argument" section, summarize Thompson's central claim.

vector: means for carrying or transmitting something
resurgence: comeback or rise to prominence
parable: short story with a moral
fallow: inactive

Paragraphs	What the Author Says and Does	
1	Says	
	Does	
2–3	Says	
	Does	
4–5	Says	
	Does	
6	Says	
	Does	
7	Says	
	Does	
8–10	Says	
	Does	

Paragraphs	What the Author Says and Does
11–12	**Says**
	Does

Main Argument:

2. Where does Thompson use words to mirror the claims you predicted based on the essay's title, the subtitle, and the data from the four graphs in Activity 3.8?

_____

_____

_____

Appreciating the Author's Craft

Discuss the following questions with your classmates.

• Why do you think Thompson chose to place some of the supporting information for his essay in graphs rather than in the text?

• What kinds of information does Thompson include in the graphs?

• If Thompson had not used graphs with his essay, how would the essay be different? Do you think it would be as effective? Explain your answer.

Relating Evidence and Claim

Although Thompson uses direct, causal language, such as "education is to blame," rather than "education may be to blame," he is not stating fact; he is making a claim, which means that he is presenting ideas that are debatable. In order to make his claim credible, Thompson uses evidence to support it.

3. Use the following graphic organizer to show how Thompson supports his claim. Write a sentence that summarizes his claim in the pediment at the top. Then write evidence that supports that claim, including data and quotes from Thompson's essay, in each of the pillars.

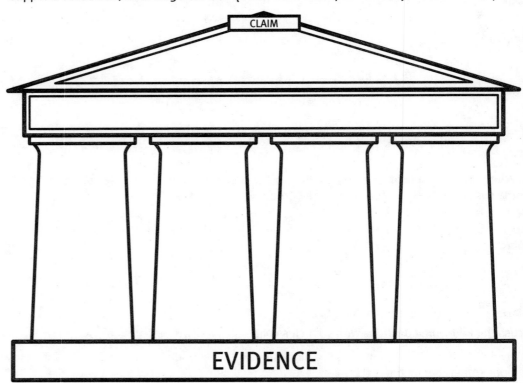

CLAIM

EVIDENCE

Check Your Understanding

According to Thompson, are summer jobs truly American or do they represent only a subset of America?

Gaining Perspectives

Over the course of the last few activities, you have been reading about teenagers getting summer jobs. The reasons why not many teenagers get summer jobs, or get jobs at all, vary from community to community across the United States, but there are trends. With a partner, monitor the numbers of teenagers getting jobs in your community as well as at the state level. Where would you look to find this type of information? How do these numbers compare to what you learned in the essays? Are you surprised with the information you are finding? Do you notice any trends? Create a brief presentation and share your data with the class.

Parsing the Essay Prompt

Learning Strategies

Graphic Organizer
Marking the Text

Learning Targets
- Analyze a writing prompt.
- Identify examples of evidence, reasoning, and stylistic and persuasive elements in an argument.

Preview

In this activity, you will begin to think about how you will write an analysis of argument about Sasse's, Lexington's, or Thompson's essay by analyzing the writing prompt, choosing a topic for your analysis, and beginning to sort through information you may want to include in it.

My Notes

📝 Explain How an Author Builds an Argument

In this unit, you have analyzed three arguments about the decline of summer work for American teenagers: one by Senator Ben Sasse, one by *The Economist's* Lexington, and one by *The Atlantic* writer Derek Thompson. Choose ONE of these articles and write an essay in which you explain how the writer builds an argument to explain the causes of the decline in summer employment among American teens and asserts what Americans should do about it, if anything. Remember to use precise language and well-chosen, concrete details in your explanation.

As you develop your essay, consider how the writer uses:

- evidence, such as facts or examples, to support claims;
- reasoning to develop ideas and connect claims and evidence; and
- stylistic or persuasive elements, such as word choice or appeals to emotion, to add power to the ideas expressed.

Note: Your essay should not explain whether you agree with the author's claims; rather, it should explain how the author builds an argument to persuade his audience.

Recognizing Good Examples of What the Writer Does

1. For your analysis of an argument, you will need to focus on what your author of choice does as a writer. With your classmates, revisit the charts you completed about what Sasse, Lexington, and Thompson say and do in their arguments. Collaborate to find examples of what these authors do with their evidence, reasoning, and stylistic and persuasive elements to make their essays more effective. Write the examples in the following chart.

Evidence	Reasoning	Stylistic and Persuasive Elements

Test-Driving Some Topics

2. Choose the argument by Sasse, by Lexington, or by Thompson that most interests you and complete the following chart with examples from that argument alone. Then return to the text to find quotes or graphic elements that could be used to illustrate your examples.

Evidence	Reasoning	Stylistic and Persuasive Elements

Outlining and Drafting

Forming a Multiple-Paragraph Outline

1. Reread the Explain How an Author Builds an Argument writing prompt in Activity 3.10. Use the following multiple-paragraph outline to plan your essay as you work through this activity.

Multiple-Paragraph Outline	
Main Idea	**Details**
Introduction Paragraph 1	• • •
Point A about what the writer does Paragraph 2	• • •
Point B about what the writer does Paragraph 3	• • •
Conclusion Paragraph 4	• • •

Developing an Analysis of Argument

2. Using your multiple-paragraph outline as a guide, draft the first paragraph of your essay. Be sure to:

- Include a general statement that addresses the summer-job topic.
- Follow the general statement with a specific statement that refers to the writer and the associated text and claim.
- Follow the specific statement with a thesis statement that relates the writer's claim to the strategies used to persuade the audience.

_____

_____

_____

_____

_____

_____

_____

_____

_____

_____

_____

_____

3. Draft the body paragraphs of your essay based on details you included in your multiple-paragraph outline. Consider which examples will be the most relevant and compelling to use. Be sure to:

- Address at least two of the author's writing strategies.
- Use quotations from the text to support your analysis of the writer's strategies.

4. Draft a conclusion for your essay. Be sure to:
- Reassert your overall claim.
- Recast your explanation in light of the evidence you have provided in your essay.

_____

_____

_____

_____

_____

_____

_____

_____

_____

_____

_____

_____

Assess and Reflect

Follow your teacher's instructions to view several graphs from the U. S. Department of Labor's website or from another source your teacher has chosen. Choose one graph to analyze and answer the following questions about it.

What do you notice? _____

_____

What do you wonder? _____

_____

What story could this graph tell? _____

_____

Complete the following sentence frame to tell about an observation you can make based on the graph you chose to interpret.

_Based on this graph, I can see there has been a trend in/toward _____ ._

Children Are the Future: Using Rhetorical Appeals

Learning Strategies

Marking the Text
Role Playing
Skimming/Scanning
SMELL
SOAPSTone

Learning Targets

- Demonstrate an understanding of the skills and knowledge necessary to successfully complete Embedded Assessment 1.
- Identify and analyze the effectiveness of rhetorical devices in a speech.
- Explain how a writer or speaker uses rhetoric to advance his or her purpose.

Preview

In this activity, as the topic shifts from work for teenagers to college, you will analyze the devices used in a speech to make it compelling, and begin planning your own argument.

Revisiting the Essential Questions

Reflect on your initial responses to the following Essential Questions. How would you adjust your responses now?

1. What makes an argument convincing?
2. What makes a piece of evidence compelling?
3. What is the value of work for teenagers?
4. What is the value of a college education?

Unpacking Embedded Assessment 1

Read the following assignment for Embedded Assessment 1: Writing an Argumentative Essay, and summarize the major elements in your Reader/Writer Notebook.

Your assignment is to write an argumentative essay about the value of a college education. Your essay must be organized as an argument in which you assert a precise claim, support it with reasons and evidence, and acknowledge and refute counterclaims fairly.

Summarize in your own words what you will need to know for the assessment. With your class, create a graphic organizer that represents the skills and knowledge you will need to accomplish this task and strategize how you will complete the assignment. To help you complete your graphic organizer, be sure to review the criteria in the Scoring Guide.

My Notes

Main Parts of an Argument

Convincing arguments have at least four main parts: a claim (or claims), reasoning, evidence, and treatment of counterarguments.

Parts of an Argument	Explanation	Helpful Questions
Claims	• offer solutions to problems • try to convince readers to change their thoughts or actions related to a problem • based on reasons	What do you think about this problem?
Reasoning	• logical grounds that show the claim is important • link between the claim and evidence	Why do you believe this?
Evidence	• data or facts that support the claim	How do you know your idea is right? What data and facts are most compelling?
Treatment of Counterarguments	• an alternate point of view that challenges the claim	What other solutions to the problem are possible?

Keep the parts of an argument in mind as you read the argumentative essays presented throughout the remainder of this unit.

As You Read

• Underline phrases or sections that seem compelling.
• Circle unknown words and phrases. Try to determine the meaning of the words by using context clues, word parts, or a dictionary.

About the Author

Barack Obama (b. 1961) became the 44th president of the United States in 2009. As a senator from Illinois, Obama rose to national prominence after giving a speech at the 2004 Democratic National Convention. He was born in Honolulu, Hawaii, attended Occidental College and Columbia University, and received a law degree from Harvard Law School in 1991. He worked as a civil rights lawyer and a teacher prior to entering politics.

Speech

Remarks by the President in a National Address to America's Schoolchildren

Wakefield High School, Arlington, Virginia, September 8, 2009

by **President Barack Obama**

GRAMMAR & USAGE

Verb Voice

Multiple verbs within a sentence should have the same voice: either active or passive.

Active voice means the subject is doing the verb's action:

The boy attended the fundraiser.

Passive voice means the subject is acted upon:

The fundraiser was attended by the boy.

Inappropriate shifts can confuse an audience. Think about what effect Obama creates by using active voice, rather than passive voice, in his speech.

1   ... I know that for many of you, today is the first day of school. And for those of you in kindergarten, or starting middle or high school, it's your first day in a new school, so it's understandable if you're a little nervous. I imagine there are some seniors out there who are feeling pretty good right now with just one more year to go. And no matter what grade you're in, some of you are probably wishing it were still summer and you could've stayed in bed just a little bit longer this morning.

2   I know that feeling. When I was young, my family lived overseas. I lived in Indonesia for a few years. And my mother, she didn't have the money to send me where all the American kids went to school, but she thought it was important for me to keep up with an American education. So she decided to teach me extra lessons herself, Monday through Friday. But because she had to go to work, the only time she could do it was at 4:30 in the morning.

3   Now, as you might imagine, I wasn't too happy about getting up that early. And a lot of times, I'd fall asleep right there at the kitchen table. But whenever I'd complain, my mother would just give me one of those looks and she'd say, "This is no picnic for me either, buster."

4   So I know that some of you are still adjusting to being back at school. But I'm here today because I have something important to discuss with you. I'm here because I want to talk with you about your education and what's expected of all of you in this new school year.

5   Now, I've given a lot of speeches about education. And I've talked about responsibility a lot. I've talked about teachers' responsibility for inspiring

My Notes

My Notes

ingenuity: ability to solve problems

students and pushing you to learn. I've talked about your parents' responsibility for making sure you stay on track, and you get your homework done, and don't spend every waking hour in front of the TV or with the Xbox. I've talked a lot about your government's responsibility for setting high standards, and supporting teachers and principals, and turning around schools that aren't working, where students aren't getting the opportunities they deserve.

6   But at the end of the day, we can have the most dedicated teachers, the most supportive parents, the best schools in the world—and none of if will make a difference, none of it will matter unless all of you fulfill your responsibilities, unless you show up to those schools, unless you pay attention to those teachers, unless you listen to your parents, and grandparents and other adults and put in the hard work it takes to succeed. That's what I want to focus on today: the responsibility each of you has for your education.

7   I want to start with the responsibility you have to yourself. Every single one of you has something that you're good at. Every single one of you has something to offer. And you have a responsibility to yourself to discover what that is. That's the opportunity an education can provide.

8   Maybe you could be a great writer—maybe even good enough to write a book or articles in a newspaper—but you might not know it until you write that English class paper that's assigned to you. Maybe you could be an innovator or an inventor—maybe even good enough to come up with the next iPhone or the new medicine or vaccine—but you might not know it until you do your project for your science class. Maybe you could be a mayor or a senator or a Supreme Court justice—but you might not know that until you join student government or the debate team.

9   And no matter what you want to do with your life, I guarantee that you'll need an education to do it. You want to be a doctor, or a teacher, or a police officer? You want to be a nurse or an architect, a lawyer or a member of our military? You're going to need a good education for every single one of those careers. You cannot drop out of school and just drop into a good job. You've got to train for it and work for it and learn for it.

10   And this isn't just important for your own life and your own future. What you make of your education will decide nothing less than the future of this country. The future of America depends on you. What you're learning in school today will determine whether we as a nation can meet our greatest challenges in the future.

11   You'll need the knowledge and problem-solving skills you learn in science and math to cure diseases like cancer and AIDS, and to develop new energy technologies and protect our environment. You'll need the insights and critical-thinking skills you gain in history and social studies to fight poverty and homelessness, crime and discrimination, and make our nation more fair and more free. You'll need the creativity and **ingenuity** you develop in all your classes to build new companies that will create new jobs and boost our economy.

12 We need every single one of you to develop your talents and your skills and your intellect so you can help us old folks solve our most difficult problems. If you don't do that—if you quit on school—you're not just quitting on yourself, you're quitting on your country.

13 Now, I know it's not always easy to do well in school. I know a lot of you have challenges in your lives right now that can make it hard to focus on your schoolwork.

14 I get it. I know what it's like. My father left my family when I was two years old, and I was raised by a single mom who had to work and who struggled at times to pay the bills and wasn't always able to give us the things that other kids had. There were times when I missed having a father in my life. There were times when I was lonely and I felt like I didn't fit in.

15 So I wasn't always as focused as I should have been on school, and I did some things I'm not proud of, and I got in more trouble than I should have. And my life could have easily taken a turn for the worse.

16 But I was—I was lucky. I got a lot of second chances, and I had the opportunity to go to college and law school and follow my dreams. My wife, our First Lady Michelle Obama, she has a similar story. Neither of her parents had gone to college, and they didn't have a lot of money. But they worked hard, and she worked hard, so that she could go to the best schools in this country.

17 Some of you might not have those advantages. Maybe you don't have adults in your life who give you the support that you need. Maybe someone in your family has lost their job and there's not enough money to go around. Maybe you live in a neighborhood where you don't feel safe, or have friends who are pressuring you to do things you know aren't right.

18 But at the end of the day, the circumstances of your life—what you look like, where you come from, how much money you have, what you've got going on at home—none of that is an excuse for neglecting your homework or having a bad attitude in school. That's no excuse for talking back to your teacher, or cutting class, or dropping out of school. There is no excuse for not trying. Where you are right now doesn't have to determine where you'll end up. No one's written your destiny for you, because here in America, you write your own destiny. You make your own future.

19 That's what young people like you are doing every day, all across America.

20 Young people like Jazmin Perez, from Roma, Texas. Jazmin didn't speak English when she first started school. Neither of her parents had gone to college. But she worked hard, earned good grades, and got a scholarship to Brown University—is now in graduate school, studying public health, on her way to becoming Dr. Jazmin Perez.

21 I'm thinking about Andoni Schultz, from Los Altos, California, who's fought brain cancer since he was three. He's had to endure all sorts of treatments and surgeries, one of which affected his memory, so it took him much longer—hundreds of extra hours—to do his schoolwork. But he never fell behind. He's headed to college this fall.

22 And then there's Shantell Steve, from my hometown of Chicago, Illinois. Even when bouncing from foster home to foster home in the toughest neighborhoods in the city, she managed to get a job at a local health care center, start a program to keep young people out of gangs, and she's on track to graduate high school with honors and go on to college.

23 And Jazmin, Andoni, and Shantell aren't any different from any of you. They face challenges in their lives just like you do. In some cases they've got it a lot worse off than many of you. But they refused to give up. They chose to take responsibility for their lives, for their education, and set goals for themselves. And I expect all of you to do the same.

24 That's why today I'm calling on each of you to set your own goals for your education—and do everything you can to meet them. Your goal can be something as simple as doing all your homework, paying attention in class, or spending some time each day reading a book. Maybe you'll decide to get involved in an extracurricular activity, or volunteer in your community. Maybe you'll decide to stand up for kids who are being teased or bullied because of who they are or how they look, because you believe, like I do, that all young people deserve a safe environment to study and learn. Maybe you'll decide to take better care of yourself so you can be more ready to learn. And along those lines, by the way, I hope all of you are washing your hands a lot, and that you stay home from school when you don't feel well, so we can keep people from getting the flu this fall and winter.

25 But whatever you resolve to do, I want you to commit to it. I want you to really work at it.

26 I know that sometimes you get that sense from TV that you can be rich and successful without any hard work—that your ticket to success is through rapping or basketball or being a reality TV star. Chances are you're not going to be any of those things.

27 The truth is, being successful is hard. You won't love every subject that you study. You won't click with every teacher that you have. Not every homework assignment will seem completely relevant to your life right at this minute. And you won't necessarily succeed at everything the first time you try.

28 That's okay. Some of the most successful people in the world are the ones who've had the most failures. J.K. Rowling's—who wrote Harry Potter—her first Harry Potter book was rejected 12 times before it was finally published. Michael Jordan was cut from his high school basketball team. He lost hundreds of games and missed thousands of shots during his career. But he once said, "I have failed over and over and over again in my life. And that's why I succeed."

29 These people succeeded because they understood that you can't let your failures define you—you have to let your failures teach you. You have to let them show you what to do differently the next time. So if you get into trouble, that doesn't mean you're a troublemaker, it means you need to try harder to act right. If you get a bad grade, that doesn't mean you are stupid, it just means you need to spend more time studying.

30 No one's born being good at all things. You become good at things through hard work. You're not a varsity athlete the first time you play a new sport. You don't hit every note the first time you sing a song. You've got to practice. The same principle applies to your schoolwork. You might have to do a math problem a few times before you get it right. You might have to read something a few times before you understand it. You definitely have to do a few drafts of a paper before it's good enough to hand in.

31 Don't be afraid to ask questions. Don't be afraid to ask for help when you need it. I do that every day. Asking for help isn't a sign of weakness, it's a sign of strength because it shows you have the courage to admit when you don't know something, and that then allows you to learn something new. So find an adult that you trust—and ask them to help you stay on track to meet your goals.

32 And even when you're struggling, even when you're discouraged, and you feel like other people have given up on you, don't ever give up on yourself, because when you give up on yourself, you give up on your country.

33 The story of America isn't about people who quit when things got tough. It's about people who kept going, who tried harder, who loved their country too much to do anything less than their best. It's the story of students who sat where you sit 250 years ago, and went on to wage a revolution and they founded this nation. Young people. Students who sat where you sit 75 years ago who overcame a Depression and won a world war; who fought for civil rights and put a man on the moon. Students who sat where you sit 20 years ago who founded Google and Twitter and Facebook and changed the way we communicate with each other.

34 So today, I want to ask all of you, what's your contribution going to be? What problems are you going to solve? What discoveries will you make? What will a President who comes here in 20 or 50 or 100 years say about what all of you did for this country?

My Notes

_____
_____
_____
_____
_____
_____
_____
_____
_____
_____
_____
_____
_____
_____
_____
_____
_____
_____
_____
_____
_____
_____
_____
_____
_____
_____
_____
_____
_____
_____
_____
_____

35 Now, your families, your teachers, and I are doing everything we can to make sure you have the education you need to answer these questions. I'm working hard to fix up your classroom and get you the books and the equipment and the computers you need to learn. But you've got to do your part, too. So I expect all of you to get serious this year. I expect you to put your best effort into everything you do. I expect great things from each of you. So don't let us down. Don't let your family down or your country down. Most of all, don't let yourself down. Make us all proud.

36 Thank you very much, everybody. God bless you. God bless America. Thank you.

Making Observations

- Which images and details in the speech stand out to you?
- What language stands out to you?

Introducing the Strategy: SOAPSTone

SOAPSTone stands for <u>S</u>peaker, <u>O</u>ccasion, <u>A</u>udience, <u>P</u>urpose, <u>S</u>ubject, and <u>T</u>one. It is a reading and writing tool for analyzing the relationships among a writer, his or her purpose, and the target audience of the text. SOAPSTone guides you in asking questions to analyze a text or to plan for writing a composition.

- **Speaker:** The speaker is the voice that tells the story.
- **Occasion:** The occasion is the context that prompted the writing.
- **Audience:** The audience is the person or persons to whom the piece is directed.
- **Purpose:** The purpose is the reason behind the text or what the writer wants the audience to think as a result of reading the text.
- **Subject:** The subject is the focus of the text.
- **Tone:** Tone is the speaker's attitude toward the subject.

5. With your group, use the SOAPSTone strategy to guide your analysis of the speech. Be prepared to discuss your analysis with the class.

SOAPSTone	Analysis	Textual Support
Speaker What does the reader know about the writer?		
Occasion What are the circumstances surrounding this text?		
Audience Who is the target audience?		
Purpose Why did the author write this text?		
Subject What is the topic?		
Tone What is the speaker's tone, or attitude, toward the subject?		

Returning to the Text

- Return to the text as you respond to the following questions. Use evidence from the text to support your responses.
- Write any additional questions you have about the text in your Reader/Writer Notebook.

6. The president begins his speech with statements about the audience's feelings and then a story about his own childhood. Why does he begin his speech in this way?

_____

_____

_____

_____

7. What is the message of this speech?

_____

_____

_____

_____

8. Reread paragraphs 13–16. Why might the speaker choose to include his own personal story here?

_____

_____

_____

_____

9. In paragraph 17, what is the effect of the president's use of repetition?

_____

_____

_____

_____

10. In paragraphs 18–24, what does the president do to overcome potential resistance (counterarguments) by his audience?

_____

_____

_____

_____

11. What is the purpose of the questions the president asks in paragraph 34?

_____

_____

_____

_____

12. Do you agree or disagree with President Obama's claim that it is important to get a good education and try your hardest in school? Defend or challenge President Obama's claim using relevant text evidence.

_____

_____

_____

_____

Elements of Rhetoric

Rhetoric is the use of words to persuade in writing or speech. There are many rhetorical devices speakers and writers use, and these include rhetorical appeals: logos, ethos, and pathos. Authors and speakers use rhetorical appeals in their arguments to persuade the intended audience that their claims are right. Together, these rhetorical appeals are central to understanding how writers and speakers appeal to their audiences and persuade them to accept their messages. It is helpful to think of them as three points of a triangle.

Logos: Text – What information, evidence, and logical reasoning are offered within the text?

Pathos: Audience – What values, beliefs, and emotions are appealed to within the text? How does the text evoke the audience's feelings?

Ethos: Speaker – What perception of the speaker is created within the text? How does the text evoke the audience's trust?

VOCABULARY

LITERARY
Writers and speakers try to connect to and persuade their audiences through the use of many devices, including rhetorical appeals. Appeals to an audience's reason or logic are called logos.

Ethos is a rhetorical appeal that focuses on the character or qualifications of the speaker. Pathos is a rhetorical appeal to the reader's or listener's senses or emotions.

SMELL is an acronym for <u>s</u>ender, <u>m</u>essage, <u>e</u>motional strategies, <u>l</u>ogical strategies, and <u>l</u>anguage. This strategy is useful for analyzing a persuasive speech or essay by asking five important questions:

- What is the sender-receiver relationship? Whom are the images and language meant to attract? Describe the speaker (or writer) of the text.
- What is the message? Summarize the thesis of the text.
- What is the desired effect of the emotional strategies?
- What logic is being used? How does it (or its absence) affect the message? Consider the logic of images as well as words.
- What does the language of the text describe? How does it affect the meaning and effectiveness of the writing? Consider the language of images as well as words.

13. Use the SMELL strategy to analyze how Obama uses the different rhetorical appeals to persuade his audience. Complete the graphic organizer and include specific quotes and textual evidence you noted while reading the speech.

Sender-Receiver Relationship: Who are the senders (speaker/writer) and receivers (audience) of the message, and what is their relationship (consider what different audiences the text may be addressing)? How does the sender attempt to establish his/her ethos?

Message: What is a literal summary of the context? What is the meaning/significance of this information?

Emotional and **Logical Strategies:** What emotional strategies (pathos) and logical arguments/appeals (logos) are included? What is their effect?

Language: What specific language supports the message? How does it affect the text's effectiveness? Consider both images (if appropriate) and actual words. What is the speaker's voice in the text?

☑ Check Your Understanding

How does President Obama use rhetoric to advance his purpose and persuade his audience to share his ideals?

📝 Explain How an Author Builds an Argument

Explain how President Obama builds the argument in his speech. In your writing, be sure to:

- Identify the claim made by the writer.
- Explain what reasons and supporting evidence the writer uses and how counterarguments are addressed. Evaluate the effectiveness of the reasons, evidence, and rebuttals of counterarguments.
- Identify the direct address to the reader toward the end of essay. In addition to the evidence that supports the writer's claim, evaluate whether or not the advice presented in that direct address helps the writer build a persuasive argument.
- Explain how the writer concludes the speech and how effective that ending is.

INDEPENDENT READING LINK

Read and Discuss

In your Independent Reading text, you are reading an argument about a topic that interests you. What makes the claim or argument in your book compelling? Share your ideas with a partner. Compare your examples, compiling a list of similarities, including strategies both authors use to build a strong argument, such as using rhetorical devices. Document your response in your Reader/Writer Notebook.

Language Checkpoint: Using Parallel Structure

- Understand the purpose of parallel structure within sentences.
- Use parallel structure correctly in writing.
- Revise writing to correct the use of parallel structure within a sentence.

Preview

In this activity, you will examine how writers use parallel structure and apply it to your own writing.

Understanding Parallel Structure Within Sentences

Parallel structure is when related ideas are expressed in the same grammatical form within the same sentence. Parallel structure can be used deliberately when arranged in sentences. It can also occur naturally in sentences when words are put together in a way that sounds clear, balanced, and even powerful.

Parallel structure can be a deliberate and convincing rhetorical technique in speeches or dramatic, powerful writing. It provides balance and repetition, allowing the audience to easily concentrate and quickly comprehend what the speaker says.

Read the following sentence from President Obama's speech.

> ...none of it will matter unless all of you fulfill your responsibilities, unless you show up to those schools, unless you pay attention to those teachers, unless you listen to your parents, and grandparents and other adults and put in the hard work it takes to succeed.

In this sentence, President Obama uses parallel structure by repeating the same clause: *unless you* [verb].

1. How does parallel structure help make the sentence clearer? Why?

Read this sentence that also includes parallel structure.

> You want to be a doctor, or a teacher, or a police officer?

This sentence includes parallel structure with the nouns that are set in a series: *doctor, teacher, police officer*.

Now reread the same sentence without parallel structure.

> You want to be a doctor, or to be a teacher, or a police officer?

2. Which version of the sentence is clearer? Why?

3. Read the following sentences and identify the parallel structure in each.

a. I've talked about your parents' responsibility for making sure you stay on track, and you get your homework done, and don't spend every waking hour in front of the TV or with the Xbox.

b. But at the end of the day, we can have the most dedicated teachers, the most supportive parents, the best schools in the world—and none of it will make a difference, none of it will matter unless all of you fulfill your responsibilities.

4. In President Obama's speech, he takes parallelism one step further to create a memorable form of repetition called *anaphora*. Read the sentences that follow. How would you describe this form of parallelism? Discuss with a partner what effect this parallelism has.

Maybe you could be a great writer—maybe even good enough to write a book or articles in a newspaper—but you might not know it until you write that English class paper that's assigned to you. Maybe you could be an innovator or an inventor—maybe even good enough to come up with the next iPhone or the new medicine or vaccine—but you might not know it until you do your project for your science class. Maybe you could be a mayor or a senator or a Supreme Court justice—but you might not know that until you join student government or the debate team.

Recognizing Parallel Structure

5. Underline the parallel clauses in these sentences from Obama's speech.

So if you get into trouble, that doesn't mean you're a troublemaker, it means you need to try harder to act right. If you get a bad grade, that doesn't mean you are stupid, it just means you need to spend more time studying.

6. Read these sentences from President Obama's speech and underline the parallel structure.

> So today, I want to ask all of you, what's your contribution going to be? What problems are you going to solve? What discoveries will you make? What will a President who comes here in 20 or 50 or 100 years say about what all of you did for this country?

Revising

Read the following paragraph. Revise the sentences to improve the paragraph's parallel structure.

You'll need knowledge and problem-solving skills you learn in science and math to work on finding cures for diseases. Insights and critical-thinking skills from history and social studies can fight against injustice. Some of you might need the creativity and ingenuity you gain in all your classes. This can help you build the companies that will help the economy grow.

☑ Check Your Understanding

What questions can you ask yourself whenever you write to ensure you are using parallel structure to enrich your writing? How can you remind yourself to correctly use parallel structure? Add the questions to your Editor's Checklist.

Practice

Reread the argument analysis you wrote in Activity 3.12 aloud. As you read, listen for where you may have used faulty parallelism. Revise any words, phrases, and clauses that you can make parallel, and strengthen your writing. Share your revisions with a partner and exchange feedback.

To Go to College or Not to Go to College?

Learning Strategies

Drafting
Marking the Text
Quickwrite
Skimming/Scanning
SMELL

Learning Targets

- Identify the treatment of counterarguments, such as concessions and rebuttals, in an argument and describe how they work.
- Examine arguments for their rhetorical devices and logical fallacies.
- Analyze the conclusion of arguments.
- Integrate ideas from multiple texts to build knowledge and vocabulary about going to college.

Preview

In this activity, you will read two argumentative pieces and analyze the elements of the arguments, including the central claims, supporting evidence, counterarguments, and treatment of counterarguments.

Rhetorical Devices and Logical Fallacies

One common consequence of using rhetorical devices to compel or persuade an audience is the accidental, or intentional, creation of a logical fallacy. When reading or listening to arguments, it is vitally important to be aware of logical fallacies and their effects to avoid being convinced by evidence that is based on faulty logic.

1. With a partner, read and discuss the Fallacies 101 graphic organizer in the Resources section. For the following fallacies, identify what makes the statement misleading. Then discuss the effect that the fallacy might have in a speech or piece of writing.

VOCABULARY

ACADEMIC
A fallacy is a false or misleading statement. A logical fallacy is a statement that is false because it is based on an error in reasoning. Logical fallacies are commonly introduced because they make good sound bites and can appeal to the audience's pathos before they have time to think about the faulty reasoning.

Fallacy Type	Why It Is Misleading
Ad Hominem/ Genetic Fallacy	
Straw Man	
Appeal to Pity	
Ad Baculum (Scare Tactics)	
Slippery Slope	

My Notes

Fallacy Type	Why It Is Misleading
Argument from Outrage	
Red Herring	
Hasty Generalization	
Post Hoc	
Ad Populum	
Either/Or	

As You Read

- Highlight words and phrases that relate to the topic of going to college.
- Circle unfamiliar words or phrases. Try to determine the meaning of the words by using context clues, word parts, or a dictionary.

About the Author

Robert Reich is the Chancellor's Professor of Public Policy at the University of California, Berkeley, as well as an author, political commentator, and political economist. Reich was the 22nd United States Secretary of Labor under President Bill Clinton from 1993 to 1997, and served in the administrations of Presidents Gerald Ford and Jimmy Carter. He has published over 12 books and is featured in the recent documentary, *Inequality for All*.

Argument

Why College Isn't (And Shouldn't Have to Be) For Everyone

by **Robert Reich**

1   I know a high school senior who's so worried about whether she'll be accepted at the college of her choice she can't sleep.

2   The parent of another senior tells me he stands at the mailbox for an hour every day waiting for a hoped-for acceptance letter to arrive.

3   Parents are also uptight. I've heard of some who have stopped socializing with other parents of children competing for admission to the same university.

4   Competition for places at top-brand colleges is absurdly intense.

5   With inequality at record levels and almost all the economic gains going to the top, there's more pressure than ever to get the golden ring.

6   A degree from a **prestigious** university can open doors to elite business schools and law schools—and to jobs paying hundreds of thousands, if not millions, a year.

7   So parents who can afford it are paying **grotesque** sums to give their kids an edge.

8   They "enhance" their kid's resumes with such things as bassoon lessons, trips to preserve the wildlife in Botswana, internships at the Atlantic Monthly.

9   They hire test preparation coaches. They arrange for consultants to help their children write compelling essays on college applications.

10   They make generous contributions to the elite colleges they once attended, to which their kids are applying —colleges that give extra points to "**legacies**" and even more to those from wealthy families that donate tons of money.

11   You might call this **affirmative action** for the rich.

12   The same intensifying competition is affecting mid-range colleges and universities that are doing everything they can to **burnish** their own brands—competing with other mid-range institutions to enlarge their applicant pools, attract good students, and inch upward on the U.S. News college rankings.

13   Every college president wants to increase the ratio of applications to admissions, thereby becoming more elite.

14   Excuse me, but this is nuts.

15   The biggest absurdity is that a four-year college degree has become the only gateway into the American middle class.

KNOWLEDGE QUEST

Knowledge Question:

What is the purpose of going to college?

Across Activities 3.13 and 3.14, you will read three arguments about going to college. While you read and build knowledge about the topic, think about your answer to the Knowledge Question.

My Notes

prestigious: respected and admired

grotesque: ridiculously inconsistent

legacies: students whose parents or other relatives attended the school

affirmative action: a policy favoring groups who have historically suffered from discrimination

burnish: polish

16 But not every young person is suited to four years of college. They may be bright and ambitious but they won't get much out of it. They'd rather be doing something else, like making money or painting murals.

17 They feel compelled to go to college because they've been told over and over that a college degree is necessary.

18 Yet if they start college and then drop out, they feel like total failures.

19 Even if they get the degree, they're stuck with a huge bill—and may be paying down their student debt for years.

20 And all too often the jobs they land after graduating don't pay enough to make the degree worthwhile.

21 Last year, according to the Federal Reserve Bank of New York, 46 percent of recent college graduates were in jobs that don't even require a college degree.

22 The biggest frauds are for-profit colleges that are raking in money even as their students drop out in droves, and whose diplomas are barely worth the ink-jets they're printed on.

23 America clings to the **conceit** that four years of college are necessary for everyone, and looks down its nose at people who don't have college degrees.

24 This has to stop. Young people need an alternative. That alternative should be a world-class system of vocational-technical education.

25 A four-year college degree isn't necessary for many of tomorrow's good jobs.

26 For example, the emerging economy will need **platoons** of technicians able to install, service, and repair all the high-tech machinery filling up hospitals, offices, and factories.

27 And people who can upgrade the software embedded in almost every gadget you buy.

28 Today it's even hard to find a skilled plumber or electrician.

29 Yet the vocational and technical education now available to young Americans is typically underfunded and inadequate. And too often denigrated as being for "losers."

30 These programs should be creating winners.

31 Germany—whose median wage (after taxes and transfers) is higher than ours—gives many of its young people world-class technical skills that have made Germany a world leader in fields such as precision manufacturing.

32 A world-class technical education doesn't have to mean young people's fates are determined when they're fourteen.

33 Instead, rising high-school seniors could be given the option of entering a program that extends a year or two beyond high school and ends with a diploma acknowledging their technical expertise.

conceit: fanciful idea
platoons: groups of people who share particular characteristics

34 Community colleges—the under-appreciated crown jewels of America's feeble attempts at equal opportunity—could be developing these curricula. Businesses could be advising on the technical skills they'll need, and promising jobs to young people who complete their degrees with good grades.

35 Government could be investing money to make these programs thrive. (And raising taxes on top incomes enough to temper the wild competition for admission to elite colleges that grease the way to those top incomes.)

36 Instead, we continue to push most of our young people through a single funnel called a four-year college education—a funnel so narrow it's causing applicants and their parents excessive stress and worry about "getting in;" that's too often ill suited and unnecessary, and far too expensive; and that can cause college dropouts to feel like failures for the rest of their lives.

37 It's time to give up the idea that every young person has to go to college, and start offering high-school seniors an alternative route into the middle class.

🖉 Knowledge Quest

- What words and phrases about going to college stand out to you?
- What is your initial reaction to Reich's argument?

☑ Focus on the Sentence

Write "S" if the words form a complete sentence. Capitalize and punctuate the sentences. Write "F" if the words are a sentence fragment. Change the fragments into complete sentences using what you read in the article.

_____ want more applicants than can be admitted

_____

_____ community colleges are underappreciated

_____

_____ high school seniors need

_____

_____ businesses should tell students what skills they are looking for

_____

Returning to the Text

- Return to the text as you respond to the following questions. Use evidence from the text to support your responses.
- Write any additional questions you have about the text in your Reader/Writer Notebook.

My Notes

> feeble: weak

My Notes

_____
_____
_____
_____
_____
_____
_____
_____
_____
_____
_____
_____
_____
_____
_____
_____
_____
_____
_____
_____
_____
_____
_____
_____
_____
_____
_____
_____
_____
_____

VOCABULARY

ACADEMIC

Concession and **rebuttal** are two ways to deal with counterarguments. Concession is when a writer or speaker acknowledges a valid point made by an opponent. It allows for different opinions and approaches toward an issue, indicating an understanding of what causes the actual debate or controversy.

A rebuttal occurs when two people debate, one of them makes an argument, and the other person follows with a reason why the first person's argument was wrong.

2. What is the claim of the argument "Why College Isn't (And Shouldn't Have to Be) For Everyone"? How does the writer set up the claim?

_____
_____
_____
_____

3. What is the connotation of the word *absurdity* as it is used in paragraph 15? Why did the author choose that word?

_____
_____
_____
_____

4. **KQ** Based on context, what is the meaning of the word *technical* in paragraph 24?

_____
_____
_____
_____

5. **KQ** Based on the ideas in his essay, what would Robert Reich say is the purpose of college?

_____
_____
_____
_____

Working from the Text

6. With a partner, discuss some rhetorical devices you see at play in Reich's argument. Use the SMELL strategy to guide your analysis.

7. Think about the claim that Reich makes in his essay. What is your opinion? Would you defend his claim or challenge it? What **concession(s)** would you make? What **rebuttal(s)** would you offer? Use the tables that follow to plan arguments for both sides of the issue, as well as a counterargument for both. Consider valid reasons for and against the topic, find text evidence in support of the arguments, and brainstorm various rhetorical devices to help persuade the audience.

AGREE, college shouldn't be for everyone because:		
Reason 1:	Evidence:	Appeals:
Reason 2:	Evidence:	Appeals:
Counterargument:		

DISAGREE, college should be for everyone because:		
Reason 1:	Evidence:	Appeals:
Reason 2:	Evidence:	Appeals:
Counterargument:		

As You Read

- Highlight statements that explain the benefits of college.
- Circle unfamiliar words or phrases. Try to determine the meaning of the words by using context clues, word parts, or a dictionary

Knowledge Question:

What is the purpose of going to college?

My Notes

About the Author

Libby Nelson is the news editor of Vox.com, where she manages a team of reporters. Libby joined Vox in 2014 as an education reporter, but she occasionally strayed off the beat to write about other topics. She previously worked at Politico, where she launched the Morning Education newsletter, and Inside Higher Ed, where she covered federal higher education policy. Her first full-time job in journalism was as a local news reporter in Scranton, Pennsylvania.

Argument

The 'not everyone should go to college' argument is classist and wrong

by **Libby Nelson**

1   The economic return on investment for a college degree has never been higher. But the more that fact is discussed, the more some pundits seem to think the US is at risk of an **epidemic** of unnecessary college-going that can be averted by singing the praises of highly skilled trades.

2   The latest, in Businessweek, is headlined "Let's Start Telling Young People the Whole Truth About College"—the whole truth being that a four-year degree isn't the only road to a stable, even lucrative, professional life.

3   Fair enough. (Though the economic evidence still comes down heavily on the side of four-year college graduates being better off in the long run.) But the argument that "everyone shouldn't go to college"—reiterated with dozens of variations in the past few years—rests on some incorrect assumptions about higher education in the U.S.

4   Many people imagine a bright line between college and vocational education—Ph.Ds on one side, plumbers on the other. That line doesn't exist, and it hasn't for at least a generation. Particularly at two-year colleges, programs for future English majors and future auto mechanics often exist side-by-side. One path might lead to an associate degree, the other to a certificate, but they're both at a place called "college."

5   As higher education economist Sandy Baum wrote in a report for the Urban Institute: "It is common to hear the suggestion that many students should forgo college and instead seek vocational training. But most of that training takes place in community colleges or for-profit postsecondary institutions."

epidemic: widespread occurrence

6   The skilled trades are demanding workers with increasing levels of technical ability, and the market rewards those who have the credential to prove it: About 30 percent of construction workers now have some kind of professional license or credential, according to the Census Bureau. So do about 20 percent of industrial workers. Workers without a traditional college degree, but with a credential, earned more than workers with no credentials at all. They still earn less than workers with a traditional degree.

7   Where do people earn these credentials? The vast majority—82 percent—of workers with credentials other than a college degree, or in addition to a college degree, earned them from educational institutions. In other words, to get ahead in those skilled jobs so often promoted as the alternative to a college education, they went to college.

Where workers earned their credentials

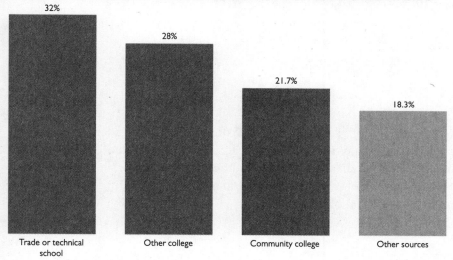

| Trade or technical school | Other college | Community college | Other sources |
| 32% | 28% | 21.7% | 18.3% |

Source: Census Bureau

8   Somehow, criticism of the cult of the college degree never pinpoints the one group where a belief that "everyone should go to college" really is pervasive: the upper middle class. Students from families in the top fifth of incomes have gone to college in disproportionately high numbers since at least the 1970s. About 80 percent of them now attend college right after high school. More than half have a bachelor's degree by age 25.

Postsecondary Enrollment Rates of Recent High School Graduates by Family Income, 1987 to 2012

9   It's more than plausible that some of those well-off students could be happy and successful with a certificate in carpentry instead of a bachelor's in business. Yet the calls to tell the truth about the value of a college degree nearly always stop short of saying where—if too many people really do go to college—that truth-telling is sorely needed.

⊘ Knowledge Quest

- What are your first thoughts about where people learn skilled trades?
- What questions do you have about Nelson's argument?

☑ Focus on the Sentence

Use information from the article to write two sentences that start with the following subordinating conjunctions.

Although _____

_____

Because _____

_____

Returning to the Text

- Return to the text as you respond to the following questions. Use evidence from the text to support your responses.
- Write any additional questions you have about the text in your Reader/Writer Notebook.

8. Nelson begins by laying out the arguments against her central claim. How does this affect the appeal of her argument?

_____

_____

_____

_____

9. **KQ** In paragraph 5, the author says many students seek training "in community colleges or for-profit postsecondary institutions." What is a "postsecondary institution"? Why would the author include this phrase in her argument?

_____

_____

_____

_____

10. What evidence does Nelson present to support her opinion that a college education is not necessarily a bad idea?

_____

_____

_____

_____

11. How does the use of the line graph support the author's claim?

_____

_____

_____

_____

12. What purpose do the graphs serve in relation to the text?

_____

_____

_____

_____

13. **KQ** Based on the ideas in her essay, what would Libby Nelson say is the purpose of college?

_____

_____

_____

_____

Working from the Text

14. With a partner, discuss some rhetorical devices you see at play in Nelson's argument. Use the SMELL strategy to guide your analysis.

15. Conduct a second read of one of the essays. As you reread, use four different colored highlighters to identify the parts of the writer's argument. Mark the writer's claim with the first color, reasons with the second color, evidence with the third color, and treatment of counterarguments with the fourth color.

16. Compare the claims made by each of these two writers. Evaluate the reasons and evidence used by each writer. What is relevant and convincing? For each text, write the claim and its most convincing supporting evidence in the chart.

"Why College Isn't (And Shouldn't Have to Be) For Everyone"	"The 'not everyone should go to college' argument is classist and wrong"
Claim: "A four-year college degree isn't necessary for many of tomorrow's good jobs."	**Claim:**
Evidence:	**Evidence:**
Counterarguments:	**Counterarguments:**
Evidence:	**Evidence:**

17. Which writer's claim do you agree with? Which do you disagree with? Use textual evidence to defend the claim you agree with. Then use textual evidence to challenge the claim you disagree with. Record your responses in the chart.

Agree	Disagree
Claim:	Claim:
Text Evidence:	Text Evidence:

18. An argument contains a conclusion that often restates the primary claim and tries to convince the reader to take an action. What is the call to action in each of these pieces?

_____

_____

_____

_____

_____

_____

_____

LANGUAGE & WRITER'S CRAFT: Effective Sentences

Effective sentences make stronger arguments. The building blocks of an effective sentence are phrases and dependent clauses. Phrases and dependent clauses cannot stand on their own as complete sentences, but they can add or clarify the information in an independent clause.

A clause is a group of words that contains a subject and a verb. A dependent clause, though it contains a subject and verb, does not express a complete thought. A phrase, on the other hand, is a group of words that does not have a subject and verb but does express some unified thought.

Dependent Clause: Although college does not seem necessary

Phrase: the unnecessary cost of college

Adding well-placed phrases and dependent clauses to sentences can help clarify the link between ideas and create a readable flow. For example:

College is necessary.

College is necessary in a technological economy. [Add a phrase.]

If you want a good career, college is necessary. [Add a dependent clause.]

PRACTICE Read the following sentences and revise them by adding a phrase or a dependent clause.

College is important.

College is not important.

INDEPENDENT READING LINK

Read and Discuss

Meet with a partner or small group to discuss the following topics.

- What claim is the author making in your independent reading?
- What is the most convincing evidence in your independent reading?
- What counterarguments has the author of your independent reading addressed? How has he or she addressed them?

✅ Check Your Understanding

Think about the conversation that would take place between Reich and Nelson on this topic. Write a counterargument each writer would pose to the other. Then write a statement each writer would use to address the other's counterargument, identifying which treatment you are using (concession, rebuttal, etc.).

College Is Still Going to Pay Off, No Matter What

Learning Strategies

Drafting
Marking the Text
Quickwrite
Skimming/Scanning

My Notes

Learning Targets

- Analyze the characteristics of informational graphics.
- Describe counterarguments and refutations, and defend and challenge a debatable claim.
- Integrate ideas from multiple texts to build knowledge and vocabulary about going to college.

Preview

In this activity, you will compare and analyze the characteristics of texts that present the same information in different mediums.

As You Read

- Highlight statistics that surprise or interest you.
- Circle unfamiliar words or phrases. Try to determine the meaning of the words by using context clues, word parts, or a dictionary

Reading Graphics

- Read the title. It tells you what the graphic is about.
- Read the labels. Headings, subheadings, and numbers tell you what the parts of the graphic are and describe the specific information given for each category.
- Follow arrows and lines to understand the direction or order of events or steps.
- Read numbers carefully, noting how amounts or intervals of time increase or decrease.
- If there is a key, pay attention to why different colors are used.

About the Author

Gillian B. White, who lives in Washington, D.C., is a senior associate editor at *The Atlantic* magazine. White focuses on topics related to economics and business, including telling stories about the economic well-being of different American cities. She has a degree in economics and political science from Columbia University and a graduate degree in journalism from Northwestern University's Medill School.

Argument

Even with Debt, College Still Pays Off

by **Gillian B. White**

A bachelor's degree can help recent graduates earn 83 percent more than peers who only completed high school.

1 Widespread unemployment among recent college graduates during, and following, the recession combined with climbing student-loan debt, has left many wondering whether or not a college education is a good or necessary investment after all.

2 In economic terms, the answer is still yes.

3 Though the cost of college is increasing, a variety of **empirical** evidence suggests that the earnings associated with a bachelor's degree still trump the debt that students incur in most cases. According to data from the New York Fed, college graduates earn 80 percent more than their peers who didn't attend, or didn't finish, undergrad—and they're also less likely to wind up unemployed than those who didn't go to college.

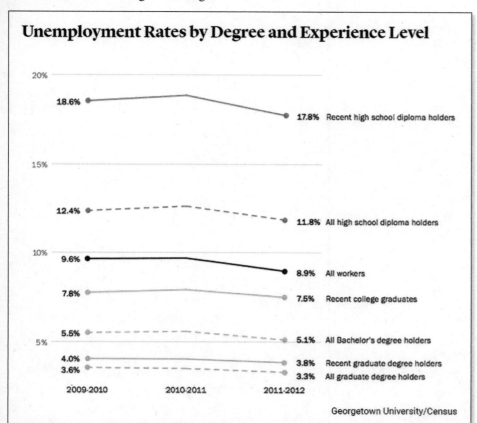

Unemployment Rates by Degree and Experience Level

- **18.6%** → **17.8%** Recent high school diploma holders
- **12.4%** → **11.8%** All high school diploma holders
- **9.6%** → **8.9%** All workers
- **7.8%** → **7.5%** Recent college graduates
- **5.5%** → **5.1%** All Bachelor's degree holders
- **4.0%** → **3.8%** Recent graduate degree holders
- **3.6%** → **3.3%** All graduate degree holders

2009-2010   2010-2011   2011-2012

Georgetown University/Census

KNOWLEDGE QUEST

Knowledge Question:
What is the purpose of going to college?

My Notes

empirical: observational or experiential

4   Researchers from Georgetown University delved further into the topic in a new study that looks at the wage advantage college grads have over those with only a high-school diploma, looking at earnings through various stages of employment, from just after graduation to decades into their careers. While unemployment rates for new grads and experienced workers alike have **fluctuated** throughout the recession and recovery, the earnings premium that college- and advanced-degree holders enjoy over their peers who didn't attend college has remained relatively stable, and in some instances, grown, according to the report that was released this week.

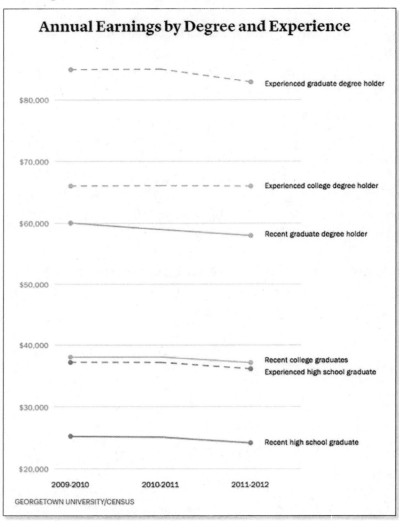

Annual Earnings by Degree and Experience

5   Overall, recent college grads aged 22 to 26 have earnings that are 83 percent higher than early-career workers who have only a high-school diploma, according to the study. But what surprised researchers the most was the premium that recent college graduates still received compared to high-school graduates who had been working in their fields for a significant period of time. According to the study, a recent college graduate has median earnings of about $37,000, which is about $1,000 more than an experienced worker aged 35 to 54 who only has a high-school education. "It's really kind of a stunner. You would have thought that all that work experience would have done the job,

fluctuated: rose and fell in number or amount

but it doesn't," says Anthony P. Carnevale, a research professor and director of the Center on Education and the Workforce at Georgetown.

6 Of course, majors and careers play a huge part in the returns of a college degree, Carnevale says. For those recent grads who majored in arts, psychology, or social work, earnings were about 29 percent more than those of peers who had only a high-school diploma, according to the report. And for those recent college grads who majored in more traditionally-lucrative subjects, like engineering, earnings were 138 percent higher than those of their high-school only peers. Attending graduate school provides an even bigger boost, earning recent, advanced-degree graduates ages 25 to 34 between 92 and 229 percent more than peers without a college degree, the study found.

7 But what happens when you factor in the growing cost of college tuition, which leaves many students to take out large sums of debt to finance their educations? In the 2012–2013 academic year, the average cumulative student-loan debt for a four-year, public-college graduate was about $25,600 according to data from the College Board. For those attending private four-year colleges, cumulative debt amounted to about $31,200. But even with those high loan totals, the value of a college degree still holds up, says Carnevale. "The truth of it is that college is still worth it. It's just that most people can't afford it." When you add up the premium that college grads benefit from, which can amount to upwards of $10,000 each year, and multiply it by a career that lasts for about 45 years, the cost of a college education is well worth it.

8 But while the long-term outcome is promising in economic terms, the realities of the financial benefits a college degree can provide are often more difficult to grasp while saddled with the burden of student-loan debt, particularly during the early portion of your career, when wages are typically at their lowest.

9 And that reflects a growing problem with the cost and structure of higher education in the U.S. In order to make smarter choices about colleges, majors, debt, and careers, students and parents alike need a lot more information and guidance, says Carnevale. "It's really a matter of building an information system, and I would argue even regulations, that make students, and institutions, and the government more responsible for giving people sensible advice about debt," he says. "I think people should talk to you about what you're going to major in and what your career prospects are. You want to make sure that people make good investments, that's the idea."

Knowledge Quest

- What is student-loan debt?
- What statistics about going to college surprise you?

Returning to the Text

- Return to the text as you respond to the following questions. Use evidence from the text to support your responses.
- Write any additional questions you have about the text in your Reader/Writer Notebook.

1. What claim does White make?

2. What kind of evidence does White primarily use to support her claim? Is the evidence compelling? Why or why not?

3. What is the source of this information? Is the data cited reliable? Why or why not?

4. How does the presentation of data in a chart aid the reader?

5. **KQ** Based on the ideas in her essay, what would Gillian B. White say is the purpose of college?

6. **KQ** In paragraph 7, how does using the word *premium* to describe the additional wages received by college graduates affect the tone of the article?

_____

_____

_____

_____

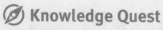 **Knowledge Quest**

Use your knowledge of the four essays you have read to consider the various arguments about whether going to college is necessary. Write an explanatory essay that responds to the question: What do we learn from the four essays about the purpose of going to college?

Be sure to:

- Quote from a variety of sources about the topic.
- Evaluate the reliability of each source.
- Integrate the sources of information to find evidence to support your opinion.

KNOWLEDGE QUEST

You can continue to build your knowledge about going to college by reading other articles at ZINC Reading Labs. Search for keywords such as *university* or *college*.

 ZINC

Working from the Text

7. Review the text and take notes on the reasons given in support of the central claim. Be as specific as possible, and include quotes as you record evidence in support of each reason.

Reason	Support/Evidence
Greater Wealth	
More Opportunities	
Less Debt	

8. Which of these reasons is the most and least convincing? Why?

_____

_____

_____

9. What do the graphs show? Do not quote the titles exactly.

_____

_____

_____

10. Why do you think the author chose to communicate the information in the form of graphs?

_____

_____

_____

11. Claims must be debatable. Use textual evidence from any of the texts you have read so far in Unit 3 to both defend and challenge White's claim. Cite at least two pieces of text evidence. Record your responses in the chart.

Defend	Challenge
Claim:	Claim:
Text Evidence:	Text Evidence:

Communicating with Visuals

Examine each of the following graphs and answer the questions.

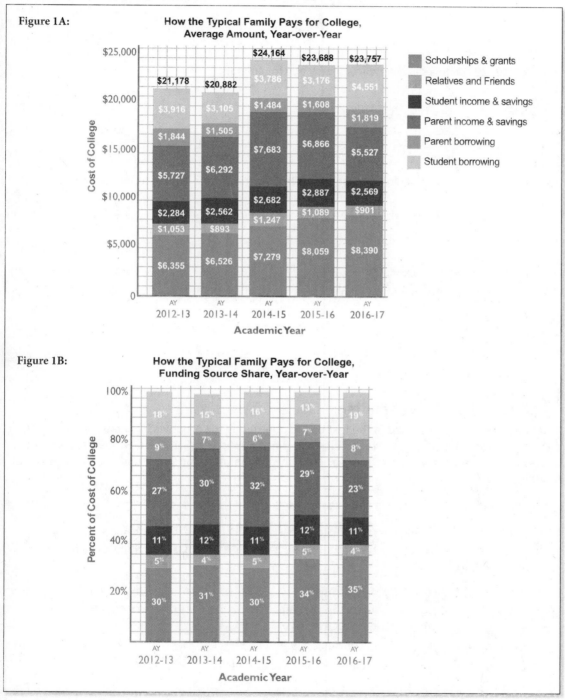

Figure 1A:

**How the Typical Family Pays for College,
Average Amount, Year-over-Year**

Legend:
- Scholarships & grants
- Relatives and Friends
- Student income & savings
- Parent income & savings
- Parent borrowing
- Student borrowing

Figure 1B:

**How the Typical Family Pays for College,
Funding Source Share, Year-over-Year**

12. What does this pair of graphs show? Do not quote the titles exactly.

_____

_____

_____

13. What do the different colors in each of the graphs represent?

_____

_____

_____

14. In 2012–2013, how did the typical family pay for college?

_____

_____

_____

15. What is being compared in these graphs? Why did the author choose to use graphs?

_____

_____

_____

16. What claim can you make from analyzing the data in these graphs?

_____

_____

_____

☑ Check Your Understanding

What arguments are presented in the text and supported by the graphics? Review the conversation you developed between Reich and Nelson in Activity 3.13. Add White's voice to the conversation. Then add your own voice by incorporating information you found in the charts about funding college.

📝 Explain How an Author Builds an Argument

Explain how the writer builds the argument in "Even with Debt, College Still Pays Off." In your writing, be sure to:

- Identify the arguable claim that is made.
- Explain what reasons and supporting evidence the writer uses and how counterarguments are addressed. Evaluate their effectiveness.
- Evaluate how convincing the conclusion is.
- Evaluate the purpose and effectiveness of the graphics the author uses.

What Do I Want to Do When I Grow Up?

Learning Strategies

Marking the Text
Skimming/Scanning

Learning Targets

- Interpret data presented in different types of graphs.
- Explain how graphic features provide information that supports a given claim or argument.

Preview

In this activity, you will analyze and explain information presented in graphs and relate that information to previous reading.

Reading a Line Graph: First Look

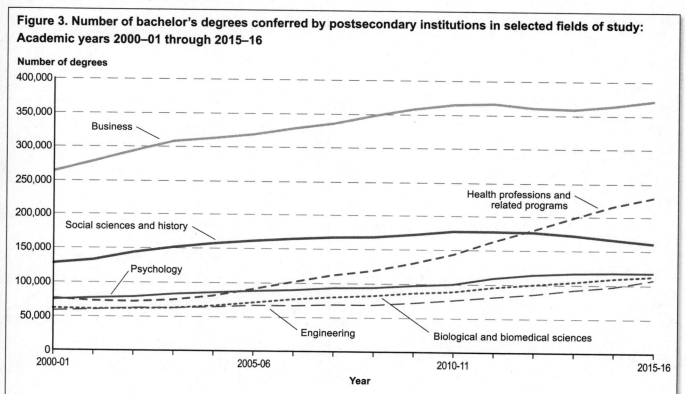

Figure 3. Number of bachelor's degrees conferred by postsecondary institutions in selected fields of study: Academic years 2000–01 through 2015–16

NOTE: The fields shown are the six programs in which the largest number of bachelor's degrees were conferred in 2015–16. Data are for postsecondary institutions participating in Title IV federal financial aid programs. Data have been adjusted where necessary to conform to the 2009–10 Classification of Instructional Programs. Some data have been revised from previously published figures.

SOURCE: U.S. Department of Education, National Center for Education Statistics, Integrated Postsecondary Education Data System (IPEDS), Fall 2001 through Fall 2016, Completions component. See *Digest of Education Statistics 2012*, table 313; and *Digest of Education Statistics 2017*, table 322.10.

Making Observations

- What are your first thoughts about the graph?
- Are you surprised by any of the data presented in this graph?

Reading a Line Graph: Second Look

1. What does this graphic show? Do not quote the title exactly.

   _____

   _____

2. What do the lines represent?

   _____

   _____

3. According to the graph, which bachelor's degree had the highest number of confirmations?

   _____

   _____

4. Which degree had the lowest number of confirmations?

   _____

   _____

5. Which degree had a decrease in confirmations between 2010–2011 and 2015–2016?

   _____

   _____

6. Which degree had an increase in confirmations between 2010–2011 and 2015–2016?

   _____

   _____

7. Why did the author choose to present this information in a line graph?

   _____

   _____

   _____

8. Think about how the information is presented in the graph. How could the graph be improved to help readers understand the information more clearly and make an informed decision about which degree to choose?

   _____

   _____

   _____

   _____

9. How does the information in the graphic support or refute the information provided in the article, "Even with Debt, College Still Pays Off." Provide textual evidence from the article to support your response.

_____

_____

_____

_____

Reading a Bar Graph: First Look

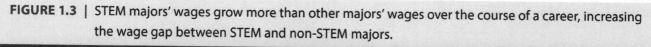

FIGURE 1.3 | STEM majors' wages grow more than other majors' wages over the course of a career, increasing the wage gap between STEM and non-STEM majors.

Median annual wages and wage growth for college-educated workers by major supergroup and age group (2013$)

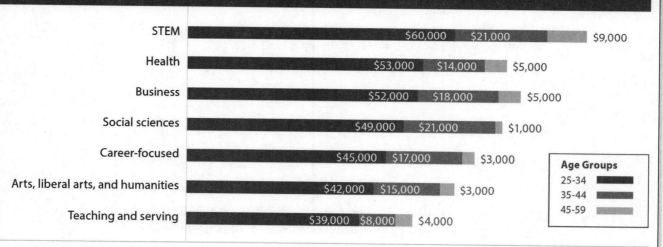

Source: Georgetown University Center on Education and the Workforce analysis of U.S. Census Bureau, *American Community Survey* micro data, 2009-2013.

Making Observations

- What data surprises you in this graph?
- What data is the most interesting to you?

Reading a Bar Graph: Second Look

10. What does this graphic show? Do not quote the title exactly.

_____

_____

_____

_____

_____

11. What do the numbers in the bars represent?

_____

_____

_____

_____

_____

_____

12. What age group earns the most money as a whole?

_____

_____

_____

_____

_____

_____

13. How does the information in the graphic support or refute the claim found in "Even with Debt, College Still Pays Off"? Provide text evidence to support your response.

_____

_____

_____

_____

_____

_____

Reading Two Bar Graphs: First Look

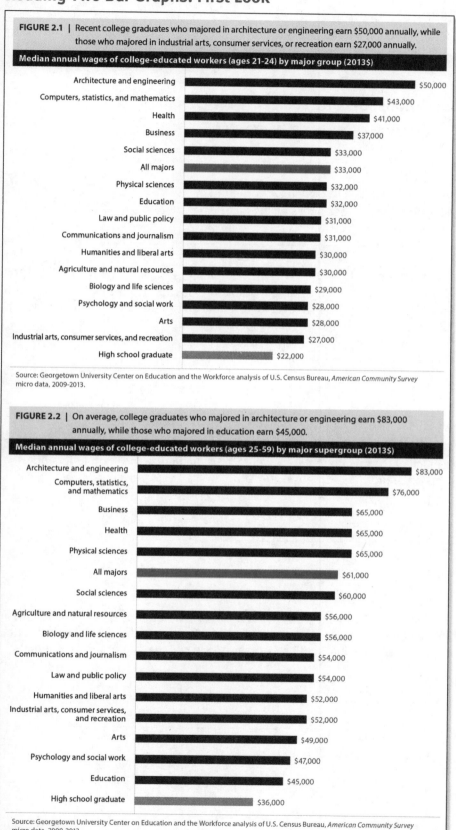

FIGURE 2.1 | Recent college graduates who majored in architecture or engineering earn $50,000 annually, while those who majored in industrial arts, consumer services, or recreation earn $27,000 annually.

Median annual wages of college-educated workers (ages 21-24) by major group (2013$)

Major group	Median annual wage
Architecture and engineering	$50,000
Computers, statistics, and mathematics	$43,000
Health	$41,000
Business	$37,000
Social sciences	$33,000
All majors	$33,000
Physical sciences	$32,000
Education	$32,000
Law and public policy	$31,000
Communications and journalism	$31,000
Humanities and liberal arts	$30,000
Agriculture and natural resources	$30,000
Biology and life sciences	$29,000
Psychology and social work	$28,000
Arts	$28,000
Industrial arts, consumer services, and recreation	$27,000
High school graduate	$22,000

Source: Georgetown University Center on Education and the Workforce analysis of U.S. Census Bureau, *American Community Survey* micro data, 2009-2013.

FIGURE 2.2 | On average, college graduates who majored in architecture or engineering earn $83,000 annually, while those who majored in education earn $45,000.

Median annual wages of college-educated workers (ages 25-59) by major supergroup (2013$)

Major supergroup	Median annual wage
Architecture and engineering	$83,000
Computers, statistics, and mathematics	$76,000
Business	$65,000
Health	$65,000
Physical sciences	$65,000
All majors	$61,000
Social sciences	$60,000
Agriculture and natural resources	$56,000
Biology and life sciences	$56,000
Communications and journalism	$54,000
Law and public policy	$54,000
Humanities and liberal arts	$52,000
Industrial arts, consumer services, and recreation	$52,000
Arts	$49,000
Psychology and social work	$47,000
Education	$45,000
High school graduate	$36,000

Source: Georgetown University Center on Education and the Workforce analysis of U.S. Census Bureau, *American Community Survey* micro data, 2009-2013.

Reading Two Bar Graphs: Second Look

14. Which career field earned the highest wages on average?

_____

_____

15. Which career field earned the lowest wages on average?

_____

_____

16. How does the information in the graphics support and/or refute the claims found in "Even with Debt, College Still Pays Off" and "The 'not everyone should go to college' argument is classist and wrong"? Provide evidence to support your response.

_____

_____

_____

_____

17. How is Figure 2.1 similar to and different from Figure 2.2? Summarize the information that is transmitted by this difference.

_____

_____

_____

_____

18. In the article, "Even with Debt, College Still Pays Off," greater wealth was given as one of the benefits of a college degree. How would your career choices and potential earnings be affected by having a college degree? Use information from the article and the four graphs to support your answer.

_____

_____

_____

_____

☑ Check Your Understanding

Do you think these graphics would persuade a student to attend college? Why or why not?

_____

_____

_____

_____

✍ Writing to Sources: Informational Text

After reviewing the data presented in the graphs, choose two of the four graphs and write a short compare/contrast paragraph about the information that is presented. Be sure to:

- Begin with a topic sentence that clearly states the comparison/contrast you plan to present.
- Explain at least one difference and one similarity between the two graphs.
- Organize your ideas logically.
- Use transitions to clarify that ideas are similar or that ideas are different.
- Support your explorations and ideas with evidence from the graphs.
- Avoid personal opinions and maintain a formal style without errors in grammar or conventions.

Don't Hate—Debate

Learning Strategies

Debate
Note-taking

INDEPENDENT READING LINK

Read and Respond

In your independent reading, look for elements of an effective argument that you have been studying in this unit, including claims, counterclaims, and supporting evidence. Note the most effective elements in your Reader/Writer Notebook.

Learning Targets

- Plan both sides of a debate by taking a stand, writing compelling reasons, identifying valid evidence, and applying persuasive rhetorical devices.

Preview

In this activity, you will prepare to debate the value of a college education as a warm-up for writing your own argument.

Introducing the Strategy: Debate

The purpose of a debate is to provide an opportunity to collect and orally present evidence supporting the affirmative and negative arguments of a proposition or issue. During a debate, participants follow a specific order of events and often have a time limit for making their points.

Preparing to Debate

A debate provides an opportunity to practice creating a reasoned argument and to identify and use appeals when trying to convince others of your point of view. In this Activity, you will engage in an informal debate.

1. Review the speeches, articles, and graphs from previous activities. Decide which side of the debate you are on: a college education is important for future success, or a college education is not important for future success.

2. Read the debate prompt.

   Debate: Is a college education important in order to be successful in life?

3. Use tables like the ones that follow to plan arguments for both sides of the issue. Consider valid reasons for and against the debate topic, find evidence in support of the arguments, and brainstorm various rhetorical devices to help you convince the audience. During the debate, you will use these notes to argue your side of the issue and address counterarguments.

YES, a college education is essential.		
Reason 1:	**Evidence:**	**Devices:**
Reason 2:	**Evidence:**	**Devices:**

NO, a college education is not essential.		
Reason 1:	**Evidence:**	**Devices:**
Reason 2:	**Evidence:**	**Devices:**

4. When it is your turn to speak, engage in the debate. Be ready to argue either claim. Keep in mind these elements of good collaborative participation:

- Be prepared and draw on that preparation by referring to text evidence.
- Respond thoughtfully to different stances.
- Adjust your speech to match the context and the task.

Sentence Frames for a Debate

- *I agree with your point about _____, but it is also important to consider _____.*
- *I disagree with your point about _____, and would like to counter with the idea that _____.*
- *You made a good point about _____, but have you considered _____?*
- *Your point about _____ is a fallacy.*

5. When it is your turn to listen, evaluate speakers' arguments for their use of rhetorical devices. Record notes in a chart similar to the one that follows as you identify examples of effective and ineffective devices, and provide a brief explanation for each example.

Use of Rhetorical Devices	Explain and Evaluate

6. After each student presents, write any comments or questions you have in your Reader/Writer Notebook. Share these questions and feedback with your classmates.

☑ Check Your Understanding

- What types of rhetorical devices provided the most effective support for the topic during the debate? Explain your answer.
- Were any devices convincing enough to make you change your mind about the issue? Explain your answer.

Planning Your Argument

Learning Strategies

Discussion Groups
Drafting
Outlining
Summarizing

Learning Targets

- Use an outline to plan an argumentative essay.
- Generate a topic sentence that includes a claim.

Preview

In this activity, you will use an outline to help you organize your argument. Then, you will draft the claim and begin gathering evidence.

Revisiting the Essential Questions

Now that you have read a variety of argumentative texts, think about the Essential Question "What makes an argument convincing?" How would you adjust your initial response? What related questions do you have?

Planning and Prewriting

Reread the assignment for Embedded Assessment 1:

Your assignment is to write an argumentative essay about the value of a college education. Your essay must be organized as an argument in which you assert a precise claim, support it with reasons and evidence, and acknowledge and refute counterarguments fairly.

1. Start a multiple-paragraph outline for your argumentative essay. Use the following frame to keep your ideas organized and clear.

Multiple-Paragraph Outline	
Main Idea	**Details**
Introduction Paragraph 1	<ul><li></li><li></li><li></li></ul>
Point A Paragraph 2	<ul><li></li><li></li><li></li></ul>
Point B Paragraph 3	<ul><li></li><li></li><li></li></ul>
Conclusion Paragraph 4	<ul><li></li><li></li><li></li></ul>

2. After you have created your multiple-paragraph outline, work with a partner to share and discuss your outline. Provide feedback to one another by asking questions and offering constructive criticism, then make any necessary changes based on the feedback you have received. The multiple-paragraph outline will be your most important tool as you begin to draft your own argumentative essay during the Embedded Assessment.

☑ Focus on the Sentence

Identify whether the following phrases are complete sentences (S) or fragments (F). Copy the complete sentences on the line beneath the text, adding correct capitalization and punctuation. Turn the fragments into complete sentences with capitalization and punctuation by using details from the texts you have read.

_____ college is valuable

_____

_____ although college graduates earn more money

_____

_____ because college is expensive

_____

_____ the benefits of a college education make it worth the cost

_____

Gathering Evidence to Support Your Claim

3. Skim through the speeches, articles, and graphs you have studied in the last few weeks. In the following table, include evidence from each of the texts that supports your claim and evidence that challenges your claim on the topic of whether or not a college education is important.

Supports My Claim	Challenges My Claim

Drafting the Embedded Assessment

Draft an essay in which you make a claim about the value of a college education. Be sure to:

- Introduce a precise claim, establishing your position.
- Use an organizing structure that will be persuasive to your audience and appropriate for the topic and context.
- Support your claim with reasons and evidence, and acknowledge and refute counterclaims fairly.
- Use quotation marks around text that comes directly from sources.

Learning Strategies

Collaborative Discussion
Generating Questions
Looping
Self-Editing/Peer-Editing
Sharing and Responding

My Notes

Learning Targets

- Revise an argumentative essay to improve and strengthen writing, focusing on purpose, organization, and language choices.
- Edit a peer's argumentative essay using collaborative feedback.

Preview

In this activity, you will revisit your argument essay to revise it, get feedback on it from a peer, and edit it.

Introducing the Strategy: Generating Questions

One way to develop a draft is by generating questions. To generate questions, a writer reads through a draft and asks questions that a reader might have about the text. The writer then finds ways to address those questions in the text.

Revising Your Draft

1. Read your draft and use the generating questions strategy to find places where you might need to add more details, supply additional evidence, write more in-depth commentary, or include better transitions to link paragraphs and create cohesion.

2. Reread your claim to make sure it is clear and arguable.

3. Reread your conclusion to make sure it is convincing and follows from the claim.

4. Reread each body paragraph to make sure each one has a reason and relevant, sufficient evidence, and relates to your claim by presenting information that is not redundant with other paragraphs. Use words and phrases to clarify the relationships between your claim, your reasons, and your evidence.

5. Skim your draft to find any rhetorical appeals you used. Determine if they are effective, and add some if you did not include any in the original draft.

6. Skim your draft to determine if your evidence is varied and sufficient.

7. Skim your draft to find your treatment of counterarguments. If you did not address any counterarguments, add some. Use words and phrases to clarify the relationships between claims and counterclaims.

8. Reread your draft and think about its organization and language. Does the essay's structure help make it more persuasive? Are your writing style and diction appropriate for your purpose and audience? Have you used sentences with parallel structures and effective placement of phrases and dependent clauses?

Peer-Editing

9. Exchange your argument essay with a peer. Identify the strengths and weaknesses of your peer's argument. Consider the following questions as you edit:

   - Is the argument clear and well developed with relevant, compelling evidence?
   - Do transitions connect paragraphs and create cohesion?
   - Are the relationships between claims, reasons, evidence, and counterclaims clear?
   - Is the commentary thoughtful?
   - Is the writer's diction appropriate for the audience and purpose?
   - Is the writing organized in a way that is persuasive?
   - Did the writer vary sentence structures to make the writing more interesting?
   - Did the writer use parallel structures properly?
   - Are there any spelling or punctuation mistakes?
   - Are there any grammar errors?

10. After reading your peer's feedback, make the appropriate revisions and edits to your argument. If you need further clarification, consider asking the following questions:

    - What do you want to know more about?
    - Which part does not make sense?
    - Which section of the text does not work?
    - How can I improve this part?

Self-Editing

11. After revising, it is essential that writers take the time to edit their own drafts to correct errors in grammar and usage, capitalization, punctuation, and spelling. Return to your draft and self-edit to strengthen the grammar and language conventions. Use your Editor's Checklist as a reference.

☑ Check Your Understanding

After editing and revising your argumentative essay draft, what areas did you determine needed improvement and were strengthened by the writing process?

INDEPENDENT READING LINK

Read and Respond

You have read a book relating to an argument about a topic that interests you. What information supports your claim? Which information counters your claim? How can you use this information to strengthen your argument? Prepare your answers in the form of a brief oral presentation.

My Notes

Writing an Argumentative Essay

 ASSIGNMENT

Your assignment is to write an argumentative essay about the value of a college education. Your essay must be organized as an argument in which you assert a precise claim, support it with reasons and evidence, and acknowledge and refute counterarguments fairly.

Planning: Make a plan for researching your topic and collecting evidence.	■ What is your claim? Is it clear? What information do you need to support it? ■ How will you use the texts you have been reading independently in your essay? ■ How will you evaluate whether you have enough information to write your draft? ■ How will you consider your audience and determine the reasons and evidence that will best convince them to support your argument?
Prewriting: Prepare to write the essay draft.	■ How will you make time to read your notes and add to, delete, or refine them as the basis for your argument? ■ What quotations will you use as evidence? ■ What information do you have to address counterarguments?
Drafting: Decide how to structure your essay.	■ What will you include in the introduction? How will you describe your claim? ■ Have you used vivid and precise language, carefully chosen diction, and formal style? ■ Have you acknowledged and addressed counterarguments? ■ Have you written a strong conclusion with a call to action?
Revising and Editing for Publication: Review and revise to make your work the best it can be.	■ Have you arranged to share your draft with a partner or with a writing group? ■ Have you consulted the Scoring Guide and the activities to prepare for revising your draft? ■ Did you use your available resources (e.g., spell check, dictionaries, Editor's Checklist) to edit for conventions and prepare your narrative for publication?

Reflection

Write an honest evaluation of your argument. Describe how you think it was effective (or not). What would you do differently next time to improve your argument?

SCORING GUIDE

Scoring Criteria	Exemplary	Proficient	Emerging	Incomplete
Ideas	The essay • includes a well-developed explanation of the issue, a claim, and a thesis statement • presents strong support for the central claim with relevant details and commentary • presents counterarguments and clearly refutes them with relevant reasoning and evidence • concludes by summarizing the main points and providing an effective call to action.	The essay • includes an explanation of the issue, a claim, and a thesis statement • presents support for the central claim but may not fully develop all evidence • presents and acknowledges counterarguments and offers some evidence to refute them • concludes by summarizing the main points and offering a call to action.	The essay • states the thesis but does not adequately explain the problem • includes some support for the claim, but it is not developed and does not provide relevant evidence or commentary • describes some counterarguments, but they are vague and are not clearly refuted • concludes by repeating main topics but ends without a suggestion for change.	The essay • states a vague or unclear thesis • contains ideas that are poorly developed or not developed at all • provides vague or no descriptions of counterarguments and refutations • concludes without summarizing main points or suggesting change.
Structure	The essay • follows a clear multiple-paragraph argumentative essay structure with a logical progression of ideas • showcases central points and uses effective transitions.	The essay • follows a multiple-paragraph argumentative structure but may not have a clearly logical progression of ideas • develops central points and uses transitions.	The essay • demonstrates an awkward, unstructured progression of ideas • spends too much time on some irrelevant details and uses few transitions.	The essay • does not follow the organization of an argumentative essay • includes some details, but the writing lacks direction and uses no transitions.
Use of Language	The essay • uses a formal style • smoothly integrates credible source material into the text (with accurate citations) • demonstrates excellent command of standard English conventions.	The essay • uses a formal style • integrates credible source material into the text (with accurate citations) • demonstrates general command of standard English conventions.	The essay • uses both informal and formal styles • may be missing citations or contain inaccurate citations • includes some grammatical weaknesses that interfere with meaning.	The essay • uses inappropriate informal style • does not include source material citations • includes several grammatical weaknesses that interfere with meaning.

Planning to Research

Learning Strategies

Brainstorming
Graphic Organizer
KWHL Chart
Note-taking

My Notes

Learning Targets

- Identify and analyze the skills and knowledge necessary to complete Embedded Assessment 2.
- Brainstorm and organize ideas, visual aids, and resources for a research presentation.

Preview

In this activity you will revisit the Essential Questions that you have been considering over the course of the unit and unpack Embedded Assessment 2. You will also begin planning your research presentation.

Revisiting the Essential Questions

1. Over the course of this unit, you have been analyzing compelling evidence and considering these four Essential Questions: *What makes an argument convincing? What makes a piece of evidence compelling? What is the value of work for teenagers? What is the value of a college education?* How do these questions relate to one another? What overarching questions could you ask that would link them together? Ask the questions and then respond to them.

Unpacking Embedded Assessment 2

Closely read the assignment for Embedded Assessment 2: Researching and Presenting a Career in order to identify and analyze the components of the assignment.

 Your assignment is to conduct research into a career that interests you. Find at least four credible sources that offer information about the requirements of that career and synthesize the information into a 5-minute presentation that includes a visual or multimedia element.

Using the assignment and Scoring Guide, work with your class to analyze the prompt and create a graphic organizer to use as a visual reminder of the required concepts (what you need to know) and skills (what you need to do). Copy the graphic organizer into your Reader/Writer Notebook. After each activity, use this graphic organizer to guide reflection about what you have learned and what you still need to learn in order to be successful on Embedded Assessment 2.

Planning for Embedded Assessment 2

2. **Brainstorm:** Start a list of careers you have been interested in at different times in your life. Add to it by discussing different careers with your classmates. Which ones sound the most interesting to you? Which one would you most like to find out about?

3. **Quickwrite:** In your Reader/Writer Notebook, write briefly about why you are interested in learning more about the career you have chosen to research.

My Notes

4. Make a list of possible sources, visual aids, and various forms of media that you could use to conduct research and present what you find. You will need to find out what qualifications and knowledge people need to work in your chosen career, what tasks are typically involved, what the working environment is generally like, etc.

5. Use the KWHL Chart in the following activity to keep track of questions you have about the career as well as what you already know about it, how you will learn about it, and what you learn about it.

Letter Writing

One of your research sources should be a person who currently works in the career you have chosen. Write this person a letter to introduce yourself and either ask your questions or set up a time to talk.

6. Write a short outline for your letter. You will need to open it with an introduction to yourself and your project, include body paragraphs that ask for specific information you want to gather, and conclude it appropriately.

7. When you are satisfied with your outline, consult a style manual to see how to format your letter. Then begin to write it using a standard letter layout and salutation.

8. After completing your letter, review it to make sure you have clearly and respectfully communicated your purpose. Your letter should include language that is appropriate for your audience and purpose, such as: *I am writing to ask you _____ . Would you please help me find information about _____?*

☑ Check Your Understanding

Meet with a partner to discuss your ideas and notes for your research project. Take turns listening, giving feedback, and asking constructive questions in order to clarify ideas and plans. Keep a list of your partner's feedback and questions in your Reader/Writer Notebook.

Diving into the Research Process

My Notes

Learning Targets

- Find and evaluate reputable sources that can be used for research.
- Generate research questions and begin to gather relevant information from multiple sources to answer them.

Preview

In this activity, you will create research questions, develop a research plan, and begin locating and evaluating sources.

Defining the Research Process

What does it mean to conduct research? You might visualize yourself sitting in front of a computer, searching for the definition of a term, information for your history paper, or the title of the latest album by your favorite artist. You may also see yourself at a library, gathering books or interviewing various people about their experiences and opinions. All these are methods of conducting research. And at the heart of all research are questions.

Identify a topic to explore or a question to answer.

Generate a major research question.

Develop a research plan.

Generate detailed questions to gain information.

Locate sources that answer your questions.

Examine your sources for credibility, bias, and faulty reasoning.

Critique your research plan and make revisions as needed.

Generate additional questions to deepen your understanding of the topic.

Locate additional sources that answer your questions.

Synthesize the information from your sources.

Present your results in an appropriate mode of delivery.

1. A KWHL chart is an effective tool to help focus and refine research by determining which of your questions need further research and where to find the information. In your Reader/Writer Notebook, create a KWHL chart similar to the one that follows. Based on your initial brainstorm from the previous activity, fill out the first three columns. Examples are provided.

K: What do I know about the career?	W: What more do I want to know about the career?	H: How will I find the information?	L: What have I learned about the career?
Chefs cook in restaurants. Different kinds of chefs prepare different kinds of foods.	Do you have to go to culinary school? What kinds of things do new chefs do in the kitchen?	Interview people who work at the new pizza place. Look at a culinary school's website.	

As you locate and examine sources, complete the KWHL chart as follows:

- In the "H" column, record the sources you have used, including URLs of web pages, book or magazine titles, and the name of the person to whom you wrote your letter.

- In the "L" column, take notes to summarize the answers to your questions.

- In the "W" column, add new questions generated by your research.

Formal vs. Informal Inquiry

Research can be formal or informal, depending on the researcher's purpose. Formal research is carefully controlled and systematic, whereas informal research is less controlled, less systematic, and sometimes quick and easy.

2. Discuss with a partner a situation in which it would be appropriate to conduct formal inquiry and one in which informal inquiry would be sufficient. Explain your ideas. Note that both lines of questioning may apply to the same general research topic.

3. Choose the major questions that you will use to guide your research. Remember, you can revise them later if necessary. Include at least one of each of the following:

- a question that explores a **need**, which is fulfilled by the career you have chosen
- a question that explores the **role** of a person who has the career
- a question that explores the **education and experience** required to be successful in the career

ACADEMIC

Credibility is the quality of being trusted or believed.

Bias is an inclination or mental leaning for or against something. Bias comes across through a writer's or speaker's choices of what to say, how to say it, and what to leave out (omission).

To be **objective** is to be based on factual information.

To be **subjective** is to be influenced by personal opinions and ideas.

My Notes

Locating and Examining Sources

In order to conduct accurate formal research for your project, you will need to examine your sources for credibility, bias, and faulty reasoning. Not all sources are created equal, particularly on the Internet. It is important to identify where each source comes from and why it was written. When looking through library catalogs or online article databases, consider the author's level of expertise as well as how long ago the article was published, or if it was sponsored by an industry or company.

4. Use the following chart to evaluate each of the digital sources you have found on the Internet.

Evaluative Question	Your Source
What is the top-level domain? .com/.net = a for-profit organization .gov = a government site .edu = an educational institution .org = a nonprofit organization	
Who is publishing the website? Is it a personal website? Is it published by an organization?	
Who is sponsoring the website? Does the website give easy access to information about the organization or group that sponsors it (such as an About Us link)?	
How timely is the website? When was the website last updated?	
What is the purpose of the website? Who is the target audience? Does it present information or opinions? Is it primarily objective or subjective?	
Who is the author of the information? What credentials does the author have? What information can you find out about this author?	
Does the website provide links? Do they work? Where do they take you? Are any additional linked sites also credible?	

Another way to check for subjectivity or bias is by cross-referencing and fact-checking the information against another source to see if the author has omitted or altered any information.

5. Choose a source to check for bias. Find three statements to verify with other sources to determine whether the statements are objective or subjective. If the author has quoted or cited a source, try to locate that source.

Statements from Your Source	Fact-Check
Statement 1:	**Cross-Reference Source:** Is your source accurate?
Statement 2:	**Cross-Reference Source:** Is your source accurate?
Statement 3:	**Cross-Reference Source:** Is your source accurate?

6. Repeat this fact-checking step with each source you intend to use.

Identifying Fallacies

One issue you may encounter in your research is finding that your sources are using fallacies or other kinds of faulty reasoning in their writing.

7. With a partner, revisit and discuss the Fallacies 101 Graphic Organizer. Write a few fallacious statements and swap them with a partner. Identify the types of fallacies that your partner's statements demonstrate and explain your reasoning.

INDEPENDENT READING LINK

Read and Discuss

Pay attention in your independent reading to how and when the author uses fallacies. Try to identify at least one fallacious statement and discuss your findings with a small group. Together, recast the statements to make them non-fallacious.

My Notes

Statement	Fallacy

8. Look back through the online sources you have examined and found credible. Reread each source for fallacious statements and highlight or annotate any you come across. Decide whether you need to replace the source or locate credible information that the faulty reasoning was based on.

Revising Your Plan or Modifying Your Question

9. Take a moment to reflect on your research process thus far. You have chosen questions and identified and evaluated sources. What has gone well? What changes might you need to make? (For example, it may be that your research has yielded very little about the career you have chosen or that your questions are not leading you to information you can use.)

_____

_____

_____

_____

_____

10. Implement necessary changes before you get any further in the development of your research presentation.

Gathering Information

11. After you have finished evaluating your sources, replace any that you have deemed unreliable. When you have selected four or more sources that are reliable and credible, use them to begin conducting thorough research in order to answer your major research questions. Use your KWHL chart to keep track of your notes and to generate new questions.

☑ Check Your Understanding

Discuss with a partner the difference between subjective and objective sources and explain why it is important to evaluate sources when conducting research.

Incorporating Sources and Synthesizing Information

Learning Targets

- Gather and synthesize information from relevant, credible source material.
- Choose which sources to quote directly and which to paraphrase.

Preview

In this activity, you will finalize your sources and begin conducting research and taking notes, modifying your research questions as needed.

Learning Strategies

Drafting
Paraphrasing
Rereading
Summarizing
Think-Pair-Share

ACADEMIC

Plagiarism is using another person's ideas without giving credit, either intentionally or unintentionally.

VOCABULARY

Using Sources Ethically

When presenting the results of your research, it is important to tell your audience which ideas and information come from your sources. This will allow them to cross-reference your information and follow the path of your research. Pretending someone else's work is your own is called plagiarism, and it is unethical. Plagiarism will hurt your credibility as a researcher. There are two ways to ethically incorporate information that comes from your sources:

- **quoting sources:** using a source's exact words
- **paraphrasing sources:** restating a source's ideas in your own words

Citing Quoted Sources

When you quote a source's exact words, you must cite the source. The most common format for citing sources in literature and language settings comes from the Modern Language Association of America (MLA). It is called the MLA format or style. In this style, in-text citations give basic information about the source of a quote in the same sentence as the quote. The citations correspond to an entry on the Works Cited page, which will include more complete information about the source.

1. Review the MLA format for in-text citations. Write any examples that help you remember the rules in your Reader/Writer Notebook.

2. In each of the following sentences, highlight the components of the in-text citation.

   And the results show that "careers for content strategists are in high demand in the 21st century" ("21st Century Careers").

   As Braeden Wong notes, "engineers are being recruited right and left for the tech industry" (8).

   "Teaching is a profession that will never become obsolete" (Whorf 22).

3. Find one quote you would like to use in your presentation. Write a sentence that incorporates the quote and includes the proper in-text citation.

My Notes

My Notes

Crediting Paraphrased Sources

How do you know when to quote a source or paraphrase it? Consider the structure of your presentation and what will best serve your audience. Paraphrasing information that is not common knowledge can help you to avoid excessive use of direct quotations, instead conveying the idea or information expressed in the source in your own words while still giving the source credit. Paraphrasing can be useful if a source is overly long or contains extra information that may not be necessary for your audience.

4. Find a chunk of text in one of your sources that you would like to paraphrase in your presentation. Read it carefully until you are confident that you understand the information and its meaning. Then write your paraphrase of the text, maintaining its meaning and giving credit to the source.

_____

_____

_____

5. Have your partner read the original quotation, then listen to you read your paraphrase. Your partner should make sure you did not use any of the specific words or phrases from the original source.

Synthesizing Information

Once you have gathered facts and research from a variety of sources, it is time to consider how you will **synthesize** the information into a logical, coherent presentation. What conclusions can you draw for your audience based on combining the information you have found? One way to do this is to look back over your quotations and summaries and group them by common ideas or the research question(s) they answer. If you do not have enough supporting information to answer one of your research questions, revise your research plan and questions.

6. Begin synthesizing your findings in a chart like the one that follows.

VOCABULARY

ACADEMIC

To **synthesize** is to combine ideas from different sources to create, express, or support a new idea or claim.

Research Question	Supporting Evidence & Quotations	My Synthesis

Creating a Bibliography

A bibliography is a tool for giving credit to your research sources. An entry typically consists of a citation that follows the guidelines of a style manual—such as MLA—for the source. A source can take many different forms: a book, an article from a magazine, a website, or other media. When you properly categorize and cite a source, you give your audience the tools to recognize your credibility and conduct research of their own. Some common rules for creating an MLA-formatted bibliography are:

- List entries alphabetically by the authors' last names.
- Alphabetize works with no known author by their titles.
- If using a website, include a URL and the date you accessed it.

Examples:

Deng, Catherine. "Finding a Career as an Artist." *The Washington Post* 23 May 2017, www.nytimes.com/2017/05/23/opinion/artist/22ander.html?_r=0. Accessed 12 May 2020.

Gowers, Richard. "The Career Trajectory of Engineers." *International Journal of Science and Engineering*, vol. 15, no. e, 2017, pp. 32–36.

Leroux, Marcel. *Global Warming: Myth Or Reality?: The Erring Ways of Climatology*. Springer, 2005.

7. In your Reader/Writer Notebook begin drafting your bibliography in MLA format. Add to it as you continue to cite sources, and alphabetize your citations in the final version.

☑ Check Your Understanding

Read the following statements from "The 'not everyone should go to college' argument is classist and wrong." Work with a partner to paraphrase the first statement. Then paraphrase the second statement on your own.

Original Statement	My Paraphrase
"But the more that fact is discussed, the more some pundits seem to think the US is at risk of an epidemic of unnecessary college-going that can be averted by singing the praises of highly skilled trades."	
"'It is common to hear the suggestion that many students should forgo college and instead seek vocational training. But most of that training takes place in community colleges or for-profit postsecondary institutions.'"	

Drafting the Embedded Assessment

Reread the assignment for Embedded Assessment 2. In your Reader/Writer Notebook, begin to organize your findings in a way that will make the most sense to your audience, noting when and how you might use various visual aids or tools to communicate information. Then start to draft your presentation. Be sure to:

- Include information from at least four relevant, credible sources that answers the major research questions you developed.
- Skillfully and ethically incorporate information and offer insightful commentary.
- Provide a clear, engaging, and appropriate introduction and conclusion.
- Avoid sources with faulty reasoning or call attention to any fallacies and incorporate a discussion of them in your presentation.

Presentation Skills and Visual Aids

Learning Targets

- Learn about and practice presentation skills.
- Give and receive feedback after practicing an informal presentation.
- Brainstorm ideas for visual aids and multimedia components.

Preview

In this activity, you will learn about and practice using presentation skills and incorporating visual aids.

My Notes

Presenting Research

Giving a presentation is more than just reading notes off a card. When you give a presentation, your audience is looking at you and listening to you. The way you deliver your information is as important as the information itself. Here are some tips to keep in mind when you are standing in front of an audience.

- Maintain good eye contact with your audience. It engages them and conveys confidence in your knowledge.
- Speak at a rate that is appropriate for the occasion and purpose, including adding pauses for effect. This will guide your audience and help them understand what you are saying.
- Speak at a volume that makes you easy to hear in the setting you are presenting in, but not so loud that you sound like you are shouting.
- Enunciate your words clearly and naturally. Look up pronunciations of technical or unfamiliar terms you will need to say aloud and practice saying them.
- Use conventional language that will communicate your ideas effectively. Combine formal, informal, and technical language to help your audience process your ideas.

1. View the presentation your teacher has selected and use the Presenting Scoring Guide in the Resources section to grade the speaker and the presentation. Explain the rationale for your grades to a small group.

Using Visual Aids

Presenting research can happen through a variety of visual media—digital slides, posters, props, diagrams, charts, videos, or other kinds of images. As you gather information and draft your presentation, consider how your audience might best be able to visualize, listen to, or interact with the information in order to understand it.

2. Revisit the presentation you viewed. What kind of multimedia did the presenter use? Was it effective? How did it enhance the presenter's point?

_____

_____

_____

INDEPENDENT READING LINK

Read and Discuss

As you read the argumentative text you have chosen, identify the author's key ideas so far. Work with a small group to present the author's argument verbally. Find or create a visual aid that helps demonstrate the argument and practice presentation skills as you present the author's ideas.

3. Apply these skills as you make an informal mini-presentation to your small group. In preparation, select one major research question that you were able to answer using online research and copy the following onto index cards:

- the research question
- the source's URL, name, or title
- a brief summary of the information you learned from that source
- at least one new question generated by the information

4. Present your findings to your group. Display the appropriate source as a visual for your audience, but use your index cards as cues while you speak. Be prepared to answer any questions your audience might have about the information you are presenting and thoughtfully listen to their feedback. Afterward, make notes about your peers' suggestions in order to improve your presentation.

5. As you listen to your peers practice presenting information, evaluate how well each presenter summarizes the information in a clear and concise manner, faces the audience, and uses eye contact. Ask clarifying questions as needed. On a separate index card for each presenter, provide feedback on the following areas.

- timing
- voice
- eye contact
- use of media
- audience engagement

6. Use the graphic organizer that follows to map out key points in your presentation and possible visual aids that can help support or demonstrate them, as well as the purpose of the visual aid (it clarifies a key point, it provides an illustrative example, it simplifies information, it engages the audience).

Key Point	Visual Aid	Purpose

Check Your Understanding

How will your visual aids help validate and expand your presentation? What other presentation skills do you need to continue to practice? How will you practice them?

Rehearsing for a Presentation

Learning Targets

- Rehearse and deliver your presentation.
- Evaluate peers' presentations.

Preview

In this activity, you will rehearse your presentation and incorporate feedback from your peers before you deliver your final presentation. You will also evaluate your peers' presentations.

Rehearsing

Rehearsing for a presentation can help you become more familiar with the information as well as help you to identify if the order of ideas needs to be changed or if additional visual aids need to be added. Be sure to practice the presentation skills you learned in the previous activity.

1. Answer the following questions in your Reader/Writer Notebook:

   - What is your plan for rehearsing your presentation delivery and getting feedback from your peers?
   - How will you use this feedback to revise and improve your presentation?
   - What presentation skills would you like to focus on?

2. In a small group, rehearse your presentation and listen to other group members' presentations. Use the following graphic organizer to give peers feedback on their rehearsals. Consider the following points as you give feedback:

   - Was the information relevant to the topic?
   - Did the visual or multimedia components emphasize the key points?
   - How engaging was the presentation? Did it feel relevant and important? Did it grab and hold your attention?
   - Did the presenter use language effectively to meet the needs of the audience, purpose, and occasion?
   - Was the speaker's evidence valid or did the speaker use any fallacious reasoning?
   - Did the presenter take advantage of technology to display information effectively?

My Notes

Presenter	Topic	Facts and Information	Visual/Multimedia Components	Effectiveness of the Presentation

My Notes

3. Use the feedback you received during your rehearsal to make any final adjustments or additions to your presentation. Based on your rehearsal, ask yourself the following questions in order to fine-tune your presentation:

- What did my audience already know about the subject? How will my presentation expand that knowledge?
- What visual or multimedia components did they find appealing? How will I use them in my presentation?
- What connections can I make between my subject and my audience to make my presentation relevant to their lives?

4. After rehearsing your presentation and listening to your classmates' presentation rehearsals, regroup to discuss which were effective and why.

☑ **Check Your Understanding**

Reflect on your own rehearsal. Did you feel prepared? How did rehearsing help you? What do you think went well? What will you do differently next time?

_____

_____

_____

_____

📖 **Independent Reading Checkpoint**

Review your independent reading. What have you learned about how to craft an effective and compelling argument? How did the author use evidence? Review any notes you took. How can you use what you have learned as you complete Embedded Assessment 2?

Researching and Presenting a Career

ASSIGNMENT

Your assignment is to conduct research into a career that interests you. Find at least four credible sources that offer information about the requirements of that career and synthesize the information into a 5-minute presentation that includes a visual or multimedia element.

Planning: Use resources, notes, and feedback to plan, conduct, and record your research.	■ Which career will you investigate? ■ What research questions will help you explore the career topic and investigate relevant information? ■ What will you do if you encounter any fallacies in the information you find? ■ How will you record citations, information, and source evaluations as you gather answers and evidence? ■ How will you record sources to create an alphabetized bibliography?
Creating and Rehearsing: Create your presentation and rehearse presenting it.	■ How will you select the most relevant facts and sufficient details to develop your presentation for your audience? ■ How will you organize your presentation in a structure and flow of information that engages the audience? ■ How will you select and incorporate visual aids or other multimedia into your presentation? ■ What is your plan for rehearsing your presentation delivery and getting feedback from peers to revise and improve your presentation?
Presenting and Listening: Use effective speaking and listening as a presenter and audience member.	■ How will you use notes for your talking points so that you can maintain eye contact with your audience? ■ During your peers' presentations, how will you use the Scoring Guide to organize your notes on each presentation?

Reflection

After completing this Embedded Assessment, think about how you planned for, organized, and accomplished the tasks for this assignment. Write a reflection explaining how evaluating and identifying sources that were valid and reliable helped you to create your research presentation. How did your visual aids enhance your presentation? How effectively did you reach your audience?

SCORING GUIDE

Scoring Criteria	Exemplary	Proficient	Emerging	Incomplete
Ideas	The presentation • includes substantial information about the subject from a variety of credible sources • skillfully and ethically incorporates information from sources and offers insightful commentary about the subject.	The presentation • includes sufficient information about the subject from a variety of credible sources • effectively and ethically incorporates information from sources and offers sufficient commentary about the subject.	The presentation • includes information about the subject from some sources • incorporates information from sources and offers commentary about the subject, but relies heavily on one or the other.	The presentation • does not include information from sources or includes information from unreliable sources • does not incorporate information from sources or offer commentary about the subject.
Structure	The presentation • provides a clear, engaging, and appropriate introduction and conclusion • is thoughtfully and appropriately paced throughout • makes use of highly engaging visuals and/or multimedia that enhance delivery.	The presentation • provides a clear and appropriate introduction and conclusion • is appropriately paced most of the time • makes use of visuals and/or multimedia that enhance delivery.	The presentation • provides an adequate introduction and conclusion • is sometimes paced inappropriately • makes use of some visuals and/or multimedia that somewhat enhance delivery.	The presentation • does not provide an introduction or conclusion • is not paced appropriately • makes use of few visuals and/or multimedia to enhance delivery.
Use of Language	The presentation • demonstrates accomplished oral communication skills (comfortable eye contact; effective speaking rate, volume, and enunciation).	The presentation • demonstrates adequate oral communication skills (some appropriate eye contact; adequate speaking rate, volume, and enunciation).	The presentation • demonstrates inadequate oral communication skills (occasional eye contact; somewhat adequate speaking rate, volume, and enunciation).	The presentation • demonstrates inadequate oral communication skills (no eye contact; inadequate speaking rate, volume, and enunciation).

POWERFUL OPENINGS

I have no idea how I untangled the complicated process of words and thought, but it happened quickly and naturally. By the time I was two, all my memories had words, and all my words had meanings.

But only in my head.

I have never spoken one single word. I am almost eleven years old.

—from "Out of My Mind," by Sharon Draper

ACTIVITY **CONTENTS**

CONTENTS

ACTIVITY

My Independent Reading List

My Independent
Reading List

Text not included in these materials.

Previewing the Unit

Learning Targets
- Preview the big ideas for the unit.
- Create a plan for reading independently.

Preview

In this activity, you will explore the big ideas and tasks of Unit 4 and make plans for your own independent reading.

My Notes

About the Unit

Instead of reading a novel in its entirety at the beginning of this unit—tracking all the twists and turns of the plot and how themes resurface and evolve over the course of the story—you will closely read the openings of several novels. In doing so, you will gain an appreciation for the captivating ways writers lure their readers in, one line at a time. Then you will settle in to read an entire novel about a young girl's coming-of-age experience and research the novel's historical and cultural context.

Essential Questions

Based on your current thinking, how would you answer these questions?

1. What makes an opening powerful?
2. What makes you want to keep reading a book?
3. How can understanding a book's context help you understand the book?

🎲 Planning Independent Reading

In this unit, you will read a novel in class that tells the story of a young girl coming of age in a real historical period. In your independent reading, you have the opportunity to read another book, either fiction or nonfiction, on a related topic that interests you. Consider finding books about people coming of age or books related to the Jim Crow era or the Civil Rights Movement. Reading other texts that relate to the theme and context of *To Kill a Mockingbird* will deepen your understanding and allow you to make meaningful connections. To find a book you will like, consider these questions.

- What kinds of books have you enjoyed reading in the past? Do you prefer fiction or nonfiction? Do you have a favorite author?

- Who are some writers and thought leaders from the Jim Crow era and the Civil Rights Movement, and what books by or about them might you be interested in reading?

- Think of some coming-of-age stories you have seen in movies or on television. Do you know if any were based on a book?

- When you find a book you might like, flip through the first section. Does it seem interesting? Does it seem too easy, too hard, or just right?

Learning Strategies

Graphic Organizer

My Notes

Learning Targets

- Analyze how filmmakers introduce a story's setting and characters.
- Draw inferences about how a novelist's process for introducing a story is similar to and different from that of a filmmaker.

Preview

In this activity, you will view the beginnings of a few different movies and then discuss some techniques the filmmakers used to hook their audiences.

Opening Writing Prompt

Imagine yourself in a movie theater—or on your own couch—waiting for a movie you have never seen to begin. Then respond to the following questions.

> What do you expect to happen in the first 3–5 minutes of the film, and why do you have these expectations? How often does the beginning of a film really hook you? What are movies you can think of that have interesting beginnings?

Watching the Beginnings

Make copies of the following chart in your Reader/Writer Notebook and fill one in for each film opening you watch with your class.

Title of Film:	
Setting	What do you know about the world, or the setting, that the film is presenting?
	What is the time period?
	What is the location?
	What is the time of day or date?
	How is the setting similar to or different from the place and time in which you live?

		My Notes
Characters	Who are the characters?	
	Which of the characters are the main characters? How do you know?	
	What do you know (or suspect you know) about each character?	
	What questions do you have about them?	
Film Techniques	How does the filmmaker use the following techniques to create a world and/or establish the characters in this film?	
	Lighting (how light is used in the scene):	
	Framing (how the object is positioned within the shot; how much of the movie screen the object occupies):	
	Camera angles (where the camera is placed in relation to the subject):	
	Editing (how different shots are connected to one another):	
Make a Prediction	What do you think will happen in the rest of the film, and what details or key words and phrases from the film's opening help you predict or infer this?	

☑ Check Your Understanding

Think about what the filmmaker did in each of the film beginnings you watched. What is the filmmaker's job at the beginning of a film? How do filmmakers draw viewers into a film? How might this process be similar to and different from that of the novelist at the beginning of a novel?

Where Am I? Orienting Yourself in a Novel's World

Learning Strategies

Close Reading
Graphic Organizer

My Notes

Learning Targets

- Analyze the settings of novels based on their opening paragraphs.
- Generate questions and draw conclusions about events that will happen in a novel.
- Integrate ideas from multiple texts to build knowledge and vocabulary about realistic novels.

Preview

In this activity, you will read excerpts from the openings of two novels and discuss how those openings hook readers.

Opening Writing Prompt

Read this opening line of a novel and jot down any telling details that indicate what kind of world you are entering.

It was a bright cold day in April, and the clocks were striking thirteen.

As You Read

- Highlight words, descriptions, and imagery that give you clues about the novel's world.
- Circle unfamiliar words or phrases. Try to determine the meaning of the words by using context clues, word parts, or a dictionary.

About the Author

George Orwell was the pseudonym of author Eric Arthur Blair (1903–1950), who took the pen name early in his writing career to avoid embarrassing his family. From boyhood, Orwell was considered both brilliant and eccentric, and his writing reflected these qualities, as well as his rejection of the social norms by which he had been raised. Although Orwell is best known for his novella *Animal Farm* and his dystopian novel *1984*, he also wrote poetry, literary criticism, news articles, and polemical essays, or essays that inspire controversy. In one such essay, "Politics and the English Language," Orwell addresses writers and argues in favor of using simple, straightforward language to boldly express ideas. He explains how clear writing correlates with clear thought, while also accusing some political leaders of using vague language, such as euphemisms, to manipulate the way people think.

Novel

from **1984**

by **George Orwell**

KNOWLEDGE QUEST

Knowledge Question:

How can a fictional setting seem real?

In Activity 4.3, you will read the openings of two novels that use realistic details to hook readers. While you read and build knowledge about the theme of realistic novels, think about your answer to the Knowledge Question.

1   It was a bright cold day in April, and the clocks were striking thirteen. Winston Smith, his chin nuzzled into his breast in an effort to escape the vile wind, slipped quickly through the glass doors of Victory Mansions, though not quickly enough to prevent a swirl of gritty dust from entering along with him.

2   The hallway **smelt** of boiled cabbage and old rag mats. At one end of it a colored poster, too large for indoor display, had been tacked to the wall. It depicted simply an enormous face, more than a meter wide: the face of a man of about forty-five, with a heavy black mustache and ruggedly handsome features. Winston made for the stairs. It was no use trying the **lift**. Even at the best of times it was seldom working, and at present the electric current was cut off during daylight hours. It was part of the economy drive in preparation for Hate Week. The **flat** was seven flights up, and Winston, who was thirty-nine and had a **varicose ulcer** above his right ankle, went slowly, resting several times on the way. On each landing, opposite the lift shaft, the poster with the enormous face gazed from the wall. It was one of those pictures which are so contrived that the eyes follow you about when you move. BIG BROTHER IS WATCHING YOU, the caption beneath it ran.

3   Inside the flat a fruity voice was reading out a list of figures which had something to do with the production of pig iron. The voice came from an oblong metal plaque like a dulled mirror which formed part of the surface of the right-hand wall. Winston turned a switch and the voice sank somewhat, though the words were still distinguishable. The instrument (the telescreen, it was called) could be dimmed, but there was no way of shutting it off completely. He moved over to the window: a smallish, frail figure, the meagerness of his body merely emphasized by the blue overalls which were the uniform of the Party. His hair was very fair, his face naturally **sanguine**, his skin roughened by coarse soap and blunt razor blades and the cold of the winter that had just ended.

4   Outside, even through the shut window pane, the world looked cold. Down in the street little eddies of wind were whirling dust and torn paper into spirals, and though the sun was shining and the sky a harsh blue, there seemed to be no color in anything, except the posters that were plastered everywhere. The black-mustachio'd face gazed down from every commanding corner. There was one on the house front immediately opposite. BIG BROTHER IS WATCHING YOU, the caption said, while the dark eyes looked deep into Winston's own. Down at street level another poster, torn at one corner, flapped fitfully in the wind, alternately covering and uncovering the single word INGSOC. In the far distance a helicopter skimmed down between the roofs, hovered for an instant like a bluebottle, and darted away again with a curving flight. It was the Police Patrol, snooping into people's windows. The patrols did not matter, however. Only the Thought Police mattered.

My Notes

smelt: smelled

lift: elevator

flat: apartment

varicose ulcer: painful, bloody sore that takes several weeks to heal

sanguine: a healthy reddish color

My Notes

_____

_____

_____

_____

_____

_____

_____

_____

_____

_____

_____

_____

_____

_____

_____

_____

_____

_____

_____

_____

_____

_____

_____

_____

_____

_____

_____

_____

_____

_____

_____

_____

⊘ Knowledge Quest

- What do the characters and events remind you of in the real world?
- Which details in the novel seem less realistic than others?

Working from the Text

1. With a partner, go back to the text and highlight the most striking examples of imagery and details that elicit the strongest emotional responses as you read.

2. How would you sum up the physical details of the novel's world? Write your one-word response in the center of the web. Then, in the surrounding ovals, write quotes from the text that support your one-word response.

3. How would you sum up the emotional effect of the novel's world? Write your one-word response in the center of the web. Then, in the surrounding ovals, write quotes from the text that support your one-word response.

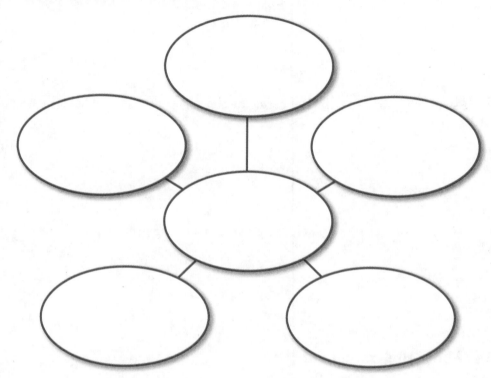

Analysis of Setting

4. Write a brief paragraph summarizing your observations and analysis of the setting of *1984*. Use the quotes from the webs you completed about the physical details and emotional effect of the novel's world to help you.

_____

_____

_____

_____

_____

_____

_____

_____

_____

Drawing Conclusions and Generating Questions

As directed by your teacher, discuss the following questions with your classmates.

- What are some questions that the excerpt from *1984* provokes?

- What are some things that seem mysterious at the beginning of the excerpt but are easier to understand later on?

- What do the details of the setting imply about the economic and political state of the novel's world?

☑ **Check Your Understanding**

How does Orwell hook readers with the first paragraphs of his novel *1984*?

📝 **Opening Writing Prompt**

Read this opening line of another novel and jot down any telling details that indicate what kind of world you are entering.

The circus arrives without warning.

As You Read

- Highlight words, descriptions, and imagery that give you clues about the novel's world.
- Circle unfamiliar words or phrases. Try to determine the meaning of the words by using context clues, word parts, or a dictionary.

About the Author

Erin Morgenstern (b. 1978) is one of a growing number of authors who wrote their first novels while participating in National Novel Writing Month, an annual writing challenge more commonly known as NaNoWriMo. During NaNoWriMo, writers try to draft 50,000 words in only 30 days. Morgenstern calls the event "magical," and she appreciates it for the company she keeps as she and other writers race toward the finish line. She also values its tight deadline, which forces her to get her ideas down quickly, without editing them as she goes. Says Morgenstern, "Before NaNoWriMo, I was the sort of person who would write a page and hate it, so I'd stop, when really you need to keep going and write more pages." Morgenstern says she explored ideas for *The Night Circus* over the course of two consecutive NaNoWriMo's, writing a different draft each time. Then she took the second draft through a heavy revision phase before finally having it published. Since then, *The Night Circus* has spent seven weeks as a *New York Times* Best Seller and won the American Library Association's Alex Award and the Locus Award for Best First Novel.

Novel

from The Night Circus

by **Erin Morgenstern**

KNOWLEDGE QUEST

Knowledge Question:
How can a fictional setting seem real?

Anticipation

1 The circus arrives without warning.

2 No announcements precede it, no paper notices on downtown posts and billboards, no mentions or advertisements in local newspapers. It is simply there, when yesterday it was not.

3 The towering tents are striped in white and black, no golds and crimsons to be seen. No color at all, save for the neighboring trees and the grass of the surrounding fields. Black-and-white stripes on grey sky; countless tents of varying shapes and sizes, with an elaborate wrought-iron fence encasing them in a colorless world. Even what little ground is visible from outside is black or white, painted or powdered, or treated with some other circus trick.

4 But it is not open for business. Not just yet.

5 Within hours everyone in town has heard about it. By afternoon news has spread several towns over. Word of mouth is a more effective method of advertisement than typeset words and exclamation points on paper pamphlets or posters. It is impressive and unusual news, the sudden appearance of a mysterious circus. People marvel at the staggering height of the tallest tents. They stare at the clock that sits just inside the gates that no one can properly describe.

crimsons: dark reds

My Notes

6 And the black sign painted in white letters that hangs upon the gates, the one that reads:

Opens at Nightfall
Closes at Dawn

7 "What kind of circus is only open at night?" people ask. No one has a proper answer, yet as dusk approaches there is a substantial crowd of spectators gathering outside the gates.

8 You are amongst them, of course. Your curiosity got the better of you, as curiosity is wont to do. You stand in the fading light, the scarf around your neck pulled up against the chilly evening breeze, waiting to see for yourself exactly what kind of circus only opens once the sun sets.

9 The ticket booth clearly visible behind the gates is closed and barred. The tents are still, save for when they ripple ever so slightly in the wind. The only movement within the circus is the clock that ticks by the passing minutes, if such a wonder of sculpture can even be called a clock.

10 The circus looks abandoned and empty. But you think perhaps you can smell caramel wafting through the evening breeze, beneath the crisp scent of the autumn leaves. A subtle sweetness at the edges of the cold.

11 The sun disappears completely beyond the horizon, and the remaining luminosity shifts from dusk to twilight. The people around you are growing restless from waiting, a sea of shuffling feet, murmuring about abandoning the endeavor in search of someplace warmer to pass the evening. You yourself are debating departing when it happens.

12 First, there is a popping sound. It is barely audible over the wind and conversation. A soft noise like a kettle about to boil for tea. Then comes the light.

13 All over the tents, small lights begin to flicker, as though the entirety of the circus is covered in particularly bright fireflies. The waiting crowd quiets as it watches this display of illumination. Someone near you gasps. A small child claps his hands with glee at the sight.

4.3

14 When the tents are all aglow, sparkling against the night sky, the sign appears.

15 Stretched across the top of the gates, hidden in curls of iron, more firefly-like lights flicker to life. They pop as they brighten, some accompanied by a shower of glowing white sparks and a bit of smoke. The people nearest to the gates take a few steps back.

16 At first, it is only a random pattern of lights. But as more of them ignite, it becomes clear that they are aligned in scripted letters. First a *C* is distinguishable, followed by more letters. A *q*, oddly, and several *e*'s. When the final bulb pops alight, and the smoke and sparks dissipate, it is finally legible, this elaborate incandescent sign. Leaning to your left to gain a better view, you can see that it reads:

Le Cirque des Rêves

17 Some in the crowd smile knowingly, while others frown and look questioningly at their neighbors. A child near you tugs on her mother's sleeve, begging to know what it says.

18 "The Circus of Dreams," comes the reply. The girl smiles delightedly.

19 Then the iron gates shudder and unlock, seemingly by their own volition. They swing outward, inviting the crowd inside.

20 Now the circus is open.

21 Now you may enter.

⊘ Knowledge Quest
- What is your first impression of the kind world the author describes?
- Which words or phrases does the author use to make the circus seem real in your mind?

⊘ Knowledge Quest
Think about the novel openings you have read. How do the writers create worlds that seem real? Write a few paragraphs to compare and contrast how the writers created realistic worlds in the openings of these novels. Be sure to:

- Include a topic sentence and cite textual evidence as support.
- Organize your ideas in a way that makes similarities and differences clear.
- Use transitions to make connections between ideas clear.
- Provide a conclusion that explains the importance of setting in the novels.

My Notes

ⓘ INDEPENDENT READING LINK
You can continue to build your knowledge about this theme by reading related fiction at ZINC Reading Labs.

Select the **fiction** filter and type keywords such as *realistic* in the **Search all ZINC articles** field.

 ZINC

volition: will

Working from the Text

5. Go back to the text and highlight the most striking examples of imagery and details that elicit the strongest emotional response as you read.

6. How would you sum up the physical details of the novel's world? Write your one-word response in the center of the web. Then, in the surrounding ovals, write quotes from the text that support your one-word response.

7. How would you sum up the emotional effect of the novel's world? Write your one-word response in the center of the web. Then, in the surrounding ovals, write quotes from the text that support your one-word response.

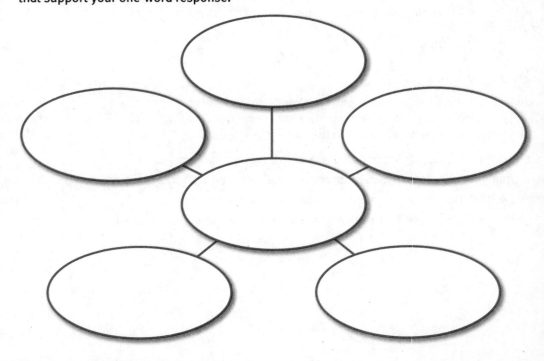

Analysis of Setting

8. Write a brief paragraph summarizing your observations and analysis of the setting of *The Night Circus*. Use the quotes from the webs you completed about the physical details and emotional effect of the novel's world to help you.

_____

_____

_____

_____

_____

_____

_____

_____

Drawing Conclusions and Generating Questions

Discuss the following questions with your classmates.

- What are some questions that the excerpt from *The Night Circus* provokes?

- What are some things that seem mysterious at the beginning of the excerpt but are easier to understand later on?

☑ Check Your Understanding

How does Morgenstern hook readers with the first paragraphs of her novel *The Night Circus*?

INDEPENDENT READING LINK

Read and Respond

Reread the opening paragraphs of the text you are reading independently. How does the author make you interested in reading more of the story or text? Does the author use any of the techniques you learned from Orwell and Morgenstern for hooking the reader? Write a paragraph that summarizes the beginning few paragraphs of the text you are reading and describes how the author uses telling details to create suspense or generate the reader's interest in the text's topic. Eliminate widow.

My Notes

_____

_____

_____

_____

_____

_____

_____

_____

_____

_____

_____

_____

_____

_____

_____

_____

_____

_____

Learning Strategies

Close Reading
Quickwrite

My Notes

Learning Targets

- Analyze an image and write a paragraph that vividly describes it.
- Use carefully chosen words to create an original opening scene.

Preview

In this activity, you will write a description of a setting in a photograph. Then you will write an original opening using techniques for hooking readers that you learned from the authors of *1984* and *The Night Circus*.

📝 Opening Writing Prompt

Describe this scene without using the word "house." You can write from any narrative point of view (first, second, or third), and you should use as many details as possible to help the reader envision and feel this scene.

Sharing Sentences and Writing Strategies

Reread the description you wrote about the house and then discuss the following questions.

1. What physical details did you provide to lead readers to infer you were describing a dilapidated house?

2. How did you use your imagination to explain what might have previously happened in this place?

3. Did you use figurative language to convey the mood?

✍ Writing Prompt: Literary

Describe an original setting by choosing a narrative point of view, picturing the scene in your mind's eye or finding an image that inspires you, and choosing an appropriate genre. Be sure to:

• Include imagery that appeals to many of the senses.

• Consider different ways you might orient your reader with telling details.

• Think about what you want your reader to feel when entering your world.

• Revisit your opening line when you are finished and assess whether it sets the appropriate tone for your setting, revising it as necessary.

Reflecting on the Writing Process: Setting

4. What physical details were you trying to communicate, and what emotional effects were you hoping the setting would have on the reader? What specific word-choice or language decisions did you make in an effort to achieve those effects?

_____

_____

_____

5. Did you include any telling details with the aim of leading the reader to make inferences? If so, what were the details and what inferences did you want the reader to make?

_____

_____

_____

6. Trade setting descriptions with a partner and read your partner's description. Then draw and complete two web graphic organizers for your partner's description. Model your webs after those you completed for the opening settings of *1984* and *The Night Circus*, basing one on a word that describes the physical details of the setting and the other on a word that describes the emotional effect of the setting.

7. Review the web graphic organizers your partner completed to describe the physical details and emotional effect of the setting you wrote about. What adjectives did your partner use to summarize your setting description? What quotes did your partner use to support his or her adjective choices? Do your reader's impressions align with your intentions as a writer?

_____

_____

_____

_____

_____

_____

Assess and Reflect

Read the following excerpt from *Harry Potter and the Sorcerer's Stone*. Then write a brief paragraph summarizing your observations and analysis of the setting it describes.

> Harry had never even imagined such a strange and splendid place. It was lit by thousands and thousands of candles that were floating in midair over four long tables, where the rest of the students were sitting. These tables were laid with glittering golden plates and goblets. At the top of the hall was another long table where the teachers were sitting. Professor McGonagall led the first years up here, so that they came to a halt in a line facing the other students, with the teachers behind them. The hundreds of faces staring at them looked like pale lanterns in the flickering candlelight. Dotted here and there among the students, the ghosts shone misty silver. Mainly to avoid all the staring eyes, Harry looked upward and saw a velvety black ceiling dotted with stars. He heard Hermione whisper, "It's bewitched to look like the sky outside. I read about it in *Hogwarts: A History*."
>
> It was hard to believe there was a ceiling there at all, and that the Great Hall didn't simply open on to the heavens.

The Role of the Narrator

Learning Targets

- Analyze character and narrative point of view based on the openings of two novels.
- Rewrite the opening of a novel from an alternative point of view.

Preview

In this activity, you will read and discuss the opening paragraphs of two novels, each of which is written from a different narrative point of view. Then you will choose a novel opening to rewrite from a different narrative point of view.

Learning Strategies

Close Reading
Marking the Text

Opening Writing Prompt

You are about to meet two very different characters: the narrator from Sharon Draper's novel *Out of My Mind*, and Montag, from Ray Bradbury's novel *Fahrenheit 451*. Find out about these characters as you read the opening of each novel. Then write a few sentences describing each character.

About the Author

Sharon Draper (b. 1948) has not only received many honors for her book writing, including five Coretta Scott King Awards and multiple recognitions for the body of work she's created for young readers, but she also has received numerous commendations for her work as an educator, including the Ohio Teacher of the Year Award and the Governor's Educational Leadership Award. Draper's love of literature and education began when she was a young girl. An avid reader by the time she started elementary school, Draper soon felt the call to instill her passion for learning in others. She followed this call and became a high school teacher, known for giving challenging writing assignments and encouraging students to enter their writing in contests. One day, the tables were turned on her when a student approached her with an ad for a short story competition and dared her to enter. She took her student's dare and won that contest—and the rest, as they say, is history.

Novel

from **Out of My Mind**

by **Sharon Draper**

Words.

1 I'm surrounded by thousands of words. Maybe millions.

2 *Cathedral. Mayonnaise. Pomegranate.*

3 *Mississippi. Neapolitan. Hippopotamus.*

4 *Silky. Terrifying. Iridescent.*

5 *Tickle. Sneeze. Wish. Worry.*

6 Words have always swirled around me like snowflakes—each one delicate and different, each one melting untouched in my hands.

7 Deep within me, words pile up in huge drifts. Mountains of phrases and sentences and connected ideas. Clever expressions. Jokes. Love songs.

8 From the time I was really little—maybe just a few months old—words were like sweet, liquid gifts, and I drank them like lemonade. I could almost taste them. They made my jumbled thoughts and feelings have substance. My parents have always blanketed me with conversation. They chattered and babbled. They verbalized and vocalized. My father sang to me. My mother whispered her strength into my ear.

9 Every word my parents spoke to me or about me I absorbed and kept and remembered. All of them.

10 I have no idea how I untangled the complicated process of words and thought, but it happened quickly and naturally. By the time I was two, all my memories had words, and all my words had meanings.

11 But only in my head.

12 I have never spoken one single word. I am almost eleven years old.

Making Observations
- How does the opening of this novel make you feel?
- What is one adjective you could use to describe the narrator, Melody?

Novel

from Fahrenheit 451

by **Ray Bradbury**

1   It was a pleasure to burn.

2   It was a special pleasure to see things eaten, to see things blackened and changed. With the brass nozzle in his fists, with this great python spitting its venomous kerosene upon the world, the blood pounded in his head, and his hands were the hands of some amazing conductor playing all the symphonies of blazing and burning to bring down the tatters and charcoal ruins of history. With his symbolic helmet numbered 451 on his stolid head, and his eyes all orange flame with the thought of what came next, he flicked the igniter and the house jumped up in a gorging fire that burned the evening sky red and yellow and black. He strode in a swarm of fireflies. He wanted above all, like the old joke, to shove a marshmallow on a stick in the furnace, while the flapping pigeon-winged books died on the porch and lawn of the house. While the books went up in sparkling whirls and blew away on a wind turned dark with burning.

3   Montag grinned the fierce grin of all men singed and driven back by flame.

Making Observations

- How does the opening of this novel make you feel?
- What is one adjective you could use to describe to Montag?

nozzle: tube at the end of a hose
tatters: old and ragged pieces

4.5

INDEPENDENT READING LINK
Read and Research

Consider conducting research into the life, work, and writing process of the author of the book you are reading independently. Before beginning your research, brainstorm some questions you have about the author. For example, *When did the author publish the book I am reading? How has this book been received by readers and critics? Why did the author write this book? What suggestions does this book's author have for other writers?* Then search for answers to your questions, using the Internet or print resources, such as biographies, magazine interviews, and encyclopedias. As you conduct research, take notes and make sure you are using credible sources and cross-checking information to make sure it is factual. After you have finished your research, write a paragraph about your author to share with your peers.

Working from the Text

1. What is the narrative point of view in the excerpt from Draper's novel, and how does it affect the way you perceive and feel about the character of Melody?

2. What is the narrative point of view in the excerpt from Bradbury's novel, and how does it affect the way you perceive and feel about the character of Montag?

 Gaining Perspectives

Melody and Montag appear to be drastically different people; however, they both display physical or mental health concerns. One doesn't speak, and the other enjoys burning things. Imagine you are a teacher and have students with mental or physical health concerns. How could you gather information to help you best understand their health and promote their well-being? Discuss the following questions with a partner: How could you make sure the information is valid? How would you protect the students' privacy? Then write a summary of your discussion in your Reader/Writer Notebook.

 Writing Prompt: Literary

Choose one of the following writing prompts:

a. Rewrite a section of the *Out of My Mind* novel opening from the third-person point of view, allowing the reader to see Melody from more of a distance.

b. Rewrite a section of the *Fahrenheit 451* novel opening from the first-person point of view, allowing the reader direct access into Montag's thoughts.

As you rewrite, keep the spirit of the passage but shift the perspective. For example, if you are writing from Montag's first-person perspective, you cannot alter the fact that he is experiencing pleasure, but you can give more detail about what he is thinking as he burns the books.

 Check Your Understanding

How does shifting narrative perspective alter the reader's feelings toward each character?

Word Study

Learning Strategies

Predicting
Previewing
Word Sort

Learning Targets

- Use print and digital resources to define words and phrases.
- Analyze the connotations of words.
- Make predictions about the tone and content of a text, based on its use of language.

Preview

In this activity, you will define and analyze a group of words to help you build background knowledge and make predictions about the opening paragraphs of a novel.

My Notes

Defining the Words

1. Work together with a group of your classmates to sort the following words into categories based on the words' meanings and relationships. Consult print and digital resources, such as a dictionary, a thesaurus, or an encyclopedia, to help you create categories. Then write the categories and each word and its definition(s) in your Reader/Writer Notebook.

paper	ramparts	cane	France
monarch	German	hum	The Channel
ink	Her Majesty	flutter	revolution
bombardier	hive	sightless	worker bees
leaflets	mortars	rattling	cannon
queen	swirl	artillery	cartwheels
Braille	drone		

Making Predictions

2. Based on your categorization of the words, answer the following questions about the opening of the novel they come from.

- What can you theorize about the novel's subject? Write your answer and tell which words support your response.

_____

_____

_____

_____

- What can you theorize about the novel's setting? Write your answer and tell which words support your response.

_____

_____

_____

_____

☑ Check Your Understanding

Make a prediction about the opening of the novel you are about to read, based on what you've inferred from words that come from it. Consider using one of the following sentence frames to help you write your prediction.

I predict that the first chapter will be set in _____ based on the author's use of the words _____ .

I predict that the first chapter will be set during _____ based on the author's use of the words _____ .

I predict that the first chapter will be about _____ based on the author's use of the words _____ .

The Power of the Omniscient Narrator

Learning Strategies

Close Reading
Graphic Organizer
Predicting

Learning Targets

- Analyze the setting of a novel based on its opening paragraphs.
- Conduct research to examine the setting of a novel.
- Visualize the setting of a novel.

Preview

In this activity, you will read an excerpt from the beginning of *All the Light We Cannot See* and then explore its setting and narrative perspective.

Opening Writing Prompt

Read the first two paragraphs from the opening of *All the Light We Cannot See* by Anthony Doerr, taking special notice of the words you sorted in the previous activity. Then answer the following question.

> Does anything about Doerr's use of these words in the passage surprise you? Explain your answer.

As You Read

- Underline clues to the novel's setting and historical context.
- Circle unfamiliar words or phrases. Try to determine the meaning of the words by using context clues, word parts, or a dictionary.

About the Author

Anthony Doerr (b. 1973) is a fiction writer whose stories often are set in places where he has lived or spent a significant amount of time. Says Doerr, "When you're working lots every day, almost everything you read or hear or see outside of those hours becomes relevant [to your writing] ... the world starts to glow with pertinence." For example, while writing *All the Light We Cannot See*, Doerr pulled inspiration from daily walks in the areas inhabited by his characters, from trips to the museum, from dozens of books on the period, as well as from musical compositions by Claude Debussy, a famous composer from the region. He is the author of both short stories and novels, and he has received multiple awards for his work, including the Pulitzer Prize and the Rome Prize from the American Academy of Arts and Letters and the American Academy in Rome.

My Notes

My Notes

Novel

from All the Light We Cannot See (Part 1)

by **Anthony Doerr**

7 August 1944

Leaflets

1   At dusk they pour from the sky. They blow across the **ramparts**, turn cartwheels over rooftops, flutter into the ravines between houses. Entire streets swirl with them, flashing white against the cobbles. *Urgent message to the inhabitants of this town*, they say. *Depart immediately to open country.*

2   The tide climbs. The moon hangs small and yellow and gibbous. On the rooftops of beachfront hotels to the east, and in the gardens behind them, a half-dozen American artillery units drop incendiary rounds into the mouths of mortars.

Bombers

3   They cross the Channel at midnight. There are twelve and they are named for songs: *Stardust* and *Stormy Weather* and *In the Mood* and *Pistol-Packin' Mama.* The sea glides along far below, spattered with the countless chevrons of whitecaps. Soon enough, the navigators can **discern** the low moonlit lumps of islands ranged along the horizon.

4   France.

5   Intercoms crackle. Deliberately, almost lazily, the bombers shed altitude. Threads of red light ascend from anti-air emplacements up and down the coast. Dark, ruined ships appear, scuttled or destroyed, one with its bow shorn away, a second flickering as it burns. On an outermost island, panicked sheep run zigzagging between rocks.

6   Inside each airplane, a bombardier peers through an aiming window and counts to twenty. Four five six seven. To the bombardiers, the walled city on its granite headland, drawing ever closer, looks like an unholy tooth, something black and dangerous, a final abscess to be lanced away.

Making Observations
- What is happening in this excerpt?
- What mood is the author building?

ramparts: walls
discern: identify or detect

Working from the Text

Work with your classmates to complete the following chart. Write text from Doerr's novel opening that gives clues about its setting or time period. Then write an assumption you can make about the novel's setting and time period, based on each clue. As needed, conduct research using the Internet or other resources to help you interpret each clue.

Clues	Assumptions or Research Findings

My Notes

☑ Check Your Understanding

Write a detailed sentence that summarizes your assumptions and findings about the setting of Doerr's novel opening.

Appreciating the Power of the Omniscient Narrator

Discuss the following questions with your classmates.

- Imagine you are a filmmaker who is trying to decide how best to represent the opening paragraphs of Doerr's novel in a movie. What visual images would you need to capture and from what perspectives would you need to film them?

- As you consider the kinds of film shots you named in response to the previous question, what does this tell you about the range of physical perspectives a third-person omniscient narrator can inhabit within just a few paragraphs?

VOCABULARY

LITERARY

An omniscient narrator is a narrator that has the power to be all-seeing and, therefore, all-knowing, as the word's etymology implies: *omni* (meaning "all") plus *scient* (meaning "knowing/knowledge").

The Omniscient Narrator as Mind Reader

Learning Targets

- Analyze characters from a novel.
- Understand the role of an omniscient narrator in a novel.

Preview

In this activity, you will read and discuss a continuation of the opening of *All the Light We Cannot See*, in which you are introduced to two of the novel's main characters.

My Notes

✍ Opening Writing Prompt

Read the following excerpt from the opening of *All the Light We Cannot See*, which includes the final paragraph from "Bombers," a section you read previously, and the first paragraph of the "The Girl," a section you will read later in this activity. Then answer the following question.

How do these two perspectives of the French walled city of Saint-Malo differ?

from All the Light We Cannot See

6   Inside each airplane, a bombardier peers through an aiming window and counts to twenty. Four five six seven. To the bombardiers, the walled city on its granite headland, drawing ever closer, looks like an unholy tooth, something black and dangerous, a final abscess to be lanced away.

The Girl

7   In a corner of the city, inside a tall, narrow house at Number 4 rue Vauborel, on the sixth and highest floor, a sightless sixteen-year-old named Marie-Laure LeBlanc kneels over a low table covered entirely with a model. The model is a miniature of the city she kneels within, and contains scale replicas of the hundreds of houses and shops and hotels within its walls. There's the cathedral with its perforated spire, and the bulky old Château de Saint-Malo, and row after row of seaside mansions studded with chimneys. A slender wooden jetty arcs out from a beach called the Plage du Môle; a delicate, reticulated atrium vaults over the seafood market; minute benches, the smallest no larger than apple seeds, dot the tiny public squares.

Relating Language to Characterization

1. Write a sentence explaining how the two depictions of Saint-Malo serve to characterize the bombardiers and Marie-Laure. Use the sentence frame to help you.

Ironically, Marie-Laure is able to see Saint-Malo as _____

whereas the bombardiers see Saint-Malo as _____ .

Aerial photograph of Saint-Malo, a French port in Brittany

As You Read

- Underline telling details about the characters of Marie-Laure and Werner.
- Circle unfamiliar words or phrases. Try to determine the meaning of the words by using context clues, word parts, or a dictionary.

Novel

from **All the Light We Cannot See** (Part 2)

by **Anthony Doerr**

The Girl

7 In a corner of the city, inside a tall, narrow house at Number 4 rue Vauborel, on the sixth and highest floor, a sightless sixteen-year-old named Marie-Laure LeBlanc kneels over a low table covered entirely with a model. The model is a miniature of the city she kneels within, and contains scale replicas of the hundreds of houses and shops and hotels within its walls. There's the cathedral with its perforated spire, and the bulky old Château de Saint-Malo, and row after row of seaside mansions studded with chimneys. A slender wooden jetty arcs out from a beach called the Plage du Môle; a delicate, reticulated atrium vaults over the seafood market; minute benches, the smallest no larger than apple seeds, dot the tiny public squares.

8 Marie-Laure runs her fingertips along the centimeter-wide parapet crowning the ramparts, drawing an uneven star shape around the entire model. She finds the opening atop the walls where four ceremonial cannons point to sea. "Bastion de la Hollande," she whispers, and her fingers walk down a little staircase. "Rue des Cordiers. Rue Jacques Cartier."

9 In a corner of the room stand two galvanized buckets filled to the rim with water. Fill them up, her great-uncle has taught her, whenever you can. The bathtub on the third floor too. Who knows when the water will go out again.

10 Her fingers travel back to the cathedral spire. South to the Gate of Dinan. All evening she has been marching her fingers around the model, waiting for her great-uncle Etienne, who owns this house, who went out the previous night while she slept, and who has not returned. And now it is night again, another revolution of the clock, and the whole block is quiet, and she cannot sleep.

11 She can hear the bombers when they are three miles away. A mounting static. The hum inside a seashell.

12 When she opens the bedroom window, the noise of the airplanes becomes louder. Otherwise, the night is dreadfully silent: no engines, no voices, no clatter. No sirens. No footfalls on the cobbles. Not even gulls. Just a high tide, one block away and six stories below, lapping at the base of the city walls.

13 And something else.

14 Something rattling softly, very close. She eases open the left-hand shutter and runs her fingers up the slats of the right. A sheet of paper has lodged there.

15 She holds it to her nose. It smells of fresh ink. Gasoline, maybe. The paper is crisp; it has not been outside long.

reticulated: net-like
galvanized: zinc coated

My Notes

_____

_____

_____

_____

_____

_____

_____

_____

_____

_____

_____

_____

_____

_____

_____

_____

_____

_____

_____

_____

_____

_____

staccato: sudden and short
diaphanous: delicate

16 Marie-Laure hesitates at the window in her stocking feet, her bedroom behind her, seashells arranged along the top of the armoire, pebbles along the baseboards. Her cane stands in the corner; her big Braille novel waits facedown on the bed. The drone of the airplanes grows.

The Boy

17 Five streets to the north, a white-haired eighteen-year-old German private named Werner Pfennig wakes to a faint **staccato** hum. Little more than a purr. Flies tapping at a far-off windowpane.

18 Where is he? The sweet, slightly chemical scent of gun oil; the raw wood of newly constructed shell crates; the mothballed odor of old bedspreads—he's in the hotel. Of course. L'hôtel des Abeilles, the Hotel of Bees.

19 Still night. Still early.

20 From the direction of the sea come whistles and booms; flak is going up.

21 An anti-air corporal hurries down the corridor, heading for the stairwell. "Get to the cellar," he calls over his shoulder, and Werner switches on his field light, rolls his blanket into his duffel, and starts down the hall.

22 Not so long ago, the Hotel of Bees was a cheerful address, with bright blue shutters on its facade and oysters on ice in its café and Breton waiters in bow ties polishing glasses behind its bar. It offered twenty-one guest rooms, commanding sea views, and a lobby fireplace as big as a truck. Parisians on weekend holidays would drink aperitifs here, and before them the occasional emissary from the republic—ministers and vice ministers and abbots and admirals—and in the centuries before them, windburned corsairs: killers, plunderers, raiders, seamen.

23 Before that, before it was ever a hotel at all, five full centuries ago, it was the home of a wealthy privateer who gave up raiding ships to study bees in the pastures outside Saint-Malo, scribbling in notebooks and eating honey straight from combs. The crests above the door lintels still have bumblebees carved into the oak; the ivy-covered fountain in the courtyard is shaped like a hive. Werner's favorites are five faded frescoes on the ceilings of the grandest upper rooms, where bees as big as children float against blue backdrops, big lazy drones and workers with **diaphanous** wings—where, above a hexagonal bathtub, a single nine-foot-long queen, with multiple eyes and a golden-furred abdomen, curls across the ceiling.

24 Over the past four weeks, the hotel has become something else: a fortress. A detachment of Austrian anti-airmen has boarded up every window, overturned every bed. They've reinforced the entrance, packed the stairwells with crates of artillery shells. The hotel's fourth floor, where garden rooms with French balconies open directly onto the ramparts, has become home to an aging high-velocity anti-air gun called an 88 that can fire twenty-one-and-a-half-pound shells nine miles.

25 *Her Majesty*, the Austrians call their cannon, and for the past week these men have tended to it the way worker bees might tend to a queen. They've fed

her oils, repainted her barrel, lubricated her wheels; they've arranged sandbags at her feet like offerings.

26 The royal *acht acht*, a deathly monarch meant to protect them all.

27 Werner is in the stairwell, halfway to the ground floor, when the 88 fires twice in quick succession. It's the first time he's heard the gun at such close range, and it sounds as if the top half of the hotel has torn off. He stumbles and throws his arms over his ears. The walls reverberate all the way down into the foundation, then back up.

28 Werner can hear the Austrians two floors up scrambling, reloading, and the receding screams of both shells as they hurtle above the ocean, already two or three miles away. One of the soldiers, he realizes, is singing. Or maybe it is more than one. Maybe they are all singing. Eight Luftwaffe men, none of whom will survive the hour, singing a love song to their queen.

29 Werner chases the beam of his field light through the lobby. The big gun detonates a third time, and glass shatters somewhere close by, and torrents of soot rattle down the chimney, and the walls of the hotel toll like a struck bell. Werner worries that the sound will knock the teeth from his gums.

30 He drags open the cellar door and pauses a moment, vision swimming. "This is it?" he asks. "They're really coming?"

31 But who is there to answer?

Making Observations

- Where is Marie-Laure when the bombing starts? Where is Werner?
- What is *Her Majesty*?

My Notes

Working from the Text

2. Prepare for an academic conversation with your classmates by completing the following chart. For each character, write a statement that uses one or two describing words that capture his or her essence. Then write quotes from the novel that support your analysis of each character.

Character	Description	Quotes from Text
Marie-Laure		
Werner		

3. Share your analysis of Marie-Laure and Werner with your classmates, following this academic-conversation protocol. Conduct the protocol twice, once for Marie-Laure and once for Werner. Take turns playing Student A, Student B, and Student C, so that every member of your group has a turn playing each role. After each round, leave time for a final "something else I noticed" opportunity for the two group members who did not make the initial claim and select evidence. This will give all members of your group a chance to revisit the quote or the larger text and find more support for or against the initial statement.

   a. **Student A:** Offer a simple statement about the character, answering the question "What's he/she like?"

   b. **Student B:** Ask Student A to supply evidence from the text by asking, "What makes you say so?"

   c. **Student A:** Offer a direct quote.

   d. **Student C:** Ask Student A to analyze the quote and how it relates back to the original statement.

   e. **Student A:** Respond by explaining how the quote supports your stance or any other reason the quote attracted you (for its word choice, literary devices, etc.).

Appreciating the Author's Craft

Discuss the following questions with your classmates.

- Think about this quote about Marie-Laure from Doerr's novel: "Something rattling softly, very close. She eases open the left-hand shutter and runs her fingers up the slats of the right. A sheet of paper has lodged there." What is the paper? How do you know?

- Why does Doerr describe the leaflet as a "sheet of paper" when he tells about Marie-Laure finding it?

☑ Check Your Understanding

When Doerr uses the phrase "sheet of paper" in place of the term "leaflet," what does he show about how an omniscient narrator can function in a story?

Writing an Analysis of Argument: Outlining and Drafting

Learning Strategies

Drafting
Outlining

My Notes

Learning Targets
- Create a plan for writing a character analysis paragraph.
- Draft a character analysis paragraph.

Preview

In this activity, you will plan and write two character-analysis paragraphs using quotes from the text and analysis that includes your own original commentary.

✍ Writing to Sources: Informational Text

Write a character analysis paragraph in your Reader/Writer Notebook. Be sure to:

- Choose a subject for your character analysis: either Marie-Laure or Werner from *All the Light We Cannot See*.
- Include a topic sentence that makes a claim about the character you are analyzing.
- Support your claim with details and quotations from the text, as well as thoughtful analysis.
- Use quotation marks around words taken directly from the novel.
- Include a concluding statement that revisits the claim without simply repeating it.

Forming a Single-Paragraph Outline

Use the following single-paragraph outline to plan your character analysis.

1. Begin your outline by revisiting your character description chart and notes to help you draft a topic sentence for your paragraph. Include in your topic sentence one of the claims you discussed with classmates about Marie-Laure's or Werner's character.

2. Develop the body of your paragraph by generating details that support your claim. Be sure to include quotations from the novel, as well as your own analysis that ties back to your claim.

3. Complete your outline by writing a concluding statement that relates the evidence you've presented back to the claim.

Single-Paragraph Outline

T.S. _____

_____

_____

1. _____

2. _____

3. _____

4. _____

C.S. _____

_____

_____

Writing a Character Analysis Paragraph

4. Use notes from your outline to help you write your character analysis. Remember to support your claim with the most compelling quotations from the novel, use quotation marks correctly, and follow each quotation with analysis that explains how the quotation relates to your claim.

_____

_____

_____

_____

_____

_____

_____

_____

_____

_____

_____

Assess and Reflect

Use your notes from the academic conversations you had about Marie-Laure and Werner as the basis for a second analytical paragraph, this time analyzing the character you did not choose to write about originally. Remember to structure your paragraph correctly and include quotations from the novel and analysis.

The Bias of the First-Person Narrator

My Notes

Learning Targets

- Analyze a character from a novel based on the opening paragraphs.
- Take part in a collaborative discussion.
- Understand how an author's use of present-tense or past-tense narration affects readers' understanding of the events of a story.

Preview

In this activity, you will read and discuss the opening of the novel *The Girl Who Fell from the Sky*, which introduces readers to two of the novel's main characters.

📝 Opening Writing Prompt

Read the opening excerpt from Heidi Durrow's novel *The Girl Who Fell from the Sky*. As the narrator Rachel tells us, the setting is "fall 1982 in Portland."

How did Rachel end up in Portland in 1982? How do you know?

As You Read

- Underline telling details about Rachel's grandmother.
- Circle unfamiliar words or phrases. Try to determine the meaning of the words by using context clues, word parts, or a dictionary.

About the Author

Although Heidi W. Durrow (b. 1969) is now a novelist, public speaker, blogger, and podcast host, she did not always have a career in the arts. For a time, she left behind her studies in English literature and journalism to be a life skills trainer for NFL and NBA athletes and, later, a corporate lawyer. Durrow spent the last 12 years of her career as a business professional working on what later would become her award-winning debut novel, *The Girl Who Fell from the Sky*. Durrow uses a variety of writing and speaking platforms to celebrate and create community for people who identify as biracial or bicultural. For *The Girl Who Fell from the Sky*, whose protagonist has a Danish mother and an African American father, Durrow received the Pen/Bellwether Prize for Socially Engaged Fiction and the NAACP Award for Outstanding Literary Debut.

Novel

from The Girl Who Fell from the Sky

by **Heidi W. Durrow**

Rachel

1   "You my lucky piece," Grandma says.

2   Grandma has walked me the half block from the hospital lobby to the bus stop. Her hand is wrapped around mine like a leash.

3   It is fall 1982 in Portland and it is raining. Puddle water has splashed up on my new shoes. My girl-in-a-new-dress feeling has faded. My new-girl feeling has disappeared.

4   My hand is in Grandma's until she reaches into a black patent leather clutch for change.

5   "Well, aren't those the prettiest blue eyes on the prettiest little girl," the bus driver says as we climb aboard. The new-girl feeling comes back and I smile.

6   "This my grandbaby. Come to live with me," Grandma can't lose Texas.

7   "Thank you, ma'am," I say. I mind my manners around strangers. Grandma is still a stranger to me.

8   I know only a few things about Grandma. She's a gardener. She has soft hands, and she smells like lavender.

9   For Christmas, Grandma always sent Robbie and me a card with a new ten-dollar bill wrapped in aluminum foil. On the back of the envelope where she pressed extra hard there'd be a small smudge. The card smelled like the lavender lotion she uses to keep her hands soft.

10   Grandma doesn't have a single wrinkle on her anywhere. She has eggplant brown skin as smooth as a plate all because of the lotion she sends for special from the South. "They got better roots down there—better dirt for making a root strong." Her body is a bullet. She is thick and short. Her dark hair is pulled back and is covered by a plastic bonnet.

11   "Well, aren't you lucky to have a special grandma," the bus driver says. "Pretty and lucky."

12   This is the picture I want to remember: Grandma looks something like pride. Like a whistle about to blow.

13   Grandma puts the change in for my fare. She wipes the rain off my face, "We almost home."

14   When we find our seats, she says something more, but I cannot hear it. She is leaning across me like a seat belt and speaks into my bad ear—it is the only lasting injury from the accident. Her hands are on me the whole ride,

across my shoulder, on my hand, stroking my hair to smooth it flat again. Grandma seems to be holding me down, as if I might fly away or fall.

15 The bus ride is seven stops and three lights. Then we are home. Grandma's home, the new girl's home in a new dress.

Making Observations
- What is your impression of Rachel's grandmother?
- What action is taking place in this excerpt?

Working from the Text

1. Prepare for an academic conversation with your classmates by completing the following chart. For the character of Grandma, write a statement that uses one or two describing words that capture her essence, as seen through Rachel's eyes. Then write quotes from the novel that support your analysis of her character.

Character	Description	Quotes from Text
Grandma		

2. Share your analysis of Grandma, as seen through Rachel's eyes, with your classmates, following this academic-conversation protocol. Conduct the protocol three times, each time focusing on a different claim about Grandma. Take turns playing Student A, Student B, and Student C, so that every member of your group has a turn playing each role. After each round, leave time for a final "something else I noticed" opportunity for the two group members who did not make the initial claim and select evidence. This will give all members of your group a chance to revisit the quote or the larger text and find more support for or against the initial statement.

   a. **Student A:** Offer a simple statement about the character, answering the question "What's he/she like?"

   b. **Student B:** Ask Student A to supply evidence from the text by asking, "What makes you say so?"

   c. **Student A:** Offer a direct quote.

   d. **Student C:** Ask Student A to analyze the quote and how it relates back to the original statement.

   e. **Student A:** Respond by explaining how the quote supports your stance or any other reason the quote attracted you (for its word choice, literary devices, etc.).

Appreciating the Author's Craft

Discuss the following questions with your classmates.

- Imagine Durrow had opened the novel with a sentence like this: "I remember when I was a little girl and went to live with my grandmother." What would have been different about Rachel's voice?

- How does Durrow's use of the present tense in her story's narration affect your experience as a reader?

☑ Check Your Understanding

Why do you think Durrow chose to tell Rachel's story in the present tense?

The Voice of Scout Finch

Learning Strategies

Close Reading
Marking the Text

Learning Targets

- Analyze the narration of a novel.
- Understand how the use of flashback can create certain effects in a story.

Preview

In this activity, you will read the first 13 paragraphs of *To Kill a Mockingbird*. Then you will compare its narration to the narration of *The Girl Who Fell from the Sky* and discuss why Harper Lee chose to structure her novel as she did.

✏️ Opening Writing Prompt

Read the first two paragraphs from the opening of Harper Lee's novel *To Kill a Mockingbird*. Then answer the following question.

> What can you learn about the narrator based on only these two paragraphs?

About the Author

Harper Lee is the pen name for Nelle Harper Lee (1926–2016), whose novel *To Kill a Mockingbird* became a classic of American literature almost immediately upon its publication in 1960. Not only did it earn Lee the Pulitzer Prize for Fiction in 1961, but its screen adaptation became an Academy Award-winning film in 1962, and the novel remains a *New York Times* Best Seller to this day. It is for this reason that many readers were incredulous when Lee chose, for many years, not to follow up this novel with another. It wasn't until 2015, shortly before her death, that Lee published her second novel, *Go Set a Watchman*. At first thought to be the sequel of *To Kill a Mockingbird*, this novel is now widely believed to be Lee's first draft of *To Kill a Mockingbird*, which started out as a series of short stories based loosely on people and events from her own life. Like its predecessor, *Go Set a Watchman* became an instant bestseller and is now appreciated for the insights it gives Lee's fans into her process as a writer.

My Notes

In the 1962 film adaptation of *To Kill a Mockingbird*, Phillip Alford (left) and Mary Badham (right) played the roles of Jem and Scout.

VOCABULARY

ACADEMIC

When people analyze events in their past, they are being **retrospective**, which means "looking back." Often people do this to learn from their mistakes or understand something from their past. The term comes from the Latin *retro* (meaning *back*, *behind*, or *backward*) and *specere* (meaning *to look at*).

Historical Background

As Scout tells the story of her family's background, she alludes to a number of people and events from English and American history. For example, Andrew Jackson was an American general who led an army of soldiers against the Creeks, a nation of Native Americans, in the Creek War of 1813–1814. Jackson's defeat of the Creeks resulted in a treaty that forced the Creeks to give up more than 21 million acres of land in the states of Georgia and Alabama. The Battle of Hastings is the name of a battle fought in England in 1066. In this battle, William the Conqueror's Norman-French army defeated King Harold II's Anglo-Saxon army, beginning the 88-year Norman occupation of England. John Wesley was a clergyman of the Church of England in the 1700s. He is credited with founding Methodism, a system of beliefs practiced within the Christian religion. "The disturbance between the North and the South" refers to the American Civil War of 1861–1865. The phrase "nothing to fear but fear itself" comes from a speech President Franklin Delano Roosevelt gave when he was inaugurated on March 4, 1933.

Reading Chapter 1: Scout's Voice

1. Like Rachel from *The Girl Who Fell from the Sky*, Scout is a first-person narrator, and she has a story from her childhood to tell. But Scout's narration of the events of her life differ from that of Rachel. How is it different? What is Scout able to do that Rachel cannot?

_____

_____

_____

_____

2. How is Scout's **retrospective** point of view evident in her voice? What words or phrases let us know she is no longer a child?

_____

_____

_____

_____

Working from the Text

3. Here are nine events mentioned in the first 13 paragraphs of *To Kill a Mockingbird*, written in the order in which they appear in the text. But in what order did they really happen? Work with your classmates to number the events chronologically. Two of the events are referenced in the Historical Background feature earlier in this activity.

   _____ Jem got his arm badly broken at the elbow.

   _____ Dill gave Scout and Jem the idea of making Boo Radley come out.

   _____ In England, Simon Finch was irritated by the persecution of those who called themselves Methodists.

   _____ Simon Finch worked his way across the Atlantic to Philadelphia, thence to Jamaica, thence to Mobile, and up the Saint Stephens.

   _____ There was a disturbance between the North and the South

   _____ Atticus Finch went to Montgomery to read law.

   _____ Atticus Finch returned to Maycomb and began his law practice.

   _____ Maycomb County (and the United States) had recently been told that it had "nothing to fear but fear itself."

   _____ Scout and Jem's mother died.

Appreciating the Author's Craft

Discuss the following questions with your classmates.

- Why do you think Lee starts *To Kill a Mockingbird* by mentioning Jem's accident in the 1930s and then flashing back to events taking place before the Civil War?

- What does Lee gain by telling readers who Simon Finch was and how Scout's immediate family is connected to him?

☑ Check Your Understanding

What is one reason an author might use flashbacks in a story?

INDEPENDENT READING LINK

Read and Discuss

Collaborate with a group of peers to discuss the books you are reading and how they connect with *To Kill a Mockingbird*. Start the discussion by presenting your book to the group. Briefly summarize its topic or plot, and then tell how you think your book relates to the coming-of-age theme or provides insights into African Americans' experiences during the era depicted in *To Kill a Mockingbird*. Then invite other peers to present their books in the same way. Finally, discuss how hearing each other's book presentations deepened your understanding of the coming-of-age theme and/or the Jim Crow era and the Civil Rights Movement.

My Notes

_____

_____

_____

_____

_____

_____

_____

_____

_____

_____

_____

_____

_____

_____

The Layers of Scout's World

Learning Strategies

Close Reading
Graphic Organizer

My Notes

_____

_____

_____

_____

_____

_____

_____

_____

_____

_____

_____

_____

_____

_____

_____

_____

_____

_____

_____

_____

_____

_____

_____

_____

_____

_____

_____

_____

_____

_____

_____

_____

Learning Targets

- Analyze the setting of a novel.
- Understand the effect of a first-person narrator's perspective on descriptions of settings and characters.

Preview

In this activity, you will continue reading Chapter 1 of *To Kill a Mockingbird* (paragraphs 14–44) and then analyze how Scout's perspective on the setting affects the way it is described.

✍ Opening Writing Prompt

Reread the part of Chapter 1 in which Scout describes her hometown of Maycomb. Then answer the following question.

What is Scout's attitude toward Maycomb? How do you know?

_____

_____

_____

_____

_____

_____

_____

Changing Word Choice to Change Tone

1. Rewrite a sentence or two from Lee's paragraphs about Maycomb with a different perspective that reveals a different attitude about the town. Be sure to keep the facts of Maycomb the same, while considering how someone who disagrees with Scout might view them. What words have to change to reveal this new attitude?

_____

_____

_____

_____

As You Read

- Underline words and phrases that tell about the setting of Scout's childhood world.
- Circle unfamiliar words or phrases. Try to determine the meaning of the words by using context clues, word parts, or a dictionary.

Novel

My Notes

from **To Kill a Mockingbird,**

Chapter 1, Paragraphs 14–44

by **Harper Lee**

14   When I was almost six and Jem was nearly ten, our summertime boundaries (within calling distance of Calpurnia) were Mrs. Henry Lafayette Dubose's house two doors to the north of us, and the Radley Place three doors to the south. We were never tempted to break them. The Radley Place was inhabited by an unknown entity the mere description of whom was enough to make us behave for days on end; Mrs. Dubose was plain hell.

15   That was the summer Dill came to us.

16   Early one morning as we were beginning our day's play in the back yard, Jem and I heard something next door in Miss Rachel Haverford's collard patch. We went to the wire fence to see if there was a puppy—Miss Rachel's rat terrier was expecting—instead we found someone sitting looking at us. Sitting down, he wasn't much higher than the collards. We stared at him until he spoke:

17   "Hey."

18   "Hey yourself," said Jem pleasantly.

19   "I'm Charles Baker Harris," he said. "I can read."

20   "So what?" I said.

21   "I just thought you'd like to know I can read. You got anything needs readin' I can do it … "

22   "How old are you," asked Jem, "four-and-a-half?"

23   "Goin' on seven."

24   "Shoot no wonder, then," said Jem, jerking his thumb at me. "Scout yonder's been readin' ever since she was born, and she ain't even started to school yet. You look right puny for goin' on seven."

25   "I'm little but I'm old," he said.

26   Jem brushed his hair back to get a better look. "Why don't you come over, Charles Baker Harris?" he said. "Lord, what a name."

27   " 's not any funnier'n yours. Aunt Rachel says your name's Jeremy Atticus Finch."

28   Jem scowled. "I'm big enough to fit mine," he said. "Your name's longer'n you are. Bet it's a foot longer."

29   "Folks call me Dill," said Dill, struggling under the fence.

30   "Do better if you go over it instead of under it," I said. "Where'd you come from?"

My Notes

31 Dill was from Meridian, Mississippi, was spending the summer with his aunt, Miss Rachel, and would be spending every summer in Maycomb from now on. His family was from Maycomb County originally, his mother worked for a photographer in Meridian, had entered his picture in a Beautiful Child contest and won five dollars. She gave the money to Dill, who went to the picture show twenty times on it.

32 "Don't have any picture shows here, except Jesus ones in the courthouse sometimes," said Jem. "Ever see anything good?"

33 Dill had seen *Dracula*, a revelation that moved Jem to eye him with the beginning of respect. "Tell it to us," he said.

34 Dill was a curiosity. He wore blue linen shorts that buttoned to his shirt, his hair was snow white and stuck to his head like duckfluff; he was a year my senior but I towered over him. As he told us the old tale his blue eyes would lighten and darken; his laugh was sudden and happy; he habitually pulled at a cowlick in the center of his forehead.

35 When Dill reduced Dracula to dust, and Jem said the show sounded better than the book, I asked Dill where his father was: "You ain't said anything about him."

36 "I haven't got one."

37 "Is he dead?"

38 "No … "

39 "Then if he's not dead you've got one, haven't you?"

40 Dill blushed and Jem told me to hush, a sure sign that Dill had been studied and found acceptable. Thereafter the summer passed in routine contentment. Routine contentment was: improving our treehouse that rested between giant twin chinaberry trees in the back yard, fussing, running through our list of dramas based on the works of Oliver Optic, Victor Appleton, and Edgar Rice Burroughs. In this matter we were lucky to have Dill. He played the character parts formerly thrust upon me—the ape in Tarzan, Mr. Crabtree in The Rover Boys, Mr. Damon in Tom Swift. Thus we came to know Dill as a pocket Merlin, whose head teemed with eccentric plans, strange longings, and quaint fancies.

41 But by the end of August our repertoire was vapid from countless reproductions, and it was then that Dill gave us the idea of making Boo Radley come out.

42 The Radley Place fascinated Dill. In spite of our warnings and explanations it drew him as the moon draws water, but drew him no nearer than the light-pole on the corner, a safe distance from the Radley gate. There he would stand, his arm around the fat pole, staring and wondering.

43 The Radley Place jutted into a sharp curve beyond our house. Walking south, one faced its porch; the sidewalk turned and ran beside the lot. The house was low, was once white with a deep front porch and green shutters, but

WORD CONNECTIONS

Content Connections

When Scout calls Dill a "pocket Merlin," she alludes to the character Merlin from the legends about King Arthur, a British leader who lived in the late fifth and early sixth centuries. Merlin was a wizard who advised King Arthur and mentored his knights.

GRAMMAR & USAGE

Metaphor

Writers use metaphor to compare two things that are different in most ways but alike in an important way. For example, when Scout calls Dill a "pocket Merlin," or a Merlin who is small enough to fit into a pocket, she uses a metaphor to help readers visualize Dill as she and Jem did—first, as a small person and constant companion, and next, as someone whose big imagination and strange ideas delighted and surprised Scout and Jem in the same way that a wizard's magic would.

had long ago darkened to the color of the slate-gray yard around it. Rain-rotted shingles drooped over the eaves of the veranda; oak trees kept the sun away. The remains of a picket drunkenly guarded the front yard—a "swept" yard that was never swept—where johnson grass and rabbit-tobacco grew in abundance.

44 Inside the house lived a malevolent phantom. People said he existed, but Jem and I had never seen him. People said he went out at night when the moon was down, and peeped in windows. When people's azaleas froze in a cold snap, it was because he had breathed on them. Any stealthy small crimes committed in Maycomb were his work. Once the town was terrorized by a series of morbid nocturnal events: people's chickens and household pets were found mutilated; although the culprit was Crazy Addie, who eventually drowned himself in Barker's Eddy, people still looked at the Radley Place, unwilling to discard their initial suspicions. A Negro would not pass the Radley Place at night, he would cut across to the sidewalk opposite and whistle as he walked. The Maycomb school grounds adjoined the back of the Radley lot; from the Radley chickenyard tall pecan trees shook their fruit into the schoolyard, but the nuts lay untouched by the children: Radley pecans would kill you. A baseball hit into the Radley yard was a lost ball and no questions asked.

WORD CONNECTIONS

Etymology
A **swept yard** is an outdoor area in front of the home where people wash clothes and cook food over an open fire. The area is swept with a broom, so as to keep it bare of grass and free of pests. The idea for having a swept yard came from West Africa, where heat and cramped living conditions made it more practical and pleasant to do cooking and laundry outside. Although a swept yard is outdoors, it is treated like an additional room of the home.

My Notes

The role of Dill was played by John Megna (right) in the 1962 film adaptation of *To Kill a Mockingbird*. Here he is joined by Jem (Phillip Alford, center) and Scout (Mary Badham, left).

Making Observations
- Who is Dill, and why do Jem and Scout like him?
- Why is Dill fascinated by the Radley Place?

Working from the Text

2. Paragraph 14 of *To Kill a Mockingbird* marks a shift in Scout's voice, from that of an adult who has had experiences outside of Maycomb to that of a little girl, whose world has strictly defined boundaries.

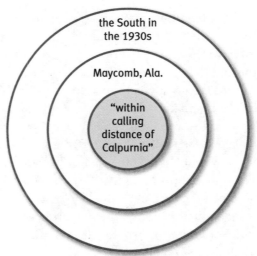

Paraphrase paragraph 14 to tell what readers learn here about the boundaries of Scout's childhood world.

_____

_____

_____

_____

3. How would you sum up the physical state of the Radley Place? Think of a word and write it in the center oval. Then write quotes from the text that support your word choice in the surrounding ovals.

4. How would you sum up Scout's emotional impression of the Radley Place? Write your one-word response in the center oval, and in each surrounding oval write a different quote from the text that supports your one-word response.

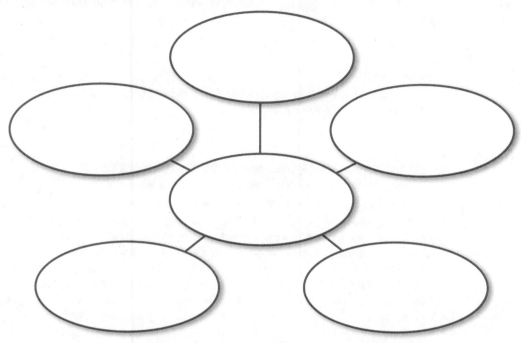

Crafting an Analytical Paragraph About Setting

5. Write a brief paragraph summarizing your analysis of the Radley Place, based on your reading thus far. As you write, be sure to do the following.

- Take into account Scout's narrative point of view, as she describes the setting. Is Scout describing the Radley Place from an older, more mature perspective or from her perspective as a superstitious child?

- Refer to the quotes in the webs you created about the Radley Place to help you write claims about Scout's impression of the setting and to find quotations to support those claims.

_____

_____

_____

_____

_____

_____

_____

☑ **Check Your Understanding**

In a first-person narrative, are the narrator's impressions about things, such as settings and characters, always completely reliable? Why or why not?

Writing a Literary Analysis Essay

Learning Strategies

Brainstorming
Drafting
Graphic Organizer
Outlining

My Notes

Learning Targets

- Choose a topic for a literary analysis essay and gather information to support a claim.
- Plan for and draft a literary analysis essay.

Preview

In this activity, you will plan and draft a literary analysis essay about the first chapter of *To Kill a Mockingbird*.

Writing to Sources: Informational Text

Because *To Kill a Mockingbird* is a novel written in the first person, readers are never given an outside view of its narrator, Scout Finch. Instead, we meet her and get to know how she thinks and what she feels through her narration, dialogue, and descriptions of the characters and setting around her. In a well-organized and developed essay, explain how Harper Lee characterizes the narrator Scout Finch and how that characterization shapes the reader's perceptions of either one of the novel's settings or one of the other characters introduced in the opening chapter.

Note: Do not merely summarize the plot of Chapter 1.

Analyzing the Text

1. Review the settings and characters you brainstormed as possible essay topics with your classmates. Choose one setting or character to write about. Then use the following chart to collect information for your literary analysis essay. Find quotes from the novel about the setting or character you chose. Then tell what each quote reveals about the setting or character. Finally, tell what each quote reveals about Scout and her relationship to the setting or character.

Quote	What the quote says about _____	What the quote says about Scout's relationship to _____

Quote	What the quote says about _____	What the quote says about Scout's relationship to _____

Quote	What the quote says about _____	What the quote says about Scout's relationship to _____

☑ Check Your Understanding

As you read through the information you collected in your chart about Scout's character and her perception of another character or setting in *To Kill a Mockingbird*, what recurring ideas or themes do you find?

Planning the Structure

2. Reread the writing prompt for your literary analysis essay. Then answer the question: *If you were writing a four- or five-paragraph essay, what would be the focus of the two or three body paragraphs?*

_____

_____

_____

Forming a Multiple-Paragraph Outline

Use the following multiple-paragraph outline to plan your literary analysis essay.

3. Begin your outline by generating details for an introductory paragraph. Include a thesis statement that focuses on the dynamic between Scout and another character or on Scout's feelings about a particular setting in *To Kill a Mockingbird*.

4. Develop more paragraphs of your outline by generating details that support your claim. Use paragraphs 2 and 3 to discuss points you want to make about Scout's character and how it is revealed through her relationship or feelings about a place.

5. Use paragraph 4 to write a conclusion that revisits your thesis in a new light.

Main Idea	Details
Introduction Paragraph 1	• • •
Point A supported by quote from text Paragraph 2	• • •
Point B supported by quote from text Paragraph 3	• • •
Conclusion Paragraph 4	• • •

Writing the Essay

6. Use notes from your chart about Scout's character and her perception of another character or setting in *To Kill a Mockingbird* to help you write your literary analysis essay. As you develop your draft, be sure to:

- Write an introduction that includes a general statement about the first-person narration of *To Kill a Mockingbird*; a specific statement that refers to Lee, her text, and her topic; and a thesis statement that conveys Lee's characterization of Scout and how it shapes the reader's perceptions of a setting or another character.

- Support your claim with the most relevant and compelling quotations from your chart about Scout's character and her relationship to another character or setting from the novel.

- Use quotation marks around text that comes directly from the novel.

- Use a variety of phrases and clauses to convey your thoughts and ideas and add interest to your writing.

- Write a conclusion that revisits your thesis in a new light.

- Meet all the criteria in the writing prompt for your essay.

Assess and Reflect

Read the following paragraph. Then write a paragraph analyzing how Boo is being characterized by Jem and explaining why you think Scout chose to include this description from Jem's perspective. Be sure to refer to telling details and word choice in your analysis.

> Jem gave a reasonable description of Boo: Boo was about six-and-a-half feet tall, judging from his tracks; he dined on raw squirrels and any cats he could catch, that's why his hands were bloodstained—if you ate an animal raw, you could never wash the blood off. There was a long jagged scar that ran across his face; what teeth he had were yellow and rotten; his eyes popped, and he drooled most of the time.

Learning Strategies

Discussion Groups
Double-Entry Journal
Marking the Text
Note-taking
Summarizing

INDEPENDENT READING LINK

Read and Respond

Set up a double-entry journal for your independent reading and use it to keep track of your reactions, your connections, memorable quotes, your predictions, and your conclusions. This will help develop your note-taking skills. Make a goal of writing at least one entry for every three pages you read.

My Notes

Learning Targets

- Identify and analyze the knowledge and skills needed to complete Embedded Assessment 1 successfully.
- Revise, refine, and reflect on an understanding of the Essential Questions.
- Apply a strategy for active reading and note-taking.

Preview

In this activity, you will set up a double-entry journal to write notes as you continue reading *To Kill a Mockingbird*, and familiarize yourself with Embedded Assessment 1.

Revisiting the Essential Questions

Based on what you learned in the first part of this unit, how would you respond to these questions now?

1. What makes an opening powerful?
2. What makes you want to keep reading a book?
3. How can understanding a book's context help you understand the book?

Unpacking Embedded Assessment 1

Read the assignment for Embedded Assessment 1: Writing a Literary Analysis Essay.

 Your assignment is to write a passage analysis of a key coming-of-age scene from *To Kill a Mockingbird*. After annotating the text to analyze Harper Lee's use of literary elements in your selected passage, write an essay explaining how the literary elements in this passage help develop a theme of the novel.

In your own words, summarize what you will need to know to complete this assessment successfully. With your class, create a graphic organizer to represent the skills and knowledge you will need to complete the tasks identified in the Embedded Assessment.

Coming-of-Age Stories

In this set of activities, you will continue to read and analyze *To Kill a Mockingbird*, which is a coming-of-age story. "Coming of age" refers to the transition between childhood and adulthood and includes going through life-changing experiences, or milestones. In some cultures, coming of age is determined at a certain age when a child is no longer a minor, but coming of age also refers to gaining a new, deeper understanding of the world.

4. The following words are related to the concept of coming of age. For each word listed, write another word that uses the same root but has a different meaning or part of speech. Explain how you changed the word. Read and discuss the example before completing the task.

a. transition (noun) <u>transitional (adjective): I added -al to change the noun to an adjective.</u>

b. child (noun) _____

_____

c. innocent (adjective) _____

_____

d. develop (verb) _____

_____

e. culture (noun) _____

_____

f. identity (noun) _____

_____

5. Quickwrite: In your own words, what does it mean to come of age?

_____

_____

6. What are some of the coming-of-age milestones you are anticipating in the upcoming years?

_____

_____

7. What are some books and movies that have a coming-of-age theme?

_____

_____

_____

Forming Opinions

8. Coming of age is a time when people learn to formulate their own opinions. Respond to the following statements by writing either *A* (Agree) or *D* (Disagree) to the left of each one to indicate your initial reaction. You can also jot down comments about the statement or mixed feelings you have about the statement.

Initial Reactions		After Reading
	1. All people are treated equally in society.	
	2. In society, it's okay to be different from what others consider normal.	
	3. People are either all good or all evil; there is no in-between.	
	4. Some words are so offensive that they should never be stated or written.	
	5. All citizens are treated fairly in our courts of law.	
	6. Speaking in grammatically correct sentences proves that a person is smart.	
	7. A hero is born, not made.	
	8. We should follow only the laws that make sense to us.	
	9. When the law does not succeed in punishing a criminal, citizens should be able to punish the criminal themselves.	
	10. Killing under any circumstances is wrong.	
	11. Good parents set limits for their children.	
	12. Every individual is prejudiced about something.	

Introducing the Strategy: Double-Entry Journal

A double-entry journal is a note-taking strategy for actively reading a text. In your journal, capture quotes and evidence from the text and write commentary. You can connect your own experiences to those of the characters, share your opinions about what is happening, trace the development of the characters, and comment on the effects of the writer's choices.

9. A double-entry journal can be used with any reading. In the upcoming activities, you will continue reading *To Kill a Mockingbird*. As you read the novel, use the following format as a model for recording notes in a double-entry journal. Take one page of notes per chapter. In the left column, copy the following: one quote about a character, one quote about the setting, and one quote that connects to your life, society, or an idea in another text. Cite the page number with the quotation. In the right column, write your thoughts about the passage. You may also use this journal to:

- Analyze the development of a theme or a character over the course of a longer story or novel.

- Jot down questions that will help deepen your understanding as you read.

- Leave notes to track your understanding of a word, a phrase, or a larger section of the text and verify or refine your understanding based on context as you continue reading.

Vivid Text (*The book says ...*)	Analysis/Question (*I say ...*)

Conflict with Miss Caroline

INDEPENDENT READING LINK

Read and Connect

What conflicts have arisen in your independent reading? How do they relate to the conflicts in *To Kill a Mockingbird*? Are they primarily internal or external? Write an entry in your double-entry journal that deals with a conflict.

Learning Targets

- Analyze conflicts that are developing between characters in a novel.
- Make a variety of connections to a novel in order to analyze how a main character develops.
- Demonstrate understanding of conflict in writing.

Preview

In this activity, you will read Chapters 2 and 3 of *To Kill a Mockingbird* and explore the conflicts that are developing.

Exploring Conflict

1. Think about the different kinds of conflict you have studied. Internal conflict occurs when a character struggles between opposing needs, desires, or emotions within his or her own mind. External conflict occurs when a character struggles against an outside force, such as another character, society, or nature. Using the following graphic organizer, brainstorm examples of conflicts from your life, the world, books, television, or movies.

Internal Conflict: *Person vs. Self* (struggles against one's own opposing needs, desires, or emotions)	External Conflict: *Person vs. Person* (struggles against another person)	External Conflict: *Person vs. Society* (struggles against laws or expectations)	External Conflict: *Person vs. Nature* (struggles against the physical world)

Working from the Text

Read Chapter 2 and then answer the following questions.

2. Work with a partner or small group to locate textual evidence of the conflict between Scout and Miss Caroline. Write quotes in the chart with commentary to explain why these two are "starting off on the wrong foot in every way."

Scout's Side	Miss Caroline's Side

3. Fill in the ovals in the web, making connections to Scout's first-day-of-school experiences. As you read Chapter 3, fill in the ovals with more connections:

- Text-to-Self: when the text makes you think of your personal experiences
- Text-to-Text: when the text makes you think of ideas in other texts
- Text-to-World: when the text makes you think of society

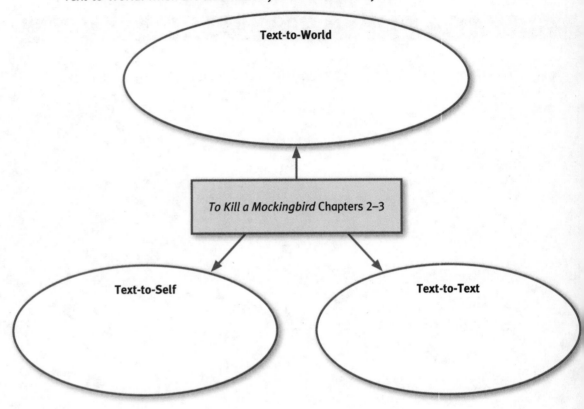

☑ Check Your Understanding

What type of conflict is happening between Scout and Miss Caroline? Support your answer with text evidence.

Getting to Know Boo

Learning Strategies

Discussion Groups
Double-Entry Journal
Graphic Organizer
Marking the Text

Learning Targets

- Analyze subplot and motif in a novel to determine how characters develop through coming-of-age experiences.
- Make predictions, form inferences, draw conclusions, and find evidence to support an analysis of a novel.

Preview

In this activity, you will continue reading *To Kill a Mockingbird* and determine how characters develop through their experiences, drawing conclusions based on textual evidence.

Facts and Rumors

1. Return to the pages in Chapter 1 that introduce the story of Boo Radley. Complete the following graphic organizer with facts, rumors, and textual evidence of each. Add your own questions and commentary about Boo's story.

Boo Radley's Story	Textual Evidence	Questions/Commentary
Facts:		
Rumors:		

As You Read

- Underline details about Boo or the Radley Place.
- Circle unknown words and phrases. Try to determine the meaning of the words by using context clues, word parts, or a dictionary.

My Notes

Novel

from To Kill a Mockingbird,
Chapter 4, Paragraphs 2–40

by **Harper Lee**

2 As the year passed, released from school thirty minutes before Jem, who had to stay until three o'clock, I ran by the Radley Place as fast as I could, not stopping until I reached the safety of our front porch. One afternoon as I raced by, something caught my eye and caught it in such a way that I took a deep breath, a long look around, and went back.

3 Two live oaks stood at the edge of the Radley lot; their roots reached out into the side-road and made it bumpy. Something about one of the trees attracted my attention.

4 Some tinfoil was sticking in a knot-hole just above my eye level, winking at me in the afternoon sun. I stood on tiptoe, **hastily** looked around once more, reached into the hole, and withdrew two pieces of chewing gum minus their outer wrappers.

5 My first impulse was to get it into my mouth as quickly as possible, but I remembered where I was. I ran home, and on our front porch I examined my loot. The gum looked fresh. I sniffed it and it smelled all right. I licked it and waited for a while. When I did not die I crammed it into my mouth: Wrigley's Double-Mint.

6 When Jem came home he asked me where I got such a wad. I told him I found it.

7 "Don't eat things you find, Scout."

8 "This wasn't on the ground, it was in a tree."

9 Jem growled.

10 "Well it was," I said. "It was sticking in that tree yonder, the one comin' from school."

11 "Spit it out right now!"

12 I spat it out. The tang was fading, anyway. "I've been chewin' it all afternoon and I ain't dead yet, not even sick."

13 Jem stamped his foot. "Don't you know you're not supposed to even touch the trees over there? You'll get killed if you do!"

14 "You touched the house once!"

15 "That was different! You go gargle—right now, you hear me?"

16 "Ain't neither, it'll take the taste outa my mouth."

17 "You don't 'n' I'll tell Calpurnia on you!"

hastily: quickly

18 Rather than risk a tangle with Calpurnia, I did as Jem told me. For some reason, my first year of school had **wrought** a great change in our relationship: Calpurnia's **tyranny**, unfairness, and meddling in my business had faded to gentle grumblings of general disapproval. On my part, I went to much trouble, sometimes, not to **provoke** her.

19 Summer was on the way; Jem and I awaited it with impatience. Summer was our best season: it was sleeping on the back screened porch in cots, or trying to sleep in the treehouse; summer was everything good to eat; it was a thousand colors in a **parched** landscape; but most of all, summer was Dill.

20 The authorities released us early the last day of school, and Jem and I walked home together. "Reckon old Dill'll be coming home tomorrow," I said.

21 "Probably day after," said Jem. "Mis'sippi turns 'em loose a day later."

22 As we came to the live oaks at the Radley Place I raised my finger to point for the hundredth time to the knot-hole where I had found the chewing gum, trying to make Jem believe I had found it there, and found myself pointing at another piece of tinfoil.

23 "I see it, Scout! I see it—"

24 Jem looked around, reached up, and **gingerly** pocketed a tiny shiny package. We ran home, and on the front porch we looked at a small box patchworked with bits of tinfoil collected from chewing-gum wrappers. It was the kind of box wedding rings came in, purple velvet with a minute catch. Jem flicked open the tiny catch. Inside were two scrubbed and polished pennies, one on top of the other. Jem examined them.

25 "Indian-heads," he said. "Nineteen-six and Scout, one of 'em's nineteen-hundred. These are real old."

26 "Nineteen-hundred," I echoed. "Say—"

27 "Hush a minute, I'm thinkin'."

28 "Jem, you reckon that's somebody's hidin' place?"

29 "Naw, don't anybody much but us pass by there, unless it's some grown person's—"

30 "Grown folks don't have hidin' places. You reckon we ought to keep 'em, Jem?"

31 "I don't know what we could do, Scout. Who'd we give 'em back to? I know for a fact don't anybody go by there—Cecil goes by the back street an' all the way around by town to get home."

32 Cecil Jacobs, who lived at the far end of our street next door to the post office, walked a total of one mile per school day to avoid the Radley Place and old Mrs. Henry Lafayette Dubose. Mrs. Dubose lived two doors up the street from us; neighborhood opinion was **unanimous** that Mrs. Dubose was the meanest old woman who ever lived. Jem wouldn't go by her place without Atticus beside him.

My Notes

wrought: brought about
tyranny: absolute rule
provoke: anger
parched: dry
gingerly: carefully
unanimous: agreed on by everyone

My Notes

33 "What you **reckon** we oughta do, Jem?"

34 Finders were keepers unless title was proven. Plucking an occasional camellia, getting a squirt of hot milk from Miss Maudie Atkinson's cow on a summer day, helping ourselves to someone's scuppernongs was part of our **ethical** culture, but money was different.

35 "Tell you what," said Jem. "We'll keep 'em till school starts, then go around and ask everybody if they're theirs. They're some bus child's, maybe—he was taken up with gettin' outa school today an' forgot 'em. These are somebody's, I know that. See how they've been **slicked up**? They've been saved."

36 "Yeah, but why should somebody wanta put away chewing gum like that? You know it doesn't last."

37 "I don't know, Scout. But these are important to somebody …"

38 "How's that, Jem…?"

39 "Well, Indian-heads—well, they come from the Indians. They're real strong magic, they make you have good luck. Not like fried chicken when you're not lookin' for it, but things like long life 'n' good health, 'n' passin' six-weeks tests … these are real valuable to somebody. I'm gonna put 'em in my trunk."

40 Before Jem went to his room, he looked for a long time at the Radley Place. He seemed to be thinking again.

reckon: think
ethical: moral
slicked up: polished

Making Observations

- What is your impression of Scout and Jem?
- What details stand out to you?

Returning to the Text

- Return to the text as you respond to the following questions. Use evidence from the text to support your responses.
- Write any additional questions you have about the text in your Reader/Writer Notebook.

2. What does Scout's changing relationship with Calpurnia suggest about Scout's coming of age?

_____

_____

_____

_____

3. Why do the children struggle with what to do with the pennies they find? What does this suggest about their character?

_____

_____

_____

_____

4. At the end of this excerpt, Jem is "thinking again." What might Jem be considering that the younger Scout hasn't thought of? Use evidence to support your response.

_____

_____

_____

_____

5. How does the author use language to help characterize the children?

_____

_____

_____

_____

Working from the Text

6. Continue reading Chapters 4–6, either in your group or independently. As you read, take notes in your double-entry journal.

VOCABULARY

LITERARY

A motif is a recurring image, symbol, theme, character type, subject, or detail that is a unifying element in an artistic work.

The plot, or sequence of events that make up a story, is often accompanied by a subplot, or secondary story, that develops from and supports the main plot. Subplots often involve minor characters.

7. The character of Boo Radley is a motif in *To Kill a Mockingbird*, and the incidents involving the children's fascination with him form one of the major subplots of the novel. In a discussion group, self-assign the following passages that explore this motif and subplot in further depth.

    Passage 1: Chapter 4 (from "Let's roll in the tire ..." to the end of Chapter 4)

    Passage 2: Chapter 5 (from "Next morning when I ..." to the end of Chapter 5)

    Passage 3: Chapter 6 (from "What are you gonna do?" to "Settle it yourselves.")

8. Form an expert group with other students who have selected the same passage. Conduct a close reading of your passage, using sticky notes to mark textual evidence and record your questions, commentary, inferences, and conclusions. Work together to complete the appropriate row of a graphic organizer like the one that follows.

Objective Summary of the Passage	Statement About How This Is a Coming-of-Age Experience	Key Textual Evidence to Support Your Interpretation
Passage 1:		
Passage 2:		
Passage 3:		

9. Return to your discussion group and share your expert group's observations, interpretations, and evidence. Take notes in the appropriate row as you listen to the other group members analyze their passages.

☑ Check Your Understanding

Write a statement about how the experience of finding gifts in the knothole of the Radley live oak tree helps Jem and Scout come of age.

Questions and Conclusions

Learning Targets

- Use various levels of questions to identify themes in a novel.
- Write thematic statements and a concluding paragraph.

Preview

In this activity, you will read Chapters 7–9 of *To Kill a Mockingbird* and work collaboratively to identify the themes explored in each chapter.

INDEPENDENT READING LINK

Read and Discuss

Choose three chunks of text from your independent reading selection. As you answer the following questions for each chunk, notice how each level adds a layer of complexity to your connection to the material. (Level 1) What does the text say? (Level 2) What does the text mean? (Level 3) Why does it matter?

First Read: Chapter 7

1. Review the Questioning the Text strategy and read the first chunk of Chapter 7 with your class, generating questions at all three levels. Share your responses to the questions in a class discussion.

Chunk 1: From the start of Chapter 7 to "I'd have the facts."

Level 1 Question: Literal Question ("What does the text say?")

Level 2 Question: Interpretive Question ("What does the text mean?")

Level 3 Question: Universal Question ("Why does it matter?")

2. Read the second and third chunks with a small group and generate questions at all three levels for each chunk. Share your responses to the questions in a group discussion.

Chunk 2: From "There are no clearly defined seasons ..." to "Huh?"

Level 1 Question: Literal Question ("What does the text say?")

Level 2 Question: Interpretive Question ("What does the text mean?")

Level 3 Question: Universal Question ("Why does it matter?")

Chunk 3: From "You reckon we oughta write a letter ..." to the end of the chapter.

Level 1 Question: Literal Question ("What does the text say?")

Level 2 Question: Interpretive Question ("What does the text mean?")

Level 3 Question: Universal Question ("Why does it matter?")

My Notes

Working from the Text

3. Work with your discussion group to identify several topics and thematic statements that can be made by examining the character of Boo Radley and how the children interact with him. What coming-of-age lessons have the children learned from these experiences?

4. As you read Chapters 8–9, chunk each chapter into at least three sections and use sticky notes to generate questions at all three levels for each chunk.

☑ Check Your Understanding

Exchange your questions with a partner and respond to the questions he or she wrote.

✍ Writing to Sources: Informational Text

Choose one of Scout's coming-of-age experiences from thus far in the novel and write a literary analysis paragraph in which you explain how that event contributes to a theme that is developing in the text. Be sure to:

- Use a single-paragraph outline to plan your draft.
- Include factual, interpretive, and universal statements that develop the idea.
- Use the present tense, literary vocabulary, and formal style consistently.

Learning Targets

- Identify and correct sentence fragments, run-on sentences, and splices.
- Edit writing to correct errors in sentence formation and strengthen writing.
- Analyze a writer's use of fragments, run-ons, and splices for stylistic effect.

Preview

In this activity, you will investigate intentional and unintentional sentence fragments, run-on sentences, and splices. You will also review the literary analysis that you wrote in Activity 4.17 for correct sentence structure.

Good and Bad Sentence Variety

Skilled writers use a variety of sentence types to establish a tone and voice, engage the reader, and convey precisely what they want to say. Sometimes they use splices, run-ons, and fragments for specific, controlled effects. But good writers are also able to identify unintentional splices, fragments, and run-on sentences in their writing, and can correct them.

Recognizing Fragments

A sentence fragment is not a complete sentence. A complete sentence has at least one independent clause—a subject and a verb that expresses a complete thought. A sentence fragment is only a partial thought.

1. Read the following text from *To Kill a Mockingbird*. Circle the subject and underline the verb, if applicable.

    I ran to him.

2. Does the text express a complete thought?

3. Read the following text from *To Kill a Mockingbird*. Circle the subject and underline the verb, if applicable.

    After while.

4. Does the text express a complete thought?

5. This excerpt from *To Kill a Mockingbird* includes fragments:

    He held them down to me. They were almost perfect miniatures of two children. The boy had on shorts. Red shorts. A shock of soapy hair fell to his eyebrows. I looked up at Jem. But not too long. A point of straight brown hair kicked downwards from his part. I had never noticed it before. Jem looked from the girl-doll to me. The girl-doll wore bangs. So did I.

    a. Which word groups are sentence fragments?

b. Explain how you identified the fragments.

c. Why might the writer have chosen to use fragments? What effect do they create?

Recognizing Run-On Sentences

Sometimes two or more complete sentences run together as if they are a single sentence, which creates a run-on sentence. This is not like a compound sentence, which includes complete sentences joined with conjunctions. As with sentence fragments, writers usually avoid using run-on sentences, although some writers use them stylistically for effect.

6. Highlight the run-on sentence in this passage about *To Kill a Mockingbird*.

> Jem and Scout keep finding things in a tree near their house they don't know where they come from. They find soap carvings of themselves, gum, and a broken watch on a chain with a knife attached.

7. With a partner, brainstorm possible ways the writer could correct the run-on sentence.

Recognizing Comma Splices

One specific kind of run-on sentence is called a **comma splice**. A comma splice occurs when two complete sentences are run together with only a comma between them.

> Scout doesn't know Boo Radley, his helpfulness surprises her.

Breaking the run-on sentences into two separate sentences, adding a conjunction after the comma, or replacing the comma with a semicolon can correct a comma splice.

8. Rewrite the sentence using a semicolon to fix the comma splice.

9. Read the following paragraph. Underline sentence fragments, draw brackets around run-on sentences, and circle the commas in comma splices.

Although the people who live in Maycomb are known for their kindness. Scout and Jem start to understand that prejudice plays a role in the community. From Atticus, they learn about tolerance and courage if a friend disagrees with him, he still considers that person a friend, he also won't allow that friend's opinions stop him from fighting for what's right.

Editing

10. Rewrite the following paragraph, correcting fragments, run-on sentences, and splices.

To Kill a Mockingbird is a coming-of-age story, it is an unforgettable novel of a childhood in a sleepy Southern town and the crisis of conscience that rocked it. It takes readers to the roots of human behavior. Both good and incredibly ugly. It shifts between innocence and experience, kindness and cruelty, love and hatred it is regarded as a masterpiece of American literature.

☑ Check Your Understanding

What questions can you add to your Editor's Checklist to help you remember to check for sentence fragments?

What questions can you add to your Editor's Checklist to help you remember to check for run-ons in your work?

What questions can you add to your Editor's Checklist to help you remember to check for comma splices in your work?

Add the questions to your Editor's Checklist.

Practice

Look back at the literary analysis you wrote in Activity 4.17. Correct any sentence fragments, run-on sentences, or comma splices you find.

Learning Strategies

Close Reading
Discussion Groups
Double-Entry Journal
Graphic Organizer

My Notes

Learning Targets

- Analyze how an author uses multiple literary elements in one passage to develop a theme.
- Use details and text evidence to identify an author's purpose.

Preview

In this activity, you will read a chapter from *To Kill a Mockingbird* and explore the author's use of various literary elements.

As You Read

- Highlight evidence that identifies direct and indirect characterization.
- Circle unknown words and phrases. Try to determine the meaning of the words by using context clues, word parts, or a dictionary.

Novel

from To Kill a Mockingbird,
Chapter 10, Paragraphs 1–9

by **Harper Lee**

1   Atticus was feeble: he was nearly fifty. When Jem and I asked him why he was so old, he said he got started late, which we felt reflected upon his abilities and manliness. He was much older than the parents of our school contemporaries, and there was nothing Jem or I could say about him when our classmates said, "My father—"

2   Jem was football crazy. Atticus was never too tired to play keep-away, but when Jem wanted to tackle him Atticus would say, "I'm too old for that, son."

3   Our father didn't do anything. He worked in an office, not in a drugstore. Atticus did not drive a dump-truck for the county, he was not the sheriff, he did not farm, work in a garage, or do anything that could possibly arouse the admiration of anyone.

4   Besides that, he wore glasses. He was nearly blind in his left eye, and said left eyes were the tribal curse of the Finches. Whenever he wanted to see something well, he turned his head and looked from his right eye.

5   He did not do the things our schoolmates' fathers did: he never went hunting, he did not play poker or fish or drink or smoke. He sat in the living room and read.

6   With these attributes, however, he would not remain as inconspicuous as we wished him to: that year, the school buzzed with talk about him defending Tom Robinson, none of which was complimentary. After my bout with Cecil Jacobs when I committed myself to a policy of cowardice, word got around

that Scout Finch wouldn't fight any more, her daddy wouldn't let her. This was not entirely correct: I wouldn't fight publicly for Atticus, but the family was fair ground. I would fight anyone from a third cousin upwards tooth and nail. Francis Hancock, for example, knew that.

7   When he gave us our air rifles Atticus wouldn't teach us to shoot. Uncle Jack instructed us in the **rudiments** thereof; he said Atticus wasn't interested in guns. Atticus said to Jem one day, "I'd rather you shot at tin cans in the back yard, but I know you'll go after birds. Shoot all the bluejays you want, if you can hit 'em, but remember it's a sin to kill a mockingbird."

8   That was the only time I ever heard Atticus say it was a sin to do something, and I asked Miss Maudie about it.

9   "Your father's right," she said. "Mockingbirds don't do one thing but make music for us to enjoy. They don't eat up people's gardens, don't nest in corncribs, they don't do one thing but sing their hearts out for us. That's why it's a sin to kill a mockingbird."

Making Observations

- What captures your attention in this excerpt?
- What do you notice about how Jem and Scout feel about Atticus?
- What do you notice about Atticus's advice?

rudiments: basics

Working from the Text

1. Work with a small group to conduct a close reading of the rest of Chapter 10. Focus first on how characters are developed, and then think about what events are advancing the plot. Use sticky notes to mark the text for evidence that directly relates to both of these literary elements.

2. After reading Chapter 10, choose two examples of characterization and plot events that stand out to you. Record them in your double-entry journal. Then share your reactions with your group and discuss how these details directly relate to a theme of the novel.

3. Based on your understanding of Atticus's character, why do you think he isn't interested in guns?

4. How does Miss Maudie's information about mockingbirds add to Atticus's comment that "it's a sin to kill a mockingbird"?

5. Based on your understanding of Chapter 10, what might a mockingbird symbolize? How does the author's use of language help you come to this conclusion?

6. What does the mad dog symbolize? What is a possible theme introduced in this chapter?

☑ Check Your Understanding

Consider the following thesis statement:

Harper Lee uses the killing of the mad dog to develop the theme that racism is a dangerous threat to a peaceful community.

Write your own thesis statement about how one literary element that you analyzed from Chapter 10 contributes to a theme.

_____

_____

✍ Writing to Sources: Informational Text

Revisit the thesis statement you wrote about the literary element you focused on. Write body paragraphs to develop your ideas. Be sure to:

- Include relevant details and examples to support your commentary.
- Maintain a formal tone and write in the literary present tense.

Learning Strategies

Diffusing
Discussion Groups
Double-Entry Journal
Drafting
Marking the Text
Skimming/Scanning

Learning Targets

- Write an interpretive statement about the significance of literary elements.
- Gather textual evidence to generate thematic statements.

Preview

In this activity, you will read an excerpt from Chapter 11 and analyze how the author creates a believable character.

As You Read

- Underline vivid descriptions of characters.
- Circle unknown words and phrases. Try to determine the meaning of the words by using context clues, word parts, or a dictionary.

Novel

from To Kill a Mockingbird,
Chapter 11, Paragraphs 1–5

by **Harper Lee**

GRAMMAR & USAGE

Independent Clauses
An independent clause is a group of words that contains a subject and a verb and can stand alone as a sentence. A sentence having more than one independent clause is a compound sentence. One way to combine two such clauses is to use a coordinating conjunction: *and, or, but*. Most sentences with multiple independent clauses need a comma before the coordinating conjunction.
Example: I did not remember our mother, but Jem did.

1 When we were small, Jem and I **confined** our activities to the southern neighborhood, but when I was well into the second grade at school and tormenting Boo Radley became **passé**, the business section of Maycomb drew us frequently up the street past the real property of Mrs. Henry Lafayette Dubose. It was impossible to go to town without passing her house unless we wished to walk a mile out of the way. Previous minor encounters with her left me with no desire for more, but Jem said I had to grow up some time.

2 Mrs. Dubose lived alone except for a Negro girl in constant attendance, two doors up the street from us in a house with steep front steps and a dog-trot hall. She was very old; she spent most of each day in bed and the rest of it in a wheelchair. It was rumored that she kept a CSA pistol concealed among her numerous shawls and wraps.

3 Jem and I hated her. If she was on the porch when we passed, we would be raked by her **wrathful** gaze, subjected to ruthless interrogation regarding our behavior, and given a **melancholy** prediction on what we would amount to when we grew up, which was always nothing. We had long ago given up the idea of walking past her house on the opposite side of the street; that only made her raise her voice and let the whole neighborhood in on it.

4 We could do nothing to please her. If I said as sunnily as I could, "Hey, Mrs. Dubose," I would receive for an answer, "Don't you say hey to me, you ugly girl! You say good afternoon, Mrs. Dubose!"

confined: restricted
passé: out of fashion
wrathful: angry
melancholy: gloomy

5   She was vicious. Once she heard Jem refer to our father as "Atticus" and her reaction was **apoplectic**. Besides being the sassiest, most disrespectful mutts who ever passed her way, we were told that it was quite a pity our father had not remarried after our mother's death. A lovelier lady than our mother never lived, she said, and it was heartbreaking the way Atticus Finch let her children run wild. I did not remember our mother, but Jem did—he would tell me about her sometimes—and he went **livid** when Mrs. Dubose shot us this message.

Making Observations

- What are your first thoughts after reading this part of the novel?
- What words or phrases stand out to you?

apoplectic: extremely angry
livid: enraged

Working from the Text

1. Consider the significance of character, conflict, and setting in the passage you just read. Ask yourself: Why are these literary elements significant in this passage? How do they connect to the larger issues in the novel?

   Use the following sentence frames to generate an interpretive statement about each of these elements.

   - *The character of Mrs. Dubose represents _____ .*
   - *The conflict between the children and Mrs. Dubose is similar to _____ .*
   - *The setting of Mrs. Dubose's house is significant because _____ .*

2. In the following quotation, Atticus gives Jem advice on how to deal with Mrs. Dubose. Consider what this advice might be foreshadowing.

   > "You just hold your head high and be a gentleman. Whatever she says to you, it's your job not to let her make you mad."

   Rewrite Atticus's advice as a statement, or "life lesson."

3. As you read the rest of Chapter 11, use sticky notes to record textual evidence of Atticus's advice to Jem and Scout concerning Mrs. Dubose.

Identifying Themes

4. Work with your class to gather evidence of Atticus's "life lessons" from other chapters. Create and illustrate a poster with the quotes and life lessons.

5. Use the quotes to identify themes based on the lessons Atticus wants his children to learn as they come of age. Create a web of these and other themes Harper Lee explores in the first half of *To Kill a Mockingbird*. When identifying themes, keep in mind the following:

   - A theme is a message, not just a topic, and it cannot be just a word, such as *prejudice*. A theme from *To Kill a Mockingbird* would be "Prejudice is based on fear."
   - Avoid clichés such as "Blood is thicker than water."
   - Don't state a theme as an order: "People must not be racist."
   - Themes should be universal, not limited to the characters in a novel. "Scout is a tomboy" is not a theme.

   Use the following web as a model.

_____   _____

_____   **Part One:**   _____

_____   Themes Connected to   _____
                            Coming of Age

_____   _____

LANGUAGE & WRITER'S CRAFT: Incorporating Quotations

Quotations are powerful pieces of text evidence that can be used to support your literary analysis. You must, however, integrate quotations into the body of your analysis smoothly and carefully, so that it is clear how the quoted text relates to the logical flow of ideas in your writing. Use the **TLQC** (Transition, Lead-in, Quote, Commentary) method to integrate your quotes with commentary in a literary analysis essay:

- **Transition:** A transitional word, phrase, or clause can be used to begin introducing your quote. The type of transition will depend on how the quotation follows from the previous ideas. Some commonly used transitions are *for example, in addition, as a result, regardless*, and *after all*.

- **Lead-in:** Give background for the quote by identifying the situation in which it occurs, who is speaking, or any other information necessary to set the quote in context.

- **Quote:** Place quoted text in quotation marks, and remember to include a parenthetical citation. Consult a style manual, such as the *MLA Handbook*, for correct formatting of citations.

- **Commentary:** Follow up the quote with an explanation of what the quote shows or how it is relevant to the point you are making.

PRACTICE Identify the transition, lead-in, quote, and commentary in the following example:

For example, Jem never loses his calm as he reads to Mrs. Dubose. Scout observes that "Through the weeks he had cultivated an expression of polite and detached interest, which he would present to her in answer to her most blood-curdling inventions." Jem is taking his father's advice and growing into the kind of man who will not get dragged down by other people's anger.

☑ Check Your Understanding

Choose one of the events in Chapter 11 to reexamine. Think about which detail offers you the most information about a theme of the story. Write a sentence that connects this detail to traits you know about the main characters in the story.

You can use the following sentence frame to help you write your sentence:

_____ *is a detail that reveals* _____ .

_____

_____

_____

_____

_____

_____

INDEPENDENT READING LINK

Read and Respond

Think about the themes that are emerging in the text you are reading independently, whether it is fiction or nonfiction. Choose one and write a thematic statement that states the theme and briefly explains how the author is developing the theme.

✍ Writing to Sources: Informational Text

Analyze how character, plot and conflict, or setting contribute to a coming-of-age theme in Chapter 11. Be sure to:

- Use an organizing structure that points to the theme.
- Include textual evidence in the form of direct quotations.
- Explain how your quotes support your analysis.
- Write objectively, using a formal style.

Shifting Perspectives

Learning Strategies

Brainstorming
Close Reading
Double-Entry Journal
Marking the Text

Learning Targets

- Create an outline for an analytical essay about how literary elements contribute to a theme.

Preview

In this activity, you will conduct a close reading of Chapter 12, marking the text for evidence of how setting, character, and conflict contribute to the theme: *Coming of age involves recognizing different perspectives*.

My Notes

Close Reading: Chapters 12–14

1. Part of coming of age is understanding that your perspective of the world is not the only one—that other perspectives based on different cultures, nationalities, religions, political beliefs, customs, languages, and values are just as real and valid as your own. Brainstorm experiences you have had that have exposed you to different perspectives.

2. Work with your class to complete the outline that follows for an essay about how literary elements and Harper Lee's use of language in Chapter 12 contribute to the theme "Coming of age involves recognizing different perspectives."

Outline for a Passage-Analysis Essay

I. Introduction:

    Hook: Anecdote, Quote, Question, or Statement of Intrigue

    Thesis:

II. Body (Supporting Paragraph):

    Topic Sentence:

    Textual Evidence:

III. Body (Supporting Paragraph):

    Topic Sentence:

    Textual Evidence:

IV. Body (Supporting Paragraph):

    Topic Sentence:

    Textual Evidence:

V. Conclusion:

    Restate Thesis:

    Literal/Interpretive/Universal Statements:

3. Look for more textual evidence in Chapter 12 to support the topic sentences in your outline.

4. Read Chapters 13–14. After you finish reading, choose a passage to reread and mark for at least two different literary elements. Use the outline as a model for your passage analysis.

☑ Focus on the Sentence

Write three sentences about how perspective and context enhance your understanding of the novel, each using a different sentence structure.

Statement: _____

_____

Question: _____

_____

Exclamation: _____

_____

✍ Drafting the Embedded Assessment

Draft an explanatory paragraph that analyzes two different literary elements from the text. Consider the purpose the author had in using those literary elements and the effect they have on readers. Be sure to:

- Plan your writing by rereading the text and discussing it with your group.
- Develop a focused and structured paragraph.
- Use text evidence in your paragraph.

Learning Strategies

Close Reading
Discussion Groups
Double-Entry Journal
Visualizing

Learning Targets

- Conduct a close reading and analyze significant literary elements.
- Analyze how an author's specific language choices create mood, voice, and tone.

Close Reading: Chapter 15

1. Read Chapter 15 with your group. Work with your group to record textual evidence of significant literary elements in the graphic organizer.

Setting	Conflict	Character	Other (Plot, symbol, motif)

2. What coming-of-age lesson could Scout, Dill, or Jem learn from the experience in Chapter 15, even if they may not recognize it yet? How does this point to a theme in the novel?

_____

_____

_____

_____

_____

Working from the Text

3. Recall that authors create the mood, voice, and tone of a text by carefully selecting words (diction) and deliberately crafting sentences (syntax). Create a double-entry journal entry about the mood, voice, and tone of several sections of this chapter by quoting important words and sentences in the left column and describing the effect they create in the right column. Use the following example as a guide.

Textual Evidence	Mood, Voice, or Tone Created
Atticus lowered the paper and gazed at Jem. "What have you been reading?" he asked. Then he said gently, "No son, those were our friends."	The word "gazed" implies a more intent look than just the word "look." This creates a mood of comfort between father and son. The son is worried, and his father is trying to calm him.

Appreciating the Author's Craft

Discuss the following questions with your classmates.

- How do Lee's specific language choices contribute to the overall suspense of Chapter 15?

- What if the events of Chapter 15 occurred today? How might they be written differently?

☑ Check Your Understanding

State your analysis of Lee's craft in one sentence using the following sentence frame.

Lee's use of the [word/phrase] _____ creates a [mood, voice, tone] of _____ because _____ .

Learning Strategies

Double-Entry Journal
Drafting
Marking the Text
Rereading
SMELL

GRAMMAR & USAGE

Parallel Structure

Parallel structure is often used in persuasive speech because it emphasizes an important aspect of the related ideas, creates a pleasing rhythm, and helps the speaker build to a point. Consider this part of Atticus's argument: "the assumption ... that *all* Negroes lie, that *all* Negroes are basically immoral beings, that *all* Negro men are not to be trusted ..." This sentence uses parallel relative clauses with *that*. Consider how Atticus's use of parallel structure adds to the force of his argument.

Learning Targets

- Recognize the rhetorical appeals used in a speech.
- In a written paragraph, analyze the use of rhetorical appeals in a key scene.

Preview

In this activity, you will explore Chapters 17–19 and an excerpt from Chapter 20, noting rhetorical appeals and analyzing Atticus's closing argument.

Close Reading: Chapters 17–19

1. Read Chapters 17–19 as a class or in small groups. After you finish reading, think about the testimony presented in the chapters. Which rhetorical appeals do the lawyers and witnesses use? Find textual evidence of each of the following:

    Logos: an appeal to logic or reason

    Ethos: an appeal to ethics or the character of the speaker

    Pathos: an appeal to senses or emotions

My Notes

_____
_____
_____
_____
_____
_____
_____
_____
_____
_____
_____
_____
_____
_____

2. Discuss the following questions with your class.
    - Which speakers rely primarily on pathos?
    - Which speakers would have had difficulty appealing to ethos?
    - What evidence comes to light through appeals to logos?

As You Read

- Highlight text that is a rhetorical appeal.
- Circle unknown words and phrases. Try to determine the meaning of the words by using context clues, word parts, or a dictionary.

Novel

from To Kill a Mockingbird,
Chapter 20, Paragraphs 40–54

by **Harper Lee**

40 "Gentlemen," he was saying. "I shall be brief, but I would like to use my remaining time with you to remind you that this case is not a difficult one, it requires no **minute sifting** of complicated facts, but it does require you to be sure beyond all reasonable doubt as to the guilt of the defendant. To begin with, this case should never have come to trial. This case is as simple as black and white.

41 "The state has not produced one **iota** of medical evidence to the effect that the crime Tom Robinson is charged with ever took place. It has relied instead upon the testimony of two witnesses whose evidence has not only been called into serious question on cross-examination, but has been flatly contradicted by the defendant. The defendant is not guilty, but somebody in this courtroom is.

42 "I have nothing but pity in my heart for the chief witness for the state, but my pity does not extend so far as to her putting a man's life at stake, which she has done in an effort to get rid of her own guilt.

43 "I say guilt, gentlemen, because it was guilt that motivated her. She has committed no crime, she has merely broken a rigid and time-honored code of our society, a code so severe that whoever breaks it is hounded from our midst as unfit to live with. She is the victim of cruel poverty and ignorance, but I cannot pity her: she is white. She knew full well the enormity of her offense, but because her desires were stronger than the code she was breaking, she **persisted** in breaking it. She persisted, and her subsequent reaction is something that all of us have known at one time or another. She did something every child has done—she tried to put the evidence of her offense away from her. But in this case she was no child hiding stolen **contraband**: she struck out at her victim—of necessity she must put him away from her—he must be removed from her presence, from this world. She must destroy the evidence of her offense. ...

46 "Her father saw it, and the defendant has testified as to his remarks. What did her father do? We don't know, but there is circumstantial evidence to indicate that Mayella Ewell was beaten savagely by someone who led almost exclusively with his left. We do know in part what Mr. Ewell did: he did what any God-fearing, persevering, respectable white man would do under the circumstances—he swore out a warrant, no doubt signing it with his left hand, and Tom Robinson now sits before you, having taken the oath with the only good hand he possesses—his right hand.

minute: precise
sifting: sorting
iota: small quantity
persisted: continued with determination
contraband: objects forbidden by the law

47 "And so a quiet, respectable, humble Negro who had the unmitigated **temerity** to 'feel sorry' for a white woman has had to put his word against two white people's. I need not remind you of their appearance and conduct on the stand—you saw them for yourselves. The witnesses for the state, with the exception of the sheriff of Maycomb County, have presented themselves to you gentlemen, to this court, in the **cynical** confidence that their testimony would not be doubted, confident that you gentlemen would go along with them on the assumption—the evil assumption—that *all* Negroes lie, that *all* Negroes are basically immoral beings, that *all* Negro men are not to be trusted around our women, an assumption one associates with minds of their **caliber**.

48 "Which, gentlemen, we know is in itself a lie as black as Tom Robinson's skin, a lie I do not have to point out to you. You know the truth, and the truth is this: some Negroes lie, some Negroes are immoral, some Negro men are not to be trusted around women—black or white. But this is a truth that applies to the human race and to no particular race of men. There is not a person in this courtroom who has never told a lie, who has never done an immoral thing, and there is no man living who has never looked upon a woman without desire."

49 Atticus paused and took out his handkerchief. Then he took off his glasses and wiped them, and we saw another "first": we had never seen him sweat—he was one of those men whose faces never **perspired**, but now it was shining tan.

50 "One more thing, gentlemen, before I quit. Thomas Jefferson once said that all men are created equal, a phrase that the Yankees and the distaff side of the Executive branch in Washington are fond of hurling at us. There is a **tendency** in this year of grace, 1935, for certain people to use this phrase out of context, to satisfy all conditions. The most ridiculous example I can think of

temerity: recklessness
cynical: distrustful
caliber: quality
perspired: sweat
tendency: inclination to do something

In the 1962 film adaptation of *To Kill a Mockingbird*, Gregory Peck (left) and Brock Peters (right) portrayed Atticus Finch and Tom Robinson.

is that the people who run public education promote the stupid and idle along with the industrious—because all men are created equal, educators will gravely tell you, the children left behind suffer terrible feelings of inferiority. We know all men are not created equal in the sense some people would have us believe—some people are smarter than others, some people have more opportunity because they're born with it, some men make more money than others, some ladies make better cakes than others—some people are born gifted beyond the normal scope of most men.

51   "But there is one way in this country in which all men are created equal— there is one human institution that makes a pauper the equal of a Rockefeller, the stupid man the equal of an Einstein, and the ignorant man the equal of any college president. That institution, gentlemen, is a court. It can be the Supreme Court of the United States or the humblest J.P. court in the land, or this honorable court which you serve. Our courts have their faults, as does any human institution, but in this country our courts are the great levelers, and in our courts all men are created equal.

52   "I'm no idealist to believe firmly in the integrity of our courts and in the jury system—that is no ideal to me, it is a living, working reality. Gentlemen, a court is no better than each man of you sitting before me on this jury. A court is only as sound as its jury, and a jury is only as sound as the men who make it up. I am confident that you gentlemen will review without passion the evidence you have heard, come to a decision, and restore this defendant to his family. In the name of God, do your duty."

53   Atticus's voice had dropped, and as he turned away from the jury he said something I did not catch. He said it more to himself than to the court. I punched Jem. "What'd he say?"

54   "'In the name of God, believe him,' I think that's what he said."

Making Observations
- What details stick with you after the first reading?
- What first impression do you get about the author's feelings about the topic of Atticus's closing argument?

idle: lazy
pauper: very poor person
idealist: person who pursues noble principles

Returning to the Text

- Return to the text as you respond to the following questions. Use evidence from the text to support your responses.
- Write any additional questions you have about the text in your Reader/Writer Notebook.

3. What does Atticus mean when he says, "This case is as simple as black and white"?

_____

_____

_____

_____

4. What tone does Atticus use when describing Mayella to the court?

_____

_____

_____

_____

5. Why is it significant that Atticus is sweating while delivering his closing statement?

_____

_____

_____

_____

6. According to Atticus, what is the one way that all men are created equal?

_____

_____

_____

_____

7. How does Atticus feel about Tom Robinson? How can you tell?

_____

_____

_____

_____

Working from the Text

8. Use the SMELL strategy to analyze Atticus's closing statement.

S = Sender-receiver relationship Atticus is the sender. The jury and the audience are the receivers. What is the relationship among Atticus, the jury, and the audience? Whom does Atticus mean to influence with his statement? What attitudes and assumptions does his target audience hold toward his subject? Toward Atticus himself?	
M = Message What is Atticus's message? Summarize the statements made in his closing argument.	
E = Emotional strategies Does Atticus use any statements that are meant to get an emotional reaction from his audience? Explain. If so, what is the desired effect?	
L = Logical strategies Does Atticus use any statements or appeals that are logical? Explain. How does the logic (or its absence) affect the message?	
L = Language Look for specific words and phrases used by Atticus, and consider how the language affects his message.	

INDEPENDENT READING LINK

Read and Discuss

Find a section of your independent reading where the writer or a character is crafting an argument. What rhetorical strategy is the writer or character using to make the argument? Is it effective? Summarize the passage, prepare your responses to the questions, and share them in a group discussion.

☑ **Check Your Understanding**

Which rhetorical appeal does Atticus rely on most heavily for his closing argument? Why?

_____

_____

_____

_____

_____

_____

_____

Aftermath and Reflection

Learning Targets

- Analyze the significance of literary elements in a passage in relation to a theme of the novel.
- Write a thesis statement and topic sentences for an essay that explains how literary elements contribute to a theme of the novel.

Preview

In this activity, you will participate in a Socratic Seminar and analyze literary elements that contribute to a theme of the novel.

Learning Strategies

Double-Entry Journal
Questioning the Text
Revising
Socratic Seminar

My Notes

Introducing the Strategy: Socratic Seminar

A Socratic Seminar is a type of collaborative discussion designed to explore a complex question, topic, or text. Participants engage in meaningful and respectful discourse by asking one another questions, listening actively, and responding thoughtfully, citing textual evidence for support. The goal is for participants to arrive at a deeper understanding of a concept or idea by the end of the discussion. A Socratic Seminar is not a debate.

Socratic Seminar

1. Your teacher will lead you in a Socratic Seminar in which you discuss the verdict of the trial. Read the questions and write your responses. Then, generate at least one question at each level to use in the discussion.

- Why is Jem so optimistic before he hears the verdict?

- How and why is Scout's reaction to the verdict different from Jem's?

Original Level 1 Question(s):

Original Level 2 Question(s):

_____

_____

Original Level 3 Question(s):

_____

_____

2. After your discussion, work with your group to co-construct a statement synthesizing your response(s) to the question(s).

_____

_____

_____

3. Work with your class to co-construct a statement about how the trial was a coming-of-age experience for Jem.

_____

_____

_____

Working from the Text

4. As you read Chapter 24, consider the significance of the chapter to the meaning of the novel as a whole. Complete the graphic organizer that follows by analyzing how different literary elements contribute to a recurring theme of the novel.

Analysis of a Literary Element in Chapter 24	Textual Evidence (Quote from text)	Theme of the Novel as a Whole	Evidence of This Theme in Another Chapter
Character: Grace Merriweather's character represents the irony of someone who claims to be religious but is actually a hypocrite.		Racism is a disease that infects a person's mind and soul.	

Analysis of a Literary Element in Chapter 24	Textual Evidence (Quote from text)	Theme of the Novel as a Whole	Evidence of This Theme in Another Chapter
Setting: The setting of the missionary tea in the Finches' living room			
Conflict:			
Plot event:			

5. **Discuss:** How does Scout's perspective on what it means to be a lady evolve during this scene? How are the events in this chapter a coming-of-age experience for her?

LANGUAGE & WRITER'S CRAFT: Topic Sentences and Transitions

When used effectively, topic sentences and transitions bring structure and flow to your writing. Your thesis—your assertion about the topic—will be stated in the introduction of your essay. Body paragraphs then explain the main ideas that work together to support your thesis. The topic sentence of a body paragraph states the main idea of that paragraph.

Transitions guide readers through your essay by showing how ideas are connected. Some transitions work to provide coherence among sentences, linking one sentence to the next.

Similarity	Contrast	Cause/Effect	Introduction
Likewise	In contrast	As a result	For example
Similarly	However	Therefore	For instance
In the same way	Conversely	Consequently	In particular
		Accordingly	To illustrate

Other transitions help link paragraphs and main ideas to a thesis. A **three-fold transition** is an example of this type of transition.

Three-fold transitions help you make logical connections between your points in the essay. They are typically used to introduce the second, third, and remaining body paragraphs, as a way to call the reader's mind back to the thesis. A three-fold transition sentence does the following:

- refers subtly to the idea discussed in the previous paragraph;
- refers briefly to the overall thesis idea; and
- refers more specifically to the new idea to be discussed in this paragraph.

PRACTICE Add at least two transitions to the following paragraph.

To Kill a Mockingbird highlights the difference between two methods of education. Miss Caroline favors a structured, inflexible method in which students must all meet the same set of expectations. "We don't write in the first grade, we print. You won't learn to write until you're in the third grade." Atticus favors a flexible approach to education that reflects the unique gifts of each child.

6. Work with your discussion group to write a thesis statement and topic sentences for an essay about how Chapter 24 contributes to a theme of the work as a whole. Consider literary elements such as character, plot, and setting.

Thesis:

Topic Sentence:

Topic Sentence:

Topic Sentence:

7. Work with your group to revise at least one of your topic sentences using three-fold transitions. For example: *After recognizing the irony in her society, Scout matures even further as she recognizes the strength of Miss Maudie's quiet, calm responses to her conflict with Grace Merriweather.*

☑ Check Your Understanding

Briefly explain the significance of Chapter 24 and how it relates to the novel as a whole.

_____

_____

_____

_____

✍ Drafting the Embedded Assessment

Draft an introductory paragraph for your essay about how the literary elements in Chapter 24 contribute to a theme of the work as a whole. Be sure to:

- State your thesis clearly in the first sentence.
- Present your main supporting details.
- Provide a transition to the body paragraphs.

Standing in Borrowed Shoes

Learning Strategies

Double-Entry Journal
Graphic Organizer
Quickwrite
Visualizing

LITERARY

A static character (or flat character) is uncomplicated, staying the same without changing or growing during the story. A dynamic character (or round character) evolves and grows in the story and has a complex personality. The word *dynamic* comes from the Greek word meaning "powerful." The root *dyna* appears in *dynamo*, *dynamite*, and *dynasty*. *Static* also comes from a Greek word, *statikos*, referring to something firm or fixed. Another English word with the root *stat* is *statistics*.

Learning Targets

- Identify character traits and create a character profile poster collaboratively.
- Evaluate how primary and secondary characters and their interactions contribute to the development of a novel's themes.

Preview

In this activity, as you read Chapter 28 of *To Kill a Mockingbird*, you will be exploring the various characters' traits and creating a profile poster of your findings.

Analyzing Characters

1. **Quickwrite:** Consider the following quote from the novel:

   "Atticus was right. One time he said you never really know a man until you stand in his shoes and walk around in them." –*Scout*

   When have Scout, Jem, or Dill had to look at the world from other people's perspectives? What have they learned from other residents of Maycomb?

   _____

   _____

   _____

   _____

   _____

   _____

   _____

2. Working in a small group, use the following graphic organizer to list the *primary* (major) and *secondary* (minor) characters you can identify from the novel. Indicate whether the primary characters are static or dynamic. When you have finished, make notes on the thematic subjects that secondary characters might represent in the novel.

My Notes

_____

_____

_____

_____

_____

_____

_____

_____

_____

_____

_____

_____

Primary Characters	Static or Dynamic	Secondary Characters	Thematic Topics They Represent

3. Working with a partner, create a character profile poster. Your poster should include the following elements:

- a picture or graphic representation of the character;
- a physical description from the novel;
- a list of several adjectives describing the character's personality, values, and/or motives;
- a description of the plot events in which this character is involved;
- a quotation about him or her from another character; and
- a quotation by the character that reveals his or her values.

4. As you view the posters your class created, use the following graphic organizer to write notes on at least two characters other than your own.

Character and Description	Events Involving the Character	Textual Evidence	Theme Related to This Character

☑ **Check Your Understanding**

Work with a partner to review the Events column of your graphic organizer. Choose an event that you think is important and locate the most significant passage describing that event. Explain why this passage is important, citing text evidence to support your answer.

> **Writing to Sources: Informational Text**
>
> Explain how Lee uses the voices of her characters to develop and distinguish their personalities. Be sure to:
>
> - Describe the voice of each character you write about.
> - Include multiple direct quotations from the text to support your claims.
> - Include transitions between points and a concluding statement.

Controversy in Context

Learning Targets

- Analyze a nonfiction text about various controversies surrounding the novel *To Kill a Mockingbird*.
- Evaluate the techniques and effectiveness of an argument.
- Use the RAFT strategy to organize and draft an argument.

Preview

In this activity, you will read an essay about the controversies in *To Kill a Mockingbird* and analyze the historical context in which it's set.

Literal and Figurative

1. **Quickwrite:** Chapter 27 ends with the line "Thus began our longest journey together." What are the literal and figurative meanings of the word "journey"? How is reading a novel similar to and different from taking a journey?

_____

_____

_____

_____

As You Read

- Underline the evidence in the arguments for and against the novel.
- Circle unknown words and phrases. Try to determine the meaning of the words by using context clues, word parts, or a dictionary.

About the Author

Jill P. May was a professor of children's literature, storytelling, multicultural literature, Jewish studies, and women's studies at Purdue University. She has received many honors for her work in researching children's stories. Dr. May retired from teaching in 2011.

Learning Strategies

Double-Entry Journal
Marking the Text
Quickwrite
RAFT

My Notes

GRAMMAR & USAGE

Active & Passive Voice

Verbs have active and passive voice in all six tenses. When the subject of the verb does the acting, the verb is in the active voice: "Lyndon Johnson gained the presidency: blacks began to seek and win political offices." Using active voice emphasizes the person or group who does the action.

When the subject of the verb receives the action, the verb is in the passive voice. A passive-voice verb always contains a form of *to be* along with the past participle of the verb: "When John F. Kennedy was killed in Texas on November 27, 1963, many southerners were shocked." Using the passive voice emphasizes the receiver of the action.

My Notes

melodramatic: emotionally exaggerated

wit: intelligent humor

restrained: understated

sporadic: occasional

espoused: supported

assassinated: murdered

Essay

from In Defense of *To Kill a Mockingbird*

by **Jill May**

1   The critical career of *To Kill a Mockingbird* is a late twentieth-century case study of censorship. When Harper Lee's novel about a small southern town and its prejudices was published in 1960, the book received favorable reviews in professional journals and the popular press. Typical of that opinion, Booklist's reviewer called the book "melodramatic" and noted "traces of sermonizing," but the book was recommended for library purchase, commending its "rare blend of wit and compassion." Reviewers did not suggest that the book was young-adult literature, or that it belonged in adolescent collections; perhaps that is why no one mentioned the book's language or violence. In any event, reviewers seemed inclined to agree that *To Kill a Mockingbird* was a worthwhile interpretation of the South's existing social structures during the 1930s. In 1961 the book won the Pulitzer Prize Award, the Alabama Library Association Book Award, and the Brotherhood Award of the National Conference of Christians and Jews. It seemed that Harper Lee's blend of family history, local custom, and restrained sermonizing was important reading, and with a young girl between the ages of six and nine as the main character, *To Kill a Mockingbird* moved rapidly into junior and senior high school libraries and curriculum. The book was not destined to be studied by college students. Southern literature's critics rarely mentioned it; few university professors found it noteworthy enough to "teach" as an exemplary southern novel.

2   By the mid-sixties *To Kill a Mockingbird* had a solid place in junior and senior high American literature studies. Once discovered by southern parents, the book's solid place became shaky indeed. Sporadic lawsuits arose. In most cases the complaint against the book was by conservatives who disliked the portrayal of whites. Typically, the Hanover County School Board in Virginia first ruled the book "immoral," then withdrew their criticism and declared the ruckus "was all a mistake" (*Newsletter on Intellectual Freedom* 1966). By 1968 the National Education Association listed the book among those which drew the most criticism from private groups. Ironically it was directly behind *Little Black Sambo* (*Newsletter* 1968). And the seventies arrived.

3   Things had changed in the South during the sixties. Two national leaders who had supported integration and had espoused the ideals of racial equality were assassinated in southern regions. When John F. Kennedy was killed in Texas on November 27, 1963, many southerners were shocked. Populist attitudes of racism were declining, and in the aftermath of the tragedy southern politics began to change. Lyndon Johnson gained the presidency: blacks began to seek and win political offices. Black leader Martin Luther King had stressed the importance of racial equality, always using Mahatma Gandhi's strategy

of nonviolent action and civil disobedience. A brilliant orator, King grew up in the South; the leader of the [Southern Christian Leadership Conference], he lived in Atlanta, Georgia. In 1968, while working on a garbage strike in Memphis, King was killed. The death of the 1965 Nobel Peace Prize winner was further embarrassment for white southerners. Whites began to look at public values anew, and gradually southern blacks found experiences in the South more tolerable. In 1971 one Atlanta businessman observed [in *Ebony*], "The liberation thinking is here. Blacks are more together. With the doors opening wider, this area is the mecca …" Southern arguments against *To Kill a Mockingbird* subsided. *The Newsletter on Intellectual Freedom* contained no record of southern court cases during the seventies or eighties. The book had sustained itself during the first period of sharp criticism; it had survived regional protests from the area it depicted.

4   The second onslaught of attack came from new groups of censors, and it came during the late seventies and early eighties. Private sectors in the Midwest and suburban East began to demand the book's removal from school libraries. Groups, such as the Eden Valley School Committee in Minnesota, claimed that the book was too laden with profanity (Newsletter 1978). In Vernon, New York, Reverend Carl Hadley threatened to establish a private Christian school because public school libraries contained such "filthy, trashy sex novels" as *A Separate Peace* and *To Kill a Mockingbird* (Newsletter 1980). And finally, blacks began to censor the book. In Warren, Indiana, three blacks resigned from the township Human Relations Advisory Council when the Warren County school administration refused to remove the book from Warren junior high school classes. They contended that the book "does psychological damage to the positive integration process and represents institutionalized racism" (Newsletter 1982). Thus, censorship of *To Kill a Mockingbird* swung from the conservative right to the liberal left. Factions representing racists, religious sects, concerned parents, and minority groups vocally demanded the book's removal from public schools. …

5   The censors' reactions to *To Kill a Mockingbird* were reactions to issues of race and justice. Their moves to ban the book derive from their own perspectives of the book's theme. Their "reader response" criticism, usually based on one reading of the book, was personal and political. They needed to ban the book because it told them something about American society that they did not want to hear. That is precisely the problem facing any author of realistic fiction. Once the story becomes real, it can become grim. An author will use first-person flashback in a story in order to let the reader lie in another time, another place. Usually the storyteller is returning for a second view of the scene. The teller has experienced the events before and the story is being retold because the scene has left the storyteller uneasy. As the storyteller recalls the past, both the listener and the teller see events in a new light. Both are working through troubled times in search of meaning. In the case of *To Kill a Mockingbird* the first-person retelling is not pleasant, but the underlying significance is with the narrative. The youthful personalities who are recalled are hopeful. Scout tells us of a time past when white people would lynch or convict a man because of the color of his skin. She also shows us three children

My Notes

orator: speaker
tolerable: bearable
sustained: kept alive
laden: filled
profanity: swearing
sects: small groups

who refuse to believe that the system is right, and she leaves us with the thought that most people will be nice if seen for what they are: humans with **frailties**. When discussing literary criticism, Theo D'Haen suggested [in *Text to Reader*] that the good literary work should have a life within the world and be "part of the ongoing activities of that world." *To Kill a Mockingbird* continues to have life within the world; its ongoing activities in the **realm** of censorship show that it is a book which deals with regional moralism. The children in the story seem very human; they worry about their own identification, they **defy** parental rules, and they cry over injustices. They mature in Harper Lee's novel, and they lose their innocence. So does the reader. If the readers are young, they may believe Scout when she says, "nothin's real scary except in books." If the readers are older they will have learned that life is scary, and they will be prepared to meet some of its realities.

Making Observations

- What information grabs your attention?
- What do you notice about the author's voice or tone?

Returning to the Text

- Return to the text as you respond to the following questions. Use evidence from the text to support your responses.
- Write any additional questions you have about the essay in your Reader/Writer Notebook.

2. How does the author open the argument?

3. What is the central claim of the essay?

4. What are the main reasons why white critics felt *To Kill a Mockingbird* should be banned in schools?

frailties: weaknesses
realm: world
defy: disobey

5. Why is it significant to note that there was a large population of black audiences who felt the novel should be banned?

6. How does *To Kill a Mockingbird* remain "part of the ongoing activities" of our world?

Working from the Text

7. Use the RAFT strategy to develop an argument defending or challenging the use of the novel *To Kill a Mockingbird* in your high school curriculum.

Role: Student

Audience: Parent, teacher, censor, administrator, school board member

Format: Letter, speech, or email

Topic: Whether or not the novel *To Kill a Mockingbird* should be part of the high school curriculum

As you write your argument, be sure to do the following:

- Start with a claim defending or challenging the use of *To Kill a Mockingbird* in the high school curriculum.
- Cite textual evidence from your research, your reading of the novel, and/or the May essay.
- Raise at least one counterargument and rebut it.
- Use a formal writing style.

☑ Check Your Understanding

Using evidence from the essay, explain how the experience of reading *To Kill a Mockingbird* in the 1960s would have been different from the experience of reading it now.

INDEPENDENT READING LINK

Read and Respond

Think about how your independent reading relates to the topics, themes, setting, or characters in *To Kill a Mockingbird*. Create a Venn diagram that shows the relationships between the two books. Then create a second Venn diagram in which you analyze similarities and differences between the authors' styles. How does each author craft the text to achieve his or her purpose for writing?

Writing a Literary Analysis Essay

 ASSIGNMENT

Your assignment is to write a passage analysis of a key coming-of-age scene from *To Kill a Mockingbird*. After annotating the text to analyze Harper Lee's use of literary elements in your selected passage, write an essay explaining how the literary elements in this passage help develop a theme of the novel.

Planning and Prewriting: Take time to select and annotate a passage.	■ Which passage from the novel will you choose to illustrate a significant coming-of-age moment? ■ How will you be sure you understand all the literary elements that you have studied in this unit? ■ How can you be sure readers know what passage you have chosen to mark and annotate to analyze literary elements? ■ How will you use your annotations to generate a working thesis that shows the significance of the passage to a theme of the book?
Drafting: Determine the structure of your essay and how to incorporate necessary elements.	■ How will you organize your essay? What tools will you use to help you organize? ■ What is your thesis? Do your topic sentences support your thesis? ■ What textual evidence do you need to support your thesis and topic sentences? ■ What elements do you need to include in your introduction and conclusion?
Evaluating and Revising: Create opportunities to review and gain feedback for revisions.	■ How will you ask for feedback on your draft? Whom will you ask? ■ How will you revise your draft for seamless integration of quotations using the TLQC method (transition, lead in, quote, and commentary)?
Editing for Publication: Confirm that the final draft is ready for publication.	■ How you will proofread and edit your draft to demonstrate a command of the conventions of standard English (capitalization, punctuation, spelling, grammar, and usage)? ■ How will you use the Scoring Guide to be sure you have met all the criteria for this assignment?

Reflection

After completing this Embedded Assessment, think about how you went about accomplishing this task, and respond to the following question: What makes you want to keep reading a book?

Writing a Literary Analysis Essay

SCORING GUIDE

Scoring Criteria	Exemplary	Proficient	Emerging	Incomplete
Ideas	The essay • includes a well-chosen passage that reveals the complex relationship between the literary elements and the major ideas and concepts of the entire work • provides supporting details to enhance understanding of the writer's position • relates commentary directly to the thesis.	The essay • reflects a careful choice of passage to show the relationship between a scene and the major ideas and concepts of the novel • provides relevant details to explain the writer's position • uses appropriate commentary.	The essay • attempts to link a passage to a major theme of the novel • presents supporting details that may be fully developed or provide an understanding of the writer's position • has commentary that may not relate directly to the thesis or may be a plot summary.	The essay • includes a passage that does not represent a major theme of the novel • is missing supporting details or presents undeveloped ideas • is missing commentary or includes commentary that does not relate directly to the thesis.
Structure	The essay • has multiple paragraphs and a clear and precise thesis that directs the organization of the body • uses transitions to clarify and connect ideas • provides relevant and insightful commentary; the conclusion follows from the ideas presented.	The essay • has multiple paragraphs and is organized with an introduction, detailed body paragraphs, and a conclusion • uses transitions to establish connections between ideas. • provides relevant commentary; the conclusion summarizes ideas.	The essay • attempts to organize ideas, but key pieces are lacking • may be missing an introduction, detailed body paragraphs, and/or a conclusion • uses few or no transitions to connect ideas. • provides little to no relevant commentary; the conclusion is weak.	The essay • does not have a focus with a clear organization of introduction, body paragraphs, and conclusion • does not use transitions to connect paragraphs and/or ideas. • provides no commentary; the conclusion is not present.
Use of Language	The essay • uses a formal style • seamlessly incorporates literary analysis vocabulary • is mostly error-free, with proper punctuation and capitalization to embed quotations in the text.	The essay • uses diction that is appropriate for an academic topic • incorporates some literary analysis vocabulary • has few errors.	The essay • uses simple language that is not appropriate for an academic topic • includes little literary analysis vocabulary • has errors that interfere with meaning.	The essay • uses slang or informal words that are not appropriate for an academic topic • includes little or no literary analysis vocabulary • has numerous errors that interfere with meaning.

Learning Strategies

Brainstorming

Discussion Groups

My Notes

Learning Targets

- Reflect on previous learning about the research process and make connections to new learning.
- Identify and analyze the skills and knowledge necessary to complete Embedded Assessment 2.

Preview

In this activity, you will revisit the Essential Questions, familiarize yourself with Embedded Assessment 2, and create a plan for your Historical Investigation and Presentation.

Revisiting the Essential Questions

Based on what you have read and discussed during Unit 4, how would you answer these questions now? What other questions do you have about the historical, cultural, and social context of *To Kill a Mockingbird*?

1. What makes an opening powerful?
2. What makes you want to keep reading a book?
3. How can understanding a book's context help you understand the book?

Unpacking Embedded Assessment 2

Closely read the assignment for Embedded Assessment 2: Historical Investigation and Presentation.

Your assignment is to research the historical, cultural, social, or geographical context in which the novel *To Kill a Mockingbird* was written. You will investigate how individuals, organizations, and events contributed to change in the United States during the Civil Rights Movement. You will work collaboratively to create an oral presentation of your findings with multimedia support and guiding questions for your audience.

In your own words, summarize what you will need to know to complete this assessment successfully. With your class, create a graphic organizer to represent the skills and knowledge you will need to complete the tasks identified in the assignment.

Working Collaboratively

You have read *To Kill a Mockingbird* over the past few weeks, and now you will form research project groups to investigate the real-life history behind the novel. It will be important that you work together as a group to conduct your investigation, create your presentation, and present your findings in an engaging way, using language that effectively meets the needs of your audience. Some important steps in working collaboratively are:

- **Develop a plan for building consensus.** Listen actively, debate respectfully, and share ideas in order to decide what individual, organization, or event your group will investigate.

- **Divide up the duties.** Settle on ground rules for decision making. After deciding on research questions, figure out each person's role in researching, recording information, and organizing the oral presentation.

- **Share resources.** Work as a team to keep track of sources, information, and citations in order to ensure that everyone has access to the same sources.

- **Assess and record sources.** Agree as a group how to find relevant sources and assess their credibility. Make sure that each group member keeps track of his or her sources to contribute to the annotated bibliography.

Discuss these steps with your project group and confirm your understanding of each one.

☑ Check Your Understanding

Which aspects of conducting research and giving a presentation have been successful for you in the past? What are some research and presentation skills you would like to develop over the course of this project?

Picturing the Past

Learning Strategies

Close Reading
Discussion Groups
Graphic Organizer

VOCABULARY

ACADEMIC

A **primary source** is an original document or image created by someone who experienced an event first-hand or is reporting about it at the time it occurs. Primary sources can include artifacts, diaries, letters, news articles, autobiographies, and photographs.

Learning Targets

- Analyze a text in order to discuss its explicit and implicit meanings.
- Cite evidence from a text that provides historical, social, and political context for *To Kill a Mockingbird*.
- Summarize observations about context after viewing images.

Preview

In this activity, you will read, view, and analyze primary-source documents and photographs from the Jim Crow era and the Civil Rights Movement in order to understand the context of *To Kill a Mockingbird*.

What Is Context?

The novel *To Kill a Mockingbird* is set in the southern United States during the Jim Crow era, when laws and perceptions regarding race had been the same for decades; however, Harper Lee wrote it during the Civil Rights Movement, when those laws and perceptions were beginning to change. In order to grasp the deeper significance of the story, it is important to analyze the context of the novel. Understanding its context can enrich your understanding of the story, including its characters, setting, and themes.

Civil Rights Timeline

- **1861** — The Civil War begins.
- **1863** — Abraham Lincoln delivers the Emancipation Proclamation, which frees slaves in the rebelling territories.
- **1865** — The Civil War ends. The 13th Amendment to the U.S. Constitution is ratified, prohibiting slavery.
- **1866** — Tennessee passes its first "Jim Crow" law segregating students.
- **1868** — The 14th Amendment to the U.S. Constitution is ratified, defining citizenship.
- **1870** — The 15th Amendment to the U.S. Constitution is ratified, giving African American men the right to vote.
- **1896** — In *Plessy v. Ferguson*, the Supreme Court rules that segregation is constitutional.
- **1954** — In *Brown v. Board of Education*, the Supreme Court rules that segregation is unconstitutional.
- **1955** — Rosa Parks is arrested for breaking a city ordinance, and the Civil Rights Movement begins.
- **1964** — The Civil Rights Act is signed, prohibiting all discrimination.
- **1965** — The Voting Rights Act is signed, outlawing practices that disenfranchise black voters.
- **1968** — Dr. Martin Luther King Jr. is assassinated.

My Notes

1. To consider the context of your own life and story, read and answer the following questions in your Reader/Writer Notebook:

   - What is the context of where you live? What are some unique and identifiable things about it and its history and geography?

   - What is the context of the time you are living in? What is happening politically, socially, and culturally that might give someone from another time a greater understanding of your life?

2. Draw a web organizer like this one. Add ovals for the historical, cultural, social, and geographical contexts of your life. With a partner, compare answers and discuss them in relation to their contexts. Then discuss how understanding the context of *To Kill a Mockingbird* might help shape your understanding of its characters, setting, and themes.

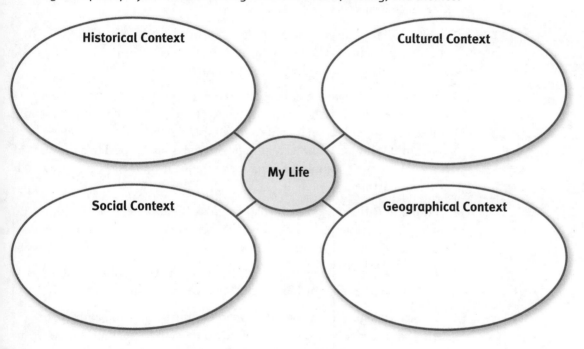

Historical Context

Cultural Context

My Life

Social Context

Geographical Context

About the Document

Black people in the 1930s were subject to Jim Crow laws, which were state and local laws in the South that enforced racial segregation. Jim Crow laws—named for an offensive slang term for a black person—were not changed until the Civil Rights Movement in the 1960s. Until then black people and white people attended separate schools, sat on different parts of public transportation, ate in separate sections of restaurants, and drank out of separate water fountains. In 1954 the Supreme Court declared segregation in public schools—and by extension, other public facilities—unconstitutional. The following text is a collection of Jim Crow laws from various states compiled by the Martin Luther King, Jr. National Historic Site.

As You Read

- Place a question mark next to information that raises questions.

- Circle unknown words and phrases. Try to determine the meaning of the words by using context clues, word parts, or a dictionary.

Informational Text

Jim Crow Laws

Martin Luther King, Jr. National Historic Site

Compiled by **the National Park Service, U.S. Department of the Interior**

1 **Nurses** No person or corporation shall require any white female nurse to nurse in **wards** or rooms in hospitals, either public or private, in which negro men are placed. *Alabama*

2 **Buses** All passenger stations in this state operated by any motor transportation company shall have separate waiting rooms or space and separate ticket windows for the white and colored races. *Alabama*

3 **Restaurants** It shall be unlawful to conduct a restaurant or other place for the serving of food in the city, at which white and colored people are served in the same room, unless such white and colored persons are **effectually** separated by a solid **partition** extending from the floor upward to a distance of seven feet or higher, and unless a separate entrance from the street is provided for each compartment. *Alabama*

4 **Pool and Billiard Rooms** It shall be unlawful for a negro and white person to play together or in company with each other at any game of pool or billiards. *Alabama*

5 **Intermarriage** The marriage of a person of Caucasian blood with a Negro, Mongolian, Malay, or Hindu shall be **null** and void. *Arizona*

6 **Intermarriage** All marriages between a white person and a negro, or between a white person and a person of negro descent to the fourth generation inclusive, are hereby forever **prohibited**. *Florida*

7 **Education** The schools for white children and the schools for negro children shall be conducted separately. *Florida*

8 **Mental Hospitals** The Board of Control shall see that proper and distinct apartments are arranged for said patients, so that in no case shall Negroes and white persons be together. *Georgia*

9 **Barbers** No colored barber shall serve as a barber [to] white women or girls. *Georgia*

10 **Burial** The officer in charge shall not bury, or allow to be buried, any colored persons upon ground set apart or used for the burial of white persons. *Georgia*

11 **Restaurants** All persons licensed to conduct a restaurant shall serve either white people **exclusively** or colored people exclusively and shall not sell to the two races within the same room or serve the two races anywhere under the same license. *Georgia*

wards: large hospital rooms housing several patients
effectually: adequately
partition: barrier; wall
null: without value
prohibited: not allowed
exclusively: only

12 Amateur Baseball It shall be unlawful for any amateur white baseball team to play baseball on any vacant lot or baseball diamond within two blocks of a playground devoted to the Negro race, and it shall be unlawful for any amateur colored baseball team to play baseball in any vacant lot or baseball diamond within two blocks of any playground devoted to the white race. *Georgia*

13 Parks It shall be unlawful for colored people to frequent any park owned or maintained by the city for the benefit, use and enjoyment of white persons ... and unlawful for any white person to frequent any park owned or maintained by the city for the use and benefit of colored persons. *Georgia*

14 Reform Schools The children of white and colored races committed to the houses of reform shall be kept entirely separate from each other. *Kentucky*

15 Circus Tickets All circuses, shows, and tent exhibitions, to which the attendance of ... more than one race is invited or expected to attend shall provide for the convenience of its patrons not less than two ticket offices with individual ticket sellers, and not less than two entrances to the said performance, with individual ticket takers and receivers, and in the case of outside or tent performances, the said ticket offices shall not be less than twenty-five (25) feet apart. *Louisiana*

16 The Blind The board of trustees shall ... maintain a separate building ... on separate ground for the admission, care, instruction, and support of all blind persons of the colored or black race. *Louisiana*

17 Railroads All railroad companies and corporations, and all persons running or operating cars or coaches by steam on any railroad line or track in the State of Maryland, for the transportation of passengers, are hereby required to provide separate cars or coaches for the travel and transportation of the white and colored passengers. *Maryland*

18 Promotion of Equality Any person ... who shall be guilty of printing, publishing or circulating printed, typewritten or written matter urging or presenting for public acceptance or general information, arguments or suggestions in favor of social equality or of intermarriage between whites and negroes, shall be guilty of a misdemeanor and subject to fine not exceeding five hundred (500.00) dollars or imprisonment not exceeding six (6) months or both. *Mississippi*

19 Intermarriage The marriage of a white person with a negro or mulatto or person who shall have one-eighth or more of negro blood, shall be unlawful and void. *Mississippi*

20 Hospital Entrances There shall be maintained by the governing authorities of every hospital maintained by the state for treatment of white and colored patients separate entrances for white and colored patients and visitors, and such entrances shall be used by the race only for which they are prepared. *Mississippi*

My Notes

amateur: non professional
vacant: unused
patrons: customers
urging: pushing forward
mulatto: a person with both black and white ancestors (derogatory term)

My Notes

WORD CONNECTIONS

Roots and Affixes

The word transportation means "a method of moving passengers or goods from one place to another." The Latin prefix *trans-* means "across" or "beyond." The Latin root *port* means "to carry" or "to bear."

The root *port* is found in many other English words, such as *portable, portfolio, import, export, report,* and *support.*

Some of the words in which the prefix *trans-* appears are *transfer, transform, translate,* and *transparent.*

pupils: students
periodicals: magazines or newspapers
segregation: separation
vicinity: nearby area
furnish: provide

21 **Prisons** The warden shall see that the white convicts shall have separate apartments for both eating and sleeping from the negro convicts. *Mississippi*

22 **Education** Separate free schools shall be established for the education of children of African descent; and it shall be unlawful for any colored child to attend any white school, or any white child to attend a colored school. *Missouri*

23 **Intermarriage** All marriages between ... white persons and negroes or white persons and Mongolians ... are prohibited and declared absolutely void. ... No person having one-eighth part or more of negro blood shall be permitted to marry any white person, nor shall any white person be permitted to marry any negro or person having one-eighth part or more of negro blood. *Missouri*

24 **Education** Separate rooms [shall] be provided for the teaching of pupils of African descent, and [when] said rooms are so provided, such pupils may not be admitted to the school rooms occupied and used by pupils of Caucasian or other descent. *New Mexico*

25 **Textbooks** Books shall not be interchangeable between the white and colored schools, but shall continue to be used by the race first using them. *North Carolina*

26 **Libraries** The state librarian is directed to fit up and maintain a separate place for the use of the colored people who may come to the library for the purpose of reading books or periodicals. *North Carolina*

27 **Transportation** The ... Utilities Commission ... is empowered and directed to require the establishment of separate waiting rooms at all stations for the white and colored races. *North Carolina*

28 **Teaching** Any instructor who shall teach in any school, college or institution where members of the white and colored race are received and enrolled as pupils for instruction shall be deemed guilty of a misdemeanor, and upon conviction thereof, shall be fined in any sum not less than ten dollars ($10.00) nor more than fifty dollars ($50.00) for each offense. *Oklahoma*

29 **Fishing, Boating, and Bathing** The [Conservation] Commission shall have the right to make segregation of the white and colored races as to the exercise of rights of fishing, boating and bathing. *Oklahoma*

30 **Telephone Booths** The Corporation Commission is hereby vested with power and authority to require telephone companies ... to maintain separate booths for white and colored patrons when there is a demand for such separate booths. That the Corporation Commission shall determine the necessity for said separate booths only upon complaint of the people in the town and vicinity to be served after due hearing as now provided by law in other complaints filed with the Corporation Commission. *Oklahoma*

31 **Lunch Counters** No persons, firms, or corporations, who or which furnish meals to passengers at station restaurants or station eating houses, in times limited by common carriers of said passengers, shall furnish said meals to white and colored passengers in the same room, or at the same table, or at the same counter. *South Carolina*

32 Libraries Any white person of such county may use the county free library under the rules and regulations prescribed by the commissioners court and may be entitled to all the privileges thereof. Said court shall make proper provision for the negroes of said county to be served through a separate branch or branches of the county free library, which shall be administered by [a] custodian of the negro race under the supervision of the county librarian. *Texas*

33 Education [The County Board of Education] shall provide schools of two kinds; those for white children and those for colored children. *Texas*

34 Railroads The conductors or managers on all such railroads shall have power, and are hereby required, to assign to each white or colored passenger his or her **respective** car, coach or compartment. If the passenger fails to disclose his race, the conductor and managers, acting in good faith, shall be the sole judges of his race. *Virginia*

35 Theaters Every person ... operating ... any public hall, theatre, opera house, motion picture show or any place of public entertainment or public **assemblage** which is attended by both white and colored persons, shall separate the white race and the colored race and shall set apart and **designate** ... certain seats therein to be occupied by white persons and a portion thereof, or certain seats therein, to be occupied by colored persons. *Virginia*

36 Intermarriage All marriages of white persons with Negroes, Mulattos, Mongolians, or Malayans hereafter contracted in the State of Wyoming are and shall be illegal and void. *Wyoming*

Making Observations
- What is your first reaction to reading these laws?
- Which law or laws stand out to you most, and why?

---

respective: separate
assemblage: gathering
designate: specify

Returning to the Text

- Return to the text as you respond to the following questions. Use text evidence to support your responses.
- Write any additional questions you have about the text in your Reader/Writer Notebook.

3. Why do you think Mississippi made it illegal to promote racial equality?

_____

_____

_____

_____

4. Each Jim Crow law in this text includes the name of the state where the law was put into effect. What can you deduce about how far-reaching Jim Crow laws were when you look at the names of the states that are listed?

_____

_____

_____

_____

5. What is the effect of using words such as "persons," "corporation," "white," and "colored" in these laws? What are the denotations of these words, and what connotations do they have based on the context of these laws?

_____

_____

_____

_____

Working from the Text

6. How did Jim Crow laws affect black citizens' basic human rights?

_____

_____

_____

_____

7. Identify three examples of Jim Crow laws that would have presented financial hardships to local governments and institutions. What can you infer from the fact that these laws went unchallenged for many years?

_____

_____

_____

_____

8. You have read the Jim Crow laws exactly as they were written (a primary source). If you had read a summary of the laws instead, how might your understanding of them be different?

_____

_____

_____

_____

9. In a group, sort the Jim Crow laws into three or four categories. Select one category and envision a setting where a peaceful protest against those Jim Crow laws is taking place. Work with your group to create a poster that could be used at the protest. State your specific stance and add graphics to make your poster more powerful. Using formal language and effective presentation skills, present your poster to another group.

Analyzing Visual Context: America in the 1930s and 1940s

Another way to gain context about a historical event or time period is to view photographs and other visual media from the time, place, or event itself.

10. Examine the following photographs taken in the 1930s and 1940s, the time period in which *To Kill a Mockingbird* is set. Make observations about the political, social, cultural, or geographical contexts you notice, paying particular attention to which details are emphasized in each account. Then write your observations, reflections, and questions in the following table.

1. White students are sitting in a classroom at the University of Oklahoma while George W. McLaurin, a black student, is sitting in the anteroom, 1948.

2. A first-grade classroom in Gees Bend, Alabama, with a wide range of ages of students. Photograph by Marion Post Wolcott, 1939.

3. A store's door is marked "White Ladies Only" in Durham, North Carolina. Photograph by Jack Delano, May 1940.

4. A water fountain is labeled "Colored" in Oklahoma City, Oklahoma. Photograph by Russell Lee, 1939.

Photo	Observations What details do you see?	Reflection What is your response to the photograph?	Questions What questions come to mind that might lead to further exploration or research?
1			
2			
3			
4			

11. How does viewing these photographs provide context for the setting of *To Kill a Mockingbird*? How do the photographs compare to the mental images you created while reading? What new information can you glean?

_____

_____

_____

_____

_____

_____

_____

_____

_____

_____

_____

_____

_____

Analyzing Visual Context: America in the 1950s and 1960s

Harper Lee wrote *To Kill a Mockingbird* during a time when people were openly questioning the justice of the Jim Crow laws. In the case of *Brown v. Board of Education*, the U.S. Supreme Court ruled in 1954 that segregation in public schools was unconstitutional; however, many people in the South disagreed. The 1960s saw the Civil Rights Movement, during which black people and their supporters organized boycotts, protests, and acts of civil disobedience to highlight the ongoing injustice of Jim Crow laws.

12. Examine the following photographs, making observations about the political, social, cultural, or geographical contexts you notice and comparing them to the photographs from the Jim Crow era. Write your observations, reflections, and questions in the table that follows. Then discuss your notes and questions about both sets of photographs with your project group. During your discussion, revisit the question about which details are emphasized in each account: the novel and both sets of photos.

5. A group of people protest the admission of the Little Rock Nine to Central High School in Little Rock, Arkansas. Photograph by John T. Bledsoe, 1959.

6. Lunch counter employees at a Peoples Drug Store in Arlington, Virginia, prepare to close early while black and white customers stage a sit-in demonstration, 1960.

7. Freedom Rider civil-rights activists in Anniston, Alabama, watch as their bus burns. Photograph by Joe Postiglione, 1961.

8. Participants in the march from Selma to Montgomery, Alabama, March 1965.

Photo	Observations What details do you see?	Reflection What is your response to the photograph?	Questions What questions come to mind that might lead to further exploration or research?
5			
6			
7			
8			

13. Look back at the images and jot down a summary sentence for each set. What similarities do you see across the two sets? What are the major differences?

_____

_____

_____

_____

_____

INDEPENDENT READING LINK

Read and Research

Generate questions and conduct informal research into the context of your independent reading text—both the context of the book's setting(s) and the context in which it was written. Think about how, if at all, that context is reflected in the contents of the book. What do you understand more clearly about the book with this new information?

☑ Check Your Understanding

How does analyzing the context of a novel help you gain a greater understanding of the story?

📝 Writing to Sources: Informational Text

After viewing and discussing the details and implications of both sets of primary-source photographs as well as the list of Jim Crow laws, write an essay explaining how *To Kill a Mockingbird* could be viewed as a commentary on the time in which it was written. Be sure to:

- Begin with a topic sentence summarizing what you learned from the photographs and Jim Crow laws.
- Include specific, relevant details about the images and laws that stood out or informed your understanding of the author's purpose.
- Provide original commentary to express your ideas.

🌱 Gaining Perspectives

You have analyzed the Jim Crow laws from the 1930s and examined photographs showing people working to change those laws during the Civil Rights Movement. With a partner, analyze current conflicts in the media over civil rights in your state and across the country. Does it surprise you that people still have to fight to protect their civil rights? What laws have been created after the Civil Rights Movement to help protect people's civil rights? Share your findings with the class, providing visuals to aid your presentation.

Research Project: Writing Research Questions

To successfully complete Embedded Assessment 2, your group will need to develop research questions.

14. Revisit the first two sentences of the assignment for Embedded Assessment 2. Then rewrite them as potential questions to guide your research. Continue to revisit these questions throughout your project's development.

My Notes

Learning Targets

- Analyze a historical document for its purpose, audience, claims, and evidence.
- Identify how a primary source provides context.

Preview

In this activity, you will read a letter by Dr. Martin Luther King Jr. and analyze the rhetorical devices and appeals he uses to convey his message.

My Notes

As You Read

- Draw a star by phrases that grab your attention.
- Circle unknown words and phrases. Try to determine the meaning of the words by using context clues, word parts, or a dictionary.

About the Author

Dr. Martin Luther King Jr. (1929–1968) was an American clergyman, activist, and leader in the Civil Rights Movement. In 1964, the Reverend Dr. King became the youngest person to receive the Nobel Peace Prize for his work to end racial segregation and racial discrimination through civil disobedience and other nonviolent means. King wrote "Letter from Birmingham Jail" in response to a statement made by eight white Alabama clergymen on April 12, 1963, titled "A Call for Unity." The clergymen agreed that social injustices existed but argued that the battle against racial segregation should be fought solely in the courts, not in the streets.

Letter

from Letter from Birmingham Jail

by **Martin Luther King Jr.**

16 April, 1963

My Dear Fellow **Clergymen**:

1   While confined here in the Birmingham city jail, I came across your recent statement calling my present activities "unwise and untimely." Seldom do I pause to answer criticism of my work and ideas. If I sought to answer all the criticisms that cross my desk, my secretaries would have little time for anything other than such correspondence in the course of the day, and I would have no time for constructive work. But since I feel that you are men of genuine good will and that your criticisms are sincerely set forth, I want to try to answer your statement in what I hope will be patient and reasonable terms.

2   I think I should indicate why I am here in Birmingham, since you have been influenced by the view which argues against "outsiders coming in." I have the honor of serving as president of the Southern Christian Leadership Conference, an organization operating in every southern state, with headquarters in Atlanta, Georgia. We have some eighty five affiliated organizations across the South, and one of them is the Alabama Christian Movement for Human Rights. Frequently we share staff, educational and financial resources with our **affiliates**. Several months ago the affiliate here in Birmingham asked us to be on call to engage in a nonviolent direct action program if such were deemed necessary. We readily consented, and when the hour came we lived up to our promise. So I, along with several members of my staff, am here because I was invited here. I am here because I have organizational ties here.

3   But more basically, I am in Birmingham because injustice is here. Just as the prophets of the eighth century B.C. left their villages and carried their "thus saith the Lord" far beyond the boundaries of their home towns, and just as the Apostle Paul left his village of Tarsus and carried the gospel of Jesus Christ to the far corners of the Greco Roman world, so am I compelled to carry the gospel of freedom beyond my own home town. Like Paul, I must constantly respond to the Macedonian call for aid.

clergymen: religious leaders
affiliates: close connections or members

My Notes

_____
_____
_____
_____
_____
_____
_____
_____
_____
_____

cognizant: aware
interrelatedness: connectedness
provincial: unsophisticated
agitator: person who stirs up public feelings
deplore: hate
superficial: shallow
oppressor: person or organization that crushes others by abusing power
affluent: rich
ominous: threatening
inferiority: having a lower status than others

4   Moreover, I am **cognizant** of the **interrelatedness** of all communities and states. I cannot sit idly by in Atlanta and not be concerned about what happens in Birmingham. Injustice anywhere is a threat to justice everywhere. We are caught in an inescapable network of mutuality, tied in a single garment of destiny. Whatever affects one directly, affects all indirectly. Never again can we afford to live with the narrow, **provincial** "outside **agitator**" idea. Anyone who lives inside the United States can never be considered an outsider anywhere within its bounds.

5   You **deplore** the demonstrations taking place in Birmingham. But your statement, I am sorry to say, fails to express a similar concern for the conditions that brought about the demonstrations. I am sure that none of you would want to rest content with the **superficial** kind of social analysis that deals merely with effects and does not grapple with underlying causes. It is unfortunate that demonstrations are taking place in Birmingham, but it is even more unfortunate that the city's white power structure left the Negro community with no alternative. ...

6   We know through painful experience that freedom is never voluntarily given by the **oppressor**; it must be demanded by the oppressed. Frankly, I have yet to engage in a direct action campaign that was "well timed" in the view of those who have not suffered unduly from the disease of segregation. For years now I have heard the word "Wait!" It rings in the ear of every Negro with piercing familiarity. This "Wait" has almost always meant "Never." We must come to see, with one of our distinguished jurists, that "justice too long delayed is justice denied."

7   We have waited for more than 340 years for our constitutional and God given rights. The nations of Asia and Africa are moving with jetlike speed toward gaining political independence, but we still creep at horse and buggy pace toward gaining a cup of coffee at a lunch counter. Perhaps it is easy for those who have never felt the stinging darts of segregation to say, "Wait." But when you have seen vicious mobs lynch your mothers and fathers at will and drown your sisters and brothers at whim; when you have seen hate filled policemen curse, kick and even kill your black brothers and sisters; when you see the vast majority of your twenty million Negro brothers smothering in an airtight cage of poverty in the midst of an **affluent** society; when you suddenly find your tongue twisted and your speech stammering as you seek to explain to your six year old daughter why she can't go to the public amusement park that has just been advertised on television, and see tears welling up in her eyes when she is told that Funtown is closed to colored children, and see **ominous** clouds of **inferiority** beginning to form in her little mental sky, and see her beginning to distort her personality by developing an unconscious bitterness toward white people; when you have to concoct an answer for a five year old son who is asking: "Daddy, why do white people treat colored people so mean?"; when you take a cross country drive and find it necessary to sleep night after night in the uncomfortable corners of your automobile because no motel will accept you; when you are humiliated day in and day out by nagging signs reading "white"

and "colored"; when your first name becomes "nigger," your middle name becomes "boy" (however old you are) and your last name becomes "John," and your wife and mother are never given the respected title "Mrs."; when you are **harried** by day and haunted by night by the fact that you are a Negro, living constantly at tiptoe stance, never quite knowing what to expect next, and are plagued with inner fears and outer resentments; when you are forever fighting a degenerating sense of "nobodiness"—then you will understand why we find it difficult to wait. There comes a time when the cup of endurance runs over, and men are no longer willing to be plunged into the abyss of despair. I hope, sirs, you can understand our **legitimate** and unavoidable impatience. You express a great deal of anxiety over our willingness to break laws. This is certainly a legitimate concern. Since we so **diligently** urge people to obey the Supreme Court's decision of 1954 outlawing segregation in the public schools, at first glance it may seem rather paradoxical for us consciously to break laws. One may well ask: "How can you advocate breaking some laws and obeying others?" The answer lies in the fact that there are two types of laws: just and unjust. I would be the first to advocate obeying just laws. One has not only a legal but a moral responsibility to obey just laws. Conversely, one has a moral responsibility to disobey unjust laws. I would agree with St. Augustine that "an unjust law is no law at all." ...

8   I wish you had commended the Negro sit-inners and demonstrators of Birmingham for their **sublime** courage, their willingness to suffer and their amazing discipline in the midst of great **provocation**. One day the South will recognize its real heroes. They will be the James Merediths, with the **noble** sense of purpose that enables them to face jeering and hostile mobs, and with the agonizing loneliness that characterizes the life of the pioneer. They will be old, oppressed, battered Negro women, symbolized in a seventy two year old woman in Montgomery, Alabama, who rose up with a sense of dignity and with her people decided not to ride segregated buses, and who responded with ungrammatical **profundity** to one who inquired about her weariness: "My feets is tired, but my soul is at rest." They will be the young high school and college students, the young ministers of the gospel and a host of their elders, courageously and nonviolently sitting in at lunch counters and willingly going to jail for conscience' sake. One day the South will know that when these disinherited children of God sat down at lunch counters, they were in reality standing up for what is best in the American dream and for the most sacred values in our Judaeo Christian heritage, thereby bringing our nation back to those great wells of democracy which were dug deep by the founding fathers in their formulation of the Constitution and the Declaration of Independence.

9   Never before have I written so long a letter. I'm afraid it is much too long to take your precious time. I can assure you that it would have been much shorter if I had been writing from a comfortable desk, but what else can one do when he is alone in a narrow jail cell, other than write long letters, think long thoughts and pray long prayers?

harried: harassed
legitimate: genuine
diligently: persistently
sublime: awe-inspiring
provocation: irritation or instigation
noble: honorable
profundity: depth

10 ... Let us all hope that the dark clouds of racial prejudice will soon pass away and the deep fog of misunderstanding will be lifted from our fear drenched communities, and in some not too distant tomorrow the radiant stars of love and brotherhood will shine over our great nation with all their **scintillating** beauty.

Yours for the cause of Peace and Brotherhood,
Martin Luther King, Jr.

Making Observations

- How does Dr. King open his letter?
- What are some of the phrases Dr. King uses to grab your attention?

scintillating: brilliant

Working from the Text

1. Analyze Dr. King's letter as a primary source by using the SOAPSTone strategy.

SOAPSTone	Analysis	Textual Evidence
Speaker: Not just who is speaking but what kind of person he/she is		
Occasion: The circumstances surrounding the creation of this text		
Audience: The intended audience and perhaps the larger audience		
Purpose: Why the author wrote this text		
Subject: The topic of the text		
Tone: The author's attitude toward the subject		

Powerful Openings

Much like a novelist, the writer of an argumentative text must create an effective introduction in which she or he grabs the reader's attention and impresses upon the reader the position of or purpose for the writing. "Letter from Birmingham Jail" is an example of an argument that weaves together effective diction, imagery, and appeals in order to create a dramatic effect on its reader.

2. Revisit the opening paragraph of the letter and the phrases you starred. What makes them stand out to you? What effect do they have on you?

_____

_____

_____

_____

_____

3. Reread the opening paragraph again to determine Dr. King's purpose for writing. What language does he use to communicate it?

_____

_____

_____

_____

4. Revisit the text to find examples of the connotative diction that Dr. King uses. In the chart that follows, analyze the effects of his diction on the tone of his argument.

Connotative Diction	Effect on the Tone

Powerful Arguments

5. Return to the text and use the My Notes section to note characteristics of argumentative text, such as claims, appeals, evidence, concessions, and rebuttals.

6. What is Dr. King's claim? What conclusion does he provide? Is his use of appeals effective in supporting his claim and conclusion?

_____

_____

_____

_____

_____

_____

_____

7. What evidence does Dr. King provide for anticipated rebuttals? What concessions does he make? How does this help or hurt his argument?

_____

_____

_____

_____

_____

_____

Rhetorical Devices

8. Revisit Dr. King's letter and the examples of strong diction and imagery you found in it. Then highlight appeals to pathos, ethos, and logos. Record your findings and analyze their effectiveness in the following chart.

Device	Examples	Analysis
Diction and Imagery		

Device	Examples	Analysis
Appeals to Pathos		
Appeals to Ethos		
Appeals to Logos		

9. With a partner, discuss your responses to the following questions:

- How does Dr. King use different kinds of rhetorical elements to achieve his purpose? Share the examples you found.

- How might you use rhetorical devices and an understanding of your audience to enhance your oral presentation, especially its opening?

☑ Check Your Understanding

What context does "Letter from Birmingham Jail" provide for understanding the time period during which *To Kill a Mockingbird* was published and how its audience might have received it at that time?

_____

_____

_____

_____

_____

✒ Writing Prompt: Argumentative

Dr. Martin Luther King Jr. uses several rhetorical devices in "Letter from Birmingham Jail." Choose one rhetorical device you think he uses to great effect. State Dr. King's purpose for using this device and explain its effectiveness. Be sure to:

- Begin with a clear thesis statement, including a precise description of the rhetorical device.
- Support your claim of the device's effectiveness with relevant evidence from the text.
- Include transitions between points and a concluding statement.

Learning Strategies

Close Reading
Diffusing
Marking the Text
Paraphrasing

VOCABULARY

ACADEMIC
A secondary source is a discussion about or commentary on a primary source. The key feature of a secondary source is that it offers an interpretation of the information gathered from primary sources.

Learning Targets

- Synthesize information and cite text evidence in response to questions about the context of the Civil Rights Movement.
- Paraphrase and summarize sources in annotations for an annotated bibliography.
- Integrate ideas from multiple texts to build knowledge and vocabulary about the Civil Rights Movement.

Preview

In this activity, you will read and analyze secondary sources and primary sources to understand how the Civil Rights Movement prompted the publication of *To Kill a Mockingbird*.

As You Read

- Underline words or phrases that describe Rosa Parks's actions and the reasons for them.
- Circle unknown words and phrases. Try to determine the meaning of the words by using context clues, word parts, or a dictionary.

KNOWLEDGE QUEST

Knowledge Question:
How and why did people protest during the Civil Rights Movement?
In Activity 4.29, you will read secondary sources and primary sources about the Civil Rights Movement. While you read and build knowledge about the topic, think about your answer to the Knowledge Question.

Article

An Act of Courage:
The Arrest Records of Rosa Parks

National Archives

1   On December 1, 1955, during a typical evening rush hour in Montgomery, Alabama, a 42-year-old woman took a seat on the bus on her way home from the Montgomery Fair department store where she worked as a seamstress. Before she reached her destination, she quietly set off a social revolution when the bus driver instructed her to move back, and she refused. Rosa Parks, an African American, was arrested that day for violating a city law requiring racial segregation of public buses.

2   On the city buses of Montgomery, Alabama, the front 10 seats were permanently reserved for white passengers. The diagram shows that Mrs. Parks was seated in the first row behind those 10 seats. When the bus became crowded, the bus driver instructed Mrs. Parks and the other three passengers seated in that row, all African Americans, to vacate their seats for the white passengers boarding. Eventually, three of the passengers moved, while Mrs. Parks remained seated, arguing that she was not in a seat reserved for whites. James Blake, the driver, believed he had the **discretion** to move the line separating black and white passengers. The law was actually somewhat murky

discretion: power to decide

on that point, but when Mrs. Parks defied his order, he called the police. Officers Day and Mixon came and promptly arrested her.

3   In police custody, Mrs. Parks was booked, fingerprinted, and briefly **incarcerated**. The police report shows that she was charged with "refusing to obey orders of bus driver." For openly challenging the racial laws of her city, she remained at great physical risk while held by the police, and her family was terrified for her. When she called home, she spoke to her mother, whose first question was "Did they beat you?"

4   Mrs. Parks was not the first person to be prosecuted for violating the segregation laws on the city buses in Montgomery. She was, however, a woman of unchallenged character who was held in high **esteem** by all those who knew her. At the time of her arrest, Mrs. Parks was active in the local National Association for the Advancement of Colored People (NAACP), serving as secretary to E. D. Nixon, president of the Montgomery chapter. Her arrest became a rallying point around which the African American community organized a bus boycott in protest of the discrimination they had endured for years. Martin Luther King, Jr., the 26-year-old minister of the Dexter Avenue Baptist Church, emerged as a leader during the well-coordinated, peaceful boycott that lasted 381 days and captured the world's attention. It was during the boycott that Reverend Martin Luther King, Jr., first achieved national fame as the public became acquainted with his powerful oratory.

5   After Mrs. Parks was convicted under city law, her lawyer filed a notice of appeal. While her appeal was tied up in the state court of appeals, a panel of three judges in the U.S. District Court for the region ruled in another case that racial segregation of public buses was unconstitutional. That case, called *Browder v. Gayle*, was decided on June 4, 1956. The ruling was made by a three-judge panel that included Frank M. Johnson, Jr., and upheld by the United States Supreme court on November 13, 1956.

6   For a quiet act of **defiance** that **resonated** throughout the world, Rosa Parks is known and revered as the "Mother of the Civil Rights Movement."

This diagram of the bus Rosa Parks rode on December 1, 1955, was included in the evidence presented in *Browder v. Gayle*. The seat in which she was seated is labeled with her name.

⊘ Knowledge Quest

- Which fact about Rosa Parks' protest do you find surprising?
- Which words or phrases stand out to you as they relate to protests during the Civil Rights Movement?

incarcerated: put in jail
esteem: respect
defiance: opposition
resonated: struck a chord

Returning to the Text

- Return to the article as you respond to the following questions. Cite text evidence to support your responses.
- Write any additional questions or insights you have about the article in your Reader/Writer Notebook.

1. How is this article, a secondary source, different from a primary source? How does the addition of the bus diagram lend perspective?

_____

_____

_____

_____

2. What context does the article provide for the Civil Rights Movement?

_____

_____

_____

_____

3. Revisit the opening paragraph of the article. What words or phrases grab your attention and make you want to continue reading? Why?

_____

_____

_____

_____

4. How is the purpose of the article communicated in the opening paragraph?

_____

_____

_____

_____

5. KQ Based on context, what is the meaning of the word *oratory* in paragraph 4, and how does it relate to the Civil Rights Movement?

_____

_____

_____

_____

6. KQ Why was Rosa Parks's protest so effective?

_____

_____

_____

_____

As You Read

- Underline details about the results of the bus boycott.
- Circle unknown words and phrases. Try to determine the meaning of the words by using context clues, word parts, or a dictionary.

News Article

Negroes' Boycott Cripples Bus Line

from **The New York Times**

Carrier in Montgomery, Ala., Increases Fares to Offset Loss of Business

Special to The New York Times
MONTGOMERY, Ala., Jan. 7, 1956

1   —The boycott of Montgomery bus lines by Negro riders entered its second month this week with no **conciliation** in sight.

2   As a result of the bus company's loss of revenue in the boycott, the City Commission Wednesday raised fares 50 per cent: adult fares from 10 to 15 cents, school fares from 5 to 8 cents. The commission also authorized a 5 cent charge for transfers, which have **heretofore** been free.

3   Asking for the increase, the bus company cited losses averaging 22 cents a mile since the boycott began Dec. 5. The losses would run even higher, company spokesmen said, except for a **curtailment** in service that has reduced mileage by 31 per cent.

> **My Notes**
>
> _____
>
> _____
>
> _____
>
> _____
>
> _____
>
> _____
>
> _____
>
> _____
>
> _____
>
> _____
>
> _____
>
> _____
>
> _____
>
> _____
>
> _____

> **KNOWLEDGE QUEST**
>
> **Knowledge Question:**
> How and why did people protest during the Civil Rights Movement?

> conciliation: resolution
> heretofore: before this
> curtailment: decrease

My Notes

4   Shortly after the boycott began, virtually all service to Negro communities was **abolished**. Two routes, serving predominantly Negro areas, were abandoned entirely and other routes revised so as to exclude Negro neighborhoods along them.

Negro Woman Convicted

5   The boycott began with the arrest and conviction of Mrs. Rosa Parks, a Negro seamstress employed by a downtown department store. Mrs. Parks had refused to give up her seat when told to do so by the bus driver.

6   At the time the incident occurred, there were twenty-six Negroes and ten white persons seated in the thirty-six-passenger bus. Law requires the bus driver to segregate the passengers but leaves it within his discretion where the line is to be drawn. Thus, on many routes serving populous Negro areas it is not uncommon to see Negroes occupying all but a few seats.

7   When the driver asked Mrs. Parks and three other Negroes to give up their seats, a number of white persons were about to board. There were already some white persons standing as well as a number of Negroes. The driver explained later in court that he was "equalizing" seating facilities.

8   Mrs. Parks refused to yield her seat and was arrested for violation of a city segregation **ordinance**. Later the charge was changed to read a violation of state law, which gives bus drivers the power to assign and reassign seating. The law makes it a **misdemeanor** for anyone to disobey the driver's orders.

9   Mrs. Parks was found guilty in City Recorder's Court and fined $10. Her attorneys filed notice of appeal. At a mass meeting in a local Negro church the night following the court hearing, Negro citizens were urged not to ride the buses. The following morning Negro **patronage** was down by an estimated 90 per cent. Today it is close to 100 per cent off.

Conditions Laid Down

10   Negro citizens, led by virtually all the city's Negro ministers, have demanded that three conditions be met before they resume riding the buses. These are:

11   Adoption of a "first-come-first-served" rule as is in effect in other Alabama cities such as Mobile and Huntsville. Under this plan Negroes would continue to load from the rear and whites from the front, but the seating, once established, would remain fixed.

12   Greater courtesy on the part of drivers. Negro bus riders have complained of rude, insulting treatment.

13   Employment of Negro drivers on routes serving predominantly Negro areas.

14   A bi-racial committee, appointed by the City Commission, has so far failed to resolve any of the differences. The company contends that it cannot adopt a "first-come-first-served" policy and comply with the segregation laws. Negotiations have been broken off, for the time at least.

abolished: stopped
ordinance: law
misdemeanor: minor crime
patronage: customer support
for a business

⌀ Knowledge Quest

- What is a boycott?
- What is most interesting to you about the way the community responds to Parks' arrest?

Returning to the Text

- Return to the news article as you respond to the following questions. Use text evidence to support your responses.
- Write any additional questions or insights you have about the article in your Reader/ Writer Notebook.

7. What is the denotation of the word "cripples?" Based on the content of the news article, what is the connotation of the word in the headline?

_____

_____

_____

_____

8. KQ How does using the word *incident* in paragraph 6 affect the tone of the article?

_____

_____

_____

_____

9. KQ Why was the bus boycott a form of protest?

_____

_____

_____

_____

10. How does this article connect to, support, or contradict "An Act of Courage: The Arrest Records of Rosa Parks"?

_____

_____

_____

_____

11. How does this news article connect to the ideas and arguments in Dr. Martin Luther King Jr.'s "Letter from Birmingham Jail"?

_____

_____

_____

_____

Powerful Openings in the News

When we read print or online newspapers, we skim headlines, sometimes reading a paragraph or two before moving on. For this reason, newspaper articles typically open with the most compelling and important information, often written with succinct, attention-grabbing language. In Unit 2, you learned the terms _lede_ and _nut graf_. Both of those terms refer to the openings of news articles.

12. Revisit the opening paragraphs of the news article. What words or phrases grab your attention and what are they designed to communicate? Why does the author open the text this way?

_____

_____

_____

_____

Letter

Re: Visit to Edisto Beach State Park

by **Donald B. Cooler**

KNOWLEDGE QUEST

Knowledge Question:
How and why did people protest during the Civil Rights Movement?

May 21, 1955

Mr. J. Arthur Brown
270 ½ Ashley Ave.
Charleston, S.C.

Re: Visit to Edisto Beach State Park—Your letter of 5-12-55.

Dear Mr. Brown:

I have been instructed by our central office in Columbia to advise you that the Forestry Commission is not empowered with the authority to grant you permission to visit Edisto Beach State Park. This park was established in 1935 for the exclusive use of white persons, and based on custom and precedence we will have to deny your request.

Several of the state parks in South Carolina are designated for Negro use only. One park in this area, Hunting Island, has separate areas for whites and Negroes. I suggest that you visit that park where you will be most welcome.

If you have any questions pertaining to the above, please contact our Columbia office direct. This correct name and address is:

      S.C. State Commission of Forestry
      P.O. Box 357
      Columbia, S.C.

                 Yours very truly,

           Donald B. Cooler, Supt.
           Edisto Beach State Park
           Edisto Island, S.C.

cc: Charles H. Flory, State Forester
       C. West Jacocks, Parks Director

My Notes

Returning to the Text

- Return to the letter as you respond to the following questions. Use text evidence to support your responses.
- Write any additional insights or questions you have about the letter in your Reader/Writer Notebook.

13. Reread the first paragraph of the letter to Mr. J. Arthur Brown. What is the purpose of the letter? What language does the author use to communicate this purpose? Why?

_____

_____

_____

_____

14. KQ The letter indicates that the Commission of Forestry is not "empowered with the authority" to let Mr. Brown visit the park. What does *authority* mean in this context? Why might the author have included this phrase in the letter?

_____

_____

_____

_____

15. How does the author's use of language impact the tone of the letter?

_____

_____

_____

_____

16. KQ What details from the letter indicate why people protested during the Civil Rights Movement? Use evidence from previous, relevant readings in your answer.

_____

_____

_____

_____

17. Consider the other letter you have read on the topic of just and unjust laws—Dr. Martin Luther King Jr.'s "Letter from Birmingham Jail." How does the purpose of this letter differ, and how is its diction different? What might Dr. King's response to it have been?

_____

_____

_____

_____

⬙ Knowledge Quest

Think about the language that was used to describe the events and ideas in the letter and the articles that you just read. How and why did people protest during the Civil Rights Movement? What makes a protest effective? Discuss your opinion with a small group. Be sure to:

- Build on others' ideas during the discussion.
- Challenge each other's conclusions on the topic.
- Justify your views by citing text evidence.

Working from the Text

18. What are the benefits and drawbacks of primary and secondary sources?

_____

_____

_____

_____

⬛ INDEPENDENT READING LINK

You can continue to build your knowledge about the Civil Rights Movement by reading other articles at ZINC Reading Labs. Search for keywords such as *civil rights* or *activism*.

ZINC

19. With a partner, look at the following chart and discuss whether to categorize each source as primary or secondary. Then fill out only the "Primary or Secondary" column.

Source	Primary or Secondary	Annotation
"An Act of Courage: The Arrest Records of Rosa Parks," National Archives		
"Negroes' Boycott Cripples Bus Line," *The New York Times*		
"Re: Visit to Edisto Beach State Park," Donald B. Cooler		

Citing Sources in an Annotated Bibliography

An annotated bibliography is a tool for tracking and giving credit to sources used in research. Entries typically consist of two parts: a citation that follows the guidelines of a style manual—such as the *MLA Handbook*—for the source, and an annotation, or brief summary of and commentary about the source.

20. With your partner, turn to the third column of the chart and write annotations that could appear in an annotated bibliography of the sources. Check your annotations by reviewing them against examples provided by your teacher to make sure you have used the correct format.

☑ Focus on the Sentence

Write two statements that describe information you learned from the sources in this activity. Then write two questions that could guide further inquiry into a topic raised in these texts.

Statement: _____

_____

Statement: _____

_____

Question: _____

_____

Question: _____

_____

INDEPENDENT READING LINK

Read and Discuss

As you read the book you have chosen, look for similar themes and contexts to that of *To Kill a Mockingbird*. Discuss your observations with a group: What recurring themes and issues do you notice? What are the differences? How has reading about the context of Jim Crow laws and the Civil Rights Movement helped you to better understand the events in your independent reading?

Creating a Research Plan and Using Sources

Learning Targets

- Develop research questions and create a research plan.
- Locate, examine, and evaluate sources of information.

Preview

In this activity, you will work collaboratively to generate research questions and plan and research information to present during your oral presentation.

Developing Research Questions

Recall that for Embedded Assessment 2, your assignment is to research the historical, cultural, social, or geographical context in which the novel *To Kill a Mockingbird* was written. You will investigate how individuals, organizations, and events contributed to the change in the United States during the Civil Rights Movement. You will work collaboratively to create an oral presentation of your findings with multimedia support and guiding questions for your audience.

1. Work collaboratively with your project group to brainstorm some of the people, organizations, and events that contributed to positive social change in the United States during the Civil Rights Movement. As your group brainstorms, ask and answer relevant questions and encourage other group members to participate. Write your notes in the following graphic organizer.

People	Organizations	Events

2. Come to a consensus on the subject of your investigation by voting or by a less formal method. Then begin to fill out the "K" column of the following KWHL chart together.

K: What do we **know** about the subject?	W: What more do we **want to know** about the subject?	H: **How** will we find information?	L: What have we **learned** about the subject?

3. Revisit the list of research questions you began earlier based on the Embedded Assessment 2 assignment. Modify your list—keeping in mind that it will guide your investigation into your subject's contribution to change—by choosing at least three research questions and writing them in the "W" column. Include at least one of each of the following:

   • a question that explores a **caus**e by setting the context; for example, *What factors influenced what life was like for black people in Birmingham, Alabama, before the Civil Rights Movement?*

   • a question that explores your **subject**; for example, *What were sit-ins, and where did they take place?*

   • a question that explores an **effect** by evaluating the change; for example, *How did the "Freedom Riders" help enforce anti-segregation laws?*

4. Decide who in your group will contribute research to which question. As you conduct your research, you will complete the graphic organizer as follows:

   • In the "H" column, record the URLs of the web page or pages where you find information to answer your questions so that you can easily find them again.

   • In the "L" column, take notes to summarize the answers to your questions.

   • In the "W" column, add new questions generated by your research.

5. To paraphrase the work you have done thus far, write a research plan that includes the following:

   • your group members' names and their roles in the project;

   • the subject of your research; and

   • a list of your major research questions.

Locating and Examining Sources

6. When seeking answers to your research questions and looking for additional facts to support your conclusions, you will need to examine your sources to make sure that they are reliable, credible, and free from bias. For example, although a text's rhetoric might be striking and impactful, it is important to cite the facts it presents rather than its rhetoric to support your claims and provide substantive information in answer to your research questions.

   Recall what you learned in Unit 3 about finding and evaluating online sources:

   - Check if the author cited sources to validate facts and whether those sources provide enough evidence.
   - Ensure that if something is written anonymously, the organization publishing it is reputable.
   - Determine whether sources are objective (based on fact) or subjective (based on personal opinions and ideas).

7. For Internet articles, use the Evaluating Online Sources graphic organizer to analyze sources. You may also analyze online or print sources using the Fallacies 101 graphic organizer to help you determine whether a source contains misleading information.

Evaluating and Modifying the Research Process

8. As a group, revisit your major research questions and the sources you have located and evaluated. Evaluate your own research by asking yourselves:

   - Are we asking broad or narrow enough questions to address the assignment?
   - Are the sources we have found proving to be useful as we seek answers to our questions?
   - Do we need to seek out different or additional sources to answer our questions?

9. Implement changes where you identify them, including modifying and reassigning your research questions, if necessary. If your group decides to find new sources, you will need to evaluate them for validity, credibility, bias, and fallacious reasoning before incorporating them into your research presentation.

☑ Check Your Understanding

Describe the steps your group has taken so far in developing your historical research presentation.

📝 Drafting the Embedded Assessment

Draft an essay that explains how an individual, an organization, or an event facilitated the changes that occurred during the Civil Rights Movement. Remember to take the historical, cultural, social, and geographical contexts of *To Kill a Mockingbird* into account as you write. Be sure to:

- Identify the individual, organization, or event in your first sentence.
- Write with appropriate academic vocabulary to discuss and analyze inferences.
- Cite relevant evidence from a variety of primary and secondary sources.
- Create an attention-grabbing opener and a satisfying conclusion.

Creating an Oral Presentation

Learning Targets

- Contribute relevant information to a collaborative group presentation.
- Integrate information from a variety of sources in order to develop a well-organized and coherent oral presentation.

Preview

In this activity, you will work with your project team to create and organize your oral presentation.

My Notes

Preparing Presentation Materials

1. Revisit your research plan and sources. Create a note card for each source you use to answer your research question(s). On one side of the card, include the research question and the citation for the source according to the MLA guidelines or other appropriate guide provided by your teacher. On the other side of the card, include the following:

   - quotes, paraphrases, and summaries of the information from the source;
   - a description of the type of source; and
   - ideas for how to use the source in a presentation, including specific notes about integrating images and digital media.

2. Before creating your own note cards, collaborate with your group and create a sample note card for one of the primary or secondary sources you read in this unit.

Creating a Powerful Opening

Recall the openings or introductions of the various texts you have studied in this unit. The unifying element in all the openings is the purpose: to communicate what the entire text will be about and to grab the reader's attention. When giving an oral presentation, effective openings are also key. In this case, you might deliver your opening both orally and visually, using digital media to grab the audience's attention and draw them in.

3. With your group, revisit your note cards and determine one or two pieces of information that stand out as being particularly remarkable or important in introducing your presentation. With your purpose in mind, discuss how the group member(s) might use the information to open your presentation.

Practicing Presentation Skills

4. Use this opportunity to practice your presentation skills by presenting findings for your part of the project to at least two other members of your group. Display the appropriate web page or other source as a visual for your audience but use your index card as you speak so that you maintain eye contact and communicate your ideas effectively. Give your audience instructions in what to listen for during your presentation, and be prepared to respond to audience questions about the information you are presenting.

5. As you listen actively to your peers' mini presentations of their sources, evaluate how well each presenter summarizes the information from the source and uses presentation skills. To provide feedback, take notes in the following graphic organizer. After each group member gives his or her mini presentation, be sure to ask questions to clarify your understanding or request more information to be included in the final presentation.

Presenter Name and Research Question	Information Learned from the Investigation	My Thoughts and Questions	Evaluation of Presentation Skills

Organizing Your Presentation

6. Now that your group has gathered resources and information to answer your research questions, it is time to select the most relevant facts and details to develop your presentation. As a group, decide the best order in which to present your research. As your group answers the following questions collaboratively, contribute relevant information, and build on the ideas of others. Together fill out the chart that follows.

- How will you open your presentation?
- How will you select the most relevant facts and sufficient details?
- How will you show a cause-and-effect relationship between the 1930s context of *To Kill a Mockingbird* and the Civil Rights Movement?
- How will you divide the speaking responsibilities?
- How will you select and incorporate multimedia components into your presentation?

Presenter	Research Question	Cause/Effect	Presentation Components	Resources Needed

Citing Sources

7. Independently and then as a group, compile the list of resources you have used for your project and create an annotated bibliography. Remember that each entry should contain an annotation that has:

   • a description of the type of source, including its relevance and authority;

   • an evaluation of the source's usefulness in answering the research questions;

   • specific information learned from the source, including key details; and

   • correct formatting and content that conforms to the guidelines in a style manual, such as the *MLA Handbook*.

☑ Check Your Understanding

What are the key features of a successful research group? How do you interact with your group members? How do you gather, organize, and present your information?

Rehearsing and Revising an Oral Presentation

Learning Targets

- Give an oral presentation using techniques that meet the needs of the audience and purpose and communicate those ideas effectively.
- Listen respectfully and actively to oral presentations and respond appropriately.

Preview

In this activity, your group will rehearse your oral presentation and make revisions based on peer feedback.

Reviewing Your Presentation

1. When you have finished researching and organizing your part of the project, review your work thoroughly for clarity, development, organization, style, diction, and sentence effectiveness.

2. Partner with a group member to peer-edit each other's work using the following checklist.

Questions	Advice for Revision
Is the opening powerful and compelling?	
Is the presentation clear and well thought out?	
Does the presentation include logical reasoning and valid evidence?	
Are the multimedia components effective?	
Is the structure of the presentation organized?	
Are word choices, style, and sentence structures effective?	
Does the presentation include formal English?	

3. Use your partner's feedback and advice to revise your work as needed.

4. After revising, come back together as a group to finalize the presentation. Use the following questions and the graphic organizer to guide you.

- What is the best order for you to present the research?
- How will you smoothly transition from one part to another?
- How will you prepare for audience questions?

Order of the Parts of the Presentation	Introductions or Transitions

5. Work with your group to analyze an audience of your peers based on evaluations. Include answers to the following questions:

- What does my audience already know about the subject, and how is my presentation going to expand on that knowledge?
- What digital media components appeal to my audience, and how will I use these in my presentation?
- What connections can I make between my subject and my target audience to make my presentation relevant to their lives?

Creating Guiding Questions

6. Before delivering your presentation, create guiding questions that your audience can use to take notes during your presentation. You will write the questions on a poster for display during your presentation, make copies for the class, or incorporate them into the media you choose. Make sure to address these three levels of questions:

- **Level 1: Literal** (Questions of Fact)

  Example: *In what ways did Jim Crow laws affect schools?*

  For my subject:

- **Level 2: Interpretive** (Questions of Meaning)

  Example: *Why was* Brown v. Board of Education *considered a landmark case?*

  For my subject:

- **Level 3: Universal** (Questions of Relevance)

  Example: *Does everyone in the United States today receive the same quality of education? If not, what needs to change to make that happen?*

  For my subject:

Rehearsing Your Presentation

7. Keep the following in mind as you deliver your presentation in rehearsal:

- Use appropriate, formal language to meet the needs of your audience and fulfill the purpose of the assignment.
- While speaking, maintain eye contact with your audience and speak at an appropriate rate.
- Enunciate and use conventions of language to communicate your ideas effectively.

Listening to a Presentation

8. Before you view your partner group's oral presentation, listen to the group's questions. Answer the questions after the presentation and provide feedback to the presenters.

Conducting a Question-and-Answer Session

9. Conduct a short question-and-answer session with your partner group after each group has rehearsed its entire presentation. The presenting group should ask guiding questions and allow time for the audience members to respond. Then the presenting group should allow time for audience members to ask and receive answers to their own questions about the presentation.

Revising Your Presentation

10. Meet with your project group and discuss your thoughts about the delivery and content of your presentation during your final rehearsal. Discuss the feedback you received from your peers. Acknowledge the most successful parts of your presentation. Then create a T-chart and list elements that need improvement in the left-hand column. Decide collaboratively how to revise your presentation so that you are sharing enough information and that the information is presented effectively. List your corresponding solutions in the right-hand column. Then work together to revise your presentation.

🎁 Independent Reading Checkpoint

Review your independent reading. What have you learned and observed about the Jim Crow era and the Civil Rights Movement during this unit? How did the events you read about connect to the texts you read independently? Were any of the events you read about referred to in your independent reading? If not, how did the theme of the text you read connect to the themes you have been reading about in this unit? Review any notes you took and discuss your findings with a small group.

My Notes

Historical Investigation and Presentation

 ASSIGNMENT

Your assignment is to research the historical, cultural, social, or geographical context in which the novel *To Kill a Mockingbird* was written. You will investigate how individuals, organizations, and events contributed to change in the United States during the Civil Rights Movement. You will work collaboratively to create an oral presentation of your findings with multimedia support and guiding questions for your audience.

Planning: Take time to plan, conduct, and record your research.	■ What individual, organization, or event will your group investigate?
	■ What research questions will help you explore the subject and investigate your subject's contribution to change (cause and effect)?
	■ How will you find relevant sources and assess their credibility?
	■ How will you record citations, information, and source evaluations as you gather answers and evidence?
	■ How will you record sources to create an alphabetized, annotated bibliography?
Creating and Rehearsing: Collaborate with your group to create and prepare a multimedia oral presentation.	■ How will you select the most relevant facts and sufficient details to develop your presentation for your audience?
	■ How will you organize your presentation to emphasize the cause-and-effect relationship between the 1930s context of the novel *To Kill a Mockingbird* and the Civil Rights Movement?
	■ How will you divide the speaking responsibilities and make smooth transitions between speakers?
	■ How will you collaborate to create an audience analysis and plan how to present your findings to your peers?
	■ How will you select and incorporate digital media components into your presentation? What is your plan for rehearsing your presentation delivery and getting feedback from your peers to revise and improve your presentation?
Presenting and Listening: Use effective speaking and listening skills as a presenter and audience member.	■ How will you use notes for your talking points so that you can maintain eye contact with your audience?
	■ During your peers' presentations, how will you use the guiding questions to organize your notes on the subject of each presentation?

Reflection

Reflect on the following question: How did the class presentations enhance your understanding and appreciation of *To Kill a Mockingbird*?

Historical Investigation and Presentation

SCORING GUIDE

Scoring Criteria	Exemplary	Proficient	Emerging	Incomplete
Ideas	The presentation • is thoughtful and well organized • demonstrates a comprehensive understanding of significant aspects of the topic and its relevance to the novel.	The presentation • is organized and displays a solid understanding of the topic • clearly connects the topic and the novel for the audience.	The presentation • is somewhat organized • contains information that shows a limited understanding of the topic or how it connects to the novel.	The presentation • is not well organized and/or does not contain relevant content • provides few or no clear facts and details to help the audience connect the topic to the novel.
Structure	The presentation • skillfully uses a variety of audio/visual resources to keep the audience engaged • includes media resources that are used creatively to enhance understanding of the topic • includes a well-organized audience guide with thoughtful questions to focus information for the audience and adequate space for recording responses.	The presentation • uses audio/visual resources to engage the audience • uses media resources effectively to support information about the topic and ideas connecting it to the novel • includes an audience guide with questions to focus information for the audience and space for recording responses.	The presentation • uses some audio/visual resources that do not engage the audience • uses media resources that are distracting and do not serve the group's purpose • includes a disorganized audience guide with overly simplistic or unthoughtful focus questions.	The presentation • does not use audio/visual resources • does not use media resources • does not include an audience guide.
Use of Language	The presentation • demonstrates accomplished oral communication skills and rehearsal to create a well-planned delivery • includes participation by all group members.	The presentation • demonstrates adequate oral communication skills and rehearsal to plan the delivery • includes participation by all group members, although some may present more than others.	The presentation • demonstrates inadequate oral communication skills and shows little evidence of rehearsal • is delivered by only some of the group members.	The presentation • shows inadequate oral communication skills and no evidence of rehearsal • is not delivered by all group members.

Resources

Independent Reading

Learning Strategies

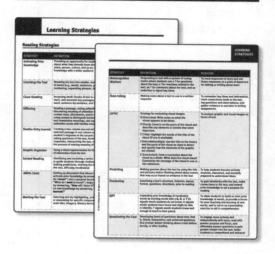

Graphic Organizers

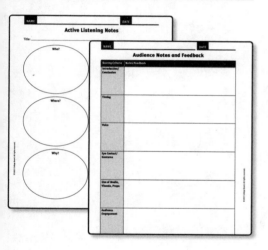

English-Spanish Glossary

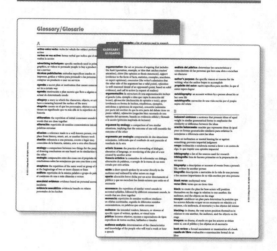

Index of Skills

Index of Authors and Titles

Suggestions for Independent Reading

This list, divided into the categories of **Literature** and **Nonfiction/Informational Text**, comprises titles related to the themes and content of the unit. For your independent reading, you can select from this wide array of titles, which have been chosen based on complexity and interest. You can do your own research and select titles that intrigue you.

Unit 1 Independent Reading List: Telling Details

Literature		
Author	**Title**	**Lexile**
Anderson, Laurie Halse	*Catalyst*	580L
Anderson, Laurie Halse	*Speak*	690L
Black, Holly and Cecil Castellucci (Editors)	*Geektastic: Stories from the Nerd Herd*	N/A
Butler, Octavia	*Kindred*	580L
Christie, Agatha	*And Then There Were None*	570L
Cormier, Robert	*The Chocolate War*	820L
Crutcher, Chris	*Athletic Shorts: Six Short Stories*	N/A
Crutcher, Chris	*Whale Talk*	1000L
Dahl, Roald	*The Umbrella Man and Other Stories*	860L
Danticat, Edwidge (Editor)	*Butterfly's Way: Voices from the Haitian Dyaspora in the United States*	N/A
Feinstein, John	*Foul Trouble*	770L
García, Cristina	*Dreaming in Cuban*	940L
Gould, Steven	*Jumper*	770L
Grover, Linda Legarde	*The Dance Boots*	N/A
Haddon, Mark	*The Curious Incident of the Dog in the Night-time*	1090L
Hinton, Susan E.	*The Outsiders*	750L
Hinton, Susan E.	*Rebeldes*	780L
Kidd, Sue Monk	*The Secret Life of Bees*	840L
Knowles, John	*A Separate Peace*	1030L
Martinez, Victor	*Parrot in the Oven: Mi Vida*	1000L
McCaffrey, Ann	*Dragonflight*	940L
McCarthy, Cormac	*All the Pretty Horses*	940L
McCarthy, Cormac	*Todos los hermosos caballos*	N/A
McDaniel, Lurlene	*Hit and Run*	610L
Montgomery, Lucy Maude	*Anne of Green Gables*	710L
Mukasonga, Scholastique	*Our Lady of the Nile*	N/A
Murphy, Julie	*Dumplin'*	710L
Myers, Walter Dean	*Slam!*	750L
Ng, Celeste	*Everything I Never Told You*	870L
Nye, Naomi Shihab	*Habibi*	850L
Paolini, Christopher	*Eragon*	710L

Ryan, Pam Munoz	Esperanza Rising	750L
Ryan, Pam Munoz	Esperanza renace	740L
Spinelli, Jerry	Stargirl	590L
Steinbeck, John	Tortilla Flats	N/A
Tan, Amy	The Joy Luck Club	930L
Trueman, Terry	Stuck in Neutral	820L
Wesselhoeft, Conrad	Dirt Bikes, Drones, and Other Ways to Fly	590L

Nonfiction/Informational Text

Author	Title	Lexile
Álvarez, Julia	Once Upon a Quincenera: Coming of Age in America	N/A
Beyer, Ramsey	Little Fish: A Memoir of a Different Kind of Year	N/A
Bonney, Grace	In the Company of Women: Inspiration and Advice from over 100 Makers, Artists, and Entrepreneurs	N/A
Huebner, Mark and Brad Wilson	Sports Bloopers: All-star Flubs and Fumbles	N/A
Jiminez, Francisco	The Circuit: Stories from the Life of a Migrant Farm Child	N/A
Jiminez, Francisco	Cajas de carton	N/A
Knisley, Lucy	Relish: My Life in the Kitchen	970L
Myers, Walter Dean	Just Write: Here's How!	970L
Yep, Lawrence (Editor)	American Dragons: Twenty-Five Asian American Voices	990L

Unit 2 Independent Reading List: Pivotal Words and Phrases

Literature

Author	Title	Lexile
Bruchac, Joseph	Code Talker: A Novel About the Navajo Marines of World War Two	910L
Cisneros, Sandra	The House on Mango Street	870L
Cisneros, Sandra	La casa en Mango Street	890L
Crane, Hart	The Complete Poems	NP
Cummings, E.E.	Selected Poems	NP
Dickinson, Emily	The Complete Poems of Emily Dickinson	NP
Gaiman, Neil	Coraline	740L
Giovanni, Nikki	Ego-Tripping and Other Poems for Young People	NP
Goldman, William	The Princess Bride	870L
Green, John	The Fault in Our Stars	850L
Grimes, Nikki	Bronx Masquerade	670L
Hansberry, Lorraine	A Raisin in the Sun	NP
Hart, Moss and George S. Kaufman	You Can't Take it With You	NP
Heppermann, Christine	Poisoned Apples: Poems for You, My Pretty	NP
Hughes, Langston	Selected Poems of Langston Hughes	NP

Levithan, David	*The Realm of Possibility*	NP
Lorde, Audre	*The Collected Poems*	NP
Millay, Edna St. Vincent	*Renascence and Other Poems*	NP
Myers, Walter Dean	*Here in Harlem: Poems in Many Voices*	NP
Myers, Walter Dean	*Street Love*	NP
Neruda, Pablo	*The Essential Neruda: Selected Poems*	NP
Oliver, Lauren	*Delirium*	920L
Rostand, Edmond	*Cyrano de Bergerac*	NP
Sánchez, Erika L.	*I Am Not Your Perfect Mexican Daughter*	HL730L
Sexton, Anne	*The Complete Poems*	NP
Silko, Leslie Marmon	*Ceremony*	890L
Soto, Gary	*Buried Onions*	850L
Soto, Gary	*Cebollas enterradas*	N/A
Wilde, Oscar	*The Importance of Being Earnest*	NP
Wilder, Thornton	*Our Town*	NP
Wilson, August	*Fences*	NP
Zindel, Paul	*The Effect of Gamma Rays on Man-in-the-Moon Marigolds*	NP

Nonfiction/Informational Text

Author	Title	Lexile
Ackroyd, Peter	*Shakespeare: The Biography*	N/A
Angelou, Maya	*I Know Why the Caged Bird Sings*	1330L
Anothony, David and Stephanie Kuligowski	*Langston Hughes: Harlem Renaissance Writer*	710L
Beah, Ishmael	*A Long Way Gone: Memoirs of a Boy Soldier*	920L
Engle, Margarita	*Enchanted Air: Two Cultures, Two Wings: A Memoir*	1120L
Heiligman, Deborah	*Vincent and Theo: The Van Gogh Brothers*	900L
Lau, Alan Chong	*Blues and Greens: A Produce Worker's Journal*	N/A
Perry, Imani	*The Radiant and Radical Life of Lorraine Hansberry*	N/A
Rodriguez, Luis	*Always Running*	830L
Rodriguez, Luis	*La vida loca: el testimonio de un pandillero en Los Angeles*	N/A
Soto, Gary	*Living Up the Street*	1140L
Woodson, Jacqueline	*Brown Girl Dreaming*	990L

Unit 3 Independent Reading List: Compelling Evidence

Literature

Author	Title	Lexile
Doyle, Arthur Conan	*The Hound of the Baskervilles*	980L
Lowry, Lois	*The Giver*	760L
Alvarez, Julia	*Return to Sender*	890L
Austen, Jane	*Pride and Prejudice*	1070L
Chbosky, Stephen	*The Perks of Being a Wallflower*	720L
Fitzgerald, F. Scott	*The Great Gatsby*	820L
Flores-Galbis, Enrique	*90 Miles to Havana*	790L
Orwell, George	*1984*	950L
Roth, Veronica	*Divergent*	HL700L
Sachar, Louis	*Holes*	660L
Twain, Mark	*Adventures of Huckleberry Finn*	980L
Twain, Mark	*The Adventures of Tom Sawyer*	950L
Vizzini, Ned	*Be More Chill*	HL700L

Nonfiction/Informational Text

Author	Title	Lexile
Balko, Radley and Tucker Carrington	*The Cadaver King and the Country Dentist: A True Story of Injustice in the American South*	N/A
Barry, Dave	*My Teenage Son's Goal in Life is to Make me Feel 3,500 Years Old*	N/A
Bhutto, Benazir	*Daughter of Destiny: An Autobiography*	N/A
Bilas, Jay	*Toughness: Developing True Strength On and Off the Court*	N/A
Brown, David O.	*Called to Rise: A Life in Faithful Service to the Community that Created Me*	N/A
Bruchac, Joseph	*Jim Thorpe, Original All-American*	950L
Cham, Jorge and Daniel Whiteson	*We Have No Idea: A Guide to the Unknown Universe*	1110L
Crowe, Chris	*Getting Away with Murder: The True Story of the Emmett Till Case*	1210L
Kaye, Cathryn Berger	*Going Blue: A Teen Guide to Saving our Oceans and Waterways*	1170L
Leland, Melvin	*Chasing Space: An Astronaut's Story of Grit, Grace, and Second Chances*	1020L
McCormick, Patricia	*Plot to Kill Hitler: Dietrich Bonhoeffer, Pastor, Spy, Unlikely Hero*	N/A
Morgan, Genevieve	*Undecided: Navigating Life and Learning After High School*	N/A
Platt, Richard	*Crime Scene: The Ultimate Guide to Forensic Science*	1190L
Pollan, Michael	*The Omnivore's Dilemma*	930L
Prinstein, Mitchell J.	*Popular: The Power of Likability in a Status Obsessed World*	N/A
Sheinkin, Steve	*Most Dangerous: Daniel Ellsberg and the Secret History of the Vietnam War*	890L
Sheinkin, Steve	*Undefeated: Jim Thorpe and the Carlisle Indian School Football Team*	N/A

Shetterly, Margot Lee	Hidden Figures: The Untold True Story of Four African-American Women Who Launched Our Nation Into Space	1120L
Vernon, Naomi ReNa	A Teen's Guide to Finding a Job	N/A
Watts, Duncan	Six Degrees: The Science of a Connected Age	N/A

Unit 4 Independent Reading List: Powerful Openings

Literature

Author	Title	Lexile
Alexie, Sherman	The Absolute True Diary of a Part-Time Indian	600L
Blum, Jenna	Those Who Save Us	N/A
Bray, Libba	A Great and Terrible Beauty	760L
Burns, Olive Ann	Cold Sassy Tree	930L
Cheva, Cherry	She's So Money	920L
Condie, Ally	Matched	680L
Danticat, Edwidge	Behind the Mountains	940L
Draper, Sharon	Tears of a Tiger	700L
Ellison, Ralph	Invisible Man	950L
Ellison, Ralph	El hombre invisible	N/A
Erdrich, Louise	Tracks	780L
Forman, Gayle	If I Stay	830L
Gibbons, Kaye	Ellen Foster	870L
Green, John	Paper Towns	850L
Hornby, Nick	Fever Pitch	1340L
Ihimaera, Witi	Whale Rider	N/A
Kluger, Steve	Last Days of Summer	900L
Kogawa, Joy	Obasan	990L
Salinger, J.D.	Catcher in the Rye	790L
Salinger, J.D.	El guardian entre el centeno	N/A
Sánchez, Erika L.	I Am Not Your Perfect Mexican Daughter	HL730L
Stockett, Kathryn	The Help	730L
Stockett, Kathryn	Criadas y señoras	N/A
Taylor, Mildred D.	Roll of Thunder, Hear My Cry	920L

Nonfiction/Informational Text

Author	Title	Lexile
Baldwin, James	The Fire Next Time	1300L
Fisher, Antwone Quenton	Finding Fish	1080L
Freedman, Russell	Freedom Walkers: The Story of the Montgomery Bus Boycott	1110L
Griffin, John Howard	Black Like Me	990L

Jenkins, George, Sampson Davis, and Rameck Hunt	*We Beat the Street: How a Friendship Pact Led to Success*	860L
Jermaine, Suzanne	*Freedom's Sons: The True Story of the Amistad Mutiny*	1030L
Lewis, John and others	*March: Book One*	GN760L
Lewis, John and others	*March: Book Two*	GN850L
Litwack, Leon F.	*Trouble in Mind: Black Southerners in the Age of Jim Crow*	N/A
Margolick, David	*Elizabeth and Hazel: Two Women of Little Rock*	N/A
Moody, Anne	*Coming of Age in Mississippi*	870L
Partridge, Elizabeth	*Marching for Freedom: Walk Together Children and Don't You Grow Weary*	960L
Williams, Jay	*Life Is Not an Accident*	N/A
Wright, Richard	*Black Boy*	950L
Wright, Simeon and Herb Boyd	*Simeon's Story: An Eyewitness Account of the Kidnapping of Emmett Till*	1050L

Independent Reading Log

Directions: This log is a place to record your progress and thinking about your independent reading during each unit. Add your log pages to your Reader/Writer Notebook or keep them as a separate place to record your reading insights.

Unit _____

Independent Reading Title _____

Author(s) _____ Text Type _____

Pages read: from _____ to _____

_____

_____

_____

_____

_____

Independent Reading Title _____

Author(s) _____ Text Type _____

Pages read: from _____ to _____

_____

_____

_____

_____

_____

_____

Independent Reading Title _____

Author(s) _____ Text Type _____

Pages read: from _____ to _____

_____

_____

_____

_____

_____

_____

Unit _____

Independent Reading Title _____

Author(s) _____ Text Type _____

Pages read: from _____ to _____

_____

_____

_____

_____

_____

Independent Reading Title _____

Author(s) _____ Text Type _____

Pages read: from _____ to _____

_____

_____

_____

_____

_____

Independent Reading Title _____

Author(s) _____ Text Type _____

Pages read: from _____ to _____

_____

_____

_____

_____

_____

Independent Reading Title _____

Author(s) _____ Text Type _____

Pages read: from _____ to _____

_____

_____

_____

_____

_____

Learning Strategies

Reading Strategies

STRATEGY	DEFINITION	PURPOSE
Activating Prior Knowledge	Providing an opportunity for students to think about what they already know about a concept, place, person, culture, and so on, and share their knowledge with a wider audience	To prepare students to encounter new concepts, places, persons, cultures, and so on, prior to reading a text; an Anticipation Guide and a Quickwrite can be used to activate and assess prior knowledge
Chunking the Text	Breaking the text into smaller, manageable units of sense (e.g., words, sentences, paragraphs) by numbering, separating phrases, drawing boxes	To reduce the intimidation factor when encountering long words, sentences, or whole texts; to increase comprehension of difficult or challenging text
Close Reading	Accessing small chunks of text to read, reread, mark, and annotate key passages, word-for-word, sentence-by-sentence, and line-by-line	To develop comprehensive understanding by engaging in one or more focused readings of a text
Diffusing	Reading a passage, noting unfamiliar words, discovering meaning of unfamiliar words using context clues, dictionaries, and/or thesauruses, using context to distinguish between denotative and connotative meanings, and replacing unfamiliar words with familiar ones	To facilitate a close reading of text, the use of resources, an understanding of synonyms, and increased comprehension of text
Double-Entry Journal	Creating a two-column journal with a student-selected passage in one column and the student's response in the second column (e.g., asking questions of the text, forming personal responses, interpreting the text, reflecting on the process of making meaning of the text)	To assist in note-taking and organizing key textual elements and responses noted during reading in order to generate textual support that can be incorporated into a piece of writing at a later time
Graphic Organizer	Using a visual representation for the organization of information from the text	To facilitate increased comprehension and discussion
Guided Reading	Identifying and modeling a series of strategies to guide students through challenging text (e.g., making predictions, marking the text, skimming the text, diffusing vocabulary)	To model for students the use of multiple strategies to make meaning of challenging texts and help them learn to apply the strategies independently
KWHL Chart	Setting up discussion that allows students to activate prior knowledge by answering, "What do I **know**?"; sets a purpose by answering, "What do I **want** to know?"; helps preview a task by answering, "**How** will I learn it?"; and reflects on new knowledge by answering, "What have I **learned**?"	To organize thinking, access prior knowledge, and reflect on learning to increase comprehension and engagement
Marking the Text	Selecting text by highlighting, underlining, and/or annotating for specific components, such as main idea, imagery, literary devices, and so on	To focus reading for specific purposes, such as author's craft, and to organize information from selections; to facilitate reexamination of a text

STRATEGY	DEFINITION	PURPOSE
Metacognitive Markers	Responding to text with a system of cueing marks where students use a ? for questions about the text; a ! for reactions related to the text; an * for comments about the text; and an underline to signal key ideas	To track responses to texts and use those responses as a point of departure for talking or writing about texts
Note-taking	Making notes about a text to use in a written response	To remember key ideas and information, track connections made to the text, log questions and observations, and gather evidence to use later in writing assignments
OPTIC	Strategy for evaluating visual images. O (Overview): Write notes on what the visual appears to be about. P (Parts): Zoom in on the parts of the visual and describe any elements or details that seem important. T (Title): Highlight the words of the title of the visual (if one is available). I (Interrelationships): Use the title as the theory and the parts of the visual as clues to detect and specify how the elements of the graphic are related. C (Conclusion); Draw a conclusion about the visual as a whole. What does the visual mean? Summarize the message of the visual in one or two sentences.	To analyze graphic and visual images as forms of text
Predicting	Making guesses about the text by using the title and pictures and/or thinking ahead about events that may occur based on evidence in the text	To help students become actively involved, interested, and mentally prepared to understand ideas
Previewing	Examining a text's structure, features, layout, format, questions, directions, prior to reading	To gain familiarity with the text, make connections to the text, and extend prior knowledge to set a purpose for reading
QHT	Expanding prior knowledge of vocabulary words by marking words with a Q, H, or T (Q signals words students do not know; H signals words students have heard and might be able to identify; T signals words students know well enough to teach to their peers)	To allow students to build on their prior knowledge of words, to provide a forum for peer teaching and learning of new words, and to serve as a prereading exercise to aid in comprehension
Questioning the Text	Developing levels of questions about text; that is, literal, interpretive, and universal questions that prompt deeper thinking about a text before, during, or after reading	To engage more actively and independently with texts, read with greater purpose and focus, and ultimately answer questions to gain greater insight into the text; helps students to comprehend and interpret

STRATEGY	DEFINITION	PURPOSE
Paraphrasing	Restating in one's own words the essential information expressed in a text, whether it be narration, dialogue, or informational text, while maintaining the original text's meaning	To encourage and facilitate comprehension of challenging text
RAFT	Primarily used to generate new text, this strategy can also be used to analyze a text by examining the role of the speaker (R), the intended audience (A), the format of the text (F), and the topic of the text (T)	To initiate reader response; to facilitate an analysis of a text to gain focus prior to creating a new text
Rereading	Encountering the same text with more than one reading	To identify additional details; to clarify meaning and/or reinforce comprehension of texts
SIFT	Analyzing a fictional text by examining stylistic elements, especially symbol, imagery, and figures of speech in order to show how all work together to reveal tone and theme	To focus and facilitate an analysis of a fictional text by examining the title and text for symbolism, identifying images and sensory details, analyzing figurative language and identifying how all these elements reveal tone and theme
Skimming/Scanning	Skimming by rapid or superficial reading of a text to form an overall impression or to obtain a general understanding of the material; scanning focuses on key words, phrases, or specific details and provides speedy recognition of information	To quickly form an overall impression prior to an in-depth study of a text; to answer specific questions or quickly locate targeted information or detail in a text
SMELL	Analyzing a persuasive speech or essay by asking five essential questions: • **S**ender-receiver relationship—What is the sender-receiver relationship? Who are the images and language meant to attract? Describe the speaker of the text. • **M**essage—What is the message? Summarize the statement made in the text. • **E**motional Strategies—What is the desired effect? • **L**ogical Strategies—What logic is operating? How does it (or its absence) affect the message? Consider the logic of the images as well as the words. • **L**anguage—What does the language of the text describe? How does it affect the meaning and effectiveness of the writing? Consider the language of the images as well as the words.	To analyze a persuasive speech or essay by focusing on five essential characteristics of the genre; analysis is related to rhetorical devices, logical fallacies, and how an author's use of language achieves specific purposes

STRATEGY	DEFINITION	PURPOSE
SOAPSTone	Analyzing text by discussing and identifying **S**peaker, **O**ccasion, **A**udience, **P**urpose, **S**ubject, and **Tone**	To facilitate the analysis of specific elements of nonfiction, literary, and informational texts, and show the relationship among the elements to an understanding of the whole
Summarizing	Giving a brief statement of the main points or essential information expressed in a text, whether it be narration, dialogue, or informational text	To facilitate comprehension and recall of a text
Think Aloud	Talking through a difficult passage or task by using a form of metacognition whereby the reader expresses how he/she has made sense of the text	To reflect on how readers make meaning of challenging texts and to facilitate discussion
TP-CASTT	Analyzing a poetic text by identifying and discussing **T**itle, **P**araphrase, **C**onnotation, **A**ttitude, **S**hift, **T**heme, and **T**itle again	To facilitate the analysis of specific elements of a literary text, especially poetry. To show how the elements work together to create meaning
Visualizing	Forming a picture (mentally and/or literally) while reading a text to deepen understanding	To increase reading comprehension, deepen understanding, and promote active engagement with text
Word Maps	Using a clearly defined graphic organizer such as concept circles or word webs to identify and reinforce word meanings	To provide a visual tool for identifying and remembering multiple aspects of words and word meanings
Word Sort	Organizing and sorting words into categories designated by the teacher or selected by the student and providing a written or oral justification for the classifications	To solidify understanding of word meanings by considering the multiple uses, meanings, and relationships of word parts, words, and groups of words

Writing Strategies

STRATEGY	DEFINITION	PURPOSE
Adding `	Enhancing a text by finding areas to add facts, details, examples, and commentary; smoothing out transitions; and clarifying and strengthening ideas and assertions	To improve, refine, and clarify the writer's thoughts during drafting and/ or revision
Brainstorming	Using a flexible but deliberate process of listing multiple ideas in a short period of time without excluding any idea from the preliminary list	To generate ideas, concepts, or key words that provide a focus and/or establish organization as part of the prewriting or revision process
Deleting	Enhancing a text by eliminating words, phrases, sentences, or ideas that inhibit clarity and cohesiveness	To improve, refine, and clarify the writer's thoughts during drafting and/ or revision
Drafting	Composing a text in its initial form before developing it	To incorporate brainstormed or initial ideas into a written format
Freewriting	Writing freely without constraints in order to generate ideas and capture thinking	To generate ideas when planning a piece of writing, or to refine and clarify thoughts, spark new ideas, and/or generate content during drafting and/or revision
Generating Questions	Clarifying and developing ideas by asking questions of the draft. May be part of self-editing or peer editing	To clarify and develop ideas in a draft; used during drafting and as part of writer response
Graphic Organizer	Organizing ideas and information visually (e.g., Venn diagrams, flowcharts, cluster maps)	To provide a visual system for organizing multiple ideas, details, and/or textual support to be included in a piece of writing
Guided Writing	Modeling the writing that students are expected to produce by guiding students through the planning, generation of ideas, organization, drafting, revision, editing, and publication of texts before students are asked to perform the same process; co-constructing texts with students as part of guided writing	To demonstrate the writing process

Speaking and Listening Strategies

STRATEGY	DEFINITION	PURPOSE
Choral Reading	Reading text lines aloud in student groups and/or individually to present an interpretation	To develop fluency; differentiate between the reading of statements and questions; practice phrasing, pacing, and reading dialogue; show how a character's emotions are captured through vocal stress and intonation
Debate	Engaging in a structured argument to examine both sides of an issue	To provide students with an opportunity to collect and orally present evidence supporting the affirmative and negative arguments of a proposition or issue
Drama Games	Participating in creative dramatics (e.g., pantomime, tableau, role-playing) to reinforce an oral literacy skill or develop a deeper understanding of a concept	To engage students in the reading and presenting of text and to create meaning through a kinesthetic approach
Fishbowl (Inner/outer circles)	Discussing specific topics within groups; some students will form the inner circle and model appropriate discussion techniques while an outer circle of students listen to and evaluate the discussion process of the inner circle in order to respond effectively	To provide students with an opportunity to engage in a formal discussion and to experience roles both as participant and active listener; students also have the responsibility of supporting their opinions and responses using specific textual evidence
Note-taking	Creating a record of information while listening to a speaker or reading a text	To facilitate active listening or close reading; to record and organize ideas that assist in processing information
Oral Reading	Reading aloud one's own text or the texts of others (e.g., echo reading, choral reading, paired readings)	To share one's own work or the work of others; build fluency and increase confidence in presenting to a group
Rehearsal	Encouraging multiple practices of a piece of text prior to a performance	To provide students with an opportunity to clarify the meaning of a text prior to a performance as they refine the use of dramatic conventions (e.g., gestures, vocal interpretations, facial expressions)
Role-Playing	Assuming the role or persona of a character	To develop the voice, emotions, and mannerisms of a character to facilitate improved comprehension of a text
Socratic Seminar	Tying a focused discussion to an essential question, topic, or selected text in which students ask questions of each other; questions initiate a conversation that continues with a series of responses and additional questions	To help students formulate questions that address issues (in lieu of simply stating their opinions) to facilitate their own discussion and arrive at a new understanding; students also have the responsibility of supporting their opinions and responses using specific textual evidence

Collaborative Strategies

STRATEGY	DEFINITION	PURPOSE
Discussion Groups	Engaging in an interactive, small-group discussion, often with an assigned role; to consider a topic, text, or question	To gain new understanding of or insight into a text from multiple perspectives
Jigsaw	In groups, students read different texts or passages from a single text, then share and exchange information from their reading with another group. They then return to their original groups to share their new knowledge.	To summarize and present information to others in a way that facilitates an understanding of a text (or multiple texts) without having each student read the text in its entirety
Literature Circles	Groups of students read the same text to participate in a mutual reading experience; based on the objective(s) of the lesson, students take on a variety of roles throughout the reading experience; texts may be selected based on individual preferences or on the demands of the text.	To provide opportunities for students to interact with one another as they read, respond to, and interpret a common text
Think-Pair-Share	Pairing with a peer to share ideas before sharing ideas and discussion with a larger group	To construct meaning about a topic or question; to test thinking in relation to the ideas of others; to prepare for a discussion with a larger group

Graphic Organizer Directory

Contents

Active Listening Feedback

Presenter's name: _____

Content

What is the presenter's purpose? _____

What is the presenter's main point? _____

Do you agree with the presenter? Why or why not? _____

_____

_____

Form

Did the presenter use a clear, loud voice? ☐ yes ☐ no

Did the presenter make eye contact? ☐ yes ☐ no

One thing I really liked about the presentation:

_____

_____

_____

One question I still have:

_____

_____

_____

Other comments or notes:

Active Listening Notes

Title: _____

Who?

What?

Where?

When?

Why?

How?

Audience Notes and Feedback

Scoring Criteria	Notes/Feedback
Introduction/ Conclusion	
Timing	
Voice	
Eye Contact/ Gestures	
Use of Media, Visuals, Props	
Audience Engagement	

Cause and Effect

Title: _____

Cause: What happened?	→	**Effect:** An effect of this is

Cause: What happened?	→	**Effect:** An effect of this is

Cause: What happened?	→	**Effect:** An effect of this is

Cause: What happened?	→	**Effect:** An effect of this is

Character Map

Character name: _____

What does the character look like?

How does the character act and feel?

What do other characters say or think about the character?

Collaborative Dialogue

Topic: _____

Use the space below to record ideas.

"Wh-" Prompts
Who?   What?   Where?   When?   Why?

Speaker 1

Speaker 2

Conclusion Builder

Evidence

Evidence

Evidence

Based on this evidence, I can conclude

Conflict Map

Title: _____

What is the main conflict in this story?

What causes this conflict?

How is the conflict resolved?

What are some other ways the conflict could have been resolved?

Conversation for Quickwrite

1. Turn to a partner and restate the prompt in your own words.

2. Brainstorm key words to use in your quickwrite response.

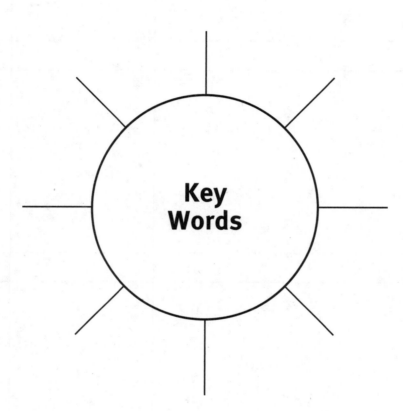

3. Take turns explaining your ideas to your partner. Try using some of the key words you brainstormed.

4. On your own, write a response to the quickwrite.

Definition and Reflection

Academic Vocabulary Word
Definition in own words
Illustration (literal or symbolic)

My experiences with this concept:

- I haven't really thought about this concept.

  _____

- I have only thought about this concept in English Language Arts class.

  _____

- I have applied this concept in other classes.

  _____

- I have applied this concept outside of school.

  _____

My level of understanding:

- I am still trying to understand this concept.

  _____

- I am familiar with this concept, but I am not comfortable applying it.

  _____

- I am very comfortable with this concept and I know how to apply it.

  _____

- I could teach this concept to another classmate.

  _____

Discourse Starters

Questioning and Discussing a Text

One question I have is _____.

Could this mean _____?

Why do you think the author _____?

I understand _____, but I wonder _____.

I notice that _____.

I think this (word/sentence/paragraph) means _____.

I think _____ because the text says _____.

In paragraph _____, the author says _____.

According to the text, _____.

One way to interpret _____ is _____.

Summarizing

The main events that take place are _____.

The major points of the text are _____.

The main idea of _____ is _____.

One central idea of this text is _____.

Another central idea is _____.

All in all, the message is _____.

The author's main purpose is to _____.

Basically, the author is saying that _____.

Comparing and Contrasting

_____ and _____ are similar because _____.

_____ and _____ are similar in that they both ____.

_____ is _____. Similarly, _____ is _____.

One thing _____ and _____ have in common is ____.

_____ and _____ are different because _____.

_____ and _____ are different in that _____.

_____ is _____. On the other hand, _____ is ____.

One difference between _____ and _____ is ____.

Clarifying

I'm not sure I understand the instructions.

Could you repeat that please?

I have a question about _____.

I am having trouble with _____.

Will you explain that again?

Could you clarify _____?

Would you mind helping me with _____?

Which (page/paragraph/section) are we reading?

How do you spell/pronounce _____?

Discourse Starters

Agreeing and Disagreeing

I agree with the idea that _____ because _____.

I share your point of view because _____.

You made a good point when you said _____.

I agree with (a person) that _____.

Although I agree that _____, I also think _____.

I understand where you're coming from, but _____.

I disagree with the idea that _____ because _____.

I see it a different way because _____.

You have a point, but the evidence suggests _____.

Arguing and Persuading with Evidence

I believe that _____ because _____.

It is clear that _____ because _____.

One reason I think _____ is _____.

Based on evidence in the text, I think _____.

Evidence such as _____ suggests that _____.

An example to support my position is _____.

This is evident because _____.

What evidence supports the idea that _____?

Can you explain why you think _____?

Evaluating

This is effective because _____.

The evidence _____ is strong because _____.

This is convincing because _____.

I see why the author _____, but I think _____.

This is not very effective because _____.

The evidence _____ is weak because _____.

This would have been better if _____.

What do you think about the writer's choice to _____?

Why do you think _____ (is/isn't) effective?

Giving Feedback and Suggesting

The part where you _____ is strong because _____.

What impressed me the most is how you _____.

This is a good start. Maybe you should add _____.

I like how you _____, but I would try _____.

You might consider changing _____.

I would suggest revising _____ so that _____.

One suggestion would be to _____.

Why did you choose _____?

A better choice might be _____.

This would be clearer if _____.

Editor's Checklist

Over the course of the year with SpringBoard, customize this Editor's Checklist as your knowledge of language conventions grows. The three examples below show you how to write a good checklist item.

	Are all the sentences complete?
	Do the subject and verb of each sentence agree?
	Do all the sentences have correct punctuation?

Writer's Checklist

	Ideas	
Ideas		
	Does your first paragraph hook the reader?	
	Is the purpose of your writing clear (to inform, to make an argument, etc.)?	
	Is the genre of writing appropriate for your purpose?	
	Is your main idea clear and easy to summarize?	
	Does your text contain details and information that support your main idea?	
	Are the ideas in the text well organized?	
	Do you connect your ideas by using transitions?	
	Do you use parallel structure to keep your ideas clear?	
	Does each paragraph have a conclusion that transitions to the next paragraph?	
	Does your writing end with a strong conclusion that restates the original purpose of the text?	
Language		
	Do you keep a consistent point of view throughout?	
	Do you use the present tense when writing about a text?	
	Are any shifts in verb tense easy to follow and necessary?	
	Have you removed unnecessary or confusing words?	
	Do you use vivid verbs and descriptive adjectives when appropriate?	
	Do you use different styles of language (like figurative or sensory) when appropriate?	
	Do you use a variety of sentence types?	
	Do you vary the way you begin your sentences?	
	Did you split up run-on sentences?	
	Are your pronoun references clear?	

Evaluating Online Sources

The URL
• What is its domain?
    • .com = a for-profit organization
    • .gov, .mil, .us (or other country code) = a government site
    • .edu = affiliated with an educational institution
    • .org = a nonprofit organization
• Is this URL someone's personal page?
• Do you recognize who is publishing this page?	

Sponsor: • Does the website give information about the organization or group that sponsors it? • Does it have a link (often called "About Us") that leads you to that information? • What do you learn?	
Timeliness: • When was the page last updated (usually this is posted at the top or bottom of the page)? • Is the topic something that changes frequently, like current events or technology?	
Purpose: • What is the purpose of the page? • What is its target audience? • Does it present information, opinion, or both? • Is it primarily objective or subjective? • How do you know?	
Author: • What credentials does the author have? • Is this person or group considered an authority on the topic?	
Links • Does the page provide links? • Do they work? • Are they helpful? • Are they objective or subjective?	

Fallacies 101

Ad Baculum (Scare Tactics)	If you don't support the party's tax plan, you and your family will be reduced to poverty. Chairman of the Board: "All those opposed to my arguments for the opening of a new department, signify by saying, 'I resign.'"
Ad hoc	Person 1: I should have gotten an A on that test. Person 2: You didn't study for that test at all. Person 1: That class is useless!
Ad Hominem (Against the Man)/ Genetic Fallacy	"My opponent, a vicious and evil person, should absolutely never be elected to office." The Volkswagen Beetle is an evil car because it was originally designed by Hitler's army.
Ad Populum	You should turn to channel 6. It's the most watched channel this year. There is always a long line at that restaurant, so the food must be really good.
Appeal To Pity	"Jonathan couldn't have cheated! He's such a nice boy and he tries so hard."
Argument from Outrage	The airline cancelled my flight an hour before takeoff and wouldn't tell me why. This is an outrage! We should all boycott the company.
Circular Reasoning	Emotional support animals should be allowed on airplanes, so the airline should change its policy. The policy should be changed because emotional support animals should be allowed on planes!
Either/Or (False Dilemma)	We can either stop using cars or destroy Earth. We must drill now or we'll remain dependent on foreign oil suppliers.
Faulty Analogies	Buying into the stock market is the same as betting on a horse race.
Hasty Generalization	They hit two home runs in the first inning of the season. This team is going all the way to the World Series!
Non-sequitur	I always see her with a book in her hands. She must hate watching TV.
Post Hoc	I ate a turkey sandwich and now I feel tired, so the turkey must have made me tired.
Red Herring	The new dress code banning t-shirts isn't fair. Students have the right to free speech just like anyone else.
Slippery Slope Fallacy	"If I don't study for the test, then I'm going to get a bad grade. If I get a bad grade on the test, I'll get a bad grade in the class, and I won't get into a good college. Getting into a good college is the most important part of getting a good job; so if I don't study for the test, I won't get a good job!"
Straw Man	People say that Mark Twain was a good author, but I disagree. If he was such a good author, why didn't he write using his own name?

Idea and Argument Evaluator

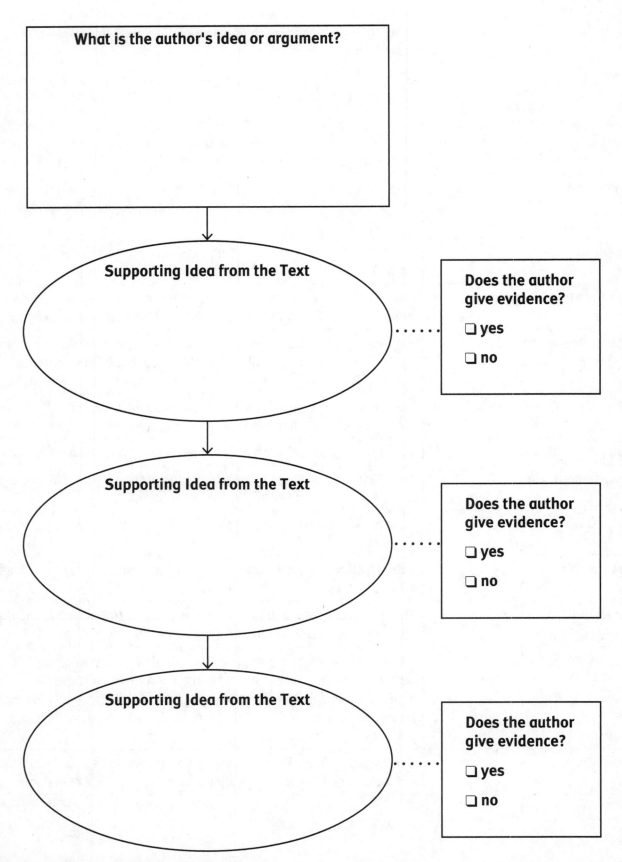

What is the author's idea or argument?

Supporting Idea from the Text

Does the author give evidence?

❏ yes

❏ no

Supporting Idea from the Text

Does the author give evidence?

❏ yes

❏ no

Supporting Idea from the Text

Does the author give evidence?

❏ yes

❏ no

Idea Connector

Directions: Write two simple sentences about the same topic. Next, write transition words around the Idea Connector. Then, choose an appropriate word to connect ideas in the two sentences. Write your combined sentence in the space below.

Sentence One

Sentence Two

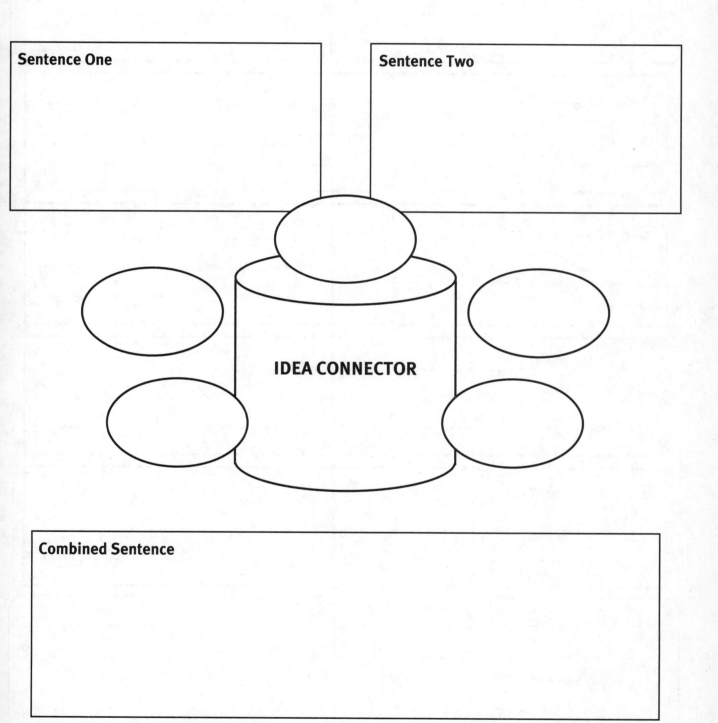

IDEA CONNECTOR

Combined Sentence

Key Idea and Details Chart

Title/Topic _____

Key Idea _____
_____
_____

Supporting detail 1 _____
_____
_____

Supporting detail 2 _____
_____
_____

Supporting detail 3 _____
_____
_____

Supporting detail 4 _____
_____
_____

Restate topic sentence: _____
_____

Concluding sentence: _____
_____
_____

Narrative Analysis and Writing

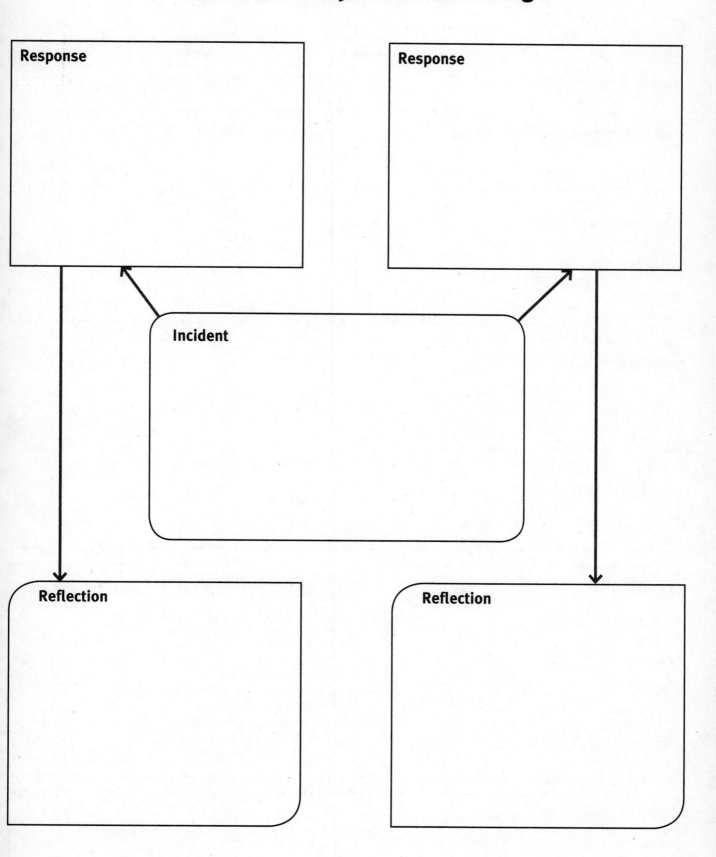

Response

Response

Incident

Reflection

Reflection

Notes for Reading Independently

Fiction

Title: _____

Author: _____

Something interesting I noticed:

A question I have:

Summary:

Illustration:

Connections to my life/other texts I've read:

How challenging this text was:
Easy   1   2   3   4   5   6   7   8   9   10   _Challenging_

Notes for Reading Independently
Nonfiction

Title: _____

Author: _____

Main idea:

Facts I learned:

Summary:

Questions I still have:

Connections to my life/other texts I've read:

How challenging this text was:

Easy   1   2   3   4   5   6   7   8   9   10   *Challenging*

Opinion Builder

Reason

Reason

Based on these reasons, my opinion is

Reason

Reason

OPTIC

Title of Piece:

Artist: _____ **Type of artwork:** _____

Overview	Look at the artwork for at least 10 seconds. Generate questions; e.g., What is the subject? What strikes you as interesting, odd, etc.? What is happening?
Parts	Look closely at the artwork, making note of important elements and details. Ask additional questions, such as: Who are the figures? What is the setting and time period? What symbols are present? What historical information would aid understanding of this piece?
Title	Consider what the title and any written elements of the text suggest about meaning. How does the title relate to what is portrayed?
Interrelationships	Look for connections between and among the title, caption, and the parts of the art. How are the different elements related?
Conclusion	Form a conclusion about the meaning/theme of the text. Remember the questions you asked when you first examined it. Be prepared to support your conclusions with evidence.

Paragraph Frame for Conclusions

Conclusion Words and Phrases

shows that

based on

suggests that

leads to

indicates that

influences

The _____ *(story, poem, play, passage, etc.)*
shows that *(helps us to conclude that)* _____
_____
_____

There are several reasons why. First, _____
_____
_____
_____
_____

A second reason is _____
_____
_____
_____
_____

Finally, _____
_____
_____
_____
_____

In conclusion, _____
_____
_____
_____
_____

Paragraph Frame for Sequencing

Sequence Words and Phrases

at the beginning

in the first place

as a result

later

eventually

in the end

lastly

In the _____ (story, poem, play, passage, etc.)
there are three important _____
(events, steps, directions, etc.)

First, _____

_____

_____

_____

Second, _____

_____

_____

_____

Third, _____

_____

_____

_____

Finally, _____

_____

_____

_____

Paraphrasing and Summarizing Map

What does the text say?	How can I say it in my own words?

How can I use my own words to summarize the text?

Peer Editing

Writer's name: _____

Did the writer answer the prompt? ☐ yes ☐ no

Did the writer use appropriate details or evidence to develop their writing? ☐ yes ☐ no

Is the writing organized in a way that makes sense? ☐ yes ☐ no

Did the writer use a variety of sentence types to make the writing more interesting? ☐ yes ☐ no

Are there any spelling or punctuation mistakes? ☐ yes ☐ no

Are there any grammar errors? ☐ yes ☐ no

Two things I really liked about the writer's story:

1. _____
   _____
   _____

2. _____
   _____
   _____

One thing I think the writer could do to improve the writing:

1. _____
   _____
   _____

Other comments or notes:

Persuasive/Argument Writing Map

Thesis

Reason

Reason

Reason

Evidence

Evidence

Evidence

Evidence

Evidence

Evidence

Evidence

Evidence

Evidence

Conclusion

Presenting Scoring Guide

Scoring Criteria	Exemplary	Proficient	Emerging	Incomplete
Introduction / Conclusion	The presentation • provides a clear, engaging, and appropriate introduction to the topic or performance • provides a clear, engaging, and appropriate conclusion that closes, summarizes, draws connections to broader themes, or supports the ideas presented.	The presentation • provides a clear and appropriate introduction to the topic or performance • provides a clear and appropriate conclusion that closes, summarizes, draws connections to broader themes, or supports the ideas presented.	The presentation • provides an adequate introduction to the topic or performance • provides an adequate conclusion that closes, summarizes, draws connections to broader themes, or supports the ideas presented.	The presentation • does not provide an introduction to the topic or performance • does not provide a conclusion that closes, summarizes, draws connections to broader themes, or supports the ideas presented.
Timing	The presentation • thoroughly delivers its intended message within the allotted time • is thoughtfully and appropriately paced throughout.	The presentation • mostly delivers its intended message within the allotted time • is appropriately paced most of the time.	The presentation • delivers some of its intended message within the allotted time • is sometimes not paced appropriately.	The presentation • does not deliver its intended message within the allotted time • is not paced appropriately.
Voice (Volume, Enunciation, Rate)	The presentation • is delivered with adequate volume enabling audience members to fully comprehend what is said • is delivered with clear enunciation.	The presentation • is delivered with adequate volume enabling audience members to mostly comprehend what is said • is delivered with mostly clear enunciation.	The presentation • is delivered with somewhat adequate volume enabling audience members to comprehend some of what is said • is delivered with somewhat clear enunciation.	The presentation • is not delivered with adequate volume, so that audience members are unable to comprehend what is said • is delivered with unclear enunciation.
Eye Contact / Gestures	The presentation • is delivered with appropriate eye contact that helps engage audience members • makes use of natural gestures and/or body language to convey meaning.	The presentation • is delivered with some appropriate eye contact that helps engage audience members • makes use of gestures and/or body language to convey meaning.	The presentation • is delivered with occasional eye contact that sometimes engages audience members • makes some use of gestures and/or body language to convey meaning.	The presentation • is not delivered with eye contact to engage audience members • makes little or no use of gestures and/or body language to convey meaning.
Use of Media, Visuals, Props	The presentation • makes use of highly engaging visuals, multimedia, and/or props that enhance delivery.	The presentation • makes use of visuals, multimedia, and/or props that enhance delivery.	The presentation • makes use of some visuals, multimedia, and/or props that somewhat enhance delivery.	The presentation • makes use of few or no visuals, multimedia, and/or props that enhance delivery.
Audience Engagement	The presentation • includes thoughtful and appropriate interactions with and responses to audience members.	The presentation • includes appropriate interactions with and responses to audience members.	The presentation • includes a few interactions with and responses to audience members.	The presentation • does not include interactions with and responses to audience members.

RAFT

Role	Who or what are you as a writer?
Audience	As a writer, to whom are you writing?
Format	As a writer, what format would be appropriate for your audience (essay, letter, speech, poem, etc.)?
Topic	As a writer, what is the subject of your writing? What points do you want to make?

Roots and Affixes Brainstorm

Directions: Write the root or affix in the circle. Brainstorm or use a dictionary to find the meaning of the root or affix and add it to the circle. Then, find words that use that root or affix. Write one word in each box. Write a sentence for each word.

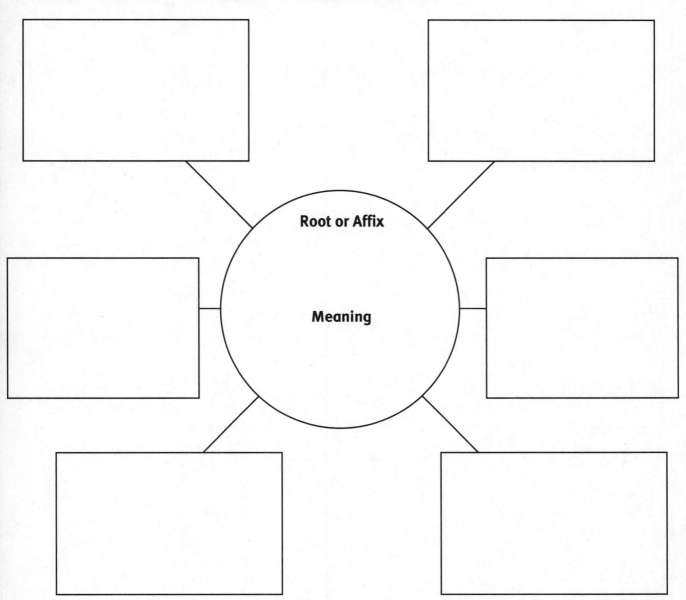

Root or Affix

Meaning

Round Table Discussion

Directions: Write the topic in the center box. One student begins by stating his or her ideas while the student to the left takes notes. Then the next student speaks while the student to his or her left takes notes, and so on.

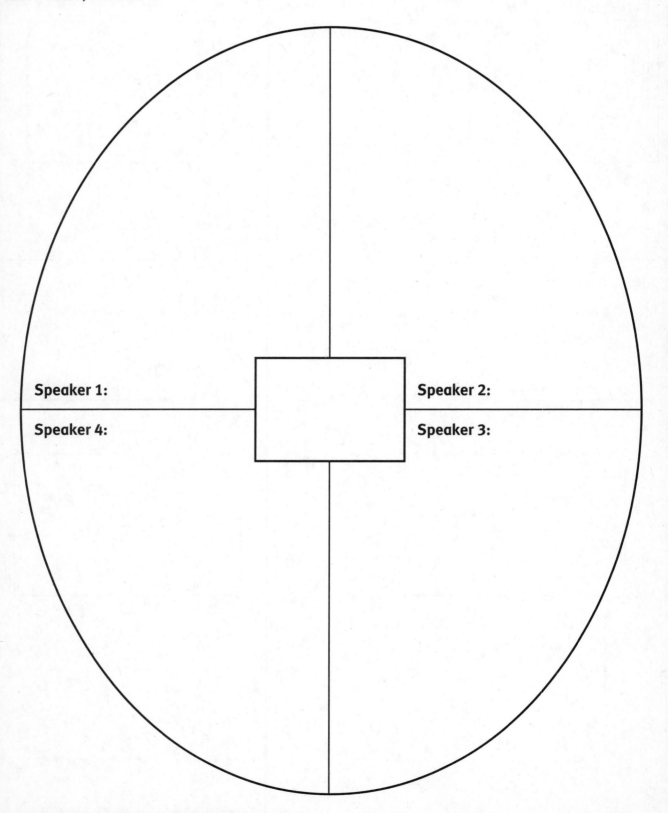

Speaker 1:

Speaker 2:

Speaker 4:

Speaker 3:

Sequence of Events Time Line

Title: _____

What happened first?

Next?

Beginning ○———————————————○ Middle ————————————————○ End →

Then?

Finally?

SMELL

Sender-Receiver Relationship—Who are the senders and receivers of the message, and what is their relationship (consider what different audiences the text may be addressing)?

Message—What is a literal summary of the content? What is the meaning/significance of this information?

Emotional Strategies—What emotional appeals (*pathos*) are included? What seems to be their desired effect?

Logical Strategies—What logical arguments/appeals (*logos*) are included? What is their effect?

Language—What specific language is used to support the message? How does it affect the text's effectiveness? Consider both images and actual words.

SOAPSTone

SOAPSTone	Analysis	Textual Support
Subject What does the reader know about the writer?		
Occasion What are the circumstances surrounding this text?		
Audience Who is the target audience?		
Purpose Why did the author write this text?		
Subject What is the topic?		
Tone What is the author's tone, or attitude?		

Text Structure Stairs

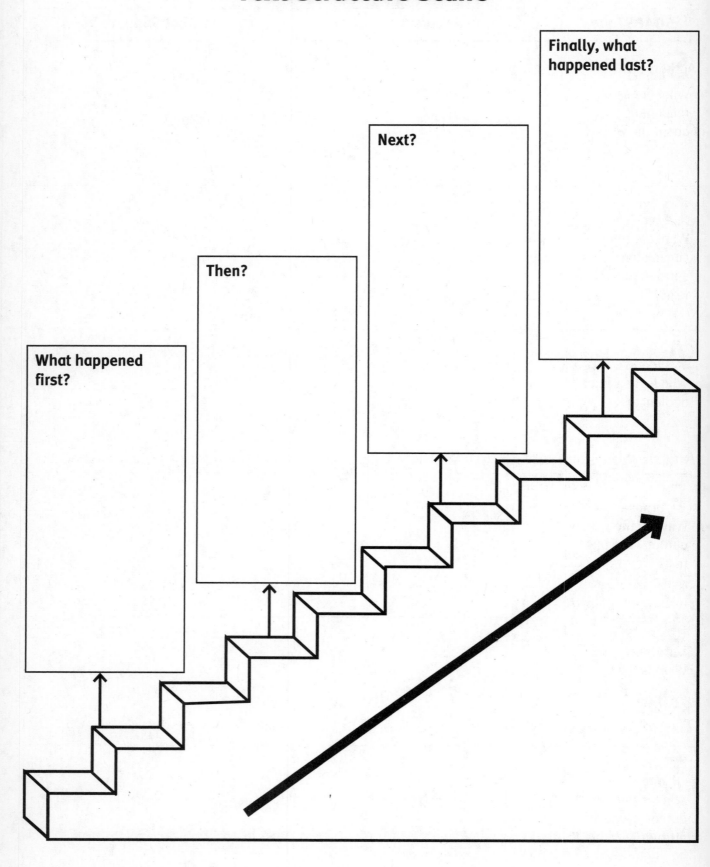

Finally, what happened last?

Next?

Then?

What happened first?

TP-CASTT Analysis

Poem Title:

Author:

Title: Make a Prediction. What do you think the title means before you read the poem?

Paraphrase: Translate the poem in your own words. What is the poem about? Rephrase difficult sections word for word.

Connotation: Look beyond the literal meaning of key words and images to their associations.

Attitude: What is the speaker's attitude? What is the author's attitude? How does the author feel about the speaker, about other characters, about the subject?

Shifts: Where do the shifts in tone, setting, voice, etc., occur? Look for time and place, keywords, punctuation, stanza divisions, changes in length or rhyme, and sentence structure. What is the purpose of each shift? How do they contribute to effect and meaning?

Title: Reexamine the title. What do you think it means now in the context of the poem?

Theme: Think of the literal and metaphorical layers of the poem. Then determine the overall theme. The theme must be written in a complete sentence.

TP-CASTT

Poem Title:

Author:

Title		
Paraphrase		
Connotation		
Attitude		
Shifts		
Title		
Theme		

Unknown Word Solver

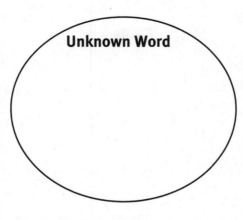

Unknown Word

Can you find any context clues? List them.

Do you recognize any word parts?

Prefix:

Root Word:

Suffix:

Do you know another meaning of this word that does not make sense in this context?

Does it look or sound like a word in another language?

What is the dictionary definition?

How can you define the word in your own words?

Venn Diagram for Writing a Comparison

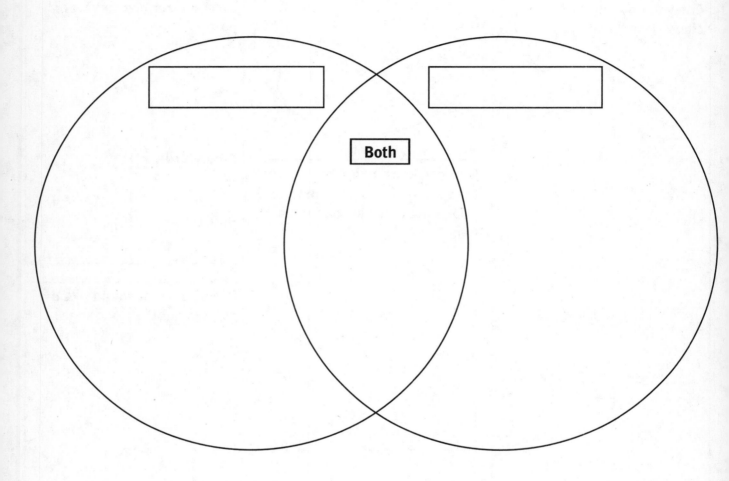

Both

They are similar in that _____

_____

_____

_____

_____

_____

They are different in that _____

_____

_____

_____

_____

_____

Verbal & Visual Word Association

Definition in Your Own Words	Important Elements

Academic Vocabulary Word

Visual Representation	Personal Association

Web Organizer

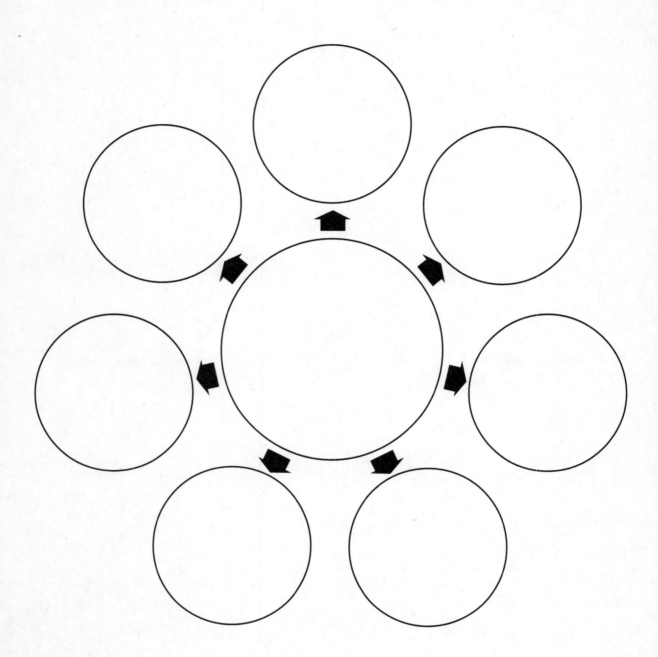

Word Choice Analyzer

Word or phrase from the text	Definition of word or phrase	How can I restate the definition in my own words?	What effect did the author produce by choosing these words?

Explain Your Analysis

The author uses the word or phrase _____ , which means

_____

Another way to say this is _____

_____

I think the author chose these words to _____

_____

_____

One way I can modify this sentence to add detail is to _____

_____

Word Map

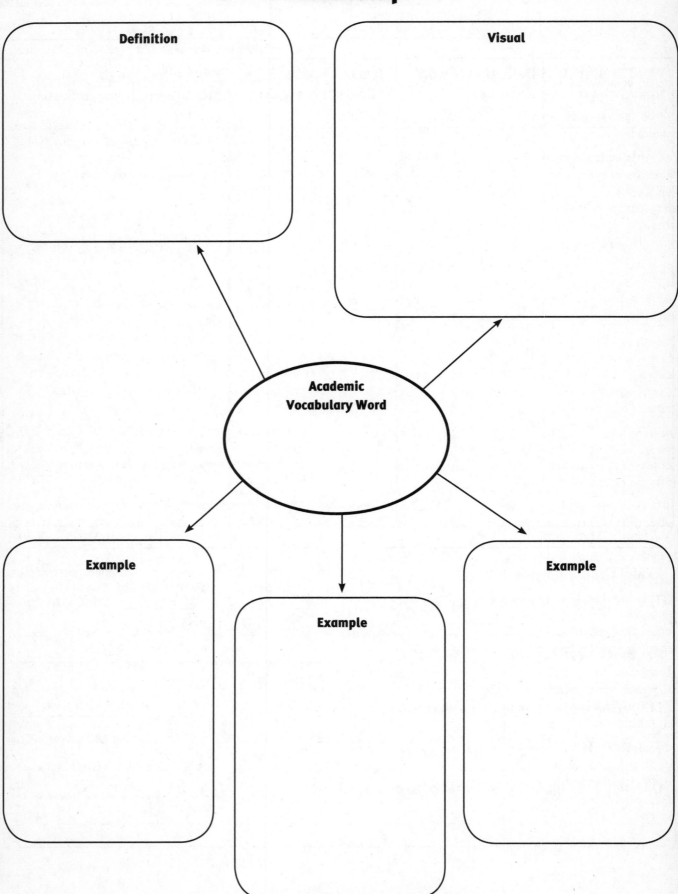

Definition

Visual

Academic Vocabulary Word

Example

Example

Example

Glossary/Glosario

A

active-voice verbs: verbs for which the subject performs the action
verbos en voz activa: forma verbal que indica que el sujeto realiza la acción

advertising techniques: specific methods used in print, graphics, or videos to persuade people to buy a product or use a service
técnicas publicitarias: métodos específicos usados en impresos, gráfica o videos para persuadir a las personas a comprar un producto o usar un servicio

agenda: a secret plan or motivation that causes someone to act in a certain way
agenda: motivación o plan secreto que lleva a alguien a actuar de determinado modo

allegory: a story in which the characters, objects, or actions have a meaning beyond the surface of the story
alegoría: cuento en el que los personajes, objetos o acciones tienen un significado que va más allá de la superficie de la historia

alliteration: the repetition of initial consonant sounds in words that are close together
aliteración: repetición de sonidos consonánticos iniciales en palabras cercanas

allusion: a reference made to a well-known person, event, or place from history, music, art, or another literary work
alusión: referencia a una persona, evento o lugar muy conocidos de la historia, música, arte u otra obra literaria

analogy: a comparison between two things for the purpose of drawing conclusions on one based on its similarities to the other
analogía: comparación entre dos cosas con el propósito de sacar conclusiones sobre las semejanzas que una cosa tiene a otra

anaphora: the repetition of the same word or group of words at the beginnings of two or more clauses or lines
anáfora: repetición de la misma palabra o grupo de palabras al comienzo de una o más cláusulas o versos

anecdotal evidence: evidence based on personal accounts of incidents
evidencia anecdótica: evidencia basada en relatos personales de los hechos

annotated bibliography: a list of sources used in research along with comments or summaries about each source
bibliografía anotada: lista de fuentes utilizadas en la investigación, junto con comentarios o resúmenes acerca de cada fuente

antagonist: the character who opposes or struggles against the main character
antagonista: personaje que se opone o lucha contra el personaje principal

aphorism: a short statement expressing an opinion or general truth
aforismo: afirmación corta que expresa una opinión o verdad general

appeals: the efforts to persuade an audience that a certain concept is true by directing statements toward reasoning or logic, character, or senses and emotions
llamados: serie de esfuerzos que alguien realiza con el fin de convencer a una audiencia de que determinado concepto es verdadero, persuadiéndola de ello mediante el uso del razonamiento o la lógica o bien apelando a su carácter, sentidos o emociones

Archetypal Criticism: criticism that deals with symbols and patterns that recur in the literature of widely diverse cultures
crítica de arquetipos: examinación de la literature basada en símbolos y diseño

archetypes: universal symbols—images, characters, motifs, or patterns—that recur in the myths, dreams, oral traditions, songs, literature, and other texts of peoples widely separated by time and place
arquetipos: símbolos universales—imágenes, personajes, motivos o patrones—reiterativos en los mitos, el arte y la literatura alrededor del mundo

archival footage: film footage taken from another, previously recorded, source
cortometraje de archivo: fragmento de película tomada de otra fuente grabada previamente

argument: a form of writing that presents a particular claim or idea and supports it with evidence
argumento: forma de redacción que presenta una opinión o idea particular y la apoya con evidencia

argumentation: the act or process of arguing that includes the *hook* (quotation, example, or idea that catches readers' attention), *claim* (the opinion or thesis statement), *support* (evidence in the form of facts, statistics, examples, anecdotes, or expert opinions), *concession* (the writer's admission that the other side of the argument has a valid point), *refutation* (a well-reasoned denial of an opponent's point, based on solid evidence), and *call to action* (a request of readers)

argumentación: la estructura de una argumentación incluye el *gancho* (cita, ejemplo o idea que capta la atención del lector), *afirmación* (declaración de opinión o tesis), *apoyo* (evidencia en forma de hechos, estadísticas, ejemplos, anécdotas u opiniones de expertos), *concesión* (admisión por parte del escritor de que la otra parte del debate tiene un punto válido), *refutación* (negación bien razonada de una opinión del oponente, basada en evidencia sólida) y *llamado a la acción* (petición inspirada de lectores)

argument by analogy: a comparison of two similar situations, implying that the outcome of one will resemble the outcome of the other

argumento por analogía: comparación de dos situaciones semejantes, infiriendo que el resultado de será parecido al resultado de la otra

artistic license: the practice of rewording of dialogue, alteration of language, or reordering of the plot of a text created by another artist

licencia artística: la costumbre de reformular un diálogo, aliteración de palabras, o arreglo de la trama de un texto creado por otro artista

aside: a short speech spoken by an actor directly to the audience and unheard by other actors on stage

aparte: alocución breve dicha por un actor directamente al público y que no escuchan los demás actores que están en el escenario

assonance: the repetition of similar vowel sounds in accented syllables, followed by different consonant sounds, in words that are close together

asonancia: repetición de sonidos vocálicos similares en sílabas acentuadas, seguida de diferentes sonidos consonánticos, en palabras que están cercanas

audience: the intended readers, listeners, or viewers of specific types of written, spoken, or visual texts

público: lectores objetivo, oyentes o espectadores de tipos específicos de textos escritos, hablados o visuales

audience analysis: determination of the characteristics and knowledge of the people who will read a work or hear a speech

análisis del público: determinar las características y conocimiento de las personas que leen una obra o escuchan un discurso

author's purpose: the specific reason or reasons for the writing; what the author hopes to accomplish

propósito del autor: razón específica para escribir; lo que el autor espera lograr

autobiography: an account written by a person about his or her own life

autobiografía: narración de una vida escrita por el propio sujeto del relato

B

balanced sentence: a sentence that presents ideas of equal weight in similar grammatical forms to emphasize the similarity or difference between the ideas

oración balanceada: oración que representa ideas de igual peso en formas gramaticales similares para enfatizar la semejanza o diferencia entre las ideas

bias: an inclination or mental leaning for or against something; prevents impartial judgment

sesgo: inclinación o tendencia mental a favor o en contra de algo, lo que impide una opinión imparcial

bibliography: a list of the sources used for research

bibliografía: lista de fuentes primarias en la preparación de un texto

biography: a description or account of events from a person's life, written by another person

biografía: descripción o narración de la vida de una persona o los sucesos importantes de su vida escritos por otra persona

blank verse: unrhymed verse

verso libre: verso que no tiene rima

block: to create the plan for how actors will position themselves on the stage in relation to one another, the audience, and the objects on the stage

ensayar: establecer un plan para determinar la posición que los actores deberán ocupar en un escenario en relación a sí mismos, a la audiencia, al escenario y a los objetos del mismo

blocking: in drama, the way actors position themselves in relation to one another, the audience, and the objects on the stage

bloqueo: en drama, el modo en que los actores se sitúan entre sí, con el público y los objetos en el escenario

book review: a formal assessment or examination of a book

reseña de libro: evaluación o examinación formal de un libro

C

cacophonous: harsh and unpleasant sounding
cacofónico: sonidos molestos y desagradables

call to action: a restatement of the claim and what the writer wants the reader to do
llamado a la acción: repetición de la afirmación y lo que el escritor quiere que el lector responda

caricature: a visual or verbal representation in which characteristics or traits are exaggerated or distorted for emphasis
caricatura: representación visual o verbal en la que las características o rasgos se exageran o se distorsionan para dar énfasis

catalog poem: a poem that uses repetition and variation in the creation of a list, or catalog, of objects or desires, plans, or memories
lista en poema: poema que usa repetición y variación en la creación de una lista o catálogo, de objetos o deseos o planes o memorias

cause: an action, event, or situation that brings about a particular result
causa: acción, suceso o situación que produce un resultado particular

caveat: a cautionary detail to be thought through carefully when analyzing something
exhortación: advertencia o consejo a tener muy en cuenta a la hora de interpretar o analizar algo

censor: to examine materials for objectionable content
censurar: examinar materiales por contenido desagradable

censorship: the act of suppressing public speech or publication of materials deemed to be offensive by the censor
censura: acto de suprimir un discurso público o publicación de materiales considerados ofensivos por un censor

challenge: to oppose or refute a statement that has been made
poner en duda: oponerse a algo o refutar una declaración que alguien ha hecho

characterization: the methods a writer uses to develop characters
caracterización: métodos que usa un escritor para desarrollar personajes

characters: people, animals, or imaginary creatures that take part in the action of a story. A short story usually centers on a *main character* but may also contain one or more *minor characters*, who are not as complex, but whose thoughts, words, or actions move the plot along. A character who is *dynamic* changes in response to the events of the narrative; a character who is *static* remains the same throughout the narrative. A *round* character is fully developed—he or she shows a variety of traits; a *flat* character is one-dimensional, usually showing only one trait.
personajes: personas, animales o criaturas imaginarias que participan en la acción de un cuento. Un cuento corto normalmente se centra en un *personaje principal*, pero puede también contener uno o más *personajes secundarios*, que no son tan complejos, pero cuyos pensamientos, palabras o acciones hacen avanzar la trama. Un personaje que es *dinámico* cambia según los eventos del relato; un personaje que es *estático* permanece igual a lo largo del relato. Un personaje *complejo* está completamente desarrollado: muestra una diversidad de rasgos; un personaje *simple* es unidimensional, mostrando normalmente sólo un rasgo.

character foil: a character whose actions or thoughts are juxtaposed against those of a major character in order to highlight key attributes of the major character
antagonista: personaje cuyas acciones o pensamientos se yuxtaponen a los de un personaje principal con el fin de destacar atributos clave del personaje principal

character sketch: a brief description of a literary character
reseña del personaje: breve descripción de un personaje literario

chorus: in traditional or classic drama, a group of performers who speak as one and comment on the action of the play
coro: en el drama tradicional o clásico, grupo de actores que hablan al unísono y comentan la acción de la obra teatral

cinematic elements: the features of cinema—movies, film, video—that contribute to its form and structure: *angle* (the view from which the image is shot), *framing* (how a scene is structured), *lighting* (the type of lighting used to light a scene), *mise en scène* (the composition, setting, or staging of an image, or a scene in a film), and *sound* (the sound effects and music accompanying each scene)
elementos cinematográficos: las características del cine—películas, filmaciones, video—que contribuyen a darle forma y estructura: *angulación* (vista desde la cual se toma la imagen), *encuadre* (cómo se estructura una escena), iluminación (tipo de *iluminación* que se usa para una escena), y *montaje* (composición, ambiente o escenificación de una imagen o escena en una película), y *sonido* (efectos sonoros y música que acompañan cada escena)

cinematic techniques: the methods a director uses to communicate meaning and to evoke particular emotional responses from viewers

técnicas cinematográficas: métodos que emplea un director para comunicar un significado y evocar cierta respuesta emocional de los videntes

claim: a thesis statement describing the position the writer is taking on an issue

afirmación: declaración de opinión (o tesis) que asevera una idea o establece un debate hacia una posición específica

cliché: an overused expression or idea

cliché: expresión o idea que se usa en exceso

climax: the point at which the action reaches its peak; the point of greatest interest or suspense in a story; the turning point at which the outcome of a conflict is decided

clímax: punto en el que la acción alcanza su punto culminante; punto de mayor interés en un cuento; punto de inflexión en el que se decide el resultado del conflicto

coherence: the quality of unity or logical connection among ideas; the clear and orderly presentation of ideas in a paragraph or essay

coherencia: calidad de unidad o relación lógica entre las ideas; presentación clara y ordenada de las ideas en un párrafo o ensayo

commentary: the expression of opinions or explanations about an event or situation

comentario: expresión oral o escrita de opiniones o explicaciones sobre una situación, tema o suceso

commentary: explanations about the significance or importance of supporting details or examples in an analysis

comentario: explicaciones acerca de la importancia de los detalles que tienen apoyo o ejemplos en un análisis

complementary: combined in a way that enhances all elements combined

complementario: combinar dos o más elementos de una manera que mejora los dos

complex character: a character that has multiple or conflicting motivations

personaje complejo: personaje que tiene motivaciones multiples o conflictivas

complex sentence: a sentence containing one independent clause and one or more subordinate clauses

oración compleja: oración que contiene una cláusula independiente y una o más cláusulas subordinadas

complications: the events in a plot that develop a conflict; the complications move the plot forward in its rising action

complicaciones: sucesos de una trama que desarrollan el conflicto; las complicaciones hacen avanzar la trama en su acción ascendente

components: the parts or elements of a whole

componentes: partes o elementos que conforman un todo

compound sentence: a sentence containing two independent clauses

oración compuesta: oración que contiene dos cláusulas independientes

concession: an admission in an argument that the opposing side has valid points

concesión: admitir en un debate que el lado opositor tiene opiniones válidas

concluding statement: a statement that follows from and supports the claim made in an argument

declaración concluyente: declaración que sigue de la afirmación, o la apoya, en un argumento

conflict: a struggle or problem in a story. An *internal conflict* occurs when a character struggles between opposing needs or desires or emotions within his or her own mind. An *external conflict* occurs when a character struggles against an outside force. This force may be another character, a societal expectation, or something in the physical world.

conflicto: lucha o problema en un cuento. Un *conflicto interno* ocurre cuando un personaje lucha entre necesidades o deseos o emociones que se contraponen dentro de su mente. Un *conflicto externo* ocurre cuando un personaje lucha contra una fuerza externa. Esta fuerza puede ser otro personaje, una expectativa social o algo del mundo físico.

connotation: the associations and emotional overtones attached to a word beyond its literal definition, or denotation; a connotation may be positive, negative, or neutral

connotación: asociaciones y alusiones emocionales unidas a una palabra más allá de su definición literal o denotación; una connotación puede ser positiva, negativa, o neutra

consonance: the repetition of final consonant sounds in stressed syllables with different vowel sounds

consonancia: repetición de sonidos consonánticos finales en sílabas acentuadas con diferentes sonidos vocálicos

context: the circumstances or conditions in which something exists or takes place

contexto: circunstancias o condiciones en las que algo ocurre

conventions: standard features, practices, and forms associated with the way something is usually done

convenciones: prácticas y formas usuales asociadas con las costumbres de hacer algo

counterarguments: the arguments that can be made to oppose a viewpoint
contraargumentos: argumentos que se presentan para rebatir un punto de vista

counterclaim: a position taken by someone with an opposing viewpoint
contrarreclamación: posición que toma una persona con un punto de vista contrario

couplet: two consecutive lines of verse with end rhyme; a couplet usually expresses a complete unit of thought
copla: dos líneas de versos consecutivos con rima final; una copla normalmente expresa una unidad de pensamiento completa

credibility: the quality of being trusted or believed
credibilidad: calidad de ser confiable o creíble

critical lens: a particular identifiable perspective as in Reader Response Criticism, Cultural Criticism, etc., through which a text can be analyzed and interpreted
ojo crítico: punto de vista particular identificable como por ejemplo Teoría de la recepción, Crítica sociocultural, etc., por medio del que se puede analizar e interpretar un texto

cultural conflict: a struggle that occurs when people with different cultural expectations or attitudes interact
conflicto cultural: lucha que ocurre cuando interactúan personas con diferentes expectativas o actitudes culturales

Cultural Criticism: criticism that focuses on the elements of culture and how they affect one's perceptions and understanding of texts
crítica cultural: analizar un texto basándose en elementos culturales y como ellos afectan la percepción y lacomprensión de textos

culture: the shared set of arts, ideals, skills, institutions, customs, attitude, values, and achievements that characterize a group of people, and that are passed on or taught to succeeding generations
cultura: conjunto de artes, ideas, destrezas, instituciones, costumbres, actitud, valores y logros compartidos que caracterizan a un grupo de personas, y que se transfieren o enseñan a las generaciones siguientes

cumulative (or loose) sentence: a sentence in which the main clause comes first, followed by subordinate structures or clauses
oración acumulativa (o frases sueltas): oración cuya cláusula principal viene primero, seguida de estructuras o cláusulas subordinadas

D

deductive reasoning: a process of drawing a specific conclusion from general information
razonamiento deductivo: proceso en que se usa información general para sacar una conclusión específica

defend: to support a statement that has been made
defender: dar apoyo a una declaración que alguien ha hecho

denotation: the precise meaning of a word
denotación: significado literal de una palabra

detail: a specific fact, observation, or incident; any of the small pieces or parts that make up something else
detalle: hecho, observación o incidente específico; cualquiera de las pequeñas piezas o partes que constituyen otra cosa

dialect: the distinctive language—including the sounds, spelling, grammar, and diction—of a specific group or class of people
dialecto: lenguaje distintivo, incluyendo sonidos, ortografía, gramática y dicción, de un grupo o clase específico de personas

dialogue: the words spoken by characters in a narrative or film
diálogo: palabras que dicen los personajes en un relato o película

dialogue tags: the phrases that attribute a quotation to the speaker, for example, *she said* or *he bellowed*
marcas del diálogo: frases que atribuyen la cita de un hablante, por ejemplo, *dijo ella* o *bramó él.*

diction: a writer's word choices, which often convey voice and tone
dicción: selección de palabras por parte del escritor; elemento estilístico que ayuda a transmitir voz y tono

diegetic sound: any sound that can logically be heard by characters on screen
sonido diegético: sonidos lógicos que los personajes pueden oír en una escena en la pantalla

direct characterization: specific information about a character provided by the narrator or author
caracterización directa: información específica sobre un personaje creada por un narrador o autor

discourse: the language or speech used in a particular context or subject
discurso: lenguaje o habla usada en un contexto o tema en particular

documentary or nonfiction film: a genre of filmmaking that provides a visual record of actual events using photographs, video footage, and interviews

documental o película de no-ficción: género cinematográfico que realiza un registro visual de sucesos basados en hechos por medio del uso de fotografías, registro en videos y entrevistas

dominant group: a more powerful group that may perceive another group as marginalized or subordinate

grupo dominante: un grupo más poderoso que puede percibir a otro grupo como maginado o subordinado

drama: a play written for stage, radio, film, or television, usually about a serious topic or situation

drama: obra teatral escrita para representar en un escenario, radio, cine o televisión, normalmente sobre un tema o situación seria

dramatic irony: a form of irony in which the reader or audience knows more about the circumstances or future events than the characters within the scene

ironía dramática: una forma de la ironía en que los lectores o el público sabe más sobre las circunstancias o sucesos futuros que los personajes en la escena

dramaturge: a member of an acting company who helps the director and actors make informed decisions about the performance by researching information relevant to the play and its context

dramaturgo: socio de una compañía teatral que ayuda al director y a los actores tomar decisiones informadas sobre la interpretación investigando información relevante a la obra teatral y su contexto

dynamic (or round) character: evolves and grows in the story and has a complex personality

personaje dinámico: personaje complejo que evoluciona a lo largo de la trama literaria

E

editorial: an article in a newspaper or magazine expressing the opinion of its editor or publisher

editorial: artículo de periódico o revista, que expresa la opinión de su editor

effect: the result or influence of using a specific literary or cinematic device; a result produced by a cause

efecto: resultado o influencia de usar un recurso literario o cinematográfico específico; resultado o producto de una causa

elaborate: to expand on or add information or detail about a point and thus to develop the point more fully

elaborar: extender o agregar información o detalles sobre un asunto, y asi desarrollar el asunto de manera más completa

empirical evidence: evidence based on experiences and direct observation through research

evidencia empírica: evidencia basada en experiencias y en la observación directa por medio de la investigación

emulate: to imitate an original work or person

emular: imitar una obra original

enfranchisement: having the rights of citizenship, such as the right to vote

emancipación: tener los derechos de la ciudananía, tales como el derecho al voto

epigram: a short, witty saying

epigrama: dicho corto e ingenioso

epigraph: a phrase, quotation, or poem that is set at the beginning of a document or component

epígrafe: frase, cita, o poema que aparece al comienzo de un documento o componente

epithet: a descriptive word or phrase used in place of or along with a name

epíteto: palabra o frase descriptiva usada en lugar de o junto con un nombre

ethos: (ethical appeal) a rhetorical appeal that focuses on the character or qualifications of the speaker

ethos: (recurso ético) recurso retórico centrado en la ética o en el carácter o capacidades del orador

euphonious: a harmonious or pleasing sound

eufónico: un sonido armonioso y agradable

evaluate: to make a judgment based on an analysis about the value or worth of the information, idea, or object

evaluar: dar una opinión basándose en un análisis sobre el valor o mérito de la información, idea, u objeto

evidence: the information that supports a position in an argument; forms of evidence include facts, statistics (numerical facts), expert opinions, examples, and anecdotes; *see also* anecdotal, empirical, and logical evidence

evidencia: información que apoya o prueba una idea o afirmación; formas de evidencia incluyen hechos, estadística (datos numéricos), opiniones de expertos, ejemplos y anécdotas; *ver también* evidencia anecdótica, empírica y lógica

exaggeration: a statement that represents something as larger, better, or worse than it really is

exageración: representar algo como más grande, mejor o peor que lo que realmente es

exemplification: the act of defining by example by showing specific, relevant examples that fit a writer's definition of a topic or concept

ejemplificación: definir por ejemplo mostrando ejemplos específicos y relevantes que se ajustan a la definición de un tema o concepto del escritor

explanatory writing: a form of writing whose purpose is to explain, describe, or give information about a topic in order to inform a reader

escrito explicativo: forma de la escritura cuyo propósito es explicar, describir o dar información sobre un tema para informar al lector

explicit theme: a theme that is clearly stated by the writer

tema explícito: tema que está claramente establecido por el escritor

exposition: events that give a reader background information needed to understand a story (characters are introduced, the setting is described, and the conflict begins to unfold)

exposición: sucesos que dan al lector los antecedentes necesarios para comprender un cuento. Durante la exposición, se presentan los personajes, se describe el ambiente y se comienza a revelar el conflicto.

extended metaphor: a comparison between two unlike things that continues throughout a series of sentences in a paragraph or lines in a poem

metáfora extendida: metáfora que se extiende por varios versos o a través de un poema completo

external coherence: unity or logical connection between paragraphs with effective transitions and transitional devices

coherencia externa: unidad o conexión lógica entre párrafos con transiciones efectivas y recursos transicionales

eye rhymes: words that appear to rhyme because of identical spelling patterns but do not actually rhyme, for example, *cough* and *through*

falsas rimas: palabras, en inglés, que poseen una terminación idéntica y, por tanto, nos llevan erróneamente a pensar que riman, tales como *cough* y *through*

F

fallacy: a false or misleading argument

falacia: argumento o poema falso o engañoso

falling action: the events in a play, story, or novel that follow the climax, or moment of greatest suspense, and lead to the resolution

acción descendente: sucesos de una obra teatral, cuento o novela posteriores al clímax, o momento de mayor suspenso, y que conllevan a la resolución

faux pas: an embarrassing act or remark in a social situation (borrowed from French)

metedura de pata: comportamiento o comentario embarazoso en el marco de una situación social

Feminist Criticism: criticism that focuses on relationships between genders and examines a text based on the patterns of thought, behavior, values, enfranchisement, and power in relations between and within the sexes

crítica feminista: se enfoca en la relación entre los sexos y examina un texto basándose en el diseño de pensamiento, comportamiento, valores, emancipación, y poder en las relaciones entre los sexos

figurative: symbolic or emblematic; not literal

figurativo: simbólico o emblemático, no literal

figurative language: the use of words to describe one thing in terms of another

lenguaje figurativo: lenguaje imaginativo o figuras retóricas que no pretenden ser tomados literalmente; el lenguaje figurativo usa figuras literarias

film techniques: the methods a director uses to communicate meaning and to evoke particular emotional responses in viewers

técnicas cinematográficas: metodos que usa un director en la comunicación del significado y evocar una respuesta emocional específica en los videntes

fixed form: a form of poetry in which the length and pattern are determined by established usage of tradition, such as a sonnet

forma fija: forma de poesía en la que la longitud y el patrón están determinados por el uso de la tradición, como un soneto

flashback: an interruption or transition to a time before the current events in a narrative

flashback: interrupción en la secuencia de los sucesos para relatar sucesos ocurridos en el pasado

flat (or static) character: a character who is uncomplicated and stays the same without changing or growing during the story

personaje estático: personaje no complicado que permanence del mismo caracter y que no cambia a lo largo de una historia

folktale: a story without a known author that has been preserved through oral retellings

cuento folclórico: cuento sin autor conocido que se ha conservado por medio de relatos orales

footage: literally, a length of film; the expression is still used to refer to digital video clips

metraje: literalmente, la longitud de una película; la expresión aún se usa para referirse a video clips digitales

foreshadowing: the use of hints or clues in a narrative to suggest future action

presagio: uso de claves o pistas en un relato para sugerir una acción futura

form: the particular structure or organization of a work

forma: estructura o organización particular de una obra

found poem: a poem consisting of words, phrases, and/or lines that come directly from another text

poema encontrado: poema compuesto de palabras, frases o pasajes sacados directamente de otros textos

free verse: poetry without a fixed pattern of meter and rhyme

verso libre: poesía que no sigue ningún patrón, ritmo o rima regular

G

genre: a kind or style of literature or art, each with its own specific characteristics. For example, poetry, short story, and novel are literary genres. Painting and sculpture are artistic genres.

género: tipo o estilo de literatura o arte, cada uno con sus propias características específicas. Por ejemplo, la poesía, el cuento corto y la novela son géneros literarios. La pintura y la escultura son géneros artísticos.

genre conventions: the essential features and format that characterize a particular genre, or style of literature or art

convenciones genéricas: características básicas y el formato que caracterizan un género específico

graphic novel: a book-length narrative, or story, in the form of a comic strip rather than words

novela gráfica: narrativa o cuento del largo de un libro, en forma de tira cómica más que palabras

graphics: images or text used to provide information on screen

gráfica: imágenes o texto que se usa para dar información en pantalla

H

hamartia: a tragic hero's fatal flaw; an ingrained character trait that causes a hero to make decisions leading to his or her death or downfall

hamartia: error fatal de un héroe trágico; característica propia de un personaje que causa que un héroe tome decisiones que finalmente llevan a su muerte o caída

hero: the main character or protagonist of a play, with whom audiences become emotionally invested

héroe: personaje principal o protagonista de una obra teatral, con el que el público se involucra emocionalmente

historical context: the circumstances or conditions in which something takes place

contexto historico: circuntancias o condiciones en las cuales algo sucede o pasa

Historical Criticism: criticism used to uncover meaning in a literary text by examining the text in the context of the time period in which it was created

historicismo: método crítico que se usa para revelar el significado de un texto literario mediante el examen de dicho texto en el contexto de la época en que fue escrito

hook: an opening in an argument or a piece of writing that grabs the reader's attention

gancho: cita, anécdota o ejemplo interesante al comienzo de un escrito, que capta la atención del lector

Horatian satire: satire that pokes fun at human foibles and folly with a witty, gentle, even indulgent tone

sátira de Horacio: sátira en que se burla de las debilidades y locuras con un tono suave, ingenioso, hasta indulgente

humor: the quality of being amusing

humor: calidad de ser divertido

hyperbole: exaggeration used to suggest strong emotion or create a comic effect

hipérbole: exageración que se usa para sugerir una emoción fuerte o crear un efecto cómico

I

iamb: a metrical foot that consists of an unstressed syllable followed by a stressed syllable

yambo: pie métrico que consta de una sílaba átona seguida de una sílaba acentuada

iambic pentameter: a rhythmic pattern of five feet (or units), each consisting of one unstressed syllable followed by a stressed syllable

pentámetro yámbico: patrón rítmico de cinco pies (o unidades) de una sílaba átona seguida de una sílaba acentuada

image: a word or phrase that appeals to one of more of the five senses and creates a picture

imagen: palabra o frase que apela a uno o más de los cinco sentido y crea un cuadro

imagery: the verbal expression of sensory experience; descriptive or figurative language used to create word pictures; imagery is created by details that appeal to one or more of the five senses

imaginería: lenguaje descriptivo o figurativo utilizado para crear imágenes verbales; la imaginería es creada por detalles que apelan a uno o más de los cinco sentidos

imperialism: a policy of extending the rule or influence of acountry over other countries or colonies; the political, military, or economic domination of one country by another

imperialismo: política de extender el dominio o la influencia de un país sobre otros países o colonias; dominio político; militar o económico de un país sobre otro(s)

implied theme: a theme that is understood through the writer's diction, language construction, and use of literary devices

tema implícito: tema que se entiende a través de la dicción del escritor, construcción lingüística y uso de recursos literarios

indirect characterization: a narrator's or author's development of a character through the character's interactions with others, thoughts about circumstances, or speaking his or her thoughts aloud

caracterización indirecta: el desarrollo de un personaje según un narrador o autor por las interacciones del personaje con otros, pensamientos sobre las circunstancias, o su habilidad de enunciar sus pensamientos en voz alta

inductive reasoning: a process of looking at individual facts to draw a general conclusion

razonamiento inductivo: proceso de observación de hechos individuales para sacar una conclusión general

inference: a conclusion about ideas or information not directly stated

inferencia: conclusión sobre las ideas o información no presentadas directamente

interior monologue: a literary device in which a character's internal emotions and thoughts are presented

monólogo interior: recurso literario en el que se presentan las emociones internas y pensamientos de un personaje

interpretation: the act of making meaning from something, such as a text

interpretación: acto de interpretar un significado de algo, tal como un texto

internal coherence: unity or logical connection within paragraphs

coherencia interna: unidad o conexión lógica entre párrafos

irony: a literary device that exploits readers' expectations; irony occurs when what happens turns out to be quite different from what was expected. *Dramatic irony* is a form of irony in which the reader or audience knows more about the circumstances or future events in a story than the characters within it; *verbal irony* occurs when a speaker or narrator says one thing while meaning the opposite; *situational irony* occurs when an event contradicts the expectations of the characters or the reader.

ironía: recurso literario que explota las expectativas de los lectores; la ironía ocurre cuando lo que se espera resulta ser bastante diferente de lo que realmente ocurre. La *ironía dramática* es una forma de ironía en la que el lector o la audiencia saben más acerca de las circunstancias o sucesos futuros de un cuento que los personajes del mismo; la *ironía verbal* ocurre cuando un orador o narrador dice una cosa queriendo decir lo contrario; la *ironía situacional* ocurre cuando un suceso contradice las expectativas de los personajes o del lector.

J

justice: the quality of being reasonable and fair in the administration of the law; the ideal of rightness or fairness

justicia: calidad de ser razonable e imparcial en la administración de la ley; ideal de rectitud o equidad

Juvenalian satire: satire that denounces, sometimes harshly, human vice and error in dignified and solemn tones

sátira de Juvenal: sátira de denuncia, a veces con aspereza, los vicios y errores humanos con tonos dignos y solemnes

juxtaposition: the arrangement of two or more things for the purpose of comparison

yuxtaposición: ordenamiento de dos o más cosas con el objeto de compararlas

L

lede: an alternative spelling of lead; the opening of a news article or a single sentence that describes the main point of the article

entradilla: comienzo de una información periodística que resume lo más importante de ella

lining out: the process of creating line breaks to add shape and meaning in free verse poetry

llamada y respuesta: proceso de crear rupturas de lineas para dar forma y significado en la poesía del verso libre

literal: explicitly stated in a text; exact

literal: algo expresado de modo explícito y exacto en un texto

literal language: the exact meanings, or denotations, of words

lenguaje literal: los signficados y denotaciones exactos de las palabras

Literary Criticism: the formal practice of interpreting, evaluating, and explaining the meaning and significance of literary works

crítica literaria: práctica formal de interpretar, evaluar y explicar el significado y el valor de obras literarias

literary theory: a systematic study of literature using various methods to analyze texts

teoría literaria: intento de establecer principios para interpretar y evaluar textos literarios

logical evidence: evidence based on facts and a clear rationale

evidencia lógica: evidencia basada en hechos y una clara fundamentación

logical fallacy: a statement that is false because it is based on an error in reasoning

argumento falaz: afirmación de carácter falso por el hecho de estar basada en un error de razonamiento

logos: (logical appeal) a rhetorical appeal to reason or logic

logos: (apelación lógica) apelación retórica que usa la evidencia factual y la lógica para apelar al sentido de la razón

M

main idea: a statement (often one sentence) that summarizes the key details of a text

idea principal: declaración (con frecuencia una oración) que resume los detalles claves de un texto

marginalize: to relegate or confine a person to a lower or outer limit

marginar: relegar o confinar a una persona a un límite bajo o ajeno

Marxist Criticism: criticism that asserts that economics provides the foundation for all social, political, and ideological reality

crítica marxista: ver un text a través de la perspectiva en que la economía proporciona la fundación de toda realidad social, política, e ideológica

media: collectively refers to the organizations that communicate information to the public

medios de comunicación: colectivamente refiere a las organizaciones que comunican información al público

media channel: a method an organization uses to communicate, such as radio, television, website, newspaper, or magazine

canales mediaticos: método que usa una organización en la comunicación como radio, televisión, sitios de web, periódico, o revista

metacognition: the ability to know and be aware of one's own thought processes; self-reflection

metacognición: capacidad de conocer y estar consciente de los propios procesos del pensamiento; introspección

metaphor: a comparison between two unlike things in which one thing is spoken of as if it were another, for example, the moon was a crisp white cracker

metáfora: comparación entre dos cosas diferentes en la que se habla de una cosa como si fuera otra, por ejemplo, la luna era una galletita blanca crujiente

meter: a pattern of stressed and unstressed syllables in poetry

métrica: patrón de sílabas acentuadas y átonas en poesía

mise en scène: the composition, or setting, of a stage

puesta en escena: la composición o el lugar de un escenario

monologue: a dramatic speech delivered by a single character in a play

monólogo: discurso dramático que hace un solo personaje en una obra teatral

montage: a composite picture that is created by bringing together a number of images and arranging them to create a connected whole

montaje: cuadro compuesto que se crea al reunir un número de imágenes y que al organizarlas se crea un todo relacionado

mood: the atmosphere or predominant emotion in a literary work, the effect of the words on the audience

carácter: atmósfera o sentimiento general en una obra literaria

motif: a recurrent image, symbol, theme, character type, subject, or narrative detail that becomes a unifying element in an artistic work or text

motivo: imagen, símbolo, tema, tipo de personaje, tema o detalle narrativo recurrente que se convierte en un elemento unificador en una obra artística

motive: a character's reason for behaving in a certain way
motivación: razón esgrimida por un personaje para obrar de determinado modo

musical (or sound) device: the use of sound to convey and reinforce the meaning or experience of poetry
aparatos musicales: uso del sonido para transmitir y reforzar el significado o experiencia de la poesía

myth: a traditional story that explains the actions of gods or heroes or the origins of the elements of nature
mito: cuento tradicional que explica las acciones de dioses o héroes, o los orígenes de los elementos de la naturaleza

N

narration: the act of telling a story
narración: acto de contar un cuento

narrative: a story about a series of events that includes character development, plot structure, and theme; can be a work of fiction or nonfiction
narrativa: narración sobre una serie de sucesos que incluye el desarrollo de personajes, estructora del argumento, y el tema; puede ser una obra de ficción o no ficción

narrative arc: the story line of a text, including a beginning (*exposition*), a middle (the *rising action*), a high point (*climax*), and an end (the *falling action* and *resolution*)
arco narrativo: línea argumental de un texto, que consta de un comienzo (*exposición*), una parte media (*acción creciente*), un punto culminante (*clímax*) y un final (*acción decreciente y resolución*)

narrative pacing: the speed at which a narrative moves
compás de la narrativa: la rapidez en que una narrativa pasa

narrator: the person telling the story
narrador: persona que cuenta una historia

non-diegetic sound: sound that cannot logically be heard by the characters on screen; examples include mood music and voice-overs
sonido no diegético: voces y comentarios superpuestos; sonidos que no provienen de la acción en pantalla.

nut graf: an abbreviation of the expression *nutshell paragraph*; a statement that tells readers of a news article why they should care about what happened
epítome: texto introductorio que hace entender a los lectores por qué debería importarles la noticia que se relata a continuación

O

objective: based on factual information
objetivo: basado en información de hechos

objective tone: a tone that is more clinical and that is not influenced by emotion
tono objetivo: tono que es mas aséptico y que no se deja influir por la emoción

objectivity: the representation of facts or ideas without injecting personal feelings or biases
objetividad: representación de los hechos o ideas sin agregar sentimientos o prejuicios personales

ode: a lyric poem expressing feelings or thoughts of a speaker, often celebrating a person, event, or thing
oda: poema lírico que expresa sentimientos o pensamientos de un orador, que frecuentemente celebra a una persona, suceso o cosa

omniscient narrator: a narrator who knows all and tells a story from the perspective of multiple characters
narrador omnisciente: narrador que conoce todo lo sucedido sobre un determinado acontecimiento y relata la historia desde la perspectiva de varios personajes

onomatopoeia: the occurrence of a word whose sound suggests its meaning
onomatopeya: palabras cuyo sonido sugiere su significado

oral interpretation: a planned oral reading that expresses the meaning of a written text
interpretación oral: lectura oral planeada que interpreta el signficado de un text escrito

oral tradition: the passing down of stories, tales, proverbs, and other culturally important ideas through oral retellings
tradición oral: traspaso de historias, cuentos, proverbios y otras historias de importancia cultural por medio de relatos orales

oxymoron: words that appear to contradict each other; for example, cold fire
oxímoron: palabras que parecen contradecirse mutuamente; por ejemplo, fuego frío

P

paradox: a statement that contains two seemingly incompatible points
paradoja: declaración que contiene dos asuntos aparentemente incompatibles

parallel structure (parallelism): refers to a grammatical or structural similarity between sentences or parts of a sentence, so that elements of equal importance are equally developed and similarly phrased for emphasis

estructura paralela (paralelismo): se refiere a una similitud gramatical o estructural entre oraciones o partes de una oración, de modo que los elementos de igual importancia se desarrollen por igual y se expresen de manera similar para dar énfasis

paraphrase: to briefly restate ideas from another source in one's own words

parafrasear: volver a presentar las ideas de otra fuente en nuestras propias palabras

parenthetical citations: used for citing sources directly in an essay

citas parentéticas: usadas en citas de fuentes primarias en un ensayo

parody: a literary or artistic work that imitates the characteristic style of an author or a work for comic effect or ridicule

parodia: obra literaria o artística que imita el estilo característico de un autor o una obra para dar un efecto cómico o ridículo

passive-voice verbs: verb form in which the subject receives the action; the passive voice consists of a form of the verb *be* plus a past participle of the verb

verbos en voz pasiva: forma verbal en la que el sujeto recibe la acción; la voz pasiva se forma con el verbo *ser* más el participio pasado de un verbo

pathos: (emotional appeal) a rhetorical appeal to the reader's or listener's senses or emotions

pathos: (apelación emocional) apelación retórica a los sentidos o emociones de los lectores u oyentes

patriarchal: having the male as head of the household and with authority over women and children

patriarcal: sociedad en que el varón es jefe del hogar en el cual mantiene autoridad sobre las mujeres y niños

perception: one person's interpretation of sensory or conceptual information

percepción: interpretación de una persona en cuanto a información sensorial o conceptual

periodic sentence: a sentence that makes sense only when the end of the sentence is reached, that is, when the main clause comes last

oración periódica: oración que tiene sentido sólo cuando se llega al final de la oración, es decir, cuando la cláusula principal viene al final

persona: the voice assumed by a writer to express ideas or beliefs that may not be his or her own

personaje: voz que asume un escritor para expresar ideas o creencias que pueden no ser las propias

personification: a figure of speech that gives human qualities to an animal, object, or idea

personificación: figura literaria que da características humanas a un animal, objeto o idea

perspective: a way of looking at the world or a mental concept about things or events, one that judges relationships within or among things or events

perspectiva: manera de visualizar el mundo o concepto mental de las cosas o sucesos, que juzga las relaciones dentro o entre cosas o sucesos

persuasive argument: an argument that convinces readers to accept or believe a writer's perspective on a topic

argumento persuasivo: argumento que convence a los lectores a aceptar o creer en la perspectiva de un escritor acerca de un tema

photo essay: a collection of photographic images that reveal the author's perspective on a subject

ensayo fotográfico: recolección de imágenes fotográficas que revelan la perspectiva del autor acerca de un tema

plagiarism: the unattributed use of another writer's words or ideas

plagio: usar como propias las palabras o ideas de otro escritor

plot: the sequence of related events that make up a story

trama: secuencia de sucesos relacionados que conforman un cuento o novela

poetic structure: the organization of words, lines, and images as well as ideas

estructura poética: organización de las palabras, versos e imágenes, así como también de las ideas

poetry: language written in lines and stanzas

poesía: género literario que se concreta en un poema y está sujeto a medida o cadencia

point of view: the perspective from which a narrative is told, that is, first person, third-person limited, or third-person omniscient

punto de vista: perspectiva desde la cual se cuenta un relato, es decir, primera persona, tercera persona limitada o tercera persona omnisciente

precept: a rule, instruction, or principle that guides a person's actions and/or moral behavior

precepto: regla, instrucción o principio que guía las acciones de una persona y/o conducta moral de alguien

primary footage: film footage shot by the filmmaker for the text at hand
metraje principal: filmación hecha por el cineasta para el texto que tiene a mano

primary source: an original document or image created by someone who experiences an event first hand
fuente primaria: documento original que contiene información de primera mano acerca de un tema

prologue: the introduction or preface to a literary work
prólogo: introducción o prefacio de una obra literaria

prose: ordinary written or spoken language, using sentences and paragraphs, without deliberate or regular meter or rhyme; not poetry or song
prosa: forma común del lenguaje escrito o hablado, usando oraciones y párrafos, sin métrica o rima deliberada o regular; ni poesía ni canción

prosody: the pattern and rhythm of sounds in poetry, including stress and intonation
prosodia: rasgos fónicos de la métrica de la poesía, incluidos el énfasis y la entonación

protagonist: the central character in a work of literature, the one who is involved in the main conflict in the plot
protagonista: personaje central de una obra literaria, el que participa en el conflicto principal de la trama

proverb: a short saying about a general truth
proverbio: dicho corto sobre una verdad general

Q

qualify: to consider to what extent a statement is true or untrue (to what extent you agree or disagree)
calificar: consider hasta qué punto una declaración es verdadera o falsa

quatrain: a four-line stanza in a poem
cuarteta: en un poema, estrofa de cuatro versos

R

rationale: an explanation for a belief, statement, or behavior
fundamento: cimientos o bases en los que se apoya una creencia, afirmación o comportamiento

Reader Response Criticism: criticism that focuses on a reader's active engagement with a piece of print or nonprint text; shaped by the reader's own experiences, social ethics, moral values, and general views of the world

crítica de reacción del lector: análisis de un texto basado en las experiencias, ética social, valores, y percepciones generales del mundo

reasoning: the thinking or logic used to make a claim in an argument
razonamiento: pensamiento o lógica que se usa para hacer una afirmación en un argumento

rebuttal: a reason why a counterargument is wrong
refutación: razón por la cual un contraargumento es erróneo

refrain: a regularly repeated line or group of lines in a poem or song, usually at the end of a stanza
estribillo: verso o grupo de versos que se repiten con regularidad en un poema o canción, normalmente al final de una estrofa

refutation: the reasoning used to disprove an opposing point
refutación: razonamiento que se usa para rechazar una opinión contraria

reliability: the extent to which a source provides quality and trustworthy information
confiabilidad: grado en el que una fuente da información confiable y de buena calidad

renaissance: a rebirth or revival
renacimiento: un volver a nacer o una reanimación

repetition: the use of any element of language—a sound, a word, a phrase, a line, or a stanza—more than once
repetición: uso de cualquier elemento del lenguaje—un sonido, una palabra, una frase, un verso o una estrofa—más de una vez

resolution (denouement): the end of a text, in which the main conflict is finally resolved
resolución (desenlace): final de una obra teatral, cuento o novela, en el que el conflicto principal finalmente se resuelve

résumé: a document that outlines a person's skills, education, and work history
currículum vitae: documento que resume las destrezas, educación y experiencia laboral de una persona

retrospective: looking back to analyze the events in one's past
retrospectiva: mirar atrás en el tiempo para analizar los acontecimientos del pasado de una persona

revise: to rework or reorganize a piece of writing to improve its logic and flow after completing a first draft
revisar: rehacer o reorganizar un escrito para mejorar su lógica y fluidez tras haber terminado un primer borrador

rhetoric: the art of using words to persuade in writing or speaking

retórica: arte de usar las palabras para persuadir por escrito o de manera hablada

rhetorical appeals: emotional, ethical, and logical arguments used to persuade an audience to agree with the writer or speaker

recursos retóricos: uso de argumentos emocionales, éticos y lógicos para persuadir por escrito o de manera hablada

rhetorical context: the subject, purpose, audience, occasion, or situation in which writing or speaking occurs

contexto retórico: sujeto, propósito, audiencia, ocasión o situación en que ocurre el escrito

rhetorical devices: specific techniques used in writing or speaking to create a literary effect or enhance effectiveness

dispositivos retóricos: técnicas específicas que se usan al escribir o al hablar para crear un efecto literario o mejorar la efectividad

rhetorical question: a question that is asked for effect or one for which the answer is obvious

pregunta retórica: pregunta hecha para producir un efecto o cuya respuesta es obvia

rhetorical slanters: rhetorical devices used to present a subject in a biased way

sesgos retóricos: recursos retóricos que se usan para presentar un determinado asunto de un modo tendencioso

rhyme: the repetition of sounds at the ends of words
rima: repetición de sonidos al final de las palabras

rhyme scheme: a consistent pattern of rhyme throughout a poem
esquema de la rima: patrón consistente de una rima a lo largo de un poema

rhythm: the pattern of stressed and unstressed syllables in spoken or written language, especially in poetry
ritmo: patrón de sílabas acentuadas y no acentuadas en lenguaje hablado o escrito, especialmente en poesía

rising action: the movement of a plot toward a climax or moment of greatest excitement; the rising action is fueled by the characters' responses to the conflict

acción ascendente: movimiento de una trama hacia el clímax o momento de mayor emoción; la acción ascendente es impulsada por las reacciones de los personajes ante el conflicto

dynamic (or round) character: a character who evolves and grows in the story and has a complex personality

personaje dinámico: personaje que evoluciona y crece en la historia y que tiene una personalidad compleja

S

sarcasm: deliberate, often ironic ridicule
sarcasmo: burla deliberada, de carácter generalmente irónico

satire: a manner of writing that mocks social conventions, actions, or attitudes with wit and humor
sátira: manera de escribir en que se burla de convenciones sociales, acciones, o actitudes con ingenio y humor

scenario: an outline, a brief account, a script, or a synopsis of a proposed series of events
escenario: bosquejo, relato breve, libreto o sinopsis de una serie de sucesos propuestos

secondary audience: a group that may receive a message intended for a target audience
audiencia secundaria: grupo que puede recibir un mensaje orientado a una audiencia específica

secondary source: a discussion about or commentary on a primary source; the key feature of a secondary source is that it offers an interpretation of information gathered from primary sources
fuente secundaria: discusión o comentario acerca de una fuente primaria; la característica clave de una fuente secundaria es que ofrece una interpretación de la información recopilada en las fuentes primarias

sensory details: details that appeal to or evoke one or more of the five senses—sight, sound, smell, taste, and touch
detalles sensoriales: detalles que apelan o evocan uno o más de los cinco sentidos—vista, oído, gusto, olfato, y tacto

sensory images: images that appeal to the reader's senses—sight, sound, smell, taste, and touch
imágenes sensoriales: imágenes que apelan a los sentidos del lector—vista, oído, olfato, gusto, y tacto

sequence of events: the order in which things happen in a story
secuencia de eventos: orden en que los sucesos de una historia pasan:

setting: the time and place in which a story happens
ambiente: tiempo y lugar en el que ocurre un relato

simile: a comparison of two different things or ideas using the words *like* or *as*, for example, the moon was as white as milk
símil: comparación entre dos o más cosas o ideas diferentes usando las palabras *como* o *tan*, por ejemplo, la luna estaba tan blanca como la leche

situational irony: a form of irony that occurs when an event contradicts the expectations of the characters or the reader
ironía situacional: ocurre cuando un evento contradice las espectativas de los personajes o el lector

slanters: rhetorical devices used to present the subject in a biased way
soslayo: recursos retóricos para presentar el tema de modo sesgado

slogan: a short, catchy phrase used for advertising by a business, club, or political party
eslogan: frase corta y tendenciosa que usa como publicidad para un negocio, club o partido político

social commentary: an expression of an opinion with the goal of promoting change by appealing to a sense of justice
comentario social: expresión de una opinión con el objeto de promover el cambio al apelar a un sentido de justicia

soliloquy: a long speech delivered by an actor alone on the stage; represents the character's internal thoughts
soliloquio: discurso largo realizado por un actor sobre el escenario que representa sus pensamientos internos

sonnet: a 14-line lyric poem, usually written in iambic pentameter and following a strict pattern of rhyme
soneto: poema lírico de catorce versos, normalmente escrito en un pentámetro yámbico y que sigue un patrón de rima estricto

sound bite: a short excerpt from the recording of a speech or piece of music which captures the essence of the longer recording
cuña: corto fragmento de una grabación o de una pieza musical que capta la esencia de la grabación completa

speaker: the imaginary voice or persona of the writer or author
orador: voz o persona imaginaria del escritor o autor

stage directions: instructions written into the script of a play that indicate stage actions, movements of performers, or production requirements
direcciones escénicas: instrucciones escritas en un guión o drama que indican acción, movimiento de actors, or requisitos de la producción

stakeholder: a person motivated or affected by a course of action
participante: persona motivada o afectada por el curso de una acción

stanza: a group of lines, usually similar in length and pattern, that form a unit within a poem

estrofa: grupo de versos, normalmente similares en longitud y patrón, que forman una unidad dentro de un poema

static (or flat) character: a character who is uncomplicated and remains the same without changing or growing throughout a narrative
personaje estático: personaje que no cambia a lo largo de una narrativa

stereotype: an oversimplified, generalized conception, opinion, and/or image about particular groups of people
estereotipo: concepto generalizado, opinión y/o imagen demasiado simplificada acerca de grupos específicos de personas

stichomythia: in drama, the delivery of dialogue in a rapid, fast-paced manner, with actors speaking emotionally and leaving very little time between speakers
esticomitia: en el drama, es la rendición del diálogo de una manera rápida con actores que hablan con emoción, dejando espacio muy breve entre los hablantes

storyboard: a tool to show images and sequencing for the purpose of visualizing a film or a story
guión gráfico: método de mostrar imágenes y secuencias con el propósito de visualizar una película o historia

strategize: to plan the actions one will take to complete a task
estrategizar: planear las acciones de uno para complir una tarea

structure: the way a literary work is organized; the arrangement of the parts in a literary work
estructura: manera en que la obra literaria está organizada; disposición de las partes en una obra literaria

style: the distinctive way a writer uses language, characterized by elements of diction, syntax, imagery, organization, and so on
estilo: manera distintiva en que un escritor usa el lenguaje, caracterizada por elementos de dicción, sintaxis, lenguaje figurado, etc.

subculture: a smaller subsection of a culture, for example, within the culture of a high school may be many subcultures
subcultura: subsección más pequeña de una cultura, por ejemplo, dentro de la cultura de una escuela secundaria puede haber muchas subculturas

subjective: based on a person's point of view, opinions, values, or emotions
subjetivo: basado en el punto de vista, las opiniones, los valores o las emociones de alguien

subjective tone: a tone that is obviously influenced by the author's feelings or emotions

tono subjetivo: tono obviamente influído por los sentimientos o emociones del autor

subjectivity: judgment based on one's personal point of view, opinion, or values

subjetividad: en base en nuestro punto de vista, opinión o valores personales

subordinate: a person or group that is perceived as having a lower social or economic status

subordinado: persona o grupo percibido de ser de rango social o estado económico bajo

subplot: a secondary or side story that develops from and supports the main plot and usually involves minor characters

argumento secundario: una historia secundaria o periférica que apoya el argumento principal y que suele involucrar a personajes secundarios o menores

subtext: the underlying or implicit meaning in dialogue or the implied relationship between characters in a book, movie, play, or film; the subtext of a work is not explicitly stated

subtexto: significado subyacente o implícito en el diálogo o la relación implícita entre los personajes de un libro, película, u obra teatral. El subtexto de una obra no se establece de manera explícita.

survey: a method of collecting data from a group of people; it can be written, such as a print or online questionnaire, or oral, such as an in-person interview

encuesta: método para recolectar datos de un grupo de personas; puede ser escrita, como un impreso o cuestionario en línea, u oral, como en una entrevista personal

symbol: anything (object, animal, event, person, or place) that represents itself but also stands for something else on a figurative level

símbolo: cualquier cosa (objeto, animal, evento, persona o lugar) que se representa a sí misma, pero también representa otra cosa a nivel figurativo

symbolic: serving as a symbol; involving the use of symbols or symbolism

simbólico: que sirve como símbolo; que implica el uso de símbolos o simbolismo

synecdoche: a figure of speech in which a part is used to represent the whole or vice versa

sinécdoque: figura retórica en que una parte se usa para representar el todo, o vice-versa

syntax: the arrangement of words and the order of grammatical elements in a sentence; the way in which words are put together to make meaningful elements, such as phrases, clauses, and sentences

sintaxis: disposición de las palabras y orden de los elementos gramaticales en una oración; manera en que las palabras se juntan para formar elementos significativos como frases, cláusulas y oraciones

synthesis: the act of combining ideas from different sources to create, express, or support a new idea

síntesis: acto de combinar ideas de diferentes fuentes para crear, expresar o apoyar una nueva idea

synthesize: to combine ideas from different sources to create, express, or support a new idea or claim

sintetizar: combinar ideas procedentes de distintas fuentes para crear, expresar o sustentar una nueva idea o afirmación

T

target audience: the intended group for which a work is designed to appeal or reach

público objetivo: grupo al que se pretende apelar o llegar con una obra

tenor: the intent, tone, or attitude conveyed by the words in a text

tenor: intención, tono o actitud transmitida por las palabras de un texto

textual evidence: the details, quotations, and examples from a text that support the analysis or argument presented

evidencia textual: detalles, citas, y ejemplos de un texto que apoyan el análisis o la argumentación presentada

theatrical elements: elements used by dramatists and directors to tell a story on stage. Elements include *costumes* (the clothing worn by actors to express their characters), *makeup* (cosmetics used to change actors' appearances and express their characters), *props* (objects used to help set the scene, advance a plot, and make a story realistic), *set* (the place where the action takes place, as suggested by objects, such as furniture, placed on a stage), and *acting choices* (gestures, movements, staging, and vocal techniques actors use to convey their characters and tell a story).

elementos teatrales: elementos utilizados por los dramaturgos y directores para contar una historia en el escenario. Los elementos incluyen *vestuario* (ropa que usan los actores para expresar sus personajes), *maquillaje* (cosméticos que se usan para cambiar la apariencia de los actores y expresar sus personajes), *elementos* (objetos que se usan para ayudar a montar la escena, avanzar la trama y crear una historia realista), *plató* (lugar donde tiene lugar la acción, según lo sugieren los objetos, como muebles, colocados sobre un escenario), y *opciones de actuación* (gestos, movimientos, representación y técnicas vocales que se usan para transmitir sus personajes y narrar una historia).

thematic statement: an interpretive statement articulating the central meaning or message of a text
oración temática: afirmación interpretativa que articula el significado o mensaje central de un texto

theme: a writer's central idea or main message; *see also* explicit theme, implied theme
tema: idea central o mensaje principal acerca de la vida de un escritor; *véase también* tema explícito, tema implícito

thesis: the main idea or point of an essay or article; in an argumentative essay the thesis is the writer's position on an issue
tesis: idea o punto principal de un ensayo o artículo; en un ensayo argumentativo, la tesis es la opinión del autor acerca de un tema

thumbnail sketch: a small drawing made to plan the composition of a more detailed or finished image that will be created later
boceto en miniatura: pequeño dibujo realizado para planificar la composición de una imagen más amplia o detallada que será posteriormente creada

tone: a writer's (or speaker's) attitude toward a subject, character, or audience
tono: actitud de un escritor u orador acerca de un tema

topic sentence: a sentence that states the main idea of a paragraph; in an essay, the topic sentence also makes a point that supports the thesis statement
oración principal: oración que establece la idea principal de un párrafo; en un ensayo, la oración principal también establece una proposición que apoya el enunciado de la tesis

tragedy: a dramatic play that tells the story of a character, usually of a noble class, who meets an untimely and unhappy death or downfall, often because of a specific character flaw or twist of fate

tragedia: obra teatral dramática que cuenta la historia de un personaje, normalmente de origen noble, que encuentra una muerte o caída imprevista o infeliz, con frecuencia debido a un defecto específico del personaje o una vuelta del destino

tragic hero: an archetypal hero based on the Greek concept of tragedy; the tragic hero has a flaw that makes him or her vulnerable to downfall or death
héroe trágico: héroe arquetípico basado en el concepto griego de la tragedia; el héroe trágico tiene un defecto que lo hace vulnerable a la caída o a la muerte

transcript: a written copy or record of a conversation that takes place between two or more people
transcripción: copia escrita de una conversación que sucede entre dos o más personas

U

unconventional: eccentric; unusual; original
no convencional: excéntrico; inusual; original

understatement: the representation of something as smaller or less significant than it really is; the opposite of exaggeration or hyperbole
subestimación: representación de algo como más pequeño o menos importante de lo que realmente es; lo opuesto a la exageración o hipérbole

V

valid: believable or truthful
válido: creíble o verídico

validity: the quality of truth or accuracy in a source
validez: calidad de verdad o precisión en una fuente

verbal irony: a form of irony that occurs when a speaker or narrator says one thing while meaning the opposite
ironía verbal: ocurre cuando un hablante o narrador dice una cosa mientras quiere decir lo opuesto

verbatim: in the exact words of a source
textualmente: palabras citadas exactamente como fueron expresadas

verify: to prove or confirm that something is true
verificar: probar o confirmar que algo es verdadero

vignette: a picture or visual or a brief descriptive literary piece
viñeta: ilustración o representación visual o pieza literaria descriptiva breve

visual delivery: the way a performer on stage interprets plot, character, and conflict through movement, gestures, and facial expressions

presentación visual: manera en que un actor en un escenario interpreta trama, carácter, y conflicto a través de movimiento, gestos, y expresiones de la cara

visual rhetoric: an argument or points made by visuals such as photographs or by other visual features of a text

retórica visual: argumentos o asuntos representados en visuales como fotos u otros rasgos visuales de un texto

visualize: to form a mental picture of something

visualizar: formarse una imagen mental de algo

vocal delivery: the way a performer on stage expresses the meaning of a text through volume, pitch, rate or speed of speech, pauses, pronunciation, and articulation

presentación vocal: manera en que se expresan las palabras en el escenario, por medio del volumen, tono, rapidez o velocidad del discurso, pausas, pronunciación y articulación

voice: a writer's (or speaker's) distinctive use of language to express ideas as well as his or her persona

voz: manera en que el escritor u orador usa las palabras y el tono para expresar ideas, así como también su personaje o personalidad

Index of Skills

Literary Skills

Acronym, 387

Allusion, 93, 340, 502

Anaphora, 393

Attitude, 273, 277, 300

Audience, 1, 14, 76, 86, 111, 155, 169, 173, 196, 222, 259, 300, 336, 341, 351, 364, 379, 387, 388, 395, 447, 585, 589

Author's background, 7, 14, 21, 33, 40, 46, 65, 86, 100, 111, 120, 134, 155, 160, 184, 193, 201, 222, 271, 275, 280, 285, 289, 298, 316, 325, 337, 351, 364, 381, 396, 402, 410, 460, 465, 473, 479, 492, 557, 580

Author's craft, 20, 21, 28, 33, 37, 38, 39, 40, 45, 46, 51, 58, 65, 70, 74, 75, 76, 82, 83, 84, 85, 86, 92, 95, 110, 111, 120, 128, 134, 155, 160, 165, 169, 170, 171, 173, 178, 180, 184, 191, 193, 196, 201, 208, 229, 269, 271, 279, 293, 337, 341, 342, 343, 351, 355, 356, 370, 371, 372, 373, 377, 391, 409, 418, 484, 489, 496, 499, 530, 536, 538, 541, 580, 598

Author's purpose, 7, 14, 21, 29, 33, 39, 40, 46, 51, 65, 76, 86, 95, 100, 111, 155, 169, 173, 185, 193, 198, 201, 208, 271, 298, 324, 336, 340, 341, 351, 364, 369, 370, 371, 379, 387, 530, 538, 579, 580, 585, 586, 598, 599

Characterization, 5, 21, 27, 33, 46, 57, 58, 71, 107, 151, 166, 168, 260, 265, 484, 489, 549, 554

  direct, 531, 532

  indirect, 530, 531, 532

Characters, 91, 100, 116, 126, 134, 139, 140, 141, 142, 143, 154, 211, 212, 213, 214, 218, 219, 220, 221, 225, 232, 236, 240, 241, 250, 464, 473, 475, 476, 484, 488, 490, 491, 492, 495, 497, 506, 507, 508, 509, 519, 535, 537, 538, 540, 550, 554

  actions, 141, 142

  appearance, 141, 142

  backstories, 151

  character tableaus, 232

  conflict, 166, 516

  development, 128

  dynamic, 554, 555

  emotions, 100, 101, 106, 149, 235, 248, 257, 260, 261, 263, 548

  foils, 143, 166, 252, 253, 530

  main (primary), 70, 71, 76, 80, 81, 86, 92, 166, 167, 555

  mood, 235

  motivation, 150, 151, 173, 221, 252, 257, 260, 261, 263

  movement, 224

  physical descriptions, 461

  profile posters, 555, 556

  protagonists, 252

  secondary, 555

  static, 554, 555

  traits, 100, 127

  transformation, 43, 44, 45

  visual representation, 253

  voice, 556, 558

Coming-of-age stories, 512, 513, 514, 516, 517, 518, 519, 524, 530, 531, 532, 533, 534, 535, 537, 538, 550, 551, 554, 555, 556, 557, 560, 561

Conflicts, 154, 163, 233, 516, 517, 518, 535, 537, 538, 540, 551

  external, 166, 168, 170, 516

  internal, 166, 168, 170, 516

Description, 46, 65, 76, 81, 117, 119, 134, 185, 195, 330, 461, 465

  language of sensation, 76

Details, 1, 5, 7, 8, 9, 10, 11, 12, 14, 21, 25, 33, 35, 39, 43, 44, 46, 49, 50, 57, 65, 68, 71, 73, 80, 83, 86, 100, 106, 107, 111, 116, 118, 120, 126, 128, 134, 139, 140, 141, 142, 143, 144, 149, 159, 185, 194, 211, 230, 262, 264, 275, 316, 324, 330, 340, 353, 369, 386, 404, 429, 458, 460, 461, 462, 464, 465, 468, 492, 500, 506, 519, 525, 538, 554, 590

Dialogue, 144, 180, 221, 225, 250, 263

Diction, 43, 65, 86, 111, 155, 169, 171, 172, 180, 183, 184, 200, 259, 280, 282, 285, 289, 298, 300, 304, 319, 320, 479, 500, 541, 580, 586, 587, 599

Drama, 178, 211, 212, 214–217, 218, 219, 220, 224, 225

  asides, 221, 226, 254

  dialogue, 221, 224, 225, 250, 263

  director's role, 227

  dramaturgy, 239

  lighting, 257

  monologues, 237, 238, 258

  music, 257

  prologues, 229, 230

  set design, 257

  soliloquies, 221, 254, 258, 259

  stage directions, 222, 224

Essays, 15–16, 154, 155, 184, 316, 324, 325, 337, 395, 402, 410, 557, 560, 561

Essential questions, 46, 50, 57, 83, 91, 154, 180, 266, 269, 315, 379, 390, 429, 436, 457, 512, 513, 564

Figurative language, 111, 118, 127, 181, 271, 285, 290

Flashbacks, 71, 128, 129, 163, 164, 165, 497, 499

Foreshadowing, 71, 128, 163, 164, 165, 535

Genre characteristics, 7, 46, 63, 71, 155, 163, 178, 181, 198, 228, 280, 298, 341, 344–345, 350, 458, 459, 500

  performance vs. written text, 208

  science fiction, 111

  tragedy vs. comedy, 180

Images/imagery, 8, 9, 11, 21, 31, 34, 65, 70, 73, 81, 83, 100, 106, 108, 118, 119, 195, 250, 264, 275, 285, 287, 288, 289, 290, 330, 461, 587

  SIFT, 93, 94, 111, 118, 237, 238

Irony, 86, 93, 95, 111, 117, 120, 143, 152

  dramatic, 58, 93, 254, 256, 264, 265, 266

  situational, 93

  verbal, 93

Literary terms, 21, 86, 93, 143, 154, 163, 166, 169, 171, 178, 224, 239, 242, 258, 260, 265, 271, 274, 280, 288, 291, 292, 389, 482, 524, 554

Metaphor, 502

Mood, 65, 86, 87, 111, 128, 155, 169, 172, 280, 285, 298, 541, 580

Motif, 540

Narratives, 25, 70, 82, 119, 163, 476

  present tense, 496

Narrators, 25, 27, 28, 52, 65, 86, 126, 128, 325

  first-person bias, 492, 494, 495, 496, 498, 504, 505

  gaze, 65, 70

Reading Skills

Writing Skills

Media Skills

Vocabulary Skills

Index of Authors and Titles

Credits

Unit 1

Epstein, Mitch. "Quiet Places." New York Times, December 21, 2016.https://www. nytimes.com/interactive/2016/12/21/magazine/the-lives-they-livedphoto-essay-spaces. html. All photographs copyright Black River Productions, Ltd./Mitch Epstein.

Bread from GOOD BONES AND SIMPLE MURDERS by Margaret Atwood, copyright © 1983, 1992, 1994, by O.W. Toad Ltd. Used by permission of Nan A. Talese, an imprint of the Knopf Double-day Publishing Group, a division of Penguin Random House LLC. All rights re-served.

"The First Day" from LOST IN THE CITY by Edward P. Jones, copyright © 1992 by Edward P. Jones. Reprinted by permission of HarperCollins Publishers.

"What Happened During the Ice Storm" by Jim Heynen from YOU KNOW WHAT IS RIGHT, copyright © 1985 by Jim Heynen. Used by permission of the author.

"The Red Fox Fur Coat" by Teolinda Gersão from The Threepenny Review, copyright © 2004 by Teolinda Gersão. Used by permissions of the author.

"Lamb to the Slaughter" by Roald Dahl, copyright The Roald Dahl Story Company Limited © 1953 By Roald Dahl. Reprinted by permission of David Higham Associates Ltd.

"Games at Twilight" from Games at Twilight by Anita Desai, copyright Penguin Books ©1978 by Anita Desai.

"There Will Come Soft Rains" by Ray Bradbury, copyright The Crowell-Collier Publishing Company ©1948 by Ray Bradbury.

"The Leap" from The Red Convertible by Louise Erdrich, copyright HarperCollins Publishers ©2009 by Louise Erdrich.

from "Martha, Martha" by Zadie Smith, from "Granta 81: Best of Young British Novelists 2003." https://granta.com/martha-martha/, copyright Granta Publications ©2003 by Zadie Smith.

McPhee, John. Excerpt from "Draft No. 4." The New Yorker, April 29, 2013. Copyright Condé Nast ©2013 by John McPhee.

"Write Badly to Write Well" from Write to Learn by Donald M. Murray. Copyright Thomson Wadsworth ©2005 by Donald M. Murray.

Unit 2

"Lottery" by Rasma Haidri from Poem, Revised: 54 Poems, Revisions, Discussions by Marion Street Press, copyright © 2004 by Rasma Haidri. Used by permission of Rasma Haidri.

"The Fight" by John Montague from Collected Poems, copyright © 1995 Wake Forest University Press. Used by permission of Wake Forest University Press.

"Tamara's Opus" by Joshua Bennett from Disability Studies Quarterly, vol. 32, no. 3, copyright © 2012 by Joshua Bennett. Used by permission of Joshua Bennett.

From West Side Story by Arthur Laurents, Leonard Bernstein, Stephen Sondheim, and Jerome Robbins. Copyright © 1956. Reprinted by permission of Random House, Inc.

"Some Like Poetry" by Wislawa Szymborska from Ambers Aglow: An Anthology of Contemporary Polish Women's Poetry, translated and edited by Regina Grol, copyright Host Publications © 2016 by Wislawa Szymborska.

"Prayer to the Pacific" from Storyteller by Leslie Marmon Silko. 2d ed. New York: Penguin, 2012.

Elizabeth Bishop, "Sestina" from The Complete Poems 1926-1979. Copyright © 1979, 1983 by Alice Helen Methfessel.

Rhina P. Espaillat, "Bilingual/Bilingüe" from Where Horizons Go (Kirksville, MO: New Odyssey Books, 1998).

"Abuelito Who" from My Wicked Wicked Ways. Copyright © 1987 by Sandra Cisneros. By special arrangement with Third Woman Press. Published in hardcover by Alfred A. Knopf and originally by Third Woman Press.

Unit 3

"The Work You Do, the Person You Are." Copyright © 2017 by Toni Morrison. Reprinted by permission of ICM Partners.

"Drowning in Dishes, but Finding a Home" from The New York Times, Oct. 11, 2014, copyright © 2014 The New York Times. All rights reserved. Used by permission and protected by the copyright laws of the United States.

"What to Do with the Kids This Summer? Put 'Em to Work" from The New York Times, July 28, 2017, copyright © 2017 Ben Sasse.

"The Decline of the American Teenager's Summer Job." © The Economist Group Limited, London. July 6th, 2017.

"Teenagers Have Stopped Getting Summer Jobs—Why?" © 2017 The Atlantic Media Co., as first published in The Atlantic magazine. All rights reserved. Distributed by Tribune Content Agency, LLC.

"Why College Isn't (And Shouldn't Have to Be) For Everyone" by Robert Reich, Huffington Post (April 9, 2012). Copyright © 2012 Bloomberg L.P.

"The 'not everyone should go to college' argument is classist and wrong" by Libby Nelson, https://www.vox.com/2014/7/16/5904661/yes-everyone-should-go-to-college, 16 July 2014, from Vox Media. Used with permission from Vox Media.

"Even With Debt, College Still Pays Off" By Gillian B. White, The Atlantic, Feb. 20, 2015

Unit 4

Orwell, George. 1984. New York: Houghton Mifflin Harcourt, 2017.

Morgenstern, Erin. The Night Circus. New York: Anchor Books, 2011.

Draper, Sharon M. Out of My Mind. New York: Simon & Schuster, 2010.

Bradbury, Ray. Fahrenheit 451. New York: Simon & Schuster Paperbacks, 2018.

Doerr, Anthony. All the Light We Cannot See. New York: Scribner, 2014.

Durrow, Heidi W. The Girl Who Fell from the Sky. Chapel Hill, NC: Algonquin Books of Chapel Hill, 2010.

From To Kill a Mockingbird by Harper Lee. Copyright © 1960 by Harper Lee. Foreword copyright © 1993 by Harper Lee. Reprinted by permission of HarperCollins Publishers.

From "In Defense of To Kill a Mockingbird" by Nicholas J. Karolides, Lee Burress, and John M. Keam, 1993, Scarecrow Press. Used by permission.

"Letter from Birmingham Jail" by Martin Luther King, Jr. Reprinted by arrangement with The Heirs to the Estate of Martin Luther King, Jr. c/o Writers House as agent for the proprietor New York, NY. Copyright 1963 Dr. Martin Luther King, Jr.; copyright renewed 1991 Coretta Scott King.

"NEGROES' BOYCOTT CRIPPLES BUS LINE; Carrier in Montgomery, Ala., Increases Fares to Offset Loss of Business Negro Woman Convicted Conditions Laid Down" New York Times, 8 January 1956. https://www.nytimes.com/1956/01/08/archives/negroes-boycott-cripples-bus-line-carrier-in-montgomery-ala.html. All photographs copyright Black River Productions, Ltd./Mitch Epstein.

Image Credits

n/a egon69 / iStock; 1 "Cakewalk" © 1987 Carmen Lomas Garza Acrylic Painting, 36x48 inches; 7 © Nina Subin; 8 © Black River Productions, Ltd. / Mitch Epstein. Courtesy of Sikkema Jenkins & Co., New York. Used with permission. All rights reserved.; 9 © Black River Productions, Ltd. / Mitch Epstein. Courtesy of Sikkema Jenkins & Co., New York. Used with permission. All rights reserved.; 10 © Black River Productions, Ltd. / Mitch Epstein. Courtesy of Sikkema Jenkins & Co., New York. Used with permission. All rights reserved.; 11 © Black River Productions, Ltd. / Mitch Epstein. Courtesy of Sikkema Jenkins & Co., New York. Used with permission. All rights reserved.; 14 Shaun Higson / Portraits / Alamy Stock Photo; 15 Professor25 /iStock; 21 Album / Alamy Stock Photo; 31 MPVHistory / Alamy Stock Photo; 33 Jim Heynen, Author © 2008 Doug Kurata; 34 Steven R Smith / Shutterstock; 40 © António Pedro Ferreira; 43 Sandra Standbridge / Getty Images; 46 Ronald Dumont/Daily Express/Getty Images; 49 George Marks / Getty Images; 65 Chronicle / Alamy Stock Photo; 67 Nordic Photos/SuperStock; 73 travelview / Shutterstock; 86 World History Archive / Alamy Stock Photo; 91 Zvonimir Atletic / Shutterstock; 100 Raphael GAILLARDE/Gamma-Rapho via Getty Images; 103 Fiona Osbaldstone © The CollegeBoard; 111 Everett Collection Inc; 111 Martin Bustamante © The CollegeBoard 120 Agence Opale / Alamy Stock Photo; 122 Christie's Images Ltd. / SuperStock; 134 Brian Dowling/ Getty Images; 155 Photo by Office of Communications, Princeton University; 160 © UNH Magazine; 160 Dorling Kindersley / Getty Images; 177 It is love at first sight for Juliet {Emma ladji) and Romeo {Nate Santana) in Chicago Shakespeare Theater's Short Shakespeare! Romeo and Juliet, adapted and directed by Marti Lyons, in the Courtyard Theater, February 22-April 28, 2017. Photo by Liz Laure 184 © Rasma Haidri; 193 Ulf Andersen/Getty Images; 194 Jim Nicholson / Alamy Stock Photo; 201 © Joshua Bennett; 203 mirzamlk / Shutterstock; 217 © Geraint Lewis; 222 Photo by Stock Montage/Getty Images; 239 Farewell - one kiss, and I'll descend (oil on canvas), Fortescue-Brickdale, Eleanor (1871-1945) / Private Collection / Photo © The Maas Gallery, London / Bridgeman Images; 244 Carolyn Cole / Contributor/Getty Images; 248 WEST SIDE STORY de JeromeRobbins et RobertWise avec Richard Beymer et Natalie Wood 1961/Bridgeman Images; 255 Juliet, Friar Lawrence and Romeo, from Shakespeare's Romeo and Juliet (colour litho), European School, (20th century) / Private Collection / © Look and Learn / Bridgeman Images; 262 Juliet and Her Nurse, 1935/6 (oil on canvas), Sickert, Walter Richard (1860-1942) / Leeds Museums and Galleries (Leeds Art Fund) / Bridgeman Images; 264 The Reconciliation of the Montagues and the Capulets over the Dead Bodies of Romeo and Juliet (oil on canvas), Leighton, Frederic (1830-96) / Private Collection / Photo © Christie's Images / Bridgeman Images; 275 Everett Collection Inc / Alamy Stock Photo; 276 Niday Picture Library / Alamy Stock Photo; 280 Chris Felver/Getty Images; 281 Lorri Kajenna / Shutterstock; 282 IntergalacticDesignStudio / Shutterstock; 285 © Josef Breitenbach Archive Center for Creative Photography, Tucson; 287 Carlo Molinari © The CollegeBoard; 298 Archive PL / Alamy Stock Photo; 311 Squaredpixels / iStock; 316 Deborah Feingold/Corbis via Getty Images; 324 Koren Shadmi ©The New York Times; 327 webphotographeer / iStock; 337 dpa picture alliance / Alamy Stock Photo; 338 © The State Journal-Register; 353 ArtWell / Shutterstock; 361 n/a 362 n/a 365 n/a 366 n/a 367 n/a 368 n/a 381 Thomas Imo/Photothek via Getty Images; 383 Hero Images / Getty Images; 396 Photo by Dimitrios Kambouris/Getty Image; 402 Libby Nelson/Vox Media, Inc. 403 n/a 404 n/a 411 n/a 412 n/a 417 © Sallie Mae; 419 McFarland, J., Hussar, B., Wang, X., Zhang, J., Wang, K., Rathbun, A., Barmer, A., Forrest Cataldi, E., and Bullock Mann, F. (2018). The Condition